JOHN WESLEY'S
F·I·F·T·Y-
T·H·R·E·E
SERMONS

edited by

EDWARD H. SUGDEN

Abingdon
Press
Nashville

JOHN WESLEY'S FIFTY-THREE SERMONS

Published by Abingdon Press 1983

Third Printing 1988

In Wesley's proposals for printing three volumes of Sermons by subscription dated September 7, 1745, the price is fixed at 2s. 6d. each volume 'in quires.' He hopes that the first volume will be in the press by Michaelmas, and delivered to subscribers by or before Christmas.

The volume is dated 1746. It is 12mo, pp. xii, 250. It has no Table of Contents or Index, but has 12 Sermons (Nos. I–XII) and a list of 'Books published by Mr. John and Charles Wesley' which fills two pages and contains seventy items, the last of which is 'Sermons on Several Occasions,' vol. I, price 2s. 6d.

Second Edition, London: W. Bowyer, 1754 (identical with first edition); Third, Bristol: W. Pine, 1769; Fourth, Paramore, 1787; Fifth, 1796.

ISBN 0-687-20493-3

MANUFACTURED BY PARTHENON PRESS,
NASHVILLE, TENNESSEE, UNITED STATES OF AMERICA

PUBLISHER'S PREFACE

This volume of John Wesley's sermons is a republication of E. H. Sugden's edition of *Wesley's Standard Sermons,* first issued in 1921 in two volumes. Sugden's introductory comments have been retained, but his footnotes have been omitted. The scheme of numbering Wesley's sermons is unique in Sugden's work; the corresponding numbering in most editions of Wesley's *Works* can be found in the chart on the next page.

NUMERATION OF SERMONS IN THIS EDITION
COMPARED WITH MOST EDITIONS
OF WESLEY'S *WORKS*

Old	New	Old	New	Old	New
I	I	XIX	XV	XXXVII	XXXII
II	II	*XX*	*XLIX*	XXXVIII	XXXIII
III	III	XXI	XVI	XXXIX	XXXIV
IV	IV	XXII	XVI	XL	XXV
V	V	XXIII	XVIII	XLI	XXXVI
VI	VI	XXIV	XIX	XLII	XXXVII
VII	VII	XXV	XX	*XLIII*	*L*
VIII	VIII	XXVI	XXI	XLIV	XXXVIII
IX	IX	XXVII	XXII	XLV	XXXIX
X	X	XXVIII	XXIII	XLVI	XL
XI	*XLV*	XXIX	XXIV	XLVII	XLI
XII	XI	XXX	XXV	XLVIII	XLII
XIII	*XLVI*	XXXI	XXVI	XLIX	XLIII
XIV	*XLVII*	XXXII	XXVII	L	XLIV
XV	*XLVIII*	XXXIII	XXVIII	*LI*	*LI*
XVI	XII	XXXIV	XXIX	*LII*	*LII*
XVII	XIII	XXXV	XXX	*LIII*	*LIII*
XVIII	XIV	XXXVI	XXXI		

The numbers of the non-standard Sermons are printed in italics.

PREFACE

IT is remarkable that though John Wesley's Four Volumes of Sermons are part of the standard of Methodist doctrine, and have to be read and approved by all our ministers, no edition of them with annotations has hitherto been issued. I have endeavoured to supply this lack.

The text has been founded on Thomas Jackson's revised and corrected edition of 1825, for which he received the special thanks of the Conference. In its Preface he says, 'Copies of the most authentic editions of Mr. Wesley's Sermons, printed in his lifetime, have been carefully collated throughout; and every effort has been made to present an edition at once complete and correct.' A comparison of Jackson's volumes with the earlier editions, especially with the fourth, issued in 1787-8, proves that Jackson took the latter as the basis of his text, and not the edition of the Sermons published as part of the *Works* in 1771. This is somewhat strange, as he was responsible for the statement that the number of Standard Sermons was fifty-three and that they were those contained in the 1771 edition (see below, vol. ii, p. 336). Stranger still is the fact that in the third edition of the *Works,* published under Jackson's supervision in 1829, the less correct 1771 text was reverted to, and has been used ever since. The most important insertions and alterations now made are enclosed in square brackets, and will be found as follows: Vol. I, pp. 41, 43, 45, 46, 48, 51, 62, 63, 72, 77, 80, 100, 123, 207, 285, 289, 294, 360, 456, 519; Vol. II, 20, 32, 185, 248, 359, 517, 518, 520. In this matter Mr. A. Wallington his rendered me valuable service in comparing the various editions.

The notes include—

(1) Some account of the occasion of the first preaching of each sermon, as far as that could be ascertained from the *Journal* and other sources;

(2) An attempt to show the relation of Wesley's teaching to more modern developments of theology;

(3) Corrections of his exegesis, where the progress of biblical study has made them necessary;

(4) Identification of the many quotations from classical and English literature which occur in the Sermons;

(5) Occasional interpretations of words and usages which have become more or less obsolete.

(6) Some indication of the development of Wesley's own views, as shown by differences between the earlier and later sermons.

I am solely responsible for the opinions expressed, and I need hardly say that they have no official authority.

My hope is that this work will attract fresh attention to these wonderful discourses, and cause them to be more widely read and studied. I have found them full of spiritual blessing and stimulus; and I am convinced that it will be of the greatest service to our beloved Church that our ministers and people should recover Wesley's theological standpoint, and should especially be inspired by his passion for souls.

I desire to acknowledge my indebtedness, first of all, to the Standard edition of the *Journal,* and Mr. Curnock's invaluable notes therein contained; and to the publications of the Wesley Historical Society. Then I have consulted from time to time Tyerman's *Life of Wesley,* with its excellent index; the older and more recent lives of Wesley; and the various histories of Methodism. Dr. W. B. Pope's *Theology* has always been at my elbow; and Dr. Osborn's monumental edition of the Hymns and Poems of the Wesleys has helped me to identify many of the quotations. I have used the 1872 edition of the Collected *Works,* and also the 1771 edition issued by Wesley. The collection of original editions of Wesley's publications in our Queen's College Library, numbering some 400, has of course been constantly referred to.

E. H. S.

CONTENTS

INTRODUCTION

I

THE STANDARD SERMONS

John Wesley published four volumes of Sermons, dated respectively 1746, 1748, 1750, and 1760. In 1763 he prepared a Model Deed for his preaching-houses, in which it was provided that persons appointed by the Conference should 'have and enjoy the premises' only on condition 'that the said persons preach no other doctrine than is contained in Mr. Wesley's Notes upon the New Testament and four volumes of sermons.' This clause must necessarily refer to the four volumes already published. In a second undated edition of the 1750 volume a sermon is added on 'Wandering Thoughts,' bringing the total number up to forty-four. In 1771 he published an edition of his collected *Works,* the first four volumes of which contained the above forty-four sermons (including 'Wandering Thoughts') and nine others, viz.:

XI.	The Witness of the Spirit—Discourse II dated	1767
XIII.	On Sin in Believers.................................... "	1763
XIV.	The Repentance of Believers...................... "	1767
XV.	The Great Assize... "	1758
XX.	The Lord our Righteousness........................ "	1765
XLIII.	The Scripture Way of Salvation................... "	1765
LI.	The Good Steward... "	1768
LII.	The Reformation of Manners...................... "	1763
LIII.	On the Death of Mr. Whitefield................. "	1770

This makes a total of fifty-three.

In 1787-8 an edition in eight volumes was published, the first four of which were identical with the volumes of 1746, 1748, 1750, and 1760, including the sermon on 'Wandering Thoughts'; but did not contain the nine sermons added in the edition of 1771. After 1787 the form of the words in the Model Deed was altered to 'the first four volumes of sermons.' The text of the present Model Deed makes the standard to be 'what is contained in certain Notes on the New Testament commonly reputed to be the Notes of the said John Wesley and . . . the First Four Volumes of Sermons commonly reputed to be written and published by him.'

For a long time it was assumed that the Fifty-three sermons in the first four volumes of the *Works* were intended; but the question was raised by the Rev. R. Green in 1894 as to which sermons really

1

constituted the Standard; and after obtaining Counsel's opinion, the
Conference of 1914 placed on record that the phrase in the Model
Deed applies to the first four volumes of Wesley's Sermons, published
in eight volumes in 1787-8; and that the total number of sermons is
forty-four. The case submitted to Counsel, and the opinion of Mr.
Owen Thompson, are given below, Vol. II, pp. 331-40.

The legal position is now therefore settled; but it is interesting to
inquire why Wesley introduced the nine additional sermons in the 1771
edition. That he reverted to the original editions in the four volumes of
1787-8 only shows that he realized the legal difficulty that would have
arisen had he changed the standard of doctrine set out in the deeds
executed before 1771; not that he had changed his mind as to the
importance of the added sermons. Why then did he add them? In the
preface to the 1771 *Works* (I quote here and elsewhere from a copy of
the original edition presented to the Library of our Theological Hall in
Melbourne by the late Dr. Osborn in 1870), par. 2, he says: 'I wanted to
methodize these tracts, to range them under proper heads, placing
those together which were on similar subjects and in such order that
one might illustrate another. This it is easy to see may be of use to the
serious reader, who will then readily observe that there is scarce any
subject of importance, either in practical or controversial divinity,
which is not treated of more or less, either professedly or occasionally.'
His aims were thus elucidation and completeness of presentation. He
knew that the previous four volumes formed part of the legal standard
of doctrine for his preachers; and he could not alter that without
creating difficulties. Moreover, he had already said in the preface to the
volume of 1746, 'I am not conscious that there is any one point of
doctrine, on which I am accustomed to speak in public, which is not
here, incidentally, if not professedly, laid before every Christian
reader.' But the twenty-five years which had passed since their first
publication had brought out certain objections, and certain new proofs,
in regard to doctrines dealt with in the first editions; and there was no
reason why he should not in this 1771 edition—which he might
reasonably expect to be the last, seeing that he was now in his
sixty-eighth year—introduce in their proper place additional sermons,
not as changing the standard, but as making clearer and more explicit
what was already there. Hence he inserted after the first sermon on the
Witness of the Spirit a second discourse on the same subject. Time had
shown it to be 'a grand part of the testimony which God has given' to the
Methodists; the experience of a great multitude had confirmed its
truth; the preaching of it had aroused violent and determined
opposition; and there had been some dangerous misunderstandings as
to its meaning. These points are all dealt with in the second discourse.
The strong teaching of No. XI, in which it might seem to be argued that
no one who ever committed sin could be called a Christian, needed
some qualification; and at its conclusion in the 1771 edition Wesley
says, 'It may easily be observed that the preceding discourse describes
the experience of those that are *strong* in faith. But hereby those that are

weak in faith may be discouraged: to prevent which the following discourse may be of use.' Then is added No. XLVI, on Sin in Believers, and No. XLVII, on The Repentance of Believers, which is the natural corollary of No. XLVI. There was no sermon in the original forty-four treating explicitly of the Last Judgement; hence is inserted for the sake of completeness No. XLVIII, The Great Assize. The next addition to the original list is No. XLIX, The Lord our Righteousness, which is inserted, as pars. 6-9 declare, to show the consistency of Wesley's teaching in 1765 with all that he has said 'for near eight-and-twenty years'; and to make clear his attitude towards the Mystics, Quakers, Presbyterians, and Independents; and specifically towards Law, Barclay, and Taylor (par. 16). No. L, The Scripture Way of Salvation, is on the old topic of justification by Faith; but it is especially intended to vindicate Wesley from the charge which 'has been roundly and vehemently affirmed for these five-and-twenty years' that he taught sanctification by works (par. iii. 3). In the fourth volume of the *Works*, after including the remaining sermons of the 1760 edition, and the tracts which there follow, he found that he had still about 80 pages to fill, in order to make the volume uniform in size with the first three, which have respectively 350, 354, and 355 pages; he therefore inserted after the sermons and before the tracts, three sermons preached on special occasions, Nos. LI, LII, and LIII, which bring the number of pages up to 353. A similar consideration serves to show why the Great Assize sermon was placed where it stands (No. XV in the first volume). Wesley wished to make the volumes in the *Works* correspond, as closely as he could, with the four volumes previously published. Now the second volume (of 1748) begins with the sermon preached at St. Mary's, Oxford, on The Circumcision of the Heart on January 1, 1733, as the first had begun with the Oxford sermon on Salvation by Faith; and it includes exactly the sermons in the second volume of the *Works*, excepting No. XLIX, The Lord our Righteousness. Unless The Circumcision of the Heart were put into the first volume, or some other sermon added in its place, the first volume would have been twenty-four pages short, in comparison with the remaining three; by inserting The Great Assize in Vol. I, the pages are made up to 350; and The Circumcision of the Heart is retained as the first in Vol. II. The insertion of No. L (The Scripture Way of Salvation) in Vol. III of the 1771 edition is to be accounted for in the same way; it brings Vol. III up to 355 pages.

Our conclusion, therefore, is—

(1) Nos. LI, LII, and LIII have nothing to do with the Standard of Doctrine:

(2) Nos. XLVI and XLVII are intended as a qualification of the teaching of No. XI, and whilst not part of the Standard, are important as an authoritative interpretation of No. XI; and No. XLV stands in the same relation to No. X.

(3) No. XLVIII is not an addition to the Standard of Doctrine; for its teaching is quite clearly contained in the Notes on the New Testament;

but it is intended to secure that the doctrine of the Last Things shall be definitely recognized as part of Wesley's teaching.

(4) Nos. XLIX and L are intended to show that Wesley had not changed his views during the twenty-five years since the publication of the first volume of the Sermons on the questions therein treated.

Therefore, whilst I fully concur in the decision of the Conference of 1914, I have thought it best to include all the fifty-three sermons in the 1771 edition: the earlier additions because they help to interpret the Standard Sermons; and the last three, partly for the sake of completeness, and partly for the special interest of the occasions on which they were preached.

The Forty-four Sermons are given below in the order in which they appeared in the volumes of 1746, 1748, 1750, and 1760, and the remaining nine are placed at the end, and renumbered accordingly.

II

THE EXACT RELATION OF THE STANDARDS TO THE MINISTRY AND MEMBERSHIP OF THE METHODIST CHURCH

Methodism had originally no doctrinal test (except by implication) for church, or rather, society membership. 'There is only one condition previously required in those who desire admission into these societies, viz.: "a desire to flee from the wrath to come, to be saved from their sins," ' and this is to be proved by their avoiding evil, doing good, and attending upon the ordinances of God. As regards our members, therefore, no doctrinal test is imposed, save in so far as a desire to be saved from sin and the wrath to come, and a saving faith in Jesus Christ, imply certain doctrinal beliefs. But for our ministers, local preachers, and office-bearers certain doctrinal tests are prescribed, and these are safeguarded, first, by the trustees of the churches, second, by the Conference and its subordinate courts, and, third, by the conscience of the individual concerned.

First, then, as to the powers and duties of trustees. The doctrinal standard to which every minister of the Methodist Church is required to conform is legally defined in the Model Deed as follows: 'No person or persons whomsoever shall . . . be permitted to preach . . . who shall maintain, promulgate, or teach any doctrine or practice contrary to what is contained in certain Notes on the New Testament, commonly reputed to be the notes of the said John Wesley, and in the first four volumes of sermons commonly reputed to be written and published by him.' This formula goes back to the original Model Deed prepared by Wesley and incorporated by him in the *Large Minutes,* where the words run: 'Provided always that the said persons preach no other doctrine than is contained in Mr. Wesley's Notes upon the New Testament and four volumes of sermons.' Consequently it is one of the duties of trustees 'to permit no person to preach or conduct worship on the trust property who maintains, promulgates, or teaches any doctrine or practice contrary to what is contained in John Wesley's Notes on the New Testament, and in the first four volumes of his sermons as at present published.'

So far the position is clear. No minister or local preacher can legally preach any doctrine contrary to the Notes and Sermons (hereinafter referred to as the Standards). No question is raised as to his personal belief; so far as the Model Deed is concerned, he may believe what he likes, provided he does not preach anything contrary to the Standards, and he is at perfect liberty to preach new doctrines, provided they are not contrary to the Standards. As to whether he violates this condition or not, the trustees of the churches are judges, and it is obvious that no further power could reasonably be given to them. They cannot exclude any one from the pulpit on suspicion or even on certainty that he is not orthodox in his *belief*. They can only judge by what he says in the pulpit, and if that is not contrary to the Standards, they cannot take any action.

The Conference, however, must, and does, go further than this. Every candidate for the ministry must be certified by the superintendent who proposes him that he 'has read and approves' the Standards. Before ordination he is required 'to pass an oral theological examination, including his acquaintance with Wesley's works, especially the first fifty-three Sermons and the Notes on the New Testament,' and, further, 'to be examined as to . . . his belief in the doctrines of the Church, and to promise that if his views of doctrine change he will quietly retire from the ministry.' At his ordination he is asked two doctrinal questions—(1) 'Are you persuaded that the Holy Scriptures contain sufficiently all doctrine required of necessity for eternal salvation through faith of Jesus Christ? and are you determined to teach nothing as required of necessity to eternal salvation but that which you shall be persuaded may be concluded and proved by the Scripture?' (2) 'I have further to inquire whether you have read the first four volumes of Mr. Wesley's Sermons and his Notes on the New Testament, and whether you believe that the system of doctrine therein contained is in accordance with the Holy Scriptures.' Subsequently every minister must answer for himself the question asked annually at the District Synod, 'Does he believe and preach our doctrines?'

It will be observed, however, that no law is laid down as to what action the Conference shall take in case the answers to any of these questions are in the negative. As the law stands no candidate can be brought forward who does not 'approve' the Standards; subsequently inquiry is made annually as to his belief in them, but it is nowhere said that the Conference must remove him from full power to deal with each case as it may judge best, provided, always, that the legal requirement of the Model Deed is not violated. At the same time the onus of responsibility is laid upon each individual by his promise that if he changes his views of doctrine he will quietly retire. If, therefore, a minister is clear that his view of any doctrine is contrary to that contained in the Standards, he is bound by his promise to resign, though it would apparently be competent for the Conference to decline to accept his resignation. If, however, his views change. but in such a way that he still believes them to be not contrary to the Standards, he is not bound to resign, though it is in the power of the Conference to examine into his views and to act upon its own judgement accordingly.

The two important questions therefore to determine are: (1) What exactly are the doctrines taught in the Standards in which belief is obligatory? and (2) what is meant by a belief being 'contrary to the Standards'?

As to the first point, the phrases used vary; the candidate must approve the Standards; the man who is to be ordained is asked whether he believes that the system of doctrine contained in them is in accordance with the Holy Scripture which he has just declared to contain all doctrine required of necessity for eternal salvation; the ordained minister is asked whether he believes 'our doctrines'; and it must be presumed that these various phrases—'the doctrine contained in' the Standards, 'the system of doctrine contained in the Standards,' 'our doctrines'—were intended to be practically synonymous, and each phrase must be allowed to throw light upon the others. The second phrase shows that it is the system of doctrine in the Standards, not isolated statements to be found in them, that is intended; and the third phrase, which Wesley constantly used—'our doctrines'—is defined in the original edition of the *Large Minutes* under question 59 ('What can be done in order to the future union of the Methodists?'), where Wesley suggests that all the ministers should sign an agreement 'to preach the old Methodist doctrines, and no other, contained in the Minutes of the Conference.' Reference to the Minutes shows that these doctrines are justification by faith, entire sanctification, the atonement of our Lord, assurance of pardon by the witness of the Spirit, the impossibility of a sincere seeker after the Truth being lost, and free grace as opposed to predestinarianism.

The eternal punishment of the finally impenitent is also affirmed, but it is expressly stated that it only applies to those who have heard the Gospel. The phrase 'our doctrines,' therefore, does not mean the whole round of Christian orthodoxy, but specifically the doctrines concerned with sin and salvation, which marked out the early Methodists. And this is the system of doctrine contained in the sermons, as a study of their titles at once demonstrates. Other doctrines are incidentally mentioned, but only these are systematically treated, and it was of these and no others that Wesley was thinking when he demanded from his helpers that they should believe and preach 'our doctrines.' He would never have described the Thirty-nine Articles as 'our' doctrines; they contain the doctrines of the Church of England, and Wesley, of course, accepted them himself; but by 'our' doctrines he meant the Methodist teaching peculiar to himself and his followers at that time in regard to salvation by faith and Christian holiness. That this is so is shown by the fact that two questions are asked in the Ordination Service; if the second question had been intended to cover the whole ground of the

Christian faith, it would be unnecessary to ask the first as well. But the inspiration and sufficiency of Scripture is not a specifically Methodist doctrine; it belongs to the whole Protestant Church; and so the question on the system of doctrine in the Standards does not include it, and it is therefore separately asked. 'Our main doctrines,' says Wesley, 'which include all the rest, are repentance, faith, and holiness. The first of these we account, as it were, the porch of religion; the next, the door; the third, religion itself.' As Dr. Fitchett, in his chapter on 'The Effective Doctrines of Methodism,' has said, 'The enduring controversies which have torn asunder the Christian Church lie in what may be called the realm of metaphysical theology. And the working theology of Methodism, since it is supremely occupied with a great cluster of evangelical doctrines, has escaped these controversies.'

John Wesley was a Pragmatist before Professor James had popularized that term. 'His theology,' if I may again quote Dr. Fitchett, 'is one which links doctrine to conduct. It has the salt of reality. Here are doctrines realized in human experience and tested by that experience.' 'Our' doctrines include no such metaphysical theory of the Trinity as is embodied in the Athanasian Creed. 'I dare not insist,' says Wesley in his sermon on the Trinity, 'upon any one's using the word Trinity or Person. I use them myself because I know of none better, but if any man has any scruple concerning them, who shall constrain him to use them? I cannot.' The fact of original sin Wesley strongly maintains, but he expressly disclaims any specific theory about it. 'It is quite beyond my understanding; it is a depth which I cannot fathom.' And, again, 'Some have attempted to explain this intricate affair. I do not commend their wisdom. I do not attempt to explain even how I at this moment stretch out my hand or move my finger.' And in the same paragraph is a profound sentence, applying to much more than this particular doctrine: 'Our perception of truth cannot be false; our understanding or apprehension of things may.' As to the misleading connotation of the phrase 'total' depravity, he says (*Minutes*, 1745): 'How can we maintain that all works done before we have a sense of the pardoning love of God are sin, and as such an abomination to Him? The works of him who has heard the Gospel and does not believe are not done as God hath willed and commanded them to be done. And yet we know not how to say that they are an abomination to the Lord in him who feareth God, and from that principle does the best he can.' The fact of the atonement shines luminously in every sermon; but there is no attempt to frame a systematic theory even of this great central truth. There is no theory of the hypostatic union of the two natures in our Lord, though the facts of His true deity and perfect manhood are definitely taught.

Every one knows Wesley's profession that he was *homo unius libri*—'a man of one book'; but, as Dr Fitchett has pointed out in the chapter above referred to, 'Methodism is committed to no special theory as to the inspiration of Scripture.' Indeed, Wesley was a critic, both higher and lower, before those much misunderstood terms were invented. In the preface to the Notes on the New Testament he says: 'Those various readings which have a vast majority of ancient copies and translations on their side, I have without scruple incorporated with the text; which I have divided all along according to the matter it contains.' In his preface to the Notes on the Old Testament he declares it to be his purpose 'to give the direct literal meaning of every verse, of every sentence, and, as far as I am able, of every word in the oracles of God. My intention is to make men think and assist them in thinking.' And in the preface to the Book of Joshua he states almost exactly the modern critical view: 'These books (Joshua to Esther) were probably collections of the authentic records of the nation which some of the prophets were divinely directed and assisted to put together. It seems the substance of the several histories was written under divine direction when the events had just happened, and long after put into the form wherein they stand now, perhaps all by the same hand.' His suggestion that these books may not have taken their present form until after the time of Ahasuerus (the Greek Xerxes) goes as far as anything that the modern critics have suggested. But it is at least clear that the documentary theory of the origin of these books was the one which he adopted.

As to the subject of the final doom of the impenitent, he repeats and applies with the utmost earnestness the Scriptural doctrine of eternal punishment; but he expressly says in one of his latest sermons (on Living without God): 'I do not conceive that any man living has a right to sentence all the heathen and Mahometan world to damnation.' And again: 'I believe the merciful God regards the lives and tempers of men more than their ideas. I believe He respects the goodness of the heart rather than the clearness of the head; and that if the heart of a man be filled with the humble, gentle, patient love of God and man, God will not cast him into everlasting fire because his ideas are not clear or because his conceptions are confused.'

This was the state of the case at Wesley's death; every candidate for the ministry was required to satisfy the Conference as to his belief in Methodist doctrine; but after he had been once received into full connexion, no further inquiry was made unless some charge of failure in orthodoxy was brought against him. But at the Conference of 1812 it was directed that at the annual District Meeting certain questions should be asked in regard to each minister; amongst them being this, 'Does he believe and preach our doctrines?' and in the year 1814 the Conference, feeling the need of more exact definition, made a list of the doctrines to which the 'unequivocal assent' of every candidate for ordination is required. 'A Trinity of Persons in the unity of the Godhead; the total depravity of all men by nature in consequence of Adam's fall; the atonement made by Christ for the sins of all the human race; justification by faith; the absolute necessity of holiness both in heart and life; the direct-witness of the Spirit; and the proper eternity of future rewards and punishments.' And in 1827, in consequence of Dr. Adam Clarke's teaching in his Commentary, the doctrine of the Eternal Sonship of Christ was added to the list, and it was directed that every candidate for ordination should be expressly examined on this point, in spite of Dr. Clarke's protest. 'Such tests of church fellowship and ministerial communion,' he said, 'never disgraced Methodism until now. Mr. Wesley would have abhorred such, as he would have abhorred the devil, whatever attachment he might have had to the general sense of the doctrine.' However, the resolution was passed, and has never been repealed. It was an unfortunate step, taken in a moment of panic, which happily has had no successors, and, I trust, never will.

The actual law, then, is as follows:

(1) Negatively, that it is illegal for any one, minister or layman, to preach in our pulpits any doctrine contrary to the Standards.

(2) Positively, that every minister shall be asked annually whether he believes and preaches our doctrines, the meaning and content of that somewhat vague expression being determined by Wesley's usage and by the list above quoted from the *Minutes* of 1814, plus the Doctrine of the Eternal Sonship of our Lord.

(3) That the procedure to be taken in the event of a negative answer to that question is nowhere determined by our laws, but is left in the hands of the Conference.

(4) That any minister who changes his views on doctrine, presumably in such a way that his new views are contrary to the Standards, is bound by his promise given before his ordination quietly to retire.

It is necessary now to inquire what is intended by a doctrine 'contrary' to the Standards. We must carefully distinguish between 'difference' and 'contrariety.' Things may be different without being contrary. The flower is different from the bud, but not contrary to it. The man is different from the child, but not contrary to him. And so our statements, even of the peculiar Methodist doctrines, may be different from, without being contrary to, John Wesley's. There is a development in doctrine as well as in life; indeed, life without development, whether in Nature or in thought, is inconceivable. For example, the wonderfully enlightening theory of the Atonement worked out in Dr. Scott Lidgett's Fernley Lecture is different from any view that is formulated by Wesley; but it is a development, not a contradiction, of Wesley's teaching. Similarly, the view of eternal punishment which eliminates from it the idea of physical torture differs from that suggested in the Standards, but does not contradict it. The essential deity of our Lord is not contradicted when the voluntary limitations which His humanity imposed upon Him are emphasized more strongly than they are in Wesley's writings.

To deny the legitimacy of such developments is to take our stand with Pius X and the encyclical named with unconscious irony *Pascendi gregis;* we cannot allow that the development of theology ceased with John Wesley, any more than with that prince of theologians, St. Thomas Aquinas. To think such a thing possible comes perilously near to blasphemy against the Holy Spirit, who has been given to guide the Church into all truth, and assuredly did not close His work in 1791 when Wesley died. For this sin there is no forgiveness; the Church that finalizes its doctrines at any point in its history has sealed its own death-warrant.

That Wesley would never have dreamed of blocking by the dead hand of his personal authority all future developments in theology is clear from his own definite statement in the preface to the Sermons: 'But some may say, I have mistaken the way myself, although I take upon me to teach it to others. It is very possible that I have. But I trust, whereinsoever I have been mistaken, my mind is open to conviction. I sincerely desire to be better informed.' This is not the language of a man who believes that he has finalized the truth, or who would desire to impose his own conclusions as infallible and unchangeable upon the whole future Church.

So far I have been dealing purely with what may be called 'Statute Law.' But evidently this law needs some authoritative interpretation; for many questions may reasonably be raised as to its precise meaning. Now, such interpretation can only be given by the supreme court of the Church, and, just as the common law of England is absolutely authoritative as an interpretation by the courts of the meaning of the Acts of Parliament, so the decisions of our Supreme Doctrinal Court, the British Wesleyan Conference, must govern our interpretation of our Standards of Doctrine.

Such decisions may be given explicitly, when a charge of want of orthodoxy is made against some minister; as e.g. in the case of Dr. Adam Clarke in 1827 (a summary of all such decisions of Conference would be a valuable addition to our Methodist literature); or implicitly, by publication in such a series as the Fernley Lectures; or by failure to institute proceedings against a minister whose published views do not accord with the hitherto usual interpretations of our doctrines.

Finally, it is of interest to determine precisely what power the Conference has to deal with our Standards of Doctrine. It could not, without an Act of Parliament, alter the provisions of the Model Deed, or permit any doctrine contrary to the Standards to be preached in our pulpits. It has, however, power to define what our doctrines are, as was done in 1814; and to decide whether any specific doctrine is or is not contrary to the Standards. It has also full power to determine its own action in the case of any minister who does not believe and preach our doctrines, or any one of them; save that it cannot permit him to preach any doctrine ruled to be contrary to the Standards in any of our trust properties. Assuming that the Conference ruled that a given doctrine was not so contrary, and any body of trustees disagreed with that ruling, the ultimate decision would rest with the Courts of Law, and finally with the House of Lords.

Methodism, then, has on the one hand a very definite body of doctrines to which she rejoices to be bound. 'It asserts the liberty of the moral agent, and indicates the spiritual nature and essential royalty of man. It is very clear as to the atoning work of Christ and the office and work of the Spirit; it insists on the necessity of personal holiness, and holds out the possibility of a victory over the apostate nature by affirming a sanctification which is entire, and a perfection in love which is not ultimate and final, but progressive in its development for ever. It looks on man as utterly lost on account of sin. But warm and generous as the sunlight of God, it looks every man in the face, and says, "Christ died for you." It preaches the glad news that to every believer in Christ the invited Spirit will come and enthrone Himself in the heart as a witness of Sonship and the living Comforter. It preaches the dreadful truth of eternal punishment, and warns men to flee from the wrath to come; and it makes known the everlasting blessedness of those who fight the good fight of faith, and obtain the crown of righteousness.' To this eloquent summary given by Rev. Charles H. Kelly I need not add a word.

On the other hand, the utmost freedom of thought is granted to us on subjects which, however important, do not essentially touch these vital doctrines. To quote a witty American Bishop, we do not believe that no one can enter the kingdom of God except through the mouth of Jonah's whale; nor do we hold that the fact that our fathers looked at things with their own eyes binds us never to look at them with ours. I am bold to affirm that no Church combines so happily security as to the essential doctrines of salvation with liberty of thought as to all questions of speculative theology. 'In this age of intellectual daring,' to quote from Dr. Clifford's address at the Wesley Centenary celebrations, 'we must not alienate the young mind by mental cowardice.' We must on occasion be ready to give sympathy and guidance to our young people, who are disturbed and perplexed by the discussions which they find in every newspaper and magazine. But the main part of our ministry we shall be wise to devote to those great doctrines of sin and salvation by which men live. Let us never forget that we are set in the Church 'for the perfecting of the saints, for the work of ministering, for the building up of the body of Christ, till we all attain unto the unity of the faith and of the knowledge of the Son of God, unto a full-grown man, unto the measure of the stature of the fullness of Christ.'

PREFACE TO THE SERMONS

I. The following Sermons contain the substance of what I have been preaching for between eight and nine years last past. During that time I have frequently spoken in public, on every subject in the ensuing collection; and I am not conscious that there is any one point of doctrine, on which I am accustomed to speak in public, which is not here, incidently, if not professedly, laid before every Christian reader. Every serious man who peruses these will therefore see, in the clearest manner, what these doctrines are which I embrace and teach as the essentials of true religion.

2. But I am thoroughly sensible, these are not proposed in such a manner as some may expect. Nothing here appears in an elaborate, elegant, or oratorical dress. If it had been my desire or design to write thus, my leisure would not permit. But, in truth, I, at present, designed nothing less; for I now write, as I generally speak, *ad populum*—to the bulk of mankind, to those who neither relish nor understand the art of speaking; but who, notwithstanding, are competent judges of those truths which are necessary to present and future happiness. I mention this, that curious readers may spare themselves the labour of seeking for what they will not find.

3. I design plain truth for plain people: therefore, of set purpose, I abstain from all nice and philosophical speculations; from all perplexed and intricate reasonings; and, as far as possible, from even the show of learning, unless in sometimes citing the original Scripture. I labour to avoid all words which are not easy to be understood, all which are not used in common life; and, in particular, those kinds of technical terms that so frequently occur in Bodies of Divinity; those modes of speaking which men of reading are intimately acquainted with, but which to common people are an unknown tongue. Yet, I am not

assured, that I do not sometimes slide into them unawares; it is so extremely natural to imagine that a word which is familiar to ourselves is so to all the world.

4. Nay, my design is, in some sense, to forget all that ever I have read in my life. I mean to speak, in the general, as if I had never read one author, ancient or modern (always excepting the inspired). I am persuaded, that, on the one hand, this may be a means of enabling me more clearly to express the sentiments of my heart, while I simply follow the chain of my own thoughts, without entangling myself with those of other men; and that, on the other, I shall come with fewer weights upon my mind, with less of prejudice and prepossession, either to search for myself, or to deliver to others, the naked truths of the gospel.

5. To candid, reasonable men, I am not afraid to lay open what have been the inmost thoughts of my heart. I have thought, I am a creature of a day, passing through life as an arrow through the air. I am a spirit come from God, and returning to God: just hovering over the great gulf; till, a few moments hence, I am no more seen; I drop into an unchangeable eternity! I want to know one thing—the way to heaven; how to land safe on that happy shore. God Himself has condescended to teach the way; for this very end He came from heaven. He hath written it down in a book. O give me that book! At any price, give me the book of God! I have it: here is knowledge enough for me. Let me be *homo unius libri*. Here then I am, far from the busy ways of men. I sit down alone: only God is here. In His presence I open, I read His book; for this end, to find the way to heaven. Is there a doubt concerning the meaning of what I read? Does anything appear dark or intricate? I lift up my heart to the Father of Lights: 'Lord, is it not Thy word, "If any man lack wisdom, let him ask of God"? Thou "givest liberally, and upbraidest not." Thou hast said, "If any be willing to do Thy will, he shall know." I am willing to do, let me know, Thy will.' I then search after and consider parallel passages of Scripture, 'comparing spiritual things with spiritual.' I meditate thereon with all the attention and earnestness of which my mind is capable. If any doubt still remains, I consult those who are experienced in the things of God; and then the writings whereby, being dead, they yet speak. And what I thus learn, that I teach.

6. I have accordingly set down in the following sermons what I find in the Bible concerning the way to heaven; with a view to distinguish this way of God from all those which are the inventions of men. I have endeavoured to describe the true, the scriptural, experimental religion, so as to omit nothing which is a real part thereof, and to add nothing thereto which is not. And herein it is more especially my desire, first, to guard those who are just setting their faces toward heaven (and who, having little acquaintance with the things of God, are the more liable to be turned out of the way), from formality, from mere outside religion, which has almost driven heart-religion out of the world; and, secondly, to warn those who know the religion of the heart, the faith which worketh by love, lest at any time they make void the law through faith, and so fall back into the snare of the devil.

7. By the advice and at the request of some of my friends, I have prefixed to the other sermons contained in this volume, three sermons of my own, and one of my brother's, preached before the University of Oxford. My design required some discourses on those heads; and I preferred these before any others, as being a stronger answer than any which can be drawn up now, to those who have frequently asserted that we have changed our doctrine of late, and do not preach now what we did some years ago. Any man of understanding may now judge for himself, when he has compared the latter with the former sermons.

8. But some may say, I have mistaken the way myself, although I take upon me to teach it to others. It is probable many will think this; and it is very possible that I have. But I trust, whereinsoever I have mistaken, my mind is open to conviction. I sincerely desire to be better informed. I say to God and man, 'What I know not, teach thou me!'

9. Are you persuaded you see more clearly than me? It is not unlikely that you may. Then treat me as you would desire to be treated yourself upon a change of circumstances. Point me out a better way than I have yet known. Show me it is so, by plain proof of Scripture. And if I linger in the path I have been accustomed to tread, and am therefore unwilling to leave it, labour with me a little; take me by the hand, and lead me as I am able to bear. But be not displeased if I entreat you not to beat me down in order to

quicken my pace: I can go but feebly and slowly at best; then, I should not be able to go at all. May I not request of you, further, not to give me hard names, in order to bring me into the right way? Suppose I were ever so much in the wrong, I doubt this would not set me right. Rather, it would make me run so much the farther from you, and so get more and more out of the way.

10. Nay, perhaps, if you are angry, so shall I be too; and then there will be small hopes of finding the truth. If once 'anger arise, ηυτε καπωος (as Homer somewhere expresses it), this smoke will so dim the eyes of my soul, that I shall be able to see nothing clearly. For God's sake, if it be possible to avoid it, let us not provoke one another to wrath. Let us not kindle in each other this fire of hell; much less blow it up into a flame. If we could discern truth by that dreadful light, would it not be loss, rather than gain? For, how far is love, even with many wrong opinions, to be preferred before truth itself without love! We may die without the knowledge of many truths, and yet be carried into Abraham's bosom. But, if we die without love, what will knowledge avail? Just as much as it avails the devil and his angels.

The God of love forbid we should ever make the trial! May He prepare us for the knowledge of all truth, by filling our hearts with all His love, and with all joy and peace in believing!

SERMON I

SALVATION BY FAITH

PREACHED AT ST. MARY'S, OXFORD, BEFORE THE UNIVERSITY, ON JUNE 11, 1738

Five of the Standard Sermons were preached in St. Mary's before the University of Oxford; viz. Nos. I, II, IV, and XIII by John and III by Charles Wesley. The preachers were appointed from the various colleges in turn by the Vice-Chancellor, and all Masters of Arts of two or more years' standing, who were presbyters or deacons of the Church of England, were liable to be called upon to officiate. Wesley tells us (*Journal*, July 25, 1741) that his turn came about once in three years. The sermons were preached at two in the afternoon on all Sundays and at 10 a.m. on saints' days, except in the Long Vacation, and had to be delivered in English, except on certain special occasions, on which Latin was to be used. Notice of at least two months had to be given to the preacher, and he received a fee of three guineas. If any statement was made in the sermon contrary to the doctrine or discipline of the Church of England, the Vice-Chancellor had authority to demand a copy of the sermon, which was submitted to the Professors of Theology; and they had power to suspend the preacher from preaching again within the precincts of the University unless he recanted his statements. This power was exercised in the case of Wesley's Sermon IV, on Scriptural Christianity (q.v.). All Doctors, Masters, graduates, and scholars were required diligently to attend these services, unless they could find some reasonable excuse for their absence. See *Statuta Universitatis Oxoniensis Titulus XII, De Concionibus.*

This sermon was preached on June 11, 1738 (not June 18, as stated in the note to the sermon in *Works*, 1771). The *Journal* only says, under date June 8, 'On Saturday came to Stanton Harcourt' (a village in Oxfordshire, about six miles due west of Oxford, with a population of about 500 souls). 'Having preached faith in Christ there on Sunday the 11th, I went on to Oxford; and thence on Monday to London.' Apparently he tried over his discourse at Stanton Harcourt in the morning, and then went on to Oxford, and preached it there in the afternoon. The meeting in Aldersgate Street where Paul, Luther, and Wesley appear in such a significant conjunction, and where Wesley felt 'my heart strangely warmed. I felt I did trust in Christ, Christ alone for salvation, and an assurance was given me that He had taken away my sins, even *mine,* and saved *me* from the law of sin and death,' took place on May 24. His new experience was thus only eighteen days old when he uttered this great manifesto before the University. The Church of

17

the Blessed Virgin Mary in the High Street of Oxford has reverberated to many epoch-making utterances. Here Cranmer witnessed a good confession, before he went out to seal his faith with his blood at the stake near Balliol, where Latimer and Ridley had already suffered; here Newman and Pusey preached those sermons which led to the Catholic revival in the Church of England in the nineteenth century; but never have its ancient walls re-echoed words of more far-reaching importance in the history of religion than when on this day John Wesley blew the first trumpet-call of the Evangelical Revival.

This was not a new sermon composed for the occasion; Wesley had preached on May 14 at St. Ann's, Aldersgate, and at the Savoy Chapel, on 'free salvation by faith in the blood of Christ'—doubtless this sermon. Indeed, it was probably written in America. Note the denial of the possibility of good works before justification, the lack of personal passion in the definition of faith, the uncompromising statement in ii. 6 of the complete absence of sin in the believer, and the confusion of justification with regeneration—all marks of Wesley's earlier period. Still, it was a favourite discourse of his; and there are several records of his having preached it in the *Journal,* and in the sermon list up to the end of 1760: notably on his father's tombstone at Epworth on June 7, 1742. He re-wrote it entirely in 1765 and published it under the title of 'The Scripture Way of Salvation,' and placed it as No. XLIII in the 1771 edition. It is interesting to compare the two sermons. The divisions are the same; but in the second salvation is taken to include prevenient grace, justification, and sanctification, which is spoken of as identical with regeneration in its beginning but as going on gradually to entire sanctification. It is allowed that good works may be done before conversion, and are indeed remotely necessary to it, though not properly a condition of salvation. The doctrine that there is no sin in a believer is declared to be extremely mischievous, as blocking the way to the seeking of entire sanctification, with which the rest of the sermon is concerned.

By grace are ye saved through faith.—EPH. ii. 8.

I. ALL the blessings which God hath bestowed upon man are of His mere grace, bounty, or favour; His free, undeserved favour; favour altogether undeserved; man having no claim to the least of His mercies. It was free grace that 'formed man of the dust of the ground, and breathed into him a living soul,' and stamped on that soul the image of God, and 'put all things under his feet.' The same free grace continues to us, at this day, life, and breath, and all things. For there is nothing we are, or have, or do, which can deserve the least thing at God's hand. 'All our works, Thou, O God, hast wrought in us.' These, therefore, are so many more instances of free mercy: and whatever righteousness may be found in man, this is also the gift of God.

2. Wherewithal then shall a sinful man atone for any the least of his sins? With his own works? No. Were they ever so many or holy, they are not his own, but God's. But indeed they are all unholy and sinful themselves, so that every one of them needs a fresh atonement. Only corrupt fruit grows on a corrupt tree. And his heart is altogether corrupt and abominable; being 'come short of the glory of God,' the glorious righteousness at first impressed on his soul, after the image of his great Creator. Therefore, having nothing, neither righteousness nor works, to plead, his mouth is utterly stopped before God.

3. If then sinful men find favour with God, it is 'grace upon grace!' If God vouchsafe still to pour fresh blessings upon us, yea, the greatest of all blessings, salvation; what can we say to these things, but, 'Thanks be unto God for His unspeakable gift!' And thus it is. Herein 'God commendeth His love toward us, in that, while we were yet sinners, Christ died' to save us. 'By grace' then 'are ye saved through faith.' Grace is the source, faith the condition, of salvation.

Now, that we fall not short of the grace of God, it concerns us carefully to inquire—

I. WHAT FAITH IT IS THROUGH WHICH WE ARE SAVED.
II. WHAT IS THE SALVATION WHICH IS THROUGH FAITH.
III. HOW WE MAY ANSWER SOME OBJECTIONS.

I. What faith it is through which we are saved.

1. And, first, it is not barely the faith of a Heathen.

Now, God requireth of a Heathen to believe, 'that God is; that He is a rewarder of them that diligently seek Him'; and that He is to be sought by glorifying Him as God, by giving Him thanks for all things, and by a careful practice of moral virtue, of justice, mercy, and truth, toward their fellow creatures. A Greek or Roman, therefore, yea, a Scythian or Indian, was without excuse if he did not believe thus much: the being and attributes of God, a future state of reward and punishment, and the obligatory nature of moral virtue. For this is barely the faith of a Heathen.

2. Nor, secondly, is it the faith of a devil, though this goes much farther than that of a Heathen. For the devil believes not

only that there is a wise and powerful God, gracious to reward, and just to punish; but also, that Jesus is the Son of God, the Christ, the Saviour of the world. So we find him declaring, in express terms, 'I know Thee who Thou art; the Holy One of God' (Luke iv. 34). Nor can we doubt but that unhappy spirit believes all those words which came out of the mouth of the Holy One; yea, and whatsoever else was written by those holy men of old, of two of whom he was compelled to give that glorious testimony, 'These men are the servants of the most high God, who show unto you the way of salvation.' Thus much, then, the great enemy of God and man believes, and trembles in believing, —that God was made manifest in the flesh; that He will 'tread all enemies under His feet'; and that 'all Scripture was given by inspiration of God.' Thus far goeth the faith of a devil.

3. Thirdly. The faith through which we are saved, in that sense of the word which will hereafter be explained, is not barely that which the Apostles themselves had while Christ was yet upon earth; though they so believed on Him as to 'leave all and follow Him'; although they had then power to work miracles, to 'heal all manner of sickness, and all manner of disease'; yea, they had then 'power and authority over all devils'; and, which is beyond all this, were sent by their Master to 'preach the kingdom of God.'

4. What faith is it then through which we are saved? It may be answered, first, in general, it is a faith in Christ: Christ, and God through Christ, are the proper objects of it. Herein, therefore, it is sufficiently, absolutely distinguished from the faith either of ancient or modern Heathens. And from the faith of a devil it is fully distinguished by this: it is not barely a speculative, rational thing, a cold, lifeless assent, a train of ideas in the head; but also a disposition of the heart. For thus saith the Scripture, 'With the heart man believeth unto righteousness'; and, 'If thou shalt confess with thy mouth the Lord Jesus, and shalt believe with thy heart that God hath raised Him from the dead, thou shalt be saved.'

5. And herein does it differ from that faith which the Apostles themselves had while our Lord was on earth, that it acknowledges the necessity and merit of His death, and the power of His resurrection. It acknowledges His death as the only sufficient means of redeeming man from death eternal, and His resurrection as the restoration of us all to life and immortality; inasmuch as

He 'was delivered for our sins, and rose again for our justification.' Christian faith is, then, not only an assent to the whole gospel of Christ, but also a full reliance on the blood of Christ; a trust in the merits of His life, death, and resurrection; a recumbency upon Him as our atonement and our life, *as given for us,* and *living in us.* [It is a sure confidence which a man hath in God, that through the merits of Christ, *his* sins are forgiven, and *he* reconciled to the favour of God;] and, in consequence hereof, a closing with Him, and cleaving to Him, as our 'wisdom, righteousness, sanctification, and redemption,' or, in one word, our salvation.

II. What salvation it is, which is through this faith, is the second thing to be considered.

1. And, first, whatsoever else it imply, it is a present salvation. It is something attainable, yea, actually attained, on earth, by those who are partakers of this faith. For thus saith the Apostle to the believers at Ephesus, and in them to the believers of all ages, not, *Ye shall be* (though that also is true), but, '*Ye are saved* through faith.'

2. *Ye are saved* (to comprise all in one word) from sin. This is the salvation which is through faith. This is that great salvation foretold by the angel, before God brought His First-begotten into the world: 'Thou shalt call His name Jesus; for He shall save His people from their sins.' And neither here, nor in other parts of holy writ, is there any limitation or restriction. All His people, or, as it is elsewhere expressed, 'all that believe in Him,' He will save from all their sins; from original and actual, past and present sin, 'of the flesh and of the spirit.' Through faith that is in Him, they are saved both from the guilt and from the power of it.

3. First, from the guilt of all past sin: for, whereas all the world is guilty before God, insomuch that should He 'be extreme to mark what is done amiss, there is none that could abide it': and whereas, 'by the law is' only 'the knowledge of sin,' but no deliverance from it, so that, 'by' fulfilling 'the deeds of the law, no flesh can be justified in His sight': now, 'the righteousness of God, which is by faith of Jesus Christ, is manifested unto all that believe.' Now, 'they are justified freely by His grace, through the redemption that is in Jesus Christ.' 'Him God hath set forth to be a propitiation through faith in His blood, to declare His righteousness for (or by) the

remission of the sins that are past.' Now hath Christ taken away 'the curse of the law, being made a curse for us.' He hath 'blotted out the handwriting that was against us, taking it out of the way, nailing it to His cross.' 'There is therefore no condemnation now to them which' believe 'in Christ Jesus.'

4. And being saved from guilt, they are saved from fear. Not indeed from a filial fear of offending; but from all servile fear; from that fear which hath torment; from fear of punishment; from fear of the wrath of God, whom they now no longer regard as a severe Master, but as an indulgent Father. 'They have not received again the spirit of bondage, but the Spirit of adoption, whereby they cry, Abba Father: the Spirit itself also bearing witness with their spirits, that they are the children of God.' They are also saved from the fear, though not from the possibility, of falling away from the grace of God, and coming short of the great and precious promises. [They are sealed with the Holy Spirit of Promise, which is the earnest of their inheritance (Eph. i. 13).] Thus have they 'peace with God through our Lord Jesus Christ. They rejoice in hope of the glory of God. And the love of God is shed abroad in their hearts, through the Holy Ghost, which is given unto them.' And hereby they are persuaded (though perhaps not at all times, nor with the same fullness of persuasion), that 'neither death, nor life, nor things present, nor things to come, nor height, nor depth, nor any other creature shall be able to separate them from the love of God, which is in Christ Jesus our Lord.'

5. Again: through this faith they are saved from the power of sin, as well as from the guilt of it. So the Apostle declares, 'Ye know that He was manifested to take away our sins; and in Him is no sin. Whosoever abideth in Him sinneth not' (1 John iii. 5, &c.). Again: 'Little children, let no man deceive you. He that committeth sin is of the devil. Whosoever believeth is born of God. And whosoever is born of God doth not commit sin; for His seed remaineth in him: and he cannot sin, because he is born of God.' Once more: 'We know that whosoever is born of God sinneth not; but he that is begotten of God keepeth himself, and that wicked one toucheth him not' (I John v. 18).

6. He that is, by faith, born of God sinneth not (1) by any habitual sin; for all habitual sin is sin reigning: but sin cannot reign in any that believeth. Nor (2) by any wilful sin; for his will, while he

abideth in the faith, is utterly set against all sin, and abhorreth it as deadly poison. Nor (3) by any sinful desire; for he continually desireth the holy and perfect will of God; and any tendency to an unholy desire, he by the grace of God, stifleth in the birth. Nor (4) doth he sin by infirmities, whether in act, word, or thought; for his infirmities have no concurrence of his will; and without this they are not properly sins. Thus, 'he that is born of God doth not commit sin': and though he cannot say he hath not sinned, yet now 'he sinneth not.'

7. This then is the salvation which is through faith, even in the present world: a salvation from sin, and the consequences of sin, both often expressed in the word *justification*; which, taken in the largest sense, implies a deliverance from guilt and punishment, by the atonement of Christ actually applied to the soul of the sinner now believing on Him, and a deliverance from the [whole body] of sin, through Christ *formed in his heart*. So that he who is thus justified, or saved by faith, is indeed *born again*. He is *born again of the Spirit* unto a new life, which 'is hid with Christ in God.' [He is a new creature: old things are passed away: all things in him are become new.] And as a new-born babe he gladly receives the αδολον, '*sincere* milk of the word, and grows thereby'; going on in the might of the Lord his God, from faith to faith, from grace to grace, until at length, he comes unto 'a perfect man, unto the measure of the stature of the fullness of Christ.'

III. The first usual objection to this is,

1. That to preach salvation, or justification, by faith only, is to preach against holiness and good works. To which a short answer might be given: 'It would be so, if we spake, as some do, of a faith which was separate from these; but we speak of a faith which is not so, but [necessarily] productive of all good works, and all holiness.'

2. But it may be of use to consider it more at large; especially since it is no new objection, but as old as St. Paul's time: for even then it was asked, 'Do we not make void the law through faith?' We answer, first, all who preach not faith do manifestly make void the law; either directly and grossly, by limitations and comments that eat out all the spirit of the text; or indirectly, by not pointing out the only means whereby it is possible to perform it. Whereas, secondly, 'we establish the law,' both by

showing its full extent and spiritual meaning; and by calling all
to that living way, whereby 'the righteousness of the law may be
fulfilled in them.' These, while they trust in the blood of Christ
alone, use all the ordinances which He hath appointed, do all the
'good works which He had before prepared that they should
walk therein,' and enjoy and manifest all holy and heavenly
tempers, even the same mind that was in Christ Jesus.

3. But does not preaching this faith lead men into pride? We
answer, Accidentally it may: therefore ought every believer to be
earnestly cautioned, in the words of the great Apostle, 'Because
of unbelief,' the first branches 'were broken off; and thou
standest by faith. Be not high-minded, but fear. If God spared
not the natural branches, take heed lest He spare not thee.
Behold therefore the goodness and severity of God! On them
which fell, severity; but towards thee, goodness, if thou continue
in His goodness; otherwise thou also shalt be cut off.' And while
he continues therein, he will remember those words of St. Paul,
foreseeing and answering this very objection (Rom. iii. 27),
'Where is boasting then? It is excluded. By what law? of works?
Nay: but by the law of faith.' If a man were justified by his works,
he would have whereof to glory. But there is no glorying for him
'that worketh not, but believeth on Him that justifieth the
ungodly' (Rom. iv. 5). To the same effect are the words both
preceding and following the text (Eph. ii. 4, &c.): 'God, who is
rich in mercy, even when we were dead in sins, hath quickened
us together with Christ (by grace ye are saved), that He might
show the exceeding riches of His grace in His kindness toward
us through Christ Jesus. For by grace are ye saved through faith;
and that not of yourselves.' Of yourselves cometh neither your
faith nor your salvation: 'it is the gift of God'; the free,
undeserved gift; the faith through which ye are saved, as well as
the salvation which He of His own good pleasure, His mere
favour, annexes thereto. That ye believe, is one instance of His
grace; that believing ye are saved, another. 'Not of works, lest
any man should boast.' For all our works, all our righteousness,
which were before our believing, merited nothing of God but
condemnation; so far were they from deserving faith, which
therefore, whenever given, is not of works. Neither is salvation
of the works we do when we believe; for it is then God that
worketh in us: and, therefore, that He giveth us a reward for

what He Himself worketh, only commendeth the riches of His mercy, but leaveth us nothing whereof to glory.

4. However, may not the speaking thus of the mercy of God, as saving or justifying freely by faith only, encourage men in sin? Indeed, it may and will: many will 'continue in sin that grace may abound'; but their blood is upon their own head. The goodness of God ought to lead them to repentance; and so it will those who are sincere of heart. When they know there is yet forgiveness with Him, they will cry aloud that He would blot out their sins also, through faith which is in Jesus. And if they earnestly cry, and faint not; if they seek Him in all the means He hath appointed; if they refuse to be comforted till He come; 'He will come, and will not tarry.' And He can do much work in a short time. Many are the examples, in the Acts of the Apostles, of God's [shedding abroad] this faith in men's hearts, even like lightning falling from heaven. So in the same hour that Paul and Silas began to preach, the jailer repented, believed, and was baptized; as were three thousand, by St. Peter, on the day of Pentecost, who all repented and believed at his first preaching. And blessed be God, there are now many living proofs that He is still 'mighty to save.'

5. Yet to the same truth, placed in another view, a quite contrary objection is made: 'If a man cannot be saved by all that he can do, this will drive men to despair.' True, to despair of being saved by their own works, their own merits or righteousness. And so it ought; for none can trust in the merits of Christ, till he has utterly renounced his own. He that 'goeth about to establish his own righteousness' cannot receive the righteousness of God. The righteousness which is of faith cannot be given him while he trusteth in that which is of the law.

6. But this, it is said, is an uncomfortable doctrine. The devil spoke like himself, that is, without either truth or shame, when he dared to suggest to men that it is such. It is the only comfortable one, it is 'very full of comfort,' to all self-destroyed, self-condemned sinners. That 'whosoever believeth on Him shall not be ashamed: that the same Lord over all is rich unto all that call upon Him': here is comfort, high as heaven, stronger than death! What! Mercy for all? For Zacchaeus, a public robber? For Mary Magdalene, a common harlot? Methinks I hear one say, 'Then I, even I, may hope for mercy!' And so thou

mayest, thou afflicted one, whom none hath comforted! God will not cast out thy prayer. Nay, perhaps He may say the next hour, 'Be of good cheer, thy sins are forgiven thee'; so forgiven, that they shall reign over thee no more; yea, and that 'the Holy Spirit shall bear witness with thy spirit that thou art a child of God.' O glad tidings! tidings of great joy, which are sent unto all people! 'Ho, every one that thirsteth, come ye to the waters: come ye, and buy, without money and without price.' Whatsoever your sins be, 'though red like crimson,' though more than the hairs of your head, 'return ye unto the Lord, and He will have mercy upon you; and to our God, for He will abundantly pardon.'

7. When no more objections occur, then we are simply told that salvation by faith only ought not to be preached as the first doctrine, or, at least, not to be preached to all. But what saith the Holy Ghost? 'Other foundation can no man lay than that which is laid, even Jesus Christ.' So then, that 'whosoever believeth on Him shall be saved,' is, and must be, the foundation of all our preaching; that is, must be preached first. 'Well, but not to all.' To whom then are we not to preach it? Whom shall we except? The poor? Nay; they have a peculiar right to have the gospel preached unto them. The unlearned? No. God hath revealed these things unto unlearned and ignorant men from the beginning. The young? By no means. 'Suffer these,' in any wise, to come unto Christ, 'and forbid them not.' The sinners? Least of all. 'He came not to call the righteous, but sinners to repentance.' Why then, if any, we are to except the rich, the learned, the reputable, the moral men. And, it is true, they too often except themselves from hearing; yet we must speak the words of our Lord. For thus the tenor of our commission runs, 'Go and preach the gospel to every creature.' If any man wrest it, or any part of it, to his destruction, he must bear his own burden. But still, 'as the Lord liveth, whatsoever the Lord saith unto us, that we will speak.'

8. At this time, more especially, will we speak, that 'by grace are ye saved through faith': because, never was the maintaining this doctrine more seasonable than it is at this day. Nothing but this can effectually prevent the increase of the Romish delusion among us. It is endless to attack, one by one, all the errors of that Church. But salvation by faith strikes at the root, and all fall at

once where this is established. It was this doctrine, which our Church justly calls *the strong rock and the Christian religion,* that first drove Popery out of these kingdoms; and it is this alone can keep it out. Nothing but this can give a check to that immorality which hath 'overspread the land as a flood.' Can you empty the great deep, drop by drop? Then you may reform us by dissuasives from particular vices. But let the 'righteousness which is of God by faith' be brought in, and so shall its proud waves be stayed. Nothing but this can stop the mouths of those who 'glory in their shame, and openly deny the Lord that bought them.' They can talk as sublimely of the law, as he that hath it written by God in his heart. To hear them speak on this head might incline one to think they were not far from the kingdom of God: but take them out of the law into the gospel; begin with the righteousness of faith; with Christ, 'the end of the law to every one that believeth'; and those who but now appeared almost, if not altogether, Christians, stand confessed the sons of perdition; as far from life and salvation (God be merciful unto them!) as the depth of hell from the height of heaven.

9. For this reason the adversary so rages whenever 'salvation by faith' is declared to the world: for this reason did he stir up earth and hell, to destroy those who first preached it. And for the same reason, knowing that faith alone could overturn the foundations of his kingdom, did he call forth all his forces, and employ all his arts of lies and calumny, to affright [that champion of the Lord of hosts,] Martin Luther, from reviving it. Nor can we wonder thereat; for, as that man of God observes, 'How would it enrage a proud, strong man armed, to be stopped and set at nought by a little child coming against him with a reed in his hand!' especially when he knew that little child would surely overthrow him, and tread him under foot. Even so, Lord Jesus! Thus hath Thy strength been ever 'made perfect in weakness'! Go forth then, thou little child that believest in Him, and His 'right hand shall teach thee terrible things!' Though thou art helpless and weak as an infant of days, the strong man shall not be able to stand before thee. Thou shalt prevail over him, and subdue him, and overthrow him, and trample him under thy feet. Thou shalt march on, under the great Captain of thy salvation 'conquering and to conquer,' until all thine

enemies are destroyed, and 'death is swallowed up in victory.'

Now, thanks be to God, which giveth us the victory through our Lord Jesus Christ; to whom, with the Father and the Holy Ghost, be blessing, and glory, and wisdom, and thanksgiving, and honour, and power, and might, for ever and ever. Amen.

SERMON II

THE ALMOST CHRISTIAN

PREACHED AT ST. MARY'S, OXFORD, BEFORE THE UNIVERSITY ON JULY 25, 1741

This sermon was preached on Sunday afternoon at two o'clock. Wesley says (*Journal* of this date): 'It being my turn (which comes about once in three years) I preached at St. Mary's before the University. So numerous a congregation (from whatever motives they came) I have seldom seen at Oxford. My text was the confession of poor Agrippa.' He had already preached the same sermon in Charles Square, London. In the open air on June 28. He had intended to preach before the University the sermon on Isaiah i. 21, 'How is the faithful city become a harlot!' which is published in the later editions of Wesley's *Works* as No. CXXXIV. It was found after his death in English, dated June 24, 1741; and also in Latin. Dr. Adam Clarke supplemented the imperfect English copy from the Latin for publication. Wesley read it on June 28 to Lady Huntingdon; but she dissuaded him from preaching it at St. Mary's. It was an outspoken attack on the doctrine and practice of the University, covering much the same ground as Section IV of the sermon on Scriptural Christianity, preached in 1744, for which John Wesley was excluded thereafter from the pulpit of St. Mary's, but expressed in much more violent language. The Deists are branded as 'the first-born of Satan'; Tillotson and Bull are criticized by name as having endeavoured to 'sap the very foundation of our Church' by their teaching on justification and holiness; 'the faith of a devil and the life of a heathen make up what most men call a *good Christian*' in Oxford. Levity in College chapel, Sabbath-breaking, novel-reading and gambling, idleness ('O what is so scarce as learning save religion!' he exclaims), non-observance of the Statutes, perjury in the subscription to the Articles and Homilies of the Church, are all vehemently denounced, to say nothing of the loss of the very notion of religion. There was much justification for what Wesley proposed to say; but undoubtedly her ladyship's advice was prudent. Consequently he decided to preach The Almost Christian and re-wrote it for the occasion in his rooms at Lincoln College. He published it later in the year.

No wonder there was a large congregation. Since his last appearance in St. Mary's three years before, John Wesley had become the best known and the most abused man in England. He had been excluded from all the churches in London save four; he had begun the practice of preaching in the open air; he had founded the 'Societies' which were the germ of the Methodist Church; his preaching had been attended by strange bodily convulsions both in London and Bristol; he had acquired and opened for worship the Foundery on Windmill Hill, north-west of Finsbury Square; love-feasts (the very name of which suggested all sorts of filthy attacks), and watch-night services had been started; laymen had been permitted to exhort and preach; the papers were full of abuse of both Wesley and the Methodists. It is surprising that the University authorities allowed him to preach in St. Mary's; it is not at all surprising that Oxford flocked to see and hear him.

It is hardly necessary to point out that the text will not bear Wesley's interpretation; it may mean 'With but little persuasion thou wouldest fain make me a Christian'; or 'In a little time, &c.'; but certainly not 'Almost.' And, even accepting the A.V. translation, Agrippa does not say 'Thou persuadest me to be an almost Christian,' but 'Almost thou persuadest me to be a Christian'—a very different thing. However, Wesley attempts no exposition of his text; it is used merely as a motto, and 'poor Agrippa' is thrown overboard before the vessel has weighed anchor, and is never picked up again. The phrase itself is doubtful English; though Southey adopted the idiom and called himself 'an almost Quaker.'

Almost thou Persuadest me to be a Christian.—ACTS xxvi. 28.

AND many there are who go thus far: ever since the Christian religion was in the world, there have been many in every age and nation who were almost persuaded to be Christians. But seeing it avails nothing before God to go *only thus far,* it highly imports us to consider,—

I. WHAT IS IMPLIED IN BEING ALMOST
II. WHAT IN BEING ALTOGETHER, A CHRISTIAN.

I. (i.) 1. Now, in the being *almost a Christian* is implied, first, heathen honesty. No one, I suppose, will make any question of this; especially, since by heathen honesty here, I mean, not that which is recommended in the writings of their philosophers only, but such as the common Heathens expected one of another, and many of them actually practised. By the rules of this they were taught that they ought not to be unjust; not to take away their neighbour's goods, either by robbery or theft; not to oppress the poor, neither to use extortion toward any; not to cheat or overreach either the poor or rich, in whatsoever commerce they had with them; to defraud no man of his right; and, if it were possible, to owe no man anything.

2. Again: the common Heathens allowed, that some regard was to be paid to truth, as well as to justice. And, accordingly,

they not only held him in abomination who was foresworn, who called God to witness to a lie; but him also who was known to be a slanderer of his neighbour, who falsely accused any man. And, indeed, little better did they esteem wilful liars of any sort; accounting them the disgrace of human kind, and the pests of society.

3. Yet again: there was a sort of love and assistance which they expected one from another. They expected whatever assistance any one could give another, without prejudice to himself. And this they extended not only to those little offices of humanity which are performed without any expense or labour, but likewise to the feeding the hungry, if they had food to spare; the clothing the naked with their own superfluous raiment; and, in general, the giving, to any that needed, such things as they needed not themselves. Thus far, in the lowest account of it, heathen honesty went; the first thing implied in the being *almost a Christian.*

(ii.) 4. A second thing implied in the being *almost a Christian* is, the having a form of godliness; of that godliness which is prescribed in the gospel of Christ; the having the *outside of a real Christian.* Accordingly, the *almost Christian* does nothing which the gospel forbids. He taketh not the name of God in vain; he blesseth, and curseth not; he sweareth not at all, but his communication is, yea, yea; nay, nay. He profanes not the day of the Lord, nor suffers it to be profaned, even by the stranger that is within his gates. He not only avoids all actual adultery, fornication, and uncleanness, but every word or look that either directly or indirectly tends thereto; nay, and all idle words, abstaining both from all detraction, backbiting, talebearing, evil speaking, and from 'all foolish talking and jesting'—ευτραπελια, a kind of virtue in the heathen moralist's account—briefly, from all conversation that is not 'good to the use of edifying,' and that, consequently, 'grieves the Holy Spirit of God, whereby we are sealed to the day of redemption.'

5. He abstains from 'wine wherein is excess'; from revellings and gluttony. He avoids, as much as in him lies, all strife and contention, continually endeavouring to live peaceably with all men. And, if he suffer wrong, he avengeth not himself, neither returns evil for evil. He is no railer, no brawler, no scoffer, either at the faults or infirmities of his neighbour. He does not willingly

wrong, hurt, or grieve any man; but in all things acts and speaks by that plain rule, 'Whatsoever thou wouldest not he should do unto thee, that do not thou to another.'

6. And in doing good he does not confine himself to cheap and easy offices of kindness, but labours and suffers for the profit of many, that by all means he may help some. In spite of toil or pain, 'whatsoever his hand findeth to do, he doeth it with all his might'; whether it be for his friends, or for his enemies; for the evil, or for the good. For being 'not slothful' in this, or in any 'business,' as he 'hath opportunity' he doeth 'good,' all manner of good, 'to all men'; and to their souls as well as their bodies. He reproves the wicked, instructs the ignorant, confirms the wavering, quickens the good, and comforts the afflicted. He labours to awaken those that sleep; to lead those whom God hath already awakened to the 'Fountain opened for sin and for uncleanness,' that they may wash therein and be clean; and to stir up those who are saved through faith, to adorn the gospel of Christ in all things.

7. He that hath the form of godliness uses also the means of grace; yea, all of them, and at all opportunities. He constantly frequents the house of God; and that, not as the manner of some is, who come into the presence of the Most High, either loaded with gold and costly apparel, or in all the gaudy vanity of dress, and either by their unseasonable civilities to each other, or the impertinent gaiety of their behaviour, disclaim all pretensions to the form as well as to the power of godliness. Would to God there were none even among ourselves who fall under the same condemnation! who come into this house, it may be, gazing about, or with all the signs of the most listless, careless indifference, though sometimes they may *seem* to use a prayer to God for His blessing on what they are entering upon; who, during that awful service, are either asleep, or reclined in the most convenient posture for it; or, as though they supposed God was asleep talking with one another, or looking round, as utterly void of employment. Neither let these be accused of the form of godliness. No; he who has even this, behaves with seriousness and attention, in every part of that solemn service. More especially, when he approaches the table of the Lord, it is not with a light or careless behaviour, but with an air, gesture, and deportment which speaks nothing else but 'God be merciful to me a sinner!'

8. To this, if we add the constant use of family prayer, by those who are masters of families, and the setting times apart for private addresses to God, with a daily seriousness of behaviour; he who uniformly practises this outward religion has the form of godliness. There needs but one thing more in order to his being *almost a Christian,* and that is, sincerity.

(iii.) 9. By sincerity I mean, a real, inward principle of religion, from whence these outward actions flow. And, indeed, if we have not this, we have not heathen honesty; no, not so much of it as will answer the demand of a heathen Epicurean poet. Even this poor wretch, in his sober intervals, is able to testify,

> *Oderunt peccare boni, virtutis amore;*
> *Oderunt peccare mali, formidine poenae,*

So that, if a man only abstains from doing evil in order to avoid punishment, *Non pasces in cruce corvos* saith the Pagan; there, 'thou hast thy reward.' But even he will not allow such a harmless man as this to be so much as a *good Heathen.* If, then, any man, from the same motive, viz. to avoid punishment, to avoid the loss of his friends, or his gain, or his reputation, should not only abstain from doing evil, but also do ever so much good; yea, and use all the means of grace; yet we could not with any propriety say, this man is even *almost a Christian!* If he has no better principle in his heart, he is only a hypocrite altogether.

10. Sincerity, therefore, is necessarily implied in the being *almost a Christian;* a real design to serve God, a hearty desire to do His will. It is necessarily implied, that a man have a sincere view of pleasing God in all things; in all his conversation; in all his actions; in all he does or leaves undone. This design, if any man be *almost a Christian,* runs through the whole tenor of his life. This is the moving principle, both in his doing good, his abstaining from evil, and his using the ordinances of God.

11. But here it will probably be inquired, 'Is it possible that any man living should go so far as this, and, nevertheless, be *only almost a Christian?* What more than this can be implied in the being *a Christian altogether?* I answer, first, that it is possible to go thus far, and yet be but *almost a Christian,* I learn, not only from the oracles of God, but also from the sure testimony of experience.

12. Brethren, great is 'my boldness towards you in this behalf.' And 'forgive me this wrong,' if I declare my own folly upon the house-top, for yours and the gospel's sake.—Suffer me, then, to speak freely of myself, even as of another man. I am content to be abased, so ye may be exalted, and to be yet more vile for the glory of my Lord.

13. I did go thus far for many years, as many of this place can testify; using diligence to eschew all evil, and to have a conscience void of offence; redeeming the time; buying up every opportunity of doing all good to all men; constantly and carefully using all the public and all the private means of grace; endeavouring after a steady seriousness of behaviour, at all times and in all places; and God is my record, before whom I stand, doing all this in sincerity; having a real design to serve God; a hearty desire to do His will in all things; to please Him who had called me to 'fight the good fight,' and to 'lay hold on eternal life.' Yet my own conscience beareth me witness in the Holy Ghost, that all this time I was but *almost a Christian*.

II. If it be inquired, 'What more than this is implied in the being *altogether a Christian?*' I answer,

(i.) 1. First, The love of God. For thus saith His word, 'Thou shalt love the Lord thy God with all thy heart, and with all thy soul, and with all thy mind, and with all thy strength.' Such a love [of God] is this, as engrosses the whole heart, as takes up all the affections, as fills the entire capacity of the soul, and employs the utmost extent of all its faculties. He that thus loves the Lord his God, his spirit continually 'rejoiceth in God his Saviour.' His delight is in the Lord, his Lord and his All, to whom 'in everything he giveth thanks. All his desire is unto God, and to the remembrance of His name.' His heart is ever crying out, 'Whom have I in heaven but Thee? and there is none upon earth that I desire beside Thee.' Indeed, what can he desire beside God? Not the world, or the things of the world: for he is crucified to the world, and the world crucified to him.' He is crucified to 'the desire of the flesh, the desire of the eye, and the pride of life.' Yea, he is dead to pride of every kind: for 'love is not puffed up'; but 'he that dwelling in love, dwelleth in God, and God in him,' is less than nothing in his own eyes.

(ii.) 2. The second thing implied in the being *altogether a*

Christian is, the love of our neighbour. For thus said our Lord, in the following words, 'Thou shalt love thy neighbour as thyself.' If any man ask, 'Who is my neighbour?' we reply, Every man in the world; every child of His who is the Father of the spirits of all flesh. Nor may we in any wise except our enemies, or the enemies of God and their own souls. But every Christian loveth these also as himself, yea, 'as Christ loved us.' He that would more fully understand what manner of love this is, may consider St. Paul's description of it. It is 'long-suffering and kind.' It 'envieth not.' It is not rash or hasty in judging. It 'is not puffed up'; but maketh him that loves, the least, the servant, of all. Love 'doth not behave itself unseemly'; but becometh 'all things to all men.' She 'seeketh not her own'; but only the good of others, that they may be saved. 'Love is not provoked.' It casteth out wrath, which he who hath is [not made perfect] in love. 'It thinketh no evil. It rejoiceth not in iniquity, but rejoiceth in the truth. It covereth all things, believeth all things, hopeth all things, endureth all things.'

(iii.) 3. There is yet one thing more that may be separately considered, though it cannot actually be separate from the preceding, which is implied in the being *altogether a Christian*; and that is the ground of all, even faith. Very excellent things are spoken of this throughout the oracles of God. 'Every one,' saith the beloved disciple, 'that believeth is born of God.' 'To as many as received Him, gave He power to become the sons of God, even to them that believe in His name.' And 'this is the victory that overcometh the world, even our faith.' Yea, our Lord Himself declares, 'He that believeth in the Son hath everlasting life; and cometh not into condemnation, but is passed from death unto life.'

4. But here let no man deceive his own soul. 'It is diligently to be noted, the faith which bringeth not forth repentance, and love, and all good works, is not that right living faith [which is here spoken of] but a dead and devilish one. For even the devils believe that Christ was born of a virgin; that He wrought all kinds of miracles, declaring Himself very God; that, for our sakes, He suffered a most painful death, to redeem us from death everlasting; that He rose again the third day; that He ascended into heaven, and sitteth at the right hand of the Father, and at the end of the world shall come again to judge

both the quick and dead. These articles of our faith the devils believe, and so they believe all that is written in the Old and New Testament. And yet for all this faith, they be but devils. They remain still in their damnable estate, lacking the very true Christian faith.'

5. 'The right and true Christian faith is' (to go on in the words of our own Church), 'not only to believe that Holy Scripture and the Articles of our Faith are true, but also to have a sure trust and confidence to be saved from everlasting damnation by Christ. It is a sure trust and confidence which a man hath in God, that, by the merits of Christ, his sins are forgiven, and he reconciled to the favour of God; whereof doth follow a loving heart, to obey His commandments.'

6. Now, whosoever has this faith, which 'purifies the heart' (by the power of God, who dwelleth therein) from pride, anger, desire, 'from all unrighteousness,' from 'all filthiness of flesh and spirit'; which fills it with love stronger than death, both to God and to all mankind; love that doeth the works of God, glorying to spend and to be spent for all men, and that endureth with joy, not only the reproach of Christ, the being mocked, despised, and hated of all men, but whatsoever the wisdom of God permits the malice of men or devils to inflict,—whosoever has this faith, thus working by love, is not almost only, but altogether, a Christian.

7. But who are the living witnesses of these things? I beseech you, brethren, as in the presence of that God before whom 'hell and destruction are without a covering—how much more the hearts of the children of men?'—that each of you would ask his own heart, 'Am I of that number? Do I so far practise justice, mercy, and truth, as even the rules of heathen honesty require? If so, have I the very *outside* of a Christian? the form of godliness? Do I abstain from evil—from whatsoever is forbidden in the written Word of God? Do I, whatever good my hand findeth to do, do it with my might? Do I seriously use all the ordinances of God at all opportunities? And is all this done with a sincere design and desire to please God in all things?'

8. Are not many of you conscious that you never came thus far; that you have not been even *almost a Christian;* that you have not come up to the standard of heathen honesty; at least, not to the form of Christian godliness?—much less hath God seen

sincerity in you, a real design of pleasing Him in all things. You never so much as intended to devote all your words and works, your business, studies, diversions, to His glory. You never even designed or desired, that whatsoever you did should be done 'in the name of the Lord Jesus,' and as such should be 'a spiritual sacrifice, acceptable to God through Christ.'

9. But, supposing you had, do good designs and good desires make a Christian? By no means, unless they are brought to good effect. 'Hell is paved,' saith one, 'with good intentions.' The great question of all, then, still remains. Is the love of God shed abroad in your heart? Can you cry out, 'My God, and my All'? Do you desire nothing but Him? Are you happy in God? Is He your glory, your delight, your crown of rejoicing? And is this commandment written in your heart,' That he who loveth God love his brother also'? Do you then love your neighbour as yourself? Do you love every man, even your enemies, even the enemies of God, as your own soul? as Christ loved you? Yea, dost thou believe that Christ loved thee, and gave Himself for thee? Hast thou faith in His blood? Believest thou the Lamb of God hath taken away thy sins, and cast them as a stone into the depth of the sea? that He hath blotted out the handwriting that was against thee, taking it out of the way, nailing it to His cross? Hast thou indeed redemption through His blood, even the remission of thy sins? And doth His Spirit bear witness with thy spirit, that thou art a child of God?

10. The God and Father of our Lord Jesus Christ, who now standeth in the midst of us, knoweth, that if any man die without this faith and this love, good it were for him that he had never been born. Awake, then, thou that sleepest, and call upon thy God: call in the day when He may be found. Let Him not rest, till He make His 'goodness to pass before thee'; till He proclaim unto thee the name of the Lord, 'The Lord, the Lord God, merciful and gracious, long-suffering, and abundant in goodness and truth, keeping mercy for thousands, forgiving iniquity, and transgression, and sin.' Let no man persuade thee, by vain words, to rest short of this prize of thy high calling. But cry unto Him day and night, who, 'while we were without strength, died for the ungodly,' until thou knowest in whom thou hast believed, and canst say, 'My Lord, and my God!' Remember, 'always to pray, and not to faint,' till thou also canst

lift up thy hand unto heaven, and declare to Him that liveth for ever and ever, 'Lord, Thou knowest all things, Thou knowest that I love Thee.'

11. May we all thus experience what it is to be, not almost only, but altogether Christians; being justified freely by His grace, through the redemption that is in Jesus; knowing we have peace with God through Jesus Christ; rejoicing in hope of the glory of God; and having the love of God shed abroad in our hearts, by the Holy Ghost given unto us!

SERMON III

AWAKE, THOU THAT SLEEPEST

PREACHED ON SUNDAY, APRIL 4, 1742, BEFORE THE UNIVERSITY OF OXFORD

BY THE REV. CHARLES WESLEY, M.A.,
STUDENT OF CHRIST CHURCH

We may be thankful that Wesley included this sermon in his first four volumes, although it was not preached by him but by his brother Charles. It is the only sermon by Charles Wesley that was published during his lifetime, except that on The Cause and Cure of Earthquakes, written in 1750 (No. CXXIX in the later editions of *Wesley's Sermons*), and the only other examples of his pulpit eloquence are a dozen sermons published by his widow in 1816. On Trinity Sunday, May 28, 1738, a week after his conversion, he records in his journal, 'I then began writing my first sermon in the name of Christ my Prophet'—that is, his first sermon after his new experience; for he had been preaching frequently since his ordination in 1735, and some of his Frederica discourses are contained in Mrs. Wesley's volume. Until October 20, 1738, he always wrote his sermons in full, and read them from the manuscript; but on that day, being at St. Antholin's church at the corner of Budge Row and Watling Street, and finding the congregation very small, he 'thought of preaching extempore; and spake on Justification from Rom. iii. for three-quarters of an hour, without hesitation.' On February 11 of the next year he repeated the experiment at Islington Church, and preached on blind Bartimaeus 'without notes.' After he began his itinerant work, he almost always preached extempore; and, if Adam Clarke is to be trusted, he occasionally had his 'bad times'; but usually he spoke with great freedom and power, and Whitehead testifies that 'his sermons were generally more awakening and useful' than those of his brother John. Henry Moore thinks that even his University sermon 'falls short of many discourses which he delivered in the highways'; and says: 'Where only God and conscious sinners were before him, it seemed as if nothing could withstand the wisdom and power with which he spake: to use the expression of a pious man, "It was all thunder and lightning." ' Again he says: 'John's preaching was all principles; Charles's was all aphorisms.' In 1766 John wrote to him: 'In connexion I beat you; but in strong, pointed sentences you beat me.' In other words, John was a logician; Charles a poet. In this and the Earthquake sermon no one can fail to admire the power of vivid description, the continuous and most telling use of scriptural phrases, the vehement note of personal appeal, the tremendous culminative effect of the successive short sentences, which come like a spray of bullets from a machine-gun. The bewildering swiftness of his rapier-play beats down his opponent's guard and does not allow him an instant to recover himself. He gains his point, not by dint of argument, but by the irresistible rush of the torrent of his emotion.

We have from the pen of Joseph Williams, a pious dissenter of Kidderminster, a description of a sermon preached in the open air at Bristol by Charles Wesley in September 1739: 'Standing on a table in a field, the preacher, with eyes and hands lifted up to heaven, prayed with uncommon fervour and fluency. He then preached about an hour in such a manner as I scarce ever heard any man preach. Though I have heard many a finer sermon according to the common taste or acceptation of sermons, I never heard any man discover such evident signs of a vehement desire, or labour so earnestly to convince his hearers, that they were all by nature in a sinful, lost, undone state. He showed how great a change faith in Christ would produce in the whole man. . . . With uncommon fervour he acquitted himself as an ambassador of Christ. . . . And although he used no notes, nor had anything in his hand but a Bible, yet he delivered his thoughts in a rich, copious variety of expression, and with so much propriety, that I could not observe anything incoherent or inanimate through the whole performance, which he concluded with singing, prayer, and the usual benediction.' He goes on to describe the evening meeting, in which Charles Wesley expounded part of the twelfth chapter of St. John 'in a sweet, savoury, spiritual manner,' and is filled with admiration of the fervent prayers and the heavenly singing which concluded the service. (*Meth. Mag.*, 1815, p. 457.)

This sermon was preached in St. Mary's before the University of Oxford on Sunday afternoon, April 4, 1742. Unfortunately, Charles's Journal is missing just at this time, but from John's we learn that Charles left London for Oxford on the previous Wednesday. John remained in London, and records: 'About two in the afternoon, being the time my brother was preaching at Oxford, before the University, I desired a few persons to meet with me and join in prayer.' Vicesimus Knox, in his *Lucubrations*, No. 131 (1780), complains of the dullness of the University sermons; 'and yet,' he says, 'when it is considered that the greater part of the audience in the University church always consists of very young men and of the common parishioners, I know not whether this apology' (viz. that these sermons are merely didactic) 'can fully justify the languor of a pulpit dissertation'; he thinks a 'lively and more energetic address to the hearers' would be an improvement; and laments that 'eloquence is less aimed at in academical pulpits than ingenious, erudite, and *inoffensive* disquisition.' He would not have found anything to complain of on this score in Charles Wesley's sermon!

In 1748 was published the *Foreigner's Companion through the Universities of Oxford and Cambridge*, by Matthew Salmon, one of the original members of the Holy Club, who later quarrelled with the Wesleys. On p. 25 he says: 'The times of the day the University go to this church, are ten in the morning and two in the afternoon on Sundays and holidays, the sermon usually lasting about half an hour. But when I happened to be in Oxford in 1742, Mr. Wesley, the Methodist, of Christ Church, entertained his audience two hours, and, having insulted and abused all degrees, from the highest to the lowest, was in a manner hissed out of the pulpit by the lads.' Charles Wesley in his Journal, April 15, 1750, quotes this passage; and adds: 'And high time for them to do so, if the historian said true; but, unfortunately for him, I measured the time by my watch, and it was within the hour; I abused neither high nor low, as my sermon, in print, will prove; neither was I hissed out of the pulpit, or treated with the least incivility, either by young or old. What, then, shall I say to my old high-Church friend, whom I once so much admired? I must rank him among the apocryphal writers, such as the judicious Dr. Mather, the wary Bishop Burnet, and the most modest Mr. Oldmixon.' (Apparently Charles had been reading Pope's *Epistle to Arbuthnot,* published 1735:

> 'From these the world will judge of men and books,
> Not from the Burnets, Oldmixons, and Cooks.')

The sermon was published by Strahan the same year and went through at least thirty-six editions. Thomas Jackson says: 'It is doubtful whether any sermon in the English language, or in any language upon earth, has passed through so many editions, or has been a means of so much spiritual good.'

Awake, thou that sleepest, and arise from the dead, and Christ shall give you light.—EPH. v. 14.

IN discoursing on these words, I shall, with the help of God—

   I. DESCRIBE THE SLEEPERS, TO WHOM THEY ARE SPOKEN:
  II. ENFORCE THE EXHORTATION, 'AWAKE, THOU THAT SLEEPEST, AND ARISE FROM THE DEAD': AND,
III. EXPLAIN THE PROMISE MADE TO SUCH AS DO AWAKE AND ARISE: 'CHRIST SHALL GIVE THEE LIGHT.'

I. 1. And first, as to the sleepers here spoken to. By sleep is signified the natural state of man; that deep sleep of the soul, into which the sin of Adam hath cast all who spring from his loins; that supineness, indolence, and stupidity, that insensibility of his real condition, wherein every man comes into the world, and continues till the voice of God awakes him.

2. Now, 'they that sleep, sleep in the night.' The state of nature is a state of utter darkness; a state wherein 'darkness covers the earth, and gross darkness the people.' The poor unawakened sinner, how much knowledge soever he may have

apathy

as to other things, has no knowledge of himself: in this respect 'he knoweth nothing yet as he ought to know.' He knows not that he is a fallen spirit, whose only business in the present world is, to recover from his fall, to regain that image of God wherein he wascreated. He sees *no necessity* for the *one thing needful,* even that inward universal change, that 'birth from above,' figured out by baptism, which is the beginning of that total renovation, that sanctification of spirit, soul, and body, 'without which no man shall see the Lord.'

3. Full of all diseases as he is, he fancies himself in perfect health. Fast bound in misery and iron, he dreams that he is [happy and] at liberty. He says, 'Peace! Peace!' while the devil, as 'a strong man armed,' is in full possession of his soul. He sleeps on still, and takes his rest, though hell is moved from beneath to meet him; though the pit from whence there is no return hath opened its mouth to swallow him up. A fire is kindled around him, yet he knoweth it not; yea, it burns him, yet he lays it not to heart.

4. By one who sleeps, we are, therefore, to understand (and would to God we might all understand it!) a sinner satisfied in his sins; contented to remain in his fallen state, to live and die without the image of God; one who is ignorant both of his disease, and of the only remedy for it; one who never was warned, or never regarded the warning voice of God, 'to flee from the wrath to come'; one that never yet saw he was in danger of hell-fire, or cried out in the earnestness of his soul, 'What must I do to be saved?'

5. If this sleeper be not outwardly vicious, his sleep is usually the deepest of all: whether he be of the Laodicean spirit, 'neither cold nor hot,' but a quiet, rational, inoffensive, good-natured professor of the religion of his fathers; or whether he be zealous and orthodox, and, 'after the most straitest sect of our religion,' live 'a Pharisee'; that is, according to the scriptural account, one that justifies himself; one that labours to establish his own righteousness, as the ground of his acceptance with God.

6. This is he, who, 'having a form of godliness, denies the power thereof'; yea, and probably reviles it, wheresoever it is found, as mere extravagance and delusion. Meanwhile, the wretched self-deceiver thanks God, that he is 'not as other men are; adulterers, unjust, extortioners'; no, he doeth no wrong to

any man. He 'fasts twice in a week,' uses all the means of grace, is constant at church and sacrament; yea, and 'gives tithes of all that he has'; does all the good that he can: 'touching the righteousness of the law,' he is 'blameless': he wants nothing of godliness, but the power; nothing of religion, but the spirit; nothing of Christianity, but the truth and the life.

7. But know ye not, that, however highly esteemed among men such a Christian as this may be, he is an abomination in the sight of God, and an heir of every woe which the Son of God, yesterday, to-day, and for ever, denounces against 'scribes and Pharisees, hypocrites'? He hath 'made clean the outside of the cup and the platter,' but within is full of all filthiness. 'An evil disease cleaveth still unto him, so that his inward parts are very wickedness.' Our Lord fitly compares him to a 'painted sepulchre,' which 'appears beautiful without'; but, nevertheless, is 'full of dead men's bones, and of all uncleanness.' The bones indeed are no longer dry; the sinews and flesh are come upon them, and the skin covers them above: but there is no breath in them, no Spirit of the living God. And, 'if any man have not the Spirit of Christ, he is none of His.' 'Ye are Christ's, if so be that the Spirit of God dwell in you': but, if not, God knoweth that ye abide in death, even until now.

8. This is another character of the sleeper here spoken to. He abides in death, though he knows it not. He is dead unto God, 'dead in trespasses and sins.' For, 'to be carnally minded is death.' Even as it is written, 'By one man sin entered into the world, and death by sin; and so death passed upon all men'; not only temporal death, but likewise spiritual and eternal. 'In that day that thou eatest,' said God to Adam, 'thou shalt surely die': not bodily (unless as he then became mortal), but spiritually: thou shalt lose the life of thy soul; thou shalt die to God; shalt be separated from Him, thy essential life and happiness.

9. Thus first was dissolved the vital union of our soul with God; insomuch that 'in the midst of' natural 'life, we are' now in spiritual 'death.' And herein we remain till the Second Adam becomes a quickening Spirit to us; till He raises the dead, the dead in sin, in pleasure, riches, or honours. But, before any dead soul can live, he 'hears' (hearkens to) 'the voice of the Son of God': he is made sensible of his lost estate, and receives the sentence of death in himself. He knows himself to be 'dead while

he liveth'; dead to God, and all the things of God; having no more power to perform the actions of a living Christian, than a dead body to perform the functions of a living man.

10. And most certain it is, that one dead in sin has not 'senses exercised to discern spiritual good and evil.' 'Having eyes, he sees not; he hath ears, and hears not.' He doth not 'taste and see that the Lord is gracious.' He 'hath not seen God at any time,' nor 'heard His voice,' nor 'handled the word of life.' In vain is the name of Jesus 'like ointment poured forth, and all His garments smell of myrrh, aloes, and cassia.' The soul that sleepeth in death hath no perception of any objects of this kind. His heart is 'past feeling,' and understandeth none of these things.

11. And hence, having no spiritual senses, no inlets of spiritual knowledge, the natural man receiveth not the things of the Spirit of God; nay, he is so far from receiving them, that whatsoever is spiritually discerned is mere foolishness unto him. He is not content with being utterly ignorant of spiritual things, but he denies the very existence of them. And spiritual sensation itself is to him the foolishness of folly. 'How,' saith he, 'can these things be? How can any man *know* that he is alive to God?' Even as you know that your body is now alive. Faith is the life of the soul; and if ye have this life abiding in you, ye want no marks to evidence it *to yourself,* but ελεγχος Πνευματος, that divine consciousness, that *witness of* God which is more and greater than ten thousand human witnesses.

12. If He doth not now bear witness with thy spirit, that thou art a child of God, O that He might convince thee, thou poor unawakened sinner, by His demonstration and power, that thou art a child of the devil! O that, as I prophesy, there might now be 'a noise and a shaking'; and may 'the bones come together, bone to his bone!' Then 'come from the four winds, O Breath! and breathe on these slain, that they may live!' And do not ye harden your hearts, and resist the Holy Ghost, who even now is come to convince you of sin, 'because you believe not on the name of the only begotten Son of God.'

II. 1. Wherefore, 'awake, thou that sleepest, and arise from the dead.' God calleth thee now by my mouth; and bids thee know thyself, thou fallen spirit, thy true state and only concern

below. 'What meanest thou, O sleeper? Arise! Call upon thy
God, if so be thy God will think upon thee, that thou perish not.'
A mighty tempest is stirred up round about thee and thou art
sinking into the depths of perdition, the gulf of God's
judgements. If thou wouldest escape them, cast thyself into
them. 'Judge thyself, and thou shalt not be judged of the Lord.'

2. Awake, awake! Stand up this moment, lest thou 'drink at
the Lord's hand the cup of His fury.' Stir up thyself to lay hold
on the Lord, the Lord thy Righteousness, mighty to save! 'Shake
thyself from the dust.' At least, let the earthquake of God's
threatenings shake thee. Awake, and cry out with the trembling
jailer, 'What must I do to be saved?' And never rest till thou
believest on the Lord Jesus, with a faith which is His gift, by the
operation of His Spirit.

3. If I speak to any one of you, more than to another, it is to
thee who thinkest thyself unconcerned in this exhortation. 'I
have a message from God unto thee.' In His name, I warn thee
'to flee from the wrath to come.' Thou unholy soul, see thy
picture in condemned Peter, lying in the dark dungeon,
between the soldiers, bound with two chains, the keepers before
the door keeping the prison. The night is far spent, the morning
is at hand, when thou art to be brought forth to execution. And
in these dreadful circumstances, thou art fast asleep; thou art
fast asleep in the devil's arms, on the brink of the pit, in the jaws
of everlasting destruction!

4. O may the Angel of the Lord come upon thee, and the light
shine into thy prison! And mayest thou feel the stroke of an
Almighty Hand, raising thee, with, 'Arise up quickly, gird
thyself, and bind on thy sandals, cast thy garment about thee,
and follow Me.'

5. Awake, thou everlasting spirit, out of thy dream of worldly
happiness! Did not God create thee for Himself? Then thou
canst not rest till thou restest in Him. Return, thou wanderer!
Fly back to thy ark. This is not thy home. Think not of building
tabernacles here. Thou art but a stranger, a sojourner upon
earth; a creature of a day, but just launching out into an
unchangeable state. Make haste. Eternity is at hand. Eternity
depends on this moment. An eternity of happiness, or an
eternity of misery!

6. In what state is thy soul? Was God, while I am yet speaking,

to require it of thee, art thou ready to meet death and judgement? Canst thou stand in His sight, who is of 'purer eyes than to behold iniquity'? Art thou 'meet to be partaker of the inheritance of the saints in light'? Hast thou 'fought a good fight, and kept the faith'? Hast thou secured the one thing needful? Hast thou recovered the image of God, even righteousness and true holiness? Hast thou put off the old man, and put on the new? Art thou clothed upon with Christ?

7. Hast thou oil in thy lamp? grace in thy heart? Dost thou 'love the Lord thy God with all thy heart, and with all thy mind, and with all thy soul, and with all thy strength'? Is that mind in thee, which was also in Christ Jesus? Art thou a Christian indeed; that is, a new creature? Are old things passed away, and all things become new?

8. Art thou a 'partaker of the divine nature'? Knowest thou not that 'Christ is in thee, except thou be reprobate'? Knowest thou that God 'dwelleth in thee, and thou in God, by His Spirit, which He hath given thee'? Knowest thou not that 'thy body is a temple of the Holy Ghost, which thou hast of God'? Hast thou the witness in thyself? the earnest of thine inheritance? [Art thou sealed by that Spirit of Promise, unto the day of redemption?] Hast thou 'received the Holy Ghost'? Or dost thou start at the question, not knowing 'whether there be any Holy Ghost'?

9. If it offends thee, be thou assured, that thou neither art a Christian, nor desirest to be one. Nay, thy very prayer is turned into sin; and thou hast solemnly mocked God this very day, by praying for the inspiration of His Holy Spirit, when thou didst not believe there was any such thing to be received.

10. Yet, on the authority of God's Word, and our own Church, I must repeat the question, 'Hast thou received the Holy Ghost?' If thou hast not, thou art not yet a Christian. For a Christian is a man that is 'anointed with the Holy Ghost and with power.' Thou art not yet made a partaker of pure religion and undefiled. Dost thou know what religion is?—that it is a participation of the divine nature; the life of God in the soul of man; Christ formed in the heart; 'Christ in thee, the hope of glory'; happiness and holiness; heaven begun upon earth; 'a kingdom of God within thee; not meat and drink,' no outward thing; 'but righteousness, and peace, and joy in the Holy Ghost'; an everlasting kingdom brought into thy soul; a 'peace of God,

that passeth all understanding'; a 'joy unspeakable, and full of glory'?

11. Knowest thou, that 'in Jesus Christ, neither circumcision availeth anything, nor uncircumcision; but faith that worketh by love'; but a new creation? Seest thou the necessity of that inward change, that spiritual birth, that life from the dead, that holiness? And art thou thoroughly convinced, that without it no man shall see the Lord? Art thou labouring after it?—'giving all diligence to make thy calling and election sure,' 'working out thy salvation with fear and trembling,' 'agonizing to enter in at the strait gate'? Art thou in earnest about thy soul? And canst thou tell the Searcher of hearts, 'Thou, O God, art the thing that I long for! Lord, Thou knowest all things; Thou knowest that I *would* love Thee!'

12. Thou hopest to be saved; but what reason hast thou to give of the hope that is in thee? Is it because thou hast done no harm? or, because thou hast done much good? or, because thou art not like other men; but wise, or learned, or honest, and morally good; esteemed of men, and of a fair reputation? Alas! all this will never bring thee to God. It is in His account lighter than vanity. Dost thou know Jesus Christ, whom He hath sent? Hath He taught thee, that 'by grace we are saved through faith; and that not of ourselves: it is the gift of God: not of works, lest any man should boast'? Hast thou received the faithful saying, as the whole foundation of thy hope, 'that Jesus Christ came into the world to save sinners'? Hast thou learned what that meaneth, 'I came not to call the righteous, but sinners to repentance? I am not sent, but unto the lost sheep'? Art thou (he that heareth, let him understand!) lost, dead, *damned already*? Dost thou know thy deserts? Dost thou feel thy wants? Art thou 'poor in spirit'? mourning for God, and refusing to be comforted? Is the prodigal 'come to himself,' and well content to be therefore thought 'beside himself' by those who are still feeding upon the husks which he hath left? Art thou willing to live godly in Christ Jesus? And dost thou therefore suffer persecution? Do men say all manner of evil against thee falsely, for the Son of Man's sake?

13. O that in all these questions ye may hear the voice that wakes the dead; and feel that hammer of the Word, which breaketh the rocks in pieces! 'If ye will hear His voice to-day, while it is called to-day, harden not your hearts.' Now, 'awake,

thou that sleepest' in spiritual death, that thou sleep not in death eternal! Feel thy lost estate, and 'arise from the dead.' Leave thine old companions in sin and death. Follow thou Jesus, and let the dead bury their dead. 'Save thyself from this untoward generation.' 'Come out from among them, and be thou separate, and touch not the unclean thing, and the Lord shall receive thee.' 'Christ shall give thee light.'

III. 1. This promise, I come, lastly, to explain. And how encouraging a consideration is this, that whosoever thou art who obeyest His call, thou canst not seek His face in vain! If thou even now 'awakest, and arisest from the dead,' He hath bound Himself to 'give thee light.' 'The Lord shall give thee grace and glory'; the light of His grace here, and the light of His glory when thou receivest the crown that fadeth not away. 'Thy light shall break forth as the morning, and thy darkness be as the noon-day.' 'God, who commanded the light to shine out of darkness, shall shine in thy heart; to give the knowledge of the glory of God in the face of Jesus Christ.' 'On them that fear the Lord shall the Sun of Righteousness arise with healing in His wings.' And in that day it shall be said unto thee, 'Arise, shine; for thy light is come, and the glory of the Lord is risen upon thee.' For Christ shall reveal Himself in thee: and He is the true Light.

2. God is light, and will give Himself to every awakened sinner that waiteth for Him; and thou shalt then be a temple of the living God, and Christ shall 'dwell in thy heart by faith': and, 'being rooted and grounded in love, thou shalt be able to comprehend with all saints, what is the breadth, and length, and depth, and height of that love of Christ which passeth knowledge,' [that thou mayest be filled with all the fullness of God.]

3. Ye see your calling, brethren. We are called to be 'an habitation of God through His Spirit'; and, through His Spirit dwelling in us, to be saints here, and partakers of the inheritance of the saints in light. So exceeding great are the promises which are given unto us, actually given unto us who believe! For by faith 'we receive, not the spirit of the world, but the Spirit which is of God'—the sum of all the promises—'that we may know the things that are freely given to us of God.'

4. The Spirit of Christ is that great gift of God which, at sundry times, and in divers manners, He hath promised to man, and hath fully bestowed since the time that Christ was glorified. Those promises, before made to the fathers, He hath thus fulfilled: 'I will put My Spirit within you, and cause you to walk in My statutes' (Ezek. xxxvi. 27). 'I will pour water upon him that is thirsty, and floods upon the dry ground: I will pour My Spirit upon thy seed, and My blessing upon thine offspring' (Isa. xliv. 3).

5. Ye may all be living witnesses of these things; of remission of sins, and the gift of the Holy Ghost. 'If thou canst believe, all things are possible to him that believeth.' 'Who among you is there that feareth the Lord, and' yet walketh 'in darkness, and hath no light'? I ask thee, in the name of Jesus, Believest thou that His arm is not shortened at all? that He is still mighty to save? that He is the same yesterday, to-day, and for ever? that He hath now power on earth to forgive sins? 'Son, be of good cheer; thy sins are forgiven.' God, for Christ's sake, hath forgiven thee. Receive this, 'not as the word of man; but as it is indeed, the word of God'; and thou art justified freely through faith. Thou shalt be sanctified also through faith which is in Jesus, and shalt set to thy seal, even thine, that 'God hath given unto us eternal life, and this life is in His Son.'

6. Men and brethren, let me freely speak unto you; and suffer ye the word of exhortation, even from one the least esteemed in the Church. Your conscience beareth you witness in the Holy Ghost, that these things are so, if so be ye have tasted that the Lord is gracious. 'This is eternal life, to know the only true God, and Jesus Christ, whom He hath sent.' This experimental knowledge, and this alone, is true Christianity. He is a Christian who hath received the Spirit of Christ. He is not a Christian who hath not received Him. Neither is it possible to have received Him, and not know it. 'For, at that day' (when He cometh, saith our Lord), 'ye shall know that I am in My Father, and you in Me, and I in you.' This is that 'Spirit of Truth, whom the world cannot receive, because it seeth Him not, neither knoweth Him: but ye know Him; for He dwelleth with you, and shall be in you' (John xiv. 17).

7. The world cannot receive Him, but utterly rejecteth the Promise of the Father, contradicting and blaspheming. But every spirit which confesseth not this is not of God. Yea, 'this is

that spirit of Antichrist, whereof ye have heard that it should come into the world; and even now it is in the world.' He is Antichrist whosoever denies the inspiration of the Holy Ghost, or that the indwelling Spirit of God is the common privilege of all believers, the blessing of the gospel, the unspeakable gift, the universal promise, the criterion of a real Christian.

8. It nothing helps them to say, 'We do not deny the *assistance* of God's Spirit; but only this *inspiration,* this *receiving the Holy Ghost,* and being *sensible* of it. It is only this *feeling* of the Spirit, this being *moved* by the Spirit, or *filled* with it, which we deny to have any place in sound religion.' But, in *only denying this,* you deny the whole Scriptures; the whole truth, and promise, and testimony of God.

9. Our own excellent Church knows nothing of this devilish distinction; but speaks plainly of 'feeling the Spirit of Christ'; of being 'moved by the Holy Ghost' and knowing and 'feeling there is no other name than that of Jesus,' whereby we can receive life and salvation. She teaches us all to pray for the 'inspiration of the Holy Spirit'; yea that we may be 'filled with the Holy Ghost.' Nay, and every Presbyter of hers professes to receive the Holy Ghost by the imposition of hands. Therefore, to deny any of these, is, in effect, to renounce the Church of England, as well as the whole Christian revelation.

10. But 'the wisdom of God' was always 'foolishness with men.' No marvel, then, that the great mystery of the gospel should be now also 'hid from the wise and prudent,' as well as in the days of old; that it should be almost universally denied, ridiculed, and exploded, as mere frenzy; and that all who dare avow it still are branded with the names of madmen and enthusiasts! This is 'that falling away' which was to come; that general apostasy of all orders and degrees of men, which we even now find to have overspread the earth. 'Run to and fro in the streets of Jerusalem, and see if ye can find a man,' a man that loveth the Lord his God with all his heart, and serveth Him with all his strength. How does our own land mourn (that we look no farther) under the overflowings of ungodliness! What villanies of every kind are committed day by day; yea, too often with impunity, by those who sin with a high hand, and glory in their shame! Who can reckon up the oaths, curses, profaneness, blasphemies; the lying, slandering, evil-speaking; the Sabbath-

breaking, gluttony, drunkenness, revenge; the whoredoms, adulteries, and various uncleanness; the frauds, injustice, oppression, extortion, which overspread our land as a flood?

11. And even among those who have kept themselves pure from these grosser abominations, how much anger and pride, how much sloth and idleness, how much softness and effeminacy, how much luxury and self-indulgence, how much covetousness and ambition, how much thirst of praise, how much love of the world, how much fear of man, is to be found! Meanwhile, how little of true religion! For, where is he that loveth either God or his neighbour, as He hath given us commandment? On the one hand, are those who have not so much as the form of godliness; on the other, those who have the form only: there stands the *open*, there the *painted*, sepulchre. So that in very deed, whosoever were earnestly to behold any public gathering together of the people (1 fear those in our churches are not to be excepted), might easily perceive, 'that the one part were Sadducees, and the other Pharisees': the one having almost as little concern about religion, as if there were 'no resurrection, neither angel nor spirit'; and the other making it a mere lifeless form, a dull round of external performances, without either true faith, or the love of God, or joy in the Holy Ghost!

12. Would to God I could except *us* of this place! 'Brethren, my heart's desire, and prayer to God, for you is, that ye may be saved' from this overflowing of ungodliness; and that here may its proud waves be stayed! But is it so indeed? God knoweth, yea, and our own consciences, it is not. Ye have not kept yourselves pure. Corrupt are we also and abominable; and few are there that understand any more; few that worship God in spirit and in truth. We, too, are 'a generation that set not our hearts aright, and whose spirit cleaveth not steadfastly unto God.' He hath appointed us indeed to be 'the salt of the earth: but if the salt hath lost its savour, it is thenceforth good for nothing; but to be cast out, and to be trodden underfoot of men.'

13. And 'shall I not visit for these things, saith the Lord? Shall not My soul be avenged on such a nation as this?' Yea, we know not how soon He may say to the sword, 'Sword, go through this land!' He hath given us long space to repent. He lets us alone this year also: but He warns and awakens us by thunder. His judgements are abroad in the earth; and we have all reason to

expect the heaviest of all, even that He 'should come unto us quickly, and remove our candlestick out of its place, except we repent and do the first works'; unless we return to the principles of the Reformation, the truth and simplicity of the gospel. Perhaps we are now resisting the last effort of divine grace to save us. Perhaps we have wellnigh 'filled up the measure of our iniquities,' by rejecting the counsel of God against ourselves, and casting out His messengers.

14. O God, 'in the midst of wrath, remember mercy'! Be glorified in our reformation, not in our destruction! Let us 'hear the rod, and Him that appointed it'! Now that Thy 'judgements are abroad in the earth,' let the inhabitants of the world 'learn righteousness'!

15. My brethren, it is high time for us to awake out of sleep before the 'great trumpet of the Lord be blown,' and our land become a field of blood. O may we speedily see the things that make for our peace, before they are hid from our eyes! 'Turn Thou us, O good Lord, and let Thine anger cease from us. O Lord, look down from heaven, behold and visit this vine'; and cause us to know 'the time of our visitation.' 'Help us, O God of our salvation, for the glory of Thy name! O deliver us, and be merciful to our sins, for Thy name's sake! And so we will not go back from Thee. O let us live, and we shall call upon Thy name. Turn us again, O Lord God of Hosts! Show the light of Thy countenance, and we shall be whole.'

'Now unto Him that is able to do exceeding abundantly above all that we can ask or think, according to the power that worketh in us, unto Him be glory in the Church by Christ Jesus throughout all ages, world without end. Amen!

SERMON IV

SCRIPTURAL CHRISTIANITY

PREACHED AT ST. MARY'S OXFORD, BEFORE THE UNIVERSITY, ON AUGUST 24, 1744

This was the last sermon preached before the University by Wesley. The Sunday sermons were preached at two in the afternoon, but the service on saints' days began at ten in the morning. As the hour booms from the Tom Tower of Christ Church on August 24 (St. Bartholomew's Day) 1744 a stately procession enters the venerable Church of St. Mary the Virgin, headed by the Esquire Bedel carrying the insignia of the Vice-Chancellor; next comes the Vice-Chancellor himself in his robes, followed by the preacher in full canonicals; after him walks the Proctors, and the Doctors of Divinity in all the glory of their scarlet—*capa et caputio coccineo induti*—bring up the rear. The vast congregation rises as they enter; and when they reach the centre of the church, the Vice-Chancellor bows to the preacher and moves to his throne, whilst John Wesley ascends the pulpit opposite. A hymn is sung, and the 'bidding prayer' is offered; and with no further preface the text is announced. 'And they were all filled with the Holy Ghost.' We have four accounts by eye-witnesses of this memorable service, which shall be now given in full.

First let the preacher himself speak. In *Journal*, Tuesday, August 21, he says:

'I set out with a few friends for Oxford. On Wednesday my brother met us from Bristol.' Friday 24 (St. Bartholomew's Day): 'I preached, I suppose the last time, at St. Mary's. Be it so. I am now clear of the blood of these men. I have fully delivered my own soul. The Beadle came to me afterwards and told me the Vice-Chancellor had sent him for my notes. I sent them without delay, not without admiring the wise providence of God. Perhaps few men of note would have given a sermon of mine the reading if I had put it into their hands; but by this means it came to be read, probably more than once by every man of eminence in the University. I left Oxford about noon, preached at Wycombe [twenty-five miles south-east of Oxford] in the evening; and on Saturday, the 25th, returned to London.'

In *A Short History of the Methodists* (1781) he adds to the record from the *Journal*:

'And I am well pleased that it should be the very day on which, in the last century, near two thousand burning and shining lights were put out at one stroke [the reference is to the ejectment from their livings on August 24, 1662, of

53

2,000 clergymen, of whom Wesley's grandfather, John Westley, was one, because they refused to take the oath prescribed in the Act of Uniformity]. Yet what a wide difference is there between their case and mine! They were turned out of house and home, and all that they had; whereas I am only hindered from preaching, without any other loss; and that in a kind of honourable manner; it being determined that, when my next turn to preach came, they would pay another person to preach for me. And so they did twice or thrice, even to the time that I resigned my fellowship' [which he did in 1751].

Charles Wesley, in his Journal, August 23, says:

'I went to Christ Church prayers with several of the brethren, who thought it strange to see men in surplices talking, laughing, and pointing, as in a play-house, the whole time of service. I got two or three hours' conference with my brother; and found the spirit which had drawn us formerly in this place. I preached to a multitude of the brethren, gownsmen, and gentry from the races [it was the Oxford race-week] who filled our inn and yard. The strangers that intermeddled not with our joy seemed struck and astonished with it, whilst we admonished one another in psalms and hymns, &c. O that all the world had a taste for *our* diversion!! Friday, August 24.—I joined my brother in stirring up the Society. They did run well, till the Moravians turned them out of the way of God's ordinances. At ten I walked with my brother and Mr. Piers and Meriton [two clergymen who had just taken part in Wesley's first Conference in London] to St. Mary's, where my brother bore his testimony before a crowded audience, much increased by the racers. Never have I seen a more attentive congregation. They did not let a word slip them. Some of the Heads stood up the whole time, and fixed their eyes on him. If they can endure sound doctrine like his, he will surely leave a blessing behind him. The Vice-Chancellor sent after him, and desired his notes; which he scaled up and sent immediately. We walked back in form, the little band of us four, for of the rest durst none join himself to us. I was a little diverted at the coyness of an old friend, Mr. Wells, who sat just before me, but took great care to turn his back upon me all the time, which did not hinder my seeing through him. At noon my brother set out for London, and I for Bristol.'

In the undergraduates' gallery was a student of Wadham, called Benjamin Kennicott, who through financial difficulties had come somewhat late to the University and was now twenty-five years of age. He afterwards became one of the most eminent of English Hebrew and Oriental scholars; was Fellow of Exeter, Keeper of the Radcliffe Library, and Canon of Christ Church. His *Vetus Testamentum Hebraicum cum variis lectionibus* (1776-80) embodied the results of the collation of 615 MSS. and 52 printed editions of the Hebrew Bible, and gave a great impetus to the study of the text of the Old Testament. He wrote a full description of this service in a letter which was published in the *Methodist Magazine*, January 1866, and from which I here copy:

'On Friday last, being St. Bartholomew's Day, the famous Methodist, Mr. John Wesley, Fellow of Lincoln College, preached before the University; which being a matter of great curiosity at present, and may possibly be greater in its consequences, I shall be particular in the account of it. All that are Masters of

Arts, and on the foundation of any College, are set down in a roll, as they take their degree, and in that order preach before the University, or pay three guineas for a preacher in their stead, and as no clergyman can avoid his turn, so the University can refuse none; otherwise Mr. Wesley would not have preached. He came to Oxford some time before [three days only], and preached frequently every day in courts, public-houses, and elsewhere. On Friday morning, having held forth twice in private, at five and at eight [I fear most of us degenerate moderns with such a service before us, would have stayed in bed to breakfast], he came to St. Mary's at ten o'clock. There were present the Vice-Chaacellor, the proctors, most of the heads of houses, a vast number of gownsmen, and a multitude of private people, with many of his followers, both brethren and sisters, who, with general [this cannot be right; I conjecture it is 'funeral'] faces and plain attire, came from around to attend their master and teacher. When he mounted the pulpit, I fixed my eyes on him and his behaviour. He is neither tall nor fat; for the latter would ill become a Methodist. His black hair quite smooth, and parted very exactly' [yes, Mr. Kennicott; this man had a way of doing everything 'very exactly], added to a peculiar composure in his countenance, showed him to be an uncommon man. His prayer was soft, short, and conformable to the rules of the University. [This rather suggests that he used a brief extempore prayer after the formal bidding prayer.] His text, Acts iv. 31: "And they were all filled with the Holy Ghost." And now he began to exalt his voice. He spoke the text very slowly, and with an agreeable emphasis. His introduction was to prove that the word *all* in the text was meant, not only of the apostles and those who received the extraordinary, but of others who received the ordinary influences (only) of the Holy Spirit; and that of such there were many in the infancy of the gospel, persons who had no business to perform besides the reformation of their own lives, and therefore wanted the ordinary divine influences only, to refresh them in their conversion and complete their Christianity. And this he chose to do, because, if the Holy Ghost was necessary for men as private persons at first, it must be so in all ages. His division of the text was, first, to show the influence of Christianity in its infancy on individuals; secondly, in its progress from one period to another; thirdly. In its final completion in the universal conversion of the world to the Christian faith. Under these three heads he expressed himself like a very good scholar, but a rigid zealot; and then he came to what he called his plain, practical conclusion. Here was what he had been preparing for all along; and he fired his address with so much zeal and unbounded satire as quite spoiled what otherwise might have been turned to great advantage; for as I liked some, so I disliked other parts of his discourse extremely. Having under his third head, displayed the happiness of the world under it—complete final reformation—"Now," says he, "where is this Christianity to be found? Is this a Christian nation? Is this a Christian city?" asserting the contrary to both. I liked some of his freedom; such as calling the generality of young gownsmen "a generation of triflers," and many other just invectives. But, considering how many shining lights are here that are the glory of the Christian cause, his sacred censure was much too flaming and strong, and his charity much too weak in not making large allowances. But so far from allowances, that, after having summed up the measure of our iniquities, he concluded with a lifted-up eye in this most solemn form: "It is time for Thee, Lord, to lay to Thine hand"—words full of such presumption and seeming imprecation, that they gave an universal shock. This, and the assertion that Oxford was not a Christian city, and this country not a Christian nation, were the most offensive parts of the sermon, except when he accused the whole body (and confessed himself to be one of the number) of the sin of perjury; and for this reason, because, upon becoming members of a College, every person takes an oath to observe the statutes of the University, and no one observes them in all things. But this gave me no uneasiness; for in every oath the intention of the legislator is the only thing you swear to observe; and the legislators here mean that you shall observe all their laws, or upon the violation of them submit to the punishment if required; and this being explained in the statute-book given to every member, does, I think, solve the whole difficulty. Had these things been omitted, and his censures moderated, I think his discourse, as to style and delivery, would have been uncommonly pleasing to others as well as to myself. He is allowed to be a man of great parts, and that by the excellent Dean of Christ Church (Dr. Conybeare); for the day he preached, the dean generously said of him, "John Wesley will always be thought a man of sound sense, though an enthusiast." However, the Vice-Chancellor sent for the sermon, and I hear the heads of colleges intend to show their resentment.'

Another youth was sitting in the body of the church amongst the Dons; for though only twenty years of age, he had a year before this been elected a Fellow of All Souls. His name was William Blackstone, destined to fame as the author of the *Commentaries on the Laws of England* and a Judge of the realm. In a letter dated August 28, 1744, and reproduced in facsimile in Hurst's *History of Methodism,* vol ii. p. 602, he says:

'We were last Friday entertained at St. Mary's by a curious sermon from Wesley the Methodist. Among other equally modest particulars he informed us, 1st That there was not one Christian among all the Heads of Houses; 2dly, that pride, gluttony, avarice, luxury, sensuality, and drunkenness were the general characteristicks of all Fellows of Colleges, who were useless to a proverbial uselessness. Lastly, that the younger part of the University were a generation of triflers, all of them perjured, and not one of them of any religion at all. His notes were demanded by the Vice-Chancellor, but on mature deliberation it has been thought proper to punish him by a mortifying neglect.'

It is pleasant to find Wesley, quoting from his quondam critic, thirty years afterwards, in his *Thoughts upon Slavery,* and describing him as 'that great ornament of his profession, Judge Blackstone.'

The sermon was published in October by Strahan, with a short preface, omitted in the collected editions: 'It was not my design, when I wrote, ever to print the latter part of the following sermon. But the false and scurrilous accounts of it which have been published, almost in every corner of the nation, constrain me to publish the whole, just as it was preached; that men of reason may judge for themselves.' Ezekiel xxxiii. 4 was prefixed to the sermon, 'Whosoever heareth the sound of the trumpet, and taketh not warning,' &c.; but was omitted in the 1771 edition. Many separate editions of the sermon were issued; there are eleven in the Wesleyan Conference Office Library.

I do not know where to find in religious literature anything to rival the portrayal in the first three divisions of this sermon of Christian experience, Christian activity, and a Christian world. There is hardly a sentence which is not directly derived from the Scriptures; but the arrangement is so skilful that the impression is not of a pasticcio of texts, but of a full flood of impassioned eloquence. It is an example of the finest oratory, controlled by a strong logical sense, absolutely free from artificial ornaments, sincere as the light, but glowing with divine fire and fervour. And if the application is outspoken and severe, it never degenerates into vulgar abuse; there is no feeling as we read that Wesley is exploiting the sins of the University for the sake of an advertisement of himself; he must be faithful, but there is a strain of tenderness that is unmistakable; and it must not be forgotten that he did not mean to publish this part of his sermon. 'I love the very sight of Oxford,' he says, in *Plain Account of Kingswood School* (1781); 'I love the manner of life; I love and esteem many of its institutions.'

But his love did not blind him to its faults. In this same pamphlet, whilst he admits the learning of the professors, he points out that all that they do is to 'read now and then an ingenious lecture, perhaps three or four times a year. They read it in the public schools; but who hears? Often *vel duo vel nemo.*' Some of the tutors 'are men of eminent learning' and are persons 'of piety and diligence'; but there are many of another sort who are both ignorant and careless of the welfare of their students. The examinations and exercises are 'an idle, useless interruption of useful studies.' They are 'horribly, shockingly superficial,' 'an execrable insult upon common sense.' The undergraduates for the most part 'no more concern themselves with learning than with religion'; they are 'loungers and triflers.' The posthumously published Sermon CXXXIV, which was not actually preached, contains an even severer indictment. The evidence from the literature of the eighteenth century abundantly justifies Wesley's criticisms. Things were at their worst just at this time (1744); and towards the end of the century they had begun to improve; possibly in part through the influence of his faithful dealing. The best commentary on this part of the sermon will be found in Godley's *Oxford in the Eighteenth Century* (1908); especially chapters iii–vi.

The Vice-Chancellor who sent for the notes of the sermon was William Hodges, Provost of Oriel, and 'a good scholar.' His objection to the sermon was probably not based on doctrinal grounds, but on the attack made in the presence of the undergraduates on the authorities of the University.

History repeats itself. Morley, *Life of Gladstone,* i. 58, says: 'Gladstone always remembered among the wonderful sights of his life, St. Mary's crammed in all parts by all orders when Mr. Bulteel, an outlying Calvinist, preached an accusatory sermon (some of it all too true) against the University.' Bulteel, like Wesley, was an open-air preacher; and lost his living on that account.

And they were all filled with the Holy Ghost.—ACTS iv. 31.

I. The same expression occurs in the second chapter, where we read, 'When the day of Pentecost was fully come, they were all' (the Apostles, with the women, and the mother of Jesus, and His brethren) 'with one accord in one place. And suddenly there came a sound from heaven as of a rushing mighty wind. And there appeared unto them cloven tongues like as of fire, and it sat upon each of them. And they were all filled with the Holy Ghost': one immediate effect whereof was, they 'began to speak with other tongues'; insomuch that both the Parthians, Medes, Elamites, and the other strangers who 'came together, when this was noised abroad, heard them speak, in their several tongues, the wonderful works of God' (Acts ii. 1-6).

2. In this chapter we read, that when the Apostles and brethren had been praying, and praising God, 'the place was shaken where they were assembled together, and they were all filled with the Holy Ghost.' Not that we find any visible appearance here, such as had been in the former instance: nor are we informed that the *extraordinary gifts* of the Holy Ghost were then given to all or any of them; such as the gifts of 'healing, of working' other 'miracles, of prophecy, of discerning spirits, the speaking with divers kinds of tongues, and the interpretation of tongues' (1 Cor. xii. 9, 10).

3. Whether these gifts of the Holy Ghost were designed to remain in the Church throughout all ages, and whether or no they will be restored at the nearer approach of the 'restitution of all things,' are questions which it is not needful to decide. But it is needful to observe this, that, even in the infancy of the Church, God divided them with a sparing hand. Were all even then prophets? Were all workers of miracles? Had all the gifts of healing? Did all speak with tongues? No, in no wise. Perhaps not one in a thousand. Probably none but the teachers in the Church, and only some of them (1 Cor. xii. 28-30). It was, therefore, for a more excellent purpose than this, that 'they were all filled with the Holy Ghost.'

4. It was, to give them (what none can deny to be essential to all Christians in all ages) the mind which was in Christ, those holy fruits of the Spirit, which whosoever hath not, is none of His; to fill them with 'love, joy, peace, long-suffering, gentleness, goodness' (Gal. v. 22-24); to endue them with faith (perhaps it might be rendered *fidelity*), with meekness and temperance; to enable them to crucify the flesh, with its affections and lusts, its passions and desires; and in consequence of that inward change,

to fulfil all outward righteousness; to 'walk as Christ also walked,' in 'the work of faith, in the patience of hope, the labour of love' (1 Thess. i. 3).

5. Without busying ourselves, then, in curious, needless inquiries, touching those *extraordinary* gifts of the Spirit, let us take a nearer view of these His *ordinary* fruits, which we are assured will remain throughout all ages;—of that great work of God among the children of men, which we are used to express by one word, 'Christianity'; not as it implies a set of opinions, a system of doctrines, but as it refers to men's hearts and lives. And this Christianity it may be useful to consider under three distinct views:

I. AS BEGINNING TO EXIST IN INDIVIDUALS:
II. AS SPREADING FROM ONE TO ANOTHER:
III. As COVERING THE EARTH.

I design to close these considerations with a plain, practical application.

I. 1. And, first, let us consider Christianity in its rise, as beginning to exist in individuals.

Suppose, then, one of those who heard the Apostle Peter preaching repentance and remission of sins, was pricked to the heart, was convinced of sin, repented, and then believed in Jesus. By this faith of the operation of God, which was the very substance, or subsistence, of things hoped for (Heb. xi. 1), the demonstrative evidence of invisible things, he instantly received the Spirit of adoption, whereby he now cried, 'Abba, Father' (Rom. viii. 15). Now first it was that he could call Jesus Lord, by the Holy Ghost (1 Cor. xii. 3), the Spirit itself bearing witness with his spirit, that he was a child of God (Rom. viii. 16). Now it was that he could truly say, 'I live not, but Christ liveth in me; and the life which I now live in the flesh, I live by faith in the Son of God, who loved me, and gave Himself for me' (Gal. ii. 20).

2. This, then, was the very essence of his faith, a divine ελεγχος (*evidence* or *conviction*) of the love of God the Father, through the Son of His love, to him a sinner, now accepted in the Beloved. And 'being justified by faith, he had peace with God' (Rom. v. 1) yea, 'the peace of God ruling in his heart'; a peace

which passing all understanding (παντα νουν, all barely rational
conception), kept his heart and mind from all doubt and fear,
through the knowledge of Him in whom he had believed. He
could not, therefore, 'be afraid of any evil tidings'; for his 'heart
stood fast, believing in the Lord.' He feared not what man could
do unto him, knowing the very hairs of his head were all
numbered. He feared not all the powers of darkness, whom God
was daily bruising under his feet. Least of all was he afraid to die;
nay, he desired to 'depart, and to be with Christ' (Phil. i. 23);
who, 'through death, had destroyed him that had the power of
death, even the devil; and delivered them who, through fear of
death, were all their life-time,' till then, 'subject to bondage'
(Heb. ii. 15).

3. His soul, therefore, magnified the Lord, and his spirit
rejoiced in God his Saviour. 'He rejoiced in Him with joy
unspeakable,' who had reconciled him to God, even the Father;
'in whom he had redemption through His blood, the forgiveness
of sins.' He rejoiced in that witness of God's Spirit with his spirit,
that he was a child of God; and more abundantly,' in hope of the
glory of God'; in hope of the glorious image of God, and full
renewal of his soul in righteousness and true holiness; and in
hope of that crown of glory that 'inheritance, incorruptible,
undefiled, and that fadeth not away.'

4. 'The love of God was also shed abroad in his heart by the
Holy Ghost which was given unto him' (Rom. v. 5). 'Because he
was a son, God had sent forth the Spirit of His Son into his heart,
crying, Abba, Father!' (Gal. iv. 6). And that filial love of God was
continually increased by the witness he had in himself (1 John v.
10) of God's pardoning love to him; by 'beholding what manner
of love it was which the Father had bestowed upon him, that he
should be called a child of God' (1 John iii. 1). So that God was
the desire of his eyes, and the joy of his heart; his portion in time
and in eternity.

5. He that thus *loved* God could not but love his brother also;
and 'not in word only but in deed and in truth.' 'If God,' said he,
'so loved us we ought also to love one another' (1 John iv. II); yea,
every soul of man, as 'the mercy of God is over all His works' (Ps.
cxlv. 9). Agreeably hereto, the affection of this lover of God
embraced all mankind for His sake; not excepting those whom
he had never seen in the flesh, or those of whom he knew

nothing more than that they were 'the offspring of God,' for whose souls His Son had died; not excepting the 'evil' and 'unthankful,' and least of all his enemies, those who hated, or persecuted, or despitefully used him for his Master's sake. These had a peculiar place, both in his heart and in his prayers. He loved them 'even as Christ loved us.'

6. And 'love is not puffed up' (1 Cor. xiii. 4). It abases to the dust every soul wherein it dwells. Accordingly, he was lowly of heart, little, mean, and vile in his own eyes. He neither sought nor received the praise of men, but that which cometh of God only. He was meek and long-suffering, gentle to all, and easy to be entreated. Faithfulness and truth never forsook him; they were 'bound about his neck, and wrote on the table of his heart.' By the same spirit he was enabled to be temperate in all things, refraining his soul even as a weaned child. He was 'crucified to the world, and the world crucified to him'; superior to 'the desire of the flesh, the desire of the eye, and the pride of life.' By the same almighty love was he saved, both from passion and pride; from lust and vanity; from ambition and covetousness; and from every temper which was not in Christ.

7. It may easily be believed, he who had this love in his heart would work no evil to his neighbour. It was impossible for him, knowingly and designedly to do harm to any man. He was at the greatest distance from cruelty and wrong, from any unjust or unkind action. With the same care did he 'set a watch before his mouth, and keep the door of his lips 'lest he should offend in tongue either against justice, or against mercy or truth. He put away all lying falsehood, and fraud; neither was guile found in his mouth. He spake evil of no man; nor did an unkind word ever come out of his lips.

8. And as he was deeply sensible of the truth of that word, 'Without Me ye can do nothing,' and, consequently, of the need he had to be watered of God every moment; so he continued daily in all the ordinances of God, the stated channels of His grace to man: 'in the Apostles' doctrine,' or teaching, receiving that food of the soul with all readiness of heart; in 'the breaking of bread,' which he found to be the communion of the body of Christ; and 'in the prayers' and praises offered up by the great congregation. And thus, he daily 'grew in grace,' increasing in strength, in the knowledge and love of God.

9. But it did not satisfy him, barely to abstain from doing evil. His soul was athirst to do good. The language of his heart continually was, ' "My Father worketh hitherto, and I work." My Lord went about doing good; and shall not I tread in His steps?' As he had opportunity, therefore, if he could do no good of a higher kind, he fed the hungry, clothed the naked, helped the fatherless or stranger, visited and assisted them that were sick or in prison. He gave all his goods to feed the poor. He rejoiced to labour or to suffer for them; and whereinsoever he might profit another, there especially to 'deny himself.' He counted nothing too dear to part with for them, as well remembering the word of his Lord, 'Inasmuch as ye have done it unto one of the least of these My brethren, ye have done it unto Me' (Matt. xxv. 40).

10. Such was Christianity in its rise. Such was a Christian in ancient days. Such was every one of those who, when they heard the threatenings of the chief priests and elders, 'lifted up their voice to God with one accord, and were all filled with the Holy Ghost. The multitude of them that believed were of one heart and of one soul': so did the love of Him in whom they had believed constrain them to love one another. 'Neither said any of them that aught of the things which he possessed was his own; but they had all things common': so fully were they crucified to the world, and the world crucified to them. 'And they continued steadfastly with one accord in the Apostles' doctrine, and in the breaking of bread, and in prayer' (Acts ii. 42). 'And great grace was upon them all: neither was there any among them that lacked: for as many as were possessors of lands or houses sold them, and brought the prices of the things that were sold, and laid them down at the Apostles' feet: and distribution was made unto every man according as he had need' (Acts iv. 31-35).

II. 1. Let us take a view, in the second place, of this Christianity, as spreading from one to another, and so gradually making its way into the world: for such was the will of God concerning it, who did not 'light a candle to put it under a bushel, but that it might give light to all that were in the house.' And this our Lord had declared to His first disciples, 'Ye are the salt of the earth,' 'the light of the world'; at the same time that He gave that general command, 'Let your light so shine before men that they may see your good works, and glorify your Father which is in heaven' (Matt. v. 13-16).

2. And, indeed, supposing a few of these lovers of mankind to see 'the whole world lying in wickedness,' can we believe they would be unconcerned at the sight, at the misery of those for whom their Lord died? Would not their bowels yearn over them, and their hearts melt away for very trouble? Could they then stand idle all the day long, even were there no command from Him whom they loved? Rather, would they not labour, by all possible means, to pluck some of these brands out of the burning? Undoubtedly they would: they would spare no pains to bring back whomsoever they could of those poor 'sheep that had gone astray, to the great Shepherd and Bishop of their souls' (1 Pet. ii. 25).

3. So the Christians of old did. They laboured, having opportunity, 'to do good unto all men' (Gal. vi. 10), warning them to flee from the wrath to come; now, now to escape the damnation of hell. They declared, 'The times of ignorance God winked at; but now He calleth all men everywhere to repent' (Acts xvii. 30). They cried aloud, Turn ye, turn ye, from your evil ways; 'so iniquity shall not be your ruin' (Ezek. xviii. 30). They 'reasoned' with them of 'temperance, and righteousness,' or justice—of the virtues opposite to their reigning sins; 'and of judgement to come'—of the wrath of God which would surely be executed on evil-doers in that day when He should judge the world (Acts xxiv. 25).

4. They endeavoured herein to speak to every man severally as he had need. To the careless, to those who lay unconcerned in darkness and in the shadow of death, they thundered, 'Awake, thou that sleepest; arise from the dead, and Christ shall give thee light.' But to those who were already awakened out of sleep, and groaning under a sense of the wrath of God, their language was, 'We have an Advocate with the Father; He is the propitiation for our sins.' Meantime, those who had believed, they provoked to love and to good works; to patient continuance in well-doing; and to abound more and more in that holiness without which no man can see the Lord (Heb, xii. 14).

5. And their labour was not in vain in the Lord. His word ran and was glorified. It grew mightily and prevailed. But so much the more did offences prevail also. The world in general were

offended, 'because they testified of it, that the works thereof
were evil' (John vii. 7). The men of pleasure were offended, not
only because these men were made, as it were, to reprove their
thoughts.' He professeth,' said they, 'to have the knowledge of
God; he calleth himself the child of the Lord; his life is not like
other men's; his ways are of another fashion; he abstaineth from
our ways, as from filthiness; he maketh his boast, that God is his
Father' (Wis. ii. 13-16); but much more, because so many of their
companions were taken away, and would no more 'run with
them to the same excess of riot' (1 Pet. iv. 4). The men of
reputation were offended, because, as the gospel spread, they
declined in the esteem of the people; and because many no
longer dared to give them flattering titles, or to pay man the
homage due to God only. The men of trade called one another
together, and said, 'Sirs, ye know that by this craft we have our
wealth: but ye see and hear that these men have persuaded and
turned away much people; so that this our craft is in danger to be
set at nought' (Acts xix. 25, &c.). Above all, the men of religion,
so called, the men of *outside* religion ' the saints of the world,'
were offended, and ready at every opportunity to cry out, 'Men
of Israel, help! We have found these men pestilent fellows,
movers of sedition throughout the world' (Acts xxiv. 5). 'These
are the men that teach all men everywhere against the people,
and against [the law]' (Acts xxi. 28).

6. Thus it was that the heavens grew black with clouds, and
the storm gathered amain. For the more Christianity spread, the
more hurt was done, in the account of those who received it not;
and the number increased of those who were more and more
enraged at these men who thus 'turned the world upside down'
(Acts xvii. 6); insomuch that more and more cried out, 'Away
with such fellows from the earth; it is not fit that they should
live'; yea, and sincerely believed that whosoever should kill them
would do God service.

7. Meanwhile they did not fail to 'cast out their name as evil'
(Luke vi. 22); so that 'this sect was everywhere spoken against'
(Acts xxviii. 22). Men said all manner of evil of them, even as had
been done of the prophets that were before them (Matt. v. 12).
And whatsoever any would affirm, others would believe; so that
offences grew as the stars of heaven for multitude. And hence
arose, at the time foreordained of the Father, persecution in all

its forms. Some, for a season, suffered only shame and reproach; some, 'the spoiling of their goods'; 'some had trial of mocking and scourging; some of bonds and imprisonment'; and others 'resisted unto blood' (Heb. x. 34; xi. 36, &c.).

8. Now it was that the pillars of hell were shaken, and the kingdom of God spread more and more. Sinners were everywhere 'turned from darkness to light, and from the power of Satan unto God.' He gave His children 'such a mouth, and such wisdom, as all their adversaries could not resist'; and their lives were of equal force with their words. But above all, their sufferings spake to all the world. They 'approved themselves the servants of God, in afflictions, in necessities, in distresses, in stripes, in imprisonments, in tumults, in labours; in perils in the sea, in perils in the wilderness, in weariness and painfulness, in hunger and in thirst, in cold and nakedness' (2 Cor. vi. 4, &c.). And when, having fought the good fight, they were led as sheep to the slaughter, and offered up on the sacrifice and service of their faith, then the blood of each found a voice, and the Heathen owned, 'He being dead, yet speaketh.'

9. Thus did Christianity spread itself in the earth. But how soon did the tares appear with the wheat, and the *mystery of iniquity* work, as well as the *mystery of godliness*! How soon did Satan find a seat, even *in the temple of God,* 'till the woman fled into the wilderness,' and 'the faithful were again minished from the children of men'! Here we tread a beaten path: the still increasing corruptions of the succeeding generations have been largely described, from time to time, by those witnesses God raised up, to show that He had 'built His Church upon a rock, and the gates of hell should not' wholly 'prevail against her' (Matt. xvi. 18).

III. 1. But shall we not see greater things than these? Yea, greater than have been yet from the beginning of the world. Can Satan cause the truth of God to fail, or His promises to be of none effect? If not, the time will come when Christianity will prevail over all, and cover the earth. Let us stand a little, and survey (the third thing which was proposed) this strange sight, a *Christian world*. Of this the prophets of old inquired and searched diligently (1 Pet. i. 10, 11, &c.): of this the Spirit which was in them testified: 'It shall come to pass in the last days, that the mountain of the Lord's house shall be established in the top of the mountains, and shall be exalted above the hills; and all nations shall flow unto it. . . . And they shall beat their swords into ploughshares, and their spears into pruning-hooks: nation shall not lift up sword against nation, neither shall they learn war any more' (Isa. ii. 2, 4). 'In that day there shall be a Root of Jesse, which shall stand for an Ensign of the people; to it shall the Gentiles seek: and His rest shall be glorious. And it shall come to pass in that day, that the Lord shall set His hand again to recover the remnant of His people; and He shall set up an Ensign for the nations, and shall assemble the outcasts of Israel, and gather together the dispersed of Judah from the four corners of the earth' (Isa. xi. 10-12). 'The wolf shall then dwell with the lamb, and the leopard shall lie down with the kid; and the calf and the young lion and the fatling together; and a little child shall lead them. They shall not hurt nor destroy, saith the Lord, in all My holy mountain: for the earth shall be full of the knowledge of the Lord, as the waters cover the sea' (Isa. xi. 6-9).

2. To the same effect are the words of the great Apostle, which it is evident have never yet been fulfilled. 'Hath God cast away His people? God forbid. But through their fall salvation is come to the Gentiles. And if the diminishing of them be the riches of the Gentiles how much more their fullness? For I would not brethren that ye should be ignorant of this mystery; that blindness in part is happened to Israel, until the fullness of the Gentiles be come in: and so all Israel shall be saved' (Rom. xi. 1, 11, 12, 25, 26).

3. Suppose now the fullness of time to be come, and the prophecies to be accomplished. What a prospect is this! All is peace, 'quietness, and assurance for ever.' Here is no din of arms, no 'confused noise,' no 'garments rolled in blood.' 'Destructions are come to a perpetual end': wars are ceased from the earth. Neither are there any intestine jars remaining; no brother rising up against brother; no country or city divided against itself, and tearing out its own bowels. Civil discord is at an end for evermore, and none is left either to destroy or hurt his neighbour. Here is no oppression to 'make' even 'the wise man mad'; no extortion to 'grind the face of the poor'; no robbery or wrong; no rapine or injustice; for all are 'content with such things as they possess.' Thus 'righteousness and peace have

kissed each other' (Ps. lxxxv. 10); they have 'taken root and filled the land'; 'righteousness flourishing out of the earth'; and 'peace looking down from heaven.'

4. And with righteousness or justice, mercy is also found. The earth is no longer full of cruel habitations. The Lord hath destroyed both the blood-thirsty and malicious, the envious and revengeful man. Were there any provocation, there is none that now knoweth to return evil for evil; but indeed there is none that doeth evil, no, not one: for all are harmless as doves. And being filled with peace and joy in believing, and united in one body, by one Spirit, they all love as brethren, they are all of one heart and of one soul. 'Neither saith any of them, that aught of the things which he possesseth is his own.' There is none among them that lacketh; for every man loveth his neighbour as himself. And all walk by one rule: 'Whatever ye would that men should do unto you, even so do unto them.'

5. It follows, that no unkind word can ever be heard among them, no strife of tongues, no contention of any kind, no railing or evil-speaking, but every one 'opens his mouth with wisdom, and in his tongue there is the law of kindness.' Equally incapable are they of fraud or guile: their love is without dissimulation: their words are always the just expression of their thoughts, opening a window into their breast, that whosoever desires may look into their hearts, and see that only love and God are there.

6. Thus, where the Lord Omnipotent taketh to Himself His mighty power and reigneth, doth He 'subdue all things to Himself,' cause every heart to overflow with love, and fill every mouth with praise. 'Happy are the people that are in such a case: yea, blessed are the people who have the Lord for their God' (Ps. cxliv. 15). 'Arise, shine,' saith the Lord; 'for thy light is come, and the glory of the Lord is risen upon thee. Thou hast known that I the Lord am thy Saviour and thy Redeemer, the mighty God of Jacob. I have made thy officers peace, and thy exactors righteousness. Violence shall no more be heard in thy land, wasting nor destruction within thy borders; but thou shalt call thy walls Salvation and thy gates Praise. Thy people are all righteous; they shall inherit the land for ever, the branch of My planting, the work of My hands, that I may be glorified. The sun shall be no more thy light by day; neither for brightness shall the

Does not exist

moon give light unto thee; but the Lord shall be unto thee an
everlasting light, and thy God thy glory' (Isa. lx. 1, 16-19, 21).

IV. Having thus briefly considered Christianity, as beginning, as going on, and as covering the earth, it remains only that
I should close the whole with a plain, practical application.

1. And, first, I would ask, Where does this Christianity now
exist? Where, I pray, do the Christians live? Which is the
country, the inhabitants whereof are all thus filled with the Holy
Ghost?—are all of one heart and of one soul; cannot suffer one
among them to lack anything, but continually give to every man
as he hath need; who, one and all, have the love of God filling
their hearts, and constraining them to love their neighbour as
themselves; who have all 'put on bowels of mercy, humbleness of
mind, gentleness, long-suffering'—who offend not in any kind,
either by word or deed, against justice, mercy, or truth; but in
every point do unto all men, as they would these should do unto
them? With what propriety can we term any a Christian country,
which does not answer this description? Why then, let us confess
we have never yet seen a Christian country upon earth.

2. I beseech you, brethren, by the mercies of God, if ye do
account me a madman or a fool, yet, *as a fool bear with me*. It is
utterly needful that some one should use great plainness of
speech towards you. It is more especially needful at *this* time; for
who knoweth but it is the *last*? Who knoweth how soon the
righteous Judge may say, 'I will no more be entreated for this
people'? 'Though Noah, Daniel, and Job were in this land, they
should but deliver their own souls.' And who will use this
plainness, if I do not? Therefore I, even I, will speak. And I
adjure you, by the living God, that ye steel not your breasts
against receiving a blessing at *my* hands. Do not say in your
hearts, *Non Persuadebis, etiamsi persuaseris*; or, in other words,
Lord, Thou shalt not *send by whom Thou will send*; let me rather
perish in my blood, than be saved by this man!

3. Brethren, 'I am persuaded better things of you, though I
thus speak.' Let me ask you then, in tender love, and in the spirit
of meekness, Is this city a Christian city? Is Christianity,
scriptural Christianity, found here? Are we, considered as a
community of men, so 'filled with the Holy Ghost,' as to enjoy in
our hearts, and show forth in our lives, the genuine fruits of that

Spirit? Are all the Magistrates, all Heads and Governors of Colleges and Halls, and their respective Societies (not to speak of the inhabitants of the town), 'of one heart and one soul'? Is 'the love of God shed abroad in our hearts'? Are our tempers the same that were in Him? And are our lives agreeable thereto? Are we 'holy as He who hath called us is holy in all manner of conversation'?

4. I entreat you to observe, that here are no peculiar notions now under consideration; that the question moved is not concerning *doubtful opinions* of one kind or another, but concerning the undoubted, fundamental branches (if there be any such) of our common Christianity. And for the decision thereof, I appeal to your own consciences, guided by the Word of God. He therefore that is not condemned by his own heart, let him go free.

5. In the fear, then, and in the presence of the great God, before whom both you and I shall shortly appear, I pray you that are in authority over us, whom I reverence for your office' sake, to consider (and not after the manner of dissemblers with God), are you 'filled with the Holy Ghost'? Are you lively portraitures of Him whom ye are appointed to represent among men? 'I have said, Ye are Gods,' ye magistrates and rulers; ye are by office so nearly allied to the God of heaven! In your several stations and degrees, ye are to show forth unto us 'the Lord our Governor.' Are all the thoughts of your hearts, all your tempers and desires suitable to your high calling? Are all your words like unto those which come out of the mouth of God? Is there in all your actions dignity and love?—a greatness which words cannot express, which can flow only from a heart 'full of God'; and yet consistent with the character of 'man that is a worm, and the son of man that is a worm'?

6. Ye venerable men, who are more especially called to form the tender minds of youth, to dispel thence the shades of ignorance and error, and train them up to be wise unto salvation, are you 'filled with the Holy Ghost'? with all those 'fruits of the Spirit,' which your important office so indispensably requires? Is your heart whole with God? full of love and zeal to set up His kingdom on earth? Do you continually remind those under your care, that the one rational end of all our studies, is to know, love, and serve 'the only true God, and Jesus

Christ whom He hath sent'? Do you inculcate upon them day by day, that love alone never faileth (whereas, whether there be tongues, they shall fail, or philosophical knowledge, it shall vanish away); and that without love, all learning is but splendid ignorance, pompous folly, vexation of spirit? Has all you teach an actual tendency to the love of God, and of all mankind for His sake? Have you an eye to this end in whatever you prescribe, touching the kind, the manner, and the measure of their studies; desiring and labouring that, wherever the lot of these young soldiers of Christ is cast, they may be so many burning and shining lights, adorning the gospel of Christ in all things? And permit me to ask, Do you put forth all your strength in the vast work you have undertaken? Do you labour herein with all your might? exerting every faculty of your soul, using every talent which God hath lent you, and that to the uttermost of your power?

7. Let it not be said, that I speak here, as if all under your care were intended to be clergymen. Not so; I only speak as if they were all intended to be Christians. But what example is set them by us who enjoy the beneficence of our forefathers? by Fellows, Students, Scholars; more especially those who are of some rank and eminence? Do ye, brethren, abound in the fruits of the Spirit, in lowliness of mind, in self-denial and mortification, in seriousness and composure of spirit, in patience, meekness, sobriety, temperance; and in unwearied, restless endeavours to do good in every kind unto all men, to relieve their outward wants, and to bring their souls to the true knowledge and love of God? Is this the general character of Fellows of Colleges? I fear it is not. Rather, have not pride and haughtiness of spirit, impatience and peevishness, sloth and indolence, gluttony and sensuality, and even a proverbial uselessness, been objected to us, perhaps not always by our enemies, nor wholly without ground? O that God would roll away this reproach from us, that the very memory of it might perish for ever!

8. Many of us are more immediately consecrated to God, called to minister in holy things. Are we then patterns to the rest, 'in word, in conversation, in charity, in spirit, in faith, in purity' (1 Tim. iv. 12)? Is there written on our forehead and on our heart, 'Holiness to the Lord'? From what motives did we enter upon this office? Was it indeed with a single eye 'to serve God,

trusting that we were inwardly moved by the Holy Ghost to take upon us this ministration, for the promoting of His glory, and the edifying of His people'? And have we 'clearly determined, by God's grace, to give ourselves wholly to this office'? Do we forsake and set aside, as much as in us lies, all worldly cares and studies? Do we apply ourselves wholly to this one thing, and draw all our cares and studies this way? Are we apt to teach? Are we taught of God, that we may be able to teach others also? Do we know God? Do we know Jesus Christ? Hath 'God revealed His Son in us'? And hath He 'made us able ministers of the new covenant'? Where then are the 'seals of our apostleship'? Who, that were dead in trespasses and sins, have been quickened by our word? Have we a burning zeal to save souls from death, so that for their sake we often forget even to eat our bread? Do we speak plain, 'by manifestation of the truth commending ourselves to every mans conscience in the sight of God' (2 Cor. iv. 2)? Are we dead to the world, and the things of the world, 'laying up all our treasure in heaven'? Do we lord over God's heritage? Or are we the least, the servants of all? When we bear the reproach of Christ, does it sit heavy upon us? Or do we rejoice therein? When we are smitten on the one cheek, do we resent it? Are we impatient of affronts? Or do we turn the other also; not resisting the evil, but overcoming evil with good? Have we a bitter zeal, inciting us to strive sharply and passionately with them that are out of the way? Or is our zeal the flame of love, so as to direct all our words with sweetness, lowliness, and meekness of wisdom?

9. Once more: what shall we say concerning the youth of this place? Have you either the form or the power of Christian godliness? Are you humble, teachable, advisable; or stubborn, self-willed, heady, and high-minded? Are you obedient to your superiors as to parents? Or do you despise those to whom you owe the tenderest reverence? Are you diligent in your easy business, pursuing your studies with all your strength? Do you redeem the time, crowding as much work into every day as it can contain? Rather, are ye not conscious to yourselves, that you waste away day after day, either in reading what has no tendency to Christianity, or in gaming, or in—you know not what? Are you better managers of your fortune than of your time? Do you, out of principle, take care to owe no man anything? Do you

'remember the Sabbath-day, to keep it holy'; to spend it in the more immediate worship of God? When you are in His house, do you consider that God is there? Do you behave 'as seeing Him that is invisible'? Do you know how to 'possess your bodies in sanctification and honour'? Are not drunkenness and uncleanness found among you? Yea, are there not of you who 'glory in their shame'? Do not many of you 'take the name of God in vain,' perhaps habitually, without either remorse or fear? Yea, are there not a multitude of you that are forsworn? I fear, a swiftly-increasing multitude. Be not surprised, brethren. Before God and this congregation, I own myself to have been of the number, solemnly swearing to observe all those customs, which I then knew nothing of; and those statutes, which I did not so much as read over, either then, or for some years after. What is perjury, if this is not? But if it be, O what a weight of sin, yea, sin of no common dye, lieth upon us! And doth not the Most High regard it?

10. May it not be one of the consequences of this, that so many of you are a generation of triflers; triflers with God, with one another, and with your own souls? For, how few of you spend, from one week to another, a single hour in private prayer! How few have any thought of God in the general tenor of your conversation! Who of you is in any degree acquainted with the work of His Spirit, His supernatural work in the souls of men? Can you bear, unless now and then in a church, any talk of the Holy Ghost? Would you not take it for granted, if one began such a conversation, that it was either hypocrisy or enthusiasm? In the name of the Lord God Almighty, I ask, what religion are you of? Even the talk of Christianity, ye cannot, will not bear. O my brethren, what a Christian city is this! 'It is time for Thee, Lord, to lay to Thine hand!'

11. For, indeed, what probability, what possibility, rather (speaking after the manner of men), is there that Christianity, scriptural Christianity, should be again the religion of this place? that all orders of men among us should speak and live as men 'filled with the Holy Ghost'? By whom should this Christianity be restored? By those of you that are in authority? Are you convinced then that this is scriptural Christianity? Are you desirous it should be restored? And do ye not count your fortune, liberty, life, dear unto yourselves, so ye may be

instrumental in the restoring of it? But suppose ye have this desire, who hath any power proportioned to the effect? Perhaps some of you have made a few faint attempts, but with how small success! Shall Christianity then be restored by young, unknown, inconsiderable men? I know not whether ye yourselves could suffer it, would not some of you cry out, 'Young man, in so doing thou reproachest us'? But there is no danger of your being put to the proof; so hath iniquity overspread us like a flood. Whom then shall God send?—the famine, the pestilence (the last messengers of God to a guilty land), or the sword, 'the armies of the Romish 'aliens,' to reform us into our first love? Nay, 'rather let us fall into Thy hand, O Lord, and let us not fall into the hand of man.'

Lord, save, or we perish! Take us out of the mire, that we sink not! O help us against these enemies! for vain is the help of man. Unto Thee all things are possible. According to the greatness of Thy power, preserve Thou those that are appointed to die; and preserve us in the manner that seemeth to Thee good; not as we will, but as Thou wilt!

SERMON V

JUSTIFICATION BY FAITH

This sermon was first published in the volume of 1746. The *Journal* entry for October 6, 1739, at Gloucester, suggests, though it does not prove, that the sermon was first preached then: 'At five in the evening, I explained to about a thousand people the nature, the cause, and the condition or instrument of justification, from these words: "To him that worketh not," ¢c.' It was preached again at Markfield June 13, 1741, from his father's tombstone at Epworth on June 8, 1742, and doubtless on many subsequent occasions. It is a clear exposition of the doctrine of justification as held by St. Paul, by Luther, by the Reformed Church of England, and substantially by all the Protestant Churches. The only point on which it needs some restatement in order to bring it into harmony with modern thought is its teaching as to the origin of sin. Wesley accepts the story of the third chapter of Genesis as literal history, and St. Paul's interpretation of it in Romans v. as final and authoritative. Indeed, he rather goes beyond anything that is actually stated in this old story in his picture of primitive man in I. 1 as a being morally and spiritually 'perfect as his Father in heaven is perfect.' Biology and anthropology will not allow of this literal interpretation. What they indicate is that the primitive pair, or primitive race, from which humanity took its origin, had gradually developed in physical structure and psychical characteristics from the lower animals of the vertebrate type. It had reached a point when the instincts of hunger and thirst and sex and so forth were fully developed; when also admiration of colour and sound and proportion had begun to be felt; and when curiosity and the desire for knowledge stirred man to activities of various kinds. Last of all came the growth of a moral sense, and the idea of duty; and then only could the race be properly described as human. Before the coming of the moral sense man was not sinful, neither was he holy; he was simply non-moral, innocent as a dog or a horse is innocent. But the moral sense involved a conflict with the older instincts and motives; and these, through their long tenure and their consequent crystallization into habit, were necessarily stronger than the nascent new-comer; yet, though defeated, the moral sense revenged itself by inspiring in the sinner shame and remorse, and a dread of the God who was conceived as the ultimate source of the moral instincts. All this is symbolically indicated in the story of the Fall. A command is given which has a divine sanction, disobedience to which is wrong. The temptation to disobey comes from the serpent, the most subtle of all the lower animals, which therefore stands for the lower nature in its highest development. (There is no suggestion in Genesis that the serpent was an incarnation of the devil—that is quite a later addition; and its popular acceptance in England is due more to Mllton than to the Bible.) The temptation is accordingly addressed to the older physical and psychical motives. 'The tree was good for food'—there is the appeal to the animal instinct of hunger; 'it was pleasant to the eyes'—there is the appeal to the aesthetic sentiment; 'it was a tree to be desired to make one wise'—there is the appeal to intellectual curiosity. In St. Paul's language it was a challenge to man to 'fulfil the desires of the flesh and the mind' rather than the new impulse of the spirit. The result was inevitable—the older habits and instincts prevailed; but with the defeat of conscience came the sense of shame, manifesting itself symbolically in special relation to the most imperious of the instincts, and the dread of God and the separation from Him, which is spiritual death. The human race is involved in the sin of Adam, because it has received from him that human nature which in its very constitution makes sin inevitable. The story of the Fall is repeated, recapitulated, in the history of every individual of the race. In the infant we find only the purely animal instincts at work; it eats and sleeps and nestles to the warmth of its mother's embrace. Then gradually we see the beginnings of aesthetic feelings, as it stretches out its hands to a brightly-coloured toy, or stops crying to listen to the sound of music. Later still comes curiosity, and it wants to grasp in its fingers or put into its mouth every new object of vision; and as it gains the power of speech, it pours out question on question, to the distraction of its parents and friends. Last of all, after a long interval, arises the dim consciousness that some things which are desirable are naughty, and must not be done; and the conflict begins in which, sooner or later, every man discovers that there is a law in his members, his bodily and intellectual outfit, warring with the law of his better self, and bringing him into a slavery from which he cannot free himself. The author of the Apocalypse of Baruch hit on a profound truth when he said (liv. 19), 'Adam is therefore not the cause [of sin] save only of his own soul, but each one of us has been the Adam of his own soul.' Sin is universal, because human nature is universal; we derive it from Adam, only as we derive from him through heredity all the predispositions to disease and physical decay which are our common lot. As partakers of the Adamic or human nature, we are born in sin; but as partakers of the deutero-Adamaic or divine nature, we may be so led by the Spirit that we shall not fulfil the desires of the flesh, having been born again, 'not of corruptible seed but of incorruptible, through the word of God, which liveth and abideth for ever.'

It is admitted that St. Paul in Romans v. interpreted the story of Genesis literally; but in this he followed the methods of exegesis in which he had been trained. As Tennant says (*Fall and Original Sin,* p. 250): 'His ideas of the first man, the temptation of Eve, the Fall and its results, were derived from the Jewish schools.' We are no more bound

to accept the details of his interpretation here than in his treatment in
Gal. iv. 21-31 of the story of Sarah and Hagar.

Wesley naturally accepted St. Paul's view; but in his *Treatise on
Original Sin* he frankly says: 'That all men are liable to these [penalties]
for Adam's sin alone I do not assert; but they are so, for their own
outward and inward sins, which, through their own fault, spring from
the infection of their nature.' And again, on the question of the justice
of God in punishing all mankind for the sin of Adam, he says: 'I do not
understand it. It is quite beyond my understanding. It is a depth which
I cannot fathom.' Nor does his view as to the origin of sin affect the
argument of this sermon in any degree. The ground of the doctrine of
justification is the universality of sin. How it came to be so, how it came
into the world at all, is irrelevant; it is here, and therefore some way of
salvation from it must be found. Underlying the whole argument,
though not expressed in so many words, there is the feeling that God
needed, not only to justify the ungodly, but to justify Himself; and this
He does by the gift of His Son.

O felix culpa, quae talem meruit salvatorem!

*To him that worketh not, but believeth on Him that justifieth the ungodly, his
faith is counted to him for righteousness.*—ROM. iv. 5.

1. How a sinner may be justified before God, the Lord and
Judge of all, is a question of no common importance to every
child of man. It contains the foundation of all our hope,
inasmuch as while we are at enmity with God, there can be no
true peace, no solid joy, either in time or in eternity. What peace
can there be, while our own heart condemns us; and much
more, He that is 'greater than our heart, and knoweth all
things'? What solid joy, either in this world or that to come, while
'the wrath of God abideth on us'?

2. And yet how little hath this important question been
understood? What confused notions have many had concerning
it! Indeed, not only confused, but often utterly false; contrary to
the truth, as light to darkness; notions absolutely inconsistent
with the oracles of God, and with the whole analogy of faith.
And hence, erring concerning the very foundation, they could
not possibly build thereon; at least, not 'gold, silver, or precious
stones,' which would endure when tried as by fire; but only 'hay
and stubble,' neither acceptable to God, nor profitable to man.

3. In order to do justice, as far as in me lies, to the vast
importance of the subject, to save those that seek the truth in

sincerity from 'vain jangling and strife of words,' to clear the confusedness of thought into which so many have already been led thereby, and to give them true and just conceptions of this great mystery of godliness, I shall endeavour to show.—

I. WHAT IS THE GENERAL GROUND OF THIS WHOLE DOCTRINE OF JUSTIFICATION;
II. WHAT JUSTIFICATION IS;
III. WHO THEY ARE THAT ARE JUSTIFIED; AND,
IV. ON WHAT TERMS THEY ARE JUSTIFIED.

I. I am first to show, what is the general ground of this whole doctrine of justification.

1. In the image of God was man made; holy as He that created him is holy; merciful as the Author of all is merciful; perfect as his Father in heaven is perfect. As God is love, so man, dwelling in love, dwelt in God, and God in him. God made him to be an 'image of His own eternity,' an incorruptible picture of the God of glory. He was accordingly pure, as God is pure, from every spot of sin. He knew not evil in any kind or degree, but was inwardly and outwardly sinless and undefiled. He 'loved the Lord his God with all his heart, and with all his mind, and soul, and strength.'

2. To man, thus upright and perfect, God gave a perfect law, to which He required full and perfect obedience. He required full obedience in every point, and this to be performed without any intermission, from the moment man became a living soul, till the time of his trial should be ended. No allowance was made for any falling short. As, indeed, there was no need of any; man being altogether equal to the task assigned, and thoroughly furnished for every good word and work.

3. To the entire law of love which was written in his heart (against which, perhaps, he could not sin directly), it seemed good to the sovereign wisdom of God to superadd one positive law: 'Thou shalt not eat of the fruit of the tree that groweth in the midst of the garden'; annexing that penalty thereto, 'In the day that thou eatest thereof thou shalt surely die.'

4. Such then was the state of man in Paradise. By the free, unmerited love of God, he was holy and happy: he knew, loved, enjoyed God, which is, in substance, life everlasting. And in this life of love he was to continue for ever, if he continued to obey

God in all things; but if he disobeyed Him in any, he was to forfeit all. 'In that day,' said God, 'thou shalt surely die.'

5. Man did disobey God. He 'ate of the tree, of which God commanded him, saying, Thou shalt not eat of it.' And in that day he was condemned by the righteous judgement of God. Then also the sentence, whereof he was warned before, began to take place upon him. For the moment he tasted that fruit, he died. His soul died, was separated from God; separate from whom the soul has no more life than the body has when separate from the soul. His body, likewise, became corruptible and mortal; so that death then took hold on this also. And being already dead in spirit, dead to God, dead in sin, he hastened on to death everlasting; to the destruction both of body and soul, in the fire never to be quenched.

6. Thus 'by one man sin entered into the world, and death by sin. And so death passed upon all men,' as being contained in him who was the common father and representative of us all. Thus, 'through the offence of one,' all are dead, dead to God, dead in sin, dwelling in a corruptible, mortal body, shortly to be dissolved, and under the sentence of death eternal. For as 'by one man's disobedience' all 'were made sinners; so, by that offence of one 'judgement came upon all men to condemnation' (Rom. v. 12, &c.).

7. In this state we were, even all mankind, when 'God so loved the world, that He gave His only begotten Son, to the end we might not perish, but have everlasting life.' In the fullness of time He was made man, another common Head of mankind, a second general Parent and Representative of the whole human race. And as such it was that 'He bore our griefs,' 'the Lord laying upon Him the iniquities of us all.' Then was He 'wounded for our transgressions, and bruised for our iniquities.' 'He made His soul an offering for sin': He poured out His blood for the transgressors; He 'bare our sins in His own body on the tree,' that by His stripes we might be healed: and by that one oblation of Himself, once offered, He hath redeemed me and all mankind; having thereby 'made a full, perfect, and sufficient sacrifice and satisfaction for the sins of the whole world.'

8. In consideration of this, that the Son of God hath 'tasted death for every man,' God hath now 'reconciled the world to Himself, not imputing to them their' former 'trespasses.' And

thus, 'as by the offence of one judgement came upon all men to condemnation; even so by the righteousness of one the free gift came upon all men unto justification.' So that, for the sake of His well-beloved Son, of what He hath done and suffered for us, God now vouchsafes, on one only condition (which Himself also enables us to perform), both to remit the punishment due to our sins, to reinstate us in His favour, and to restore our dead souls to spiritual life, as the earnest of life eternal.

9. This, therefore, is the general ground of the whole doctrine of justification. By the sin of the first Adam, who was not only the father, but likewise the representative, of us all, we all fell short of the favour of God; we all became children of wrath; or, as the Apostle expresses it, 'judgement came upon all men to condemnation.' Even so, by the sacrifice for sin made by the second Adam, as the representative of us all, God is so far reconciled to all the world, that He hath given them a new covenant; the plain condition whereof being once fulfilled, 'there is no more condemnation' for us, but 'we are justified freely by His grace, through the redemption that is in Jesus Christ.'

II. 1. But what is it to be *justified*? What is *justification*? This was the second thing which I proposed to show. And it is evident, from what has been already observed, that it is not the being made actually just and righteous. This is *sanctification*; which is, indeed, in some degree, the immediate fruit of justification, but, nevertheless, is a distinct gift of God, and of a totally different nature. The one implies, what God does for us through His Son; the other, what He works in us by His Spirit. So that, although some rare instances may be found, wherein the term *justified* or *justification* is used in so wide a sense as to include *sanctification* also; yet, in general use, they are sufficiently distinguished from each other, both by St. Paul and the other inspired writers.

2. Neither is that far-fetched conceit, that justification is the clearing us from accusation, particularly that of Satan, easily proveable from any clear text of holy writ. In the whole scriptural account of this matter, as above laid down, neither that accuser nor his accusation appears to be at all taken in. It cannot indeed be denied, that he is the 'accuser' of men, emphatically so called. But it does in no wise appear, that the

great Apostle hath any reference to this, more or less, in all that he hath written touching justification, either to the Romans or the Galatians.

3. It is also far easier to take for granted, than to prove from any clear scripture testimony, that justification is the clearing us from the accusation brought against us by the law: at least, if this forced, unnatural way of speaking mean either more or less than this, that whereas we have transgressed the law of God, and thereby deserved the damnation of hell, God does not inflict on those who are justified the punishment which they had deserved.

4. Least of all does justification imply, that God is deceived in those whom He justifies; that He thinks them to be what, in fact, they are not; that He accounts them to be otherwise than they are. It does by no means imply, that God judges concerning us contrary to the real nature of things; that He esteems us better than we really are, or believes us righteous when we are unrighteous. Surely no. The judgement of the all-wise God is always according to truth. Neither can it ever consist with His unerring wisdom, to think that I am innocent, to judge that I am righteous or holy, because another is so. He can no more, in this manner, confound me with Christ, than with David or Abraham. Let any man, to whom God hath given understanding, weigh this without prejudice; and he cannot but perceive, that such a notion of justification is neither reconcileable to reason nor Scripture.

5. The plain scriptural notion of justification is pardon, the forgiveness of sins. It is that act of God the Father, whereby, for the sake of the propitiation made by the blood of His Son, He 'showeth forth His righteousness' (or mercy) 'by the remission of the sins that are past.' This is the easy, natural account of it given by St. Paul, throughout this whole epistle. So he explains it himself, more particularly in this, and in the following chapter. Thus, in the next verses but one to the text, 'Blessed are they,' saith he, 'whose iniquities are forgiven, and whose sins are covered: blessed is the man to whom the Lord will not impute sin.' To him that is justified or forgiven, God 'will not impute sin' to his condemnation. He will not condemn him on that account, either in this world or in that which is to come. His sins, all his past sins, in thought, word and deed, are covered, are blotted

out, shall not be remembered or mentioned against him, any more than if they had not been. God will not inflict on that sinner what he deserved to suffer, because the Son of His love hath suffered for him. And from the time we are 'accepted through the Beloved,' 'reconciled to God through His blood,' He loves, and blesses, and watches over us for good, even as if we had never sinned.

Indeed the Apostle in one place seems to extend the meaning of the word much farther, where he says, 'Not the hearers of the law, but the doers of the law, shall be justified.' Here he appears to refer our justification to the sentence of the great day. And so our Lord Himself unquestionably doth, when He says, 'By thy words thou shalt be justified'; proving thereby that 'for every idle word men shall speak, they shall give an account in the day of judgement'; but perhaps we can hardly produce another instance of St. Paul's using the word in that distant sense. In the general tenor of his writings, it is evident he doth not; and least of all in the text before us, which undeniably speaks, not of those who have already 'finished their course,' but of those who are now just *setting out,* just beginning to 'run the race which is set before them.'

III. 1. But this is the third thing which was to be considered, namely, Who are they that are justified? And the Apostle tells us expressly, the ungodly: 'He' (that is, God) 'justifieth the ungodly'; the ungodly of every kind and degree; and none but the ungodly. As 'they that are righteous need no repentance,' so they need no forgiveness. It is only sinners that have any occasion for pardon: it is sin alone which admits of being forgiven. Forgiveness, therefore, has an immediate reference to sin, and, in this respect, to nothing else. It is our *unrighteousness* to which the pardoning God is *merciful:* it is our *iniquity* which He 'remembereth no more.'

2. This seems not to be at all considered by those who so vehemently contend that a man must be sanctified, that is, holy, before he can be justified; especially by such of them as affirm, that universal holiness or obedience must precede justification. (Unless they mean that justification at the last day which is wholly out of the present question.) So far from it, that the very supposition is not only flatly impossible (for where there is no

love of God, there is no holiness, and there is no love of God but from a sense of His loving us), but also grossly, intrinsically absurd, contradictory to itself. For it is not a saint but a sinner that is forgiven, and under the notion of a sinner. God justifieth not the godly, but the ungodly; not those that are holy already, but the unholy. Upon what condition He doeth this, will be considered quickly: but whatever it is, it cannot be holiness. To assert this, is to say the Lamb of God takes away only those sins which were taken away before.

3. Does then the Good Shepherd seek and save only those that are found already? No. He seeks and saves that which is lost. He pardons those who need His pardoning mercy. He saves from the guilt of sin (and, at the same time, from the power) sinners of every kind, of every degree; men who, till then, were altogether ungodly; in whom the love of the Father was not; and, consequently, in whom dwelt no good thing, no good or truly Christian temper; but all such as were evil and abominable— pride, anger, love of the world, the genuine fruits of that *carnal mind* which is 'enmity against God.'

4. These who are sick, the burden of whose sins is intolerable, are they that need a Physician; these who are guilty, who groan under the wrath of God, are they that need a pardon. These who are *condemned already,* not only by God, but also by their own conscience, as by a thousand witnesses, of all their ungodliness, both in thought, and word, and work, cry aloud for him that 'justifieth the ungodly,' through the redemption that is in Jesus,—the ungodly, and 'him that worketh not'; that worketh not, before he is justified, anything that is good, that is truly virtuous or holy, but only evil continually. For his heart is necessarily, essentially evil, till the love of God is shed abroad therein. And while the tree is corrupt, so are the fruits; 'for an evil tree cannot bring forth good fruit.'

5. If it be objected, 'Nay, but a man, before he is justified, may feed the hungry, or clothe the naked; and these are good works,'—the answer is easy: He may do these, even before he is justified; and these are, in one sense, 'good works'—they are 'good and profitable to men.' But it does not follow, that they are, strictly speaking, good in themselves, or good in the sight of God. All truly *good works* (to use the words of our Church) *follow after justification;* and they are therefore good and 'acceptable to

God in Christ,' because they 'spring out of a true and living faith.' By a parity of reason, all *works done before justification are not good,* in the Christian sense, *forasmuch as they spring not of faith in Jesus Christ* (though [often] from some kind of faith in God they may spring); 'yea rather, for that they are not done as God hath willed and commanded them to be done, we doubt not' (how strange soever it may appear to some) 'but they have the nature of sin.'

6. Perhaps those who doubt of this have not duly considered the weighty reason which is here assigned, why no works done before justification can be truly and properly good. The argument plainly runs thus:—

No works are good, which are not done as God hath willed and commanded them to be done:

But no works done before justification are done as God hath willed and commanded them to be done:

Therefore, no works done before justification are good.

The first proposition is self-evident; and the second—that no works done before justification are done as God hath willed and commanded them to be done—will appear equally plain and undeniable, if we only consider, God hath willed and commanded, that *all our works* should *be done in charity* (εν αγαπη), in love, in that love to God which produces love to all mankind. But none of our works can be done in this love, while the love of the Father (of God as our Father) is not in us; and this love cannot be in us till we receive the 'Spirit of adoption, crying in our hearts, Abba, Father.' If, therefore, God doth not *justify the ungodly,* and him that (in this sense) *worketh not,* then hath Christ died in vain; then, notwithstanding His death, can no flesh living be justified.

IV. 1. But on what terms, then, is he justified, who is altogether *ungodly,* and till that time *worketh not?* On one alone, which is faith: he 'believeth in Him that justifieth the ungodly.' And 'he that believeth is not condemned'; yea, he is 'passed from death unto life.' 'For the righteousness' (or mercy) 'of God is by faith of Jesus Christ unto all and upon all them that believe: whom God hath set forth for a propitiation, through faith in His blood; that He might be just, and' (consistently with His justice) 'the justifier of him which believeth in Jesus': 'therefore, we conclude, that a man is justified by faith, without the deeds of the law'; without previous obedience to the moral law, which, indeed, he could not, till now, perform. That it is the moral law, and that alone, which is here intended, appears evidently from the words that follow: 'Do we then make void the law through faith? God forbid! Yea, we establish the law.' What law do we establish by faith? Not the ritual law: not the ceremonial law of Moses. In no wise; but the great, unchangeable law of love, the holy love of God and of our neighbour.

2. Faith in general is a divine, supernatural ελεγχος, *evidence* or *conviction*, 'of things not seen,' not discoverable by our bodily senses, as being either past, future, or spiritual, justifying faith implies, not only a divine evidence or conviction that 'God was in Christ, reconciling the world unto Himself,' but a sure trust and confidence that Christ died for *my* sins, that He loved *me*, and gave Himself for *me*. And at what time soever a sinner thus believes, be it in early childhood, in the strength of his years, or when he is old and hoary-haired, God justifieth that ungodly one: God, for the sake of His Son, pardoneth and absolveth him who had in him, till then, no good thing. Repentance, indeed, God had given him before; but that repentance was neither more nor less than a deep sense of the want of all good, and the presence of all evil. And whatever good he hath, or doeth, from that hour, when he first believes in God through Christ, faith does not *find*, but *bring*. This is the fruit of faith. First the tree is good, and then the fruit is good also.

3. I cannot describe the nature of this faith better than in the words of our own Church: 'The only instrument of salvation' (whereof justification is one branch) 'is faith; that is, a sure trust and confidence that God both hath and will forgive our sins, that He hath accepted us again into His favour, for the merits of Christ's death and passion. But here we must take heed that we do not halt with God through an inconstant, wavering faith: Peter, coming to Christ upon the water, because he fainted in faith, was in danger of drowning; so we, if we begin to waver or doubt, it is to be feared that we shall sink as Peter did, not into the water, but into the bottomless pit of hell-fire.'

'Therefore, have a sure and constant faith, not only that the death of Christ is available for all the world, but that He hath made a full and sufficient sacrifice for *thee*, a perfect cleansing of *thy* sins, so that thou mayest say, with the Apostle, He loved *thee*, and gave Himself for *thee*. For this is to make Christ *thine own*, and to apply His merits unto *thyself*.'

4. By affirming that this faith is the term or *condition of justification*, I mean, first, that there is no justification without it. 'He that believeth not is condemned already'; and so long as he believeth not, that condemnation cannot be removed, but 'the wrath of God abideth on him.' As 'there is no other name given under heaven' than that of Jesus of Nazareth, no other merit whereby a condemned sinner can ever be saved from the guilt of sin, so there is no other way of obtaining a share in His merit, than *by faith in his name*. So that as long as we are without this faith, we are 'strangers to the covenant of promise,' we are 'aliens from the commonwealth of Israel, and without God in the world.' Whatsoever virtues (so called) a man may have—I speak of those unto whom the gospel is preached; for 'what have I to do to judge them that are without?'—whatsoever good works (so accounted) he may do, it profiteth not; he is still a *child of wrath*, still under the curse, till he believes in Jesus.

5. Faith, therefore, is the *necessary* condition of justification; yea, and the *only necessary* condition thereof. This is the second point carefully to be observed; that, the very moment God giveth faith (for *it is the gift of God*) to the 'ungodly' that 'worketh not,' that 'faith is counted to him for righteousness.' He hath no righteousness at all, antecedent to this; not so much as negative righteousness, or innocence. But 'faith is imputed to him for righteousness' the very moment that he believeth. Not that God (as was observed before) thinketh him to be what he is not. But as 'He made Christ to be sin for us,' that is, treated Him as a sinner, punishing Him for our sins, so He counteth us righteous, from the time we believe in Him: that is, He doth not punish us for our sins; yea, treats us as though we were guiltless and righteous.

6. Surely the difficulty of assenting to this proposition, that 'faith is the *only condition* of justification,' must arise from not understanding it. We mean thereby thus much, that it is the only thing without which no one is justified; the only thing that is immediately, indispensably, absolutely requisite in order to pardon. As, on the one hand, though a man should have everything else without faith, yet he cannot be justified; so, on the other, though he be supposed to want everything else, yet if

he hath faith, he cannot but be justified. For suppose a sinner of any kind or degree, in a full sense of his total ungodliness, of his utter inability to think, speak, or do good, and his absolute meetness for hell-fire; suppose, I say, this sinner, helpless and hopeless, casts himself wholly on the mercy of God in Christ (which indeed he cannot do but by the grace of God), who can doubt but he is forgiven in that moment? Who will affirm that any more is *indispensably required*, before that sinner can be justified?

Now, if there ever was one such instance from the beginning of the world (and have there not been, and are there not, ten thousand times ten thousand?), it plainly follows, that faith is, in the above sense, the sole condition of justification.

7. It does not become poor, guilty, sinful worms, who receive whatsoever blessings they enjoy (from the least drop of water that cools our tongue, to the immense riches of glory in eternity), of grace, of mere favour, and not of debt, to ask of God the reasons of His conduct. It is not meet for us to call Him in question, 'who giveth account to none of His ways'; to demand, Why didst Thou make faith the condition, the only condition, of justification? Wherefore didst Thou decree, *He that believeth*, and he only, *shall be saved*? This is the very point on which St. Paul so strongly insists in the ninth chapter of this Epistle, viz. that the terms of pardon and acceptance must depend, not on us, but *on Him that calleth us*: that there is no *unrighteousness with God*, in fixing His own terms, not according to ours, but His own good pleasure; who may justly say, 'I will have mercy on whom I will have mercy,' namely, on him who believeth in Jesus. 'So then it is not of him that willeth, nor of him that runneth,' to choose the condition on which he shall find acceptance, 'but of God that showeth mercy'; that accepteth none at all, but of His own free love, His unmerited goodness. 'Therefore hath He mercy on whom He will have mercy,' viz. on those who believe on the Son of His love; 'and whom He will,' that is, those who believe not, 'He hardeneth,' leaves at last to the hardness of their hearts.

8. One reason, however, we may humbly conceive, of God's fixing this condition of justification, 'If thou believest in the Lord Jesus Christ, thou shalt be saved,' was to *hide pride from man*. Pride had already destroyed the very angels of God, had cast down 'a third part of the stars of heaven.' It was likewise in great

measure owing to this, when the tempter said, 'Ye shall be as gods,' that Adam fell from his own steadfastness, and brought sin and death into the world. It was therefore an instance of wisdom worthy of God, to appoint such a condition of reconciliation for him and all his posterity, as might effectually humble, might abase them to the dust. And such is faith. It is peculiarly fitted for this end: for he that cometh unto God by this faith, must fix his eye singly on his own wickedness, on his guilt and helplessness, without having the least regard to any supposed good in himself, to any virtue or righteousness whatsoever. He must come as a *mere sinner*, inwardly and outwardly, self-destroyed and self-condemned, bringing nothing to God but ungodliness only, pleading nothing of his own but sin and misery. Thus it is, and thus alone, when his *mouth is stopped*, and he stands utterly *guilty before God*, that he can *look unto Jesus*, as the whole and sole *propitiation for his sins*. Thus only can he be *found in Him*, and receive the 'righteousness which is of God by faith.'

9. Thou ungodly one, who hearest or readest these words! thou vile, helpless, miserable sinner! I charge thee before God the Judge of all, go straight unto Him, with all thy ungodliness. Take heed thou destroy not thy own soul by pleading thy righteousness, more or less. Go as altogether ungodly, guilty, lost, destroyed, deserving and dropping into hell; and thou shalt then find favour in His sight, and know that He justifieth the ungodly. As such thou shalt be brought unto the *blood of sprinkling*, as an undone, helpless, damned sinner. Thus *look unto Jesus*! There is *the Lamb of God*, who *taketh away* thy *sins*! Plead thou no works, no righteousness of thine own! no humility, contrition, sincerity! In no wise. That were, in very deed, to deny the Lord that bought thee. No: plead thou singly the blood of the covenant, the ransom paid for thy proud, stubborn, sinful soul. Who art thou, that now seest and feelest both thine inward and outward ungodliness? Thou art the man! I want thee for my Lord! I challenge *thee* for a child of God by faith! The Lord hath need of thee. Thou who feelest thou art just fit for hell, art just fit to advance His glory; the glory of His free grace, justifying the ungodly and him that worketh not. O come quickly! Believe in the Lord Jesus, and thou, even thou, art reconciled to God.

SERMON VI

THE RIGHTEOUSNESS OF FAITH

In *Journal,* June 12, 1742, Wesley says, 'I preached on the righteousness of the law and the righteousness of faith.' [This was at Epworth.] 'While I was speaking, several dropped down as dead, and among the rest such a cry was heard of sinners groaning for the righteousness of faith as almost drowned my voice. But many of these soon lift up their heads with joy, and broke out into thanksgiving, being assured they now had the desire of their souls—the forgiveness of their sins.' On June 17 he preached on the same subject at Sheffield, and 'had not half finished my discourse when I was constrained to break off in the midst, our hearts were so filled with a sense of the love of God, and our mouths with prayer and thanksgiving. When we were somewhat satisfied herewith, I went on to call sinners to the salvation ready to be revealed.'

It seems a pity that a sermon so clear, convincing, and effective should have been based on a misinterpretation of the text. But so it is. To begin with, Wesley affirms that the first verse refers to an alleged covenant of works made with Adam while in Paradise, and not to the covenant given by Moses. The passage occurs in Lev. xviii. 5, and runs, 'Ye shall therefore keep My statutes, and My judgements; which, if a man do, he shall live in them.' The phrase 'My statutes and judgements' is used several times in Leviticus, and refers always to the laws which are there laid down. The Covenant of Works is a theological fiction, which made its first appearance about the beginning of the seventeenth century. It is not found in any of the creeds or symbols, except the Westminster Confession (1648), in which chap. vii. sec. 2 runs: 'The first covenant made with man was a covenant of works, wherein life was promised to Adam, and in him to his posterity, upon condition of perfect and personal obedience.' Wesley admits that both passages 'were spoken by Moses himself to the people of Israel, and that concerning the covenant which then was.' Yet all through the sermon he takes the first passage as referring to the covenant of works. He rightly says that the second passage also had its original reference to the law of Moses; but he fails to notice, at any rate explicitly, that St. Paul does not quote the exact words of Moses (Deut. xxx. 11-14), but modifies them to suit his purpose, and puts them into the mouth of 'the righteousness which is of faith' personified. What Moses said was that the law was not too hard for the people to observe; it had not to be fetched from heaven, or from over the sea; on the contrary, it was actually in their mouth and heart. St. Paul adapts this saying, which had already become proverbial (see 4 Esdras iv. 8, Baruch iii. 29, Jubilees xxiv. 32), and makes the Righteousness of Faith say, 'It is not necessary to bring Christ down from above; He has already become incarnate amongst men: nor to bring Him back from the dead; He has already been raised from the grave; there are no impossibilities required of thee; the word of salvation is in thy mouth and heart. Thou hast but to believe on Christ in thy heart, and confess Him with thy mouth, and thou art saved.' St. Paul's argument is that the gospel, like the law, is clearly revealed to men by the preaching of himself and his fellow apostles; but, unlike the law, it demands not a perfect and unbroken obedience to precepts, but a faith which makes righteousness possible. Thus Wesley's premisses are all wrong, but his conclusions are all right; which happened sometimes even to St. Paul himself, as in 1 Cor. ix. 9.

Moses describeth the righteousness which is of the law, That the man which doeth those things shall live by them.
But the righteousness which is of faith speaketh on this wise, Say not in thine heart, Who shall ascend into heaven (that is, to bring Christ down from above)?
Or, Who shall descend onto the deep (that is, to bring up Christ again from the dead)?
But what saith it? The work is nigh thee, even in thy mouth, and in thy heart: that is, the word of faith which we preach.—ROM. x. 5-8.

1. The Apostle does not here oppose the covenant given by Moses, to the covenant given by Christ. If we ever imagined this, it was for want of observing, that the latter as well as the former part of these words were spoken by Moses himself to the people of Israel, and that concerning the covenant which then was (Deut. xxx. 11, 12, 14). But it is the covenant of grace, which God, through Christ, hath established with men in all ages (as well before and under the Jewish dispensation, as since God was manifest in the flesh), which St. Paul here opposes to the covenant of works, made with Adam while in paradise, but commonly supposed to be the only covenant which God had made with man, particularly by those Jews of whom the Apostle writes.

2. Of these it was that he so affectionately speaks in the beginning of this chapter: 'My heart's desire and prayer to God for Israel is, that they may be saved. For I bear them record, that they have a zeal for God, but not according to knowledge. For they being ignorant of God's righteousness' (of the justification that flows from His mere grace and mercy, freely forgiving our

sins through the Son of His love, through the redemption which is in Jesus) 'and seeking to establish their own righteousness' (their own holiness, antecedent to faith in 'Him that justifieth the ungodly,' as the ground of their pardon and acceptance), 'have not submitted themselves unto the righteousness of God,' and consequently, seek death in the error of their life.

3. They were ignorant that 'Christ is the end of the law for righteousness to every one that believeth,'—that, by the oblation of Himself once offered, He had put an end to the first law or covenant (which, indeed, was not given by God to Moses, but to Adam in his state of innocence), the strict tenor whereof, without any abatement, was, 'Do this, and live'; and, at the same time, purchased for us that better covenant, 'Believe, and live'; believe, and thou shalt be saved; now saved, both from the guilt and power of sin, and, of consequence, from the wages of it.

4. And how many are equally ignorant now, even among those who are called by the name of Christ! How many who have now 'a zeal for God,' yet have it not 'according to knowledge'; but are still seeking 'to establish their own righteousness' as the ground of their pardon and acceptance; and therefore vehemently refuse to 'submit themselves unto the righteousness of God'! Surely my heart's desire, and prayer to God for you, brethren, is, that ye may be saved. And, in order to remove this grand stumbling-block out of your way, I will endeavour to show, first, what the righteousness *is* which is of the law, and what 'the righteousness which is of faith'; secondly, the folly of trusting in the righteousness of the law, and the wisdom of submitting to that which is of faith.

I. 1. And, first, 'the righteousness which is of the law saith, The man which doeth these things shall live by them.' Constantly and perfectly observe all these things to do them, and then thou shalt live for ever. This law, or covenant (usually called the covenant of works), given by God to man in paradise, required an obedience perfect in all its parts, entire and wanting nothing, as the condition of his eternal continuance in the holiness and happiness wherein he was created.

2. It required that man should fulfil all righteousness, inward and outward, negative and positive: that he should not only abstain from every idle word, and avoid every evil work, but

should keep every affection, every desire, every thought, in obedience to the will of God; that he should continue holy as He which had created him was holy, both in heart, and in all manner of conversation; that he should be pure in heart, even as God is pure; perfect as his Father in heaven was perfect: that he should love the Lord his God with all his heart, with all his soul, with all his mind, and with all his strength; that he should love every soul which God had made, even as God had loved him: that by this universal benevolence, he should dwell in God (who is love), and God in him: that he should serve the Lord his God with all his strength, and in all things singly aim at His glory.

3. These were the things which the righteousness of the law required, that he who did them might live thereby. But it farther required, that this entire obedience to God, this inward and outward holiness, this conformity both of heart and life to His will, should be perfect in *degree*. No abatement, no allowance could possibly be made, for falling short in any degree, as to any jot or tittle, either of the outward or the inward law. If every commandment relating to outward things was obeyed, yet that was not sufficient, unless every one was obeyed with all the strength, in the highest measure, and most perfect manner. Nor did it answer the demand of this covenant to love God with every power and faculty, unless He were loved with the full capacity of each, with the whole possibility of the soul.

4. One thing more was indispensably required by the righteousness of the law, namely, that this universal obedience, this perfect holiness both of heart and life, should be perfectly uninterrupted also, should continue without any intermission, from the moment wherein God created man, and breathed into his nostrils the breath of life, until the days of his trial should be ended, and he should be confirmed in life everlasting.

5. The righteousness, then, which is of the law, speaketh on this wise: 'Thou, O man of God, stand fast in love, in the image of God wherein thou art made. If thou wilt remain in life, keep the commandments, which are now written in thy heart. Love the Lord thy God with all thy heart. Love, as thyself, every soul that He hath made. Desire nothing but God. Aim at God in every thought, in every word and work. Swerve not in one motion of body or soul, from Him, thy mark, and the prize of thy high calling; and let all that is in thee praise His holy name, every

power and faculty of thy soul, in every kind, in every degree, and at every moment of thine existence. "This do, and thou shalt live": thy light shall shine, thy love shall flame, more and more, till thou art received up into the house of God in the heavens, to reign with Him for ever and ever.'

6. 'But the righteousness which is of faith speaketh on this wise: Say not in thine heart, Who shall ascend into heaven? that is, to bring down Christ from above' (as though it were some impossible task which God required thee previously to perform, in order to thine acceptance); 'or, Who shall descend into the deep? that is, to bring up Christ from the dead' (as though that were still remaining to be done, for the sake of which thou wert to be accepted); 'but what saith it? The word,' according to the tenor of which thou mayest now be accepted as an heir of life eternal, 'is nigh thee, even in thy mouth, and in thy heart: that is, the word of faith, which we preach'—the new covenant which God hath now established with sinful man through Christ Jesus.

7. By 'the righteousness which is of faith' is meant, that condition of justification (and, in consequence, of present and final salvation, if we endure therein unto the end) which was given by God to _fallen man,_ through the merits and mediation of His only-begotten Son. This was in part revealed to Adam, soon after his fall; being contained in the original promise, made to him, and his seed, concerning the Seed of the woman, who should 'bruise the serpent's head' (Gen. iii. 15). It was a little more clearly revealed to Abraham, by the Angel of God from heaven, saying, 'By Myself have I sworn, saith the Lord, that in thy Seed shall all the nations of the world be blessed' (Gen. xxii. 16, 18). It was yet more fully made known to Moses, to David, and to the prophets that followed; and, through them, to many of the people of God in their respective generations. But still the bulk even of these were ignorant of it; and very few understood it clearly. Still 'life and immortality' were not so 'brought to light' to the Jews of old, as they are now unto us 'by the gospel.'

8. Now this covenant saith not to sinful man, 'Perform unsinning obedience, and live.' If this were the term, he would have no more benefit by all which Christ hath done and suffered for him, than if he was required, in order to life, to 'ascend into heaven, and bring down Christ from above'; or to 'descend into the deep,' into the invisible world, and 'bring up Christ from the

dead.' It doth not require any impossibility to be done (although, to mere man, what it requires would be impossible; but not to man assisted by the Spirit of God): this were only to mock human weakness. Indeed, strictly speaking, the covenant of *grace* doth not require us to *do* anything at all, as absolutely and indispensably necessary in order to our justification; but only to *believe* in Him who, for the sake of His Son, and the propitiation which He hath made, 'justifieth the ungodly that worketh not,' and imputes his faith to him for righteousness. Even so Abraham 'believed in the Lord, and He counted it to him for righteousness' (Gen. xv. 6). 'And he received the sign of circumcision, a seal of the righteousness of faith . . . that he might be the father of all them that believe . . . that righteousness might be imputed unto them also' (Rom. iv. 11). 'Now it was not written for his sake alone, that it,' i.e. faith, 'was imputed to him; but for us also, to whom it shall be imputed,' to whom faith shall be imputed for righteousness, shall stand in the stead of perfect obedience, in order to our acceptance with God, 'if we believe on Him who raised up Jesus our Lord from the dead; who was delivered' to death 'for our offences, and was raised again for our justification' (Rom. iv. 23-25): for the assurance of the remission of our sins, and of a second life to come, to them that believe.

9. What saith then the covenant of forgiveness, of unmerited love, of pardoning mercy? 'Believe in the Lord Jesus Christ, and thou shalt be saved.' In the day thou believest, thou shalt surely live. Thou shalt be restored to the favour of God; and in His pleasure is life. Thou shalt be saved from the curse, and from the wrath, of God. Thou shalt be quickened from the death of sin into the life of righteousness. And if thou endure to the end, believing in Jesus, thou shalt never taste the second death; but, having suffered with thy Lord, shalt also live and reign with Him for ever and ever.

10. Now 'this word is nigh thee.' This condition of life is plain, easy, always at hand. 'It is in thy mouth, and in thy heart,' through the operation of the Spirit of God. The moment 'thou believest in thine heart' in Him whom God 'hath raised from the dead,' and 'confessest with thy mouth the Lord Jesus,' as *thy* Lord and *thy* God, 'thou shalt be saved' from condemnation, from the guilt and punishment of thy former sins, and shalt

have power to serve God in true holiness all the remaining days of thy life.

11. What is the difference then between the 'righteousness which is of the law,' and the 'righteousness which is of faith'? between the first covenant, or the covenant of works, and the second, the covenant of grace? The essential, unchangeable difference is this: the one supposes him to whom it is given, to be already holy and happy, created in the image and enjoying the favour of God; and prescribes the condition whereon he may continue therein, in love and joy, life and immortality: the other supposes him to whom it is given, to be now unholy and unhappy, fallen short of the glorious image of God, having the wrath of God abiding on him, and hastening, through sin, whereby his soul is dead, to bodily death, and death everlasting; and to man in this state it prescribes the condition whereon he may regain the pearl he has lost, may recover the favour and image of God, may retrieve the life of God in his soul, and be restored to the knowledge and the love of God, which is the beginning of life eternal.

12. Again: the covenant of works, in order to man's *continuance* in the favour of God, in His knowledge and love, in holiness and happiness, required of perfect man a *perfect* and uninterrupted *obedience* to every point of the law of God. Whereas, the covenant of grace, in order to man's *recovery* of the favour and the life of God, requires only *faith*; living faith in Him who, through God, justifies him that obeyed not.

13. Yet, again: the covenant of works required of Adam, and all his children, to pay the price themselves, in consideration of which they were to receive all the future blessings of God. But in the covenant of grace, seeing we have nothing to pay. God 'frankly forgives us all': provided only, that we believe in Him who hath paid the price for us; who hath given Himself a 'propitiation for our sins, for the sins of the whole world.'

14. Thus the first covenant required what is now *afar off* from all the children of men; namely, unsinning obedience, which is far from those who are 'conceived and born in sin.' Whereas, the second requires what is nigh at hand; as though it should say, 'Thou art sin! God is love! Thou by sin art fallen short of the glory of God; yet there is mercy with Him. Bring then all thy sins to the pardoning God, and they shall vanish away as a cloud. If

thou wert not ungodly, there would be no room for Him to justify thee as ungodly. But now draw near, in full assurance of faith. He speaketh, and it is done. Fear not, only believe; for even the just God justifieth all that believe in Jesus.'

II. 1. These things considered, it will be easy to show, as I proposed to do in the second place, the folly of trusting in the 'righteousness which is of the law,' and the wisdom of submitting to the 'righteousness which is of faith.'

The folly of those who still trust in the 'righteousness which is of the law,' the terms of which are, 'Do this, and live,' may abundantly appear from hence: they set out wrong; their very first step is a fundamental mistake: for, before they can ever think of claiming any blessing on the terms of this covenant, they must suppose themselves to be in his state with whom this covenant was made. But how vain a supposition this is; since it was made with Adam in a state of innocence! How weak, therefore, must that whole building be, which stands on such a foundation! And how foolish are they who thus build on the sand; who seem never to have considered, that the covenant of works was not given to man when he was 'dead in trespasses and sins,' but when he was alive to God, when he knew no sin, but was holy as God is holy; who forget, that it was never designed for the *recovery* of the favour and life of God once lost, but only for the *continuance* and increase thereof, till it should be complete in life everlasting.

2. Neither do they consider, who are thus seeking to establish their 'own righteousness, which is of the law,' what manner of obedience or righteousness that is which the law indispensably requires. It must be perfect and entire in every point, or it answers not the demand of the law. But which of you is able to perform such obedience? or, consequently, to live thereby? Who among you fulfils every jot and tittle even of the outward commandments of God? doing nothing, great or small, which God forbids? leaving nothing undone which He enjoins? speaking no *idle word*? having your conversation always 'meet to minister grace to the hearers'? and, 'whether you eat or drink, or whatever you do, doing all to the glory of God'? And how much less are you able to fulfil all the inward commandments of God; those which require, that every temper and motion of your soul

should be holiness unto the Lord! Are you able to 'love God with all your heart'? to love all mankind as your own soul? to 'pray without ceasing? in everything to give thanks'? to have God always before you? and to keep every affection, desire, and thought, in obedience to His law?

3. You should farther consider, that the righteousness of the law requires not only the obeying every command of God, negative and positive, internal and external, but likewise in the perfect degree. In every instance whatever, the voice of the law is, 'Thou shalt serve the Lord thy God with all thy strength.' It allows no abatement of any kind: it excuses no defect: it condemns every coming short of the full measure of obedience, and immediately pronounces a curse on the offender: it regards only the invariable rules of justice, and saith, 'I know not to show mercy.'

4. Who then can appear before such a Judge, who is 'extreme to mark what is done amiss'? How weak are they who desire to be tried at the bar where 'no flesh living can be justified'!—none of the offspring of Adam. For, suppose we did now keep every commandment with all our strength; yet one single breach, which ever was, utterly destroys our whole claim to life. If we have ever offended in any one point, this righteousness is at an end. For the law condemns all who do not perform uninterrupted as well as perfect obedience. So that, according to the sentence of this, for him who hath once sinned, in any degree, 'there remaineth only a fearful looking for of fiery indignation, which shall devour the adversaries' of God.

5. Is it not then the very foolishness of folly, for fallen man to seek life by this righteousness? for man, who was 'shapen in wickedness, and in sin did his mother conceive him'? man, who is, by nature, all 'earthly, sensual, devilish'; altogether 'corrupt and abominable'; in whom, till he find grace, 'dwelleth no good thing'; nay, who cannot of himself think one good thought; who is indeed all sin, a mere lump of ungodliness, and who commits sin in every breath he draws; whose actual transgressions, in word and deed, are more in number than the hairs of his head? What stupidity, what senselessness, must it be for such an unclean, guilty, helpless worm as this, to dream of seeking acceptance by his own righteousness, of living by 'the righteousness which is of the law'!

6. Now, whatsoever considerations prove the folly of trusting in the 'righteousness which is of the law,' prove equally the wisdom of submitting to the 'righteousness which is of God by faith.' This were easy to be shown with regard to each of the preceding considerations. But, to waive this, the wisdom of the first step hereto, the disclaiming our own righteousness plainly appears from hence, that it is acting according to truth to the real nature of things. For, what is it more, than to acknowledge with our heart as well as lips, the true state wherein we are? to acknowledge, that we bring with us into the world a corrupt, sinful nature; more corrupt, indeed, than we can easily conceive, or find words to express? that hereby we are prone to all that is evil, and averse from all that is good: that we are full of pride, self-will, unruly passions, foolish desires, vile and inordinate affections; lovers of the world, lovers of pleasure more than lovers of God? that our lives have been no better than our hearts, but many ways ungodly and unholy; insomuch that our actual sins, both in word and deed, have been as the stars of heaven for multitude; that, on all these accounts, we are displeasing to Him who is of purer eyes than to behold iniquity, and deserve nothing from Him but indignation and wrath and death, the due wages of sin? that we cannot, by any of our righteousness (for indeed we have none at all), nor by any of our works (for they are as the tree upon which they grow), appease the wrath of God, or avert the punishment we have justly deserved; yea, that, if left to ourselves, we shall only wax worse and worse, sink deeper and deeper into sin, offend God more and more, both with our evil works, and with the evil tempers of our carnal mind, till we fill up the measure of our iniquities, and bring upon ourselves swift destruction? And is not this the very state wherein by nature we are? To acknowledge this, then, both with our heart and lips, that is, to disclaim our own righteousness, 'the righteousness which is of the law,' is to act according to the real nature of things, and, consequently, is an instance of true wisdom.

7. The wisdom of submitting to 'the righteousness of faith' appears, farther, from this consideration, that it is the righteousness of God: I mean here, it is that method of reconciliation with God which hath been chosen and established by God Himself, not only as He is the God of wisdom, but as He

is the sovereign Lord of heaven and earth and of every creature which He hath made. Now, as it is not meet for man to say unto God, 'What doest Thou?'—as none, who is not utterly void of understanding, will contend with One that is mightier than he, with Him whose kingdom ruleth over all: so it is true wisdom, it is a mark of sound understanding, to acquiesce in whatever He hath chosen; to say in this, as in all things, 'It is the Lord: let Him do what seemeth Him good.'

8. It may be farther considered, that it was of mere grace, of free love, of undeserved mercy, that God hath vouchsafed to sinful man any way of reconciliation with Himself; that we were not cut away from His hand, and utterly blotted out of His remembrance. Therefore, whatever method He is pleased to appoint, of His tender mercy, of His unmerited goodness, whereby His enemies, who have so deeply revolted from Him, so long and obstinately rebelled against Him, may still find favour in His sight, it is doubtless our wisdom to accept it with all thankfulness.

9. To mention but one consideration more. It is wisdom to aim at the best end by the best means. Now the best end which any creature can pursue is, happiness in God. And the best end a fallen creature can pursue is, the recovery of the favour and image of God. But the best, indeed the only means under heaven given to a man, whereby he may regain the favour of God, which is better than life itself, or the image of God, which is the true life of the soul, is the submitting to the 'righteousness which is of faith,' the believing in the only-begotten Son of God.

III. 1. Whosoever therefore thou art, who desirest to be forgiven and reconciled to the favour of God, do not say in thy heart, 'I must *first do this;* I must *first* conquer every sin; break off every evil word and work, and do all good to all men; or, I must *first* go to church, receive the Lord's supper, hear more sermons, and say more prayers.' Alas, my brother! thou art clean gone out of the way. Thou art still 'ignorant of the righteousness of God,' and art 'seeking to establish thy own righteousness' as the ground of thy reconciliation. Knowest thou not, that thou canst do nothing but sin, till thou art reconciled to God? Wherefore, then, dost thou say, 'I must do this and this *first,* and then I shall believe'? Nay, but *first believe!* Believe in the Lord Jesus Christ, the propitiation for thy sins. Let this good foundation first be laid, and then thou shalt do all things well.

2. Neither say in thy heart, 'I cannot be accepted yet, because I am not *good enough.*' Who is *good enough,* who ever was, to merit acceptance at God's hands? Was ever any child of Adam *good enough* for this? or will any till the consummation of all things? And, as for thee, thou art not good at all: there dwelleth in thee no good thing. And thou never wilt be, till thou believe in Jesus. Rather thou wilt find thyself worse and worse. But is there any need of being worse, in order to be accepted? Art thou not *bad enough* already? Indeed thou art; and that God knoweth. And thou thyself canst not deny it. Then delay not. All things are now ready. 'Arise, and wash away thy sins.' The fountain is open. Now is the time to wash thee white in the blood of the Lamb. Now He shall 'purge' thee as 'with hyssop,' and thou shalt 'be clean': He shall 'wash' thee, and thou shalt 'be whiter than snow.'

3. Do not say, 'But I am not *contrite enough*: I am not *sensible enough* of my sins.' I know it. I would to God thou wert more *sensible* of them, more *contrite* a thousand fold than thou art. But do not stay for this. It may be, God will make thee so, not before thou believest, but by believing. It may be, thou wilt not weep much, till thou lovest much because thou hast had much forgiven. In the meantime look unto Jesus. Behold, how He loveth thee! What could He have done more for thee which He hath not done?

> O Lamb of God, was ever pain,
> Was ever love like Thine?

Look steadily upon Him, till He looks on thee, and breaks thy hard heart. Then shall thy 'head' be 'waters' and thy 'eyes fountains of tears.'

4. Nor yet do thou say, 'I must *do* something more *before* I come to Christ.' I grant, supposing thy Lord should delay His coming, it were meet and right to wait for His appearing, in doing, so far as thou hast power, whatsoever He hath commanded thee. But there is no necessity for making such a supposition. How knowest thou that He will delay? Perhaps He will appear, as the dayspring from on high, before the morning light. O do not set Him a time! Expect Him every hour. Now He is nigh! even at the door!

5. And to what end wouldest thou wait for *more sincerity before* thy sins are blotted out? To make thee more worthy of the grace of God? Alas, thou art still 'establishing thy own righteousness.' He will have mercy, not because thou art worthy of it, but because His compassions fail not; not because thou art righteous, but because Jesus Christ hath atoned for thy sins.

Again: if there be anything good in *sincerity*, why dost thou expect it *before* thou hast faith?—seeing faith itself is the only root of whatever is really good and holy.

Above all, how long wilt thou forget, that whatsoever thou doest, or whatsoever thou hast, before thy sins are forgiven thee, it avails nothing with God toward the procuring of thy forgiveness! yea, and that it must all be cast behind thy back, trampled under foot, made no account of, or thou wilt never find favour in God's sight; because, until then, thou canst not ask it as a mere sinner, guilty, lost, undone, having nothing to plead, nothing to offer to God, but only the merits of His well-beloved Son, 'who loved *thee,* and gave Himself for *thee*'!

6. To conclude. Whosoever thou art, O man, who hast the sentence of death in thyself, who feelest thyself a condemned sinner, and hast the wrath of God abiding on thee: unto thee saith the Lord, not, 'Do this'—perfectly obey all my commands—'and live'; but, 'Believe in the Lord Jesus Christ, and thou shalt be saved.' 'The word of faith is nigh unto thee': now, at this instant, in the present moment, and in thy present state, sinner as thou art, just as thou art, believe the gospel; and 'I will be merciful unto *thy* unrighteousness, and *thy* iniquities will I remember no more.'

SERMON VII

THE WAY TO THE KINGDOM

The structure of this sermon is peculiar. The first part of it is an exposition of Rom. xiv. 17, 'The kingdom of God is not meat and drink,' &c.; the second is an application based on the second clause of Mark i. 15, 'Repent ye, and believe the gospel.' On Sunday, June 6, 1742, Wesley was at Epworth, and offered his services to Mr. Romley the curate, 'but he did not care to accept of my assistance. The church was exceeding full in the afternoon, a rumour being spread that I was to preach. But the sermon on Quench not the Spirit was not suitable to the expectation of many of the hearers. Mr. Romley told them that one of the most dangerous ways of quenching the Spirit was by enthusiasm; and enlarged on the character of an enthusiast in a very florid and oratorical manner. After sermon John Taylor stood in the churchyard, and gave notice, as the people were coming out, "Mr. Wesley, not being permitted to preach in the church, designs to preach here at six o'clock." Accordingly at six I came, and found such a congregation as I believe Epworth never saw before. I stood near the east end of the church, upon my father's tombstone, and cried, "The kingdom of heaven is not meat and drink; but righteousness, and peace, and joy in the Holy Ghost." ' He remained eight days at Epworth, preaching every day from his father's tombstone, his texts being, on Monday, Eph. ii. 8—the Oxford Sermon No. I; on Tuesday Rom. iv. 5 (Sermon V); on Wednesday Luke xviii. 10; on Thursday Rom. viii. 15 (Sermon IX); on Friday Ezek. xxxvii. 1 seq.; on Saturday Rom. x. 5 (Sermon VI), and on Sunday Matt. v. 1 (Sermon XVI). In a letter to Mr. John Smith, dated March 25, 1747, he says, 'I am well assured I did far more good by preaching three days on my father's tomb than I did by preaching three years in his pulpit.' The Rev. John Whitelamb, who was for a time Samuel Wesley's curate at Epworth, and married poor deformed Mary (Molly) Wesley in 1734, but lost her in November of the same year, came over from Wroot, where he was still rector, though his grief at the death of his wife and her baby had driven him into unbelief, and heard John preach on the Tuesday. He wrote on the Friday to Wesley: 'I saw you at Epworth on Tuesday evening. Your way of thinking is so extraordinary that your presence creates an awe, as though you were an inhabitant of another world. . . . I cannot refrain from tears when I reflect, this is the man who at Oxford was more than a father to me; this is he whom I have heard expound, or dispute publicly, or preach at St.

Mary's, with such applause; and—oh, that I should ever add—whom I
have lately heard preach at Epworth, on his father's tombstone!'

There is little doubt that this sermon, or at any rate the first part of it,
was the first of this series of 'tombstone' sermons. It was a favourite of
Wesley's, and is often mentioned in the *Journal* during this and the
following years; and also in the sermon list at the end of the Standard
Edition of the *Journal*. It is quite different from the one on the same
text, No. XLVII, on The Repentance of Believers, which was written in
April 1767.

To the modern reader it seems strange that a sermon on The
kingdom of God should make no reference at all to the social
reconstruction demanded by Christianity; but Wesley was right in
thinking that the only way to social salvation is through the salvation of
individual men and women. The kingdom in the heart must come
before the kingdom in society can be realized. Schemes for social
reform will never work until the men who constitute society are
themselves saved.

The kingdom of God is at hand: repent ye, and believe the gospel.—MARK i. 15.

These words naturally lead us to consider, first, the nature of
true religion, here termed by our Lord 'the kingdom of God,'
which, saith He, 'is at hand'; and, secondly, the way thereto,
which He points out in those words, 'Repent ye, and believe the
gospel.'

I. 1. We are, first, to consider the nature of true religion, here
termed by our Lord 'the kingdom of God.' The same expression
the great Apostle uses in his Epistle to the Romans, where he
likewise explains his Lord's words saying, 'The kingdom of God
is not meat and drink; but righteousness, and peace, and joy in
the Holy Ghost' (Rom. xiv. 17).

2. 'The kingdom of God,' or true religion 'is not meat and
drink.' It is well known, that not only the unconverted Jews, but
great numbers of those who had received the faith of Christ,
were, notwithstanding, 'zealous of the law' (Acts xxi. 20), even
the ceremonial law of Moses. Whatsoever, therefore, they found
written therein, either concerning meat and drink offerings, or
the distinction between clean and unclean meats, they not only
observed themselves, but vehemently pressed the same, even on
those 'among the Gentiles' (or Heathens) 'who were turned to
God'; yea, to such a degree, that some of them taught,

wheresoever they came among them, 'Except ye be circumcised, and keep the law' (the whole ritual law), 'ye cannot be saved' (Acts xv. 1, 24).

3. In opposition to these, the Apostle declares, both here and in many other places, that true religion does not consist in *meat* and *drink*, or in any ritual observances; nor, indeed, in any outward thing whatever; in anything exterior to the heart; the whole substance thereof lying in 'righteousness, peace, and joy in the Holy Ghost.'

4. Not in any *outward thing*; such as *forms* or *ceremonies*, even of the most excellent kind. Supposing these to be ever so decent and significant, ever so expressive of inward things: supposing them ever so helpful, not only to the vulgar, whose thought reaches little farther than their sight; but even to men of understanding, men of stronger capacities, as doubtless they may sometimes be; yea, supposing them, as in the case of the Jews, to be appointed by God Himself; yet even during the period of time wherein that appointment remains in force, true religion does not principally consist therein; nay, strictly speaking, not at all. How much more must this hold concerning such rites and forms as are only of human appointment! The religion of Christ rises infinitely higher, and lies immensely deeper, than all these. These are good in their place; just so far as they are in fact subservient to true religion. And it were superstition to object against them, while they are applied only as occasional helps to human weakness. But let no man carry them farther. Let no man dream that they have any intrinsic worth; or that religion cannot subsist without them. This were to make them an abomination to the Lord.

5. The nature of religion is so far from consisting in these, in forms of worship, or rites and ceremonies, that it does not properly consist in any outward actions, of what kind soever. It is true, a man cannot have any religion who is guilty of vicious, immoral actions; or who does to others what he would not they should do unto him, if he were in the same circumstances. And it is also true, that he can have no real religion who 'knows to do good, and doeth it not.' Yet may a man both abstain from outward evil, and do good, and still have no religion. Yea, two persons may do the same outward work; suppose feeding the hungry, or clothing the naked; and, in the meantime, one of

these may be truly religious, and the other have no religion at all; for the one may act from the love of God, and the other from the love of praise. So manifest it is, that although true religion naturally leads to every good word and work, yet the real nature thereof lies deeper still, even in 'the hidden man of the heart.'

6. I say of *the heart*. For neither does religion consist in orthodoxy, or right opinions; which, although they are not properly outward things, are not in the heart, but the understanding. A man may be orthodox in every point; he may not only espouse right opinions, but zealously defend them against all opposers; he may think justly concerning the incarnation of our Lord, concerning the ever-blessed Trinity, and every other doctrine contained in the oracles of God; he may assent to all the three creeds—that called the Apostles', the Nicene, and the Athanasian; and yet it is possible he may have no religion at all, no more than a Jew, Turk, or Pagan. He may be almost as orthodox—as the devil (though indeed not altogether; for every man errs in something; whereas we cannot well conceive him to hold any erroneous opinion), and may, all the while, be as great a stranger as he to the religion of the heart.

7. This alone is religion, truly so called: this alone is in the sight of God of great price. The Apostle sums it all up in three particulars, 'righteousness, and peace, and joy in the Holy Ghost.' And, first, *righteousness*. We cannot be at a loss concerning this, if we remember the words of our Lord, describing the two grand branches thereof, on which 'hang all the Law and the Prophets': 'Thou shalt love the Lord thy God with all thy heart, and with all thy mind, and with all thy soul, and with all thy strength: this is the first and great commandment' (Mark xii. 30); the first and great branch of Christian righteousness. Thou shalt delight thyself in the Lord thy God; thou shalt seek and find all happiness in Him. He shall be 'thy shield, and thy exceeding great reward,' in time and in eternity. All thy bones shall say, 'Whom have I in heaven but Thee? And there is none upon earth that I desire beside Thee.' Thou shalt hear and fulfil His word, who saith, 'My son, give me thy heart.' And, having given Him thy heart, thy inmost soul, to reign there without a rival, thou mayest well cry out, in the fullness of thy heart, 'I will love Thee, O Lord, my strength. The Lord is my strong rock, and my defence; my Saviour, my God, and my

might, in whom I will trust; my buckler, the horn also of my salvation, and my refuge.'

8. And the second commandment is like unto this; the second great branch of Christian righteousness is closely and inseparably connected therewith; even, 'Thou shalt love thy neighbour as thyself.' *Thou shalt love*—thou shalt embrace with the most tender good-will, the most earnest and cordial affection, the most inflamed desires of preventing or removing all evil, and of procuring for him every possible good. *Thy neighbour*—that is, not only thy friend, thy kinsman, or thy acquaintance; not only the virtuous, the friendly, him that loves thee, that prevents or returns thy kindness; but every child of man, every human creature, every soul which God hath made; not excepting him whom thou never hast seen in the flesh, whom thou knowest not, either by face or name; not excepting him whom thou knowest to be evil and unthankful, him that still despitefully uses and persecutes thee: him thou shalt love *as thyself*; with the same invariable thirst after his happiness in every kind; the same unwearied care to screen him from whatever might grieve or hurt either his soul or body.

9. Now is not this love 'the fulfilling of the law'? the sum of all Christian righteousness? of all inward righteousness,—for it necessarily implies 'bowels of mercies, humbleness of mind' (seeing 'love is not puffed up'), 'gentleness, meekness, longsuffering' (for love 'is not provoked,' but 'believeth, hopeth, endureth all things'): and of all outward righteousness,—for 'love worketh no evil to his neighbour,' either by word or deed. It cannot willingly hurt or grieve any one. And it is zealous of good works. Every lover of mankind, as he hath opportunity, 'doeth good unto all men,' being (without partiality, and without hypocrisy) 'full of mercy and good fruits.'

10. But true religion, or a heart right toward God and man, implies happiness as well as holiness. For it is not only 'righteousness,' but also 'peace and joy in the Holy Ghost.' What peace? 'The peace of God,' which God only can give, and the world cannot take away; the peace which' passeth all understanding,' all barely rational conception; being a supernatural sensation, a divine taste, of 'the powers of the world to come'; such as the natural man knoweth not, how wise soever in the things of this world; nor, indeed, can he know it, in his present

state, 'because it is spiritually discerned.' It is a peace that banishes all doubt, all painful uncertainty; the Spirit of God bearing witness with the spirit of a Christian, that he is 'a child of God.' And it banishes fear, all such fear as hath torment: the fear of the wrath of God; the fear of hell; the fear of the devil; and, in particular, the fear of death: he that hath the peace of God, desiring, if it were the will of God, 'to depart, and to be with Christ.'

11. With this peace of God, wherever it is fixed in the soul, there is also 'joy in the Holy Ghost'; joy wrought in the heart by the Holy Ghost, by the ever-blessed Spirit of God. He it is that worketh in us that calm, humble rejoicing in God, through Christ Jesus, 'by whom we have now received the atonement,' καταλλαγην, the reconciliation with God; and that enables us boldly to confirm the truth of the royal Psalmist's declaration, 'Blessed is the man' (or rather, *happy*) 'whose unrighteousness is forgiven and whose sin is covered.' He it is that inspires the Christian soul with that even, solid joy, which arises from the testimony of the Spirit that he is a child of God; and that gives him to 'rejoice with joy unspeakable, in hope of the glory of God'; hope both of the glorious image of God, which is in part, and shall be fully, 'revealed in him'; and of that crown of glory which fadeth not away, reserved in heaven for him.

12. This holiness and happiness, joined in one, are sometimes styled, in the inspired writings, 'the kingdom of God' (as by our Lord in the text), and sometimes, 'the kingdom of heaven.' It is termed, 'the kingdom of God,' because it is the immediate fruit of God's reigning in the soul. So soon as ever He takes unto Himself His mighty power, and sets up His throne in our hearts, they are instantly filled with this 'righteousness, and peace, and joy in the Holy Ghost.' It is called 'the kingdom of heaven,' because it is (in a degree) heaven opened in the soul. For whosoever they are that experience this, they can aver before angels and men,

> Everlasting life is won,
> Glory is on earth begun;

according to the constant tenor of Scripture, which everywhere bears record, God 'hath given unto us eternal life, and this life is in His Son. He that hath the Son' (reigning in his heart) 'hath life,' even life everlasting (1 John v. 11, 12). For 'this is life eternal, to know Thee the only true God, and Jesus Christ whom Thou hast sent' (John xvii. 3). And they to whom this is given may confidently address God, though they were in the midst of a fiery furnace,—

> Thee, Lord, safe-shielded by Thy power,
> Thee, Son of God, JEHOVAH, we adore;
> In form of man descending to appear:
> To Thee be censeless hallelujahs given,
> Praise, as in heaven Thy throne, we offer here;
> For where Thy presence is display'd, is heaven.

13. And this 'kingdom of God,' or of heaven, 'is at hand.' As these words were originally spoken, they implied that 'the time' was then fulfilled, God being 'made manifest in the flesh,' when He would set up His kingdom among men, and reign in the hearts of His people. And is not the time now fulfilled? For, 'Lo,' (saith He), 'I am with you always,' you who preach remission of sins in My name, 'even unto the end of the world' (Matt. xxviii. 20). Wheresoever, therefore, the gospel of Christ is preached, this His 'kingdom is nigh at hand.' It is not far from every one of you. Ye may this hour enter thereinto, if so be ye hearken to His voice, 'Repent ye, and believe the gospel.'

II. 1. This is the way; walk ye in it. And, first, 'repent'; that is, know yourselves. This is the first repentance, previous to faith; even conviction, or self-knowledge. Awake, then, thou that sleepest. Know thyself to be a sinner, and what manner of sinner thou art. Know that corruption of thy inmost nature, whereby thou art very far gone from original righteousness, whereby 'the flesh lusteth' always 'contrary to the Spirit,' through that 'carnal mind' which 'is enmity against God,' which 'is not subject to the law of God indeed can be.' Know that thou art corrupted in every power, in every faculty of thy soul; that thou art totally corrupted in every one of these, all the foundations being out of course. The eyes of thine understanding are darkened, so that they cannot discern God, or the things of God. The clouds of ignorance and error rest upon thee, and cover thee with the shadow of death. Thou knowest nothing yet as thou oughtest to know, neither God, nor the world, nor thyself. Thy will is no longer the will of God, but is utterly perverse and distorted, averse from all good, from all which God loves, and prone to all evil, to every abomination which God hateth. Thy affections are alienated from God, and scattered abroad over all the earth. All thy passions, both thy desires and aversions, thy joys and sorrows, thy hopes and fears, are out of frame, are either undue in their degree, or placed on undue objects. So that there is no soundness in thy soul; but 'from the crown of the head, to the sole of the foot' (to use the strong expression of the prophet), there are only 'wounds, and bruises, and putrefying sores.'

2. Such is the inbred corruption of thy heart, of thy very inmost nature. And what manner of branches canst thou expect to grow from such an evil root? Hence springs unbelief; ever departing from the living God; saying, 'Who is the Lord, that I should serve Him? Tush! Thou God carest not for it.' Hence independence; affecting to be like the Most High. Hence pride, in all its forms; teaching thee to say, 'I am rich, and increased in goods, and have need of nothing.' From this evil fountain flow forth the bitter streams of vanity, thirst of praise, ambition, covetousness, the lust of the flesh, the lust of the eye, and the pride of life. From this arise anger, hatred, malice, revenge, envy, jealousy, evil surmisings: from this, all the foolish and hurtful lusts that now 'pierce thee through with many sorrows,' and, if not timely prevented, will at length drown thy soul in everlasting perdition.

3. And what fruits can grow on such branches as these? Only such as are bitter and evil continually. Of pride cometh contention, vain boasting, seeking and receiving praise of men, and so robbing God of that glory which He cannot give unto another. Of the lust of the flesh come gluttony or drunkenness, luxury or sensuality, fornication, uncleanness; variously defiling that body which was designed for a temple of the Holy Ghost: of unbelief, every evil word and work. But the time would fail, shouldest thou reckon up all; all the idle words thou hast spoken, provoking the Most High, grieving the Holy One of Israel; all the evil works thou hast done, either wholly evil in themselves, or, at least, not done to the glory of God. For thy actual sins are more than thou art able to express, more than the hairs of thy head. Who can number the sands of the sea, or the drops of rain, or thy iniquities?

4. And knowest thou not that 'the wages of sin is death'?—death, not only temporal, but eternal. 'The soul that sinneth, it shall die'; for the mouth of the Lord hath spoken it. It shall die the second death. This is the sentence, to 'be punished' with never-ending death, 'with everlasting destruction from the presence of the Lord, and from the glory of His power.' Knowest thou not that every sinner ενοχος εστι τη γεεννη του πυρος, not properly 'is in danger of hell-fire'; that expression is far too weak; but rather 'is under the sentence of hell-fire'; doomed already, just dragging to execution. Thou art guilty of everlasting death. It is the just reward of thy inward and outward wickedness. It is just that the sentence should now take place. Dost thou see, dost thou feel this? Art thou thoroughly convinced that thou deservest God's wrath, and everlasting damnation? Would God do thee no wrong, if He now commanded the earth to open, and swallow thee up?—if thou wert now to go down quick into the pit, into the fire that never shall be quenched? If God hath given thee truly to repent, thou hast a deep sense that these things are so; and that it is of His mere mercy thou art not consumed, swept away from the face of the earth.

5. And what wilt thou do to appease the wrath of God, to atone for all thy sins, and to escape the punishment thou hast so justly deserved? Alas, thou canst do nothing; nothing that will in any wise make amends to God for one evil work, or word, or thought. If thou couldest now do all things well, if from this very hour till thy soul should return to God thou couldest perform perfect, uninterrupted obedience, even this would not atone for what is past. The not increasing thy debt would not discharge it. It would still remain as great as ever. Yea, the present and future obedience of all the men upon earth, and all the angels in heaven, would never make satisfaction to the justice of God for one single sin. How vain, then, was the thought of atoning for thy own sins, by anything thou couldest do! It costeth far more to redeem one soul, than all mankind is able to pay. So that were there no other help for a guilty sinner, without doubt he must have perished everlastingly.

6. But suppose perfect obedience, for the time to come, could atone for the sins that are past, this would profit thee nothing; for thou art not able to perform it; no, not in any one point.

Begin now: make the trial. Shake off that outward sin that so
easily besetteth thee. Thou canst not. How then wilt thou change
thy life from all evil to all good? Indeed, it is impossible to be
done, unless first thy heart be changed. For, so long as the tree
remains evil, it cannot bring forth good fruit. But art thou able
to change thy own heart, from all sin to all holiness? to quicken a
soul that is dead in sin—dead to God, and alive only to the
world? No more than thou art able to quicken a dead body, to
raise to life him that lieth in the grave. Yea, thou art not able to
quicken thy soul in any degree, no more than to give any degree
of life to the dead body. Thou canst do nothing, more or less, in
this matter; thou art utterly without strength. To be deeply
sensible of this, how helpless thou art, as well as how guilty and
how sinful,—this is that 'repentance not to be repented of,'
which is the forerunner of the kingdom of God.

7. If to this lively conviction of thy inward and outward sins, of
thy utter guiltiness and helplessness, there be added suitable
affections,—sorrow of heart, for having despised thy own
mercies; remorse, and self-condemnation, having thy mouth
stopped; shame to lift up thine eyes to heaven; fear of the wrath
of God abiding on thee, of His curse hanging over thy head, and
of the fiery indignation ready to devour those who forget God,
and obey not our Lord Jesus Christ; earnest desire to escape
from that indignation, to cease from evil, and learn to do
well,—then I say unto thee, in the name of the Lord, 'Thou art
not far from the kingdom of God.' One step more, and thou
shalt enter in. Thou dost 'repent.' Now, 'believe the gospel.'

8. *The gospel* (that is, good tidings, good news for guilty,
helpless sinners), in the largest sense of the word, means, the
whole revelation made to men by Jesus Christ; and sometimes
the whole account of what our Lord did and suffered while He
tabernacled among men. The substance of all is, 'Jesus Christ
came into the world to save sinners'; or, 'God so loved the world,
that He gave His only-begotten Son, to the end we might not
perish, but have everlasting life'; or, 'He was bruised for our
transgressions, He was wounded for our iniquities; the
chastisement of our peace was upon Him; and with His stripes
we are healed.'

9. *Believe* this, and the kingdom of God is thine. By faith thou
attainest the promise. 'He pardoneth and absolveth all that truly

repent, and unfeignedly believe His holy gospel.' As soon as ever God hath spoken to thy heart, 'Be of good cheer, thy sins are forgiven thee,' His kingdom comes: thou hast 'righteousness, and peace, and joy in the Holy Ghost.'

10. Only beware thou do not deceive thy own soul, with regard to the nature of this faith. It is not, as some have fondly conceived, a bare assent to the truth of the Bible, of the articles of our Creed, or of all that is contained in the Old and New Testament. The devils believe this, as well as I or thou! And yet they are devils still. But it is, over and above this, a sure trust in the mercy of God, through Christ Jesus. It is a confidence in a pardoning God. It is a divine evidence or conviction that 'God was in Christ, reconciling the world to Himself, not imputing to them their' former 'trespasses'; and in particular, that the Son of God hath loved *me*, and given Himself for *me*; and that I, even I, am now reconciled to God by the blood of the cross.

11. Dost thou thus believe? Then the peace of God is in thy heart, and sorrow and sighing flee away. Thou art no longer in doubt of the love of God; it is clear as the noon-day sun. Thou criest out, 'My song shall be always of the loving-kindness of the Lord: with my mouth will I ever be telling of Thy truth, from one generation to another.' Thou art no longer afraid of hell, or death, or him that had once the power of death, the devil; no, nor painfully afraid of God Himself; only thou hast a tender, filial fear of offending Him. Dost thou believe? Then thy 'soul doth magnify the Lord,' and thy 'spirit rejoiceth in God thy Saviour.' Thou rejoicest in that thou hast 'redemption through His blood, even the forgiveness of sins.' Thou rejoicest in that 'Spirit of adoption,' which crieth in thy heart, 'Abba, Father!' Thou rejoicest in a 'hope full of immortality'; in reaching forth unto the 'mark for the prize of thy high calling'; in an earnest expectation of all the good things which God hath prepared for them that love Him.

12. Dost thou now believe? Then 'the love of God is' now 'shed abroad in thy heart.' Thou lovest Him, because He first loved us. And, because thou lovest God, thou lovest thy brother also. And being filled with 'love, peace, joy,' thou art also filled with 'long-suffering, gentleness, fidelity, goodness, meekness, temperance,' and all the other fruits of the same Spirit; in a word, with whatever dispositions are holy, are heavenly, or divine. For

while thou 'beholdest with open,' uncovered 'face' (the veil now being taken away) 'the glory of the Lord,' His glorious love, and the glorious image wherein thou wast created, thou art 'changed into the same image from glory to glory, by the Spirit of the Lord.'

13. This repentance, this faith, this peace, joy, love; this change from glory to glory, is what the wisdom of the world has voted to be madness, mere enthusiasm, utter distraction. But thou, O man of God, regard them not; be thou moved by none of these things. Thou knowest in whom thou hast believed. See that no man take thy crown. Whereunto thou hast already attained, hold fast, and follow, till thou attain all the great and precious promises. And thou who hast not yet known Him, let not vain men make thee ashamed of the gospel of Christ. Be thou in nothing terrified by those who speak evil of the things which they know not. God will soon turn thy heaviness into joy. Oh, let not thy hands hang down! Yet a little longer, and He will take away thy fears, and give thee the spirit of a sound mind. He is nigh 'that justifieth: who is he that condemneth? It is Christ that died, yea rather, that rose again, who is even now at the right hand of God, making intercession' for thee.

Now cast thyself on the Lamb of God, with all thy sins, how many soever they be; and 'an entrance shall' now 'be ministered unto thee into the kingdom of our Lord and Saviour Jesus Christ'!

SERMON VIII

THE FIRST-FRUITS OF THE SPIRIT

In the *Journal,* June 25, 1745, Wesley says: 'We rode to St. Just. I preached at seven to the largest congregation I have seen since my coming. At the meeting of the earnest, loving society all our hearts were in a flame: and again at five in the morning, while I explained "There is no condemnation to them which are in Christ Jesus." ' On July 15 he read prayers and preached on this text at Laneast church. From the nature of its contents, this sermon was not suitable for general use; it needed a congregation of believers, and there are few records cf its being preached either in the *Journal* or the Sermon List. But no doubt the substance of it was part of the continuous exposition of the Epistle to the Romans which was often given by Wesley to his societies. It shows a distinct advance on his views of the nature of sin and its continuance in believers suggested in some of the earlier sermons; indeed, it is a sort of first sketch for Sermon XLVI on Sin In Believers.

There is therefore now no condemnation to them which are in Christ Jesus who walk not after the flesh but after the Spirit.—Rom. viii. 1.

1. By 'them which are in Christ Jesus,' St. Paul evidently means, those who truly believe in Him; those who, 'being justified by faith, have peace with God through our Lord Jesus, Christ.' They who thus believe do no longer 'walk after the flesh,' no longer follow the motions of corrupt nature, but 'after the Spirit'; both their thoughts, words, and works are under the direction of the blessed Spirit of God.

2. 'There is therefore now no condemnation to' these. There is no condemnation to them from God; for He hath *justified* them 'freely by His grace through the redemption that is in Jesus.' He hath forgiven all their iniquities, and blotted out all their sins. And there is no condemnation to them from within; for they 'have received, not the spirit of the world, but the Spirit which is of God; that they might know the things which are freely given to them of God' (1 Cor. ii. 12); which Spirit 'beareth witness with their spirits, that they are the children of God.' And

to this is added the testimony of their conscience, 'that in simplicity and godly sincerity, not with fleshly wisdom, but by the grace of God, they have had their conversation in the world' (2 Cor. i. 12).

3. But because this scripture has been so frequently misunderstood, and that in so dangerous a manner; because such multitudes of 'unlearned and unstable men' (οι αμαθεις και αστηρικτοι, men untaught of God, and consequently unestablished in the truth which is after godliness) have wrested it to their own destruction; I propose to show, as clearly as I can, first, who those are 'which are in Christ Jesus,' and 'walk not after the flesh, but after the Spirit'; and, secondly, how 'there is no condemnation to' these. I shall conclude with some practical inferences.

I. 1. First, I am to show, who those are that 'are in Christ Jesus.' And are they not those who believe in His name? those who are 'found in Him, not having their own righteousness, but the righteousness which is of God by faith'? These, 'who have redemption through His blood,' are properly said to be *in Him*; for they dwell in Christ, and Christ in them. They are joined unto the Lord in one Spirit. They are ingrafted into Him, as branches into the vine. They are united, as members to their head, in a manner which words cannot express, nor could it before enter into their hearts to conceive.

2. Now 'whosoever abideth in Him, sinneth not'; 'walketh not after the flesh.' The flesh, in the usual language of St. Paul, signifies corrupt nature. In this sense he uses the word, writing to the Galatians, 'The works of the flesh are manifest' (Gal. v. 19); and a little before, 'Walk in the Spirit, and ye shall not fulfil the lust' (or desire) 'of the flesh' (ver. 16). To prove which, namely, that those who 'walk by the Spirit' do not 'fulfil the lusts of the flesh,' he immediately adds, 'For the flesh lusteth against the Spirit, and the Spirit lusteth against the flesh (for these are contrary to each other); that ye may not do the things which ye would.' So the words are literally translated (ινα μη α αν θελητε ταυτα ποιντε), not, 'So that ye cannot do the things that ye would'; as if the flesh overcame the Spirit: a translation which hath not only nothing to do with the original text of the Apostle, but likewise makes his whole argument nothing worth; yea, asserts just the reverse of what he is proving.

3. They who are of Christ, who abide in Him, 'have crucified the flesh with its affections and lusts.' They abstain from all those works of the flesh; from 'adultery and fornication'; from 'uncleanness and lasciviousness'; from 'idolatry, witchcraft, hatred, variance'; from 'emulations, wrath, strife, sedition, heresies, envyings, murders, drunkenness, revellings'; from every design, and word, and work, to which the corruption of nature leads. Although they feel the root of bitterness in themselves, yet are they endued with power from on high to trample it continually under foot, so that it cannot 'spring up to trouble them'; insomuch that every fresh assault which they undergo only gives them fresh occasion of praise, of crying out, 'Thanks be unto God, who giveth us the victory through Jesus Christ our Lord.'

4. They now 'walk after the Spirit,' both in their hearts and lives. They are taught of Him to love God and their neighbour, with a love which is as 'a well of water, springing up into everlasting life.' And by Him they are led into every holy desire, into every divine and heavenly temper, till every thought which arises in their heart is holiness unto the Lord.

5. They who 'walk after the Spirit' are also led by Him into all holiness of conversation. Their 'speech is always in grace, seasoned with salt'; with the love and fear of God. 'No corrupt communication comes out of their mouth; but only that which is good,' that which is 'to the use of edifying,' which is 'meet to minister grace to the hearers.' And herein likewise do they exercise themselves day and night, to do only the things which please God; in all their outward behaviour to follow Him 'who left us an example that we might tread in His steps'; in all their intercourse with their neighbour, to walk in justice, mercy, and truth; and 'whatsoever they do,' in every circumstance of life, to 'do all to the glory of God.'

6. These are they who indeed 'walk after the Spirit.' Being filled with faith and with the Holy Ghost, they possess in their hearts, and show forth in their lives, in the whole course of their words and actions, the genuine fruits of the Spirit of God, namely, 'love, joy, peace, long-suffering, gentleness; goodness, fidelity, meekness, temperance,' and whatsoever else is lovely or praiseworthy. 'They adorn in all things the gospel of God our Saviour'; and give full proof to all mankind, that they are indeed

actuated by the same Spirit 'which raised up Jesus from the dead.'

II. 1. I proposed to show, in the second place, how 'there is no condemnation to them which are' thus 'in Christ Jesus,' and thus 'walk not after the flesh, but after the Spirit.'

And, first, to believers in Christ, walking thus, 'there is no condemnation' on account of their past sins. God condemneth them not for any of these: they are as though they had never been; they are cast 'as a stone into the depth of the sea' and He remembereth them no more. God, having 'set forth His Son to be a propitiation' for them 'through faith in His blood,' hath declared unto them 'His righteousness for the remission of the sins that are past.' He layeth therefore none of these to their charge; their memorial is perished with them.

2. And there is no condemnation in their own breast; no sense of guilt, or dread of the wrath of God. They 'have the witness in themselves': they are conscious of their interest in the blood of sprinkling. 'They have not received again the spirit of bondage unto fear,' unto doubt and racking uncertainty; but they 'have received the Spirit of adoption,' crying in their heart, 'Abba, Father.' Thus, being 'justified by faith,' they have the peace of God ruling in their hearts; flowing from a continual sense of His pardoning mercy, and 'the answer of a good conscience toward God.'

3. If it be said, 'But sometimes a believer in Christ may lose his sight of the mercy of God; sometimes such darkness may fall upon him that he no longer sees Him that is invisible, no longer feels that witness in himself of his part in the atoning blood; and then he is inwardly condemned, he hath again 'the sentence of death in himself'' ': I answer, supposing it so to be, supposing him not to see the mercy of God, then he is not a believer: for faith implies light; the light of God shining upon the soul. So far, therefore, as any one loses this light, he, for the time, loses his faith. And, no doubt, a true believer in Christ may lose the light of faith; and so far as this is lost, he may, for a time, fall again into condemnation. But this is not the case of them who now 'are in Christ Jesus,' who now believe in His name. For so long as they believe, and walk after the Spirit, neither God condemns them, nor their own heart.

4. They are not condemned, secondly, for any present sins, for now transgressing the commandments of God. For they do not transgress them: they do not 'walk after the flesh, but after the Spirit.' This is the continual proof of their 'love of God, that they keep His commandments'; even as St. John bears witness, 'Whosoever is born of God doth not commit sin. For His seed remaineth in him, and he cannot sin, because he is born of God': he cannot, so long as that seed of God, that loving, holy faith remaineth in him. So long as 'he keepeth himself' herein, 'that wicked one toucheth him not.' Now it is evident, he is not condemned for the sins which he doth not commit at all. They, therefore, who are thus 'led by the Spirit are not under the law' (Gal. v. 18): not under the curse or condemnation of it; for it condemns none but those who break it. Thus, that law of God, 'Thou shalt not steal,' condemns none but those who do steal. Thus, 'Remember the Sabbath-day to keep it holy,' condemns those only who do not keep it holy. But against the fruits of the Spirit 'there is no law' (ver. 23); as the Apostle more largely declares in those memorable words of his former Epistle to Timothy: 'We know that the law is good, if a man use it lawfully; knowing this' (if, while he uses the law of God, in order either to convince or direct, he know and remember this), οτι δικαιω νομος ου κειται, (not 'that the law is not made for a righteous man,' but) 'that the law does not lie against a righteous man': it has no force against him, no power to condemn him; 'but against the lawless and disobedient, against the ungodly and sinners, against the unholy and profane; according to the glorious gospel of the blessed God' (1 Tim. i. 8, 9, 11).

5. They are not condemned, thirdly, for inward sin, even though it does now remain. That the corruption of nature does still remain, even in those who are the children of God by faith; that they have in them the seeds of pride and vanity, of anger, lust, and evil desire, yea, sin of every kind; is too plain to be denied, being matter of daily experience. And on this account it is, that St. Paul, speaking to those whom he had just before witnessed to be 'in Christ Jesus' (1 Cor. i. 2, 9), to have been 'called of God into the fellowship' (or participation) 'of His Son Jesus Christ'; yet declares, 'Brethren, I could not speak unto you as unto spiritual, but as unto carnal, even as unto babes in Christ' (1 Cor. iii. 1): 'babes in Christ'; so we see they were 'in Christ';

they were believers in a low degree. And yet how much of sin remained in them! of that 'carnal mind, which is not subject to the law of God'!

6. And yet, for all this, they are not condemned. Although they feel the flesh, the evil nature, in them; although they are more sensible, day by day, that their 'heart is deceitful and desperately wicked'; yet, so long as they do not yield thereto; so long as they give no place to the devil; so long as they maintain a continual war with all sin, with pride, anger, desire, so that the flesh hath not dominion over them, but they still 'walk after the Spirit'; 'there is no condemnation to them which are in Christ Jesus.' God is well pleased with their sincere, though imperfect obedience; and they 'have confidence toward God,' knowing they are His, 'by the Spirit which He hath given' them (1 John iii. 24).

7. Nay, fourthly, although they are continually convinced of sin cleaving to all they do; although they are conscious of not fulfilling the perfect law, either in their thoughts, or words, or works; although they know they do not love the Lord their God with all their heart, and mind, and soul, and strength; although they feel more or less of pride, or self-will, stealing in and mixing with their best duties; although even in their more immediate intercourse with God, when they assemble themselves with the great congregation, and when they pour our their souls in secret to Him who seeth all the thoughts and intents of the heart, they are continually ashamed of their wandering thoughts, or of the deadness and dullness of their affections; yet there is no condemnation to them still, either from God or from their own heart. The consideration of these manifold defects only gives them a deeper sense, that they have always need of the blood of sprinkling which speaks for them in the ears of God, and that Advocate with the Father 'who ever liveth to make intercession for them.' So far are these from driving them away from Him in whom they have believed, that they rather drive them the closer to Him whom they feel the want of every moment. And, at the same time, the deeper sense they have of this want, the more earnest desire do they feel, and the more diligent they are, as they 'have received the Lord Jesus, so to walk in Him.'

8. They are not condemned, fifthly, for sins of infirmity, as they are usually called. Perhaps it were advisable rather to call

them *infirmities*, that we may not seem to give any countenance to sin, or to extenuate it in any degree, by thus coupling it with infirmity. But (if we must retain so ambiguous and dangerous an expression), by sins of infirmity I would mean, such involuntary failings as the saying a thing we believe true, though, in fact, it prove to be false; or, the hurting our neighbour without knowing or designing it, perhaps when we designed to do him good. Though these are deviations from the holy, and acceptable, and perfect will of God, yet they are not properly sins, nor do they bring any guilt on the conscience of 'them which are in Christ Jesus.' They separate not between God and them, neither intercept the light of His countenance; as being no ways inconsistent with their general character of' walking not after the flesh, but after the Spirit.'

9. Lastly. 'There is no condemnation' to them for anything whatever which it is not in their power to help; whether it be of an inward or outward nature, and whether it be doing something or leaving something undone. For instance, the Lord's supper is to be administered; but you do not partake thereof. Why do you not? You are confined by sickness; therefore you cannot help omitting it; and for the same reason you are not condemned. There is no guilt, because there is no choice. As there 'is a willing mind, it is accepted according to that a man hath, not according to that he hath not.'

10. A believer, indeed, may sometimes be *grieved*, because he cannot do what his soul longs for. He may cry out when he is detained from worshipping God in the great congregation, 'Like as the hart panteth after the water-brooks, so panteth my soul after Thee, O God. My soul is athirst for God, yea, even for the living God: when shall I come to appear in the presence of God?' He may earnestly desire (only still saying in his heart, 'Not as I will, but as Thou wilt') to 'go again with the multitude, and bring them forth into the house of God.' But still, if he cannot go, he feels no condemnation, no guilt, no sense of God's displeasure; but can cheerfully yield up those desires with, 'O my soul, put thy trust in God! for I will yet give Him thanks, who is the help of my countenance and my God.'

11. It is more difficult to determine concerning those which are usually styled sins of surprise: as when one who commonly in patience possesses his soul, on a sudden and violent temptation,

speaks or acts in a manner not consistent with the royal law,
'Thou shalt love thy neighbour as thyself.' Perhaps it is not easy
to fix a general rule concerning transgressions of this nature.
We cannot say, either that men are, or that they are not,
condemned for sins of surprise in general: but it seems,
whenever a believer is by surprise overtaken in a fault, there is
more or less condemnation, as there is more or less concurrence
of his will. In proportion as a sinful desire, or word, or action is
more or less voluntary, so we may conceive God is more or less
displeased, and there is more or less guilt upon the soul.

12. But if so, then there may be some sins of surprise which
bring much guilt and condemnation. For, in some instances, our
being surprised is owing to some wilful and culpable neglect; or
to a sleepiness of soul which might have been prevented, or
shaken of before the temptation came. A man may be previously
warned either of God or man, that trials and dangers are at
hand; and yet may say in his heart, 'A little more slumber, a little
more folding of the hands to rest.' Now, if such an one
afterwards fall, though unawares, into the snare which he might
have avoided,—that he fell unawares is no excuse; he might
have foreseen and have shunned the danger. The falling, even
by surprise, in such an instance as this, is, in effect, a wilful sin;
and, as such, must expose the sinner to condemnation, both
from God and his own conscience.

13. On the other hand, there may be sudden assaults, either
from the world, or the god of this world, and frequently from
our own evil hearts, which we did not, and hardly could, foresee.
And by these even a believer, while weak in faith, may possibly
be borne down, suppose into a degree of anger, or thinking evil
of another, with scarce any concurrence of his will. Now, in such
a case, the jealous God would undoubtedly show him that he had
done foolishly. He would be convinced of having swerved from
the perfect law, from the mind which was in Christ, and
consequently, *grieved* with a godly sorrow, and lovingly *ashamed*
before God. Yet need he not come into condemnation. God
layeth not folly to his charge, but hath compassion upon him,
'even as a father pitieth his own children.' And his heart
condemneth him not: in the midst of that sorrow and shame he
can still say, 'I will trust and not be afraid; for the Lord Jehovah
is my strength and my song; He also is become my salvation.'

III. 1. It remains only to draw some practical inferences from the preceding considerations.

And, first, if there be 'no condemnation to them which are in Christ Jesus,' and 'walk not after the flesh, but after the Spirit,' on account of their past sin; then why art thou fearful. O thou of little faith? Though thy sins were once more in number than the sand, what is that to thee, now thou art in Christ Jesus? 'Who shall lay anything to the charge of God's elect? It is God that justifieth: who is he that condemneth?' All the sins thou hast committed from thy youth up, until the hour when thou wast 'accepted in the Beloved,' are driven away as chaff, are gone, are lost, swallowed up, remembered no more. Thou art now 'born of the Spirit': wilt thou be troubled or afraid of what is done before thou wert born? Away with thy fears! Thou art not called to fear, but to the 'spirit of love and of a sound mind.' Know thy calling! Rejoice in God thy Saviour, and give thanks to God thy Father through Him.

2. Wilt thou say, 'But I have again committed sin, since I had redemption through His blood? And therefore it is, that "I abhor myself, and repent in dust and ashes." ' It is meet thou shouldest abhor thyself; and it is God who hath wrought thee to this self-same thing. But, dost thou now believe? Hath He again enabled thee to say, 'I know that my Redeemer liveth'; 'and the life which I now live, I live by faith in the Son of God'? Then that faith again cancels all that is past, and there is no condemnation to thee. At whatsoever time thou truly believest in the name of the Son of God, all thy sins, antecedent to that hour, vanish away as the morning dew. Now then, 'stand thou fast in the liberty wherewith Christ hath made thee free.' He hath once more made thee free from the power of sin, as well as from the guilt and punishment of it. O 'be not entangled again with the yoke of bondage!'—neither the vile, devilish bondage of sin, of evil desires, evil tempers, or words, or works, the most grievous yoke on this side hell; nor the bondage of slavish, tormenting fear, of guilt and self-condemnation.

3. But secondly, do all they which abide 'in Christ Jesus, walk not after the flesh, but after the Spirit'? Then we cannot but infer, that whosoever now committeth sin, hath no part or lot in this matter. He is even now condemned by his own heart. But, 'if our heart condemn us,' if our own conscience beareth witness

that we are guilty, undoubtedly God doth; for 'He is greater than our heart, and knoweth all things'; so that we cannot deceive Him, if we can ourselves. And think not to say, 'I was justified once; my sins were once forgiven me': I know not that; neither will I dispute whether they were or no. Perhaps at this distance of time, it is next to impossible to know, with any tolerable degree of certainty, whether that was a true, genuine work of God, or whether thou didst only deceive thy own soul. But this I know with the utmost degree of certainty, 'he that committeth sin is of the devil.' Therefore, thou art of thy father the devil. It cannot be denied: for the works of thy father thou doest. O flatter not thyself with vain hopes! Say not to thy soul, 'Peace, peace'! For there is no peace. Cry aloud! Cry unto God out of the deep; if haply He may hear thy voice. Come unto Him as at first, as wretched and poor, as sinful, miserable, blind and naked! And beware thou suffer thy soul to take no rest, till His pardoning love be again revealed; till He 'heal thy backslidings,' and fill thee again with the 'faith that worketh by love.'

4. Thirdly. Is there no condemnation to them which 'walk after the Spirit,' by reason of *inward sin* still remaining, so long as they do not give way thereto; nor by reason of *sin cleaving* to all they do? Then fret not thyself because of ungodliness, though it still remain in thy heart. Repine not, because thou still comest short of the glorious image of God; nor yet because pride, self-will, or unbelief, cleave to all thy words and works. And be not afraid to know all this evil of thy heart, to know thyself as also thou art known. Yea, desire of God, that thou mayest not think of thyself more highly than thou oughtest to think. Let thy continual prayer be,

> Show me, as my soul can bear,
>   The depth of inbred sin;
> All the unbelief declare,
>   The pride that lurks within.

But when He heareth thy prayer, and unveils thy heart; when He shows thee thoroughly what spirit thou art of then beware that thy faith fail thee not, that thou suffer not thy shield to be torn from thee. Be abased. Be humbled in the dust. See thyself nothing, less than nothing, and vanity. But still, 'let not thy heart be troubled, neither let it be afraid.' Still hold fast, 'I, even I, have

an Advocate with the Father, Jesus Christ the righteous.' 'And as
the heavens are higher than the earth, so is His love higher than
even my sins.' Therefore God is merciful to thee a sinner! such a
sinner as thou art! God is love; and Christ hath died! Therefore
the Father Himself loveth thee! Thou art His child! Therefore
He will withhold from thee no manner of thing that is good. Is it
good that the whole body of sin, which is now crucified in thee,
should be destroyed? It shall be done! Thou shalt be 'cleansed
from all filthiness both of flesh and spirit.' Is it good, that
nothing should remain in thy heart but the pure love of God
alone? Be of good cheer! 'Thou shalt love the Lord thy God with
all thy heart, and mind, and soul, and strength.' 'Faithful is He
that hath promised, who also will do it.' It is thy part, patiently to
continue in the work of faith, and in the labour of love; and in
cheerful peace, in humble confidence, with calm and resigned
and yet earnest, expectation, to wait till the zeal of the Lord of
hosts shall perform this.

5. Fourthly. If they that 'are in Christ,' and 'walk after the
Spirit,' are not condemned for *sins of infirmity,* as neither for
involuntary failings, nor for anything whatever which they are not
able to help; then beware, O thou that hast faith in His blood,
that Satan herein gain no advantage over thee. Thou art still
foolish and weak, blind and ignorant; more weak than any
words can express; more foolish than it can yet enter into thy
heart to conceive; knowing nothing yet as thou oughtest to
know. Yet, let not all thy weakness and folly, or any fruit thereof,
which thou art not yet able to avoid, shake thy faith, thy filial
trust in God, or disturb thy peace or joy in the Lord. The rule
which some give, as to wilful sins, and which, in that case, may
perhaps be dangerous, is undoubtedly wise and safe if it be
applied only to the case of weakness and infirmities. Art thou
fallen. O man of God? Yet, do not lie there, fretting thyself and
bemoaning thy weakness but meekly say, 'Lord, I shall fall thus
every moment, unless Thou uphold me with Thy hand.' And
then arise! Leap and walk! Go on thy way! 'Run with patience the
race that is set before thee.'

6. Lastly. Since a believer need not come into condemnation,
even though he be *surprised* into what his soul abhors (suppose
his being surprised is not owing to any carelessness or wilful
neglect of his own); if thou who believest art thus overtaken in a

fault, then grieve unto the Lord: it shall be a precious balm. Pour out thy heart before Him, and show Him of thy trouble; and pray with all thy might to Him who is 'touched with the feeling of thy infirmities,' that He would establish, and strengthen, and settle thy soul, and suffer thee to fall no more. But still He condemneth thee not. Wherefore shouldest thou fear? Thou hast no need of any 'fear that hath torment.' Thou shalt love Him that loveth thee, and it sufficeth: more love will bring more strength. And, as soon as thou lovest Him with all thy heart, thou shalt be 'perfect and entire, lacking nothing.' Wait in peace for that hour, when 'the God of peace shall sanctify thee wholly, so that thy whole spirit and soul and body may be preserved blameless unto the coming of our Lord Jesus Christ'!

SERMON IX

THE SPIRIT OF BONDAGE AND
OF ADOPTION

In the *Journal* for Sunday, October 7, 1739, Wesley says, 'A few, I trust, out of two or three thousand were awakened by the explanation of those words: "Ye have not received the spirit of bondage," &c.' This was at Gloucester, and the service was held at seven in the morning. On April 25 of the same year he records: 'To above two thousand at Baptist Mills (Bristol) I explained that glorious scripture, describing the state of every true believer in Christ—every one who by faith is born of God—"Ye have not received," &c.' This service was held at four in the afternoon. He preached it again at Bristol at 7.30 a.m. on March 10, 1741; from his father's tombstone at Epworth, June 10, 1742; and on September 17, 1743, at Morvah 'to the largest congregation I have seen in Cornwall.'

The distinction, which is the essence of this sermon, between the natural man, the awakened sinner, and the believer, is a sound and useful one; especially when the concession in iv. 2, that these states may sometimes not be mutually exclusive, is borne in mind. But it is doubtful whether St. Paul meant by 'a spirit of bondage' the temper of the convicted man; it rather refers to the condition of a Jew under the law, and of a Gentile under the sway of superstition, in contrast with the liberty of the Christian. The earnest Jew or heathen hopes to be saved by obedience to certain laws, precepts, and observances; he is a slave to these, and is constantly in fear lest he should have failed to keep them. The Pharisee, striving anxiously to observe every point in the thousand and one precepts of the Mishnah, and the savage of New Britain, hedged about at every moment of his life by tabus and the dread of witchcraft, are equally slaves, and live in constant fear of offending. This is the spirit of bondage tending to fear to which St. Paul refers; but it is perhaps justifiable to apply the phrase to the convicted sinner, who is certainly an example of this spirit, though not the only one.

Ye have not received the spirit of bondage again unto fear; but ye have received the Spirit of adoption, whereby we cry, Abba, Father.—ROM. viii. 15.

1. St. Paul here speaks to those who are the children of God by faith. 'Ye,' saith he, who are indeed His children, have drank into His Spirit; 'ye have not received the spirit of bondage

again unto fear'; but, 'because ye are sons, God hath sent forth the Spirit of His Son into your hearts.' 'Ye have received the Spirit of adoption, whereby we cry, Abba, Father.'

2. The spirit of bondage and fear is widely distant from this loving Spirit of adoption: those who are influenced only by slavish fear cannot be termed 'the sons of God'; yet some of them may be styled His servants, and are 'not far from the kingdom of heaven.'

3. But it is to be feared, the bulk of mankind, yea, of what is called the Christian world, have not attained even this; but are still afar off, 'neither is God in all their thoughts.' A few names may be found of those who love God; a few more there are that fear Him; but the greater part have neither the fear of God before their eyes, nor the love of God in their hearts.

4. Perhaps most of you, who, by the mercy of God, now partake of a better spirit may remember the time when ye were as they, when ye were under the same condemnation. But at first ye knew it not though ye were wallowing daily in your sins and in your blood; till, in due time, ye 'received the spirit of fear' (*ye received,* for this also is the gift of God); and afterwards, fear vanished away and the Spirit of love filled your hearts.

5. One who is in the first state of mind, without fear or love, is in Scripture termed a 'natural man': one who is under the spirit of bondage and fear, is sometimes said to be 'under the law' (although that expression more frequently signifies one who is under the Jewish dispensation, or who thinks himself obliged to observe all the rites and ceremonies of the Jewish law): but one who has exchanged the spirit of fear for the Spirit of love is properly said to be 'under grace.'

Now, because it highly imports us to know what spirit we are of, I shall endeavour to point out distinctly, first, the state of a 'natural man'; secondly, that of one who is 'under the law'; and, thirdly, of one who is 'under grace.'

I. 1. And, first, the state of a *natural man*. This the Scripture represents as a state of sleep: the voice of God to him is, 'Awake, thou that sleepest.' For his soul is in a deep sleep: his spiritual senses are not awake: they discern neither spiritual good nor evil. The eyes of his understanding are closed; they are sealed together, and see not. Clouds and darkness continually rest upon them; for he lies in the valley of the shadow of death. Hence, having no inlets for the knowledge of spiritual things, all the avenues of his soul being shut up, he is in gross, stupid ignorance of whatever he is most concerned to know. He is utterly ignorant of God, knowing nothing concerning Him as he ought to know. He is totally a stranger to the law of God, as to its true, inward, spiritual meaning. He has no conception of that evangelical holiness, without which no man shall see the Lord; nor of the happiness which they only find whose 'life is hid with Christ in God.'

2. And, for this very reason, because he is fast asleep, he is, in some sense, at rest. Because he is blind, he is also secure: he saith, 'Tush, there shall no harm happen unto me.' The darkness which covers him on every side, keeps him in a kind of peace; so far as peace can consist with the works of the devil, and with an earthly, devilish mind. He *sees* not that he stands on the edge of the pit; therefore he *fears* it not. He cannot *tremble* at the danger he does not *know*. He has not understanding enough to fear. Why is it that he is in no dread of God? Because he is totally ignorant of Him: if not saying in his heart, 'There is no God'; or, that 'He sitteth on the circle of the heavens, and humbleth' not 'Himself to behold the things which are done on earth'; yet satisfying himself as well, to all Epicurean intents and purposes, by saying, 'God is merciful'; confounding and swallowing up all at once in that unwieldy idea of mercy all His holiness and essential hatred of sin; all His justice, wisdom, and truth. He is in no dread of the vengeance denounced against those who obey not the blessed law of God, because he understands it not. He imagines the main point is, to *do thus,* to be *outwardly* blameless; and sees not that it extends to every temper, desire, thought, motion of the heart. Or he fancies that the obligation hereto is ceased; that Christ came to 'destroy the Law and the Prophets'; to save His people *in,* not *from,* their sins; to bring them to heaven without holiness—notwithstanding His own words. 'Not one jot or tittle of the law shall pass away, till all things are fulfilled'; and, 'Not every one that saith unto Me, Lord, Lord! shall enter into the kingdom of heaven; but he that doeth the will of My Father which is in heaven.'

3. He is secure, because he is utterly ignorant of himself. Hence he talks of 'repenting by-and-by'; he does not indeed

exactly know when, but some time or other before he dies;
taking it for granted, that this is quite in his own power. For what
should hinder his doing it, if he will? If he does but once set a
resolution, no fear but he will make it good!

4. But this ignorance never so strongly glares, as in those who
are termed *men of learning*. If a natural man be one of these, he
can talk at large of his rational faculties, of the freedom of his
will, and the absolute necessity of such freedom, in order to
constitute man a moral agent. He reads, and argues, and proves
to a demonstration, that every man may do as he will; may
dispose his own heart to evil or good, as it seems best in his own
eyes. Thus the god of this world spreads a double veil of
blindness over his heart, lest, by any means, 'the light of the
glorious gospel of Christ should shine' upon it.

5. From the same ignorance of himself and God, there may
sometimes arise, in the natural man, a kind of *joy*, in
congratulating himself upon his own wisdom and goodness; and
what the world calls joy he may often possess. He may have
pleasure in various kinds; either in gratifying the desires of the
flesh, or the desire of the eye, or the pride of life; particularly if
he has large possessions; if he enjoy an affluent fortune; then he
may 'clothe' himself 'in purple and fine linen, and fare
sumptuously every day.' And so long as he thus doeth well unto
himself, men will doubtless speak good of him. They will say,
'He is a happy man.' For, indeed, this is the sum of worldly
happiness; to dress, and visit, and talk, and eat, and drink, and
rise up to play.

6. It is not surprising, if one in such circumstances as these,
dosed with the opiates of flattery and sin, should imagine,
among his other waking dreams, that he walks in great *liberty*.
How easily may he persuade himself, that he is at liberty from all
vulgar errors, and from the *prejudice* of education; judging
exactly right, and keeping clear of all extremes. 'I am free,' may
he say, 'from all the *enthusiasm* of weak and narrow souls; from
superstition, the disease of fools and cowards, always righteous
over much; and from *bigotry*, continually incident to those who
have not a free and generous way of thinking.' And too sure it is,
that he is altogether free from the 'wisdom which cometh from
above,' from holiness, from the religion of the heart, from the
whole mind which was in Christ.

7. For all this time he is the servant of sin. He commits sin, more or less, day by day. Yet he is not troubled: he 'is in no bondage,' as some speak; he feels no condemnation. He contents himself (even though he should profess to believe that the Christian Revelation is of God) with, 'Man is frail. We are all weak. Every man has his infirmity.' Perhaps he quotes Scripture: 'Why, does not Solomon say, The righteous man falls into sin seven times a day? And, doubtless, they are all hypocrites or enthusiasts who pretend to be better than their neighbours.' If, at any time, a serious thought fix upon him, he stifles it as soon as possible, with, 'Why should I fear, since God is merciful, and Christ died for sinners?' Thus, he remains a willing servant of sin, content with the bondage of corruption; inwardly and outwardly unholy, and satisfied therewith; not only not conquering sin, but not striving to conquer, particularly that sin which doth so easily beset him.

8. Such is the state of every *natural man*; whether he be a gross, scandalous transgressor, or a more reputable and decent sinner, having the form, though not the power, of godliness. But how can such an one be *convinced of sin*? How is he brought to *repent*, to be *under the law*, to receive the *spirit of bondage unto fear*? This is the point which is next to be considered.

II. 1. By some awful providence, or by His word applied with the demonstration of His Spirit, God touches the heart of him that lay asleep in darkness and in the shadow of death. He is terribly shaken out of his sleep, and awakes into a consciousness of his danger. Perhaps in a moment, perhaps by degrees, the eyes of his understanding are opened, and now first (the veil being in part removed) discern the real state he is in. Horrid light breaks in upon his soul; such light as may be conceived to gleam from the bottomless pit, from the lowest deep, from a lake of fire burning with brimstone. He at last sees the loving, the merciful God is also 'a consuming fire'; that He is a just God and a terrible, rendering to every man according to his works, entering into judgement with the ungodly for every idle word, yea, and for the imaginations of the heart. He now clearly perceives, that the great and holy God is 'of purer eyes than to behold iniquity'; that He is an avenger of every one who rebelleth against Him, and repayeth the wicked to his face; and that 'it is a fearful thing to fall into the hands of the living God.'

2. The inward, spiritual meaning of the law of God now begins to glare upon him. He perceives 'the commandment is exceeding broad,' and there is 'nothing hid from the light thereof.' He is convinced, that every part of it relates, not barely to outward sin or obedience, but to what passes in the secret recesses of the soul, which no eye but God's can penetrate. If he now hears, 'Thou shalt not kill,' God speaks in thunder, 'He that hateth his brother is a murderer'; 'He that saith unto his brother, Thou fool, is obnoxious to hell-fire.' If the law say, 'Thou shalt not commit adultery,' the voice of the Lord sounds in his ears, 'He that looketh on a woman to lust after her hath committed adultery with her already in his heart.' And thus, in every point, he feels the Word of God 'quick and powerful, sharper than a two-edged sword.' It 'pierces even to the dividing asunder of his soul and spirit, his joints and marrow.' And so much the more, because he is conscious to himself of having neglected so great salvation; of having 'trodden under foot the Son of God,' who would have saved him from his sins, and 'counted the blood of the covenant an unholy,' a common, unsanctifying 'thing.'

3. And as he knows, 'all things are naked and open unto the eyes of Him with whom we have to do,' so he sees himself naked, stripped of all the fig-leaves which he had sewed together, of all his poor pretences to religion or virtue, and his wretched excuses for sinning against God. He now sees himself, like the ancient sacrifices, τετραχηλισμενον, *cleft in sunder,* as it were, from the neck downward, so that all within him stands confessed. His heart is bare, and he sees it is all sin, 'deceitful above all things, desperately wicked'; that it is altogether corrupt and abominable, more than it is possible for tongue to express; that there dwelleth therein no good thing, but unrighteousness and ungodliness only; every motion thereof, every temper and thought, being only evil continually.

4. And he not only sees, but feels in himself, by an emotion of soul which he cannot describe, that for the sins of his heart, were his life without blame (which yet it is not, and cannot be; seeing 'an evil tree cannot bring forth good fruit'), he deserves to be cast into the fire that never shall be quenched. He feels that 'the wages,' the just reward, 'of sin,' of his sin above all, 'is death';

even the second death, the death which dieth not, the destruction of body and soul in hell.

5. Here ends his pleasing dream, his delusive rest, his false peace, his vain security. His joy now vanishes as a cloud; pleasures, once loved, delight no more. They pall upon the taste: he loathes the nauseous sweet; he is weary to bear them. The shadows of happiness flee away, and sink into oblivion: so that he is stripped of all, and wanders to and fro, seeking rest, but finding none.

6. The fumes of those opiates being now dispelled, he feels the anguish of a wounded spirit. He finds that sin let loose upon the soul (whether it be pride, anger, or evil desire, whether self-will, malice, envy, revenge, or any other) is perfect misery: he feels sorrow of heart for the blessings he has lost, and the curse which is come upon him; remorse for having thus destroyed himself, and despised his own mercies; fear, from a lively sense of the wrath of God, and of the consequences of His wrath, of the punishment which He has justly deserved, and which he sees hanging over his head; fear of death, as being to him the gate of hell, the entrance of death eternal; fear of the devil, the executioner of the wrath and righteous vengeance of God; fear of men, who, if they were able to kill his body, would thereby plunge both body and soul into hell,—fear, sometimes arising to such a height, that the poor, sinful, guilty soul is terrified with everything, with nothing, with shades, with a leaf shaken of the wind. Yea, sometimes it may even border upon distraction, making a man 'drunken though not with wine,' suspending the exercise of the memory, of the understanding, of all the natural faculties. Sometimes it may approach to the very brink of despair; so that he who trembles at the name of death, may yet be ready to plunge into it every moment, to 'choose strangling rather than life.' Well may such a man roar, like him of old, for the very disquietness of his heart. Well may he cry out, 'The spirit of a man may sustain his infirmities; but a wounded spirit who can bear?'

7. Now he truly desires to break loose from sin, and begins to struggle with it. But though he strive with all his might, he cannot conquer: sin is mightier than he. He would fain escape; but he is so fast in prison, that he cannot get forth. He resolves against sin, but yet sins on: he sees the snare, and abhors and

runs into it. So much does his boasted reason avail—only to enhance his guilt, and increase his misery! Such is the freedom of his will, free only to evil; free to 'drink in iniquity like water'; to wander farther and farther from the living God, and do more 'despite to the Spirit of grace.'

8. The more he strives, wishes, labours to be free, the more does he feel his chains, the grievous chains of sin, wherewith Satan binds and 'leads him captive at his will'; his servant he is, though he repine ever so much; though he rebel, he cannot prevail. He is still in bondage and fear, by reason of sin: generally, of some outward sin, to which he is peculiarly disposed, either by nature, custom, or outward circumstances; but always, of some inward sin, some evil temper or unholy affection. And the more he frets against it the more it prevails; he may bite, but cannot break his chain. Thus he toils without end, repenting and sinning, and repenting and sinning again, till at length the poor, sinful, helpless wretch is even at his wit's end, and can barely groan, 'O wretched man that I am! who shall deliver me from the body of this death?'

9. This whole struggle of one who is 'under the law,' under the 'spirit of fear and bondage,' is beautifully described by the Apostle in the foregoing chapter, speaking in the person of an awakened man. 'I,' saith he, 'was alive without the law once' (verse 9): I had much life, wisdom, strength, and virtue; so I thought: 'but when the commandment came, sin revived, and I died': when the commandment, in its spiritual meaning, came to my heart, with the power of God, my inbred sin was stirred up, fretted, inflamed, and all my virtue died away. 'And the commandment, which was ordained to life, I found to be unto death. For sin, taking occasion by the commandment, deceived me, and by it slew me' (verses 10, 11): it came upon me unawares; slew all my hopes; and plainly showed, in the midst of life I was in death. 'Wherefore the law is holy, and the commandment holy, and just, and good' (verse 12): I no longer lay the blame on this, but on the corruption of my own heart. I acknowledge that 'the law is spiritual; but I am carnal, sold under sin' (verse 14): I now see both the spiritual nature of the law; and my own carnal, devilish heart 'sold under sin,' totally enslaved (like slaves bought with money, who were absolutely at their master's disposal): 'for that which I do, I allow not; for what

I would, I do not; but what I hate, that I do' (verse 15): such is the bondage under which I groan; such the tyranny of my hard master. 'To will is present with me; but how to perform that which is good I find not. For the good that I would, I do not; but the evil which I would not, that I do' (verses 18, 19): 'I find a law,' an inward constraining power, 'that, when I would do good, evil is present with me. For I delight in,' or consent to, 'the law of God, after the inward man' (verses 21, 22): in my 'mind' (so the Apostle explains himself in the words that immediately follow; and so ο εσω ανθρωπος, *the inward man*, is understood in all other Greek writers): 'but I see another law in my members,' another constraining power, 'warring against the law of my mind,' or inward man, 'and bringing me into captivity to the law' or power 'of sin' (verse 23): dragging me, as it were, at my conqueror's chariot-wheels, into the very thing which my soul abhors. 'O wretched man that I am! who shall deliver me from the body of this death?' (verse 24). Who shall deliver me from this helpless, dying life, from this bondage of sin and misery? Till this is done, 'I myself' (or rather, *that I*, αυτος εγω, that man I am now personating) 'with the mind,' or inward man, 'serve the law of God'; my mind, my conscience, is on God's side: 'but with my flesh,' with my body, 'the law of sin' (verse 25), being hurried away by a force I cannot resist.

10. How lively a portraiture is this of one 'under the law'! one who feels the burden he cannot shake off; who pants after liberty, power, and love, but is in fear and bondage still! until the time that God answers the wretched man, crying out, 'Who shall deliver me' from this bondage of sin, from this body of death?—'The grace of God through Jesus Christ thy Lord.'

III. 1. Then it is that this miserable bondage ends, and he is no more 'under the law, but under grace.' This state we are, thirdly, to consider; the state of one who has found *grace* or favour in the sight of God, even the Father, and who has the *grace* or power of the Holy Ghost reigning in his heart; who has received, in the language of the Apostle, the 'Spirit of adoption, whereby' he now cries, 'Abba, Father!'

2. 'He cried unto the Lord in his trouble, and God delivers him out of his distress.' His eyes are opened in quite another manner than before, even to see a loving, gracious God. While he is

calling, 'I beseech Thee, show me Thy glory!'—he hears a voice in his inmost soul, 'I will make all My goodness pass before thee, and I will proclaim the name of the Lord: I will be gracious to whom I will be gracious, and I will show mercy to whom I will show mercy.' And it is not long before 'the Lord descends in the cloud, and proclaims the name of the Lord.' Then he sees, but not with eyes of flesh and blood, 'The Lord, the Lord God, merciful and gracious, long-suffering, and abundant in goodness and truth; keeping mercy for thousands, and forgiving iniquities, and transgressions, and sin.'

3. Heavenly, healing light now breaks in upon his soul. He 'looks on Him whom he had pierced'; and 'God, who out of darkness commanded light to shine, shineth in his heart.' He sees the light of the glorious love of God, in the face of Jesus Christ. He hath a divine 'evidence of things not seen' by sense, even of 'the deep things of God'; more particularly of the love of God, of His pardoning love to him that believes in Jesus. Overpowered with the sight, his whole soul cries out, 'My Lord, and my God!' For he sees all his iniquities laid on Him who 'bare them in His own body on the tree': he beholds the Lamb of God taking away his sins. How clearly now does he discern, that 'God was in Christ, reconciling the world unto Himself; making Him sin for us, who knew no sin, that we might be made the righteousness of God through Him'; and that he himself is reconciled to God, by that blood of the covenant!

4. Here end both the guilt and power of sin. He can now say, 'I am crucified with Christ; nevertheless I live; yet not I, but Christ liveth in me; and the life which I now live in the flesh' (even in this mortal body), 'I live by faith in the Son of God, who loved me, and gave Himself for me.' Here end remorse, and sorrow of heart, and the anguish of a wounded spirit. 'God turneth his heaviness into joy.' He made sore, and now His hands bind up. Here ends also that bondage unto fear; for 'his heart standeth fast, believing in the Lord.' He cannot fear any longer the wrath of God; for he knows it is now turned away from him, and looks upon Him no more as an angry Judge, but as a loving Father. He cannot fear the devil, knowing he has 'no power, except it be given him from above.' He fears not hell; being an heir of the kingdom of heaven: consequently, he has no fear of death; by reason whereof he was in time past, for so many years, 'subject to

bondage.' Rather, knowing that 'if the earthly house of this tabernacle be dissolved, he hath a building of God—a house not made with hands, eternal in the heavens; he groaneth earnestly, desiring to be clothed upon with that house which is from heaven.' He groans to shake off this house of earth, that 'mortality' may be 'swallowed up of life'; knowing that God 'hath wrought him for the selfsame thing; who hath also given him the earnest of His Spirit.'

5. And 'where the Spirit of the Lord is, there is liberty'; liberty, not only from guilt and fear, but from sin, from that heaviest of all yokes, that basest of all bondage. His labour is not now in vain. The snare is broken, and he is delivered. He not only strives, but likewise prevails; he not only fights, but conquers also. 'Henceforth he does not serve sin' (chap. vi. 6, &c.). He is 'dead unto sin, and alive unto God'; 'sin doth not now reign,' even 'in his mortal body,' nor doth he 'obey it in the desires thereof.' He does not 'yield his members as instruments of unrighteousness unto sin, but as instruments of righteousness unto God.' For 'being now made free from sin, he is become the servant of righteousness.'

6. Thus 'having peace with God through our Lord Jesus Christ,' 'rejoicing in hope of the glory of God,' and having power over all sin, over every evil desire, and temper, and word, and work, he is a living witness of the 'glorious liberty of the sons of God'; all of whom, being partakers of like precious faith, bear record with one voice, 'We have received the Spirit of adoption, whereby we cry, Abba, Father!'

7. It is this Spirit which continually 'worketh in them, both to will and to do of His good pleasure.' It is He that sheds the love of God abroad in their hearts, and the love of all mankind; thereby purifying their hearts from the love of the world, from the lust of the flesh, the lust of the eye, and the pride of life. It is by Him they are delivered from anger and pride, from all vile and inordinate affections. In consequence, they are delivered from evil words and works, from all unholiness of conversation; doing no evil to any child of man, and being zealous of all good works.

8. To sum up all: the *natural* man neither fears nor loves God, one *under the law* fears, one *under grace* loves Him. The first has no light in the things of God, but walks in utter darkness; the second sees the painful light of hell; the third, the joyous light of heaven.

He that sleeps in death has a false peace; he that is awakened has no peace at all; he that believes has true peace,—the peace of God filling and ruling his heart. The Heathen, baptized or unbaptized, hath a fancied liberty, which is indeed licentiousness; the Jew, or one under the Jewish dispensation, is in heavy, grievous bondage; the Christian enjoys the true glorious liberty of the sons of God. An unawakened child of the devil sins willingly; one that is awakened sins unwillingly; a child of God 'sinneth not,' but 'keepeth himself, and the wicked one toucheth him not.' To conclude: the natural man neither conquers nor fights; the man under the law fights with sin, but cannot conquer; the man under grace fights and conquers, yea, is 'more than conqueror through Him that loveth him.'

IV. 1. From this plain account of the threefold state of man, the *natural,* the *legal,* and the *evangelical,* it appears that it is not sufficient to divide mankind into sincere and insincere. A man may be sincere in any of these states; not only when he has the 'Spirit of adoption,' but while he has the 'spirit of bondage unto fear'; yea, while he has neither this fear, nor love. For undoubtedly there may be sincere Heathens, as well as sincere Jews or Christians. This circumstance, then, does by no means prove that a man is in a state of acceptance with God.

'Examine yourselves, therefore,' not only whether ye are sincere, but 'whether ye be in the faith.' Examine narrowly (for it imports you much), what is the ruling principle in your soul? Is it the love of God? Is it the fear of God? Or is it neither one nor the other? Is it not rather the love of the world? the love of pleasure, or gain? of ease, or reputation? If so, you are not come so far as a Jew. You are but a Heathen still. Have you heaven in your heart? Have you the Spirit of adoption, ever crying, Abba, Father? Or do you cry unto God, as 'out of the belly of hell,' overwhelmed with sorrow and fear? Or are you a stranger to this whole affair, and cannot imagine what I mean? Heathen, pull off the mask! Thou hast never put on Christ! Stand barefaced! Look up to heaven; and own before Him that liveth for ever and ever, thou hast no part either among the sons or servants of God!

Whosoever thou art, Dost thou commit sin, or dost thou not? If thou dost, is it willingly or unwillingly? In either case, God hath told thee whose thou art: 'He that committeth sin is of the devil.' If thou committest it willingly, thou art his faithful servant: he will not fail to reward thy labour. If unwillingly, still thou art his servant. God deliver thee out of his hands!

Art thou daily fighting against all sin? and daily more than conqueror? I acknowledge thee for a child of God. O stand fast in thy glorious liberty! Art thou fighting, but not conquering? striving for the mastery, but not able to attain? Then thou art not yet a believer in Christ; but follow on, and thou shalt know the Lord. Art thou not fighting at all, but leading an easy, indolent, fashionable life? O how hast thou dared to name the name of Christ, only to make it a reproach among the Heathen? Awake, thou sleeper! Call upon thy God, before the deep swallow thee up!

2.Perhaps one reason why so many think of themselves more highly than they ought to think, why they do not discern what state they are in, is, because these several states of soul are often mingled together, and in some measure meet in one and the same person. Thus experience shows, that the legal state, or state of fear, is frequently mixed with the natural; for few men are so fast asleep in sin, but they are sometimes more or less awakened. As the Spirit of God does not 'wait for the call of man,' so, at some times He *will* be heard. He puts them in fear, so that, for a season at least, the Heathen 'know themselves to be but men.' They feel the burden of sin, and earnestly desire to flee from the wrath to come. But not long: they seldom suffer the arrows of conviction to go deep into their souls; but quickly stifle the grace of God, and return to their wallowing in the mire.

In like manner, the evangelical state, or state of love, is frequently mixed with the legal. For few of those who have the spirit of bondage and fear remain always without hope. The wise and gracious God rarely suffers this; 'for He remembereth that we are but dust'; and He willeth not that 'the flesh should fail before Him, or the spirit which He hath made.' Therefore at such times as He seeth good, He gives a dawning of light unto them that sit in darkness. He causes a part of His goodness to pass before them, and shows He is a 'God that heareth the prayer.' They see the promise, which is by faith in Christ Jesus, though it be yet afar off; and hereby they are encouraged to 'run with patience the race which is set before them.'

3. Another reason why many deceive themselves, is, because they do not consider how far a man may go, and yet be in a natural,

or, at best, a legal state. A man may be of a compassionate and a benevolent temper; he may be affable, courteous, generous, friendly; he may have some degree of meekness, patience, temperance, and of many other moral virtues. He may feel many desires of shaking off all vice, and of attaining higher degrees of virtue. He may abstain from much evil; perhaps from all that is grossly contrary to justice, mercy, or truth. He may do much good, may feed the hungry, clothe the naked, relieve the widow and fatherless. He may attend public worship, use prayer in private, read many books of devotion; and yet, for all this, he may be a mere natural man, knowing neither himself nor God; equally a stranger to the spirit of fear and to that of love; having neither repented, nor believed the gospel.

But suppose there were added to all this a deep conviction of sin, with much fear of the wrath of God; vehement desires to cast off every sin, and to fulfil all righteousness; frequent rejoicing in hope, and touches of love often glancing upon the soul; yet neither do these prove a man to be *under grace*, to have true, living, Christian faith, unless the Spirit of adoption abide in his heart, unless he can continually cry, 'Abba. Father!'

4. Beware, then, thou who art called by the name of Christ, that thou come not short of the mark of thy high calling. Beware thou rest not, either in a natural state, with too many that are accounted *good Christians*; or in a legal state, wherein, those who are highly esteemed of men are generally content to live and die. Nay, but God hath prepared better things for thee, if thou follow on till thou attain. Thou art not called to fear and tremble, like devils; but to rejoice and love, like the angels of God. 'Thou shalt love the Lord thy God with all thy heart, and with all thy soul, and with all thy mind, and with all thy strength.' Thou shalt 'rejoice evermore'; thou shalt 'pray without ceasing'; thou shalt 'in everything give thanks.' Thou shalt do the will of God on earth as it is done in heaven. O prove thou 'what is that good, and acceptable, and perfect will of God'! Now present thyself 'a living sacrifice holy acceptable to God'! 'Whereunto thou hast already attained hold fast,' by 'reaching forth unto those things which are before'; until 'the God of peace make thee perfect in every good work, working in thee that which is well-pleasing in His sight, through Jesus Christ: to whom be glory for ever and ever! Amen!'

SERMON X

THE WITNESS OF THE SPIRIT

DISCOURSE I

This sermon would seem to have been written for the edition of 1746. In Sermon XLV (written and published in 1767), ii. 3, Wesley quotes from this sermon, and says, 'After *twenty years'* further consideration, I see no cause to retract any part of this.' I find no record of its having been preached until August 11, 1753, where it stands in the sermon list at the end of the Standard edition of the *Journal* against St. Gennys, along with Jas. i. 27. Wesley reached St. Gennys on Saturday evening, August 11, after preaching at Camelford at noon, and getting wet through in 'such a shower of rain as I never saw before in Europe.' On Sunday the 12th, 'I never saw so many people in this church; nor did I ever before speak so plainly to them. They hear; but when will they feel?' As no texts are set down in the list for August 12, I take it that the two put down for August 11 are those that he preached from on the Sunday. 'Rom. viii. 15, &c,' is set down as the subject of the morning exercise at the society meeting at Bristol on Tuesday, March 10, 1741. Mr. Curnock says of these morning exercises: 'For this duty he prayed and robed. Usually he went fasting. Returning to his rooms, he drank chocolate or tea, and at once proceeded to write in his journal, or in sermon form, or in a paper for use in society meetings, the substance of the exposition that morning given' (*Journal*, II. p. 354 *n.*). This note refers to the meetings at the Foundery, but doubtless those at Bristol were on the same lines. This was probably the first form of this sermon, which was elaborated and revised for the edition of 1746. It is rather a tractate than a sermon, and was intended for publication, not for pulpit delivery. But whilst it does not seem to have been often preached, the doctrine which it defends formed part of almost every sermon of Wesley's in these early years. For example, in Sermon I, ii. 4, it is specified as one of the privileges of salvation by faith; and in sermon IV, i. 3, we are told that the Christian of the apostolic age 'rejoiced in that witness of God's Spirit with his spirit that he was a child of God.'

This great doctrine, the clear statement of which was one of the most important services rendered to the Church by Wesley, had been obscured by the Sacramentarian teaching of the Romish Church and exaggerated by the Mystics. The Westminster Confession had allowed it to be an ordinary gift of the Spirit to the believer; but stated that he may have to 'wait long and contend with many difficulties before he be partaker of it.' On the other hand, it taught that assurance, when once

attained, is indefectible. The Anglican Articles are vague; in Art. XVII
it is said that those who through grace obey the calling of God 'be made
sons of God by adoption'; but there is no reference to the direct witness
of the Spirit. Bishop Pearson, however, in *Exposition of Creed*, Art. VIII,
says, 'It is the office of the Holy Ghost to assure us of the adoption of
sons. . . . As, therefore, we are born again by the Spirit, and receive
from Him our regeneration, so we are also assured by the Spirit of our
adoption'; and this passage is quoted in proof thereof. It was not from
his own Church, but from the Moravians, and especially from the
teaching of Peter Bohler, that Wesley in the early part of 1738 learnt
that one of the fruits of true faith in Christ was 'constant peace, arising
from a sense of forgiveness.' 'I was quite amazed,' he says (*Journal*, May
24, 1738), 'and looked upon it as a new gospel.' Then on May 24 came
the great experience of realized salvation; 'an assurance was given me
that He had taken away my sins, even mine, and saved me from the law
of sin and death.' For more than six months, however, he suffered from
doubt and frequent darkness; but when he was once fairly embarked
on his evangelical mission, they disappeared and troubled him no
more. On September 3, 1739, he was much encouraged by his mother's
experience. At first she had been fearful that he had erred in this
matter; she told him she had scarce heard such a thing mentioned as the
having God's Spirit bearing witness with our spirit; and she had never
dared to ask it for herself. But two or three weeks before this
conversation, as she was receiving the Sacrament, she knew that God
for Christ's sake had forgiven her all her sins. Her father, Dr. Annesley,
had had this experience, she said, for over forty years, but had never
preached it to others. As early as January 25, 1740, Wesley says, 'I never
yet knew one soul thus saved without what you call the faith of
assurance; I mean a sure confidence that by the merits of Christ he was
reconciled to the favour of God.' In the *Minutes* of 1744, in answer to Q.
8, 'Does any one believe, who has not the witness in himself, or any
longer than he sees, loves, obeys God?' he says, 'We apprehend not.' In
Minutes of 1745 he dares not positively say that there are not exempt
cases, and allows that there may be infinite degrees in seeing God. In
1746 he admits that it is hard to judge of individual cases, as we do not
know all the circumstances; but he affirms that all sincere persons who
are striving for this assurance will surely find it before they die. In the
Farther Appeal (1745), part I, he defends this doctrine against the attack
of the Bishop of Lichfield at full length; and again in 1747 in his Letters
XLI and XLII to Mr. John Smith (who was probably Thomas Secker).

In 1747, a month after the Conference, he writes to Charles: 'By
justifying faith, I mean that faith which whosoever hath not is under the
wrath and curse of God. By a sense of pardon I mean a distinct, explicit
assurance that my sins are forgiven. I allow (1) That there is such an
explicit assurance; (2) That it is the common privilege of real
Christians; (3) That it is the proper Christian faith which purifies the
heart and overcomes the world. But I cannot allow that justifying faith
is such an assurance, or necessarily connected therewith. Because, if

justifying faith necessarily implies such an explicit assurance of pardon, then every one who has it not, and every one so long as he has it not, is under the wrath and curse of God. But this is a supposition contrary to Scripture and experience (Isa. i. 10 and Acts x. 34). Again, the assertion that justifying faith is a sense of pardon is contrary to reason, it is flatly absurd. For how can a sense of our having received pardon be the condition of our receiving it?' In other words, we do not believe, because we have received the witness of the Spirit; but normally we receive the witness of the Spirit as soon as we believe.

This doctrine Wesley held and preached to the end; but experience led him to discard more explicitly his first view that there could be no salvation without assurance. Thus in his answer to Prof. Rutherforth in 1768 he says: 'I believe a consciousness of being in the favour of God (which I do not term *full assurance,* since it is frequently weakened, nay, perhaps interrupted, by returns of doubt or fear) is the common privilege of Christians, fearing God and working righteousness. Yet I do not affirm there are no exceptions to this general rule. . . . Therefore I have not, for many years, thought a consciousness of acceptance to be essential to justifying faith.'

The opposition which was aroused by Wesley's teaching on this point was due to the not unnatural reaction, after the Restoration, from the extravagant claims of many of the Puritans to special divine illumination. Thus Butler in *Hudibras* i. 1 describes Ralpho, the squire, who stands for the Independents, as getting his knowledge from the New Light:

> 'Whate'er men speak by this new light
> Still they are sure to be i' th' right;
> 'Tis a dark lanthorn of the Spirit
> Which none see by but those that bear it;
> A light that falls down from on high
> For Spiritual trades to cozen by.'

If a man could claim a direct illumination of the Spirit on one point, why not on many, or all, others? Thus the door would be thrown open to all kinds of wild and extravagant ideas, against which it would be impossible to argue, because their authors held them to be the result of direct divine inspiration. Many good people, too, like Mrs. Susanna Wesley, feared to be presumptuous if they claimed such a gift. And when to this is added the unspiritual character of the period, and its passion for cold correctness and good form, It is easy to see why the early Methodists were branded as enthusiasts and madmen, chiefly because they maintained the possibillty and realization of the direct witness of the Spirit. As Dr. Cutten (*Psychological Phenomena of Christianity,* p. 234) says, 'Pentecost needed a defence against the charge of drunkenness.'

Recent studies in the psychology of the spiritual life confirm Wesley's teaching, though they do not always use his language. They agree in holding that in some way there must be a direct communication of the divine to the human spirit for the full development of the higher life. Thus Prof. Boyce Gibson, of the Melbourne University (who bears two names that will always be memorable in Methodism), says of Rudolf Eucken: 'Eucken's own explicit conviction is that the immediate revelation of this all-inclusive spiritual life to ours, and its power to maintain itself steadily in presence of the perils and limitations of our human nature, is an axiomatic fact, apart from which there can be no root of truth or of reason in our lives at all. It is in this intimacy of our life with God's that Eucken finds the new immediacy that can alone satisfy the life that has broken from the immediacy of sense, and inspire our human frailty for its redemptive mission in the world.' Bergson holds that the highest thing in man is his 'susceptibility for God,' which culminates in a 'real union of being' with God. Von Haering (*Ethics of Christian Life*, p. 197) says: 'The assurance of salvation . . . is a present experience of blessedness and a certain hope of blessedness, and is present blessedness in fellowship with God.' Dr. Cutten, in the work cited above, p. 250, says, in reference to the theory that the experience of the witness of the Spirit is due to suggestion: 'To say that it is suggestion only is doing violence to the united testimony of thousands whose evidence is as valuable as any in the land.'

The Spirit itself beareth witness with our spirit, that we are the children of God.—ROM. viii. 16.

1. How many vain men, not understanding what they spake, neither whereof they affirmed, have wrested this scripture to the great loss, if not the destruction, of their souls! How many have mistaken the voice of their own imagination for this witness of the Spirit of God, and thence idly presumed they were the children of God, while they were doing the works of the devil! These are truly and properly enthusiasts; and, indeed, in the worst sense of the word. But with what difficulty are they convinced thereof, especially if they have drank deep into that spirit of error. All endeavours to bring them to the knowledge of themselves, they will then account fighting against God; and that vehemence and impetuosity of spirit, which they call 'contending earnestly for the faith,' sets them so far above all the usual methods of conviction, that we may well say, 'With men it is impossible.'

2. Who then can be surprised, if many reasonable men, seeing the dreadful effects of this delusion, and labouring to keep at the utmost distance from it, should sometimes lean toward another extreme?—if they are not forward to believe any who

speak of having this witness, concerning which others have so grievously erred?—if they are almost ready to set all down for enthusiasts who use the expressions which have been so terribly abused?—yea, if they should question whether the witness or testimony here spoken of be the privilege of *ordinary* Christians, and not, rather, one of those *extraordinary* gifts which they suppose belonged only to the apostolic age?

3. But is there any necessity laid upon us of running either into one extreme or the other? May we not steer a middle course—keep a sufficient distance from that spirit of error and enthusiasm, without denying the gift of God, and giving up the great privilege of His children? Surely we may. In order thereto let us consider, in the presence and fear of God,—

I. WHAT IS THIS WITNESS OR TESTIMONY OF OUR SPIRIT; WHAT IS THE TESTIMONY OF GOD'S SPIRIT; AND, HOW DOES HE 'BEAR WITNESS WITH OUR SPIRIT THAT WE ARE THE CHILDREN OF GOD'?

II. HOW IS THIS JOINT TESTIMONY OF GOD'S SPIRIT AND OUR OWN, CLEARLY AND SOLIDLY DISTIN-GUISHED FROM THE PRESUMPTION OF A NATU-RAL MIND, AND FROM THE DELUSION OF THE DEVIL?

I. 1. Let us first consider, what is the witness or testimony of our spirit. But here I cannot but desire all those who are for swallowing up the testimony of the Spirit of God in the rational testimony of our own spirit, to observe, that in this text the Apostle is so far from speaking of the testimony of our own spirit *only*, that it may be questioned whether he speaks of it *at all*—whether he does not speak *only* of the testimony of God's Spirit. It does not appear but the original text may be fairly understood thus. The Apostle had just said, in the preceding verse, 'Ye have received the Spirit of adoption, whereby we cry, Abba, Father'; and immediately subjoins, Αυτο το Πνευμα (some copies read, το αυτο Πνευμα) συμμαρτυρει τω πνευματι ημων οτι εσμεν τεκνα Θεου; which may be translated, 'The same Spirit beareth witness to our spirit, that we are the children of God' (The preposition συν only denoting, that He witnesses this *at the same time* that He enables us to cry, Abba, Father). But I contend not; seeing so many other texts, with the experience of all real Christians, sufficiently evidence, that there is in every believer, both the testimony of God's Spirit, and the testimony of his own, that he is a child of God.

2. With regard to the latter, the foundation thereof is laid in those numerous texts of Scripture which describe the marks of the children of God; and that so plain, that he which runneth may read them. These are also collected together, and placed in the strongest light, by many both ancient and modern writers. If any need farther light, he may receive it by attending on the ministry of God's word; by meditating thereon before God in secret; and by conversing with those who have the knowledge of His ways. And by the reason or understanding that God has given him, which religion was designed not to extinguish, but to perfect—according to that of the Apostle, 'Brethren, be not children in understanding; in malice' or wickedness 'be ye children; but in understanding be ye men' (I Cor. xiv. 20)—every man applying those scriptural marks to himself may know whether he is a child of God. Thus, if he know, first, 'as many as are led by the Spirit of God,' into all holy tempers and actions, 'they are the sons of God' (for which he has the infallible assurance of holy writ); secondly, I am thus 'led by the Spirit of God'; he will easily conclude, 'Therefore I am a son of God.'

3. Agreeable to this are all those plain declarations of St. John, in his First Epistle: 'Hereby we know that we do know Him, if we keep His commandments' (chap. ii. 3). 'Whoso keepeth His word, in him verily is the love of God perfected: hereby know we that we are in Him'; that we are indeed the children of God (verse 5). 'If ye know that He is righteous, ye know that every one that doeth righteousness is born of Him' (verse 29). 'We know that we have passed from death unto life, because we love the brethren' (chap. iii. 14). 'Hereby we know that we are of the truth, and shall assure our hearts before Him' (verse 19); namely, because we 'love one another, not in word, neither in tongue, but in deed and in truth.' 'Hereby know we that we dwell in Him, because He hath given us of His' loving 'Spirit' (chap. iv. 13). And, 'Hereby we know that He abideth in us, by the' obedient 'Spirit which He hath given us' (chap. iii. 24).

4. It is highly probable there never were any children of God, from the beginning of the world unto this day, who were farther advanced in the grace of God, and the knowledge of our Lord

Jesus Christ, than the Apostle John, at the time when he wrote these words, and the fathers in Christ to whom he wrote. Notwithstanding which, it is evident, both the Apostle himself, and all those pillars in God's temple, were very far from despising these marks of their being the children of God; and that they applied them to their own souls for the confirmation of their faith. Yet all this is no other than rational evidence, the witness of our spirit, our reason or understanding. It all resolves into this: Those who have these marks are children of God: but we have these marks: therefore we are children of God.

5. But how does it appear, that we have these marks? This is a question which still remains. How does it appear, that we do love God and our neighbour, and that we keep His commandments? Observe, that the meaning of the question is, How does it appear to *ourselves*, not to *others*? I would ask him, then, that proposes this question, How does it appear to you, that you are alive, and that you are now in ease and not in pain? Are you not immediately conscious of it? By the same immediate consciousness, you will know if your soul is alive to God; if you are saved from the pain of proud wrath, and have the ease of a meek and quiet spirit. By the same means you cannot but perceive if you love, rejoice, and delight in God. By the same you must be directly assured if you love your neighbour as yourself; if you are kindly affectioned to all mankind, and full of gentleness and long-suffering. And with regard to the outward mark of the children of God, which is, according to St. John, the keeping His commandments, you undoubtedly know in your own breast, if, by the grace of God, it belongs to you. Your conscience informs you from day to day, if you do not take the name of God within your lips, unless with seriousness and devotion, with reverence and godly fear; if you remember the Sabbath-day to keep it holy; if you honour your father and mother; if you do to all as you would they should do unto you; if you possess your body in sanctification and honour; and if, whether you eat or drink, you are temperate therein, and do all to the glory of God.

6. Now this is properly the testimony of our own spirit; even the testimony of our own conscience, that God hath given us to be holy of heart, and holy in outward conversation. It is a consciousness of our having received, in and by the Spirit of adoption, the tempers mentioned in the Word of God, as

belonging to His adopted children; even a loving heart toward God, and toward all mankind; hanging with child-like confidence on God our Father, desiring nothing but Him, casting all our care upon Him, and embracing every child of man with earnest, tender affection, [so as to be ready to lay down our life for our brother, as Christ laid down His life for us,—] a consciousness that we are inwardly conformed, by the Spirit of God, to the image of His Son, and that we walk before Him in justice, mercy, and truth, doing the things which are pleasing in His sight.

7. But what is that testimony of God's Spirit, which is superadded to, and conjoined with, this? How does He 'bear witness with our spirit that we are the children of God'? It is hard to find words in the language of men to explain 'the deep things of God.' Indeed, there are none that will adequately express what the children of God experience. But perhaps one might say (desiring any who are taught of God to correct, to soften, or strengthen the expression), the testimony of the Spirit is an inward impression on the soul, whereby the Spirit of God directly witnesses to my spirit, that I am a child of God; that Jesus Christ hath loved me, and given Himself for me; and that all my sins are blotted out, and I, even I, am reconciled to God.

8. That this testimony of the Spirit of God must needs, in the very nature of things, be antecedent to the testimony of our own spirit, may appear from this single consideration. We must be holy of heart, and holy in life, before we can be conscious that we are so; before we can have the testimony of our spirit, that we are inwardly and outwardly holy. But we must love God, before we can be holy at all; this being the root of all holiness. Now we cannot love God, till we know He loves us. 'We love Him, because He first loved us.' And we cannot know His pardoning love to us, till His Spirit witnesses it to our spirit. Since, therefore, this testimony of His Spirit must precede the love of God and all holiness, of consequence it must precede our inward consciousness thereof, or the testimony of our spirit concerning them.

9. Then, and not till then—when the Spirit of God beareth that witness to our spirit, 'God hath loved thee, and given His own Son to be the propitiation for thy sins; the Son of God hath loved thee, and hath washed thee from thy sins in His blood'—'we love God, because He first loved us'; and, for His

sake, we love our brother also. And of this we cannot but be conscious to ourselves; we 'know the things that are freely given to us of God.' We know that we love God, and keep His commandments; and 'hereby also we know that we are of God.' This is that testimony of our own spirit, which, so long as we continue to love God and keep His commandments, continues joined with the testimony of God's Spirit, 'that we are the children of God.'

10. Not that I would by any means be understood, by anything which has been spoken concerning it, to exclude the operation of the Spirit of God, even from the testimony of our own spirit. In no wise. It is He that not only worketh in us every manner of thing that is good, but also shines upon His own work, and clearly shows what He has wrought. Accordingly, this is spoken of by St. Paul, as one great end of our receiving the Spirit, 'that we may know the things which are freely given to us of God': that He may strengthen the testimony of our conscience, touching our 'simplicity and godly sincerity'; and give us to discern in a fuller and stronger light, that we now do the things which please Him.

11. Should it still be inquired, 'How does the Spirit of God "bear witness with our spirit, that we are the children of God," so as to exclude all doubt, and evince the reality of our sonship?'—the answer is clear from what has been observed above. And first, as to the witness of our spirit: the soul as intimately and evidently perceives when it loves, delights, and rejoices in God, as when it loves and delights in anything on earth. And it can no more doubt, whether it loves, delights, and rejoices or no, than whether it exists or no. If, therefore, this be just reasoning,

He that now loves God, that delights and rejoices in Him with an humble joy, an holy delight, and an obedient love, is a child of God:

But I thus love, delight, and rejoice in God;

Therefore, I am a child of God:—

Then a Christian can in no wise doubt of his being a child of God. Of the former proposition he has as full an assurance as he has that the Scriptures are of God; and of his thus loving God, he has an inward proof, which is nothing short of self-evidence. Thus, the testimony of our own spirit is with the most intimate conviction manifested to our hearts, in such a manner, as beyond all reasonable doubt to evince the reality of our sonship.

12. The manner how the *divine* testimony is manifested to the heart, I do not take upon me to explain. Such knowledge is too wonderful and excellent for me: I cannot attain unto it. The wind bloweth, and I hear the sound thereof; but I cannot tell how it cometh, or whither it goeth. As no one knoweth the things of a man, save the spirit of a man that is in him; so the *manner* of the things of God knoweth no one, save the Spirit of God. But the fact we know; namely, that the Spirit of God does give a believer such a testimony of his adoption, that while it is present to the soul, he can no more doubt the reality of his sonship, than he can doubt of the shining of the sun, while he stands in the full blaze of his beams.

II. 1. How this joint testimony of God's Spirit and our spirit may be clearly and solidly distinguished from the presumption of a natural mind, and from the delusion of the devil, is the next thing to be considered. And it highly imports all who desire the salvation of God, to consider it with the deepest attention, as they would not deceive their own souls. An error in this is generally observed to have the most fatal consequences: the rather, because he that errs, seldom discovers his mistake, till it is too late to remedy it.

2. And, first, how is this testimony to be distinguished from the presumption of a natural mind? It is certain, one who was never convinced of sin is always ready to flatter himself, and to think of himself, especially in spiritual things, more highly than he ought to think. And hence, it is in no wise strange, if one who is vainly puffed up by his fleshly mind, when he hears of this privilege of true Christians among whom he undoubtedly ranks himself, should soon work himself up into a persuasion that he is already possessed thereof. Such instances now abound in the world, and have abounded in all ages. How then may the real testimony of the Spirit with our spirit be distinguished from this damning presumption?

3. I answer, the holy Scriptures abound with marks, whereby the one may be distinguished from the other. They describe, in the plainest manner, the circumstances which go before, which accompany, and which follow, the true, genuine testimony of

the Spirit of God with the spirit of a believer. Whoever carefully weighs and attends to these will not need to put darkness for light. He will perceive so wide a difference, with respect to all these, between the real and the pretended witness of the Spirit, that there will be no danger, I might say, no possibility, of confounding the one with the other.

4. By these, one who vainly presumes on the gift of God might surely know, if he really desired it, that he hath been hitherto 'given up to a strong delusion,' and suffered to believe a lie. For the Scriptures lay down those clear, obvious marks, as preceding, accompanying, and following that gift, which a little reflection would convince him, beyond all doubt, were never found in his soul. For instance: the Scripture describes repentance, or conviction of sin, as constantly going before this witness of pardon. So, 'Repent; for the kingdom of heaven is at hand' (Matt. iii. 2). 'Repent ye, and believe the gospel' (Mark i. 15). 'Repent, and be baptized every one of you, for the remission of sins' (Acts ii. 38). 'Repent ye therefore, and be converted, that your sins may be blotted out' (Acts iii. 19). In conformity whereto, our Church also, continually places repentance before pardon, or the witness of it. 'He pardoneth and absolveth all them that truly repent, and unfeignedly believe His holy gospel.' 'Almighty God . . . hath promised forgiveness of sins to all them who, with hearty repentance and true faith, turn unto Him.' But he is a stranger even to this repentance: he hath never known a broken and a contrite heart: 'the remembrance of his sins' was never 'grievous unto him,' nor 'the burden of them intolerable.' In repeating those words, he never meant what he said; he merely paid a compliment to God. And were it only from the want of this previous work of God, he hath too great reason to believe that he hath grasped a mere shadow, and never yet known the real privilege of the sons of God.

5. Again: the Scriptures describe the being born of God, which must precede the witness that we are His children, as a vast and mighty change; a change 'from darkness to light, as well as 'from the power of Satan unto God'; as a 'passing from death unto life,' a resurrection from the dead. Thus the Apostle to the Ephesians: 'You hath He quickened, who were dead in trespasses and sins' (ii. 1). And again, 'When we were dead in sins, He hath quickened us together with Christ; and hath raised

us up together, and made us sit together in heavenly places in
Christ Jesus' (verses 5, 6). But what knoweth he, concerning
whom we now speak, of any such change as this? He is altogether
unacquainted with this whole matter. This is a language which
he does not understand. He tells you he always was a Christian.
He knows no time when he had need of such a change. By this
also, if he give himself leave to think, may he know, that he is not
born of the Spirit; that he has never yet known God; but has
mistaken the voice of nature for the voice of God.

6. But waiving the consideration of whatever he has or has not
experienced in time past; by the present marks may we easily
distinguish a child of God from a presumptuous self-deceiver.
The Scriptures describe that joy in the Lord which accompanies
the witness of His Spirit, as an humble joy; a joy that abases to the
dust, that makes a pardoned sinner cry out, 'I am vile! What am
I, or my father's house! Now mine eye seeth Thee, I abhor
myself in dust and ashes!' And wherever lowliness is, there is
meekness, patience, gentleness, long-suffering. There is a soft,
yielding spirit; a mildness and sweetness, a tenderness of soul,
which words cannot express. But do these fruits attend that
supposed testimony of the Spirit in a presumptuous man? Just the
reverse. The more confident he is of the favour of God, the
more is he lifted up; the more does he exalt himself; the more
haughty and assuming is his whole behaviour. The stronger
witness he imagines himself to have, the more overbearing is he
to all around him; the more incapable of receiving any reproof;
the more impatient of contradiction. Instead of being more
meek, and gentle, and teachable, more 'swift to hear, and slow to
speak,' he is more slow to hear, and swift to speak; more unready
to learn of any one; more fiery and vehement in his temper, and
eager in his conversation. Yea, perhaps, there will sometimes
appear a kind of fierceness in his air, his manner of speaking, his
whole deportment, as if he were just going to take the matter out
of God's hands, and himself to 'devour the adversaries.'

7. Once more: the Scriptures teach, 'This is the love of God,'
the sure mark thereof, 'that we keep His commandments' (I
John v. 3). And our Lord Himself saith, 'He that keepeth My
commandments, he it is that loveth Me' (John xiv. 21). Love
rejoices to obey; to do, in every point, whatever is acceptable to
the beloved. A true lover of God hastens to do His will on earth

as it is done in heaven. But is this the character of the presumptuous pretender to the love of God? Nay, but His love gives him a liberty to disobey, to break, not keep, the commandments of God. Perhaps, when he was in fear of the wrath of God, he did labour to do His will. But now, looking on himself as 'not under the law,' he thinks he is no longer obliged to observe it. He is therefore less zealous of good works; less careful to abstain from evil; less watchful over his own heart; less jealous over his tongue. He is less earnest to deny himself, and to take up his cross daily. In a word, the whole form of his life is changed, since he has fancied himself to be *at liberty*. He is no longer 'exercising himself unto godliness'; 'wrestling not only with flesh and blood, but with principalities and powers,' enduring hardships, 'agonizing to enter in at the strait gate.' No; he has found an easier way to heaven; a broad, smooth, flowery path; in which he can say to his soul, 'Soul, take thy ease; eat, drink, and be merry.' It follows, with undeniable evidence, that he has not the true testimony of his own spirit. He cannot be conscious of having those marks which he hath not; that lowliness, meekness, and obedience: nor yet can the Spirit of the God of truth bear witness to a lie; or testify that he is a child of God, when he is manifestly a child of the devil.

8. Discover thyself, thou poor self-deceiver!—thou who art confident of being a child of God; thou who sayest, 'I have the witness in myself,' and therefore defiest all thy enemies. Thou art weighed in the balance and found wanting; even in the balance of the sanctuary. The word of the Lord hath tried thy soul, and proved thee to be reprobate silver. Thou art not lowly of heart; therefore thou hast not received the Spirit of Jesus unto this day. Thou art not gentle and meek; therefore thy joy is nothing worth: it is not joy in the Lord. Thou dost not keep His commandments: therefore thou lovest Him not, neither art thou partaker of the Holy Ghost. It is consequently as certain and as evident as the oracles of God can make it, His Spirit doth not bear witness with thy spirit that thou art a child of God. O cry unto Him, that the scales may fall off thine eyes; that thou mayest know thyself as thou art known; that thou mayest receive the sentence of death in thyself, till thou hear the voice that raises the dead, saying, 'Be of good cheer: thy sins are forgiven; thy faith hath made thee whole.'

9. 'But how may one who has the real witness in himself
distinguish it from presumption?' How, I pray, do you
distinguish day from night? How do you distinguish light from
darkness; or the light of a star, or a glimmering taper, from the
light of the noonday sun? Is there not an inherent, obvious,
essential difference between the one and the other? And do you
not immediately and directly perceive that difference, provided
your senses are rightly disposed? In like manner, there is an
inherent, essential difference between spiritual light and
spiritual darkness; and between the light wherewith the Sun of
Righteousness shines upon our heart, and that glimmering light
which arises only from 'sparks of our own kindling': and this
difference also is immediately and directly perceived, if our
spiritual senses are rightly disposed.

10. To require a more minute and philosophical account of
the manner whereby we distinguish these, and of the *criteria*, or
intrinsic marks, whereby we know the voice of God, is to make a
demand which can never be answered; no, not by one who has
the deepest knowledge of God. Suppose, when Paul answered
before Agrippa, the wise Roman had said, 'Thou talkest of
hearing the voice of the Son of God. How dost thou know it was
His voice? By what *criteria*, what intrinsic marks, dost thou know
the voice of God? Explain to me the *manner* of distinguishing this
from a human or angelic voice.' Can you believe, the Apostle
himself would have once attempted to answer so idle a demand?
And yet, doubtless, the moment he heard that voice, he knew it
was the voice of God. But *how* he knew this, who is able to
explain? Perhaps neither man nor angel.

11. To come yet closer: suppose God were now to speak to any
soul, 'Thy sins are forgiven thee,' He must be willing that soul
should know His voice; otherwise He would speak in vain. And
He is able to effect this; for, whenever He wills, to do is present
with Him. And He does effect it: that soul is absolutely assured,
'This voice is the voice of God.' But yet he who hath that witness
in himself cannot explain it to one who hath it not; nor indeed is
it to be expected that he should. Were there any natural medium
to prove, or natural method to explain, the things of God to
unexperienced men, then the natural man might discern and
know the things of the Spirit of God. But this is utterly contrary

to the assertion of the Apostle, that 'he cannot know them, because they are spiritually discerned'; even by spiritual senses, which the natural man hath not.

12. 'But how shall I know that my spiritual senses are rightly disposed?' This also is a question of vast importance; for if a man mistake in this, he may run on in endless error and delusion. 'And how am I assured that this is not my case; and that I do not mistake the voice of the Spirit?' Even by the testimony of your own spirit: by 'the answer of a good conscience toward God.' By the fruits which He hath wrought in your spirit, you shall know the testimony of the Spirit of God. Hereby you shall know that you are in no delusion, that you have not deceived your own soul. The immediate fruits of the Spirit, ruling in the heart, are 'love, joy, peace, bowels of mercies, humbleness of mind, meekness, gentleness, long-suffering.' And the outward fruits are, the doing good to all men; the doing no evil to any; and the walking in the light—a zealous, uniform obedience to all the commandments of God.

13. By the same fruits shall you distinguish this voice of God from any delusion of the devil. That proud spirit cannot humble thee before God. He neither can nor would soften thy heart, and melt it first into earnest mourning after God, and then into filial love. It is not the adversary of God and man that enables thee to love thy neighbour; or to put on meekness, gentleness, patience, temperance, and the whole armour of God. He is not divided against himself, or a destroyer of sin, his own work. No; it is none but the Son of God who cometh 'to destroy the works of the devil.' As surely therefore as holiness is of God, and as sin is the work of the devil, so surely the witness thou hast in thyself is not of Satan, but of God.

14. Well then mayest thou say, 'Thanks be unto God for His unspeakable gift!' Thanks be unto God, who giveth me to 'know in whom I have believed'; who hath 'sent forth the Spirit of His Son into my heart, crying, Abba, Father,' and even now, 'bearing witness with my spirit that I am a child of God'! And see, that not only thy lips, but thy life show forth His praise. He hath sealed thee for His own; glorify Him then in thy body and thy spirit, which are His. Beloved, if thou hast this hope in thyself, purify thyself, as He is pure. While thou beholdest what manner of love

the Father hath given thee, that thou shouldest be called a child of God, cleanse thyself 'from all filthiness of flesh and spirit, perfecting holiness in the fear of God'; and let all thy thoughts, words, and works be a spiritual sacrifice, holy, acceptable to God through Christ Jesus!

SERMON XI

THE WITNESS OF OUR OWN SPIRIT

I can find no record either in the *Journal* or in the sermon list of the preaching of this sermon. No doubt the substance of it was often given to the Societies in the expositions which were regularly delivered to them by Wesley; but it is rather a treatise than a sermon, and is not adapted for a general congregation. Even for believers it needs, as Wesley felt, the qualifications which he added in the two following sermons in the 1771 edition. Sermon CV, on Conscience, is from the first part of the same text.

The object of the sermon is to explain what is meant by the witness of our own spirit referred to in Rom. viii. 16, as distinguished from the witness of the Divine Spirit to our adoption; the indirect as contrasted with the direct evidence of our acceptance. The text is not the best that could have been chosen for this purpose. It is St. Paul's vindication of his conduct at Corinth, which had been attacked by his opponents on the ground that he was a designing adventurer, walking according to the flesh (i.e. actuated by motives of mere worldly shrewdness), enriching himself under pretence of a collection for the poor saints at Jerusalem, and only refusing to take a salary in order to impose on the generosity of his converts. He says in answer to this: 'The boast I make is this, as my conscience testifies to me, that my whole conduct in worldly matters was regulated by holiness and godly sincerity, not by the prudence of the natural man, but by the grace of God, and that more particularly in my relations to you.' There is no reference to his consciousness of acceptance with God, or the witness of his conscience to that. Moreover, the reading of the A.V., on which certain sections of the sermon are based, is doubtful; for απλοτητι (simplicity) the better attested reading is αγιοτητι (holiness).

With regard to this question, it may be well to turn aside for a moment from the explanations of the theologians to the actual experiences immediately following after conversion. These have been scientifically examined and tabulated by Prof. Starbuck and are summarized by Prof. James in *Varieties of Religious Experience,* Lecture X, as follows:

(1) The sense of the coming into life of a higher control; which results in the loss of all the worry, the sense that all is ultimately well with one, the peace, the harmony, the willlngness to be, even though the outer conditions should remain the same.

(2) The sense of perceiving truths not known before. The mysteries of life become lucid; and often, nay, usually, the solution is more or less unutterable in words.

(3) A sense of clean and beautiful newness within and without. This is often accompanied by a sense of brilliant light, a light ineffable in the soul and in nature.

(4) The most characteristic of all the elements of the conversion crisis is the ecstasy of happiness produced.

Normally this new experience follows a period of depression, doubt, misery, amounting often to utter despair. It is not the result of argument or logical conviction, but follows instantly on the surrender of self to Christ in faith. This is psychologically what is meant by the witness of the Spirit; but each convert will afterwards explain it in his own way. To one it is the removal of the sense of condemnation, i.e. Justification; to a second it is the realization that God is his loving Father, i.e. Adoption; to a third it is the feeling that the old self has gone, and that a new life has come into his soul, i.e. Regeneration. But all these worketh that one and the same Spirit, dividing to every man severally as He will. Therefore, though the Scripture speaks specifically of the witness of the Spirit to adoption, it would be absurd to say that the consciousness of forgiveness, and the new birth, are not equally His work; and therefore equally a witness borne by Him to what has taken place. The distinction between justification, adoption, and regeneration is the result of a sound analysis; but we must not suppose that processes which can be conceived separately in thought are necessarlly separate in fact. They are all included in the one process of conversion, and neither can exist without the others. Adoption connects itself with the work of the Father, justification with that of the Son, regeneration with that of the Holy Ghost; and like their divine authors, these three are one. Moreover, to all three our own spirit bears conjoint witness with the Holy Spirit, re-echoing to His testimony in the conscious joy of pardon, the kindling love of sonship, the pulsing power of the new life.

But all this is the starting-point of the process of sanctification; the gradual bringing of the whole thought and life into conformity with the law of God; and unless this follows, it is proof that the supposed direct witness was a delusion. The fruits of the Spirit will be produced in ever richer fullness; and of this fact both ourselves and others can judge. This is really the indirect witness with which this sermon is concerned—the testimony of a good conscience and a good life. It is not right to limit the witness of our own spirit to this confirmatory testimony; it is also a party to the direct witness. Hence Dr. Pope thinks the 'indirect witness' the preferable name (iii. 130).

This is our rejoicing, the testimony of our conscience, that in simplicity and godly sincerity, not with fleshly wisdom, but by the grace of God, we have had our conversation in the world.—2 COR. i. 12.

I. SUCH is the voice of every true believer in Christ, so long as he abides in faith and love. 'He that followeth Me,' saith our Lord, 'walketh not in darkness': and while he hath the light, he rejoiceth therein. As he hath 'received the Lord Jesus Christ,' so he walketh in Him; and while he walketh in Him, the exhortation of the Apostle takes place in his soul, day by day, 'Rejoice in the Lord always; and again I say, Rejoice.'

2. But that we may not build our house upon the sand (lest when the rains descend, and the winds blow, and the floods arise and beat upon it, it fall, and great be the fall thereof), I intend in the following discourse to show what is the nature and ground of a Christian's joy. We know, in general, it is that happy peace, that calm satisfaction of spirit which arises from such a testimony of his conscience, as is here described by the Apostle. But, in order to understand this the more thoroughly, it will be requisite to weigh all his words; whence will easily appear, both what we are to understand by *conscience,* and what by the *testimony* thereof; and also, how he that hath this testimony rejoiceth evermore.

3. And, first, what are we to understand by *conscience?* What is the meaning of this word that is in every one's mouth? One would imagine it was an exceeding difficult thing to discover this, when we consider how large and numerous volumes have been from time to time wrote on this subject; and how all the treasures of ancient and modern learning have been ransacked, in order to explain it. And yet it is to be feared, it has not received much light from all those elaborate inquiries. Rather, have not most of those writers puzzled the cause; 'darkening counsel by words without knowledge'; perplexing a subject, plain in itself and easy to be understood? For, set aside but hard words, and every man of an honest heart will soon understand the thing.

4. God has made us thinking beings, capable of perceiving what is present, and of reflecting or looking back on what is past. In particular, we are capable of perceiving whatsoever passes in our own hearts or lives; of knowing whatsoever we feel or do; and that either while it passes, or when it is past. This we mean when we say, man is a *conscious* being: he hath a *consciousness,* or inward perception, both of things present and past, relating to himself, of his own tempers and outward behaviour. But what we usually term *conscience* implies somewhat more than this. It is not barely the knowledge of our present or the remembrance of

our preceding life. To remember, to bear witness either of past
or present things, is only one, and the least office of conscience:
its main business is to excuse or accuse, to approve or
disapprove, to acquit or condemn.

5. Some late writers indeed have given a new name to this, and
have chose to style it a *moral sense*. But the old word seems
preferable to the new, were it only on this account, that it is more
common and familiar among men, and therefore easier to be
understood. And to Christians it is undeniably preferable, on
another account also; namely, because it is scriptural; because it
is the word which the wisdom of God hath chose to use in the
inspired writings.

And according to the meaning wherein it is generally used
there, particularly in the Epistles of St. Paul, we may understand
by conscience, a faculty or power, implanted by God in every
soul that comes into the world, of perceiving what is right or
wrong in his own heart or life, in his tempers, thoughts, words,
and actions.

6. But what is the rule whereby men are to judge of right and
wrong? whereby their conscience is to be directed? The rule of
Heathens, as the Apostle teaches elsewhere, is 'the law written in
their hearts.' 'These,' saith he, 'not having the' outward 'law, are
a law unto themselves: who show the work of the law,' that which
the outward law prescribes, 'written in their hearts,' by the
finger of God; 'their conscience also bearing witness,' whether
they walk by this rule or not, 'and their thoughts the meanwhile
accusing, or even excusing,' acquitting, defending them; η και
απολογουμενων (Rom. ii. 14, 15). But the Christian rule of
right and wrong is the Word of God, the writings of the Old and
New Testament; all that the prophets and 'holy men of old'
wrote 'as they were moved by the Holy Ghost'; all that Scripture
which was 'given by inspiration of God,' and which is indeed
'profitable for doctrine,' or teaching the whole will of God; 'for
reproof' of what is contrary thereto; for 'correction' of error;
and 'for instruction,' or training us up, 'in righteousness' (2
Tim. iii. 16).

This is a lantern unto a Christian's feet, and a light in all his
paths. This alone he receives as his rule of right or wrong, of
whatever is really good or evil. He esteems nothing good, but
what is here enjoined, either directly or by plain consequence;

he accounts nothing evil but what is here forbidden, either in terms, or by undeniable inference. Whatever the Scripture neither forbids nor enjoins, either directly or by plain consequence, he believes to be of an indifferent nature; to be in itself neither good nor evil; this being the whole and sole outward rule whereby his conscience is to be directed in all things.

7. And if it be directed thereby in fact, then hath he 'the answer of a good conscience toward God.' 'A good conscience' is what is elsewhere termed by the Apostle, 'a conscience void of offence.' So, what he at one time expresses thus, 'I have lived in all good conscience before God until this day' (Acts xxiii. 1); he denotes at another by that expression, 'Herein do I exercise myself, to have always a conscience void of offence toward God, and toward men' (chap, xxiv. 16). Now, in order to this there is absolutely required, first, a right understanding of the Word of God, of His 'holy, and acceptable, and perfect will' concerning us, as it is revealed therein. For it is impossible we should walk by a rule, if we do not know what it means. There is, secondly, required (which how few have attained!) a true knowledge of ourselves; a knowledge both of our hearts and lives, of our inward tempers and outward conversation: seeing, if we know them not, it is not possible that we should compare them with our rule. There is required, thirdly, an agreement of our hearts and lives, of our tempers and conversation, of our thoughts, and words, and works, with that rule, with the written Word of God. For, without this, if we have any conscience at all, it can be only an evil conscience. There is, fourthly, required, an inward perception of this agreement with our rule: and this habitual perception, this inward consciousness itself, is properly a *good conscience*; or, in the other phrase of the Apostle, 'a conscience void of offence toward God, and toward men.'

8. But whoever desires to have a conscience thus void of offence, let him see that he lay the right foundation. Let him remember, 'other foundation' of this 'can no man lay, than that which is laid, even Jesus Christ.' And let him also be mindful, that no man buildeth on Him but by a living faith; that no man is a partaker of Christ, until he can clearly testify, 'The life which I now live, I live by faith in the Son of God'; in Him who is now *revealed* in my heart; who 'loved me, and gave Himself for me.'

Faith alone is that evidence, that conviction, that demonstration of things invisible, whereby the eyes of our understanding being opened, and divine light poured in upon them, we 'see the wondrous things of God's law'; the excellency and purity of it; the height, and depth, and length, and breadth thereof, and of every commandment contained therein. It is by faith that, beholding 'the light of the glory of God in the face of Jesus Christ,' we perceive, as in a glass, all that is within ourselves, yea, the inmost motions of our souls. And by this alone can that blessed love of God be 'shed abroad in our hearts,' which enables us so to love one another as Christ loved us. By this is that gracious promise fulfilled unto all the Israel of God, 'I will put My laws into their mind, and write' (or engrave) 'them in their hearts' (Heb. viii. 10); hereby producing in their souls an entire agreement with His holy and perfect law, and 'bringing into captivity every thought to the obedience of Christ.'

And, as an evil tree cannot bring forth good fruit, so a good tree cannot bring forth evil fruit. As the heart therefore of a believer, so likewise his life, is thoroughly conformed to the rule of God's commandments; in a consciousness whereof, he can give glory to God, and say with the Apostle, 'This is our rejoicing, the testimony of our conscience, that in simplicity and godly sincerity, not with fleshly wisdom, but by the grace of God, we have had our conversation in the world.'

9. 'We have had our conversation.' The Apostle in the original expresses this by one single word, ανεστραφημεν; but the meaning thereof is exceeding broad, taking in our whole deportment, yea, every inward as well as outward circumstance, whether relating to our soul or body. It includes every motion of our heart, of our tongue, of our hands and bodily members. It extends to all our actions and words; to the employment of all our powers and faculties; to the manner of using every talent we have received, with respect either to God or man.

10. 'We have had our conversation in the world'; even in the world of the ungodly: not only among the children of God (that were comparatively a little thing); but among the children of the devil, among those that lie in wickedness, εν το πονηρω, *in the wicked one.* What a world is this! How thoroughly impregnated with the spirit it continually breathes! As our God is good, and doeth good, so the god of this world, and all his children, are

evil, and do evil (so far as they are suffered) to all the children of God. Like their father, they are always lying in wait, or 'walking about, seeking whom they may devour'; using fraud or force, secret wiles or open violence, to destroy those who are not of the world; continually warring against our souls, and, by old or new weapons, and devices of every kind, labouring to bring them back into the snare of the devil, into the broad road that leadeth to destruction.

11. 'We have had our' whole 'conversation,' in such a world, 'in simplicity and godly sincerity.' First, in simplicity: this is what our Lord recommends under the name of a 'single eye.' 'The light of the body,' saith He, is 'the eye. If therefore thine eye be single, thy whole body shall be full of light.' The meaning whereof is this: What the eye is to the body, that the intention is to all the words and actions: if, therefore, this eye of thy soul be single, all thy actions and conversation shall be 'full of light,' of the light of heaven, of love, and peace, and joy in the Holy Ghost.

We are then simple of heart, when the eye of our mind is singly fixed on God; when in all things we aim at God alone, as our God, our portion, our strength, our happiness, our exceeding great reward, our all, in time and eternity. This is simplicity; when a steady view, a single intention of promoting His glory, of doing and suffering His blessed will, runs through our whole soul, fills all our heart, and is the constant spring of all our thoughts, desires, and purposes.

12. 'We have had our conversation in the world,' secondly, in 'godly sincerity.' The difference between simplicity and sincerity seems to be chiefly this: simplicity regards the intention itself, sincerity the execution of it; and this sincerity relates not barely to our words, but to our whole conversation, as described above. It is not here to be understood in that narrow sense, wherein St. Paul himself sometimes uses it, for speaking the truth, or abstaining from guile, from craft, and dissimulation; but in a more extensive meaning, as actually hitting the mark, which we aim at by simplicity. Accordingly, it implies in this place, that we do, in fact, speak and do all to the glory of God; that all our words are not only pointed at this, but actually conducive thereto; that all our actions flow on in an even stream, uniformly subservient to this great end; and that in our whole lives, we are

moving straight toward God, and that continually; walking steadily on in the highway of holiness, in the paths of justice, mercy, and truth.

13. This sincerity is termed by the Apostle, godly sincerity, or the sincerity of God; ειλικρινεια Θεου; to prevent our mistaking or confounding it with the sincerity of the Heathens (for they had also a kind of sincerity among them, for which they professed no small veneration); likewise to denote the object and end of this, as of every Christian virtue, seeing whatever does not ultimately tend to God, sinks among 'the beggarly elements of the world.' By styling it the sincerity of God, he also points out the Author of it, the 'Father of lights, from whom every good and perfect gift descendeth'; which is still more clearly declared in the following words, 'Not with fleshly wisdom, but by the grace of God.'

14. 'Not with fleshly wisdom': as if he had said, 'We cannot thus converse in the world, by any natural strength of understanding, neither by any naturally acquired knowledge or wisdom. We cannot gain this simplicity, or practise this sincerity, by the force either of good sense, good nature, or good breeding. It overshoots all our native courage and resolution, as well as all our precepts of philosophy. The power of custom is not able to train us up to this, nor the most exquisite rules of human education. Neither could I Paul ever attain hereto, nowithstanding all the advantages I enjoyed, so long as I was *in the flesh,* in my natural state, and pursued it only by *fleshly,* natural *wisdom.*'

And yet surely, if any man could, Paul himself might have attained thereto by that wisdom: for we can hardly conceive any who was more highly favoured with all the gifts both of nature and education. Besides his natural abilities, probably not inferior to those of any person then upon the earth, he had all the benefits of learning, studying at the University of Tarsus, afterwards brought up at the feet of Gamaliel, a person of the greatest account, both for knowledge and integrity, that was then in the whole Jewish nation. And he had all the possible advantages of religious education, being a Pharisee, the son of a Pharisee, trained up in the very straitest sect or profession, distinguished from all others by a more eminent strictness. And herein he had 'profited above many' others, 'who were his equals' in years, 'being more abundantly zealous' of whatever he thought would please God, and 'as touching the righteousness of the law, blameless.' But it could not be, that he should hereby attain this simplicity and godly sincerity. It was all but lost labour; in a deep, piercing sense of which he was at length constrained to cry out, 'The things which were gain to me, those I counted loss for Christ. Yea doubtless, and I count all things but loss for the excellency of the knowledge of Christ Jesus my Lord' (Phil. iii. 7, 8).

15. It could not be that ever he should attain to this, but by the 'excellent knowledge of Jesus Christ' our Lord; or 'by the grace of God'—another expression of nearly the same import. By 'the grace of God' is sometimes to be understood that free love, that unmerited mercy, by which I a sinner, through the merits of Christ, am now reconciled to God. But in this place it rather means that power of God the Holy Ghost, which 'worketh in us both to will and to do of His good pleasure.' As soon as ever the grace of God in the former sense, His pardoning love, is manifested to our souls, the grace of God in the latter sense, the power of His Spirit, takes place therein. And now we can perform, through God, what to man was impossible. Now we can order our conversation aright. We can do all things in the light and power of that love, through Christ which strengtheneth us. We now have 'the testimony of our conscience,' which we could never have by fleshly wisdom, 'that in simplicity and godly sincerity we have our conversation in the world.'

16. This is properly the ground of a Christian's joy. We may now therefore readily conceive, how he that hath this testimony in himself rejoiceth evermore. 'My soul,' may he say, 'doth magnify the Lord, and my spirit rejoiceth in God my Saviour.' I rejoice in Him, who, of His own unmerited love, of His own free and tender mercy, 'hath called me into this state of salvation,' wherein, through His power, I now stand. I rejoice, because His Spirit beareth witness to my spirit, that I am bought with the blood of the Lamb; and that, believing in Him, 'I am a member of Christ, a child of God, and an inheritor of the kingdom of heaven.' I rejoice, because the sense of God's love to me hath, by the same Spirit, wrought in me to love Him, and to love for His sake every child of man, every soul that He hath made. I rejoice, because He gives me to feel in myself 'the mind that was in

Christ': simplicity, a single eye to Him in every motion of my heart; power always to fix the loving eye of my soul on Him who 'loved me, and gave Himself for me'; to aim at Him alone, at His glorious will, in all I think, or speak, or do: purity, desiring nothing more but God; 'crucifying the flesh with its affections and lusts'; 'setting my affections on things above, not on things of the earth': holiness, a recovery of the image of God, a renewal of soul 'after His likeness': and godly sincerity, directing all my words and works, so as to conduce to His glory. In this I likewise rejoice, yea, and will rejoice, because my conscience beareth me witness in the Holy Ghost, by the light He continually pours in upon it, that I 'walk worthy of the vocation wherewith I am called'; that I 'abstain from all appearance of evil,' fleeing from sin as from the face of a serpent; that as I have opportunity I do all possible good, in every kind, to all men; that I follow my Lord in all my steps, and do what is acceptable in His sight. I rejoice, because I both see and feel, through the inspiration of God's Holy Spirit, that all my works are wrought in Him, yea, and that it is He who worketh all my works in me. I rejoice in seeing through the light of God, which shines in my heart, that I have power to walk in His ways; and that, through His grace, I turn not therefrom, to the right hand or to the left.

17. Such is the ground and the nature of that joy whereby an adult Christian rejoiceth evermore. And from all this we may easily infer, first, that this is not a *natural* joy. It does not arise from any natural cause: not from any sudden flow of spirits. This may give a transient start of joy; but the Christian *rejoiceth always*. It cannot be owing to bodily health or ease; to strength and soundness of constitution: for it is equally strong in sickness and pain; yea, perhaps far stronger than before. Many Christians have never experienced any joy, to be compared with that which then filled their soul, when the body was wellnigh worn out with pain, or consumed away with pining sickness. Least of all can it be ascribed to outward prosperity, to the favour of men, or plenty of worldly goods; for then, chiefly, when their faith has been tried as with fire, by all manner of outward afflictions, have the children of God rejoiced in Him, whom unseen they loved, even with joy unspeakable. And never surely did men rejoice like those who were used as 'the filth and offscouring of the world'; who wandered to and fro, being in

want of all things; in hunger, in cold, in nakedness; who had trials, not only of 'cruel mockings,' but, 'moreover of bonds and imprisonments'; yea, who, at last, 'counted not their lives dear unto themselves, so they might finish their course with joy.'

18. From the preceding considerations, we may, secondly, infer, that the joy of a Christian does not arise from any blindness of conscience, from his not being able to discern good from evil. So far from it, that he was an utter stranger to this joy, till the eyes of his understanding were opéned; that he knew it not, until he had spiritual senses, fitted to discern spiritual good and evil. And now the eye of his soul waxeth not dim: he was never so sharp-sighted before: he has so quick a perception of the smallest things, as is quite amazing to the natural man. As a mote is visible in the sunbeam, so to him who is walking in the light, in the beams of the uncreated Sun, every mote of sin is visible. Nor does he close the eyes of his conscience any more: that sleep is departed from him. His soul is always broad awake: no more slumber or folding of the hands to rest! He is always standing on the tower, and hearkening what his Lord will say concerning him; and always rejoicing in this very thing, in 'seeing Him that is invisible.'

19. Neither does the joy of a Christian arise, thirdly, from any dullness or callousness of conscience. A kind of joy, it is true, may arise from this, in those whose 'foolish hearts are darkened'; whose heart is callous, unfeeling, dull of sense, and consequently, without spiritual understanding. Because of their senseless, unfeeling hearts, they may rejoice even in committing sin; and this they may probably call *liberty*!—which is indeed mere drunkenness of soul, a fatal numbness of spirit, the stupid insensibility of a seared conscience. On the contrary, a Christian has the most exquisite sensibility; such as he could not have conceived before. He never had such a tenderness of conscience as he has had since the love of God has reigned in his heart. And this also is his glory and joy, that God hath heard his daily prayer:

> O that my tender soul might fly
> The first abhorr'd approach of ill;
> Quick as the apple of an eye,
> The slightest touch of sin to feel.

20. To conclude. Christian joy is joy in obedience; joy in loving God, and keeping His commandments: and yet not in keeping them as if we were thereby to fulfil the terms of the covenant of works; as if by any works or righteousness of ours we were to procure pardon and acceptance with God. Not so: we are already pardoned and accepted through the mercy of God in Christ Jesus. Not as if we were by our own obedience to procure life, life from the death of sin: this also we have already through the grace of God. Us 'hath He quickened, who were dead in sins'; and now we are 'alive to God, through Jesus Christ our Lord.' But we rejoice in walking according to the covenant of grace, in holy love and happy obedience. We rejoice in knowing that, 'being justified through His grace,' we have 'not received that grace of God in vain'; that God having freely (not for the sake of our willing or running, but through the blood of the Lamb) reconciled us to Himself, we run, in the strength which He hath given us, the way of His commandments. He hath 'girded us with strength unto the war,' and we gladly 'fight the good fight of faith.' We rejoice, through Him who liveth in our hearts by faith, to 'lay hold of eternal life.' This is our rejoicing, that as our 'Father worketh hitherto,' so (not by our own might or wisdom, but through the power of His Spirit, freely given in Christ Jesus) we also work the works of God. And may He work in us whatsoever is well-pleasing in His sight! To whom be the praise for ever and ever!

SERMON XII

THE MEANS OF GRACE

This fine sermon was written as an antidote to the infection of 'stillness' which came upon the Societies in 1739. In the preface to the second part of the *Journal* Wesley says, 'About September 1739, while my brother and I were absent, certain men crept in among them unawares, greatly troubling and subverting their souls.' They taught that the members would never get a clean heart 'till you leave off using the means of grace, so called; till you leave off running to church and sacrament, and praying, and singing, and reading either the Bible or any other book; for you cannot use these things without trusting in them.' The chief agent in this movement was Philip Henry Molther, a Moravian missionary, who arrived in London on October 18, 1739, and at once joined the Fetter Lane Society. On December 31 Wesley had a long conversation with him, and set down the summary of his views; he taught, *inter alia,* that the way to faith is to wait on Christ and be still; that is, not to use the means of grace; not to go to church; not to communicate; not to fast; not to use so much private prayer; not to read the Scripture; because it is impossible for a man to use them without trusting in them. Spangenberg came to London about the same time and joined with Mother; and between them they converted to their 'stillness' several of the Methodists, including Brown, Bowers, George Bell, John Bray, and John Simpson. Even Charles Wesley was affected, and on January 22, 1741, he stopped preaching and said he intended to preach no more. The fit only lasted about three weeks; but it occasioned John much anxiety. Gambold, Westley Hall, and Benjamin Ingham embraced the same error.

John Wesley at once attacked this mischievous form of Mysticism. On November 15, 1739, 'I exhorted four or five thousand people at Bristol neither to neglect nor rest in the means of grace'; and on the 19th 'I exhorted the society to wait upon God in all His ordinances.' This was doubtless substantially the present sermon. He took up the several points in detail in his expositions to the society at Fetter Lane in June 1740, speaking on the 24th on 'Why are ye yet subject to ordinances?' on the 25th on 'All scripture is given by inspiration of God'; on the 26th on 'Search the Scriptures'; and on the 27th and 28th on the Lord's Supper. The result was that he and his followers left the Fetter Lane Society on July 20, and met at the Foundery on the 23rd; so providentially shaking off the Moravian connexion, which would have been a great obstacle to Wesley's work.

It must be remembered that the sermon was addressed to those who were seeking the Lord, and had not yet received the witness of the Spirit; it was these whom the Moravians exhorted to 'stillness,' not the assured believers. The only point that may be said to be still open to discussion is whether unconverted men, who are seeking salvation, should be admitted to the Lord's Supper; as we shall see, Wesley strongly held that they should be encouraged to communicate, and should take every opportunity of doing so.

The whole of the fourth part of the *Journal*, which was published in 1744, should be read in this connexion; and the two hymns by Charles Wesley which are appended to it. The first, on The Means of Grace, beginning 'Long have I seemed to serve Thee, Lord,' was first published in *Hymns and Sacred Poems*, 1740 (*Collected Works*, i. 233). Fifteen of its twenty-three verses were in the 1876 Hymn-Book as Hymns 91 and 92. The second was republished in *Hymns and Sacred Poems* (1749), 95, 'The Bloody Issue Cured' (*Collected Works*, iv. 251). Both emphasize the teaching of the sermon—that the means of grace are necessary, but that the sinner must not trust in them but in Christ.

As to the text, I have only found one reference to it; on June 22, 1741, Wesley allowed his Bible to open casually, and it opened at Mal. iii., which he forthwith proceeded to expound. But many texts would equally fit the sermon, and I imagine it was preached very often in substance in the years 1739-46.

Ye are gone away from Mine ordinances, and have not kept them. —MAL. iii. 7.

I. 1. But are there any *ordinances* now, since life and immortality were brought to light by the gospel? Are there, under the Christian dispensation, any *means ordained* of God, as the usual channels of His grace? This question could never have been proposed in the apostolical church, unless by one who openly avowed himself to be a Heathen; the whole body of Christians being agreed, that Christ had ordained certain outward means, for conveying His grace into the souls of men. Their constant practice set this beyond all dispute; for so long as 'all that believed were together, and had all things common' (Acts ii. 44), 'they continued steadfastly in the teaching of the Apostles, and in breaking of bread, and in prayers' (verse 42).

2. But in process of time, when 'the love of many waxed cold,' some began to mistake the *means* for the *end*, and to place religion, rather in doing those outward works, than in a heart renewed after the image of God. They forgot that 'the end of

'every' commandment is love, out of a pure heart,' with 'faith unfeigned': the loving the Lord their God with all their heart, and their neighbour as themselves: and the being purified from pride, anger, and evil desire, by a 'faith of the operation of God.' Others seemed to imagine, that though religion did not principally consist in these outward means, yet there was something in them wherewith God was well pleased; something that would still make them acceptable in His sight, though they were not exact in the weightier matters of the law, in justice, mercy, and the love of God.

3. It is evident, in those who abused them thus, they did not conduce to the end for which they were ordained: rather, the things which should have been for their health, were to them an occasion of falling. They were so far from receiving any blessing therein, that they only drew down a curse upon their head; so far from growing more heavenly in heart and life, that they were twofold more the children of hell than before. Others, clearly perceiving that these means did not convey the grace of God to those children of the devil, began, from this particular case, to draw a general conclusion,—that they were not means of conveying the grace of God.

4. Yet the number of those who *abused* the ordinances of God was far greater than of those who *despised* them, till certain men arose, not only of great understanding (sometimes joined with considerable learning), but who likewise appeared to be men of love, experimentally acquainted with true, inward religion. Some of these were burning and shining lights, persons famous in their generations, and such as had well deserved of the Church of Christ, for standing in the gap against the overflowings of ungodliness.

It cannot be supposed, that these holy and venerable men intended any more, at first, than to show that outward religion is nothing worth, without the religion of the heart; that 'God is a Spirit, and they who worship Him must worship Him in spirit and in truth'; that, therefore, external worship is lost labour, without a heart devoted to God; that the outward ordinances of God then profit much, when they advance inward holiness; but, when they advance it not, are unprofitable and void, are lighter than vanity; yea, that when they are used, as it were, *in the place of* this, they are an utter abomination to the Lord.

5. Yet it is not strange, if some of these, being strongly convinced of that horrid profanation of the ordinances of God, which had spread itself over the whole Church, and wellnigh driven true religion out of the world, in their fervent zeal for the glory of God, and the recovery of souls from that fatal delusion, spake as if outward religion were absolutely nothing, as if it had no place in the religion of Christ. It is not surprising at all, if they should not always have expressed themselves with sufficient caution; so that unwary hearers might believe they condemned all outward means, as altogether unprofitable, and as not designed of God to be the ordinary channels of conveying His grace into the souls of men.

Nay, it is not impossible, some of these holy men did, at length, themselves fall into this opinion: in particular those who, not by choice, but by the providence of God, were cut off from all these ordinances; perhaps wandering up and down, having no certain abiding-place, or dwelling in dens and caves of the earth. These, experiencing the grace of God in themselves, though they were deprived of all outward means, might infer that the same grace would be given to them who of set purpose abstained from them.

6. And experience shows how easily this notion spreads, and insinuates itself into the minds of men; especially of those who are thoroughly awakened out of the sleep of death, and begin to feel the weight of their sins a burden too heavy to be borne. These are usually impatient of their present state; and, trying every way to escape from it, they are always ready to catch at any new thing, any new proposal of ease or happiness. They have probably tried most outward means, and found no ease in them: it may be, more and more of remorse, and fear, and sorrow, and condemnation. It is easy, therefore, to persuade these that it is better for them to abstain from all those means. They are already weary of striving (as it seems) in vain, of labouring in the fire; and are therefore glad of any pretence to cast aside that wherein their soul has no pleasure, to give over the painful strife, and sink down into an indolent inactivity.

II. 1. In the following discourse, I propose to examine at large whether there are any means of grace.

By 'means of grace,' I understand outward signs, words, or

actions, ordained of God, and appointed for this end, to be the ordinary channels whereby He might convey to men, preventing, justifying, or sanctifying grace.

I use this expression, 'means of grace,' because I know none better; and because it has been generally used in the Christian Church for many ages—in particular by our own Church, which directs us to bless God both for the means of grace, and hope of glory; and teaches us, that a sacrament is 'an outward sign of inward grace, and a means whereby we receive the same.'

The chief of these means are prayer, whether in secret or with the great congregation; searching the Scriptures (which implies reading, hearing, and meditating thereon); and receiving the Lord's supper, eating bread and drinking wine in remembrance of Him; and these we believe to be ordained of God, as the ordinary channels of conveying His grace to the souls of men.

2. But we allow, that the whole value of the means depends on their actual subservience to the end of religion; that, consequently, all these means, when separate from the end, are less than nothing and vanity; that if they do not actually conduce to the knowledge and love of God, they are not acceptable in His sight; yea, rather, they are an abomination before Him, a stink in His nostrils; He is weary to bear them. Above all, if they are used as a kind of *commutation* for the religion they were designed to subserve, it is not easy to find words for the enormous folly and wickedness of thus turning God's arms against Himself; of keeping Christianity out of the heart by those very means which were ordained for the bringing it in.

3. We allow, likewise, that all outward means whatever, if separate from the Spirit of God, cannot profit at all, cannot conduce, in any degree, either to the knowledge or love of God. Without controversy, the help that is done upon earth, He doeth it Himself. It is He alone who, by His own almighty power, worketh in us what is pleasing in His sight; and all outward things, unless He work in them and by them, are mere weak and beggarly elements. Whosoever, therefore, imagines there is any intrinsic power in any means whatsoever, does greatly err, not knowing the Scriptures, neither the power of God. We know that there is no inherent power in the words that are spoken in prayer, in the letter of Scripture read, the sound thereof heard or the bread and wine received in the Lord's supper; but that it is

God alone who is the Giver of every good gift, the Author of all grace; that the whole power is of Him, whereby through any of these, there is any blessing conveyed to our souls. We know, likewise, that He is able to give the same grace, though there were no means on the face of the earth. In this sense, we may affirm, that, with regard to God, there is no such thing as means; seeing He is equally able to work whatsoever pleaseth Him, by any, or by none at all.

4. We allow farther, that the use of all means whatever will never atone for one sin; that it is the blood of Christ alone, whereby any sinner can be reconciled to God; there being no other propitiation for our sins, no other fountain for sin and uncleanness. Every believer in Christ is deeply convinced that there is no merit but in Him; that there is no merit in any of his own works; not in uttering the prayer, or searching the Scripture, or hearing the Word of God, or eating of that bread and drinking of that cup. So that if no more be intended by the expression some have used, 'Christ is the only means of grace,' than this,—that He is the only meritorious cause of it, it cannot be gainsaid by any who know the grace of God.

5. Yet once more: we allow, though it is a melancholy truth, that a large proportion of those who are called Christians, do to this day abuse the means of grace to the destruction of their souls. This is doubtless the case with all those who rest content in the form of godliness, without the power. Either they fondly presume they are Christians already, because they do thus and thus (although Christ was never yet revealed in their hearts, nor the love of God shed abroad therein); or else they suppose they shall infallibly be so, barely because they use these means; idly dreaming (though perhaps hardly conscious thereof), either that there is some kind of *power* therein, whereby, sooner or later (they know not when), they shall certainly be made holy; or that there is a sort of *merit* in using them, which will surely move God to give them holiness, or accept them without it.

6. So little do they understand that great foundation of the whole Christian building, 'By grace are ye saved': ye are saved from your sins, from the guilt and power thereof, ye are restored to the favour and image of God, not for any works, merits, or deservings of yours, but by the free grace, the mere mercy of God, through the merits of His well-beloved Son: ye

are thus saved, not by any power, wisdom, or strength, which is in you, or in any other creature; but merely through the grace or power of the Holy Ghost, which worketh all in all.

7. But the main question remains: 'We know this salvation is the gift and the work of God; but how (may one say who is convinced he hath it not) may I attain thereto?' If you say, 'Believe, and thou shalt be saved!' he answers, 'True; but how shall I believe?' You reply, 'Wait upon God.' 'Well; but how am I to wait? In the means of grace, or out of them? Am I to wait for the grace of God which bringeth salvation, by using these means, or by laying them aside?'

8. It cannot possibly be conceived, that the Word of God should give no direction in so important a point; or, that the Son of God, who came down from heaven for us men and for our salvation, should have left us undetermined with regard to a question wherein our salvation is so nearly concerned.

And, in fact, He hath not left us undetermined; He hath shown us the way wherein we should go. We have only to consult the oracles of God; to inquire what is written there; and, if we simply abide by their decision, there can no possible doubt remain.

III. 1. According to this, according to the decision of holy writ, all who desire the grace of God are to wait for it in the means which He hath ordained; in using, not in laying them aside.

And, first, all who desire the grace of God are to wait for it in the way of prayer. This is the express direction of our Lord Himself. In His Sermon upon the Mount, after explaining at large wherein religion consists, and describing the main branches of it, He adds, 'Ask, and it shall be given you; seek, and ye shall find; knock, and it shall be opened unto you: for every one that asketh receiveth; and he that seeketh findeth; and to him that knocketh it shall be opened' (Matt, vii. 7, 8). Here we are in the plainest manner directed to ask, in order to, or as a means of, receiving; to seek, in order to find, the grace of God, the pearl of great price; and to knock, to continue asking and seeking, if we would enter into His kingdom.

2. That no doubt might remain, our Lord labours this point in a more peculiar manner. He appeals to every man's own heart: 'What man is there of you, who, if his son ask bread, will he give

him a stone? or, if he ask a fish, will he give him a serpent? If ye then, being evil, know how to give good gifts unto your children, how much more shall your Father which is in heaven,' the Father of angels and men, the Father of the spirits of all flesh, 'give good things to them that ask Him'? (verses 9-11). Or, as He expresses Himself on another occasion, including all good things in one, 'How much more shall your heavenly Father give the Holy Spirit to them that ask Him?' (Luke xi. 13). It should be particularly observed here, that the persons directed to ask had not then received the Holy Spirit: nevertheless our Lord directs them to use this means, and promises that it should be effectual; that upon asking they should receive the Holy Spirit, from Him whose mercy is over all His works.

3. The absolute necessity of using this means, if we would receive any gift from God, yet farther appears from that remarkable passage which immediately precedes these words: 'And He said unto them,' whom He had just been teaching how to pray, 'Which of you shall have a friend, and shall go unto him at midnight, and shall say unto him, Friend, lend me three loaves: and he from within shall answer, Trouble me not; I cannot rise and give thee. I say unto you, Though he will not rise and give him, because he is his friend, yet because of his importunity he will rise and give him as many as he needeth. And I say unto you, Ask, and it shall be given you' (Luke xi. 5, 7-9). 'Though he will not give him, because he is his friend, yet because of his importunity he will rise and give him as many as he needeth.' How could our blessed Lord more plainly declare, that we may receive of God, by this means, by importunately asking, what otherwise we should not receive at all?

4. 'He spake also another parable, to this end, that men ought always to pray, and not to faint,' till through this means they should receive of God whatsoever petition they asked of Him: 'There was in a city a judge, which feared not God, neither regarded man: and there was a widow in that city; and she came unto him, saying, Avenge me of my adversary. And he would not for a while; but afterward he said within himself, Though I fear not God, nor regard man, yet because this widow troubleth me, I will avenge her, lest by her continual coming she weary me' (Luke xviii. 1-5). The application of this our Lord Himself hath made: 'Hear what the unjust judge saith!' Because she continues

to ask, because she will take no denial, therefore I will avenge her. 'And shall not God avenge His own elect, which cry day and night unto Him? I tell you He will avenge them speedily,' if they pray, and faint not.

5. A direction, equally full and express, to wait for the blessings of God in private prayer, together with a positive promise that, by this means, we shall obtain the request of our lips, He hath given us in those well-known words: 'Enter into thy closet, and when thou hast shut thy door, pray to thy Father which is in secret; and thy Father which seeth in secret shall reward thee openly' (Matt. vi. 6).

6. If it be possible for any direction to be more clear, it is that which God hath given us by the Apostle, with regard to prayer of every kind, public or private, and the blessing annexed thereto: 'If any of you lack wisdom, let him ask of God, that giveth to all men liberally' (if they ask; otherwise 'ye have not, because ye ask not,' Jas. iv. 2), 'and upbraideth not; and it shall be given him' (Jas. i. 5).

If it be objected, 'But this is no direction to unbelievers; to them who know not the pardoning grace of God: for the Apostle adds, "But let him ask in faith"; otherwise, "let him not think that he shall receive anything of the Lord"': I answer, The meaning of the word *faith*, in this place, is fixed by the Apostle himself, as if it were on purpose to obviate this objection, in the words immediately following: 'Let him ask in faith, nothing wavering,' nothing *doubting*, μηδεν διακρινομενος; not doubting but God heareth his prayer, and will fulfil the desire of his heart.

The gross, blasphemous absurdity of supposing *faith*, in this place, to be taken in the full Christian meaning, appears hence: it is supposing the Holy Ghost to direct a man who knows he has not this faith (which is here termed *wisdom*), to ask it of God, with a positive promise that 'it shall be given him'; and then immediately to subjoin, that it shall not be given him, unless he have it before he asks for it! But who can bear such a supposition? From this scripture, therefore, as well as those cited above, we must infer, that all who desire the grace of God are to wait for it in the way of prayer.

7. Secondly. All who desire the grace of God are to wait for it in searching the Scriptures.

Our Lord's direction, with regard to the use of this means, is likewise plain and clear. 'Search the Scriptures,' saith He to the unbelieving Jews, 'for they testify of Me' (John v. 39). And for this very end did He direct them to search the Scriptures, that they might believe in Him.

The objection, that 'this is not a command, but only an assertion, that they did search the Scriptures,' is shamelessly false. I desire those who urge it, to let us know how a command can be more clearly expressed, than in those terms, Επευνατε τασ γραφας. It is as peremptory as so many words can make it.

And what a blessing from God attends the use of this means, appears from what is recorded concerning the Bereans: who, after hearing St. Paul, 'searched the Scriptures daily, whether those things were so. Therefore many of them believed,'— found the grace of God, in the way which He had ordained (Acts xvii. 11, 12).

It is probable, indeed, that in some of those who had 'received the word with all readiness of mind,' 'faith came,' as the same Apostle speaks, 'by hearing,' and was only confirmed by reading the Scriptures: but it was observed above, that, under the general term of searching the Scriptures, both hearing, reading, and meditating are contained.

8. And that this is a means whereby God not only gives, but also confirms and increases, true wisdom, we learn from the words of St. Paul to Timothy: 'From a child thou hast known the holy Scriptures, which are able to make thee wise unto salvation through faith which is in Christ Jesus' (2 Tim, iii. 15). The same truth (namely, that this is the great means God has ordained for conveying His manifold grace to man) is delivered, in the fullest manner that can be conceived, in the words which immediately follow: 'All Scripture is given by inspiration of God'; consequently, all Scripture is infallibly true; 'and is profitable for doctrine, for reproof, for correction, for instruction in righteousness'; to the end 'that the man of God may be perfect, throughly furnished unto all good works' (verses 16, 17).

9. It should be observed, that this is spoken primarily and directly of the Scriptures which Timothy had known from a child; which must have been those of the Old Testament, for the New was not then wrote. How far then was St. Paul (though he was 'not a whit behind the very chief of the Apostles,' nor, therefore, I presume, behind any man now upon earth) from

making light of the Old Testament! Behold this, lest ye one day 'wonder and perish,' ye who make so small account of one half of the oracles of God! Yea, and that half of which the Holy Ghost expressly declares, that it is 'profitable,' as a means ordained of God for this very thing, 'for doctrine, for reproof, for correction, for instruction in righteousness'; to the end, 'the man of God may be perfect, throughly furnished unto all good works.'

10. Nor is this profitable only for the men of God, for those who walk already in the light of His countenance; but also for those who are yet in darkness, seeking Him whom they know not. Thus St. Peter: 'We have also a more sure word of prophecy': literally, 'And we have the prophetic word more sure': Και εχομεν βεβαιοτερον τον προφητικον λογον: confirmed by our being 'eye-witnesses of His majesty,' and 'hearing the voice which came from the excellent glory,' 'unto which'—prophetic word; so he styles the holy Scriptures—'ye do well that ye take heed, as unto a light that shineth in a dark place, until the day dawn, and the Day-star arise in your hearts' (2 Pet. i. 19). Let all therefore who desire that day to dawn upon their hearts, wait for it in searching the Scriptures.

11. Thirdly. All who desire an increase of the grace of God are to wait for it in partaking of the Lord's supper; for this also is a direction Himself hath given: 'The same night in which He was betrayed He took bread, and brake it, and said, Take, eat: this is My Body'; that is, the sacred sign of My body: 'this do in remembrance of Me.' Likewise 'He took the cup, saying, This cup is the new testament,' or covenant, 'in My blood'; the sacred sign of that covenant: 'this do ye in remembrance of Me. For as often as ye eat this bread, and drink this cup, ye do show forth the Lord's death till He come' (1 Cor. xi. 23, &c.): ye openly exhibit the same, by these visible signs, before God, and angels, and men; ye manifest your solemn remembrance of His death, till He cometh in the clouds of heaven.

Only 'let a man' first 'examine himself,' whether he understand the nature and design of this holy institution, and whether he really desire to be himself made conformable to the death of Christ; and so, nothing doubting, 'let him eat of that bread, and drink of that cup' (verse 28).

Here, then, the direction first given by our Lord is expressly repeated by the Apostle: 'Let him eat; let him drink' (εσθιετω, πινετω, both in the imperative mood); words not implying a bare permission only, but a clear, explicit command; a command to all those who either already are filled with peace and joy in believing, or can truly say, 'The remembrance of our sins is grievous unto us, the burden of them is intolerable.'

12. And that this is also an ordinary, stated means of receiving the grace of God, is evident from those words of the Apostle which occur in the preceding chapter: 'The cup of blessing which we bless, is it not the communion,' or *communication,* 'of the blood of Christ? The bread which we break, is it not the communion of the body of Christ?' (I Cor. x. 16). Is not the eating of that bread, and the drinking of that cup, the outward, visible means whereby God conveys into our souls all that spiritual grace, that righteousness, and peace, and joy in the Holy Ghost, which were purchased by the body of Christ once broken, and the blood of Christ once shed for us? Let all, therefore, who truly desire the grace of God, eat of that bread, and drink of that cup.

IV. 1. But as plainly as God hath pointed out the way wherein He will be inquired after, innumerable are the objections which men, wise in their own eyes, have from time to time raised against it. It may be needful to consider a few of these; not because they are of weight in themselves, but because they have so often been used, especially of late years, to turn the lame out of the way; yea, to trouble and subvert those who did run well, till Satan appeared as an angel of light.

The first and chief of these is, 'You cannot use these means (as you call them) without *trusting* in them.' I pray, where is this written? I expect you should show me plain Scripture for your assertion: otherwise I dare not receive it; because I am not convinced that you are wiser than God.

If it really had been as you assert, it is certain Christ must have known it. And if He had known it, He would surely have warned us; He would have revealed it long ago. Therefore, because He has not, because there is no tittle of this in the whole revelation of Jesus Christ, I am as fully assured your assertion is false, as that this revelation is of God.

'However, leave them off for a short time, to see whether you trusted in them or no.' So I am to disobey God, in order to know whether I trust in obeying Him! And do you avow this advice? Do you deliberately teach to 'do evil, that good may come'? O tremble at the sentence of God against such teachers! Their 'damnation is just.'

'Nay, if you are troubled when you leave them off, it is plain you trusted in them.' By no means. If I am troubled when I wilfully disobey God, it is plain His Spirit is still striving with me; but if I am not troubled at wilful sin, it is plain I am given up to a reprobate mind.

But what do you mean by '*trusting* in them'?—looking for the blessing of God therein? believing, that if I wait in this way, I shall attain what otherwise I should not? So I do. And so I will, God being my helper, even to my life's end. By the grace of God, I will *thus* trust in them, till the day of my death; that is, I will believe, that whatever God hath promised, He is faithful also to perform. And seeing He hath promised to bless me in this way, I *trust* it shall be according to His word.

2. It has been, secondly, objected, 'This is seeking salvation by works.' Do you know the meaning of the expression you use? What is seeking salvation by works? In the writings of St. Paul, it means, either seeking to be saved by observing the ritual works of the Mosaic law; or expecting salvation for the sake of our own works, by the merit of our own righteousness. But how is either of these implied in my waiting in the way God has ordained, and expecting that He will meet me there, because He has promised so to do?

I do expect that He will fulfil His word, that He will meet and bless me in this way. Yet not for the sake of any works which I have done, nor for the merit of my righteousness; but merely through the merits, and sufferings, and love of His Son, in whom He is always well pleased.

3. It has been vehemently objected, thirdly, 'that Christ is the only means of grace.' I answer, This is mere playing upon words. Explain your term, and the objection vanishes away. When we say, 'Prayer is a means of grace,' we understand a channel through which the grace of God is conveyed. When you say, 'Christ is the means of grace,' you understand the sole price and purchaser of it; or, that 'no man cometh unto the Father, but through Him.' And who denies it? But this is utterly wide of the question.

4. 'But does not the Scripture' (it has been objected, fourthly) 'direct us to *wait* for salvation? Does not David say, "My soul waiteth upon God; for of Him cometh my salvation"? And does not Isaiah teach us the same thing saying, "O Lord, we have waited for Thee"?' All this cannot be denied. Seeing it is the gift of God, we are undoubtedly to *wait* on Him for salvation. But how shall we wait? If God Himself has appointed a way, can you find a better way of waiting for Him? But that He hath appointed a way, hath been shown at large, and also what that way is. The very words of the prophet which you cite, put this out of all question. For the whole sentence runs thus: 'In the way of Thy judgements,' or ordinances, 'O Lord, have we waited for Thee' (lsa. xxvi. 8). And in the very same way did David wait, as his own words abundantly testify: 'I have waited for Thy saving health, O Lord, and have kept Thy law. Teach me, O Lord, the way of Thy statutes, and I shall keep it unto the end.'

5. 'Yea,' say some, 'but God has appointed another way: "Stand still, and see the salvation of God."'

Let us examine the Scriptures to which you refer. The first of them, with the context, runs thus,—

'And when Pharaoh drew nigh, the children of Israel lifted up their eyes; and they were sore afraid. And they said unto Moses, Because there were no graves in Egypt, hast thou taken us away to die in the wilderness? And Moses said unto the people, Fear ye not, stand still, and see the salvation of the Lord. And the Lord said unto Moses, Speak unto the children of Israel, that they go forward. But lift thou up thy rod, and stretch out thine hand over the sea, and divide it; and the children of Israel shall go on dry ground through the midst of the sea' (Exod. xiv. 10, &c.).

This was the *salvation of God*, which they *stood still* to see, by *marching forward* with all their might!

The other passage, wherein this expression occurs, stands thus: 'There came some that told Jehoshaphat, saying, There cometh a great multitude against thee from beyond the sea. And Jehoshaphat feared, and set himself to seek the Lord, and proclaimed a fast throughout all Judah. And Judah gathered themselves together, to ask help of the Lord: even out of all the cities they came to seek the Lord. And Jehoshaphat stood in the congregation, in the house of the Lord. . . . Then upon Jahaziel came the Spirit of the Lord. And he said, Be not dismayed by reason of this great multitude. To-morrow go ye down against them: ye shall not need to fight in this battle. Set yourselves: stand ye still, and see the salvation of the Lord. And they rose early in the morning, and went forth. And when they began to sing and to praise, the Lord set ambushments against the children of Ammon, Moab, and mount Seir; . . . and every one helped to destroy another' (2 Chron. xx. 2, &c.).

Such was the salvation which the children of Judah saw. But how does all this prove, that we ought not to wait for the grace of God in the means which He hath ordained?

6. I shall mention but one objection more, which, indeed, does not properly belong to this head: nevertheless, because it has been so frequently urged, I may not wholly pass it by.

'Does not St. Paul say, "If ye be dead with Christ, why are ye subject to ordinances"? (Col. ii. 20). Therefore, a Christian, one that is dead with Christ, need not use the ordinances any more.'

So you say, 'If I am a Christian, I am not subject to the ordinances of Christ'! Surely, by the absurdity of this, you must see at the first glance, that the ordinances here mentioned cannot be the ordinances of Christ; that they must needs be the Jewish ordinances, to which it is certain a Christian is no longer subject.

And the same undeniably appears from the words immediately following, 'Touch not, taste not, handle not': all evidently referring to the ancient ordinances of the Jewish law.

So that this objection is the weakest of all. And, in spite of all, that great truth must stand unshaken,—that all who desire the grace of God are to wait for it in the means which He hath ordained.

V. 1. But this being allowed, that all who desire the grace of God are to wait for it in the means He hath ordained; it may still be inquired, how those means should be used, both as to the order and the manner of using them.

With regard to the former, we may observe, there is a kind of order, wherein God Himself is generally pleased to use these means in bringing a sinner to salvation. A stupid, senseless wretch is going on in his own way, not having God in all his thoughts, when God comes upon him unawares, perhaps by an awakening sermon or conversation, perhaps by some awful providence, or, it may be, by an immediate stroke of His convincing Spirit, without any outward means at all. Having now a desire to flee from the wrath to come, he purposely goes to *hear* how it may be done. If he finds a preacher who speaks to the heart, he is amazed, and begins searching the Scriptures, whether these things are so. The more he *hears* and *reads*, the more convinced he is; and the more he meditates thereon day and night. Perhaps he finds some other book which explains and enforces what he has heard and read in Scripture. And by all these means, the arrows of conviction sink deeper into his soul. He begins also to *talk* of the things of God, which are ever uppermost in his thoughts; yea, and to talk with God; to *pray* to Him; although, through fear and shame, he scarce knows what to say. But whether he can speak or no, he cannot but pray, were it only in 'groans which cannot be uttered.' Yet, being in doubt, whether 'the high and lofty One that inhabiteth eternity' will regard such a sinner as him, he wants to pray with those who know God, with the faithful, in the great congregation. But here he observes others go up to the table of the Lord. He considers, 'Christ has said, "Do this!" How is it that I do not? I am too great a sinner. I am not fit. I am not worthy.' After struggling with these scruples awhile, he breaks through. And thus he continues in God's way, in hearing, reading, meditating, praying, and partaking of the Lord's supper, till God, in the manner that pleases Him, speaks to his heart, 'Thy faith hath saved thee. Go in peace.'

2. By observing this order of God, we may learn what means to recommend to any particular soul. If any of these will reach a stupid, careless sinner, it is probably hearing, or conversation. To such, therefore, we might recommend these, if he has ever any thought about salvation. To one who begins to feel the weight of his sins, not only hearing the Word of God, but reading it too, and perhaps other serious books, may be a means of deeper conviction. May you not advise him also to meditate on what he reads, that it may have its full force upon his heart? Yea, and to speak thereof, and not be ashamed, particularly among those who walk in the same path. When trouble and heaviness take hold upon him, should you not then earnestly exhort him to pour out his soul before God; 'always to pray and not to faint';

and when he feels the worthlessness of his own prayers, are you not to work together with God, and remind him of going up into the house of the Lord, and praying with all that fear Him? But if he does this, the dying word of his Lord will soon be brought to his remembrance; a plain intimation, that this is the time when we should second the motions of the blessed Spirit. And thus may we lead him, step by step, through all the means which God has ordained; not according to our own will, but just as the providence and the Spirit of God go before and open the way.

3. Yet, as we find no command in holy writ for any particular order to be observed herein, so neither do the providence and the Spirit of God adhere to any without variation; but the means into which different men are led, and in which they find the blessing of God, are varied, transposed, and combined together, a thousand different ways. Yet still our wisdom is to follow the leadings of His providence and His Spirit; to be guided herein (more especially as to the means wherein we ourselves seek the grace of God), partly by His outward providence, giving us the opportunity of using sometimes one means, sometimes another, partly by our experience, which it is whereby His free Spirit is pleased most to work in our heart. And in the meantime, the sure and general rule for all who groan for the salvation of God is this,—whenever opportunity serves, use all the means which God has ordained; for who knows in which God will meet thee with the grace that bringeth salvation?

4. As to the manner of using them—whereon indeed it wholly depends whether they shall convey any grace at all to the user—it behoves us, first, always to retain a lively sense, that God is above all means. Have a care, therefore, of limiting the Almighty. He doeth whatsoever and whensoever it pleaseth Him. He can convey His grace either in or out of any of the means which He hath appointed. Perhaps He will. 'Who hath known the mind of the Lord? or who hath been His counsellor?' Look, then, every moment for His appearing! Be it at the hour you are employed in His ordinances; or before, or after that hour; or when you are hindered therefrom. He is not hindered; He is always ready, always able, always willing to save. 'It is the Lord: let Him do what seemeth Him good!'

Secondly. Before you use any means, let it be deeply impressed on your soul,—there is no *power* in this. It is, in itself, a poor, dead, empty thing: separate from God, it is a dry leaf, a shadow. Neither is there any *merit* in my using this; nothing intrinsically pleasing to God; nothing whereby I deserve any favour at His hands, no, not a drop of water to cool my tongue. But, because God bids, therefore I do; because He directs me to wait in this way, therefore here I wait for His free mercy, whereof cometh my salvation.

Settle this in your heart, that the *opus operatum*, the mere work done, profiteth nothing; that there is no Power to save but in the Spirit of God, no *merit* but in the blood of Christ; that, consequently, even what God ordains, conveys no grace to the soul, if you trust not in Him alone. On the other hand, he that does truly trust in Him cannot fall short of the grace of God, even though he were cut off from every outward ordinance, though he were shut up in the centre of the earth.

Thirdly. In using all means, seek God alone. In and through every outward thing, look singly to the *power* of His Spirit, and the *merits* of His Son. Beware you do not stick in the *work* itself; if you do, it is all lost labour. Nothing short of God can satisfy your soul. Therefore, eye Him in all, through all, and above all.

Remember also, to use all means *as means*; as ordained, not for their own sake, but in order to the renewal of your soul in righteousness and true holiness. If, therefore, they actually tend to this, well; but, if not, they are dung and dross.

Lastly. After you have used any of these, take care how you value yourself thereon; how you congratulate yourself as having done some great thing. This is turning all into poison. Think, 'If God was not there, what does this avail? Have I not been adding sin to sin? How long? O Lord, save, or I perish! O lay not this sin to my charge!' If God was there, if His love flowed into your heart, you have forgot, as it were, the outward work. You see, you know, you feel, God is all in all. Be abased. Sink down before Him. Give Him all the praise. 'Let God in all things be glorified through Christ Jesus.' Let all your bones cry out, 'My song shall be always of the loving kindness of the Lord: with my mouth will I ever be telling of Thy truth from one generation to another!'

SERMON XIII

THE CIRCUMCISION OF THE HEART

PREACHED AT ST. MARY'S, OXFORD, BEFORE THE UNIVERSITY, ON JANUARY 1, 1733

As Wesley placed his sermon before the University on Salvation by Faith first in his first volume, so he began the second with another of his University sermons, preached at St. Mary's, Oxford, on January 1, 1733. It may be well to recall that he became a student at Christ Church in 1720; decided to take Orders, and was ordained deacon in 1725, and began to study Jeremy Taylor's *Holy Living and Holy Dying,* and Thomas à Kempis's *De Imitatione Christi,* with the result that he resolved to 'give my heart, yea, all my heart, to God'; 'to dedicate all my life to God, all my thoughts, and words, and actions'; and this he proceeded to do with characteristic thoroughness. It is not too much to speak of this as his first conversion; though it was not till May 24, 1738, that he received the consciousness that his sins were forgiven, and the witness of the Spirit that he was a child of God. But during the intervening years, though in his Georgia Journal he says that he was not a Christian, his maturer reflection led him to the more just conclusion that he was all this time a servant of God, though he had not yet the faith of a son. His first sermon, of which happily the MS. has been preserved, and was published in facsimile in 1903, was preached at South Leigh, a village near Witney, about ten miles west of Oxford, on Matt. vi. 33. A photograph of the little church may be seen in the Standard edition of the *Journal,* i. 63. On Wednesday, October 16, 1771, he says: 'I preached at South Leigh. Here it was that I preached my first sermon six and forty years ago. One man was in my present audience who heard it.' The earliest of his published sermons (in the posthumous fifth series) was a funeral discourse on the death of young Robin Griffiths, preached at Broadway (not, as is stated in the printed edition, at Epworth) on February 15, 1727. It was on 2 Sam. xii. 23, and is numbered CXXXV, and entitled On Mourning for the Dead. In 1726 he was elected a Fellow of Lincoln College, and in 1727 took his Master's degree; and in this same year he tells us, 'I read Mr. Law's *Christian Perfection* and *Serious Call,* and more explicitly resolved to be all devoted to God in body, soul, and spirit.'

From August 1727 to November 1729 he was at Epworth and Wroot, acting as his father's curate, and in 1728 was ordained priest at Oxford by Bishop Potter. One sermon from this period has been preserved on 2 Cor. ii. 17, and was published as No. CXXXVI in the fifth (posthumous) series. In November 1729 he was summoned back to

Oxford by Dr. Morley, the Rector of Lincoln, and he continued in residence there until he went to Georgia in 1735. He found that his brother Charles had gathered a few students round him at Christ Church for the cultivation of the spiritual life, and he at once became the head of this little society, which had already received the nickname of 'Methodist' from some University wag. It is not necessary to describe again their devotion, their self-sacrifice, their strict attention to all ecclesiastical rules, their diligent study of the Bible, and above all their charity to the poor and their ministrations to the prisoners in the jail. Their one guide was the Bible; and it was in 1730 that John Wesley says he 'began to be *homo unius libri*, to study (comparatively) no book but the Bible.' In 1732 he wrote a sermon for his pupils On the Duty of Constant Communion, which he afterwards published in the *Arminian Magazine*, 1787, p. 229, and republished in the edition of the sermons in 1788, No. CI, with this note: 'The following discourse was written about five and fifty years ago, for the use of my pupils at Oxford. I have added very little, but retrenched much; as I then used more words than I do now. But I thank God, I have not yet seen cause to alter my sentiments, in any point which is therein delivered.' In July 1732 he paid a visit to William Law at Putney, and no doubt their intercourse deepened the strong impression which Law's works had already produced upon him, and he began to study the *Theologia Germanica* and other writings of the Mystics. Meantime, the Oxford Methodists had come more and more into the public eye; and in *Fogg's Journal* of December 9, 1732, an abusive attack on them appeared, in which they were charged with asceticism, voluntary affliction of their bodies, fasting strictly twice a week, rising at four every morning, singing hymns for two hours every day, and in short 'practising everything contrary to the judgement of other persons.' The writer thinks their motives are poverty, hypocrisy used as a veil for vice, enthusiasm, madness, and superstitious scruples. It was immediately after this ribald attack that Wesley was called upon to preach his first sermon before the University on New Year's Day, 1733—the sermon now under consideration. He thought well of it; and in *Journal*, September 1, 1778, he says: 'I know not that I can write a better [sermon] on the Circumcision of the Heart than I did five and forty years ago. Perhaps, indeed, I may have read five or six hundred books more than I had then, and may know a little more history or natural philosophy than I did; but I am not sensible that this has made any essential addition to my knowledge in divinity. Forty years ago I knew and preached every Christian doctrine which I preach now.' It will be noted that this latter date only goes back to 1738, when he first grasped the truth of conscious salvation by faith. In a letter to a friend written in May 1765 he says: 'January 1, 1733, I preached the sermon on the Circumcision of the Heart, which contains all that I now teach concerning salvation from all sin, and loving God with an undivided heart. In the same year I printed (the first time I ventured to print anything) for the use of my pupils, *A Collection of Forms of Prayer,* and in this I spoke explicitly of giving 'the whole heart and the whole life to

God.' This was then, as it is now, my idea of perfection, though I should have started at the word.'

The sermon was not published until it appeared in the second volume of sermons in 1748; and in a footnote Wesley explains that he has added to the sermon as originally preached the latter half of i. 7, in which saving faith is defined as he came to understand it in 1738. The influence of Jeremy Taylor and William Law is very perceptible throughout, especially in the prominence given to humility, which takes precedence even of the Pauline triad, faith, hope, and love.

Wesley wrote in this same year a sermon on Eph. iv. 30, which was published in the *Arminian Magazine*, 1798, p. 607, and included as No. CXXXVIII in the fifth (posthumous) series. It is noteworthy that both in this and the previous sermon the doctrine of the wituess of the Spirit is explicitly taught. To complete the record for this period, he preached before the University on June 11, 1734, what Charles calls his 'Jacobite sermon,' of which little seems to be known, except that it was submitted to the Vice-Chancellor beforehand and allowed by him. On Sunday, September 21, 1735, he preached before the University on Job iii. 17, and at the request of several of the hearers it was published the same year by C. Rivington—Wesley's first published sermon. It appears as No. CXXVII in the fourth (posthumous) series under the title of The Trouble and Rest of Good Men; and is remarkable for its statement that perfect holiness is not found on earth, but that death shall destroy at once the whole body of sin. The original edition is a fine bit of typography; quite the best printed of any of Wesley's publications. It is mistakenly given by Heylin as from Prov. iii. 17, under the title of The Pleasantness of a Religious Life. Finally, we have Sermon CXLI, On the Holy Spirit, from 2 Cor. iii. 17, the last in the fifth (posthumous) series, which is said in the heading to have been preached at St. Mary's, Oxford, on Whit Sunday, 1736. Wesley was in Frederica on that date (June 13, 1736), meeting the first society in America; he reckons this day as the second birthday of Methodism. So either the editor of the sermon was mistaken in his date, or the sermon was read at Oxford by Wesley's substitute—which is quite possible. On internal evidence the sermon may well have been written by him before he left England.

Circumcision is that of the heart, in the spirit and not in the letter.—ROM. ii. 29.

I. IT is the melancholy remark of an excellent man, that he who now preaches the most essential duties of Christianity runs the hazard of being esteemed, by a great part of his hearers, 'a setter forth of new doctrines.' Most men have so *lived away* the substance of that religion, the profession whereof they still retain, that no sooner are any of those truths proposed which difference the Spirit of Christ from the spirit of the world, than they cry out, 'Thou bringest strange things to our ears; we would know what these things mean': though he is only preaching to them 'Jesus and the resurrection,' with the necessary consequence of it,—If Christ be risen, ye ought then to die unto the world, and to live wholly unto God.

2. A hard saying this to the natural man, who is alive unto the world, and dead unto God; and one that he will not readily be persuaded to receive as the truth of God, unless it be so qualified in the interpretation, as to have neither use nor significancy left. He 'receiveth not the' words 'of the Spirit of God,' taken in their plain and obvious meaning; 'they are foolishness unto him: neither' indeed 'can he know them, because they are spiritually discerned': they are perceivable only by that spiritual sense, which in him was never yet awakened; for want of which he must reject, as idle fancies of men, what are both the wisdom and the power of God.

3. That 'circumcision is that of the heart, in the spirit, and not in the letter'—that the distinguishing mark of a true follower of Christ, of one who is in a state of acceptance with God, is not either outward circumcision, or baptism, or any other outward form, but a right state of soul, a mind and spirit renewed after the image of Him that created it—is one of those important truths that can only be spiritually discerned. And this the Apostle himself intimates in the next words: 'Whose praise is not of men, but of God.' As if he had said, 'Expect not, whoever thou art, who thus followest thy great Master, that the world, the men who follow Him not, will say, "Well done, good and faithful servant!" Know that the circumcision of the heart, the seal of thy calling, is foolishness with the world. Be content to wait for thy applause till the day of thy Lord's appearing. In that day shalt thou have praise of God, in the great assembly of men and angels.'

I design, first, particularly to inquire, wherein this circumcision of the heart consists; and, secondly, to mention some reflections that naturally arise from such an inquiry.

I. 1. I am, first, to inquire, wherein that circumcision of the heart consists, which will receive the praise of God. In general we may observe, it is that habitual disposition of soul which, in the sacred writings, is termed holiness; and which directly implies, the being cleansed from sin, 'from all filthiness both of flesh and spirit'; and, by consequence, the being endued with those virtues which were also in Christ Jesus; the being so 'renewed in the spirit of our mind,' as to be 'perfect as our Father in heaven is perfect.'

2. To be more particular: circumcision of heart implies humility, faith, hope, and charity. Humility, a right judgement of ourselves, cleanses our minds from those high conceits of our own perfections, from that undue opinion of our own abilities and attainments, which are the genuine fruit of a corrupted nature. This entirely cuts off that vain thought, 'I am rich, and wise, and have need of nothing'; and convinces us that we are by nature 'wretched, and poor, and miserable, and blind, and naked.' It convinces us, that in our best estate we are, of ourselves, all sin and vanity; that confusion, and ignorance, and error reign over our understanding; that unreasonable, earthly, sensual, devilish passions usurp authority over our will; in a word, that there is no whole part in our soul, that all the foundations of our nature are out of course.

3. At the same time we are convinced, that we are not sufficient of ourselves to help ourselves; that, without the Spirit of God, we can do nothing but add sin to sin; that it is He alone who worketh in us by His almighty power, either to will or do that which is good; it being as impossible for us even to think a good thought, without the supernatural assistance of His Spirit, as to create ourselves, or to renew our whole souls in righteousness and true holiness.

4. A sure effect of our having formed this right judgement of the sinfulness and helplessness of our nature, is a disregard of that 'honour which cometh of man,' which is usually paid to some supposed excellency in us. He who knows himself, neither desires nor values the applause which he knows he deserves not. It is therefore 'a very small thing with him, to be judged by man's judgement.' He has all reason to think, by comparing what it has said, wither for or against him, with what he feels in his own breast, that the world, as well as the god of this world, was 'a liar from the beginning.' And even as to those who are not of the world; though he would choose, if it were the will of God, that they should account of him as of one desirous to be found a faithful steward of his Lord's goods, if haply this might be a means of enabling him to be of more use to his fellow servants,

yet as this is the one end of his wishing for their approbation, so
he does not at all rest upon it: for he is assured, that whatever
God wills, he can never want instruments to perform; since He is
able, even of these stones, to raise up servants to do His pleasure.

5. This is that lowliness of mind, which they have learned of
Christ, who follow His example and tread in His steps. And this
knowledge of their disease, whereby they are more and more
cleansed from one part of it, pride and vanity, disposes them to
embrace, with a willing mind, the second thing implied in
circumcision of the heart,—that faith which alone is able to make
them whole, which is the one medicine given under heaven to
heal their sickness.

6. The best guide of the blind, the surest light of them that are
in darkness, the most perfect instructor of the foolish, is faith.
But it must be such a faith as is 'mighty through God, to the
pulling down of strongholds'—to the overturning all the
prejudices of corrupt reason, all the false maxims revered
among men, all evil customs and habits, all that 'wisdom of the
world which is foolishness with God'; as 'casteth down
imaginations,' reasonings, 'and every high thing that exalteth
itself against the knowledge of God, and bringeth into captivity
every thought to the obedience of Christ.'

7. 'All things are possible to him that' thus 'believeth.' 'The
eyes of his understanding being enlightened,' he sees what is his
calling; even to glorify God, who hath bought him with so high a
price, in his body and in his spirit, which now are God's by
redemption, as well as by creation. He feels what is 'the
exceeding greatness of His power,' who, as He raised up Christ
from the dead, so is able to quicken us, dead in sin, 'by His Spirit
which dwelleth in us.' 'This is the victory which overcometh the
world, even our faith'; that faith, which is not only an unshaken
assent to all that God hath revealed in Scripture—and in
particular to those important truths, 'Jesus Christ came into the
world to save sinners,' 'He bare our sins in His own body on the
tree,' 'He is the propitiation for our sins, and not for ours only,
but also for the sins of the whole world,'—but likewise the
revelation of Christ in our hearts; a divine evidence or
conviction of His love, His free, unmerited love to me a sinner; a
sure confidence in His pardoning mercy, wrought in us by the
Holy Ghost; a confidence, whereby every true believer is

enabled to bear witness, 'I know that my Redeemer liveth,' that I have an 'Advocate with the Father,' and that 'Jesus Christ the righteous' is my Lord and 'the propitiation for my sins'—I know He hath 'loved me, and given Himself for me'—He hath reconciled me, even me, to God; and I 'have redemption through His blood, even the forgiveness of sins.'

8. Such a faith as this cannot fail to show evidently the power of Him that inspires it, by delivering His children from the yoke of sin and 'purging their consciences from dead works'; by strengthening them so, that they are no longer constrained to obey sin in the desires thereof; but instead of 'yielding their members unto it, as instruments of unrighteousness,' they now 'yield themselves' entirely 'unto God, as those that are alive from the dead.'

9. Those who are thus by faith born of God have also strong consolation through hope. This is the next thing which the circumcision of the heart implies; even the testimony of their own spirit with the Spirit which witnesses in their hearts that they are the children of God. Indeed it is the same Spirit who works in them that clear and cheerful confidence that their heart is upright toward God; that good assurance, that they now do, through His grace, the things which are acceptable in His sight; that they are now in the path which leadeth to life, and shall, by the mercy of God, endure therein to the end. It is He who giveth them a lively expectation of receiving all good things at God's hand; a joyous prospect of that crown of glory which is reserved in heaven for them. By this anchor a Christian is kept steady in the midst of the waves of this troublesome world, and preserved from striking upon either of those fatal rocks,—presumption or despair. He is neither discouraged by the misconceived severity of his Lord, nor does he 'despise the riches of His goodness.' He neither apprehends the difficulties of the race set before him to be greater than he has strength to conquer, nor expects them to be so little as to yield in the conquest till he has put forth all his strength. The experience he already has in the Christian warfare, as it assures him his 'labour is not in vain,' if 'whatever his hand findeth to do, he doeth it with his might'; so it forbids his entertaining so vain a thought, as that he can otherwise gain any advantage; as that any virtue can be shown, any praise attained, by faint hearts and feeble hands;

or indeed, by any but those who pursue the same course with the great Apostle of the Gentiles: 'I,' says he, 'so run, not as uncertainly; so fight I, not as one that beateth the air: but I keep under my body, and bring it into subjection; lest, by any means, when I have preached to others, I myself should be a castaway.'

10. By the same discipline is every good soldier of Christ to inure himself to endure hardship. Confirmed and strengthened by this, he will be able not only to renounce the works of darkness, but every appetite too, and every affection, which is not subject to the law of God. For 'every one,' saith St. John, 'who hath this hope, purifieth himself even as He is pure.' It is his daily care, by the grace of God in Christ, and through the blood of the covenant, to purge the inmost recesses of his soul from the lusts that before possessed and defiled it; from uncleanness, and envy, and malice, and wrath; from every passion and temper that is after the flesh, that either springs from or cherishes his native corruption: as well knowing, that he whose very body is the temple of God, ought to admit into it nothing common or unclean; and that holiness becometh that house for ever, where the Spirit of holiness vouchsafes to dwell.

11. Yet lackest thou one thing, whosoever thou art, that to a deep humility, and a steadfast faith, hast joined a lively hope and thereby in a good measure cleansed thy heart from its inbred pollution. If thou wilt be perfect, add to all these, charity; add love, and thou hast the circumcision of the heart. 'Love is the fulfilling of the law, the end of the commandment.' Very excellent things are spoken of love; it is the essence, the spirit the life of all virtue. It is not only the first and great command but it is all the commandments in one. 'Whatsoever things are just, whatsoever things are pure, whatsoever things are amiable,' or honourable; 'if there be any virtue, if there be any praise,' they are all comprised in this one word,—love. In this is perfection, and glory, and happiness. The royal law of heaven and earth is this, 'Thou shalt love the Lord thy God with all thy heart, and with all thy soul, and with all thy mind, and with all thy strength.'

12. Not that this forbids us to love anything besides God: it implies that we love our brother also. Nor yet does it forbid us (as some have strangely imagined) to take pleasure in anything but God. To suppose this, is to suppose the Fountain of holiness is directly the author of sin; since He has inseparably annexed

pleasure to the use of those creatures which are necessary to sustain the life He has given us. This, therefore, can never be the meaning of His command. What the real sense of it is, both our blessed Lord and His Apostles tell us too frequently, and too plainly, to be misunderstood. They all with one mouth bear witness, that the true meaning of those several declarations, 'The Lord thy God is one Lord'; 'Thou shalt have no other gods but Me'; 'Thou shalt love the Lord thy God with all thy strength'; 'Thou shalt cleave unto Him'; 'The desire of thy soul shall be to His name,' is no other than this: The one perfect Good shall be your one ultimate end. One thing shall ye desire for its own sake,—the fruition of Him that is All in all. One happiness shall ye propose to your souls, even an union with Him that made them; the having 'fellowship with the Father and the Son'; the being joined to the Lord in one Spirit. One design you are to pursue to the end of time,—the enjoyment of God in time and in eternity. Desire other things, so far as they tend to this. Love the creature, as it leads to the Creator. But in every step you take, be this the glorious point that terminates your view. Let every affection, and thought, and word, and work, be subordinate to this. Whatever ye desire or fear, whatever ye seek or shun, whatever ye think, speak or do, be it in order to your happiness in God, the sole End, as well as Source, of your being.

13. Have no end, no ultimate end, but God. Thus our Lord: 'One thing is needful'; and if thine eye be singly fixed on this one thing, 'thy whole body shall be full of light.' Thus St. Paul: 'This one thing I do; I press toward the mark, for the prize of the high calling in Christ Jesus.' Thus St. James: 'Cleanse your hands, ye sinners; and purify your hearts, ye double-minded.' Thus St. John: 'Love not the world, neither the things that are in the world. For all that is in the world, the lust of the flesh, the lust of the eye, and the pride of life, is not of the Father, but is of the world.' The seeking happiness in what gratifies either the desire of the flesh, by agreeably striking upon the outward senses; the desire of the eye, of the imagination, by its novelty, greatness, or beauty; or the pride of life, whether by pomp, grandeur, power, or, the usual consequence of them, applause and admiration,— 'is not of the Father,' cometh not from, neither is approved by, the Father of spirits: 'but of the world'; it is the distinguishing mark of those who will not have Him to reign over them.

II. 1. Thus have I particularly inquired, what that circumcision of heart is, which will obtain the praise of God. I am, in the second place, to mention some reflections that naturally arise from such an inquiry as a plain rule whereby every man may judge of himself, whether he be of the world or of God.

And, first, it is clear from what has been said, that no man has a title to the praise of God, unless his heart is circumcised by humility; unless he is little, and base, and vile in his own eyes; unless he is deeply convinced of that inbred 'corruption of his nature,' 'whereby he is very far gone from original righteousness,' being prone to all evil, averse to all good, corrupt and abominable; having a 'carnal mind which is enmity against God, and is not subject to the law of God, nor indeed can be'; unless he continually feels in his inmost soul, that without the Spirit of God resting upon him, he can neither think, nor desire, nor speak, nor act anything good or well-pleasing in His sight.

No man, I say, has a title to the praise of God, till he feels his want of God; nor indeed, till he seeketh that 'honour which cometh of God' only; and neither desires nor pursues that which cometh of man, unless so far only as it tends to this.

2. Another truth, which naturally follows from what has been said, is, that none shall obtain the honour that cometh of God, unless his heart be circumcised by faith; even a 'faith of the operation of God'; unless, refusing to be any longer led by his senses, appetites, or passions, or even by that blind leader of the blind, so idolized by the world, natural reason, he lives and walks by faith; directs every step, as 'seeing Him that is invisible'; 'looks not at the things that are seen, which are temporal, but at the things that are not seen, which are eternal'; and governs all his desires, designs, and thoughts, all his actions and conversations, as one who is entered in within the veil, where Jesus sits at the right hand of God.

3. It were to be wished, that they were better acquainted with this faith who employ much of their time and pains in laying another foundation; in grounding religion on the eternal *fitness* of things, on the intrinsic *excellence* of virtue, and the *beauty* of actions flowing from it; on the *reasons,* as they term them, of good and evil, and the *relations,* of beings to each other. Either these accounts of the grounds of Christian duty coincide with the scriptural, or not. If they do, why are well-meaning men

perplexed and drawn from the weightier matters of the law by a cloud of terms, whereby the easiest truths are explained into obscurity? If they are not then it behoves them to consider who is the author of this new doctrine; whether he is likely to be an angel from heaven, who preacheth another gospel than that of Christ Jesus; though, if he were God, not we, hath pronounced his sentence: 'Let him be accursed.'

4. Our gospel, as it knows no other foundation of good works than faith, or of faith than Christ, so it clearly informs us we are not His disciples while we either deny Him to be the Author, or His Spirit to be the Inspirer and Perfecter, both of our faith and works. 'If any man have not the Spirit of Christ, he is none of his.' He alone can quicken those who are dead unto God, can breathe into them the breath of Christian life, and so prevent, accompany, and follow them with His grace, as to bring their good desires to good effect. And, 'as many as are thus led by the Spirit of God, they are the sons of God.' This is God's short and plain account of true religion and virtue; and 'other foundation can no man lay.'

5. From what has been said, we may, thirdly, learn, that none is truly 'led by the Spirit,' unless that 'Spirit bear Witness with his spirit, that he is a child of God'; unless he see the prize and the crown before him, and 'rejoice in hope of the glory of God.' So greatly have they erred who have taught that, in serving God, we ought not to have a view to our own happiness! Nay, but we are often and expressly taught of God, to have 'respect unto the recompense of reward'; to balance the toil with the 'joy set before us,' these 'light afflictions' with that 'exceeding weight of glory.' Yea, we are 'aliens to the covenant of promise,' we are 'without God in the world,' until God, 'of His abundant mercy, hath begotten us again unto a living hope of the inheritance incorruptible, undefiled, and that fadeth not away.'

6. But if these things are so, it is high time for those persons to deal faithfully with their own souls, who are so far from finding in themselves this joyful assurance that they fulfil the terms, and shall obtain the promises, of that covenant, as to quarrel with the covenant itself, and blaspheme the terms of it; to complain, they are too severe; and that no man ever did or shall live up to them. What is this but to reproach God, as if He were an hard Master, requiring of His servants more than He enables them to

perform?—as if He had mocked the helpless works of His hands, by binding them to impossibilities; by commanding them to overcome, where neither their own strength nor His grace was sufficient for them?

7. These blasphemers might almost persuade those to imagine themselves guiltless, who, in the contrary extreme, hope to fulfil the commands of God without taking any pains at all. Vain hope! that a child of Adam should ever expect to see the kingdom of Christ and of God without striving, without *agonizing*, first 'to enter in at the strait gate'; that one who was 'conceived and born in sin,' and whose 'inward parts are very wickedness,' should once entertain a thought of being 'purified as his Lord is pure,' unless he tread in His steps, and 'take up his cross daily,' unless he 'cut off his right hand,' and 'pluck out the right eye, and cast it from him'; that he should ever dream of shaking off his old opinions, passions, tempers, of being 'sanctified throughout in spirit, soul, and body,' without a constant and continued course of general self-denial!

8. What less than this can we possibly infer from the above-cited words of St. Paul, who, living 'in infirmities, in reproaches, in necessities, in persecutions, in distresses' for Christ's sake; who, being full of 'signs and wonders, and mighty deeds,' who, having been 'caught up into the third heaven,'—yet reckoned, as a late author strongly expresses it, that all his virtues would be insecure, and even his salvation in danger, without this constant self-denial? 'So run I,' says he, 'not as uncertainly; so fight I, not as one that beateth the air': by which he plainly teaches us, that he who does not thus run, who does not thus deny himself daily, does run uncertainly, and fighteth to as little purpose as he that 'beateth the air.'

9. To as little purpose does he talk of 'fighting the fight of faith,' as vainly hope to attain the crown of incorruption (as we may, lastly, infer from the preceding observations), whose heart is not circumcised by love. Love, cutting off both the lust of the flesh, the lust of the eye, and the pride of life—engaging the whole man, body, soul, and spirit, in the ardent pursuit of that one object—is so essential to a child of God, that without it, whosoever liveth is counted dead before Him. 'Though I speak with the tongues of men and of angels, and have not love, I am as sounding brass, or a tinkling cymbal. Though I have the gift of

prophecy, and understand all mysteries, and all knowledge; and though I have all faith, so as to remove mountains, and have not love, I am nothing.' Nay, 'though I give all my goods to feed the poor, and my body to be burned, and have not love, it profiteth me nothing.'

10. Here, then, is the sum of the perfect law; this is the true circumcision of the heart. Let the spirit return to God that gave it, with the whole train of its affections. 'Unto the place from whence all the rivers came,' thither let them flow again. Other sacrifices from us He would not; but the living sacrifice of the heart He hath chosen. Let it be continually offered up to God through Christ, in flames of holy love. And let no creature be suffered to share with Him: for He is a jealous God. His throne will He not divide with another: He will reign without a rival. Be no design, no desire admitted there, but what has Him for its ultimate object. This is the way wherein those children of God once walked, who, being dead, still speak to us: 'Desire not to live but to praise His name: let all your thoughts, words, and works tend to His glory. Set your heart firm on Him, and on other things only as they are in and from Him. Let your soul be filled with so entire a love of Him that you may love nothing but for His sake.' 'Have a pure intention of heart, a steadfast regard to His glory in all your actions.' 'Fix your eye upon the blessed hope of your calling, and make all the things of the world minister unto it.' For then, and not till then, is that 'mind in us which was also in Christ Jesus'; when, in every motion of our heart, in every word of our tongue, in every work of our hands, we 'pursue nothing but in relation to Him, and in subordination to His pleasure'; when we, too, neither think, nor speak, nor act, to fulfil our 'own will, but the will of Him that sent us'; when, whether we 'eat, or drink, or whatever we do, we do all to the glory of God.'

Faith *hope* *Love*
power →SIN of God *Fruit*
Peace Neighbor
obedience

Marks

SERMON XIV

THE MARKS OF THE NEW BIRTH

Wesley gave a series of expositions of the earlier chapters of St. John's Gospel to the London societies in March and April 1741, this particular passage being entered as the subject for Friday, April 3. It is entered as the text of a sermon on January 2, 1743, when he preached from it at Epworth at 5 a.m. It was repeated at Evesham in the evening of January 12. It appears in the sermon list about seven times from 1750 to 1757. His favourite text on the New Birth was the previous verse (Sermon No. XXXIX, q.v.).

The text is unfortunately chosen for this sermon. The context is entirely disregarded and the passage taken merely as a motto. The 'so' obviously refers to the previous clause of the verse; and the meaning is that the processes of the new birth are as mysterious and inexplicable as the blowing of the wind. The treatment of the subject is analogous to that of the last sermon—The Circumcision of the Heart—faith, hope, and love being the marks of the new birth; and the section on Love owes a good deal to chap. xx of Law's *Serious Call*. It is related to the following sermon much as No. XI (The Witness of our own Spirit) is related to No. XLVI (Sin in Believers). The first sets out the ideal of the Christian life; the second makes the qualifications which practical experience shows to be necessary.

The teaching of the first paragraph on Baptismal Regeneration requires a fuller consideration than a footnote would permit. The Article (XXVII), Of Baptism, is not explicit. It states that baptism is not only a sign of profession, but also a sign of regeneration or new birth; and that thereby 'the promises of the forgiveness of sin and of our adoption to be the sons of God by the Holy Ghost are visibly signed and sealed'; but it does not definitely say that the baptized infant is regenerated. The Office for Baptism is, however much more definite; prayer is offered, 'Give Thy Holy Spirit to this infant, that he may be *born again,* and be made an heir of everlasting salvation'; and after the administration of the sacrament, the priest shall say, 'Seeing that this child is *regenerate* and grafted into the body of Christ's Church, let us give thanks to Almighty God'; and again, 'We yield Thee most hearty thanks, most merciful Father, that it hath pleased Thee *to regenerate* this infant with Thy Holy Spirit,' &c. Wesley was trained up in and accepted this view. In Sermon XXXIX, iv. 2, he says: 'It is certain our Church supposes that all who are baptized in their infancy are at the same time born again; and it is allowed that the whole Office for the Baptism of Infants proceeds upon this supposition. Nor is it an objection of any weight against this, that we cannot comprehend how this work can be wrought in infants. For neither can we comprehend how it is wrought in a person of riper years.' But he significantly adds, 'Whatever be the case with infants' (which implies some hesitation on his part) 'it is sure all of riper years who are baptized are not at the same time born again.' So in Sermon XV, i. 1: 'From all the passages of holy writ wherein this expression "the being born of God" occurs, we may learn that it implies not barely the being baptized, or any outward change whatever; but a vast inward change.' In *Journal*, May 24, 1738, he says: 'I believe till I was about ten years old, I had not sinned away that "washing of the Holy Ghost" which was given me in baptism.' In the *Treatise on Baptism*, published in 1756, he says 'that in baptism infants are (1) freed from the guilt of original sin, so that, if they die before committing actual sin, they will be saved; (2) admitted into the new covenant relation between God and His people, as by circumcision the children of Jews were admitted into the old covenant; (3) admitted into the Church; (4) made the children of God by adoption and grace. 'Herein,' he says, 'a principle of grace is infused, which will not be wholly taken away, unless we quench the Holy Spirit of God by long-continued wickedness.' However, in the *Sunday Service of the Methodists* (1784 and 1786), the Office for Baptism was much abridged; the three passages quoted above were omitted; the word 'regenerated' is not used, except in the quotation from John iii. 5 in the introductory exhortation; the minister at the end gives thanks 'that this child is admitted into the body of Christ's Church,' and that it hath pleased God 'to receive this infant for Thy own child by adoption, and to admit him into Thy holy Church.' In the editions of 1857 and later, the thanksgivings at the end were omitted altogether. When the *Book of Offices* was revised in 1882, there was a strenuous debate in the Conference over the alterations proposed in the Office for Baptism. The reference to John iii. 5 was left out by the Committee, as well as all phrases that might seem to suggest that the infant was born again in baptism; a prayer was added for the parents; and the short prayers, placed previously just before the act of baptism, were transferred to the end of the service, to avoid the supposition that they were meant to be answered at the time the child was baptized. I was present at the debate, and well remember how it was urged by some of the brethren that we were bound to accept the doctrine of baptismal regeneration because Mr. Wesley affirmed it in the Standard Sermons. Dr. Rigg replied that we were not bound to accept every doctrine that might be incidentally mentioned in the Standards, but only the general scheme of doctrine therein contained. The Conference supported this view, and the revised form was agreed to, with the proviso that liberty should be left to any minister to use the older form if he so desired (*Minutes*, 1882, p. 223). This, however, did not prevent two well-known ministers from resigning their connexion with the Conference and entering the Church of England. The Methodist Church has thus definitely repudiated the view that the infant is born again in baptism, though liberty of judgement is left to each minister; and it may fairly be argued that Wesley's revision of the service in 1784 proves that in his later life he altered his earlier opinion. Watson in his *Institutes (WORKS,* xii. 266) says: 'To the infant child it is a visible reception into the same covenant and church—a pledge of acceptance through Christ—the bestowment of a title to all the grace of the covenant as circumstances may require, and as the mind of the child may be capable, or made capable, of receiving it. . . . It secures, too, the gift of the Holy Spirit in those secret spiritual influences by which the actual regeneration of those children who die in infancy is effected; and which are a seed of life in those who are spared.' Dr. W. B. Pope maintains that baptism is not a mere sign or badge of Christian profession, nor only an impressive emblem of the washing away of sin; it does convey its accompanying grace to the recipient. I remember being present during the Conference of 1885 at Trinity Chapel, Southport, when Dr. Pope baptized a child; and as he handed it back to its parents, he said, 'Doubt not but your child has received in this holy sacrament all the grace of which he is now capable.' Our danger in Methodism has not been in the direction of over-estimating the value of this sacrament, but rather in regarding it as merely the recognition of the child's formal reception into the Church. Our perfunctoriness in the administration of it, and our subsequent failure to look after our baptized children and give them due pastoral attention, has been a grave cause of loss and harm to ourselves, and has given no little advantage to those who have sought to cast discredit on infant baptism and to urge our young people to be rebaptized by immersion. It is a question whether we have not made a mistake in dropping the rite of Confirmation without substituting for it some solemn service at which our baptized children could consciously take upon themselves the vows made for them at their baptism.

This sermon was first published in Vol. II of the Sermons in 1748.

So is every one that is born of the Spirit.—JOHN iii. 8.

1. How is every one that is 'born of the Spirit'—that is, born again—born of God? What is meant by the being born again, the being born of God, or being born of the Spirit? What is implied in the being a son or a child of God, or having the Spirit of adoption? That these privileges, by the free mercy of God, are ordinarily annexed to baptism (which is thence termed by our Lord in a preceding verse, the being 'born of water and of the Spirit') we know; but we would know what these privileges are: what is the new birth?

2. Perhaps it is not needful to give a definition of this, seeing the Scripture gives none. But as the question is of the deepest

concern to every child of man; since, 'except a man be born again,' born of the Spirit, 'he cannot see the kingdom of God'; I propose to lay down the marks of it in the plainest manner, just as I find them laid down in Scripture.

I. 1. The first of these, and the foundation of all the rest, is faith. So St. Paul, 'Ye are all the children of God by faith in Christ Jesus' (Gal. iii. 26). So St. John, 'To them gave He power' (εξουσιαν, *right* or *privilege,* it may rather be translated) 'to become the sons of God, even to them that believe on His name; which were born,' when they believed, 'not of blood, nor of the will of the flesh,' not by natural generation, 'nor of the will of man,' like those children adopted by men, in whom no inward change is thereby wrought, 'but of God' (John i. 12, 13). And again, in his General Epistle, 'Whosoever believeth that Jesus is the Christ is born of God' (1 John v. 1).

2. But it is not a barely notional or speculative faith that is here spoken of by the Apostles. It is not a bare assent to this proposition, 'Jesus is the Christ'; nor indeed to all the propositions contained in our creed, or in the Old and New Testament. It is not merely an assent to any or all these credible things, as credible. To say this, were to say (which who could hear?) that the devils were born of God; for they have this faith. They, trembling, believe, both that Jesus is the Christ, and that all Scripture, having been given by inspiration of God, is true as God is true. It is not only an assent to divine truth, upon the testimony of God, or upon the evidence of miracles; for *they* also heard the words of His mouth, and knew Him to be a faithful and true witness. They could not but receive the testimony He gave, both of Himself, and of the Father which sent Him. They saw likewise the mighty works which He did, and thence believed that He 'came forth from God.' Yet, notwithstanding this faith, they are still 'reserved in chains of darkness unto the judgement of the great day.'

3. For all this is no more than a dead faith. The true, living, Christian faith, which whosoever hath is born of God, is not only assent, an act of the understanding; but a disposition, which God hath wrought in his heart; 'a sure trust and confidence in God, that, through the merits of Christ, his sins are forgiven, and he reconciled to the favour of God.' This implies, that a man first

renounce himself; that, in order to be 'found in Christ,' to be accepted through Him, he totally rejects all 'confidence in the flesh'; that, 'having nothing to pay,' having no trust in his own works or righteousness of any kind, he comes to God as a lost, miserable, self-destroyed, self-condemned, undone, helpless sinner; as one whose mouth is utterly stopped and who is altogether 'guilty before God.' Such a sense of sin (commonly called 'despair' by those who speak evil of the things they know not), together with a full conviction, such as no words can express, that of Christ only cometh our salvation, and an earnest desire of that salvation, must precede a living faith, a trust in Him, who 'for us paid our ransom by His death, and [for us] fulfilled the law in His life.' This faith then, whereby we are born of God, is 'not only a belief of all the articles of our faith, but also a true confidence of the mercy of God through our Lord Jesus Christ.'

4. An immediate and constant fruit of this faith whereby we are born of God, a fruit which can in no wise be separated from it, no, not for an hour, is power over sin,—power over outward sin of every kind; over every evil word and work; for wheresoever the blood of Christ is thus applied, it 'purgeth the conscience from dead works,'—and over inward sin; for it purifieth the heart from every unholy desire and temper. This fruit of faith St. Paul has largely described, in the sixth chapter of his Epistle to the Romans. 'How shall we,' saith he, 'who' by faith 'are dead to sin, live any longer therein?' 'Our old man is crucified with Christ, that the body of sin might be destroyed, that henceforth we should not serve sin.' 'Likewise, reckon ye yourselves to be dead unto sin, but alive unto God through Jesus Christ our Lord. Let not sin therefore reign' even 'in your mortal body,' 'but yield yourselves unto God, as those that are alive from the dead.' 'For sin shall not have dominion over you. . . . God be thanked, that ye were the servants of sin . . . but being made free,'—the plain meaning is, God be thanked, that though ye were, in time past, the servants of sin, yet now, 'being free from sin ye are become the servants of righteousness.'

5. The same invaluable privilege of the sons of God is as strongly asserted by St. John; particularly with regard to the former branch of it, namely, power over outward sin. After he had been crying out, as one astonished at the depth of the riches

of the goodness of God, 'Behold, what manner of love the Father hath bestowed upon us, that we should be called the sons of God! Beloved, now are we the sons of God; and it doth not yet appear what we shall be: but we know that, when He shall appear, we shall be like Him; for we shall see Him as He is' (1 John iii. 1, &c.),—he soon adds, 'Whosoever is born of God doth not commit sin; for His seed remaineth in him: and he cannot sin, because he is born of God' (verse 9). But some men will say, 'True: whosoever is born of God doth not commit sin *habitually*.' *Habitually!* Whence is that? I read it not. It is not written in the Book. God plainly saith, 'He doth not commit sin'; and thou addest, *habitually!* Who art thou that *mendest* the oracles of God?—that 'addest to the words of this book'? Beware, I beseech thee, lest God 'add to thee all the plagues that are written therein'! especially when the comment thou addest is such as quite swallows up the text: so that by this μεθοδεια πλανης, this artful method of deceiving, the precious promise is utterly lost; by this κυβεια ανθρωπων, this tricking and shuffling of men, the Word of God is made of none effect. O beware, thou that thus takest from the words of this book, that, taking away the whole meaning and spirit from them, leavest only what may indeed be termed a dead letter, lest God take away thy part out of the book of life!

6. Suffer we the Apostle to interpret his own words, by the whole tenor of his discourse. In the fifth verse of this chapter, he had said, 'Ye know that He,' Christ, 'was manifested to take away our sins; and in Him is no sin.' What is the inference he draws from this? 'Whosoever abideth in Him sinneth not: whosoever sinneth hath not seen Him, neither known Him' (1 John iii. 6). To his enforcement of this important doctrine, he premises an highly necessary caution: 'Little children, let no man deceive you' (verse 7); for many will endeavour so to do; to persuade you that you may be unrighteous, that you may commit sin, and yet be children of God: 'He that doeth righteousness is righteous, even as He is righteous. He that committeth sin is of the devil; for the devil sinneth from the beginning.' Then follows, 'Whosoever is born of God doth not commit sin; for His seed remaineth in him: and he cannot sin, because he is born of God.' 'In this,' adds the Apostle, 'the children of God are manifest, and the children of the devil.' By this plain mark (the committing or

not committing sin) are they distinguished from each other. To the same effect are those words in his fifth chapter: 'We know that whosoever is born of God sinneth not; but he that is begotten of God keepeth himself, and that wicked one toucheth him not' (verse 18).

7. Another fruit of this living faith is peace. For, 'being justified by faith,' having all our sins blotted out, 'we have peace with God through our Lord Jesus Christ' (Rom. v. 1). This indeed our Lord Himself, the night before His death, solemnly bequeathed to all His followers: 'Peace,' saith He, 'I leave with you' (you who 'believe in God,' and 'believe also in Me'); 'My peace I give unto you: not as the world giveth, give I unto you. Let not your heart be troubled, neither let it be afraid' (John xiv. 27). And again: 'These things have I spoken unto you, that in Me ye might have peace' (John xvi. 33). This is that 'peace of God which passeth all understanding,' that serenity of soul which it hath not entered into the heart of a natural man to conceive, and which it is not possible for even the spiritual man to utter. And it is a peace which all the powers of earth and hell are unable to take from him. Waves and storms beat upon it, but they shake it not; for it is founded upon a rock. It keepeth the hearts and minds of the children of God, at all times and in all places. Whether they are in ease or in pain, in sickness or health, in abundance or want, they are happy in God. In every state they have learned to be content, yea, to give thanks unto God through Christ Jesus; being well assured, that 'whatsoever is, is best,' because it is His will concerning them: so that in all the vicissitudes of life their heart 'standeth fast, believing in the Lord.'

II. 1. A second scriptural mark of those who are born of God, is hope. Thus St. Peter, speaking to all the children of God who were then scattered abroad, saith, 'Blessed be the God and Father of our Lord Jesus Christ, which according to His abundant mercy, hath begotten us again unto a lively hope' (1 Pet. i. 3). Ελπιδα ζωσαν, a *lively* or *living* hope, saith the Apostle; because there is also a *dead* hope, as well as a dead faith; a hope which is not from God, but from the enemy of God and man;—as evidently appears by its fruits; for, as it is the offspring of pride, so it is the parent of every evil word and work; whereas, every man that hath in him this living hope, is 'holy as He that calleth him is holy'; every man that can truly say to his brethren in Christ, 'Beloved, now are we the sons of God, and we shall see Him as He is,' 'purifieth himself, even as He is pure.'

2. This hope [,—termed in the Epistle to the Hebrews (x. 22), πληροφορια πιστεως, and elsewhere πληροφοριαν ελπιδος (vi. II); in our translation 'the full assurance of faith, and the full assurance of hope,' expressions the best which our language could afford, although far weaker than those in the original,—as described in Scripture,] implies, first, the testimony of our own spirit, or conscience, that we walk 'in simplicity and godly sincerity'; secondly [and chiefly] the testimony of the Spirit of God, 'bearing witness with,' or to, 'our spirit, that we are the children of God,' 'and if children, then heirs, heirs of God, and joint-heirs with Christ.'

3. Let us well observe what is here taught us by God Himself, touching this glorious privilege of His children. Who is it that is here said to bear witness? Not our spirit only, but another; even the Spirit of God: He it is who 'beareth witness with our spirit.' What is it He beareth witness of? 'That we are the children of God; and if children, then heirs; heirs of God, and joint-heirs with Christ' (Rom. viii. 16, 17); 'if so be that we suffer with Him,' if we deny ourselves, if we take up our cross daily, if we cheerfully endure persecution or reproach for His sake, 'that we may also be glorified together.' And in whom doth the Spirit of God bear this witness? In all who are the children of God. By this very argument does the Apostle prove, in the preceding verses, that they are so: 'As many,' saith he, 'as are led by the Spirit of God, they are the sons of God.' 'For ye have not received the spirit of bondage again to fear; but ye have received the Spirit of adoption, whereby we cry Abba, Father!' It follows, 'the Spirit itself beareth witness with our spirit, that we are the children of God' (Rom. viii. 14-16).

4. The variation of the phrase in the fifteenth verse is worthy our observation: 'Ye have received the Spirit of adoption, whereby we cry, Abba, Father!' *Ye*, as many as are the sons of God, have, in virtue of your sonship, received that self-same Spirit of adoption, whereby *we* cry, Abba, Father. *We*, the apostles, prophets, teachers (for so the word may not improperly be understood), *we*, through whom you have

believed, the 'ministers of Christ, and stewards of the mysteries of God.' As *we* and *you* have one Lord, so we have one Spirit: as we have one faith, so we have one hope also. We and you are sealed with one 'Spirit of promise,' the earnest of *your* and of *our* inheritance: the same Spirit bearing witness with your and with our spirit, 'that we are the children of God.'

5. And thus is the Scripture fulfilled, 'Blessed are they that mourn; for they shall be comforted.' For it is easy to believe, that though sorrow may precede this witness of God's Spirit with our spirit (indeed *must* in some degree, while we groan under fear, and a sense of the wrath of God abiding on us); yet, as soon as any man feeleth it in himself, his 'sorrow is turned into joy.' Whatsoever his pain may have been before; yet, as soon as that 'hour is come, he remembereth the anguish no more, for joy' that he is born of God. It may be, many of *you* have now sorrow, because you are 'aliens from the commonwealth of Israel'; because you are conscious to yourselves that you have not this Spirit; that you are 'without hope and without God in the world.' But when the Comforter is come, 'then your heart shall rejoice': yea, 'your joy shall be full,' and 'that joy no man taketh from you' (John xvi. 22). 'We joy in God,' will ye say 'through our Lord Jesus Christ, by whom we have now received the atonement'; 'by whom we have access into this grace,' this state of grace, of favour, or reconciliation with God, 'wherein we stand, and rejoice in hope of the glory of God' (Rom. v. 2). 'Ye,' saith St. Peter, whom God hath 'begotten again unto a lively hope, are kept by the power of God unto salvation: wherein ye greatly rejoice, though now for a season, if need be, ye are in heaviness through manifold temptations; that the trial of your faith may be found unto praise, and honour, and glory at the appearing of Jesus Christ; in whom, though now ye see Him not, ye rejoice with joy unspeakable and full of glory' (1 Pet. i. 5, &c.). Unspeakable indeed! It is not for the tongue of man to describe this joy in the Holy Ghost. It is 'the hidden manna, which no man knoweth, save he that receiveth it.' But this we know, it not only remains, but overflows, in the depth of affliction. 'Are the consolations of God small' with His children, when all earthly comforts fail? Not so. But when sufferings most abound, the consolation of His Spirit doth much more abound; insomuch that the sons of God 'laugh at destruction when it cometh'; at

want, pain, hell, and the grave; as knowing Him who 'hath the keys of death and hell' and will shortly 'cast them into the bottomless pit'; as hearing even now the great voice out of heaven, saying, 'Behold, the tabernacle of God is with men, and He will dwell with them, and they shall be His people, and God Himself shall be with them, and be their God. And God shall wipe away all tears from their eyes; and there shall be no more death, neither sorrow, nor crying, neither shall there be any more pain; for the former things are passed away' (Rev. xxi. 3, 4).

III. 1. A third scriptural mark of those who are born of God, and the greatest of all, is love; even 'the love of God shed abroad in their hearts by the Holy Ghost which is given unto them' (Rom. v. 5). 'Because they are sons, God hath sent forth the Spirit of His Son into their hearts, crying, Abba. Father!' (Gal. iv. 6). By this Spirit, continually looking up to God as their reconciled and loving Father, they cry to Him for their daily bread, for all things needful, whether for their souls or bodies. They continually pour out their hearts before Him, knowing 'they have the petitions which they ask of Him' (1 John v. 15). Their delight is in Him. He is the joy of their heart; their 'shield,' and their 'exceeding great reward.' The desire of their soul is toward Him; it is their 'meat and drink to do His will'; and they are 'satisfied as with marrow and fatness, while their mouth praiseth Him with joyful lips' (Ps. lxiii. 5).

2. And in this sense also, 'every one who loveth Him that begat, loveth Him that is begotten of Him' (1 John v. 1). His spirit rejoiceth in God his Saviour. He 'loveth the Lord Jesus Christ in sincerity.' He is so 'joined unto the Lord,' as to be one spirit. His soul hangeth upon Him, and chooseth Him as altogether lovely, 'the chiefest among ten thousand.' He knoweth he feeleth what that means, 'My beloved is mine and I am His' (Cant. ii. 16). 'Thou art fairer than the children of men; full of grace are Thy lips, because God hath anointed Thee for ever!' (Ps. xlv. 2).

3. The necessary fruit of this love of God is the love of our neighbour; of every soul which God hath made; not excepting our enemies; not excepting those who are now 'despitefully using and persecuting us'—a love whereby we love every man as

ourselves; as we love our own souls. Nay, our Lord has expressed it still more strongly, teaching us to 'love one another, even as He hath loved us.' Accordingly, the commandment written in the hearts of all those that love God is no other than this, 'As I have loved you, so love ye one another.' Now, 'herein perceive we the love of God; in that He laid down His life for us' (1 John iii. 16). 'We ought,' then, as the Apostle justly infers, 'to lay down our lives for the brethren.' If we feel ourselves ready to do this, then do we truly love our neighbour. Then 'we know that we have passed from death unto life, because we' thus 'love the brethren' (1 John iii. 14). 'Hereby know we' that we are born of God, that we 'dwell in Him, and He in us, because He hath given us of His' loving 'Spirit' (iv. 13). For 'love is of God; and every one that' thus 'loveth is born of God, and knoweth God' (iv. 7).

4. But some may possibly ask, 'Does not the Apostle say, "This is the love of God, that we keep His commandments"?' (1 John v. 3). Yea, and this is the love of our neighbour also, in the same sense as it is the love of God. But what would you infer from hence? that the keeping the outward commandments is all that is implied in loving God with all your heart, with all your mind, and soul, and strength, and in loving your neighbour as yourself? that the love of God is not an affection of the soul, but merely an *outward service*? and that the love of our neighbour is not a disposition of heart, but barely a course of *outward works*? To mention so wild an interpretation of the Apostle's words, is sufficiently to confute it. The plain indisputable meaning of the text is,—this is the sign or proof of the love of God, of our keeping the first and great commandment, to keep all the rest of His commandments. For true love, if it be once shed abroad in our heart, will constrain us so to do; since, whosoever loves God with all his heart, cannot but serve Him with all his strength.

5. A second fruit, then, of the love of God (so far as it can be distinguished from it) is universal obedience to Him we love, and conformity to His will; obedience to all the commands of God, internal and external; obedience of the heart and of the life: in every temper, and in all manner of conversation. And one of the tempers most obviously implied herein is, the being 'zealous of good works'; the hungering and thirsting to do good, in every possible kind, unto all men; the rejoicing to 'spend and

be spent for them,' for every child of man; not looking for any recompense in this world, but only in the resurrection of the just.

IV. 1. Thus have I plainly laid down those marks of the new birth which I find laid down in Scripture. Thus doth God Himself answer that weighty question, What is it to be born of God? Such, if the appeal be made to the oracles of God, is 'every one that is born of the Spirit.' This it is, in the judgement of the Spirit of God, to be a son or a child of God: it is, so to *believe* in God, through Christ, as 'not to commit sin,' and to enjoy at all times, and in all places, that 'peace of God which passeth all understanding.' It is, so to *hope* in God through the Son of His love, as to have not only the 'testimony of a good conscience,' but also the Spirit of God 'bearing witness with your spirits, that ye are the children of God'; whence cannot but spring the rejoicing [evermore] in Him through whom ye 'have received the atonement.' It is, so to *love* God, who hath thus loved you, as you never did love any creature: so that ye are constrained to love all men as yourselves; with a love not only ever burning in your hearts, but flaming out in all your actions and conversations, and making your whole life one 'labour of love,' one continued obedience to those commands, 'Be ye merciful, as God is merciful'; 'Be ye holy, as I the Lord am holy'; 'Be ye perfect, as your Father which is in heaven is perfect.'

2. Who then are ye that are *thus* born of God? Ye 'know the things which are given to you of God.' Ye well know that ye are the children of God, and 'can assure your hearts before Him.' And every one of you who has observed these words cannot but feel, and know of a truth, whether at this hour (answer to God, and not to man!) you are thus a child of God or no. The question is not, what you was made in baptism (do not evade); but, what are you now? Is the Spirit of adoption now in your heart? To your own heart let the appeal be made. I ask not, whether you *was* born of water and of the Spirit; but are you *now* the temple of the Holy Ghost which dwelleth in you? I allow you was 'circumcised with the circumcision of Christ' (as St. Paul emphatically terms baptism); but does the Spirit of Christ and of glory *now* rest upon you? Else, 'your circumcision is become uncircumcision.'

3. Say not then in your heart, 'I *was once* baptized, therefore I *am now* a child of God.' Alas, that consequence will by no means hold. How many are the baptized gluttons and drunkards, the baptized liars and common swearers, the baptized railers and evil-speakers, the baptized whoremongers, thieves, extortioners? What think you? Are these now the children of God? Verily, I say unto you, whosoever you are, unto whom any one of the preceding characters belong, 'Ye are of your father the devil, and the works of your father ye do.' Unto you I call, in the name of Him whom you crucify afresh, and in His words to your circumcised predecessors, 'Ye serpents, ye generation of vipers, how can ye escape the damnation of hell?'

4. How, indeed, except ye be born again? For ye are now dead in trespasses and sins. To say, then, that ye cannot be born again, that there is no new birth but in baptism, is to seal you all under damnation, to consign you to hell, without help, without hope. And perhaps some may think this just and right. In their zeal for the Lord of Hosts, they may say, 'Yea, cut off the sinners, the Amalekites! Let these Gibeonites be utterly destroyed! They deserve no less.' No; nor I, nor you. Mine and your desert, as well as theirs, is hell! and it is mere mercy, free, undeserved mercy, that *we* are not now in unquenchable fire. You will say, 'But we are washed'; we were born again 'of water and of the Spirit.' So *were* they: this, therefore, hinders not at all, but that ye may *now* be even as they. Know ye not, that 'what is highly esteemed of men is an abomination in the sight of God'? Come forth, ye 'saints of the world,' ye that are honoured of men, and see who will cast the first stone at them, at these wretches not fit to live upon the earth, these common harlots, adulterers, murderers. Only learn ye first what that meaneth, 'He that hateth his brother is a murderer' (1 John iii. 15). 'He that looketh on a woman to lust after her hath committed adultery with her already in his heart' (Matt. v. 28). 'Ye adulterers and adulteresses, know ye not that the friendship of the world is enmity with God?' (Jas. iv. 4).

5. 'Verily, verily, I say unto you, ye' also 'must be born again.' 'Except ye' also 'be born again, ye cannot see the kingdom of God.' Lean no more on the staff of that broken reed, that ye *were* born again in baptism. Who denies that ye were then made children of God, and heirs of the kingdom of heaven? But,

notwithstanding this, ye are now children of the devil. Therefore, ye must be born again. And let not Satan put it into your heart to cavil at a word, when the thing is clear. Ye have heard what are the marks of the children of God: all ye who have them not on your souls, baptized or unbaptized, must needs receive them, or without doubt ye will perish everlastingly. And if ye have been baptized, your only hope is this,—that those who were made the children of God by baptism, but are now the children of the devil, may yet again receive 'power to become the sons of God'; that they may receive again what they have lost, even the 'Spirit of adoption, crying in their hearts, Abba, Father!'

Amen, Lord Jesus! May every one who prepareth his heart yet again to seek Thy face receive again that Spirit of adoption, and cry out, 'Abba, Father!' Let him now again have power so to believe in Thy name as to become a child of God; as to know and feel he hath 'redemption in Thy blood, even the forgiveness of sins'; and that he 'cannot commit sin, because he is born of God.' Let him be now 'begotten again unto a living hope,' so as to 'purify himself as Thou art pure'; and 'because he is a son,' let the Spirit of love and of glory rest upon him, cleansing him 'from all filthiness of flesh and spirit,' and teaching him to 'perfect holiness in the fear of God'!

SERMON XV

THE GREAT PRIVILEGE OF THOSE THAT
ARE BORN OF GOD

This fine practical sermon is evidently intended to modify the uncompromising teaching of the previous discourse on the sinlessness of believers. It bears many marks of being a later composition than that: for example, the clear distinction drawn between justification and regeneration in pars. 1 and 2; the more definite statement that being born again is not 'barely the being baptized'; and the frank admission that sin is possible in those 'whom we cannot deny to have been truly born of God.' Wesley preached from this text at Lambeth on September 23, 1739, 'and showed (to the amazement, it seemed, of many who were present) how "he that is born of God doth not commit sin,"' and at Kendalshire, near Bristol, on January 17, 1740; but I doubt if it was this sermon. It does not occur in the sermon list; though the previous verse is mentioned as a text in 1752. On the whole, the evidence is that it was written in the first instance for publication, and as a supplement to Sermon XIV; though the substance of it may well have been given in the series of studies in this epistle recorded in August 1740 at the Foundery, and in November 1740 at Bristol.

Whosoever is born of God doth not commit sin.—1 JOHN iii. 9.

I. It has been frequently supposed, that the being born of God was all one with the being justified; that the new birth and justification were only different expressions, denoting the same thing: it being certain, on the one hand, that whoever is justified is also born of God; and, on the other, that whoever is born of God is also justified; yea, that both these gifts of God are given to every believer in one and the same moment. In one point of time his sins are blotted out, and he is born again of God.

2. But though it be allowed, that justification and the new birth are, in point of time, inseparable from each other, yet they are easily distinguished, as being not the same, but things of a widely different nature. Justification implies only a relative, the new birth a real, change. God in justifying us does something *for* us; in begetting us again, He does the work *in* us. The former

changes our outward relation to God, so that of enemies we become children; by the latter our inmost souls are changed, so that of sinners we become saints. The one is the taking away the guilt, the other the taking away the power, of sin: so that, although they are joined together in point of time, yet are they of wholly distinct natures.

3. The not discerning this, the not observing the wide difference there is between being justified and being born again, has occasioned exceeding great confusion of thought in many who have treated on this subject; particularly when they have attempted to explain this great privilege of the children of God; to show how 'whosoever is born of God doth not commit sin.'

4. In order to apprehend this clearly, it may be necessary, first, to consider what is the proper meaning of that expression, 'Whosoever is born of God'; and, secondly, to inquire in what sense he 'doth not commit sin.'

I. 1. First, we are to consider, what is the proper meaning of that expression, 'Whosoever is born of God.' And, in general, from all the passages of holy writ wherein this expression, 'the being born of God,' occurs, we may learn that it implies not barely the being baptized, or any outward change whatever; but a vast inward change, a change wrought in the soul, by the operation of the Holy Ghost; a change in the whole manner of our existence; for, from the moment we are born of God, we live in quite another manner than we did before; we are, as it were, in another world.

2. The ground and reason of the expression is easy to be understood. When we undergo this great change, we may, with much propriety, be said to be born again, because there is so near a resemblance between the circumstances of the natural and of the spiritual birth; so that to consider the circumstances of the natural birth, is the most easy way to understand the spiritual.

3. The child which is not yet born subsists indeed by the air, as does everything which has life; but *feels* it not, nor anything else, unless in a very dull and imperfect manner. It *hears* little, if at all; the organs of hearing being as yet closed up. It *sees* nothing; having its eyes fast shut, and being surrounded with utter darkness. There are, it may be, some faint beginnings of life,

when the time of its birth draws nigh, and some motion consequent thereon, whereby it is distinguished from a mere mass of matter; but it has no *senses*; all these avenues of the soul are hitherto quite shut up. Of consequence, it has scarce any intercourse with this visible world; nor any knowledge, conception, or idea, of the things that occur therein.

4. The reason why he that is not yet born is wholly a stranger to the visible world, is not because it is afar off (it is very nigh; it surrounds him on every side); but, partly, because he has not those senses, they are not yet opened in his soul, whereby alone it is possible to hold commerce with the material world; and partly, because so thick a veil is cast between, through which he can discern nothing.

5. But no sooner is the child born into the world, than he exists in a quite different manner. He now *feels* the air with which he is surrounded, and which pours into him from every side, as fast as he alternately breathes it back, to sustain the flame of life: and hence springs a continual increase of strength, of motion, and of sensation; all the bodily senses being now awakened, and furnished with their proper objects.

His eyes are now opened to perceive the light, which, silently flowing in upon them, discovers not only itself, but an infinite variety of things, with which before he was wholly unacquainted. His ears are unclosed, and sounds rush in with endless diversity. Every sense is employed upon such objects as are peculiarly suitable to it; and by these inlets the soul, having an open intercourse with the visible world, acquires more and more knowledge of sensible things, of all the things which are under the sun.

6. So it is with him that is born of God. Before that great change is wrought, although he subsists by Him, in whom all that have life 'live, and move, and have their being,' yet he is not *sensible* of God; he does not *feel*, he has no inward consciousness of His presence. He does not perceive that divine breath of life, without which he cannot subsist a moment: nor is he sensible of any of the things of God; they make no impression upon his soul. God is continually calling to him from on high, but he heareth not; his ears are shut, so that the 'voice of the charmer' is lost on him, 'charm he never so wisely.' He seeth not the things of the Spirit of God; the eyes of his understanding being closed,

and utter darkness covering his whole soul, surrounding him on every side. It is true he may have some faint dawnings of life, some small beginnings of spiritual motion; but as yet he has no spiritual senses capable of discerning spiritual objects; consequently, he 'discerneth not the things of the Spirit of God; he cannot know them, because they are spiritually discerned.'

7. Hence he has scarce any knowledge of the invisible world, as he has scarce any intercourse with it. Not that it is afar off: no: he is in the midst of it; it encompasses him round about. The *other world*, as we usually term it, is not far from every one of us: it is above, and beneath, and on every side. Only the natural man discerneth it not; partly, because he has no spiritual senses, whereby alone we can discern the things of God; partly, because so thick a veil is interposed as he knows not how to penetrate.

8. But when he is born of God, born of the Spirit, how is the manner of his existence changed! His whole soul is now sensible of God, and he can say, by sure experience, 'Thou art about my bed, and about my path'; I feel Thee in all my ways: 'Thou besettest me behind and before, and layest Thy hand upon me.' The spirit or breath of God is immediately inspired, breathed into the new-born soul; and the same breath which comes from, returns to, God: as it is continually received by faith, so it is continually rendered back by love, by prayer, and praise, and thanksgiving; love, and praise, and prayer being the breath of every soul which is truly born of God. And by this new kind of spiritual respiration, spiritual life is not only sustained, but increased day by day, together with spiritual strength, and motion, and sensation; all the senses of the soul being now awake, and capable of discerning spiritual good and evil.

9. 'The eyes of his understanding' are now 'open,' and he 'seeth Him that is invisible.' He sees what is 'the exceeding greatness of His power' and of His love towards them that believe. He sees that God is merciful to him a sinner; that he is reconciled through the Son of His love. He clearly perceives both the pardoning love of God, and all His 'exceeding great and precious promises.' 'God, who commanded the light to shine out of darkness, hath shined,' and doth shine, 'in his heart,' to enlighten him with 'the knowledge of the glory of God in the face of Jesus Christ.' All the darkness is now passed away, and he abides in the light of God's countenance.

10. His ears are now opened, and the voice of God no longer calls in vain. He hears and obeys the heavenly calling; he knows the voice of his Shepherd. All his spiritual senses being now awakened, he has a clear intercourse with the invisible world; and hence he knows more and more of the things which before it could not 'enter into his heart to conceive.' He now knows what the peace of God is; what is joy in the Holy Ghost; what the love of God which is shed abroad in the hearts of them that believe in Him through Christ Jesus. Thus the veil being removed which before interrupted the light and voice, the knowledge and love of God, he who is born of the Spirit dwelleth in love, 'dwelleth in God, and God in him.'

II. 1. Having considered the meaning of that expression, 'Whosoever is born of God,' it remains, in the second place, to inquire, in what sense he 'doth not commit sin.'

Now one who is so born of God, as hath been above described, who continually receives into his soul the breath of life from God, the gracious influence of His Spirit, and continually renders it back; one who thus believes and loves, who by faith perceives the continual actings of God upon his spirit, and, by a kind of spiritual reaction returns the grace he receives, in unceasing love, and praise, and prayer; not only doth not commit sin, while he thus keepeth himself, but so long as this 'seed remaineth in him, he cannot sin, because he is born of God.'

2. By sin, I here understand outward sin, according to the plain, common acceptation of the word; an actual, voluntary transgression of the law; of the revealed, written law of God; of any commandment of God, acknowledged to be such at the time that it is transgressed. But 'whosoever is born of God,' while he abideth in faith and love, and in the spirit of prayer and thanksgiving, not only doth not, but cannot, thus commit sin. So long as he thus believeth in God through Christ, and loves Him, and is pouring out his heart before Him, he cannot voluntarily transgress any command of God, either by speaking or acting what he knows God hath forbidden: so long that seed which remaineth in him, that loving, praying, thankful faith, compels him to refrain from whatsoever he knows to be an abomination in the sight of God.

3. But here a difficulty will immediately occur; and one that to many has appeared insuperable, and induced them to deny the plain assertion of the Apostle, and give up the privilege of the children of God.

It is plain, in fact, that those whom we cannot deny to have been truly born of God (the Spirit of God having given us in His Word this infallible testimony concerning them), nevertheless, not only could, but did, commit sin, even gross, outward sin. They did transgress the plain known laws of God, speaking or acting what they knew He hid forbidden.

4. Thus David was unquestionably born of God or ever he was anointed king over Israel. He knew in whom he had believed; 'he was strong in faith, giving glory to God.' 'The Lord,' saith he, 'is my Shepherd; therefore can I lack nothing. He shall feed me in green pastures, and lead me forth beside the waters of comfort. Yea, though I walk through the valley of the shadow of death, I will fear no evil; for Thou art with me' (Ps. xxiii. 1, &c.). He was filled with love; such as often constrained him to cry out, 'I will love Thee, O Lord, my strength. The Lord is my stony rock, and my defence; . . . the horn also of my salvation and my refuge' (Ps. xviii. 1, 2). He was a man of prayer; pouring out his soul before God in all circumstances of life; and abundant in praises and thanksgiving: 'Thy praise,' saith he, 'shall be ever in my mouth' (Ps. xxxiv. 1): 'Thou art my God, and I will thank Thee: Thou art my God, and I will praise Thee' (Ps. cxviii. 28). And yet such a child of God could and did commit sin; yea, the horrid sins of adultery and murder.

5. And even after the Holy Ghost was more largely given, after 'life and immortality were brought to light by the gospel,' we want not instances of the same melancholy kind, which were also doubtless written for our instruction. Thus he who (probably from his selling all that he had, and bringing the price for the relief of his poor brethren) was by the Apostles themselves 'surnamed Barnabas,' that is, 'the son of consolation' (Acts iv. 36, 37); who was so honoured at Antioch, as to be selected with Saul out of all the disciples, to carry their relief unto the brethren in Judea (Acts xi. 29, 30); this Barnabas, who, at his return from Judea, was, by the peculiar direction of the Holy Ghost, solemnly 'separated from the other prophets and teachers, for the work whereunto God had called him' (xiii. 1-4) even to

accompany the great Apostle among the Gentiles, and to be his fellow labourer in every place,—nevertheless, was afterwards so sharp (xv. 35, 39), in his contention with St. Paul (because he 'thought it not good to take with them John,' in his visiting the brethren a second time, 'who had departed from them from Pamphylia, and went not with them to the work') that he himself also departed from the work; that he 'took John, and sailed unto Cyprus' (xv. 39); forsaking him to whom he had been in so immediate a manner joined by the Holy Ghost.

6. An instance more astonishing than both these is given by St. Paul in his Epistle to the Galatians. When Peter, the aged, the zealous, the first of the apostles, one of the three most highly favoured by his Lord, 'was come to Antioch, I withstood him to the face, because he was to be blamed. For before that certain came from James, he did eat with the Gentiles'—the Heathens converted to the Christian faith—as having been peculiarly taught of God, that he 'should not call any man common or unclean' (Acts x. 28). 'But when they were come he separated himself, fearing them which were of the circumcision. And the other Jews dissembled likewise with him; insomuch that Barnabas also was carried away with their dissimulation. But when I saw that they walked not uprightly according to the truth of the gospel, I said unto Peter before them all, If thou, being a Jew, livest after the manner of the Gentiles'—not regarding the ceremonial law of Moses—'why compellest thou the Gentiles to live as do the Jews'? (Gal. ii. 11, &c.). Here is also plain, undeniable sin committed by one who was undoubtedly born of God. But how can this be reconciled with the assertion of St. John, if taken in the obvious literal meaning, that 'whosoever is born of God, doth not commit sin'?

7. I answer, What has been long observed is this: so long as 'he that is born of God keepeth himself' (which he is able to do by the grace of God), 'the wicked one toucheth him not'; but if he keepeth not himself, if he abideth not in the faith, he may commit sin even as another man.

It is easy therefore to understand, how any of these children of God might be moved from his own steadfastness, and yet the great truth of God declared by the Apostle, remain steadfast and unshaken. He did not 'keep himself,' by that grace of God which was sufficient for him. He fell, step by step, first, into negative, inward sin, not 'stirring up the gift of God which was in him,' not 'watching unto prayer,' not 'pressing on to the mark of the prize of his high calling': then into positive inward sin, inclining to wickedness with his heart, giving way to some evil desire or temper: next he lost his faith, his sight of a pardoning God, and consequently his love of God; and, being then weak and like another man, he was capable of committing even outward sin.

8. To explain this by a particular instance: David was born of God, and saw God by faith. He loved God in sincerity. He could truly say, 'Whom have I in heaven but Thee? and there is none upon earth,' neither person nor thing, 'that I desire in comparison of Thee.' But still there remained in his heart that corruption of nature which is the seed of all evil.

'He was walking upon the roof of his house' (2 Sam. xi. 2), probably praising the God whom his soul loved, when he looked down, and saw Bathsheba. He felt a temptation; a thought which tended to evil. The Spirit of God did not fail to convince him of this. He doubtless heard and knew the warning voice; but he yielded in some measure to the thought, and the temptation began to prevail over him. Hereby his spirit was sullied; he saw God still; but it was more dimly than before. He loved God still; but not in the same degree; not with the same strength and ardour of affection. Yet God checked him again, though His Spirit was grieved; and His voice, though fainter and fainter, still whispered, 'Sin lieth at the door; look unto Me and be thou saved.' But he would not hear; he looked again, not unto God but unto the forbidden object; till nature was superior to grace and kindled lust in his soul.

The eye of his mind was now closed again, and God vanished out of his sight. Faith, the divine, supernatural intercourse with God and the love of God, ceased together: he then rushed on as a horse into the battle, and knowingly committed the outward sin.

9. You see the unquestionable progress from grace to sin: thus it goes on, from step to step. (1) The divine seed of loving conquering faith, remains in him that is born of God. 'He keepeth himself,' by the grace of God, and 'cannot commit sin.' (2) A temptation arises; whether from the world, the flesh, or the devil, it matters not. (3) The Spirit of God gives him warning that sin is near, and bids him more abundantly watch unto

prayer. (4) He gives way, in some degree, to the temptation, which now begins to grow pleasing to him. (5) The Holy Spirit is grieved; his faith is weakened; and his love of God grows cold. (6) The Spirit reproves him more sharply, and saith, 'This is the way; walk thou in it.' (7) He turns away from the painful voice of God, and listens to the pleasing voice of the tempter. (8) Evil desire begins and spreads in his soul, till faith and love vanish away: he is then capable of committing outward sin, the power of the Lord being departed from him.

10. To explain this by another instance: the Apostle Peter was full of faith and of the Holy Ghost; and hereby keeping himself, he had a conscience void of offence toward God and toward man.

Walking thus in simplicity and godly sincerity, 'before that certain came from James, he did eat with the Gentiles,' knowing that what God had cleansed was not common or unclean.

But 'when they were come,' a temptation arose in his heart, 'to fear those of the circumcision' (the Jewish converts, who were zealous for circumcision and the other rites of the Mosaic law), and regard the favour and praise of these men, more than the praise of God.

He was warned by the Spirit that sin was near: nevertheless, he yielded to it in some degree, even to sinful fear of man, and his faith and love were proportionably weakened.

God reproved him again for giving place to the devil. Yet he would not hearken to the voice of his Shepherd; but gave himself up to that slavish fear, and thereby quenched the Spirit.

Then God disappeared, and faith and love being extinct, he committed the outward sin: *walking not uprightly,* not 'according to the truth of the gospel,' he 'separated himself' from his Christian brethren, and by his evil example, if not advice also, 'compelled even the Gentiles to live after the manner of the Jews'; to entangle themselves again with that 'yoke of bondage,' from which 'Christ had set them free.'

Thus it is unquestionably true, that he who is born of God, keeping himself, doth not, cannot commit sin; and yet, if he keepeth not himself, he may commit all manner of sin with greediness.

III. 1. From the preceding considerations we may learn, first, to give a clear and incontestable answer to a question which has frequently perplexed many who were sincere of heart: 'Does sin precede or follow the loss of faith? Does a child of God first commit sin, and thereby lose his faith? Or does he lose his faith first, before he can commit sin?'

I answer, Some sin of omission, at least, must necessarily precede the loss of faith; some inward sin: but the loss of faith must precede the committing outward sin.

The more any believer examines his own heart, the more will he be convinced of this: that faith, working by love, excludes both inward and outward sin from a soul watching unto prayer; that nevertheless we are even then liable to temptation, particularly to the sin that did easily beset us; that if the loving eye of the soul be steadily fixed on God, the temptation soon vanishes away: but if not, if we are εξελκομενοι (as the Apostle James speaks, chap. i. 14), *drawn out* of God by our *own desire,* and δελεαζομενοι, *caught by the bait* of present or promised pleasures; then that desire, conceived in us, brings forth sin; and having by that inward sin destroyed our faith, it casts us headlong into the snare of the devil, so that we may commit any outward sin whatever.

2. From what has been said, we may learn, secondly, what the life of God in the soul of a believer is; wherein it properly consists; and what is immediately and necessarily implied therein. It immediately and necessarily implies the continual inspiration of God's Holy Spirit; God's breathing into the soul, and the soul's breathing back what it first receives from God; a continual action of God upon the soul, and a reaction of the soul upon God; an unceasing presence of God, the loving, pardoning God, manifested to the heart, and perceived by faith; and an unceasing return of love, praise and prayer, offering up all the thoughts of our hearts, all the words of our tongues, all the works of our hands, all our body, soul, and spirit, to be a holy sacrifice, acceptable unto God in Christ Jesus.

3. And hence we may, thirdly, infer the absolute necessity of this reaction of the soul (whatsoever it be called), in order to the continuance of the divine life therein. For it plainly appears, God does not continue to act upon the soul, unless the soul reacts upon God. He prevents us indeed with the blessings of His goodness. He first loves us, and manifests Himself unto us. While we are yet afar off, He calls us to Himself, and shines upon

our hearts. But if we do not then love Him who first loved us; if we will not hearken to His voice; if we turn our eye away from Him, and will not attend to the light which He pours in upon us; His Spirit will not always strive: He will gradually withdraw, and leave us to the darkness of our own hearts. He will not continue to breathe into our soul, unless our soul breathes toward Him again; unless our love, and prayer, and thanksgiving return to Him, a sacrifice wherewith He is well pleased.

4. Let us learn, lastly, to follow that direction of the great Apostle, 'Be not high-minded, but fear.' Let us fear sin, more than death or hell. Let us have a jealous (though not painful) fear, lest we should lean to our own deceitful hearts. 'Let him that standeth take heed lest he fall.' Even he who now standeth fast in the grace of God, in the faith that overcometh the world, may nevertheless fall into inward sin, and thereby 'make shipwreck of his faith.' And how easily then will outward sin regain its dominion over him! Thou, therefore, O man of God! watch always, that thou mayest always hear the voice of God! Watch, that thou mayest pray without ceasing, at all times, and in all places, pouring out thy heart before Him! So shalt thou always believe, and always love, and never commit sin.

SERMONS XVI-XXVII

As a practical manual of Christian conduct, it would be hard to find anything so good as this noble series of thirteen sermons. Nothing could prove more conclusively that Wesley's enthusiastic preaching of justification by faith gave no excuse to his followers for 'making void the law through faith.' Their ethical teaching glows throughout with spiritual fervour; and their appeal to the conscience is irresistible. They are a candle of the Lord, searching the innermost parts of the soul; and in reading them once again, I have been driven to my knees in penitence and confession, many and many a time.

As an exposition of the Sermon on the Mount, they have certain obvious deficiencies. There is no attempt to show the relation of our Lord's teaching to the Old Testament Scriptures and to the current thought of His own time. Nor is there any discussion of the relation of St. Matthew's version to that given in St. Luke's Gospel. It is now generally agreed that we have in Luke vi. 20-49 a report of the discourse as it was delivered by our Lord; and that the author of the first Gospel (Matthew or another) has incorporated with it many sayings of our Lord spoken at other times and under other circumstances, which in his judgement threw light upon various points dealt with; and made the survey of the ethics of the kingdom more complete. Moreover, he has given a deeper spiritual meaning to some of the sayings than they conveyed in their first form; as when he changes 'Blessed are ye poor' to 'Blessed are the poor in spirit.' But we who believe in the inspiration of the Scriptures recognize in these additions and modifications the comment of the Spirit of Christ upon His words; and His comments have no less authority than the text on which they are based. And if Wesley finds in the Beatitudes, as he does, a summary of the Christian life, beginning with repentance and proceeding through justification to entire sanctification, it is no real objection to say that the meaning he attaches to them cannot have been that which was suggested to the minds of the first hearers of the sermon on the hill in Galilee; for he, too, wrote under the influence of the same Spirit, who has been given to guide Christ's people into all the truth.

The foundation of these sermons was laid on the good ship *Simmonds* during Wesley's voyage to Georgia in 1735. We have Ingham's authority for saying that 'during the voyage Wesley went over our Saviour's Sermon on the Mount.' In the *Journal* for April 1, 1739.

Wesley says: 'In the evening, Mr. Whitefield being gone [i.e. to visit the Baldwin Street Society; he did not leave Bristol till the next morning], I began expounding our Lord's Sermon on the Mount (one pretty remarkable precedent of field-preaching, though I suppose there were churches at that time also) to a little society which was accustomed to meet once or twice a week in Nicholas Street.' This was in Bristol, whither he had come the day before to meet Whitefield. On February 17 Whitefield had for the first time preached in the open air to some two hundred colliers at Kingswood; and had continued his outdoor services during the intervening six weeks. Wesley heard him at the Bowling Green this same Sunday morning. 'I could scarce reconcile myself at first,' he says, 'to this strange way of preaching in the fields, . . . having been all my life (till very lately) so tenacious of every point relating to decency and order, that I should have thought the saving of souls almost a sin if it had not been done in a church.' However, on Monday, April 2, he says: 'At four in the afternoon I submitted to be more vile, and proclaimed in the highways the glad tidings of salvation, speaking from a little eminence in a ground adjoining to the city to about three thousand people. The text was Isa. lxi. 1, 2; the place was in St. Philip's Marsh near the junction of Old Bread Street and Cheese Lane, then called the Brickyard, and now occupied by the goods-yard of the Midland Railway. On Saturday, July 21, he records: 'I began expounding, a second time, our Lord's Sermon on the Mount. In the morning, Sunday the 22nd, as I was explaining "Blessed are the poor in spirit" to about three thousand people, we had a fair opportunity of showing all men what manner of spirit we were of; for in the middle of the sermon the pressgang came, and seized on one of the hearers.' This service was held on the Bowling Green in the heart of Bristol. Again in October he went through the Sermon on the Mount and the Epistles of St. John 'in Temple Backs,' still in Bristol. On Monday, June 16, 1740, he expounded Matt. v at Mr. Crouch's in London; and in September he went to get a little retirement to the vicarage at Bexley, a village in Kent, about a dozen miles south-east of London, where his old friend the Rev. Henry Piers was the incumbent; 'where in the mornings and evenings I expounded the Sermon on the Mount.' The exposition was repeated once more at Kingswood in January 1741. In June 1742, on Sunday the 13th, he relates: 'At six I preached for the last time in Epworth churchyard to a vast multitude gathered together from all points, on the beginning of our Lord's Sermon on the Mount. I continued among them for near three hours; and yet we scarce knew how to part.' There are many records of the preaching of individual sermons from the series to the end of Wesley's life. The first nine were published in Vol. II of the sermons in 1748; the remaining four in Vol. III in 1750. No. XII was published separately in 1758 under the title of *A Caution against False Prophets, particularly Recommended to the People called Methodists.*

SERMON XVI

UPON OUR LORD'S SERMON ON THE MOUNT

DISCOURSE I

This particular sermon is recorded as having been preached near Chepstow on October 15, 1739, and at Whitechapel on June 21, 1740. On September 17, 1739, Wesley preached at Plaistow on 'Blessed are they that mourn.' 'It pleased God,' he says, 'to give us in that hour two living instances of that piercing sense both of the guilt and power of sin, that dread of the wrath of God, and that full conviction of man's inability either to remove the power, or atone for the guilt, of sin (called by the world despair); in which properly consist that poverty of spirit and mourning which are the gate of Christian blessedness.' He preached again from this text at Wapping on July 11, 1740.

And seeing the multitudes, He went up into a mountain: and when He was set,
   His disciples came unto Him:
And He opened His mouth, and taught them, saying,
Blessed are the poor in spirit: for theirs is the kingdom of heaven.
Blessed are they that mourn: for they shall be comforted.—MATT. v. 1-4.

I. OUR LORD had now gone 'about all Galilee' (Matt. iv. 23), beginning at the time 'when John was cast into prison' (verse 12), not only 'teaching in their synagogues, and preaching the gospel of the kingdom,' but likewise 'healing all manner of sickness and all manner of disease among the people.' It was a natural consequence of this, that 'there followed Him great multitudes from Galilee, and from Decapolis, and from Jerusalem, and from Judea, and from the region beyond Jordan' (verse 25). 'And seeing the multitudes,' whom no synagogue could contain, even had there been any at hand, 'He went up into a mountain,' where there was room for all that came unto Him from every quarter. 'And when He was set,' as the manner of the Jews was, 'His disciples came unto Him. And He opened His mouth' (an expression denoting the beginning of a solemn discourse), 'and taught them, saying. . . .'

2. Let us observe, who it is that is here speaking, that we may

take heed how we hear. It is the Lord of heaven and earth, the
Creator of all; who, as such, has a right to dispose of all His
creatures; the Lord our Governor, whose kingdom is from
everlasting, and ruleth over all; the great Lawgiver, who can well
enforce all His laws, being 'able to save and to destroy,' yea, to
punish with 'everlasting destruction from His presence and
from the glory of His power.' It is the eternal Wisdom of the
Father, who knoweth whereof we are made and understands
our inmost frame; who knows how we stand related to God, to
one another, to every creature which God hath made, and,
consequently, how to adapt every law He prescribes to all the
circumstances wherein He hath placed us. It is He who is 'loving
unto every man, whose mercy is over all His works'; the God of
love, who, having emptied Himself of His eternal glory, is come
forth from His Father to declare His will to the children of men,
and then goeth again to the Father; who is sent of God 'to open
the eyes of the blind, and to give light to them that sit in
darkness.' It is the great Prophet of the Lord, concerning whom
God had solemnly declared long ago, 'Whosoever will not
hearken unto My words which He shall speak in My name, I will
require it of him' (Deut. xviii. 19); or, as the Apostle expresses it,
'Every soul which will not hear that Prophet shall be destroyed
from among the people' (Acts iii. 23).

3. And what is it which He is teaching? The Son of God, who
came from heaven, is here showing us the way to heaven; to the
place which He hath prepared for us; the glory He had before
the world began. He is teaching us the true way to life
everlasting; the royal way which leads to the kingdom; and the
only true way—for there is none besides: all other paths lead to
destruction. From the character of the Speaker, we are well
assured that He hath declared the full and perfect will of God.
He hath uttered not one tittle too much—nothing more than He
had received of the Father; nor too little—He hath not shunned
to declare the whole counsel of God; much less hath He uttered
anything wrong, anything contrary to the will of Him that sent
Him. All His words are true and right concerning all things, and
shall stand fast for ever and ever.

And we may easily remark, that in explaining and confirming
these faithful and true sayings, He takes care to refute not only
the mistakes of the Scribes and Pharisees, which then were the

false comments whereby the Jewish teachers of that age had perverted the Word of God, but all the practical mistakes that are inconsistent with salvation, which should ever arise in the Christian church; all the comments whereby the Christian teachers (so called) of any age or nation should pervert the Word of God, and teach unwary souls to seek death in the error of their life.

4. And hence we are naturally led to observe, whom it is that He is here teaching. Not the Apostles alone: if so, He had no need to have gone up into the mountain. A room in the house of Matthew, or any of His disciples, would have contained the twelve. Nor does it in any wise appear that the disciples who came unto Him were the twelve only. Οι μαθηται αυτου, without any force put upon the expression, may be understood of all who desired to learn of Him. But to put this out of all question, to make it undeniably plain that where it is said, 'He opened His mouth and taught them,' the word them includes all the multitudes who went up with Him into the mountain, we need only observe the concluding verses of the seventh chapter: 'And it came to pass, when Jesus had ended these sayings, the multitudes (οι οχλοι) were astonished at His doctrine,' or teaching; 'for He taught them,' the multitudes, 'as one having authority, and not as the Scribes.'

Nor was it only those multitudes who were with Him on the mount, to whom He now taught the way of salvation; but all the children of men; the whole race of mankind; the children that were yet unborn; all the generations to come, even to the end of the world, who should ever hear the words of this life.

5. And this all men allow, with regard to some parts of the ensuing discourse. No man, for instance, denies that what is said of poverty of spirit relates to all mankind. But many have supposed, that other parts concerned only the Apostles, or the first Christians, or the ministers of Christ; and were never designed for the generality of men, who, consequently, have nothing at all to do with them.

But may we not justly inquire, who told them this, that some parts of this discourse concerned only the Apostles, or the Christians of the apostolic age, or the ministers of Christ? Bare assertions are not a sufficient proof to establish a point of so great importance. Has then our Lord Himself taught us, that some parts of His discourse do not concern all mankind? Without doubt, had it been so, He would have told us; He could not have omitted so necessary an information. But has He told us so? Where? In the discourse itself? No; here is not the least intimation of it. Has He said so elsewhere? in any other of His discourses? Not one word so much as glancing this way can we find in anything He ever spoke, either to the multitudes, or to His disciples. Has any one of the Apostles, or other inspired writers, left such an instruction upon record? No such thing. No assertion of this kind is to be found in all the oracles of God. Who then are the men who are so much wiser than God—wise so far above that is written?

6. Perhaps they will say, that the reason of the thing requires such a restriction to be made. If it does, it must be on one of these two accounts; because, without such a restriction, the discourse would either be apparently absurd, or would contradict some other scripture. But this is not the case. It will plainly appear, when we come to examine the several particulars, that there is no absurdity at all in applying all which our Lord hath here delivered to all mankind. Neither will it infer any contradiction to anything else He has delivered, nor to any other scripture whatever. Nay, it will farther appear, that either all the parts of this discourse are to be applied to men in general, or no part; seeing they are all connected together, all joined as the stones in an arch, of which you cannot take one away, without destroying the whole fabric.

7. We may, lastly, observe, how our Lord teaches here. And surely, as at all times, so particularly at this, He speaks 'as never man spake.' Not as the holy men of old; although they also spoke 'as they were moved by the Holy Ghost.' Not as Peter, or James, or John, or Paul: they were indeed wise master-builders in His Church; but still in this, in the degrees of heavenly wisdom, the servant is not as his Lord. No, nor even as Himself at any other time, or on any other occasion. It does not appear, that it was ever His design, at any other time or place, to lay down at once the whole plan of His religion; to give us a full prospect of Christianity; to describe at large the nature of that holiness without which no man shall see the Lord. Particular branches of this He has indeed described, on a thousand different occasions; but never, besides here, did He give, of set purpose, a general

view of the whole. Nay, we have nothing else of this kind in all the Bible; unless one should except that short sketch of holiness delivered by God in those ten words or commandments to Moses, on mount Sinai. But even here how wide a difference is there between one and the other! 'Even that which was made glorious had no glory in this respect, by reason of the glory that excelleth' (2 Cor. iii. 10).

8. Above all, with what amazing love does the Son of God here reveal His Father's will to man! He does not bring us again 'to the mount that burned with fire, nor unto blackness, and darkness, and tempest.' He does not speak as when He 'thundered out of heaven'; when the Highest 'gave His thunder, hailstones, and coals of fire.' He now addresses us with His still, small voice,—'Blessed,' or happy, 'are the poor in spirit.' Happy are the mourners; the meek; those that hunger after righteousness; the merciful; the pure in heart: happy in the end, and in the way; happy in this life, and in life everlasting! As if He had said, 'Who is he that lusteth to live, and would fain see good days? Behold, I show you the thing which your soul longeth for! See the way you have so long sought in vain; the way of pleasantness; the path to calm, joyous peace, to heaven below, and heaven above!'

9. At the same time, with what authority does He teach! Well might they say, 'Not as the Scribes.' Observe the manner (but it cannot be expressed in words), the air, with which He speaks! Not as Moses, the servant of God; not as Abraham, His friend; not as any of the prophets; nor as any of the sons of men. It is something more than human; more than can agree to any created being. It speaks the Creator of all! A God, a God appears! Yea, 'Ο 'ΩΝ, the Being of beings. JEHOVAH, the Self-existent, the Supreme, the God who is over all blessed for ever.

10. This divine discourse, delivered in the most excellent method, every subsequent part illustrating those that precede, is commonly, and not improperly, divided into three principal branches: the first contained in the fifth, the second in the sixth, and the third in the seventh chapter. In the first, the sum of all true religion is laid down in eight particulars, which are explained, and guarded against the false glosses of man, in the following parts of the fifth chapter. In the second are rules for

that right intention which we are to preserve in all our outward actions, unmixed with worldly desires, or anxious cares for even the necessaries of life. In the third are cautions against the main hindrances of religion, closed with an application of the whole.

I. 1. Our Lord first lays down the sum of all true religion in eight particulars, which He explains and guards against the false glosses of men, to the end of the fifth chapter.

Some have supposed that He designed, in these, to point out the several stages of the Christian course—the steps which a Christian successively takes in his journey to the promised land; others, that all the particulars here set down belong at all times to every Christian. And why may we not allow both the one and the other? What inconsistency is there between them? It is undoubtedly true, that both poverty of spirit, and every other temper which is here mentioned, are at all times found, in a greater or less degree, in every real Christian. And it is equally true, that real Christianity always begins in poverty of spirit and goes on in the order here set down, till the 'man of God is made perfect.' We begin at the lowest of these gifts of God; yet so as not to relinquish this, when we are called of God to come up higher; but 'whereunto we have already attained, we hold fast,' while we press on to what is yet before, to the highest blessings of God in Christ Jesus.

2. The foundation of all is poverty of spirit: here, therefore, our Lord begins: 'Blessed,' saith He, 'are the poor in spirit; for theirs is the kingdom of heaven.'

It may not improbably be supposed, that our Lord looked on those who were round about Him, and, observing that not many rich were there, but rather the poor of the world, took occasion from thence to make a transition from temporal to spiritual things. 'Blessed,' saith He (or *happy*—so the word should be rendered, both in this and the following verses), 'are the poor in spirit.' He does not say, they that are poor as to outward circumstances, it being not impossible that some of these may be as far from happiness as a monarch upon his throne; but 'the poor in spirit'—they who, whatever their outward circumstances are, have that disposition of heart which is the first step to all real, substantial happiness, either in this world, or that which is to come.

3. Some have judged, that by the poor in spirit here, are meant those who love poverty; those who are free from covetousness, from the love of money; who fear, rather than desire, riches. Perhaps they have been induced so to judge, by wholly confining their thoughts to the very term; or by considering that weighty observation of St. Paul, that 'the love of money is the root of all evil.' And hence many have wholly divested themselves, not only of riches, but of all worldly goods. Hence also the vows of voluntary poverty seem to have arisen in the Romish Church; it being supposed that so eminent a degree of this fundamental grace must be a large step toward the 'kingdom of heaven.'

But these do not seem to have observed, first, that the expression of St. Paul must be understood with some restriction; otherwise it is not true; for the love of money is not the root, the sole root, of all evil. There are a thousand other roots of evil in the world, as sad experience daily shows. His meaning can only be, it is the root of very many evils; perhaps of more than any single vice besides. Secondly, that this sense of the expression, 'poor in spirit,' will by no means suit our Lord's present design, which is to lay a general foundation whereon the whole fabric of Christianity may be built; a design which would be in no wise answered by guarding against one particular vice: so that, if even this were supposed to be one part of His meaning, it could not possibly be the whole. Thirdly, that it cannot be supposed to be any part of His meaning, unless we charge Him with manifest tautology; seeing, if poverty of spirit were only freedom from covetousness, from the love of money, or the desire of riches, it would coincide with what He afterwards mentions, it would be only a branch of purity of heart.

4. Who then are 'the poor in spirit'? Without question, the humble; they who know themselves; who are convinced of sin; those to whom God hath given that first repentance, which is previous to faith in Christ.

One of these can no longer say, 'I am rich, and increased in goods, and have need of nothing'; as now knowing, that he is 'wretched, and poor, and miserable, and blind, and naked.' He is convinced that he is spiritually poor indeed; having no spiritual good abiding in him. 'In me,' saith he, 'dwelleth no good thing,' but whatsoever is evil and abominable. He has a deep sense of the loathsome leprosy of sin which he brought with him from his mother's womb, which overspreads his whole soul, and totally corrupts every power and faculty thereof. He sees more and more of the evil tempers which spring from that evil root: the pride and haughtiness of spirit, the constant bias to think of himself more highly than he ought to think; the vanity, the thirst after the esteem or honour that cometh from men; the hatred or envy, the jealousy or revenge, the anger, malice, or bitterness; the inbred enmity both against God and man, which appears in ten thousand shapes; the love of the world, the self-will, the foolish and hurtful desires, which cleave to his inmost soul. He is conscious how deeply he has offended by his tongue; if not by profane, immodest, untrue, or unkind words, yet by discourse which was not 'good to the use of edifying,' not 'meet to minister grace to the hearers,' which, consequently, was all corrupt in God's account, and grievous to His Holy Spirit. His evil works are now likewise ever in his sight: if he tells them, they are more than he is able to express. He may as well think to number the drops of rain, the sands of the sea, or the days of eternity.

5. His guilt is now also before his face: he knows the punishment he has deserved, were it only on account of his carnal mind, the entire, universal corruption of his nature: how much more, on account of all his evil desires and thoughts, of all his sinful words and actions! He cannot doubt for a moment, but the least of these deserves the damnation of hell—'the worm that dieth not, and the fire that never shall be quenched.' Above all, the guilt of 'not believing on the name of the only-begotten Son of God' lies heavy upon him. How, saith he, shall I escape, who 'neglect so great salvation'! 'He that believeth not is condemned already,' and 'the wrath of God abideth on him.'

6. But what shall he give in exchange for his soul, which is forfeited to the just vengeance of God? 'Wherewithal shall he come before the Lord?' How shall he pay Him that he oweth? Were he from this moment to perform the most perfect obedience to every command of God, this would make no amends for a single sin for any one act of past disobedience; seeing he owes God all the service he is able to perform, from this moment to all eternity: could he pay this, it would make no manner of amends for what he ought to have done before. He sees himself therefore utterly helpless with regard to atoning for

his past sins; utterly unable to make any amends to God, to pay any ransom for his own soul.

But if God would forgive him all that is past, on this one condition, that he should sin no more; that for the time to come he should entirely and constantly obey all His commands; he well knows that this would profit him nothing, being a condition he could never perform. He knows and feels that he is not able to obey even the outward commands of God; seeing these cannot be obeyed while his heart remains in its natural sinfulness and corruption; inasmuch as an evil tree cannot bring forth good fruit. But he cannot cleanse a sinful heart: with men this is impossible: so that he is utterly at a loss even how to begin walking in the path of God's commandments. He knows not how to get one step forward in the way. Encompassed with sin, and sorrow, and fear, and finding no way to escape, he can only cry out, 'Lord, save, or I perish!'

7. Poverty of spirit then, as it implies the first step we take in running the race which is set before us, is a just sense of our inward and outward sins, and of our guilt and helplessness. This some have monstrously styled 'the virtue of humility'; thus teaching us to be proud of knowing we deserve damnation! But our Lord's expression is quite of another kind; conveying no idea to the hearer, but that of mere want, of naked sin, of helpless guilt and misery.

8. The great apostle, where he endeavours to bring sinners to God, speaks in a manner just answerable to this. 'The wrath of God,' saith he, 'is revealed from heaven against all ungodliness and unrighteousness of men' (Rom. i. 18 &c.); a charge which he immediately fixes on the heathen world, and thereby proves they are under the wrath of God. He next shows that the Jews were no better than they, and were therefore under the same condemnation; and all this, not in order to their attaining 'the noble virtue of humility,' but 'that every mouth might be stopped, and all the world become guilty before God.'

He proceeds to show, that they were helpless as well as guilty; which is the plain purport of all those expressions: 'Therefore by the deeds of the law there shall no flesh be justified'; 'But now the righteousness of God, which is by faith of Jesus Christ, without the law, is manifested'; 'We conclude, that a man is justified by faith, without the deeds of the law,'—expressions all tending to the same point, even to 'hide pride from man'; to humble him to the dust, without teaching him to reflect upon his humility as a virtue; to inspire him with that full, piercing conviction of his utter sinfulness, guilt, and helplessness, which casts the sinner, stripped of all, lost and undone, on his strong Helper, Jesus Christ the righteous.

9. One cannot but observe here, that Christianity begins just where heathen morality ends; poverty of spirit, conviction of sin, the renouncing ourselves, the not having our own righteousness (the very first point in the religion of Jesus Christ), leaving all pagan religion behind. This was ever hid from the wise men of this world; insomuch that the whole Roman language, even with all the improvements of the Augustan age, does not afford so much as a name for *humility* (the word from whence we borrow this, as is well known, bearing in Latin a quite different meaning); no, nor was one found in all the copious language of Greece, till it was made by the great apostle.

10. O that we may feel what they were not able to express! Sinner, awake! Know thyself! Know and feel, that thou wert 'shapen in wickedness,' and that 'in sin did thy mother conceive thee'; and that thou thyself hast been heaping sin upon sin, ever since thou couldest discern good from evil! Sink under the mighty hand of God, as guilty of death eternal; and cast off, renounce, abhor, all imagination of ever being able to help thyself! Be it all thy hope to be washed in His blood, and renewed by His almighty Spirit, who Himself 'bare all our sins in His own body on the tree'! So shalt thou witness, 'Happy are the poor in spirit: for theirs is the kingdom of heaven.'

11. This is that kingdom of heaven, or of God, which is within us; even 'righteousness, and peace, and joy in the Holy Ghost.' And what is 'righteousness,' but the life of God in the soul; the mind which was in Christ Jesus; the image of God stamped upon the heart, now renewed after the likeness of Him that created it? What is it but the love of God, because He first loved us, and the love of all mankind for His sake?

And what is this 'peace,' the peace of God, but that calm serenity of soul, that sweet repose in the blood of Jesus, which leaves no doubt of our acceptance in Him; which excludes all fear, but the loving, filial fear of offending our Father which is in heaven?

This inward kingdom implies also 'joy in the Holy Ghost'; who seals upon our hearts 'the redemption which is in Jesus,' the righteousness of Christ imputed to us 'for the remission of the sins that are past'; who giveth us now 'the earnest of our inheritance,' of the crown which the Lord, the righteous Judge, will give at that day. And well may this be termed 'the kingdom of heaven'; seeing it is heaven already opened in the soul: the first springing up of those rivers of pleasure which flow at God's right hand for evermore.

12. 'Theirs is the kingdom of heaven.' Whosoever thou art, to whom God hath given to be 'poor in spirit,' to feel thyself lost, thou hast a right thereto, through the gracious promise of Him who cannot lie. It is purchased for thee by the blood of the Lamb. It is very nigh: thou art on the brink of heaven! Another step, and thou enterest into the kingdom of righteousness, and peace, and joy! Art thou all sin?—'Behold the Lamb of God, who taketh away the sin of the world!' All unholy?—see thy 'Advocate with the Father, Jesus Christ the righteous!' Art thou unable to atone for the least of thy sins?—'He is the propitiation for' all thy 'sins.' Now believe on the Lord Jesus Christ, and all thy sins are blotted out! Art thou totally unclean in soul and body?--here is the 'fountain for sin and uncleanness!' 'Arise, and wash away thy sins!' Stagger no more at the promise through unbelief! Give glory to God! Dare to believe! Now cry out, from the ground of thy heart,—

> Yes, I yield, I yield at last,
>   Listen to Thy speaking blood;
> Me, with all my sins, I cast
>   On my atoning God.

13. Then thou learnest of Him to be 'lowly of heart.' And this is the true, genuine, Christian humility, which flows from a sense of the love of God, reconciled to us in Christ Jesus. Poverty of spirit, in this meaning of the word, begins where a sense of guilt and of the wrath of God ends; and is a continual sense of our total dependence on Him, for every good thought, or word, or work; of our utter inability to all good, unless He 'water us every moment'; and an abhorrence of the praise of men,

knowing that all praise is due unto God only. With this is joined a loving shame, a tender humiliation before God, even for the sins which we know He hath forgiven us, and for the sin which still remaineth in our hearts, although we know it is not imputed to our condemnation. Nevertheless, the conviction we feel of inbred sin is deeper and deeper every day. The more we grow in grace, the more do we see of the desperate wickedness of our heart. The more we advance in the knowledge and love of God, through our Lord Jesus Christ (as great a mystery as this may appear to those who know not the power of God unto salvation), the more do we discern of our alienation from God, of the enmity that is in our carnal mind, and the necessity of our being entirely renewed in righteousness and true holiness.

II. 1. It is true, he has scarce any conception of this who now begins to know the inward kingdom of heaven. 'In his prosperity he saith, I shall never be moved; Thou, Lord, hast made my hill so strong.' Sin is so utterly bruised beneath his feet, that he can scarce believe it remaineth in him. Even temptation is silenced, and speaks not again: it cannot approach, but stands afar off. He is borne aloft in the chariots of joy and love: he soars 'as upon the wings of an eagle.' But our Lord well knew that this triumphant state does not often continue long: He therefore presently subjoins, 'Blessed are they that mourn; for they shall be comforted.'

2. Not that we can imagine this promise belongs to those who mourn only on some worldly account; who are in sorrow and heaviness merely on account of some worldly trouble or disappointment, such as the loss of their reputation or friends, or the impairing of their fortune. As little title to it have they who are afflicting themselves, through fear of some temporal evil; or who pine away with anxious care, or that desire of earthly things which 'maketh the heart sick.' Let us not think these 'shall receive anything from the Lord': He is not in all their thoughts. Therefore it is that they thus 'walk in a vain shadow, and disquiet themselves in vain.' 'And this shall ye have of Mine hand,' saith the Lord, 'ye shall lie down in sorrow.'

3. The mourners of whom our Lord here speaks, are those that mourn on quite another account: they that mourn after God; after Him in whom they did 'rejoice with joy unspeakable'

when He gave them to 'taste the good,' the pardoning 'word, and
the powers of the world to come.' But He now 'hides His face
and they are troubled'; they cannot see Him through the dark
cloud. But they see temptation and sin, which they fondly
supposed were gone never to return, arising again, following
after them amain, and holding them in on every side. It is not
strange if their soul is now disquieted within them, and trouble
and heaviness take hold upon them. Nor will their great enemy
fail to improve the occasion: to ask, 'Where is now thy God?
Where is now the blessedness whereof thou spakest? the
beginning of the kingdom of heaven? Yea, hath God said, "Thy
sins are forgiven thee?" Surely God hath not said it. It was only a
dream, a mere delusion, a creature of thy own imagination. If
thy sins are forgiven, why art thou thus? Can a pardoned sinner
be thus unholy?' And if then, instead of immediately crying to
God, they reason with him that is wiser than they, they will be in
heaviness indeed, in sorrow of heart, in anguish not to be
expressed. Nay, even when God shines again upon the soul, and
takes away all doubt of His past mercy, still he that is weak in
faith may be tempted and troubled on account of what is to
come; especially when inward sin revives, and thrusts sore at
him that he may fall. Then may he again cry out,—

> I have a sin of fear, that when I've spun
> My last thread, I shall perish on the shore!—

lest I should make shipwreck of the faith, and my last state be
worse than the first,—

> Lest all my bread of life should fail,
> And I sink down unchanged to hell!

4. Sure it is, that this 'affliction,' for the present, 'is not joyous,
but grievous; nevertheless, afterward it bringeth forth peace-
able fruit unto them that are exercised thereby.' Blessed,
therefore, are they that thus mourn, if they 'tarry the Lord's
leisure' and suffer not themselves to be turned out of the way, by
the miserable comforters of the world; if they resolutely reject
all the comforts of sin, of folly, and vanity; all the idle diversions
and amusements of the world; all the pleasures which 'perish in
the using,' and which only tend to benumb and stupefy the soul,

that it may neither be sensible of itself nor God. Blessed are they who 'follow on to know the Lord,' and steadily refuse all other comfort. They shall be comforted by the consolations of His Spirit; by a fresh manifestation of His love; by such a witness of His accepting them in the Beloved, as shall never more be taken away from them. This 'full assurance of faith' swallows up all doubt, as well as all tormenting fear; God now giving them a sure hope of an enduring substance, and 'strong consolation through grace.' Without disputing whether it be possible for any of those to 'fall away, who were once enlightened, and made partakers of the Holy Ghost,' it suffices them to say, by the power now resting upon them, 'Who shall separate us from the love of Christ? . . . I am persuaded, that neither death, nor life, nor things present, nor things to come, nor height, nor depth, shall be able to separate us from the love of God, which is in Christ Jesus our Lord' (Rom. viii. 35-39).

5. This whole process, both of mourning for an absent God, and recovering the joy of His countenance, seems to be shadowed out in what our Lord spoke to His Apostles, the night before His passion: 'Do ye inquire of that I said, A little while, and ye shall not see Me: and again, a little while and ye shall see Me? Verily, verily, I say unto you, That ye shall weep and lament'; namely, when ye do not see Me; 'but the world shall rejoice'; shall triumph over you, as though your hope were now come to an end. 'And ye shall be sorrowful,' through doubt, through fear, through temptation, through vehement desire; 'but your sorrow shall be turned into joy,' by the return of Him whom your soul loveth, 'A woman when she is in travail hath sorrow, because her hour is come: but as soon as she is delivered of the child, she remembereth no more the anguish, for joy that a man is born into the world. And ye now have sorrow': ye mourn, and cannot be comforted: 'but I will see you again, and your heart shall rejoice,' with calm inward joy, 'and your joy no man taketh from you' (John xvi. 19-22).

6. But although this mourning is at an end, is lost in holy joy, by the return of the Comforter, yet is there another, and a blessed mourning it is, which abides in the children of God. They still mourn for the sins and miseries of mankind: they 'weep with them that weep.' They weep for them that weep not for themselves, for the sinners against their own souls. They

mourn for the weakness and unfaithfulness of those that are, in some measure, saved from their sins. 'Who is weak, and they are not weak? Who is offended, and they burn not?' They are grieved for the dishonour continually done to the Majesty of heaven and earth. At all times they have an awful sense of this, which brings a deep seriousness upon their spirits; a seriousness which is not a little increased since the eyes of their understanding were opened, by their continually seeing the vast ocean of eternity, without a bottom or a shore, which has already swallowed up millions of millions of men, and is gaping to devour them that yet remain. They see here the house of God eternal in the heavens; there, hell and destruction without a covering; and thence feel the importance of every moment, which just appears, and is gone for ever!

7. But all this wisdom of God is foolishness with the world. The whole affair of mourning and poverty of spirit is with them stupidity and dullness. Nay, it is well if they pass so favourable a judgement upon it; if they do not vote it to be mere moping and melancholy, if not downright lunacy and distraction. And it is no wonder at all, that this judgement should be passed by those who know not God. Suppose, as two persons were walking together, one should suddenly stop, and with the strongest signs of fear and amazement, cry out, 'On what a precipice do we stand! See, we are on the point of being dashed in pieces! Another step, and we shall fall into that huge abyss! Stop! I will not go on for all the world!'—when the other, who seemed, to himself at least, equally sharpsighted looked forward and saw nothing of all this; what would he think of his companion, but that he was beside himself; that his head was out of order; that much religion (if he was not guilty of 'much learning') had certainly made him mad!

8. But let not the children of God, 'the mourners in Sion,' be moved by any of these things. Ye, whose eyes are enlightened, be not troubled by those who walk on still in darkness. Ye do not walk on in a vain shadow: God and eternity are real things. Heaven and hell are in very deed open before you; and ye are on the edge of the great gulf. It has already swallowed up more than words can express, nations, and kindreds, and peoples, and tongues; and still yawns to devour, whether they see it or no, the giddy, miserable children of men. O cry aloud! Spare not! Lift up your voice to Him who grasps both time and eternity, both

for yourselves and your brethren, that ye may be counted worthy to escape the destruction that cometh as a whirlwind! that ye may be brought safe through all the waves and storms, into the haven where you would be! Weep for yourselves, till He wipes away the tears from your eyes. And even then, weep for the miseries that come upon the earth, till the Lord of all shall put a period to misery and sin, shall wipe away the tears from all faces, and 'the knowledge of the Lord shall cover the earth, as the waters cover the sea.'

SERMON XVII

UPON OUR LORD'S SERMON ON THE MOUNT

DISCOURSE II

On October 19, 1739 Wesley was at Cardiff, and says: 'At six almost the whole town (I was informed) came together, to whom I explained the six last Beatitudes; but my heart was so enlarged I knew not how to give over, so that we continued three hours.' Matt. v. 6 was his text at Spitalfields on December 30, 1760.

Blessed are the meek : for they shall inherit the earth.
Blessed are they which do hunger and thirst after righteousness: for they shall be
filled.
Blessed are the merciful: for they shall obtain mercy.—MATT. v. 5-7.

I. 1. When 'the winter is past,' when 'the time of singing is come, and the voice of the turtle is heard in the land'; when He that comforts the mourners is now returned, 'that He may abide with them for ever'; when, at the brightness of His presence, the clouds disperse, the dark clouds of doubt and uncertainty, the storms of fear flee away, the waves of sorrow subside, and their spirit again rejoiceth in God their Saviour; then is it that this word is eminently fulfilled; then those whom He hath comforted can bear witness, 'Blessed,' or happy, 'are the meek; for they shall inherit the earth.'

2. But who are 'the meek'? Not those who grieve at nothing, because they know nothing; who are not discomposed at the evils that occur, because they discern not evil from good. Not those who are sheltered from the shocks of life by a stupid insensibility; who have, either by nature or art the virtue of stocks and stones, and resent nothing, because they feel nothing. Brute philosophers are wholly unconcerned in this matter. Apathy is as far from meekness as from humanity. So that one would not easily conceive how any Christians of the purer ages, especially any of the Fathers of the Church, could confound

these, and mistake one of the foulest errors of Heathenism for a branch of true Christianity.

3. Nor does Christian meekness imply, the being without zeal for God, any more than it does ignorance or insensibility. No; it keeps clear of every extreme, whether in excess or defect. It does not destroy but balance the affections, which the God of nature never designed should be rooted out by grace, but only brought and kept under due regulations. It poises the mind aright. It holds an even scale, with regard to anger, and sorrow, and fear; preserving the mean in every circumstance of life, and not declining either to the right hand or the left.

4. Meekness, therefore, seems properly to relate to ourselves: but it may be referred either to God or our neighbour. When this due composure of mind has reference to God, it is usually termed 'resignation'; a calm acquiescence in whatsoever is His will concerning us, even though it may not be pleasing to nature; saying continually, 'It is the Lord; let Him do what seemeth Him good.' When we consider it more strictly with regard to ourselves, we style it 'patience' or 'contentedness.' When it is exerted toward other men, then it is 'mildness' to the good and 'gentleness' to the evil.

5. They who are truly meek can clearly discern what is evil; and they can also suffer it. They are sensible of everything of this kind, but still, meekness holds the reins. They are exceeding 'zealous for the Lord of hosts'; but their zeal is always guided by knowledge, and tempered, in every thought, and word, and work, with the love of man, as well as the love of God. They do not desire to extinguish any of the passions which God has for wise ends implanted in their nature; but they have the mastery of all: they hold them all in subjection, and employ them only in subservience to those ends. And thus even the harsher and more unpleasing passions are applicable to the noblest purposes; even hatred, anger, and fear, when engaged against sin and regulated by faith and love, are as walls and bulwarks to the soul, so that the wicked one cannot approach to hurt it.

6. It is evident, this divine temper is not only to abide but to increase in us day by day. Occasions of exercising, and thereby increasing it, will never be wanting while we remain upon earth. 'We have need of patience, that after we have done' and suffered 'the will of God, we may receive the promise.' We have need of

resignation, that we may in all circumstances say, 'Not as I will, but as Thou wilt.' And we have need of 'gentleness toward all men'; but especially toward the evil and unthankful: otherwise we shall be overcome of evil, instead of overcoming evil with good.

7. Nor does meekness restrain only the outward act, as the Scribes and Pharisees taught of old, and the miserable teachers who are not taught of God will not fail to do in all ages. Our Lord guards against this, and shows the true extent of it, in the following words: 'Ye have heard that it was said by them of old time, Thou shalt not kill; and whosoever shall kill shall be in danger of the judgement' (Matt. v. 21, &c.): 'But I say unto you, That whosoever is angry with his brother without a cause shall be in danger of the judgement: and whosoever shall say to his brother, Raca, shall be in danger of the council: but whosoever shall say, Thou fool, shall be in danger of hell-fire.'

8. Our Lord here ranks under the head of murder, even that anger which goes no farther than the heart; which does not show itself by any outward unkindness, no, not so much as a passionate word. 'Whosoever is angry with his brother,' with any man living, seeing we are all brethren; whosoever feels any unkindness in his heart, any temper contrary to love; whosoever is angry without a cause, without a sufficient cause, or farther than that cause requires, 'shall be in danger of the judgement'; ενοχος εσται; *shall,* in that moment, *be obnoxious to* the righteous judgement of God.

But would not one be inclined to prefer the reading of those copies which omit the word εικη, *without a cause*? Is it not entirely superfluous? For if *anger at persons* be a temper contrary to love, how can there be a cause, a sufficient cause for it,—any that will justify it in the sight of God?

Anger at sin we allow. In this sense we may be angry, and yet we sin not. In this sense our Lord Himself is once recorded to have been angry: 'He looked round about upon them with anger, being grieved for the hardness of their hearts.' He was grieved at the sinners, and angry at the sin. And this is undoubtedly right before God.

9. 'And whosoever shall say to his brother, Raca'—whosoever shall give way to anger, so as to utter any contemptuous word. It is observed by commentators, that Raca is a Syriac word, which

properly signifies, *empty, vain, foolish*; so that it is as inoffensive an expression as can well be used toward one at whom we are displeased. And yet, whosoever shall use this, as our Lord assures us, 'shall be in danger of the council'; rather, shall be obnoxious thereto: he shall be liable to a severer sentence from the Judge of all the earth.

'But whosoever shall say, Thou fool'—whosoever shall so give place to the devil, as to break out into reviling, into designedly reproachful and contumelious language—'shall be obnoxious to hell-fire'; shall, in that instant, be liable to the highest condemnation. It should be observed, that our Lord describes all these as obnoxious to capital punishment. The first to strangling, usually inflicted on those who were condemned in one of the inferior courts; the second, to stoning, which was frequently inflicted on those who were condemned by the great Council at Jerusalem; the third, to burning alive, inflicted only on the highest offenders, in the 'valley of the sons of Hinnom'; Ται Εννομ, from which that word is evidently taken which we translate 'hell.'

10. And whereas men naturally imagine, that God will excuse their defect in some duties, for their exactness in others; our Lord next takes care to cut off that vain, though common imagination. He shows, that it is impossible for any sinner to *commute* with God; who will not accept one duty for another, nor take a part of obedience for the whole. He warns us, that the performing our duty to God will not excuse us from our duty to our neighbour; that works of piety as they are called, will be so far from commending us to God if we are wanting in charity, that, on the contrary that want of charity will make all those works an abomination to the Lord.

'Therefore, if thou bring thy gift to the altar and there rememberest that thy brother hath aught against thee'—on account of thy unkind behaviour toward him, of thy calling him, 'Raca,' or, 'Thou fool'—think not that thy gift will atone for thy anger; or that it will find any acceptance with God, so long as thy conscience is defiled with the guilt of unrepented sin. 'Leave there thy gift before the altar, and go thy way; first be reconciled to thy brother' (at least do all that in thee lies toward being reconciled), 'and then come and offer thy gift' (Matt. v. 23, 24).

11. And let there be no delay in what so nearly concerneth thy

soul. 'Agree with thine adversary quickly'—now; upon the spot; 'whiles thou art in the way with him'—if it be possible, before he go out of thy sight; 'lest at any time the adversary deliver thee to the judge'—lest he appeal to God the judge of all; 'and the judge deliver thee to the officer'—to Satan, the executioner of the wrath of God; 'and thou be cast into prison'—into hell, there to be reserved to the judgement of the great day. 'Verily I say unto thee, Thou shalt by no means come out thence, till thou hast paid the uttermost farthing.' But this it is impossible for thee ever to do: seeing thou hast nothing to pay. Therefore, if thou art once in that prison, the smoke of thy torment must 'ascend up for ever and ever.'

12. Meantime 'the meek shall inherit the earth.' Such is the foolishness of worldly wisdom! The wise of the world had warned them again and again, that if they did not resent such treatment, if they would tamely suffer themselves to be thus abused, there would be no living for them upon earth; that they would never be able to procure the common necessaries of life, nor to keep even what they had; that they could expect no peace, no quiet possession, no enjoyment of anything. Most true, suppose there were no God in the world; or suppose He did not concern Himself with the children of men: but 'when God ariseth to judgement, and to help all the meek upon earth,' how doth He laugh all this heathen wisdom to scorn, and turn the 'fierceness of man to His praise'! He takes a peculiar care to provide them with all things needful for life and godliness; He secures to them the provision He hath made, in spite of the force, fraud, or malice of men; and what He secures He gives them richly to enjoy. It is sweet to them, be it little or much. As in patience they possess their souls, so they truly possess whatever God hath given them. They are always content, always pleased with what they have: it pleases them, because it pleases God: so that while their heart, their desire, their joy is in heaven, they may truly be said to 'inherit the earth.'

13. But there seems to be a yet farther meaning in these words, even that they shall have a more eminent part in 'the new earth, wherein dwelleth righteousness'; in that inheritance, a general description of which (and the particulars we shall know hereafter) St. John hath given in the twentieth chapter of the Revelation: 'And I saw an angel come down from heaven, . . .

and he laid hold on the dragon, that old serpent, . . . and bound him a thousand years. . . . And I saw the souls of them that were beheaded for the witness of Jesus, and for the Word of God, and of them which had not worshipped the beast, neither his image, neither had received his mark upon their foreheads, or in their hands; and they lived and reigned with Christ a thousand years. But the rest of the dead lived not again until the thousand years were finished. This is the first resurrection. Blessed and holy is he that hath part in the first resurrection: on such the second death hath no power, but they shall be priests of God and of Christ, and shall reign with Him a thousand years.'

II. 1. Our Lord has hitherto been more immediately employed in removing the hindrances of true religion: such is pride, the first grand hindrance of all religion, which is taken away by poverty of spirit; levity and thoughtlessness, which prevent any religion from taking root in the soul, till they are removed by holy mourning: such are anger, impatience, discontent, which are all healed by Christian meekness. And when once these hindrances are removed, these evil diseases of the soul, which were continually raising false cravings therein, and filling it with sickly appetites, the native appetite of a heaven-born spirit returns; it hungers and thirsts after righteousness: and 'blessed are they which do hunger and thirst after righteousness: for they shall be filled.'

2. Righteousness, as was observed before, is the image of God, the mind which was in Christ Jesus. It is every holy and heavenly temper in one; springing from, as well as terminating in, the love of God, as our Father and Redeemer, and the love of all men for His sake.

3. 'Blessed are they which do hunger and thirst after' this: in order fully to understand which expression, we should observe, first, that hunger and thirst are the strongest of all our bodily appetites. In like manner this hunger in the soul, this thirst after the image of God, is the strongest of all our spiritual appetites, when it is once awakened in the heart; yea, it swallows up all the rest in that one great desire,—to be renewed after the likeness of Him that created us. We should, secondly, observe, that from the time we begin to hunger and thirst, those appetites do not cease, but are more and more craving and importunate, till we

either eat and drink, or die. And even so, from the time that we begin to hunger and thirst after the whole mind which was in Christ, these spiritual appetites do not cease, but cry after their food with more and more importunity; nor can they possibly cease, before they are satisfied, while there is any spiritual life remaining. We may, thirdly, observe, that hunger and thirst are satisfied with nothing but meat and drink. If you would give to him that is hungry all the world beside, all the elegance of apparel, all the trappings of state, all the treasure upon earth, yea, thousands of gold and silver; if you would pay him ever so much honour,—he regards it not: all these things are then of no account with him. He would still say, 'These are not the things I want: give me food, or else I die.' The very same is the case with every soul that truly hungers and thirsts after righteousness. He can find no comfort in anything but this: he can be satisfied with nothing else. Whatever you offer besides, it is lightly esteemed: whether it be riches, or honour, or pleasure, he still says 'This is not the thing which I want! Give me love, or else I die!'

4. And it is as impossible to satisfy such a soul, a soul that is athirst for God, the living God with what the world accounts religion, as with what they account happiness. The religion of the world implies three things: (1) The doing no harm, the abstaining from outward sin; at least from such as is scandalous, as robbery, theft, common swearing, drunkenness: (2) The doing good, the relieving the poor; the being charitable, as it is called: (3) The using the means of grace: at least the going to church and to the Lord's supper. He in whom these three marks are found is termed by the world 'a religious man.' But will this satisfy him who hungers after God? No: it is not food for his soul. He wants a religion of a nobler kind, a religion higher and deeper than this. He can no more feed on this poor, shallow, formal thing, than he can 'fill his belly with the east wind.' True, he is careful to abstain from the very appearance of evil; he is zealous of good works; he attends all the ordinances of God: but all this is not what he longs for. This is only the outside of that religion which he insatiably hungers after. The knowledge of God in Christ Jesus; the life which is hid with Christ in God'; the being 'joined unto the Lord in one spirit'; the having 'fellowship with the Father and the Son'; the 'walking in the light as God is in the light'; the being 'purified even as He is pure,'—this is the

religion, the righteousness he thirsts after; nor can he rest, till he thus rests in God.

5. 'Blessed are they who' thus 'hunger and thirst after righteousness; for they shall be filled.' They shall be filled with the things which they long for; even with righteousness and true holiness. God shall satisfy them with the blessings of His goodness, with the felicity of His chosen. He shall feed them with the bread of heaven, with the manna of His love. He shall give them to drink of His pleasures as out of the river, which he that drinketh of shall never thirst, only for more and more of the water of life. This thirst shall endure for ever.

6. Whosoever then thou art, to whom God hath given to 'hunger and thirst after righteousness,' cry unto Him that thou mayest never lose that inestimable gift—that this divine appetite may never cease. If many rebuke thee, and bid thee hold thy peace, regard them not; yea, cry so much the more, 'Jesus, Master, have mercy on me!' 'Let me not live, but to be holy as Thou art holy!' No more 'spend thy money for that which is not bread, nor thy labour for that which satisfieth not.' Canst thou hope to dig happiness out of the earth—to find it in the things of the world? O trample under foot all its pleasures, despise its honours, count its riches as dung and dross—yea, and all the things which are beneath the sun—'for the excellency of the knowledge of Christ Jesus,' for the entire renewal of thy soul in that image of God wherein it was originally created. Beware of quenching that blessed hunger and thirst, by what the world calls 'religion'; a religion of form, of outside show, which leaves the heart as earthly and sensual as ever. Let nothing satisfy thee but the power of godliness, but a religion that is spirit and life; thy dwelling in God, and God in thee—the being an inhabitant of eternity; the entering in by the blood of sprinkling 'within the veil,' and sitting 'in heavenly places with Christ Jesus.'

III. 1. And the more they are filled with the life of God, the more tenderly will they be concerned for those who are still without God in the world, still dead in trespasses and sins. Nor shall this concern for others lose its reward. 'Blessed are the merciful: for they shall obtain mercy.'

The word used by our Lord more immediately implies the compassionate, the tender-hearted; those who, far from despising, earnestly grieve for, those that do not hunger after God.

This eminent part of brotherly love is here, by a common figure, put for the whole; so that 'the merciful,' in the full sense of the term, are they who love their neighbours as themselves.

2. Because of the vast importance of this love—without which, 'though we spake with the tongues of men and angels, though we had the gift of prophecy, and understood all mysteries, and all knowledge; though we had all faith, so as to remove mountains; yea, though we gave all our goods to feed the poor, and our very bodies to be burned, it would profit us nothing'—the wisdom of God has given us, by the Apostle Paul, a full and particular account of it; by considering which we shall most clearly discern who are the merciful that shall obtain mercy.

3. 'Charity,' or love (as it were to be wished it had been rendered throughout, being a far plainer and less ambiguous word), the love of our neighbour as Christ hath loved us, 'suffereth long'; is patient towards all men: it suffers all the weakness, ignorance, errors infirmities, all the frowardness and littleness of faith, of the children of God; all the malice and wickedness of the children of the world. And it suffers all this, not only for a time, for a short season, but to the end; still feeding our enemy when he hungers; if he thirst, still giving him drink: thus continually 'heaping coals of fire,' of melting love, 'upon his head.'

4. And in every step toward this desirable end, the 'overcoming evil with good,' 'love is kind' (χρηστεύεται, a word not easily translated): it is *soft, mild, benign*. It stands at the utmost distance from moroseness, from all harshness or sourness of spirit; and inspires the sufferer at once with the most amiable sweetness, and the most fervent and tender affection.

5. Consequently, 'love envieth not': it is impossible it should; it is directly opposite to that baneful temper. It cannot be, that he who has this tender affection to all, who earnestly wishes all temporal and spiritual blessings, all good things in this world and the world to come, to every soul that God hath made, should be pained at His bestowing any good gift on any child of man. If he has himself received the same, he does not grieve, but rejoice, that another partakes of the common benefit. If he has not, he

blesses God that his brother at least has, and is herein happier than himself. And the greater his love, the more does he rejoice in the blessings of all mankind; the farther is he removed from every kind and degree of envy toward any creature.

6. Love ου περπερευεται,—not 'vaunteth not itself'; which coincides with the very next words; but rather (as the word likewise properly imports), *is not rash* or *hasty* in judging; it will not hastily condemn any one. It does not pass a severe sentence, on a slight or sudden view of things: it first weighs all the evidence, particularly that which is brought in favour of the accused. A true lover of his neighbour is not like the generality of men, who, even in cases of the nicest nature, 'see a little, presume a great deal, and so jump to the conclusion.' No: he proceeds with wariness and circumspection, taking heed to every step; willingly subscribing to that rule of the ancient Heathen (O where will the modern Christian appear!) 'I am so far from lightly believing what one man says against another, that I will not easily believe what a man says against himself. I will always allow him second thoughts, and many times counsel too.'

7. It follows, love 'is not puffed up': it does not incline or suffer any man 'to think more highly of himself than he ought to think'; but rather to think soberly: yea, it humbles the soul unto the dust. It destroys all high conceits engendering pride; and makes us rejoice to be as nothing, to be little and vile, the lowest of all, the servant of all. They who are 'kindly affectioned one to another with brotherly love' cannot but 'in honour prefer one another.' Those who, having the same love, are of one accord, do in lowliness of mind 'each esteem other better than themselves.'

8. 'It doth not behave itself unseemly'; it is not rude, or willingly offensive to any. It 'renders to all their due; fear to whom fear, honour to whom honour'; courtesy, civility, humanity to all the world; in their several degrees 'honouring all men.' A late writer defines good breeding, nay, the highest degree of it, politeness, 'A continual desire to please, appearing in all the behaviour.' But if so, there is none so well-bred as a Christian, a lover of all mankind. For he cannot but desire to 'please all men for their good to edification': and this desire cannot be hid; it will necessarily appear in all his intercourse with men. For his 'love is without dissimulation': it will appear in all

his actions and conversation: yea, and will constrain him, though without guile, 'to become all things to all men, if by any means he may save some.'

9. And in becoming all things to all men, 'love seeketh not her own.' In striving to please all men, the lover of mankind has no eye at all to his own temporal advantage. He covets no man's silver, or gold, or apparel: he desires nothing but the salvation of their souls: yea, in some sense, he may be said, *not to seek his own* spiritual, any more than temporal, advantage; for while he is on the full stretch to save their souls from death, he, as it were, forgets himself. He does not think of himself, so long as that zeal for the glory of God swallows him up. Nay, at some times he may almost seem through an excess of love, to give up himself, both his soul and his body; while he cries out, with Moses, 'O, this people have sinned a great sin; yet now, if Thou wilt forgive their sin—; and if not, blot me out of the book which Thou hast written' (Exod. xxxii. 31, 32); or, with St. Paul, 'I could wish that myself were accursed from Christ for my brethren, my kinsmen according to the flesh' (Rom. ix. 3).

10. No marvel that such 'love is not provoked'; ου παροξυν-εται. Let it be observed, the word *easily*, strangely inserted in the translation, is not in the original: St. Paul's words are absolute. 'Love is not provoked'; it is not provoked to unkindness toward any one. Occasions indeed will frequently occur; outward provocations of various kinds; but love does not yield to provocation; it triumphs over all. In all trials it looketh unto Jesus, and is more than conqueror in His love.

It is not improbable that our translators inserted that word, as it were, to *excuse* the Apostle; who, as they supposed, might otherwise appear to be wanting in the very love which he so beautifully describes. They seem to have supposed this from a phrase in the Acts of the Apostles, which is likewise very inaccurately translated. When Paul and Barnabas disagreed concerning John, the translation runs thus, 'And the contention was so sharp between them, that they departed asunder' (Acts xv. 39). This naturally induces the reader to suppose, that they were equally sharp therein; that St. Paul, who was undoubtedly right, with regard to the point in question (it being quite improper to take John with them again, who had deserted them before), was as much provoked as Barnabas, who gave such a proof of his anger, as to leave the work for which he had been set apart by the Holy Ghost. But the original imports no such thing; nor does it affirm that St. Paul was provoked at all. It simply says, Εγενετο ουν παροξυσμος,—'And there was a sharpness,' a *paroxysm* of anger; in consequence of which Barnabas left St. Paul, took John, and went his own way. Paul then 'chose Silas and departed, being recommended by the brethren to the grace of God' (which is not said concerning Barnabas); 'and he went through Syria and Cilicia,' as he had proposed, 'confirming the churches.' But to return.

11. Love prevents a thousand provocations which would otherwise arise, because it 'thinketh no evil.' Indeed, the merciful man cannot avoid knowing many things that are evil; he cannot but see them with his own eyes, and hear them with his own ears. For love does not put out his eyes, so that it is impossible for him not to see that such things are done; neither does it take away his understanding, any more than his senses, so that he cannot but know that they are evil. For instance; when he sees a man strike his neighbour, or hears him blaspheme God, he cannot either question the thing done, or the words spoken, or doubt of their being evil: yet, ου λογιζεται το κακον. The word λογιζεται, 'thinketh,' does not refer either to our seeing and hearing, or to the first and involuntary acts of our understanding; but to our *willingly thinking* what we need not; our *inferring* evil, where it does not appear; to our *reasoning* concerning things which we do not see; our *supposing* what we have neither seen nor heard. This is what true love absolutely destroys. It tears up, root and branch, all *imagining* what we have not known. It casts out all jealousies, all evil surmisings, all readiness to believe evil. It is frank, open, unsuspicious; and, as it cannot design, so neither does it fear, evil.

12. It 'rejoiceth not in iniquity'; common as this is, even among those who bear the name of Christ, who scruple not to rejoice over their enemy, when he falleth either into affliction, or error, or sin. Indeed, how hardly can they avoid this, who are zealously attached to any party! How difficult is it for them not to be pleased with any fault which they discover in those of the opposite party,—with any real or supposed blemish, either in their principles or practice! What warm defender of any cause is clear of these? Yea, who is so calm as to be altogether free? Who

does not rejoice when his adversary makes a false step, which he thinks will advantage his own cause? Only a man of love. He alone weeps over either the sin or folly of his enemy, takes no pleasure in hearing or in repeating it, but rather desires that it may be forgotten for ever.

13. But he 'rejoiceth in the truth,' wheresoever it is found; in 'the truth which is after godliness'; bringing forth its proper fruit,—holiness of heart, and holiness of conversation. He rejoices to find that even those who oppose him, whether with regard to opinions, or some points of practice, are nevertheless lovers of God, and in other respects unreprovable. He is glad to hear good of them, and to speak all he can consistently with truth and justice. Indeed, good in general is his glory and joy, wherever diffused throughout the race of mankind. As a citizen of the world he claims a share in the happiness of all the inhabitants of it. Because he is a man, he is not unconcerned in the welfare of any man; but enjoys whatsoever brings glory to God, and promotes peace and good-will among men.

14. This 'love covereth all things' (so, without all doubt, παντα στεγει should be translated; for otherwise it would be the very same with παντα υπομενει, 'endureth all things'): because the merciful man rejoiceth not in iniquity, neither does he willingly make mention of it. Whatever evil he sees, hears, or knows, he nevertheless conceals, so far as he can without making himself 'partaker of other men's sins.' Wheresoever or with whomsoever he is, if he sees anything which he approves not, it goes not out of his lips, unless to the person concerned, if haply he may gain his brother. So far is he from making the faults or failings of others the matter of his conversation, that of the absent he never does speak at all, unless he can speak well. A talebearer, a backbiter, a whisperer, an evil-speaker, is to him all one as a murderer. He would just as soon cut his neighbour's throat, as thus murder his reputation. Just as soon would he think of diverting himself by setting fire to his neighbour's house, as of thus 'scattering abroad arrows, fire-brands, and death,' and saying, 'Am I not in sport?'

He makes one only exception. Sometimes he is convinced that it is for the glory of God or (which comes to the same) the good of his neighbour, that an evil should not be covered. In this case, for the benefit of the innocent, he is constrained to declare the guilty. But even here, (1) He will not speak at all, till love, superior love, constrains him. (2) He cannot do it from a general confused view of doing good, or promoting the glory of God, but from a clear sight of some particular end, some determinate good which he pursues. (3) Still he cannot speak unless he be fully convinced that this very means is necessary to that end; that the end cannot be answered, at least not so effectually, by any other way. (4) He then doeth it with the utmost sorrow and reluctance; using it as the last and worst medicine, a desperate remedy in a desperate case, a kind of poison never to be used but to expel poison. Consequently, (5) He uses it as sparingly as possible. And this he does with fear and trembling, lest he should transgress the law of love by speaking too much, more than he would have done by not speaking at all.

15. Love 'believeth all things.' It is always willing to think the best; to put the most favourable construction on everything. It is ever ready to believe whatever may tend to the advantage of any one's character. It is easily convinced of (what it earnestly desires) the innocence and integrity of any man; or, at least, of the sincerity of his repentance, if he had once erred from the way. It is glad to excuse whatever is amiss; to condemn the offender as little as possible; and to make all the allowance for human weakness which can be done without betraying the truth of God.

16. And when it can no longer believe, then love 'hopeth all things.' Is any evil related of any man? Love hopes that the relation is not true, that the thing related was never done. Is it certain it was?—'But perhaps it was not done with such circumstances as are related; so that, allowing the fact, there is room to hope it was not so ill as it is represented.' Was the action apparently undeniably evil? Love hopes the intention was not so. Is it clear, the design was evil too?—'Yet might it not spring from the settled temper of the heart, but from a start of passion, or from some vehement temptation, which hurried the man beyond himself.' And even when it cannot be doubted, but all the actions, designs, and tempers are equally evil; still love hopes that God will at last make bare His arm, and get Himself the victory; and that there shall be 'joy in heaven over' this 'one sinner that repenteth, more than over ninety and nine just persons that need no repentance.'

17. Lastly. It 'endureth all things.' This completes the character of him that is truly merciful. He endureth not some, not many, things only; not most, but absolutely *all things.* Whatever the injustice, the malice, the cruelty of men can inflict, he is able to suffer. He calls nothing intolerable; he never says of anything, 'This is not to be borne.' No; he can not only do, but suffer, all things through Christ which strengtheneth him. And all he suffers does not destroy his love, nor impair it in the least. It is proof against all. It is a flame that burns even in the midst of the great deep. 'Many waters cannot quench 'his' love, neither can the floods drown it.' It triumphs over all. It 'never faileth,' either in time or in eternity.

> In obedience to what heaven decrees,
> Knowledge shall rail, and prophecy shall cease;
> But lasting charity's more ample sway,
> Nor bound by time, nor subject to decay,
> In happy triumph shall for ever live,
> And endless good diffuse, and endless praise receive.

So shall 'the merciful obtain mercy'; not only by the blessing of God upon all their ways, by His now repaying the love they bear to their brethren a thousand-fold into their own bosom; but likewise by 'an exceeding and eternal weight of glory,' in the 'kingdom prepared for them from the beginning of the world.'

18. For a little while you may say, 'Woe is me, that I' am constrained to 'dwell with Mesech, and to have my habitation among the tents of Kedar!' You may pour out your soul, and bemoan the loss of true, genuine love in the earth: lost indeed! You may well say (but not in the ancient sense), 'See how *these Christians* love one another!' these Christian kingdoms, that are tearing out each other's bowels, desolating one another with fire and sword! these Christian armies, that are sending each other by thousands, by ten thousands, quick into hell! these Christian nations, that are all on fire with intestine broils, party against party, faction against faction! these Christian cities, where deceit and fraud, oppression and wrong, yea robbery and murder, go not out of their streets! these Christian families, torn asunder with envy, jealousy, anger, domestic jars, without number, without end! yea, what is most dreadful, most to be lamented of all, these Christian churches!—churches ('tell it not in Gath,'—

but, alas! how can we hide it, either from Jews, Turks, or Pagans?) that bear the name of Christ, the Prince of Peace, and wage continual war with each other! that convert sinners by burning them alive! that are 'drunk with the blood of the saints'! Does this praise belong only to 'Babylon the Great, the mother of harlots and abominations of the earth'? Nay, verily; but Reformed churches (so called) have fairly learned to tread in her steps. Protestant churches too know how to persecute, when they have power in their hands, even unto blood. And meanwhile, how do they also anathematize each other! devote each other to the nethermost hell! What wrath, what contention, what malice, what bitterness, is everywhere found among them, even where they agree in essentials, and only differ in opinions, or in the circumstantials of religion! Who follows after *only* the 'things that make for peace, and things wherewith one may edify another'? O God! how long? Shall Thy promise fail? Fear it not, ye little flock! Against hope, believe in hope! It is your Father's good pleasure yet to renew the face of the earth. Surely all these things shall come to an end, and the inhabitants of the earth shall learn righteousness. 'Nation shall not lift up sword against nation, neither shall they know war any more.' 'The mountain of the Lord's house shall be established on the top of the mountains'; and 'all the kingdoms of the world shall become the kingdoms of our God.' 'They shall not' then 'hurt or destroy in all His holy mountain'; but they shall call their 'walls salvation, and their gates praise.' They shall all be without spot or blemish, loving one another, even as Christ hath loved us.—Be thou part of the first-fruits, if the harvest is not yet. Do thou love thy neighbour as thyself. The Lord God fill thy heart with such a love to every soul, that thou mayest be ready to lay down thy life for his sake! May thy soul continually overflow with love, swallowing up every unkind and unholy temper, till He calleth thee up into the region of love, there to reign with Him for ever and ever!

SERMON XVIII

UPON OUR LORD'S SERMON ON THE MOUNT

DISCOURSE III

On Sunday, August 26, 1739, Wesley preached on the Bowling Green in Bristol at a quarter to seven in the morning to a congregation of 4,000 from 'Blessed are the peace-makers,' &c.; and at Rose Green at five in the evening of the same day from Matt. v. 9-12, when he estimates the hearers at 5,000. He had heard Whitefield preach in the open air on April 1, 1739, at eight in the morning at the Bowling Green, and at 4.15 in the evening at Rose Green. The next day he followed Whitefield's example and held his first open-air service at the Brickfields, taking for his text 'The Spirit of the Lord is upon me,' &c. The Bowling Green was near the centre of the city, and he regularly preached there throughout this year. Rose Green was a flat piece of ground on the top of a high hill about two miles out of Bristol amongst the collieries. Mr. H. J. Foster and Mr. H. Arnaud Scott have identified it as the plot marked 227 on the Ordnance Map sheet lxxii. 10. It was the place where Whitefield began field-preaching on February 17 of this year. There were heaps of refuse from the coal-pits scattered over the ground, one of which made an excellent pulpit. It is sometimes referred to simply as 'The Mount,' and it is not unlikely that Wesley recognized an encouraging coincidence in the name, and took special satisfaction in choosing his text from our Lord's Sermon on the Mount on this occasion. See Foster's 'Bristol Notes' in *W.K.S.* iii. 2.

Blessed are the Pure in heart: for they shall see God.
Blessed are the Peace-makers: for they shall be called the children of God.
Blessed are they which are Persecuted for righteousness sake: for theirs is the
    kingdom of heaven.
Blessed are ye, when men shall revile you, and persecute you, and shall say all
    manner of evil against you falsely, for My sake.
Rejoice, and be exceeding glad: for great is your reward in heaven: for so
    persecuted they the prophets which were before you.—MATT. v. 8-12

I. 1. How excellent things are spoken of the love of our neighbour! It is the 'fulfilling of the law,' 'the end of the commandment.' Without this, all we have, all we do, all we suffer is of no value in the sight of God. But it is that love of our neighbour which springs from the love of God: otherwise itself is nothing worth. It behoves us, therefore, to examine well upon what foundation our love of our neighbour stands; whether it is really built upon the love of God; whether we do 'love Him because He first loved us'; whether we are pure in heart: for this is the foundation which shall never be moved. 'Blessed are the pure in heart: for they shall see God.'

2. 'The pure in heart' are they whose hearts God hath 'purified even as He is pure'; who are purified, through faith in the blood of Jesus, from every unholy affection; who, being 'cleansed from all filthiness of flesh and spirit, perfect holiness in the' loving 'fear of God.' They are, through the power of His grace, purified from pride, by the deepest poverty of spirit; from anger, from every unkind or turbulent passion, by meekness and gentleness; from every desire but to please and enjoy God, to know and love Him more and more, by that hunger and thirst after righteousness which now engrosses their whole soul: so that now they love the Lord their God with all their heart, and with all their soul, and mind, and strength.

3. But how little has this purity of heart been regarded by the false teachers of all ages! They have taught men barely to abstain from such outward impurities as God hath forbidden by name; but they did not strike at the heart; and by not' guarding against, they in effect countenanced, inward corruptions.

A remarkable instance of this, our Lord has given us in the following words: 'Ye have heard that it was said by them of old time, Thou shalt not commit adultery' (verse 27); and, in explaining this, those blind leaders of the blind only insisted on men's abstaining from the outward act. 'But I say unto You, That whosoever looketh on a woman to lust after her hath committed adultery with her already in his heart' (verse 28); for God requireth truth in the inward parts: He searcheth the heart, and trieth the reins; and if thou incline unto iniquity with thy heart, the Lord will not hear thee.

4. And God admits no excuse for retaining anything which is an occasion of impurity. Therefore, 'if thy right eye offend thee, pluck it out, and cast it from thee: for it is profitable for thee that one of thy members should perish, and not that thy whole body should be cast into hell' (verse 29). If persons as dear to thee as thy right eye be an occasion of thy thus offending God, a means of exciting unholy desire in thy soul, delay not, forcibly separate

from them. 'And if thy right hand offend thee, cut it off, and cast it from thee: for it is profitable for thee that one of thy members should perish, and not that thy whole body should be cast into hell' (verse 30). If any who seem as necessary to thee as thy right hand be an occasion of sin, of impure desire; even though it were never to go beyond the heart, never to break out in word or action; constrain thyself to an entire and final parting: cut them off at a stroke: give them up to God. Any loss, whether of pleasure, or substance, or friends, is preferable to the loss of thy soul.

Two steps only it may not be improper to take before such an absolute and final separation. First, try whether the unclean spirit may not be driven out by fasting and prayer, and by carefully abstaining from every action, and word, and look, which thou hast found to be an occasion of evil. Secondly, if thou art not by this means delivered, ask counsel of him that watcheth over thy soul, or, at least, of some who have experience in the ways of God, touching the time and manner of that separation; but confer not with flesh and blood, lest thou be 'given up to a strong delusion to believe a lie.'

5. Nor may marriage itself, holy and honourable as it is, be used as a pretence for giving a loose to our desires. Indeed, 'it hath been said, Whosoever will put away his wife, let him give her a writing of divorcement': and then all was well; though he alleged no cause, but that he did not like her, or liked another better. 'But I say unto you, That whosoever shall put away his wife, saving for the cause of fornication' (that is, adultery; the word πορνεια signifying unchastity in general, either in the married or unmarried state), 'causeth her to commit adultery,' if she marry again: 'and whosoever shall marry her that is put away committeth adultery' (verses 31, 32).

All polygamy is clearly forbidden in these words, wherein our Lord expressly declares, that for any woman who has a husband alive, to marry again is adultery. By parity of reason, it is adultery for any man to marry again so long as he has a wife alive, yea, although they were divorced; unless that divorce had been for the cause of adultery: in that only case there is no scripture which forbids [the innocent person] to marry again.

6. Such is the purity of heart which God requires, and works in those who believe on the Son of His love. And 'blessed are'

they who are thus 'pure in heart: for they shall see God.' He will
'manifest Himself unto them,' not only 'as He doth not unto the
world,' but as He doth not always to His own children. He will
bless them with the clearest communications of His Spirit, the
most intimate 'fellowship with the Father and with the Son.' He
will cause His presence to go continually before them and the
light of His countenance to shine upon them. It is the ceaseless
prayer of their heart, 'I beseech Thee, show me Thy glory'; and
they have the petition they ask of Him. They now see Him by
faith (the veil of flesh 'being made, as it were, transparent), even
in these His lowest works, in all that surrounds them, in all that
God has created and made. They see Him in the height above,
and in the depth beneath; they see Him filling all in all. The pure
in heart see all things full of God. They see Him in the
firmament of heaven; in the moon, walking in brightness; in the
sun, when he rejoiceth as a giant to run his course. They see Him
'making the clouds His chariots, and walking upon the wings of
the wind.' They see Him 'preparing rain for the earth, and
blessing the increase of it; giving grass for the cattle, and green
herb for the use of man.' They see the Creator of all, wisely
governing all, and 'upholding all things by the word of His
power.' 'O Lord our Governor, how excellent is Thy name in all
the world!'

7. In all His providences relating to themselves, to their souls
or bodies, the pure in heart do more particularly see God. They
see His hand ever over them for good; giving them all things in
weight and measure, numbering the hairs of their head, making
a hedge round about them and all that they have, and disposing
all the circumstances of their life according to the depth both of
His wisdom and mercy.

8. But in a more especial manner they see God in His
ordinances. Whether they appear in the great congregation, to
'pay Him the honour due unto His name,' 'and worship Him in
the beauty of holiness'; or 'enter into their closets,' and there
pour out their souls before their 'Father which is in secret';
whether they search the oracles of God, or hear the ambassadors
of Christ proclaiming glad tidings of salvation; or, by eating of
that bread, and drinking of that cup, 'show forth His death till
He come' in the clouds of heaven,—in all these His appointed
ways, they find such a near approach as cannot be expressed.

They see Him, as it were, face to face, and 'talk with Him, as a man talketh with his friend'—a fit preparation for those mansions above, wherein they shall see Him as He is.

9. But how far were they from seeing God who having heard 'that it had been said by them of old times, Thou shalt not forswear thyself, but shalt perform unto the Lord thine oaths' (verse 33), interpreted it thus, Thou shalt not forswear thyself, when thou swearest by the Lord Jehovah: thou 'shalt perform unto the Lord' these 'thine oaths'; but as to other oaths, He regardeth them not.

So the Pharisees taught. They not only allowed all manner of swearing in common conversation; but accounted even forswearing a little thing, so they had not sworn by the peculiar name of God.

But our Lord here absolutely forbids all common swearing as well as all false swearing; and shows the heinousness of both, by the same awful consideration, that every creature is God's, and He is everywhere present, in all, and over all. 'I say unto you, Swear not at all; neither by heaven, for it is God's throne' (verse 34); and, therefore, this is the same as to swear by Him who sitteth upon the circle of the heavens: 'Nor by the earth; for it is His footstool' (verse 35); and He is as intimately present in earth as heaven: 'Neither by Jerusalem; for it is the city of the great King'; and God is well known in her palaces. 'Neither shalt thou swear by thy head; because thou canst not make one hair white or black' (verse 36); because even this, it is plain, is not thine, but God's, the sole disposer of all in heaven and earth. 'But let your communication' (verse 37), your conversation, your discourse with each other, 'be, Yea, yea; Nay, nay!; a bare serious affirming or denying; 'for whatsoever is more than these cometh of evil': εκ του πονηρον εστιν, *is of the evil one*; proceedeth from the devil, and is a mark of his children.

10. That our Lord does not here forbid the 'swearing in judgement and truth,' when we are required so to do by a magistrate, may appear (1), From the occasion of this part of His discourse—the abuse He was here reproving—which was false swearing, and common swearing; the swearing before a magistrate being quite out of the question. (2) From the very words wherein He forms the general conclusion: 'Let your communication,' or discourse, 'be, Yea, yea; Nay, nay.' (3) From

His own example: for He answered Himself upon oath, when
required by a magistrate. When the high-priest said unto him, 'I
adjure thee by the living God, that thou tell us whether thou be
the Christ, the Son of God,' Jesus immediately answered in the
affirmative, 'Thou hast said' (that is, the truth); 'nevertheless'
(or, rather, *moreover*), 'I say unto you, Hereafter shall ye see the
Son of Man sitting on the right hand of power, and coming in
the clouds of heaven' (Matt, xxvi. 63, 64). (4) From the example
of God, even the Father, who, 'willing more abundantly to show
unto the heirs of promise the immutability of His counsel,
confirmed it by an oath' (Heb. vi. 17). (5) From the example of
St. Paul, who we think had the Spirit of God, and well
understood the mind of his Master. 'God is my witness,' saith he,
to the Romans, 'that without ceasing I make mention of you
always in my prayers' (Rom. i. 9): to the Corinthians, 'I call God
for a record upon my soul, that to spare you I came not as yet
unto Corinth' (2 Cor. i. 23): and to the Philippians, 'God is my
record, how greatly I long after you in the bowers of Jesus
Christ' (Phil. i. 8). Hence it undeniably appears, that if the
Apostle knew the meaning of his Lord's words, they do not
forbid swearing on weighty occasions even to one another: how
much less before a magistrate! And, lastly, from that assertion of
the great Apostle, concerning solemn swearing in general
(which it is impossible he could have mentioned without any
touch of blame, if his Lord had totally forbidden it): 'Men verily
swear by the greater'; by one greater than themselves; 'and an
oath for confirmation is to them an end of all strife' (Heb. vi. 16).

11. But the great lesson which our blessed Lord inculcates
here, and which He illustrates by this example, is, that God is in
all things, and that we are to see the Creator in the glass of every
creature; that we should use and look upon nothing as separate
from God, which indeed is a kind of practical Atheism; but, with
a true magnificence of thought, survey heaven and earth, and all
that is therein, as contained by God in the hollow of His hand,
who by His intimate presence holds them all in being, who
pervades and actuates the whole created frame, and is, in a true
sense, the soul of the universe.

II. 1. Thus far our Lord has been more directly employed in
teaching the religion of the heart. He has shown what Christians

are to be. He proceeds to show what they are to do also,—how inward holiness is to exert itself in our outward conversation. 'Blessed,' saith He, 'are the peace-makers; for they shall be called the children of God.'

2. 'The peace-makers': the word in the original is οι ειρηνοποιοι. It is well known that ειρηνη, in the sacred writings, implies all manner of good; every blessing that relates either to the soul or the body, to time or eternity. Accordingly, when St. Paul, in the titles of his epistles, wishes grace and peace to the Romans or the Corinthians, it is as if he had said, 'As a fruit of the free, undeserved love and favour of God, may you enjoy all blessings, spiritual and temporal; all the good things which God hath prepared for them that love Him.'

3. Hence we may easily learn, in how wide a sense the term 'peace-makers' is to be understood. In its literal meaning it implies those lovers of God and man who utterly detest and abhor all strife and debate, all variance and contention; and accordingly labour with all their might, either to prevent this fire of hell from being kindled, or, when it is kindled, from breaking out, or, when it is broke out, from spreading any farther. They endeavour to calm the stormy spirits of men, to quiet their turbulent passions, to soften the minds of contending parties, and, if possible, reconcile them to each other. They use all innocent arts, and employ all their strength, all the talents which God has given them, as well to preserve peace where it is, as to restore it where it is not. It is the joy of their heart to promote, to confirm, to increase, mutual good-will among men, but more especially among the children of God, however distinguished by things of smaller importance; that as they have all 'one Lord, one faith,' as they are all 'called in one hope of their calling,' so they may all 'walk worthy of the vocation wherewith they are called; with all lowliness and meekness, with long-suffering, forbearing one another in love; endeavouring to keep the unity of the Spirit in the bond of peace.'

4. But, in the full extent of the word, a peace-maker is one that, as he hath opportunity, 'doeth good unto all men'; one that, being filled with the love of God and of all mankind, cannot confine the expressions of it to his own family, or friends, or acquaintance, or party, or to those of his own opinions,—no, nor those who are partakers of like precious faith; but steps over all

these narrow bounds, that he may do good to every man, that he may, some way or other manifest his love to neighbours and strangers, friends and enemies. He doeth good to them all, as he hath opportunity, that is, on every possible occasion; 'redeeming the time,' in order thereto; buying up every opportunity, improving every hour, losing no moment wherein he may profit another. He does good, not of one particular kind but good in general, in every possible way; employing herein all his talents of every kind, all his powers and faculties of body and soul, all his fortune, his interest, his reputation; desiring only, that when his Lord cometh He may say, 'Well done, good and faithful servant.'

5. He doeth good to the uttermost of his power, even to the bodies of all men. He rejoices to 'deal his bread to the hungry,' and to 'cover the naked with a garment.' Is any a stranger? He takes him in, and relieves him according to his necessities. Are any sick or in prison? He visits them, and administers such help as they stand most in need of. And all this he does, not as unto man; but remembering Him that hath said, 'Inasmuch as ye have done it unto one of the least of these My brethren, ye have done it unto Me.'

6. How much more does he rejoice, if he can do any good to the soul of any man! This power, indeed, belongeth unto God. It is He only that changes the heart, without which every other change is lighter than vanity. Nevertheless it pleases Him who worketh all in all, to help man chiefly by man; to convey his own power, and blessing, and love, through one man to another. Therefore, although it be certain that, 'the help which is done upon earth, God doeth it Himself'; yet has no man need, on this account, to stand idle in his vineyard. The peace-maker cannot: he is ever labouring therein, and, as an instrument in God's hand, preparing the ground for his Master's use, or sowing the seed of the kingdom, or watering what is already sown, if haply God may give the increase. According to the measure of grace which he has received, he uses all diligence, either to reprove the gross sinner, to reclaim those who run on headlong in the broad way of destruction; or 'to give light to them that sit in darkness,' and are ready to 'perish for lack of knowledge'; or to 'support the weak, to lift up the hands that hang down and the feeble knees'; or to bring back and heal that which was lame and turned out of the way. Nor is he less zealous to confirm those who are

already striving to enter in at the strait gate; to strengthen those
that stand, that they may 'run with patience the race which is set
before them'; to build up in their most holy faith those that know
in whom they have believed; to exhort them to stir up the gift of
God which is in them, that, daily growing in grace, 'an entrance
may be ministered unto them abundantly into the everlasting
kingdom of our Lord and Saviour Jesus Christ.'

7. 'Blessed are they who are thus continually employed in the
work of faith and the labour of love; 'for they shall be called,'
that is, *shall be* (a common Hebraism),' the children of God.' God
shall continue unto them the Spirit of adoption, yea, shall pour it
more abundantly into their hearts. He shall bless them with all
the blessings of His children. He shall acknowledge them as sons
before angels and men; 'and if sons, then heirs; heirs of God,
and joint-heirs with Christ.'

III. 1. One would imagine such a person as has been above
described, so full of genuine humility, so unaffectedly serious,
so mild and gentle, so free from all selfish design, so devoted to
God, and such an active lover of men, should be the darling of
mankind. But our Lord was better acquainted with human
nature in its present state. He therefore closes the character of
this man of God with showing him the treatment he is to expect
in the world. 'Blessed,' saith He, 'are they which are persecuted
for righteousness' sake; for theirs is the kingdom of heaven.'

2. In order to understand this thoroughly, let us, first
inquire, Who are they that are persecuted? And this we may
easily learn from St. Paul: 'As of old, he that was born after the
flesh persecuted him that was born after the Spirit, even so it is
now' (Gal. iv. 29). 'Yea,' saith the Apostle, 'and all that will live
godly in Christ Jesus shall suffer persecution' (2 Tim. iii. 12).
The same we are taught by St. John: 'Marvel not, my brethren, if
the world hate you. We know that we have passed from death
unto life, because we love the brethren' (1 John iii. 13, 14). As if
he had said, The brethren, the Christians, cannot be loved, but
by them who have passed from death unto life. And most
expressly by our Lord: 'If the world hate you, ye know that it
hated Me before it hated you. If ye were of the world, the world
would love his own; but because ye are not of the world,
therefore the world hateth you. Remember the word that I said

unto you, The servant is not greater than his lord. If they have persecuted Me, they will also persecute you' (John xv. 18, &c.).

By all these scriptures it manifestly appears who they are that are persecuted; namely, the righteous: he 'that is born of the Spirit'; 'all that will live godly in Christ Jesus'; they that are 'passed from death unto life'; those who are 'not of the world'; all those who are meek and lowly in heart, that mourn for God, that hunger after His likeness; all that love God and their neighbour, and therefore, as they have opportunity, do good unto all men.

3. If it be secondly, inquired, why they are persecuted, the answer is equally plain and obvious. It is 'for righteousness' sake'; because they are righteous; because they are born after the Spirit; because they will 'live godly in Christ Jesus'; because they 'are not of the world.' Whatever may be pretended, this is the real cause: be their infirmities more or less, still, if it were not for this, they would be borne with, and the world would love its own. They are persecuted because they are *poor in spirit*; that is, say the world, 'poor-spirited, mean, dastardly souls, good for nothing, not fit to live in the world';—because they *mourn*: 'They are such dull, heavy, lumpish creatures, enough to sink any one's spirits that sees them! They are mere death-heads; they kill innocent mirth, and spoil company wherever they come';—because they are *meek*: 'Tame, passive fools, just fit to be trampled upon';—because they *hunger and thirst after righteousness*: 'A parcel of hot-brained enthusiasts, gaping after they know not what, not content with rational religion, but running mad after raptures and inward feelings' —because they are *merciful*, lovers of all, lovers of the evil and unthankful: 'Encouraging all manner of wickedness; nay tempting people to do mischief by impunity: and men who it is to be feared, have their own religion still to seek; very loose in their principles';—because they are *pure in heart*: 'Uncharitable creatures, that damn all the world, but those that are of their own sort! Blasphemous wretches, that pretend to make God a liar, to live without sin!'—Above all because they are *peace-makers*; because they take all opportunities of doing good to all men. This is the grand reason why they have been persecuted in all ages, and will be till the restitution of all things: 'If they would but keep their religion to themselves, it would be tolerable: but it is this spreading their errors, this infecting so many others, which is not to be endured. They do so

much mischief in the world, that they ought to be tolerated no longer. It is true, the men do some things well enough; they relieve some of the poor: but this, too, is only done to gain the more to their party; and so, in effect, to do the more mischief!' Thus the men of the world sincerely think and speak. And the more the kingdom of God prevails, the more the peace-makers are enabled to propagate lowliness, meekness, and all other divine tempers, the more mischief is done, in their account: consequently, the more are they enraged against the authors of this, and the more vehemently will they persecute them.

4. Let us, thirdly, inquire, Who are they that persecute them? St. Paul answers, 'He that is born after the flesh': every one who is not 'born of the Spirit,' or, at least, desirous so to be; all that do not at least labour to 'live godly in Christ Jesus'; all that are not 'passed from death unto life,' and, consequently, cannot 'love the brethren'; 'the world,' that is, according to our Saviour's account, they who 'know not Him that sent Me'; they who know not God, even the loving, pardoning God, by the teaching of His own Spirit.

The reason is plain: the spirit which is in the world is directly opposite to the Spirit which is of God. It must therefore needs be that those who are of the world will be opposite to those who are of God. There is the utmost contrariety between them, in all their opinions, their desires, designs, and tempers. And hitherto the leopard and the kid cannot lie down in peace together. The proud because he is proud, cannot but persecute the lowly; the light and airy, those that mourn: and so in every other kind; the unlikeness of disposition (were there no other) being a perpetual ground of enmity. Therefore, were it only on this account, all the servants of the devil will persecute the children of God.

5. Should it be inquired, fourthly, how they will persecute them, it may be answered in general, Just in that manner and measure which the wise Disposer of all sees will be most for His glory,—will tend most to His children's growth in grace, and the enlargement of His own kingdom. There is no one branch of God's government of the world which is more to be admired than this. His ear is never heavy to the threatenings of the persecutor, or the cry of the persecuted. His eye is ever open, and His hand stretched out to direct every the minutest

circumstance. When the storm shall begin, how high it shall rise, which way it shall point its course, when and how it shall end, are all determined by His unerring wisdom. The ungodly are only a sword of His; an instrument which He uses as it pleaseth Him and which itself, when the gracious ends of His providence are answered, is cast into the fire.

At some rare times, as when Christianity was planted first, and while it was taking root in the earth; as also when the pure doctrine of Christ began to be planted again in our nation; God permitted the storm to rise high, and His children were called to resist unto blood. There was a peculiar reason why He suffered this with regard to the Apostles, that their evidence might be the more unexceptionable. But from the annals of the Church we learn another, and a far different reason, why He suffered the heavy persecutions which arose in the second and third centuries; namely, because 'the mystery of iniquity' did so strongly 'work'; because of the monstrous corruptions which even then reigned in the Church: these God chastised, and at the same time strove to heal, by those severe but necessary visitations.

Perhaps the same observation may be made, with regard to the grand persecution in our own land. God had dealt very graciously with our nation: He had poured out various blessings upon us: He had given us peace abroad and at home; and a king, wise and good beyond his years: and, above all, He had caused the pure light of His gospel to arise and shine amongst us. But what return did He find? 'He looked for righteousness; but behold a cry'—a cry of oppression and wrong, of ambition and injustice, of malice and fraud, and covetousness. Yea, the cry of those who even then expired in the flames entered into the ears of the Lord of Sabaoth. It was then God arose to maintain His own cause against those that held the truth in unrighteousness. Then He sold them into the hands of their persecutors by a judgement mixed with mercy; an affliction to punish and yet a medicine to heal, the grievous backslidings of His people.

6. But it is seldom God suffers the storm to rise so high as torture or death, or bonds, or imprisonment. Whereas His children are frequently called to endure the lighter kinds of persecution; they frequently suffer the estrangement of kinsfolks, the loss of the friends that were as their own soul.

They find the truth of their Lord's word (concerning the *event*, though not the *design* of His coming), 'Suppose ye that I am come to give peace upon earth? I tell you, Nay; but rather division' (Luke xii. 51). And hence will naturally follow loss of business or employment, and consequently of substance. But all these circumstances likewise are under the wise direction of God who allots to every one what is most expedient for him.

7. But the persecution which attends *all* the children of God is that our Lord describes in the following words: 'Blessed are ye when men shall revile you and persecute you'—shall persecute by reviling you—'and say all manner of evil against you falsely, for My sake.' This cannot fail; it is the very badge of our discipleship; it is one of the seals of our calling; it is a sure portion entailed on all the children of God: if we have it not, we are bastards, and not sons: straight through evil report, as well as good report, lies the only way to the kingdom. The meek, serious, humble, zealous lovers of God and man are of good report among their brethren; but of evil report with the world, who count and treat them 'as the filth and offscouring of all things.'

8. Indeed, some have supposed that before the fullness of the Gentiles shall come in, the scandal of the cross will cease; that God will cause Christians to be esteemed and loved even by those who are as yet in their sins. Yea, and sure it is, that even now He at some times suspends the contempt as well as the fierceness of men; 'He makes a man's enemies to be at peace with him' for a season, and gives him favour with his bitterest persecutors. But setting aside this exempt case, the scandal of the cross is not yet ceased; but a man may say still, 'If I please men, I am not the servant of Christ.' Let no man therefore regard that pleasing suggestion (pleasing doubtless to flesh and blood), 'that bad men only *pretend* to hate and despise them that are good, but do indeed love and esteem them in their hearts.' Not so: they may employ them sometimes; but it is for their own profit. They may put confidence in them; for they know their ways are not like other men's. But still they love them not; unless so far as the Spirit of God may be striving with them. Our Saviour's words are express: 'If ye were of the world, the world would love its own; but because ye are not of the world, therefore the world hateth you.' Yea (setting aside what exceptions may be made by the

preventing grace, or the peculiar providence, of God), it hateth them as cordially and sincerely as ever it did their Master.

9. It remains only to inquire, How are the children of God to behave with regard to persecution? And, first, they ought not knowingly or designedly to bring it upon themselves. This is contrary both to the example and advice of our Lord and all His Apostles; who teach us not only not to seek, but to avoid it, as far as we can, without injuring our conscience; without giving up any part of that righteousness which we are to prefer before life itself. So our Lord expressly saith: 'When they persecute you in this city, flee ye into another'; which is indeed, when it can be taken, the most unexceptionable way of avoiding persecution.

10. Yet think not that you can always avoid it, either by this or any other means. If ever that idle imagination steals into your heart, put it to flight by that earnest caution, 'Remember the word that I said unto you, The servant is not greater than his lord. If they have persecuted Me, they will also persecute you.' 'Be ye wise as serpents, and harmless as doves.' But will this screen you from persecution? Not unless you have more wisdom than your Master, or more innocence than the Lamb of God.

Neither desire to avoid it, to escape it wholly; for if you do, you are none of His. If you escape the persecution, you escape the blessing; the blessing of those who are persecuted for righteousness' sake. If you are not persecuted for righteousness' sake, you cannot enter into the kingdom of heaven. 'If we suffer with Him, we shall also reign with Him. But if we deny Him, He will also deny us.'

11. Nay, rather, 'rejoice and be exceeding glad,' when men persecute you for His sake; when they persecute you by reviling you, and by 'saying all manner of evil against you falsely'; which they will not fail to mix with every kind of persecution: they must blacken you to excuse themselves: 'For so persecuted they the prophets which were before you,'—those who were most eminently holy in heart and life; yea, and all the righteous which ever have been from the beginning of the world. Rejoice, because by this mark also ye know unto whom ye belong; and 'because great is your reward in heaven'—the reward purchased by the blood of the covenant, and freely bestowed in proportion to your sufferings, as well as to your holiness of heart and life. 'Be exceeding glad'; knowing that these 'light afflictions, which

are but for a moment, work out for you a far more exceeding and eternal weight of glory.'

12. Meantime, let no persecution turn you out of the way of lowliness and meekness, of love and beneficence. 'Ye have heard' indeed 'that it hath been said, An eye for an eye, and a tooth for a tooth' (Matt. v. 38): and your miserable teachers have hence allowed you to avenge yourselves, to return evil for evil: 'but I say unto you, That ye resist not evil,'—not thus; not by returning it in kind. 'But,' rather than do this, 'whosoever smiteth thee on thy right cheek, turn to him the other also. And if any man will sue thee at the law, and take away thy coat, let him have thy cloak also. And whosoever shall compel thee to go a mile, go with him twain.'

So invincible let thy meekness be. And be thy love suitable thereto. 'Give to him that asketh thee, and from him that would borrow of thee turn not thou away.' Only, give not away that which is another man's, that which is not thine own. Therefore, (1) Take care to owe no man anything: for what thou owest is not thine own, but another man's. (2) Provide for those of thine own household. This also God hath required of thee; and what is necessary to sustain them in life and godliness is also not thine own. Then, (3) Give or lend all that remains, from day to day, or from year to year: only, first, seeing thou canst not give or lend to all, remember the household of faith.

13. The meekness and love we are to feel, the kindness we are to show to them which persecute us for righteousness' sake, our blessed Lord describes farther in the following verses: O that they were engraven upon our hearts! 'Ye have heard that it hath been said, Thou shalt love thy neighbor, and hate thy enemy' (Matt. v. 43, &c.): God indeed had said only the former part, 'Thou shalt love thy neighbour'; the children of the devil had added the latter, 'and hate thy enemy'; 'But I say unto you,' (1) 'Love your enemies': see that you bear a tender good-will to those who are most bitter of spirit against you; who wish you all manner of evil. (2) 'Bless them that curse you.' Are there any whose bitterness of spirit breaks forth in bitter words? who are continually cursing and reproaching you when you are present, and 'saying all evil against you' when absent? So much the rather do you bless: in conversing with them, use all mildness and softness of language. Reprove them, by repeating a better lesson

before them; by showing them how they ought to have spoken.
And, in speaking of them, say all the good you can, without
violating the rules of truth and justice. (3) 'Do good to them that
hate you': let your actions show that you are as real in love, as they
in hatred. Return good for evil. 'Be not overcome of evil, but
overcome evil with good.' (4) If you can do nothing more, at least
'pray for them that despitefully use you and persecute you.' You
can 'never be disabled from doing this; nor can all their malice or
violence hinder you. Pour out your souls to God, not only for
those who did this once, but now repent; this is a little thing: 'If thy
brother, seven times a day, turn and say unto thee, I repent' (Luke
xvii. 4); that is, if, after ever so many relapses, he give thee reason
to believe that he is really and thoroughly changed; then thou
shalt forgive him, so as to trust him, to put him in thy bosom, as if
he had never sinned against thee at all; but pray for, wrestle with
God for, those that do not repent, that now despitefully use thee
and persecute thee. Thus far forgive them, 'not until seven times
only, but, until seventy times seven' (Matt. xviii. 22).

Whether they repent or no, yea, though they appear farther
and farther from it, yet show them this instance of kindness;
'that ye may be the children,' that ye may approve yourselves the
genuine children, 'of your Father which is in heaven'; who shows
His goodness by giving such blessings as they are capable of,
even to His stubbornest enemies; 'who maketh His sun to rise on
the evil and on the good, and sendeth rain on the just and on the
unjust.' 'For if ye love them which love you, what reward have
ye? do not even the publicans the same?' (Matt. v. 46)—who
pretend to no religion; whom ye yourselves acknowledge to be
without God in the world. 'And if ye salute,' show kindness in
word or deed to, 'your brethren,' your friends or kinsfolk, 'only;
what do ye more than others?'—than those who have no religion
at all? 'do not even the publicans so?' (Matt. v. 47). Nay, but
follow ye a better pattern than them. In patience, in
long-suffering, in mercy, in beneficence of every kind, to all,
even to your bitterest persecutors; 'be ye,' Christians, 'perfect,'
in kind, thongh not in degree, 'even as your Father which is in
heaven is perfect' (Matt. v. 48).

IV. Behold Christianity in its native form, as delivered by its
great Author! This is the genuine religion of Jesus Christ! Such

He presents it to him whose eyes are opened. See a picture of God so far as He is imitable by man! a picture drawn by God's own hand. 'Behold, ye despisers, and wonder, and perish!' Or, rather, wonder and adore! Rather cry out, 'Is this the religion of Jesus of Nazareth? the religion which I persecuted? Let me no more be found even to fight against God. Lord, what wouldest Thou have me to do?' What beauty appears in the whole! How just a symmetry! What exact proportion in every part! How desirable is the happiness here described! How venerable, how lovely the holiness! This is the spirit of religion; the quintessence of it. These are indeed the fundamentals of Christianity. O that we may not be hearers of it only!—'like a man beholding his own face in a glass, who goeth his way, and straightway forgetteth what manner of man he was.' Nay, but let us steadily 'look into this perfect law of liberty, and continue therein.' Let us not rest, until every line thereof is transcribed into our own hearts. Let us watch, and pray, and believe, and love, and 'strive for the mastery,' till every part of it shall appear in our soul, graven there by the finger of God; till we are 'holy as He which hath called us is holy, perfect as our Father which is in heaven is perfect.'

SERMON XIX

UPON OUR LORD'S SERMON ON THE MOUNT

DISCOURSE IV

This sermon was preached at West Street on February 3, 1747; and the substance of it no doubt was frequently given to the societies in London and Bristol in the course of the expositions already referred to. It is Wesley's criticism of the Mystic doctrine in relation to good works, as Sermon XII is in regard to the means of grace. It should be compared with the Preface to the *Hymns and Sacred Poems* (1739), where he says that some of the hymns 'were wrote upon the scheme of the Mystic Divines. And these, it is owned, we had once in great veneration, as the best explainers of the gospel of Christ. But we are now convinced that we therein greatly erred, not knowing the Scriptures, neither the power of God.' He proceeds to criticize their teaching as to justification, their commendation of entire seclusion from men ('Holy solitaries,' he exclaims, 'is a phrase no more consistent with the gospel than holy adulterers'), and their substitution of contemplation for good works. The question became a very practical one with him when the Moravian quietism or 'stillness' began to infect the Fetter Lane society in the autumn of 1739, and ultimately led to his separation from it in July 1740. But Richard Bell and John Bray kept on tintinnabulating and hee-hawing, and it was many years before the Methodist societies quite got rid of this pernicious leaven. He was deeply grieved, too, at the later mystical developments in William Law's teaching, which began to manifest themselves about 1733. He was amazed and disgusted at the absurd crudities of his physical speculations; and he had no patience when he thought of the little divine in the pleasant retirement of his cottage at Putney, whilst he himself was running from Bristol to Newcastle, preaching every day, and on full stretch to arouse and save the souls of men. And when in 1741 Charles caught the disease, it was no wonder that he denounced the whole Mystical doctrine as 'this masterpiece of the wisdom from beneath, the fairest of all the devices wherewith Satan hath ever perverted the right ways of the Lord!'

But in his cooler moments he was quite ready to appreciate the better elements of Mysticism, and to admit that its earlier exponents were 'men of love, experimentally acquainted with true, inward religion; burning and shining lights, and such as had well deserved of the Church of Christ' (Sermon XII, i. 4). And when the passing years had mellowed him, he declares in his preface to her Life, written in 1776, that Madam Guyon, with all her mistakes, was 'good in an eminent degree.' 'So that, upon the whole,' he concludes, 'I know not whether we may not search many centuries to find another woman who was such a pattern of true holiness.' The student should read Prof. William James's chapter on 'Mysticism' in *Varieties of Religions Experience*, where its weakness and its strength are both lucidly set forth. Both types of character, the active and the contemplative, are necessary for the completeness of the Church; and Methodism has room, and a sphere of service, for both a Hugh Price Hughes and a William Burt Pope; and neither hand nor eye can say to eye or hand, 'I have no need of thee.'

Ye are the salt of the earth: but if the salt have lost his savour, wherewith shall it be salted? it is thenceforth good for nothing, but to be cast out, and to be trodden under foot of men.
Ye are the light of the world. A city that is set on an hill cannot be hid.
Neither do men light a candle, and put it under a bushel, but on a candlestick; and it giveth light unto all that are in the house.
Let your light so shine before men, that they may see your good works, and glorify your Father which is in heaven.—MATT. v. 13-16.

1. The beauty of holiness, of that inward man of the heart which is renewed after the image of God, cannot but strike every eye which God hath opened—every enlightened understanding. The ornament of a meek, humble, loving spirit, will at least excite the approbation of all those who are capable, in any degree, of discerning spiritual good and evil. From the hour men begin to emerge out of the darkness which covers the giddy, unthinking world, they cannot but perceive how desirable a thing it is to be thus transformed into the likeness of Him that created us. This inward religion bears the shape of God so visibly impressed upon it, that a soul must be wholly immersed in flesh and blood when he can doubt of its divine original. We may say of this, in a secondary sense, even as of the Son of God Himself, that it is 'the brightness of His glory, the express image of His person'—απαυγασμα της δοξης αυτου—'the beaming forth of His' eternal 'glory'; and yet so tempered and softened, that even the children of men may herein see God and live; χαρακτηρ της υποστασεως αυτου—'the character, the stamp, the living impression of His person,' who is the fountain of beauty and love, the original source of all excellency and perfection.

2. If religion, therefore, were carried no farther than this, they could have no doubt concerning it; they should have no objection against pursuing it with the whole ardour of their

souls. 'But why,' say they, 'is it clogged with other things? What need of loading it with *doing* and *suffering*? These are what damps the vigour of the soul, and sinks it down to earth again. Is it not enough to "follow after charity"; to soar upon the wings of love? Will it not suffice to worship God, who is a Spirit, with the spirit of our minds, without encumbering ourselves with outward things, or even thinking of them at all? Is it not better, that the whole extent of our thought should be taken up with high and heavenly contemplation; and that instead of busying ourselves at all about externals, we should only commune with God in our hearts?'

3. Many eminent men have spoken thus; have advised us 'to cease from all outward action'; wholly to withdraw from the world; to leave the body behind us; to abstract ourselves from all sensible things; to have no concern at all about outward religion, but *to work all virtues in the will*; as the far more excellent way, more perfective of the soul as well as more acceptable to God.

4. It needed not that any should tell our Lord of this master-piece of the wisdom from beneath, this fairest of all the devices wherewith Satan hath ever perverted the right ways of the Lord! And O! what instruments hath he found from time to time, to employ in this his service to wield this grand engine of hell against some of the most important truths of God!—men that would 'deceive, if it were possible, the very elect,' the men of faith and love; yea, that have for a season deceived and led away no inconsiderable number of them, who have fallen in all ages into the gilded snare, and hardly escaped with the skin of their teeth.

5. But has our Lord been wanting on His part? Has He not sufficiently guarded us against this pleasing delusion? Has He not armed us here with armour of proof against Satan 'transformed into an angel of light'? Yea, verily: He here defends, in the clearest and strongest manner, the active, patient religion He had just described. What can be fuller and plainer than the words He immediately subjoins to what He had said of doing and suffering? 'Ye are the salt of the earth: but if the salt have lost his savour, wherewith shall it be salted? It is thenceforth good for nothing but to be cast out, and trodden under foot of men. Ye are the light of the world. A city that is set on an hill cannot be hid. Neither do men light a candle and put it

under a bushel, but on a candlestick; and it giveth light to all that are in the house. Let your light so shine before men, that they may see your good works, and glorify your Father which is in heaven.'

In order fully to explain and enforce these important words, I shall endeavour to show, first, that Christianity is essentially a social religion; and that to turn it into a solitary one is to destroy it. Secondly, that to conceal this religion is impossible, as well as utterly contrary to the design of its Author. I shall, thirdly, answer some objections; and conclude the whole with a practical application.

I. 1. First. I shall endeavour to show, that Christianity is essentially a social religion; and that to turn it into a solitary religion, is indeed to destroy it.

By Christianity, I mean that method of worshipping God which is here revealed to man by Jesus Christ. When I say, This is essentially a social religion, I mean not only that it cannot subsist so well, but that it cannot subsist at all, without society,—without living and conversing with other men. And in showing this, I shall confine myself to those considerations which will arise from the very discourse before us. But if this be shown, then, doubtless, to turn this religion into a solitary one is to destroy it.

Not that we can in any wise condemn the intermixing solitude or retirement with society. This is not only allowable, but expedient; nay, it is necessary, as daily experience shows, for every one that either already is, or desires to be a real Christian. It can hardly be, that we should spend one entire day in a continued intercourse with men, without suffering loss in our soul, and in some measure grieving the Holy Spirit of God. We have need daily to retire from the world, at least morning and evening, to converse with God, to commune more freely with our Father which is in secret. Nor indeed can a man of experience condemn even longer seasons of religious retire-ment, so they do not imply any neglect of the worldly employ wherein the providence of God has placed us.

2. Yet such retirement must not swallow up all our time: this would be to destroy, not advance, true religion. For, that the religion described by our Lord in the foregoing words cannot

subsist without society, without our living and conversing with other men, is manifest from hence, that several of the most essential branches thereof can have no place if we have no intercourse with the world.

3. There is no disposition, for instance, which is more essential to Christianity than meekness. Now although this, as it implies resignation to God, or patience in pain and sickness, may subsist in a desert, in a hermit's cell, in total solitude; yet as it implies (which it no less necessarily does) mildness, gentleness, and long-suffering, it cannot possibly have a being, it has no place under heaven, without an intercourse with other men: so that to attempt turning this into a solitary virtue is to destroy it from the face of the earth.

4. Another necessary branch of true Christianity is peace-making, or doing of good. That this is equally essential with any of the other parts of the religion of Jesus Christ, there can be no stronger argument to evince (and therefore it would be absurd to allege any other), than that it is here inserted in the original plan He has laid down of the fundamentals of His religion. Therefore, to set aside this is the same daring insult on the authority of our Great Master as to set aside mercifulness, purity of heart, or any other branch of His institution. But this is apparently set aside by all who call us to the wilderness; who recommend entire solitude either to the babes, or the young men, or the fathers in Christ.

For will any man affirm that a solitary Christian (so called, though it is little less than a contradiction in terms) can be a merciful man,—that is, one that takes every opportunity of doing all good to all men? What can be more plain than that this fundamental branch of the religion of Jesus Christ cannot possibly subsist without society, without our living and conversing with other men?

5. 'But is it not expedient, however,' one might naturally ask, 'to converse only with good men,—only with those whom we know to be meek and merciful, holy of heart, and holy of life? Is it not expedient to refrain from any conversation or intercourse with men of the opposite character,—men who do not obey, perhaps do not believe, the gospel of our Lord Jesus Christ?' The advice of St. Paul to the Christians at Corinth may seem to favour this: 'I wrote unto you in an epistle not to company with

fornicators' (1 Cor. v. 9). And it is certainly not advisable so to company with them, or with any of the workers of iniquity, as to have any particular familiarity or any strictness of friendship with them. To contract or continue an intimacy with any such is no way expedient for a Christian. It must necessarily expose him to abundance of dangers and snares, out of which he can have no reasonable hope of deliverance.

But the Apostle does not forbid us to have any intercourse at all even with the men that know not God: 'For then,' says he ' ye must needs go out of the world'; which he could never advise them to do. But he subjoins, 'If any man that is called a brother,' that professes himself a Christian, 'be a fornicator, or covetous, or an idolater, or a railer, or a drunkard, or an extortioner' (1 Cor. v. 11); 'now I have written unto you not to keep company' with him; 'with such an one no not to eat.' This must necessarily imply, that we break off all familiarity, all intimacy of acquaintance, with him. 'Yet count him not,' saith the Apostle elsewhere, 'as an enemy, but admonish him as a brother' (2 Thess, iii. 15); plainly showing that even in such a case as this, we are not to renounce all fellowship with him. So that here is no advice to separate wholly even from wicked men. Yea, these very words teach us quite the contrary.

6. Much more the words of our Lord; who is so far from directing us to break off all commerce with the world, that without it, according to His account of Christianity, we cannot be Christians at all. It would be easy to show, that some intercourse even with ungodly and unholy men is absolutely needful, in order to the full exertion of every temper which He has described as the way to the kingdom; that it is indispensably necessary, in order to the complete exercise of poverty of spirit, of mourning, and of every other disposition which has a place here, in the genuine religion of Jesus Christ. Yea, it is necessary to the very being of several of them: of that meekness, for example, which, instead of demanding 'an eye for an eye, or a tooth for a tooth,' doth 'not resist evil,' but cause us rather, when smitten 'on the right cheek, to turn the other also'; of that mercifulness, whereby we 'love our enemies, bless them that curse us, do good to them that hate us, and pray for them which despitefully use us and persecute us'; and of that complication of love and all holy tempers which is exercised in suffering for

righteousness' sake. Now all these, it is clear, could have no being, were we to have no commerce with any but real Christians.

7. Indeed, were we wholly to separate ourselves from sinners, how could we possibly answer that character which our Lord gives us in these very words? 'Ye' (Christians, ye that are lowly, serious, and meek; ye that hunger after righteousness, that love God and man, that do good to all, and therefore suffer evil; ye) 'are the salt of the earth': it is your very nature to season whatever is round about you. It is the nature of the divine savour which is in you, to spread to whatsoever you touch; to diffuse itself, on every side, to all those among whom you are. This is the great reason why the providence of God has so mingled you together with other men, that whatever grace you have received of God may through you be communicated to others; that every holy temper and word and work of yours may have an influence on them also. By this means a check will, in some measure, be given to the corruption which is in the world; and a small part, at least, saved from the general infection, and rendered holy and pure before God.

8. That we may the more diligently labour to season all we can with every holy and heavenly temper, our Lord proceeds to show the desperate state of those who do not impart the religion they have received; which indeed they cannot possibly fail to do, so long as it remains in their own hearts. 'If the salt have lost his savour, wherewith shall it be salted? It is thenceforth good for nothing but to be cast out, and trodden under foot of men': if ye who were holy and heavenly-minded, and consequently zealous of good works, have no longer that savour in yourselves, and do therefore no longer season others; if you are grown flat, insipid, dead, both careless of your own souls, and useless to the souls of other men; wherewith shall ye be salted? How shall ye be recovered? What help? What hope? Can tasteless salt be restored to its savour? No; 'it is thenceforth good for nothing but to be cast out,' even as the mire in the streets, 'and to be trodden under foot of men,' to be overwhelmed with everlasting contempt. If ye had never known the Lord, there might have been hope,—if ye had never been 'found in Him': but what can you now say to that, His solemn declaration, just parallel to what He hath here spoken? 'Every branch in Me that beareth not

fruit, He,' the Father, 'taketh away. He that abideth in Me, and I in him, bringeth forth much fruit.' 'If a man abide not in Me,' or do not bring forth fruit, 'he is cast out as a branch, and withered; and men gather them,' not to plant them again, but 'to cast them into the fire' (John xv. 2, 5, 6).

9. Toward those who have never tasted of the good word, God is indeed pitiful and of tender mercy. But justice takes place with regard to those who have tasted that the Lord is gracious, and have afterwards turned back 'from the holy commandment' then 'delivered to them.' 'For it is impossible for those who were once enlightened' " (Heb. vi. 4, &c.), in whose hearts God had once shined, to enlighten them with the knowledge of the glory of God in the face of Jesus Christ; 'who have tasted of the heavenly gift,' of redemption in His blood, the forgiveness of sins; 'and were made partakers of the Holy Ghost,' of lowliness, of meekness, and of the love of God and man shed abroad in their hearts by the Holy Ghost which was given unto them; and 'have fallen away'—και παραπεσοντασ (here is not a supposition, but a flat declaration of matter of fact), 'to renew them again unto repentance; seeing they crucify to themselves the Son of God afresh, and put Him to an open shame.

But that none may misunderstand these awful words it should be carefully observed, (1) Who they are that are here spoken of; namely, they, and they only, who were once thus 'enlightened'; they only, 'who did taste of' that 'heavenly gift, and were' thus 'made partakers of the Holy Ghost.' So that all who have not experienced these things are wholly unconcerned in this scripture. (2) What that falling away is, which is here spoken of: it is an absolute, total apostasy. A believer may fall, and not fall away. He may fall and rise again. And if he should fall, even into sin, yet this case, dreadful as it is, is not desperate. For 'we have an Advocate with the Father, Jesus Christ the righteous; and He is the propitiation for our sins.' But let him above all things beware, lest his 'heart be hardened by the deceitfulness of sin'; lest he should sink lower and lower, till he wholly fall away, till he become as salt that hath lost its savour: for if we thus sin wilfully, after we have received the experimental' knowledge of the truth, there remaineth no more sacrifice for sins; but a certain fearful looking for of judgement and fiery indignation, which shall devour the adversaries.'

II. 1. 'But although we may not wholly separate ourselves
from mankind, although it be granted we ought to season them
with the religion which God has wrought in our hearts, yet may
not this be done insensibly? May we not convey this into others in
a secret and almost imperceptible manner, so that scarce any one
shall be able to observe how or when it is done?—even as salt
conveys its own savour into that which is seasoned thereby,
without any noise, and without being liable to any outward
observation. And if so, although we do not go out of the world,
yet we may lie hid in it. We may thus far keep our religion to
ourselves; and not offend those whom we cannot help.'

2. Of this plausible reasoning of flesh and blood our Lord was
well aware also: and He has given a full answer to it in those
words which come now to be considered; in explaining which I
shall endeavour to show, as I proposed to do in the second place,
that so long as true religion abides in our hearts, it is impossible
to conceal it, as well as absolutely contrary to the design of its
great Author.

And, first, it is impossible for any that have it, to conceal the
religion of Jesus Christ. This our Lord makes plain beyond all
contradiction, by a two-fold comparison: 'Ye are the light of the
world: a city set upon a hill cannot be hid.' Ye Christians are 'the
light of the world,' with regard both to your tempers and actions.
Your holiness makes you as conspicuous as the sun in the midst
of heaven. As ye cannot go out of the world, so neither can ye
stay in it without appearing to all mankind. Ye may not flee from
men; and while ye are among them, it is impossible to hide your
lowliness and meekness, and those other dispositions whereby
ye aspire to be perfect as your Father which is in heaven is
perfect. Love cannot be hid any more than light; and least of all,
when it shines forth in action, when ye exercise yourselves in the
labour of love, in beneficence of every kind. As well may men
think to hide a city, as to hide a Christian; yea, as well may they
conceal a city set upon a hill, as a holy, zealous, active lover of
God and man.

3. It is true, men who love darkness rather than light, because
their deeds are evil, will take all possible pains to prove, that the
light which is in you is darkness. They will say evil, all manner of
evil, falsely, of the **good** which is in you; they will lay to your
charge that which is **farthest** from your thoughts, which is the

very reverse of all you are, and all you do. And your patient continuance in well-doing, your meek suffering all things for the Lord's sake, your calm, humble joy in the midst of persecution, your unwearied labour to overcome evil with good, will make you still more visible and conspicuous than ye were before.

4. So impossible it is, to keep our religion from being seen, unless we cast it away; so vain is the thought of hiding the light, unless by putting it out! Sure it is, that a secret, unobserved religion cannot be the religion of Jesus Christ. Whatever religion can be concealed, is not Christianity. If a Christian could be hid, he could not be compared to a city set upon a hill; to the light of the world, the sun shining from heaven, and seen by all the world below. Never, therefore, let it enter into the heart of him whom God hath renewed in the spirit of his mind, to hide that light, to keep his religion to himself; especially considering it is not only impossible to conceal true Christianity, but likewise absolutely contrary to the design of the great Author of it.

5. This plainly appears from the following words: 'Neither do men light a candle to put it under a bushel.' As if he had said, As men do not light a candle, only to cover and conceal it, so neither does God enlighten any soul with His glorious knowledge and love, to have it covered or concealed, either by prudence, falsely so called, or shame, or voluntary humility; to have it hid either in a desert, or in the world; either by avoiding men, or in conversing with them. 'But they put it on a candlestick, and it giveth light to all that are in the house': in like manner, it is the design of God that every Christian should be in an open point of view; that he may give light to all around, that he may visibly express the religion of Jesus Christ.

6. Thus hath God in all ages spoken to the world, not only by precept, but by example also. He hath 'not left Himself without witness,' in any nation where the sound of the gospel hath gone forth, without a few who have testified His truth by their lives as well as their words. These have been 'as lights shining in a dark place.' And from time to time they have been the means of enlightening some, of preserving a remnant, a little seed which was 'counted unto the Lord for a generation.' They have led a few poor sheep out of the darkness of the world, and guided their feet into the way of peace.

7. One might imagine that, where both Scripture and the reason of things speak so clearly and expressly, there could not be much advanced on the other side, at least not with any appearance of truth. But they who imagine thus know little of the depths of Satan. After all that Scripture and reason have said, so exceeding plausible are the pretences for solitary religion, for a Christian's going out of the world, or at least hiding himself in it, that we need all the wisdom of God to see through the snare, and all the power of God to escape it; so many and strong are the objections which have been brought against being social, open, active Christians.

III. 1. To answer these, was the third thing which I proposed. And, first, it has been often objected, that religion does not lie in outward things, but in the heart, the inmost soul; that it is the union of the soul with God the life of God in the soul of man; that outside religion is nothing worth; seeing God 'delighteth not in burnt-offerings,' in outward services, but a pure and holy heart is the 'sacrifice He will not despise.'

I answer, It is most true, that the root of religion lies in the heart, in the inmost soul; that this is the union of the soul with God, the life of God in the soul of man. But if this root be really in the heart, it cannot but put forth branches. And these are the several instances of outward obedience, which partake of the same nature with the root; and, consequently, are not only marks or signs, but substantial parts, of religion.

It is also true, that bare outside religion, which has no root in the heart is nothing worth; that God delighteth not in such outward services, no more than in Jewish burnt-offerings; and that a pure and holy heart is a sacrifice with which He is always well pleased. But He is also well pleased with all that outward service which arises from the heart; with the sacrifice of our prayers (whether public or private), of our praises and thanksgivings; with the sacrifice of our goods, humbly devoted to Him, and employed wholly to His glory; and with that of our bodies, which He peculiarly claims, which the Apostle beseeches us, 'by the mercies of God, to present unto Him, a living sacrifice, holy and acceptable unto God.'

2. A second objection, nearly related to this, is, that love is all in all; that it is 'the fulfilling of the law,' 'the end of the

commandment,' of every commandment of God; that all we do, and all we suffer, if we have not charity or love, profiteth us nothing; and therefore the Apostle directs us to 'follow after charity,' and terms this 'the more excellent way.'

I answer, It is granted, that the love of God and man, arising from faith unfeigned, is all in all, the fulfilling of the law, the end of every commandment of God. It is true, that without this, whatever we do, whatever we suffer, profits us nothing. But it does not follow, that love is all in such a sense as to supersede either faith or good works. It is 'the fulfilling of the law,' not by releasing us from but by constraining us to obey it. It is 'the end of the commandment,' as every commandment leads to and centres in it. It is allowed, that whatever we do or suffer without love profits us nothing: but withal, whatever we do or suffer in love, though it were only the suffering reproach for Christ, or the giving a cup of cold water in His name, it shall in no wise lose its reward.

3. 'But does not the Apostle direct us to "follow after charity"? And does he not term it "a more excellent way"?'—He does direct us to 'follow after charity'; but not after that alone. His words are, 'Follow after charity, and desire spiritual gifts' (1 Cor. xiv. 1). Yea, 'follow after charity'; and desire to spend and be spent for your brethren. 'Follow after charity'; and as you have opportunity, do good to all men.

In the same verse wherein he terms this, the way of love, 'a more excellent way,' he directs the Corinthians to desire other gifts beside it; yea, to desire them earnestly. 'Covet earnestly,' saith he, 'the best gifts; and yet I show unto you a more excellent way' (1 Cor. xii. 31). More excellent than what? Than the gifts of healing, of speaking with tongues, and of interpreting, mentioned in the preceding verses; but not more excellent than the way of obedience. Of this the Apostle is not speaking; neither is he speaking of outward religion at all: so that this text is quite wide of the present question.

But suppose the Apostle had been speaking of outward as well as inward religion, and comparing them together; suppose, in the comparison, he had given the preference ever so much to the latter; suppose he had preferred (as he justly might) a loving heart, before all outward works whatever; yet it would not follow that we were to reject either one or the other. No; God hath joined them together from the beginning of the world; and let not man put them asunder.

4. 'But "God is a Spirit; and they that worship Him, must worship Him in spirit and in truth." And is not this enough? Nay, ought we not to employ the whole strength of our mind herein? Does not attending to outward things clog the soul, that it cannot soar aloft in holy contemplation? Does it not damp the vigour of our thought? Has it not a natural tendency to encumber and distract the mind? Whereas St. Paul would have us to be "without carefulness," and to "wait upon the Lord without distraction." '

I answer, 'God is a Spirit; and they that worship Him must worship Him in spirit and in truth.' Yea, and this is enough: we ought to employ the whole strength of our mind therein. But then I would ask, What is it to worship God, a Spirit, in spirit and in truth? Why, it is to worship Him with our spirit; to worship Him in that manner which none but spirits are capable of. It is to believe in Him, as a wise, just, holy Being, of purer eyes than to behold iniquity; and yet merciful gracious and longsuffering; forgiving iniquity, and transgression and sin; casting all our sins behind His delight in Him, to desire Him, with all our heart, and mind, and soul, and strength; to imitate Him we love, by purifying ourselves even as He is pure; and to obey Him whom we love, and in whom we believe, both in thought, and word, and work. Consequently, one branch of the worshipping God in spirit and in truth is, the keeping His outward commandments. To glorify Him, therefore, with our bodies as well as with our spirits; to go through outward work with hearts lifted up to Him; to make our daily employment a sacrifice to God; to buy and sell, to eat and drink, to His glory,—this is worshipping God in spirit and in truth, as much as the praying to Him in a wilderness.

5. But if so, then contemplation is only one way of worshipping God in spirit and in truth. Therefore to give ourselves up entirely to this, would be to destroy many branches of spiritual worship, all equally acceptable to God, and equally profitable, not hurtful, to the soul. For it is a great mistake to suppose that an attention to those outward things, whereto the providence of God hath called us, is any clog to a Christian, or any hindrance at all to his always seeing Him that is invisible. It

does not at all damp the ardour of his thought; it does not encumber or distract his mind; it gives him no uneasy or hurtful care, who does it all as unto the Lord; who hath learned, whatsoever he doeth in word or deed, to do all in the name of the Lord Jesus; having only one eye of the soul, which moves round on outward things, and one immovably fixed on God. Learn what this meaneth, ye poor recluses, that you may clearly discern your own littleness of faith: yea, that you may no longer judge others by yourselves, go and learn what that meaneth,—

> Thou, O Lord, in tender love,
>   Dost all my burdens bear;
> Lift my heart to things above,
>   And fix it ever there.
> Calm on tumult's wheel I sit,
>   'Midst busy multitudes alone;
> Sweetly waiting at Thy feet,
>   Till all Thy will be done.

6. But the grand objection is still behind. 'We appeal,' say they, 'to experience. Our light did shine; we used outward things many years; and yet they profited nothing. We attended on all the ordinances; but we were no better for it; nor indeed any one else: nay, we were the worse; for we fancied ourselves Christians for so doing, when we knew not what Christianity meant.'

I allow the fact: I allow that you and ten thousand more have thus abused the ordinances of God; mistaking the means for the end; supposing that the doing these, or some other outward works, either was the religion of Jesus Christ, or would be accepted in the place of it. But let the abuse be taken away, and the use remain. Now use all outward things, but use them with a constant eye to the renewal of your soul in righteousness and true holiness.

7. But this is not all: they affirm, 'Experience likewise shows, that the trying to do good is but lost labour. What does it avail to feed or clothe men's bodies, if they are just dropping into everlasting fire? And what good can any man do to their souls? If these are changed, God doeth it Himself. Besides, all men are either good, at least desirous so to be, or obstinately evil. Now the former have no need of us; let them ask help of God, and it shall

be given them: and the latter will receive no help of us. Nay, and our Lord forbids to "cast our pearls before swine." '

I answer, (1) Whether they will finally be lost or saved, you are expressly commanded to feed the hungry, and clothe the naked. If you can, and do not, whatever becomes of them, you shall go away into everlasting fire. (2) Though it is God only changes hearts yet He generally doeth it by man. It is our part to do all that in us lies, as diligently as if we could change them ourselves, and then to leave the event to Him. (3) God, in answer to their prayers, builds up His children by each other in every good gift; nourishing and strengthening the whole 'body by that which every joint supplieth.' So that 'the eye cannot say to the hand, I have no need of thee'; no, nor even 'the head to the feet, I have no need of you.' Lastly. How are you assured, that the persons before you are dogs or swine? Judge them not, until you have tried. 'How knowest thou, O man, but thou mayest gain thy brother'—but thou mayest, under God, save his soul from death? When he spurns thy love, and blasphemes the good word, then it is time to give him up to God.

8. 'We have tried; we have laboured to reform sinners; and what did it avail? On many we could make no impression at all: and if some were changed for a while, yet their goodness was but as the morning dew, and they were soon as bad, nay, worse than ever: so that we only hurt them, and ourselves too; for our minds were hurried and discomposed,—perhaps filled with anger instead of love: therefore, we had better have kept our religion to ourselves.'

It is very possible this fact also may be true; that you have tried to do good, and have not succeeded; yea, that those who seemed reformed, relapsed into sin, and their last state was worse than the first. And what marvel? Is the servant above his Master? But how often did He strive to save sinners, and they would not hear; or, when they had followed Him awhile, they turned back as a dog to his vomit! But He did not therefore desist from striving to do good: no more should you, whatever your success be. It is your part to do as you are commanded: the event is in the hand of God. You are not accountable for this: leave it to Him, who orders all things well. 'In the morning sow thy seed, and in the evening withhold not thy hand: for thou knowest not whether shall prosper' (Eccles. xi. 6).

But the trial hurries and frets your own soul. Perhaps it did so for this very reason, because you thought you was accountable for the event, which no man is, nor indeed can be; or perhaps, because you was off your guard—you was not watchful over your own spirit. But this is no reason for disobeying God. Try again: but try more warily than before. Do good (as you forgive) 'not seven times only, but until seventy times seven.' Only be wiser by experience: attempt it every time more cautiously than before. Be more humbled before God, more deeply convinced that of yourself you can do nothing. Be more jealous over your own spirit; more gentle, and watchful unto prayer. Thus 'cast your bread upon the waters, and you shall find it again after many days.'

IV. 1. Notwithstanding all these plausible pretences for hiding it, 'let your light so shine before men, that they may see your good works, and glorify your Father which is in heaven.' This is the practical application which our Lord Himself makes of the foregoing considerations.

'Let your light so shine,'—your lowliness of heart; your gentleness, and meekness of wisdom; your serious, weighty concern for the things of eternity, and sorrow for the sins and miseries of men; your earnest desire of universal holiness, and full happiness in God; your tender goodwill to all mankind, and fervent love to your supreme Benefactor. Endeavour not to conceal this light, wherewith God hath enlightened your soul; but let it shine before men, before all with whom you are, in the whole tenor of your conversation. Let it shine still more eminently in your actions, in your doing all possible good to all men; and in your suffering for righteousness' sake, while you 'rejoice and are exceeding glad,' knowing that 'great is your reward in heaven.'

2. 'Let your light so shine before men, that they may see your good works,'—so far let a Christian be from ever designing or desiring to conceal his religion! On the contrary, let it be your desire, not to conceal it; not to put the light under a bushel. Let it be your care to place it 'on a candlestick, that it may give light to all that are in the house.' Only take heed, not to seek your own praise herein, not to desire any honour to yourselves. But let it

be your sole aim, that all who see your good works may 'glorify your Father which is in heaven.'

3. Be this your one ultimate end in all things. With this view, be plain, open, undisguised. Let your love be without dissimulation: why should you hide fair, disinterested love? Let there be no guile found in your mouth: let your words be the genuine picture of your heart. Let there be no darkness or reservedness in your conversation, no disguise in your behaviour. Leave this to those who have other designs in view; designs which will not bear the light. Be ye artless and simple to all mankind; that all may see the grace of God which is in you. And although some will harden their hearts, yet others will take knowledge that ye have been with Jesus, and, by returning themselves to the great Bishop of their souls, 'glorify your Father which is in heaven.'

4. With this one design, that men may glorify God in you, go on in His name, and in the power of His might. Be not ashamed even to stand alone, so it be in the ways of God. Let the light which is in your heart shine in all good works, both works of piety and works of mercy. And in order to enlarge your ability of doing good, renounce all superfluities. Cut off all unnecessary expense in food, in furniture, in apparel. Be a good steward of every gift of God, even of these His lowest gifts. Cut off all unnecessary expense of time, all needless or useless employments; and 'whatsoever thy hand findeth to do, do it with thy might.' In a word, be thou full of faith and love; do good; suffer evil. And herein be thou 'steadfast, unmovable'; yea, 'always abounding in the work of the Lord; forasmuch as thou knowest that thy labour is not in vain in the Lord.'

SERMON XX

UPON OUR LORD'S SERMON ON THE MOUNT

DISCOURSE V

On May 15, 1739, the *Journal* records: 'As I was expounding in the Back Lane on the righteousness of the Scribes and Pharisees, many who had before been righteous in their own eyes abhorred themselves as in dust and ashes. But two, who seemed to be more deeply convinced than the rest, did not long sorrow as men without hope, but found in that hour that they had "an advocate with the Father, Jesus Christ the righteous." ' Back Lane lies in the eastern part of Bristol, between Jacob Street and Old Market Street. Wesley had preached there for the first time on Tuesday, April 17, 1739. The service was held in an upper room; and on that occasion the weight of the congregation made the floor give way; but it did not sink far, and the sermon was duly concluded. This sermon is also recorded as preached at Redriff (or Rotherhithe) on July 11, 1740; and the text, Matt. v. 20, is set down half a dozen times in the sermon list between 1747 and 1759. The favourite sermon on the Pharisee and the Publican was no doubt much on the same lines as the latter part of this discourse.

Think not that I am come to destroy the Law, or the Prophets: I am not come to destroy, but to fulfil.

For verily I say unto you, Till heaven and earth pass, one jot or one tittle shall in no wise pass from the law, till all be fulfilled.

Whosoever therefore shall break one of these least commandments, and shall teach men so, he shall be called the least in the kingdom of heaven: but whosoever shall do and teach them, the same shall be called great into the kingdom of heaven.

For I say unto you, That except your righteousness shall exceed the righteousness of the Scribes and Pharisees, ye shall in no case enter into the Kingdom of heaven.—MATT. v. 17-20.

1. Among the multitude of reproaches which fell upon Him who 'was despised and rejected of men,' it could not fail to be one, that He was a teacher of novelties, an introducer of *a new religion*. This might be affirmed with the more colour, because many of the expressions He had used were not common among the Jews: either they did not use them at all, or not in the same

sense, not in so full and strong a meaning. Add to this, that the worshipping God' in spirit and in truth 'must always appear a new religion to those who have hitherto known nothing but outside worship, nothing but the' form of godliness.'

2. And it is not improbable, some might hope it was so; that He was abolishing the old religion, and bringing in another— one which, they might flatter themselves, would be an easier way to heaven. But our Lord refutes, in these words, both the vain hopes of the one, and the groundless calumnies of the other.

I shall consider them in the same order as they lie, taking each verse for a distinct head of discourse.

I. 1. And first, 'Think not that I am come to destroy the Law, or the Prophets: I am not come to destroy, but to fulfil.'

The ritual or ceremonial law, delivered by Moses to the children of Israel, containing all the injunctions and ordinances which related to the old sacrifices and service of the temple, our Lord indeed did come to destroy, to dissolve, and utterly abolish. To this bear all the Apostles witness; not only Barnabas and Paul, who vehemently withstood those who taught that Christians ought 'to keep the law of Moses' (Acts xv. 5); not only St. Peter, who termed the insisting on this, on the observance of the ritual law, a 'tempting God,' and 'putting a yoke upon the neck of the disciples, which neither our fathers,' saith he, 'nor we, were able to bear'; but all the Apostles, elders, and brethren, being assembled with one accord (verse 22), declared, that to command them to keep this law, was to 'subvert their souls'; and that 'it seemed good to the Holy Ghost' and to them, to lay no such burden upon them (verse 28). This 'hand-writing of ordinances our Lord did blot out, take away, and nail to His cross.'

2. But the moral law, contained in the Ten Commandments, and enforced by the prophets, He did not take away. It was not the design of His coming to revoke any part of this. This is a law which never can be broken, which 'stands fast as the faithful witness in heaven.' The moral stands on an entirely different foundation from the ceremonial or ritual law, which was only designed for a temporary restraint upon a disobedient and stiffnecked people; whereas this was from the beginning of the

world, being 'written not on tables of stone,' but on the hearts of all the children of men, when they came out of the hands of the Creator. And, however the letters once wrote by the finger of God are now in a great measure defaced by sin, yet can they not wholly be blotted out, while we have any consciousness of good and evil. Every part of this law must remain in force upon all mankind, and in all ages; as not depending either on time or place, or any other circumstances liable to change, but on the nature of God, and the nature of man, and their unchangeable relation to each other.

3. 'I am not come to destroy, but to fulfil.' Some have conceived our Lord to mean I am come to fulfil this, by My entire and perfect obedience to it. And it cannot be doubted but He did, in this sense, fulfil every part of it. But this does not appear to be what He intends here, being foreign to the scope of His present discourse. Without question His meaning in this place is (consistently with all that goes before and follows after), I am come to establish it in its fullness in spite of all the glosses of men: I am come to place in a full and clear view whatsoever was dark or obscure therein: I am come to declare the true and full import of every part of it; to show the length and breadth, the entire extent, of every commandment contained therein and the height and depth, the inconceivable purity and spirituality of it in all its branches.

4. And this our Lord has abundantly performed, in the preceding and subsequent parts of the discourse before us; in which He has not introduced a new religion into the world, but the same which was from the beginning,—a religion, the substance of which is without question as old as the creation, being coeval with man and having proceeded from God at the very time when 'man became a living soul' (the *substance,* I say; for some circumstances of it now relate to man as a fallen creature); a religion witnessed to both by the law and by the prophets in all succeeding generations. Yet was it never so fully explained, nor so thoroughly understood, till the great Author of it Himself condescended to give mankind this authentic comment on all the essential branches of it; at the same time declaring it should never be changed, but remain in force to the end of the world.

II. 1. 'For verily I say unto you' (a solemn preface, which denotes both the importance and certainty of what is spoken), 'Till heaven and earth pass, one jot or one tittle shall in no wise pass from the law, till all be fulfilled.'

'One jot': it is literally, *not one iota,* not the most inconsiderable vowel. 'Or one tittle,' μια κεραια—one *corner* or *point* of a consonant. It is a proverbial expression, which signifies that no one commandment contained in the moral law, nor the least part of any one, however inconsiderable it might seem, should ever be disannulled.

'Shall in no wise pass from the law': ου μη παρελθη απο του νομου. The double negative, here used, strengthens the sense, so as to admit of no contradiction: and the word παρελθη, it may be observed, is not barely *future,* declaring what *will* be; but has likewise the force of an *imperative,* ordering what *shall* be. It is a word of authority, expressing the sovereign will and power of Him that spake; of Him whose word is the law of heaven and earth, and stands fast for ever and ever.

'One jot or one tittle shall in no wise pass, till heaven and earth pass'; or, as it is expressed immediately after, εως αν παντα γενηται,—*till all* (or rather *all things*) *be fulfilled,* till the consummation of all things. Here is therefore no room for that poor evasion (with which some have delighted themselves greatly), that 'no part of the law was to pass away, till *all the law* was fulfilled: but it has been fulfilled by Christ; and therefore now must pass, for the gospel to be established.' Not so: the word *all* does not mean all the law, but all things in the universe; as neither has the term *fulfilled* any reference to the law, but to all things in heaven and earth.

2. From all this we may learn, that there is no contrariety at all between the law and the gospel; that there is no need for the law to pass away, in order to the establishing the gospel. Indeed neither of them supersedes the other, but they agree perfectly well together. Yea, the very same words, considered in different respects, are parts both of the law and of the gospel: if they are considered as commandments, they are parts of the law; if as promises, of the gospel. Thus, 'Thou shalt love the Lord thy God with all thy heart,' when, considered as a commandment, is a branch of the law; when regarded as a promise, is an essential part of the gospel—the gospel being no other than the

commands of the law, proposed by way of promise. Accordingly, poverty of spirit, purity of heart, and whatever else is enjoined in the holy law of God, are no other, when viewed in a gospel light, than so many great and precious promises.

3. There is, therefore, the closest connexion that can be conceived between the law and the gospel. On the one hand, the law continually makes way for, and points us to, the gospel; on the other, the gospel continually leads us to a more exact fulfilling of the law. The law, for instance, requires us to love God, to love our neighbour, to be meek, humble, or holy: we feel that we are not sufficient for these things; yea, that 'with man this is impossible.' But we see a promise of God, to give us that love, and to make us humble, meek, and holy: we lay hold of this gospel, of these glad tidings: it is done unto us according to our faith; and 'the righteousness of the law is fulfilled in us,' through faith which is in Christ Jesus.

We may yet farther observe, that every command in holy writ is only a covered promise. For by that solemn declaration, 'This is the covenant I will make after those days, saith the Lord: I will put My laws in your minds, and write them in your hearts,' God hath engaged to give whatsoever He commands. Does He command us then to 'pray without ceasing,' to 'rejoice evermore,' to be 'holy as He is holy'? It is enough: He will work in us this very thing: it shall be unto us according to His word.

4. But if these things are so, we cannot be at a loss what to think of those who in all ages of the Church, have undertaken to change or supersede some commands of God, as they professed by the peculiar direction of His Spirit. Christ has here given us an infallible rule, whereby to judge of all such pretensions. Christianity, as it includes the whole moral law of God, both by way of injunction and of promise, if we will hear Him, is designed of God to be the last of all His dispensations. There is no other to come after this. This is to endure till the consummation of all things. Of consequence, all such new revelations are of Satan, and not of God; and all pretences to another more perfect dispensation fall to the ground of course. 'Heaven and earth shall pass away'; but *this* word 'shall not pass away.'

III. 1. 'Whosoever, therefore, shall break one of these least commandments, and shall teach men so, he shall be called the least in the kingdom of heaven: but whosoever shall do and teach them, the same shall be called great in the kingdom of heaven.'

Who, what are they, that make the preaching of the law a character of reproach? Do they not see on whom the reproach must fall—on whose head it must light at last? Whosoever on this ground despiseth us despiseth Him that sent us. For did ever any man preach the law like Him, even when He came not to condemn but to save the world; when He came purposely to 'bring life and immortality to light through the gospel'? Can any preach the law more expressly, more rigorously, than Christ does in these words? And who is he that shall amend them? Who is he that shall instruct the Son of God how to preach? Who will teach Him a better way of delivering the message which He hath received of the Father?

2. 'Whosoever shall break one of these least commandments,' or one of the least of these commandments. 'These commandments,' we may observe, is a term used by our Lord as an equivalent with the law, or the law and the prophets,—which is the same thing, seeing the prophets added nothing to the law, but only declared, explained, or enforced it, as they were moved by the Holy Ghost.

'Whosoever shall break one of these least commandments,' especially if it be done wilfully or presumptuously;—*one*—for 'he that keepeth the whole law, and' thus 'offends in one point, is guilty of all'; the wrath of God abideth on him, as surely as if he had broken every one. So that no allowance is made for one darling lust; no reserve for one idol; no excuse for refraining from all besides, and only giving way to one bosom sin. What God demands is, an entire obedience; we are to have an eye to all His commandments; otherwise we lose all the labour we take in keeping some, and our poor souls for ever and ever.

'One of these least,' or one of the least of these commandments: here is another excuse cut off, whereby many, who cannot deceive God, miserably deceive their own souls. 'This sin,' saith the sinner, 'is it not a little one? Will not the Lord spare me in this thing? Surely He will not be extreme to mark this, since I do not offend in the greater matters of the law.' Vain hope! Speaking after the manner of men, we may term these great, and those little, commandments; but, in reality they are not so. If we use propriety of speech there is no such thing as a little sin; every sin being a transgression of the holy and perfect law, and an affront on the great Majesty of heaven.

3. 'And shall teach men so.' In some sense it may be said, that whosoever openly breaks any commandment teaches others to do the same; for example speaks, and many times louder than precept. In this sense, it is apparent, every open drunkard is a teacher of drunkenness; every Sabbath-breaker is constantly teaching his neighbour to profane the day of the Lord. But this is not all: an habitual breaker of the law is seldom content to stop here; he generally teaches other men to do so too, by word as well as example; especially when he hardens his neck, and hateth to be reproved. Such a sinner soon commences an advocate for sin; he defends what he is resolved not to forsake; he excuses the sin which he will not leave, and thus directly teaches every sin which he commits.

'He shall be called least in the kingdom of heaven'—that is shall have no part therein. He is a stranger to the kingdom of heaven which is on earth: he hath no portion in that inheritance; no share of that 'righteousness, and peace, and joy in the Holy Ghost.' Nor, by consequence, can he have any part in the glory which shall be revealed.

4. But if those who even thus break, and teach others to break, 'one of the least of these commandments, shall be called least in the kingdom of heaven,' shall have no part in the kingdom of Christ and of God; if even these shall be cast into 'outer darkness, where is wailing and gnashing of teeth'; then where will they appear, whom our Lord chiefly and primarily intends in these words—they who, bearing the character of teachers sent from God, do nevertheless themselves break His commandments; yea, and openly teach others so to do; being corrupt both in life and doctrine?

5. These are of several sorts. Of the first sort are they who live in some wilful, habitual sin. Now, if an ordinary sinner teaches by his example, how much more a sinful minister—even if he does not attempt to defend, excuse, or extenuate his sin! If he does, he is a murderer indeed; yea, the murderer-general of his congregation. He peoples the regions of death. He is the choicest instrument of the prince of darkness. When he goes hence, 'hell from beneath is moved to meet him at his coming.'

Nor can he sink into the bottomless pit, without dragging a multitude after him.

6. Next to these are the good-natured, good sort of men; who live an easy, harmless life, neither troubling themselves with outward sin, nor with inward holiness; men who are remarkable neither one way nor the other, neither for religion nor irreligion; who are very regular both in public and private, but do not pretend to be any stricter than their neighbours. A minister of this kind breaks, not one, or a few only, of the least commandments of God: but all the great and weighty branches of His law which relate to the power of godliness, and all that require us to 'pass the time of our sojourning in fear,' to 'work out our salvation with fear and trembling,' to have our 'loins always girt, and our lights burning,' to 'strive' or agonize 'to enter in at the strait gate.' And he *teaches men so,* by the whole form of his life, and the general tenor of his preaching, which uniformly tends to soothe those in their pleasing dream who imagine themselves Christians and are not; to persuade all who attend upon his ministry to sleep on and take their rest. No marvel, therefore, if both he, and they that follow him, wake together in everlasting burnings!

7. But above all these, in the highest rank of the enemies of the gospel of Christ are they who openly and explicitly 'judge the law' itself, and 'speak evil of the law'; who teach men to break (λυσαι, to *dissolve,* to *loose,* to *untie,* the obligation of) not one only, whether of the least or of the greatest, but all the commandments at a stroke; who teach, without any cover, in so many words, 'What did our Lord do with the law? He abolished it. There is but one duty, which is that of believing. All commands are unfit for our times. From any demand of the law, no man is obliged now to go one step, or give away one farthing, to eat or omit one morsel.' This is, indeed, carrying matters with a high hand; this is withstanding our Lord to the face, and telling Him that He understood not how to deliver the message on which He was sent. O Lord, lay not this sin to their charge! Father forgive them; for they know not what they do!

8. The most surprising of all the circumstances that attend this strong delusion is, that they who are given up to it really believe that they honour Christ by overthrowing His law, and that they are magnifying His office, while they are destroying His

doctrine. Yea, they honour Him just as Judas did, when he said, 'Hail, Master!' and kissed Him. And He may as justly say to every one of them, 'Betrayest thou the Son of Man with a kiss?' It is no other than betraying Him with a kiss, to talk of His blood, and take away His crown; to set light by any part of His law, under pretence of advancing His gospel. Nor, indeed, can any one escape this charge, who preaches faith in any such a manner as either directly or indirectly tends to set aside any branch of obedience; who preaches Christ so as to disannul, or weaken in any wise, the least of the commandments of God.

9. It is impossible, indeed, to have too high an esteem for 'the faith of God's elect.' And we must all declare, 'By grace ye are saved through faith; not of works, lest any man should boast.' We must cry aloud to every penitent sinner, 'Believe in the Lord Jesus Christ, and thou shalt be saved.' But, at the same time, we must take care to let all men know, we esteem no faith but that which worketh by love; and that we are not saved by faith, unless so far as we are delivered from the power as well as the guilt of sin. And when we say, 'Believe, and thou shalt be saved,' we do not mean, 'Believe, and thou shalt step from sin to heaven, without any holiness coming between; faith supplying the place of holiness'; but, 'Believe, and thou shalt be holy; believe in the Lord Jesus, and thou shalt have peace and power together: thou shalt have power from Him in whom thou believest, to trample sin under thy feet; power to love the Lord thy God with all thy heart, and to serve Him with all thy strength; thou shalt have power, "by patient continuance in well-doing, to seek for glory, and honour, and immortality"; thou shalt both do and teach all the commandments of God, from the least even to the greatest: thou shalt teach them by thy life as well as thy words, and so "be called great in the kingdom of heaven." '

IV. 1. Whatever other way we teach to the kingdom of heaven, to glory, honour, and immortality, be it called 'the way of faith,' or by any other name, it is, in truth, the way to destruction. It will not bring a man peace at the last. For thus saith the Lord, 'I say unto you, That except your righteousness shall exceed the righteousness of the Scribes and Pharisees, ye shall in no case enter into the kingdom of heaven.'

The Scribes, mentioned so often in the New Testament, as

some of the most constant and vehement opposers of our Lord, were not secretaries, or men employed in writing only, as that term might incline us to believe. Neither were they lawyers, in our common sense of the word; although the word νομικοι is so rendered in our translation. Their employment had no affinity at all to that of a lawyer among us. They were conversant with the laws of God, and not with the laws of man. These were their study: it was their proper and peculiar business to read and expound the law and the prophets; particularly in the synagogues. They were the ordinary, stated preachers among the Jews. So that if the sense of the original word was attended to, we might render it, 'the divines.' For these were the men who made divinity their profession: and they were generally (as their name literally imports) men of letters; men of the greatest account for learning that were then in the Jewish nation.

2. The Pharisees were a very ancient sect, or body of men, among the Jews; originally so called from the Hebrew word פרש, which signifies to *separate* or *divide*. Not that they made any formal separation from, or division in, the national Church: they were only distinguished from others by greater strictness of life, by more exactness of conversation. For they were zealous of the law in the minutest points; paying tithes of mint, anise, and cummin: and hence they were had in honour of all the people, and generally esteemed the holiest of men.

Many of the Scribes were of the sect of the Pharisees. Thus St. Paul himself, who was educated for a Scribe, first at the university of Tarsus, and after that in Jerusalem, at the feet of Gamaliel (one of the most learned Scribes or Doctors of the Law that were then in the nation), declares of himself before the council, 'I am a Pharisee, the son of a Pharisee' (Acts xxiii. 6); and before King Agrippa, 'After the straitest sect of our religion I lived a Pharisee' (xxvi. 5). And the whole body of the Scribes generally esteemed and acted in concert with the Pharisees. Hence we find our Saviour so frequently coupling them together, as coming in many respects under the same consideration. In this place they seem to be mentioned together as the most eminent professors of religion; the former of whom were accounted the wisest, the latter the holiest of men.

3. What 'the righteousness of the Scribes and Pharisees' really was, it is not difficult to determine. Our Lord has preserved an

authentic account which one of them gave of himself: and he is clear and full in describing his own righteousness; and cannot be supposed to have omitted any part of it. He went up indeed 'into the temple to pray'; but was so intent upon his own virtues, that he forgot the design upon which he came. For it is remarkable, he does not properly pray at all: he only tells God how wise and good he was. 'God, I thank thee, that I am not as other men are, extortioners, unjust, adulterers; or even as this publican. I fast twice in the week; I give tithes of all that I possess.' His righteousness therefore consisted of three parts: first, saith he, 'I am not as other men are'; I am not an extortioner, not unjust, not an adulterer; not 'even as this publican': secondly, 'I fast twice in the week': and, thirdly,' I give tithes of all that I possess.'

'I am not as other men are.' This is not a small point. It is not every man that can say this. It is as if he had said, 'I do not suffer myself to be carried away by that great torrent, custom. I live not by custom, but by reason; not by the examples of men, but by the Word of God. I am not an extortioner, not unjust, not an adulterer; however common these sins are, even among those who are called the people of God (extortion, in particular—a kind of legal injustice, not punishable by any human law, the making gain of another's ignorance or necessity—having filled every corner of the land); nor even as this publican; not guilty of any open or presumptuous sin; not an outward sinner; but a fair, honest man, of blameless life and conversation.'

4. 'I fast twice in the week.' There is more implied in this than we may at first be sensible of. All the stricter Pharisees observed the weekly fasts; namely, every Monday and Thursday. On the former day, they fasted in memory of Moses receiving on that day (as their tradition taught) the two tables of stone written by the finger of God; on the latter, in memory of his casting them out of his hand, when he saw the people dancing round the golden calf. On these days, they took no sustenance at all, till three in the afternoon; the hour at which they began to offer up the evening sacrifice in the temple. Till that hour, it was their custom to remain in the temple, in some of the corners, apartments, or courts thereof; that they might be ready to assist at all the sacrifices, and to join in all the public prayers. The time between they were accustomed to employ, partly in private addresses to God, partly in searching the Scriptures, in reading

the law and the prophets, and in meditating thereon. Thus much is implied in, 'I fast twice in the week'; the second branch of the righteousness of a Pharisee.

5. 'I give tithes of all that I possess.' This the Pharisees did with the utmost exactness. They would not except the most inconsiderable thing; no, not mint, anise, and cummin. They would not keep back the least part of what they believed properly to belong to God; but gave a full tenth of their whole substance yearly, and of all their increase, whatsoever it was.

Yea, the stricter Pharisees (as has been often observed by those who are versed in the ancient Jewish writings), not content with giving one tenth of their substance to God in His priests and Levites, gave another tenth to God in the poor, and that continually. They gave the same proportion of all they had in alms, as they were accustomed to give in tithes. And this likewise they adjusted with the utmost exactness; that they might not keep back any part, but might fully render unto God the things which were God's, as they accounted this to be. So that, upon the whole, they gave away, from year to year, an entire fifth of all that they possessed.

6. This was 'the righteousness of the Scribes and Pharisees'; a righteousness which, in many respects, went far beyond the conception which many have been accustomed to entertain concerning it. But perhaps it will be said, 'It was all false and feigned; for they were all a company of hypocrites.' Some of them doubtless were; men who had really no religion at all, no fear of God, or desire to please Him; who had no concern for the honour that cometh of God, but only for the praise of men. And these are they whom our Lord so severely condemns, so sharply reproves, on many occasions. But we must not suppose, because many Pharisees were hypocrites, therefore all were so. Nor indeed is hypocrisy by any means essential to the character of a Pharisee. This is not the distinguishing mark of their sect. It is rather this, according to our Lord's account, 'They trusted in themselves that they were righteous, and despised others.' This is their genuine badge. But the Pharisee of this kind cannot be an hypocrite. He must be, in the common sense, sincere; otherwise he could not 'trust in himself that he is righteous.' The man who was here commending himself to God, unquestionably thought himself righteous. Consequently he was no hypocrite;

he was not conscious to himself of any insincerity. He now spoke to God just what he thought, that he was abundantly better than other men.

But the example of St. Paul, were there no other, is sufficient to put this out of all question. He could not only say when he was a Christian, 'Herein do I exercise myself, to have always a conscience void of offence toward God, and toward men' (Acts xxiv. 16); but even concerning the time when he was a Pharisee, 'Men and brethren, I have lived in all good conscience before God until this day' (xxiii. 1). He was therefore sincere when he was a Pharisee, as well as when he was a Christian. He was no more a hypocrite when he persecuted the church, than when he preached the faith which once he persecuted. Let this then be added to 'the righteousness of the Scribes and Pharisees'—a sincere belief that they are righteous, and in all things 'doing God service.'

7. And yet, 'except your righteousness,' saith our Lord, 'shall exceed the righteousness of the Scribes and Pharisees, ye shall in no case enter into the kingdom of heaven.' A solemn and weighty declaration, and one which it behoves all who are called by the name of Christ seriously and deeply to consider. But before we inquire how our righteousness may exceed theirs, let us examine whether at present we come up to it.

First. A Pharisee was 'not as other men are.' In externals he was singularly good. Are we so? Do we dare to be singular at all? Do we not rather swim with the stream? Do we not many times dispense with religion and reason together, because we would not *look particiular*? Are we not often more afraid of being out of the fashion, than being out of the way of salvation? Have we courage to stem the tide, to run counter to the world, 'to obey God rather than man'? Otherwise, the Pharisee leaves us behind at the very first step. It is well if we overtake him any more.

But to come closer. Can we use his first plea with God?—which is, in substance, 'I do no harm: I live in no outward sin: I do nothing for which my own heart condemns me.' Do you not? Are you sure of that? Do you live in no practice for which your own heart condemns you? If you are not an adulterer, if you are not unchaste, either in word or deed, are you not unjust? The grand measure of justice, as well as of mercy, is, 'Do unto others as thou wouldest they should do unto thee.' Do you walk by this

rule? Do you never do unto any what you would not they should
do unto you? Nay, are you not grossly unjust? Are you not an
extortioner? Do you not make a gain of any one's ignorance or
necessity; neither in buying nor selling? Suppose you were
engaged in trade: do you demand, do you receive, no more than
the real value of what you sell? Do you demand, do you receive
no more of the ignorant than of the knowing—of a little child,
than of an experienced trader? If you do, why does not your
heart condemn you? You are a barefaced extortioner. Do you
demand no more than the usual price of goods of any who is in
pressing want—who must have, and that without delay, the
things which you only can furnish him with? If you do, this also is
flat extortion. Indeed you do not come up to the righteousness
of a Pharisee.

8. A Pharisee, secondly (to express his sense in our common
way), used all the means of grace. As he fasted often and much,
twice in every week, so he attended all the sacrifices. He was
constant in public and private prayer, and in reading and
hearing the Scriptures. Do you go as far as this? Do you fast
much and often?—twice in the week? I fear not. Once at
least—'on all Fridays in the year'? (So our Church clearly and
peremptorily enjoins all her members to do; to observe all these,
as well as the vigils and the forty days of Lent, as days of fasting
or abstinence.) Do you fast twice in the year? I am afraid some
among us cannot plead even this! Do you neglect no opportunity
of attending and partaking of the Christian sacrifice? How many
are they who call themselves Christians and yet are utterly
regardless of it—yet do not eat of that bread, or drink of that
cup, for months, perhaps years together! Do you, every day,
either hear the Scriptures, or read them, and meditate thereon?
Do you join in prayer with the great congregation, daily, if you
have opportunity; if not, whenever you can; particularly on that
day which you 'remember to keep it holy'? Do you strive to *make*
opportunities? Are you glad when they say unto you, 'We will go
into the house of the Lord'? Are you zealous of, and diligent in,
private prayer? Do you suffer no day to pass without it? Rather,
are not some of you so far from spending therein (with the
Pharisee) several hours in one day, that you think one hour full
enough, if not too much? Do you spend an hour in a day, or in a
week, in praying to your Father which is in secret? yea, an hour

in a month? Have you spent one hour together in private prayer ever since you was born? Ah, poor Christian! Shall not the Pharisee rise up in the judgement against thee and condemn thee? His righteousness is as far above thine as the heaven is above the earth!

9. The Pharisee, thirdly, paid tithes and gave alms of all that he possessed. And in how ample a manner! So that he was (as we phrase it) 'a man that did much good.' Do we come up to him here? Which of us is so abundant as he was in good works? Which of us gives a fifth of all his substance to God, both of the principal and of the increase? Who of us, out of (suppose) an hundred pounds a year, gives twenty to God and the poor; out of fifty, ten; and so in a larger or a smaller proportion? When shall our righteousness, in using all the means of grace, in attending all the ordinances of God, in avoiding evil and doing good, equal at least the righteousness of the Scribes and Pharisees?

10. Although if it only equalled theirs, what would that profit? 'For verily I say unto you, Except your righteousness shall exceed the righteousness of the Scribes and Pharisees, ye shall in no case enter into the kingdom of heaven.' But how can it exceed theirs? Wherein does the righteousness of a Christian exceed that of a Scribe or Pharisee? Christian righteousness exceeds theirs, first in the extent of it. Most of the Pharisees, though they were rigorously exact in many things, yet were emboldened, by the traditions of the elders, to dispense with others of equal importance. Thus, they were extremely punctual in keeping the fourth commandment—they would not even rub an ear of corn on the Sabbath day; but not at all in keeping the third—making little account of light, or even false, swearing. So that their righteousness was partial; whereas the righteousness of a real Christian is universal. He does not observe one, or some parts of the law of God, and neglect the rest; but keeps all His commandments, loves them all, values them above gold or precious stones.

11. It may be, indeed, that some of the Scribes and Pharisees endeavoured to keep all the commandments, and consequently were, as touching the righteousness of the law, that is, according to the letter of it, blameless. But still the righteousness of a Christian exceeds all this righteousness of a Scribe or Pharisee,

by fulfilling the spirit as well as the letter of the law; by inward as
well as outward obedience. In this, in the spirituality of it, it
admits of no comparison. This is the point which our Lord has so
largely proved, in the whole tenor of this discourse. Their
righteousness was external only; Christian righteousness is in
the inner man. The Pharisee 'cleansed the outside of the cup
and the platter'; the Christian is clean within. The Pharisee
laboured to present God with a good life; the Christian with a
holy heart. The one shook off the leaves, perhaps the fruits, of
sin; the other 'lays the axe to the root'; as not being content with
the outward form of godliness, how exact soever it be, unless the
life, the Spirit, the power of God unto salvation be felt in the
inmost soul.

Thus, to do no harm, to do good, to attend the ordinances of
God (the righteousness of a Pharisee), are all external; whereas,
on the contrary, poverty of spirit, mourning, meekness, hunger
and thirst after righteousness, the love of our neighbour, and
purity of heart (the righteousness of a Christian), are all
internal. And even peace-making (or doing good), and
suffering for righteousness' sake, stand entitled to the blessings
annexed to them, only as they imply these inward dispositions,
as they spring from, exercise, and confirm them. So that
whereas the righteousness of the Scribes and Pharisees was
external only, it may be said, in some sense, that the
righteousness of a Christian is internal only: all his actions and
sufferings being as nothing in themselves, being estimated
before God only by the tempers from which they spring.

12. Whosoever therefore thou art, who bearest the holy and
venerable name of a Christian, see, first, that thy righteousness
fall not short of the righteousness of the Scribes and Pharisees.
Be not thou 'as other men are'! 'Dare to stand alone'; to be,
'against example, singularly good.' If thou 'follow a multitude' at
all, it must be 'to do evil.' Let not custom or fashion be thy guide,
but reason and religion. The practice of others is nothing to
thee: 'Every man must give an account of himself to God.'
Indeed, if thou canst save the soul of another, do; but at least
save one,—thy own. Walk not in the path of death because it is
broad, and many walk therein. Nay, by this very token thou
mayest know it. Is the way wherein thou now walkest, a broad,
well-frequented, fashionable way? Then it infallibly leads to

destruction. O be not thou 'damned for company'! Cease from
evil: fly from sin as from the face of a serpent! At least, do no
harm. 'He that committeth sin is of the devil.' Be not thou found
in that number. Touching outward sins, surely the grace of God
is even now sufficient for thee. 'Herein,' at least, 'exercise thyself
to have a conscience void of offence toward God, and toward
men.'

Secondly. Let not thy righteousness fall short of theirs with
regard to the ordinances of God. If thy labour or bodily strength
will not allow of thy fasting twice in the week, however, deal
faithfully with thy own soul, and fast as often as thy strength will
permit. Omit no public, no private opportunity of pouring out
thy soul in prayer. Neglect no occasion of eating that bread and
drinking that cup which is the communion of the body and
blood of Christ. Be diligent in searching the Scriptures; read as
thou mayest, and meditate therein day and night. Rejoice to
embrace every opportunity of hearing 'the word of reconciliation' declared by the 'ambassadors of Christ,' the 'stewards of the
mysteries of God.' In using all the means of grace, in a constant
and careful attendance on every ordinance of God, live up to (at
least till thou canst go beyond) 'the righteousness of the Scribes
and Pharisees.'

Thirdly. Fall not short of a Pharisee in doing good. Give alms
of all thou dost possess. Is any hungry? Feed him. Is he athirst?
Give him drink. Naked? Cover him with a garment. If thou hast
this world's goods, do not limit thy beneficence to a scanty
proportion. Be merciful to the uttermost of thy power. Why not
even as this Pharisee? Now 'make thyself friends,' while the time
is, 'of the mammon of unrighteousness that when thou failest,'
when this earthly tabernacle is dissolved, they 'may receive thee
into everlasting habitations.'

13. But rest not here. Let thy righteousness 'exceed the
righteousness of the Scribes and Pharisees.' Be not thou content
to 'keep the whole law and offend in one point.' Hold thou fast
all His commandments, and all 'false ways do thou utterly
abhor.' Do all the things whatsoever He hath commanded, and
that with all thy might. Thou canst do all things through Christ
strengthening thee; though without Him thou canst do nothing.

Above all, let thy righteousness exceed theirs in the purity and
spirituality of it. What is the exactest form of religion to thee? the

most perfect outside righteousness? Go thou higher and deeper than all this! Let thy religion be the religion of the heart. Be thou poor in spirit; little, and base, and mean, and vile in thy own eyes; amazed and humbled to the dust at the love of God which is in Christ Jesus thy Lord! Be serious: let the whole stream of thy thoughts, words, and works be such as flows from the deepest conviction that thou standest on the edge of the great gulf, thou and all the children of men, just ready to drop in, either into everlasting glory or everlasting burnings! Be meek: let thy soul be filled with mildness, gentleness, patience, long-suffering toward all men; at the same time that all which is in thee is athirst for God, the living God, longing to awake up after His likeness, and to be satisfied with it. Be thou a lover of God, and of all mankind. In this spirit, do and suffer all things. Thus 'exceed the righteousness of the Scribes and Pharisees,' and thou shalt be 'called great in the kingdom of heaven.'

SERMON XXI

UPON OUR LORD'S SERMON ON THE MOUNT

DISCOURSE VI

The substance of this sermon was no doubt part of the systematic expositions of the Sermon on the Mount to the Societies. The only reference to it as a distinct discourse is in the sermon-register for Monday, December 24, 1750, when it was preached in the morning at the Foundery, the text being Matt. vi. 13, &c.

The three chief duties of the Jewish religion were almsgiving, prayer, and fasting. These our Lord assumes are practised by His hearers, and He does not prescribe them, but gives directions for their acceptable performance.

The practice of almsgiving, whilst encouraged in the Old Testament, became specially prominent in the third and second centuries B.C. Tobit gives advice to Tobias (Tob. xii. 8), 'Prayer is good with fasting and alms and righteousness. . . . It is better to give alms than to lay up gold. For alms doth deliver from death, and shall purge away all sin.' So the Son of Sirach (Ecclus. iii. 3o) says, 'Alms maketh an atonement for sin.' In process of time the alms were given through the synagogue, by the officers of which the relief of the poor was organized. One of the Mishpotim in the Midrash Tanchumah runs, 'God, whose creditor you have become when you helped the helpless, will rescue you and yours from danger when it is near.' The modern Jews have maintained their nation's character in this respect, and it used to be, and probably still is, a rare thing to find a Jew in a workhouse in England.

Prayer is not a matter for legislation, and no directions for this exercise are given in the law. The essence of prayer is its spontaneity; it is the cry of a soul at the point of destruction—'Lord, save, or I perish!'—or the exchange of intimate confidences between the child and his Father in heaven. To order prayer to be offered is to make it impossible. So the law left it alone; but the whole of the Old Testament smokes with the incense of the prayers of the saints, and the Book of Psalms is the model of all devotion. By the end of the first century B.C. prayers had been regularized by the Rabbis, and three hours of prayer were prescribed—the third, the sixth, and the ninth hours; or, as Schurer thinks, the hours of the morning and evening sacrifice, and sunset. The synagogues were always open for the offering of prayer, and it was usual to go thither at each hour of prayer for that purpose; but if the hour of prayer overtook a man in his home or in the street, he would offer his prayer there. This led in many cases to ostentatious praying in the most public places possible, in order to gain credit with the crowd. Hence our Lord's criticism.

It should be noted that in verse 1 the better reading is, 'Take heed that ye do not your *righteousness* before men.' Righteousness includes the three branches cited as illustrations of the general proposition—almsgiving, prayer, and fasting. In each case the sin denounced is ostentation; the verses 7 to 15 interrupt the continuity of the sermon, and are an editorial insertion of the evangelist. The warning against 'vain repetitions' is directed not against Pharisaic but heathen prayers, and does not properly belong here. St. Luke (xi. 1-4) gives us the Lord's Prayer in its chronological place, and states the occasion on which it was dictated to the disciples; but St. Matthew's version seems to be the original one, Luke having omitted certain clauses which would not be understood by the Gentile readers for whom he was writing. Thus 'which art in heaven' is a well-known Jewish qualification of God; the reference to the angels in the third petition would have no meaning to the Gentiles; 'sins' is a more familiar word than the Jewish 'debts'; and the second part of the sixth petition may imply the Jewish belief in a personal Devil, 'Deliver us from the Evil One.' The Doxology is an early liturgical addition to the prayer, and not a part of it as delivered by our Lord. The two verses which follow occur in another connexion in Mark xi. 25, and practically in Matt. xviii. 35.

Take heed that ye do not your alms before men, to be seen of them: otherwise ye have no reward of your Father which is in heaven.

Therefore when thou doest thine alms, do not sound a trumpet before thee, as the hypocrites do in the synagogues and in the streets, that they may have glory of men. Verily I say unto you, They have their reward.

But when thou doest alms, let not thy left hand know what the right hand doeth:

That thine alms may be in secret: and thy Father which seeth in secret Himself shall reward thee openly.

And when thou Prayest, thou shall not be as the hypocrites are: for they love to Pray standing in the synagogues and in the corners of the streets that they may be seen of men. Verily I say unto you, They have have their reward.

But thou, when thou prayest, enter into thy closet, and when thou hast shut thy door, pray to thy Father which is in secret, and thy Father which seeth in secret shall reward thee openly.

But when ye pray, use not vain repetitions, as the Heathen do: for they think that they shall be heard for their much speaking.

Be not ye therefore like unto them: for your Father knoweth what things ye have need of, before ye ask Him.

After this manner therefore pray ye: Our Father which art in heaven, Hallowed by Thy name. Thy kingdom come. Thy will be done in earth, as it is in heaven. Give us this day our daily bread. And forgive us our debts, as we forgive our debtors. And lead us not into temptation, but deliver us from evil: For Thine is the kingdom, and the power, and the glory, for ever. Amen.

For if ye forgive men their trespasses, your heavenly Father will also forgive you:

But if ye forgive not men their trespasses, neither will your Father forgive your
trespasses.—MATT. vi. 1-15.

1. In the preceding chapter our Lord has described inward religion in its various branches. He has laid before us those dispositions of soul which constitute real Christianity; the inward tempers contained in that 'holiness, without which no man shall see the Lord'; the affections which, when flowing from their proper fountain, from a living faith in God through Christ Jesus, are intrinsically and essentially good, and acceptable to God. He proceeds to show, in this chapter, how all our actions likewise, even those that are indifferent in their own nature, may be made holy, and good, and acceptable to God, by a pure and holy intention. Whatever is done without this, He largely declares, is of no value before God. Whereas, whatever outward works are thus consecrated to God, they are, in His sight, of great price.

2. The necessity of this purity of intention, He shows, first, with regard to those which are usually accounted religious actions, and indeed are such when performed with a right intention. Some of these are commonly termed' works of piety'; the rest, 'works of charity' or mercy. Of the latter sort, He particularly names almsgiving; of the former, prayer and fasting. But the directions given for these are equally to be applied to every work, whether of charity or mercy.

I. 1. And, first, with regard to works of mercy. 'Take heed,' saith He, 'that ye do not your alms before men, to be seen of them: otherwise ye have no reward of your Father which is in heaven.' 'That ye do not your alms': although this only is named, yet is every work of charity included, everything which we give, or speak, or do, whereby our neighbor may be profited; whereby another man may receive any advantage, either in his body or soul. The feeding the hungry, the clothing the naked, the entertaining or assisting the stranger, the visiting those that are sick or in prison, the comforting the afflicted, the instructing the ignorant, the reproving the wicked, the exhorting and encouraging the well-doer; and if there be any other work of mercy, it is equally included in this direction.

2. 'Take heed that ye do not your alms before men, to be seen of them.' The thing which is here forbidden is not barely the

doing good in the sight of men; this circumstance alone, that others see what we do, makes the action neither worse nor better; but the doing it before men, 'to be seen of them,' with this view, from this intention only. I say, from this intention only; for this may, in some cases, be a part of our intention; we may design that some of our actions should be seen, and yet they may be acceptable to God. We may intend that our light should shine before men, when our conscience bears us witness in the Holy Ghost, that our ultimate end in designing they should see our good works is, 'that they may glorify our Father which is in heaven.' But take heed that ye do not the least thing with a view to your own glory: take heed that a regard to the praise of men have no place at all in your works of mercy. If ye seek your own glory, if you have any design to gain the honour that cometh of men, whatever is done with this view is nothing worth; it is not done unto the Lord: He accepteth it not; 'ye have no reward' for this 'of your Father which is in heaven.'

3. 'Therefore when thou doest thine alms, do not sound a trumpet before thee, as the hypocrites do in the synagogues and in the streets, that they may have praise of men.' The word synagogue does not here mean a place of worship, but any place of public resort, such as the market-place, or exchange. It was a common thing among the Jews who were men of large fortunes, particularly among the Pharisees, to cause a trumpet to be sounded before them in the most public parts of the city, when they were about to give any considerable alms. The pretended reason for this was to call the poor together to receive it; but the real design, that they might have praise of men. But be not thou like unto them. Do not thou cause a trumpet to be sounded before thee. Use no ostentation in doing good. Aim at the honour which cometh of God only. They who seek the praise of men have their reward: they shall have no praise of God.

4. 'But when thou doest alms, let not thy left hand know what thy right hand doeth.' This is a proverbial expression, the meaning of which is, Do it in as secret a manner as is possible; as secret as is consistent with the doing it at all (for it must not be left undone; omit no opportunity of doing good, whether secretly or openly), and with the doing it in the most effectual manner. For here is also an exception to be made: when you are fully persuaded in your own mind, that by your not concealing the

good which is done, either you will yourself be enabled, or others excited, to do the more good, then you may not conceal it; then let your light appear, and, 'shine to all that are in the house.' But, unless where the glory of God and the good of mankind oblige you to the contrary, act in as private and unobserved a manner as the nature of the thing will admit; 'that thy alms may be in secret; and thy Father which seeth in secret, He shall reward thee openly'; perhaps in the present world—many instances of this stand recorded in all ages; but infallibly in the world to come, before the general assembly of men and angels.

II. 1. From works of charity or mercy our Lord proceeds to those which are termed 'works of piety.' 'And when thou prayest,' saith He, 'thou shalt not be as the hypocrites are; for they love to pray standing in the synagogues, and in the corners of the streets, that they may be seen of men.' 'Thou shalt not be as the hypocrites are.' Hypocrisy, then, or insincerity, is the first thing we are to guard against in prayer. Beware not to speak what thou dost not mean. Prayer is the lifting up of the heart to God: all words of prayer, without this, are mere hypocrisy. Whenever therefore thou attemptest to pray, see that it be thy one design to commune with God, to lift up thy heart to Him, to pour out thy soul before Him; not as the hypocrites, who love, or are wont, 'to pray standing in the synagogues,' the exchange, or market-places, 'and in the corners of the streets,' wherever the most people are, 'that they may be seen of men': this was the sole design, the motive, and end, of the prayers which they there repeated. 'Verily I say unto you, They have their reward.' They are to expect none from your Father which is in heaven.

2. But it is not only the having an eye to the praise of men, which cuts us off from any reward in heaven; which leaves us no room to expect the blessing of God upon our works, whether of piety or mercy. Purity of intention is equally destroyed by a view to any temporal reward whatever. If we repeat our prayers, if we attend the public worship of God, if we relieve the poor, with a view to gain or interest, it is not a whit more acceptable to God, than if it were done with a view to praise. Any temporal view, any motive whatever on this side eternity, any design but that of promoting the glory of God, and the happiness of men for God's sake, makes every action, however fair it may appear to men, an abomination unto the Lord.

3. 'But when thou prayest, enter into thy closet, and when thou hast shut thy door, pray to thy Father which is in secret. There is a time when thou art openly to glorify God, to pray, and praise Him in the great congregation. But when thou desirest more largely and more particularly to make thy requests known unto God, whether it be in the evening, or in the morning, or at noonday, 'enter into thy closet, and shut thy door.' Use all the privacy thou canst. (Only leave it not undone, whether thou hast any closet, any privacy, or no. Pray to God, if it be possible, when none seeth but He; but if otherwise, pray to God.) Thus 'pray to thy Father which is in secret'; pour out all thy heart before Him; 'and thy Father which seeth in secret, He shall reward thee openly.'

4. 'But when ye pray,' even in secret, 'use not vain repetitions, as the Heathen do'; μη βαττολογησητε. Do not use abundance of words without any meaning. Say not the same thing over and over again; think not the fruit of your prayers depends on the length of them, like the Heathens; for 'they think they shall be heard for their much speaking.'

The thing here reproved is not simply the length, any more than the shortness, of our prayers;—but, first, length without meaning; speaking much, and meaning little or nothing; the using (not all repetitions; for our Lord Himself prayed thrice, repeating the same words; but) vain repetitions, as the Heathens did, reciting the names of their gods over and over; as they do among Christians (vulgarly so called), and not among the Papists only, who say over and over the same string of prayers, without ever feeling what they speak: secondly, the thinking to be heard for our much speaking, the fancying God measures prayers by their length, and is best pleased with those which contain the most words, which sound the longest in His ears. These are such instances of superstition and folly as all who are named by the name of Christ should leave to the Heathens, to them on whom the glorious light of the gospel hath never shined.

5. 'Be not ye therefore like unto them.' Ye who have tasted of the grace of God in Christ Jesus are thoroughly convinced, 'your Father knoweth what things ye have need of, before ye ask Him.' So that the end of your praying is not to inform God, as though He knew not your wants already; but rather to inform yourselves; to fix the sense of those wants more deeply in your

hearts, and the sense of your continual dependence on Him who only is able to supply all your wants. It is not so much to move God, who is always more ready to give than you to ask, as to move yourselves, that you may be willing and ready to receive the good things He has prepared for you.

III. 1. After having taught the true nature and ends of prayer, our Lord subjoins an example of it; even that divine form of prayer which seems in this place to be proposed by way of pattern chiefly, as the model and standard of all our prayers: 'After this manner therefore pray ye.' Whereas, elsewhere He enjoins the use of these very words: 'He said unto them, When ye pray, say . . .' (Luke xi. 2).

2. We may observe, in general, concerning this divine prayer, first, that it contains all we can reasonably or innocently pray for. There is nothing which we have need to ask of God, nothing which we can ask without offending Him, which is not included, either directly or indirectly, in this comprehensive form. Secondly, that it contains all we can reasonably or innocently desire: whatever is for the glory of God, what ever is needful or profitable, not only for ourselves, but for every creature in heaven and earth. And, indeed, our prayers are the proper test of our desires; nothing being fit to have a place in our desires which is not fit to have a place in our prayers: what we may not pray for, neither should we desire. Thirdly, that it contains all our duty to God and man; whatsoever things are pure and holy, whatsoever God requires of the children of men, whatsoever is acceptable in His sight, whatsoever it is whereby we may profit our neighbour, being expressed or implied therein.

3. It consists of three parts,—the preface, the petitions, and the doxology, or conclusion. The preface, 'Our Father which art in heaven,' lays a general foundation for prayer; comprising what we must first know of God, before we can pray in confidence of being heard. It likewise points out to us all those tempers with which we are to approach to God, which are most essentially requisite, if we desire either our prayers or our lives should find acceptance with Him.

4. 'Our Father': if He is a Father, then He is good, then He is loving, to His children. And here is the first and great reason for prayer. God is willing to bless; let us ask for a blessing. 'Our

Father,'—our Creator: the Author of our being; He who raised us from the dust of the earth; who breathed into us the breath of life, and we became living souls. But if He made us, let us ask, and He will not withhold any good thing from the work of His own hands. 'Our Father,'—our Preserver; who, day by day, sustains the life He has given; of whose continuing love we now and every moment receive life, and breath, and all things. So much the more boldly let us come to Him, and we shall 'obtain mercy, and find grace to help in time of need.' Above all, the Father of our Lord Jesus Christ, and of all that believe in Him; who justifies us 'freely by His grace, through the redemption that is in Jesus'; who hath' blotted out all our sins, and healed all our infirmities'; who hath received us for His own children, by adoption and grace; and, 'because' we 'are sons, hath sent forth the Spirit of His Son into' our 'hearts, crying, Abba, Father'; who 'hath begotten us again of incorruptible seed,' and 'created us anew in Christ Jesus.' Therefore we know that He heareth us always; therefore we pray to Him without ceasing. We pray, because we love; and 'we love Him, because He first loved us.'

5. 'Our Father': not *mine* only who now cry unto Him, but *ours* in the most extensive sense. The God and 'Father of the spirits of all flesh'; the Father of angels and men: so the very Heathens acknowledge Him to be, Πατηρ ανδρον τε Θεων τε. The Father of the universe, of all the families both in heaven and earth. Therefore with Him there is no respect of persons. He loveth all that He hath made. 'He is loving unto every man, and His mercy is over all His works.' And the Lord's delight is in them that fear Him, and put their trust in His mercy; in them that trust in Him through the Son of His love, knowing they are 'accepted in the Beloved.' But 'if God so loved us, we ought also to love one another'; yea, all mankind; seeing 'God so loved the world, that He gave His only-begotten Son,' even to die the death, that they 'might not perish, but have everlasting life.'

6. 'Which art in heaven': high and lifted up, God over all, blessed for ever; who, sitting on the circle of the heavens, beholdeth all things both in heaven and earth; whose eye pervades the whole sphere of created being, yea, and of uncreated night; unto whom 'are known all His works,' and all the works of every creature, not only 'from the beginning of the world' (a poor, low, weak translation) but απ αιωνος, from all

eternity, from everlasting to everlasting; who constrains the host
of heaven, as well as the children of men, to cry out with wonder
and amazement, O the depth! 'the depth of the riches, both of
the wisdom and of the knowledge of God'! 'Which art in
heaven': the Lord and Ruler of all, superintending and
disposing all things; who art the King of kings, and Lord of
lords, the blessed and only Potentate; who art strong and girded
about with power, doing whatsoever pleaseth Thee; the
Almighty; for whensoever Thou willest, to do is present with
Thee. 'In heaven': eminently there. Heaven is Thy throne, 'the
place where Thine honour' particularly 'dwelleth.' But not there
alone; for Thou fillest heaven and earth, the whole expanse of
space. 'Heaven and earth are full of Thy glory. Glory be to Thee,
O Lord most high!'

Therefore should we 'serve the Lord with fear, and rejoice
unto Him with reverence.' Therefore should we think, speak,
and act, as continually under the eye, in the immediate presence,
of the Lord, the King.

7. 'Hallowed be Thy name.' This is the first of the six petitions
whereof the prayer itself is composed. The name of God is God
Himself; the nature of God, so far as it can be discovered to man.
It means therefore, together with His existence, all His
attributes or perfections:—His Eternity, particularly signified
by His great and incommunicable name. JEHOVAH, as the
Apostle John translates it, Το Α και το Ω αρχη και τελος, ο ων
και ο ην και ο ερχομενος—'The Alpha and Omega, the
beginning and the end; He which is, and which was, and which is
to come';—His fullness of Being, denoted by His other great
name, *I AM THAT I AM!*—His omnipresence:—His omnipo-
tence; who is indeed the only Agent in the material world; all
matter being essentially dull and inactive, and moving only as it
is moved by the finger of God; and He is the spring of action in
every creature, visible and invisible, which could neither act nor
exist, without the continual influx and agency of His almighty
power—His wisdom, clearly deduced from the things that are
seen, from the goodly order of the universe;—His Trinity in
Unity, and Unity in Trinity, discovered to us in the very first line
of His written Word; בְּרָא אֱלֹהִים,—literally, *the Gods created*, a
plural noun joined with a verb of the singular number; as well as
in every part of His subsequent revelations, given by the mouth

of all His holy Prophets and Apostles—His essential purity and holiness;—and, above all, His love, which is the very brightness of His glory.

In praying that God, or His name, may be hallowed or glorified, we pray that He may be known, such as He is, by all that are capable thereof, by all intelligent beings, and with affections suitable to that knowledge; that He may be duly honoured, and feared, and loved, by all in heaven above and in the earth beneath; by all angels and men, whom for that end He has made capable of knowing and loving Him to eternity.

8. 'Thy kingdom come.' This has a close connexion with the preceding petition. In order that the name of God may be hallowed, we pray that His kingdom, the kingdom of Christ, may come. This kingdom then comes to a particular person, when he 'repents and believes the gospel'; when he is taught of God, not only to know himself, but to know Jesus Christ and Him crucified. As 'this is life eternal, to know the only true God, and Jesus Christ whom He hath sent'; so it is the kingdom of God begun below, set up in the believer's heart; 'the Lord God Omnipotent' then 'reigneth,' when He is known through Christ Jesus. He taketh unto Himself His mighty power, that He may subdue all things unto Himself. He goeth on in the soul conquering and to conquer, till He hath put all things under His feet, till 'every thought is brought into captivity to the obedience of Christ.'

When therefore God shall 'give His Son the heathen for His inheritance, and the uttermost parts of the earth for His possession'; when 'all kingdoms shall bow before Him, and all nations shall do Him service'; when 'the mountain of the Lord's house,' the church of Christ, 'shall be established in the top of the mountains'; when 'the fullness of the Gentiles shall come in, and all Israel shall be saved'; then shall it be seen, that 'the Lord is King, and hath put on glorious apparel,' appearing to every soul of man as King of kings and Lord of lords. And it is meet for all those who love His appearing, to pray that He would hasten the time; that this His kingdom, the kingdom of grace, may come quickly, and swallow up all the kingdoms of the earth; that all mankind, receiving Him for their King, truly believing in His name, may be filled with righteousness, and peace, and joy, with holiness and happiness; till they are removed hence into His heavenly kingdom, there to reign with Him for ever and ever.

For this also we pray in those words, 'Thy kingdom come': we pray for the coming of His everlasting kingdom, the kingdom of glory in heaven, which is the continuation and perfection of the kingdom of grace on earth. Consequently this, as well as the preceding petition, is offered up for the whole intelligent creation, who are all interested in this grand event, the final renovation of all things, by God's putting an end to misery and sin, to infirmity and death, taking all things into His own hands, and setting up the kingdom which endureth throughout all ages.

Exactly answerable to all this are those awful words in the prayer at the burial of the dead: 'Beseeching Thee, that it may please Thee of Thy gracious goodness, shortly to accomplish the number of Thine elect, and to hasten Thy kingdom: that we, with all those that are departed in the true faith of Thy holy name, may have our perfect consummation and bliss, both in body and soul, in Thy everlasting glory.'

9. 'Thy will be done in earth, as it is in heaven.' This is the necessary and immediate consequence wherever the kingdom of God is come; wherever God dwells in the soul by faith, and Christ reigns in the heart by love.

It is probable, many, perhaps the generality of men, at the first view of these words, are apt to imagine they are only an expression of, or petition for, resignation; for a readiness to suffer the will of God, whatsoever it be, concerning us. And this is unquestionably a divine and excellent temper, a most precious gift of God. But this is not what we pray for in this petition; at least, not in the chief and primary sense of it. We pray, not so much for a passive, as for an active conformity to the will of God, in saying, 'Thy will be done in earth, as it is in heaven.'

How is it done by the angels of God in heaven—those who now circle His throne rejoicing? They do it *willingly*; they love His commandments, and gladly hearken to His words. It is their meat and drink to do His will; it is their highest glory and joy. They do it *continually*; there is no interruption in their willing service. They rest not day nor night, but employ every hour (speaking after the manner of men; otherwise our measures of duration, days, and nights, and hours, have no place in eternity) in fulfilling His commands, in executing His designs, in performing the counsel of His will. And they do it *perfectly*. No sin, no defect belongs to angelic minds. It is true, 'the stars are not pure in His sight,' even the morning-stars that sing together before Him. 'In His sight,' that is, in comparison of Him, the very angels are not pure. But this does not imply, that they are not pure *in themselves*. Doubtless they are; they are without spot and blameless. They are altogether devoted to His will, and perfectly obedient in all things.

If we view them in another light, we may observe, the angels of God in heaven do *all* the will of God. And they do nothing else, nothing but what they are absolutely assured is His will. Again: they do all the will of God *as* He willeth; in the manner which pleases Him, and no other. Yea, and they do this, only *because* it is His will; for this end, and no other reason.

10. When therefore we pray, that the will of God may 'be done in earth as it is in heaven,' the meaning is, that all the inhabitants of the earth, even the whole race of mankind, may do the will of their Father which is in heaven, as *willingly* as the holy angels; that these may do it *continually*, even as they, without any interruption of their willing service; yea, and that they may do it *perfectly*—that 'the God of peace, through the blood of the everlasting covenant, may make them perfect in every good work to do His will, and work in them' all 'which is well pleasing in His sight.'

In other words, we pray that we and all mankind may do the whole will of God in all things; and nothing else, not the least thing but what is the holy and acceptable will of God: we pray that we may do the whole will of God *as* He willeth, in the manner that pleases Him: and, lastly, that we may do it *because* it is His will; that this may be the sole reason and ground, the whole and only motive, of whatsoever we think, or whatsoever we speak or do.

11. 'Give us this day our daily bread.' In the three former petitions we have been praying for all mankind. We come now more particularly to desire a supply for our own wants. Not that we are directed, even here, to confine our prayer altogether to ourselves; but this, and each of the following petitions, may be used for the whole Church of Christ upon earth.

By 'bread' we may understand all things needful, whether for our souls or bodies; τα προς ζωην και ευσεβειαν—*the things pertaining to life and godliness*: we understand not barely the outward bread, what our Lord terms 'the meat which perisheth'; but much more the spiritual bread, the grace of God, the food' which endureth unto everlasting life.' It was the judgement of many of the ancient Fathers, that we are here to understand the sacramental bread also; daily received in the beginning by the whole Church of Christ, and highly esteemed, till the love of many waxed cold, as the grand channel whereby the grace of His Spirit was conveyed to the souls of all the children of God.

'Our daily bread.' The word we render *daily* has been differently explained by different commentators. But the most plain and natural sense of it seems to be this, which is retained in almost all translations, as well ancient as modern,—what is sufficient for this day; and so for each day as it succeeds.

12. 'Give us': for we claim nothing of right, but only of free mercy. We deserve not the air we breathe, the earth that bears, or the sun that shines upon us. All our desert, we own, is hell: but God loves us freely; therefore, we ask Him to give, what we can no more procure for ourselves than we can merit it at His hands.

Not that either the goodness or the power of God is a reason for us to stand idle. It is His will that we should use all diligence in all things, that we should employ our utmost endeavours, as much as if our success were the natural effect of our own wisdom and strength; and then, as though we had done nothing, we are to depend on Him, the Giver of every good and perfect gift.

'This day': for we are to take no thought for the morrow. For this very end has our wise Creator divided life into these little portions of time, so clearly separated from each other, that we might look on every day as a fresh gift of God, another life, which we may devote to His glory; and that every evening may be as the close of life, beyond which we are to see nothing but eternity.

13. 'And forgive us our trespasses, as we forgive them that trespass against us.' As nothing but sin can hinder the bounty of God from flowing forth upon every creature, so this petition naturally follows the former; that, all hindrances being removed, we may the more clearly trust in the God of love for every manner of thing which is good.

'Our trespasses': the word properly signifies *our debts*. Thus our sins are frequently represented in Scripture; every Sin laying us under a fresh debt to God, to whom we already owe, as it were, ten thousand talents. What, then, can we answer when He shall say, 'Pay me that thou owest'? We are utterly insolvent; we have nothing to pay; we have wasted all our substance. Therefore, if He deal with us according to the rigour of His law, if He exact what He justly may, He must command us to be 'bound hand and foot, and delivered over to the tormentors.'

Indeed we are already bound hand and foot by the chains of our own sins. These considered with regard to ourselves, are chains of iron and fetters of brass. They are wounds wherewith the world the flesh, and the devil have gashed and mangled us all over. They are diseases that drink up our blood and spirits, that bring us down to the chambers of the grave. But, considered as they are here, with regard to God, they are debts immense and numberless. Well, therefore, seeing we have nothing to pay, may we cry unto Him, that He would frankly forgive us all!

The word translated *forgive,* implies either to forgive a debt, or to unloose a chain. And if we attain the former, the latter follows of course: if our debts are forgiven, the chains fall off our hands. As soon as ever, through the free grace of God in Christ, we 'receive forgiveness of sins,' we receive likewise 'a lot among those which are sanctified, by faith which is in Him.' Sin has lost its power: it has no dominion over those who are under grace, that is, in favour with God. As 'there is now no condemnation to them that are in Christ Jesus,' so they are freed from sin as well as from guilt. 'The righteousness of the law is fulfilled in' them, and they 'walk not after the flesh, but after the Spirit.'

14. 'As we forgive them that trespass against us.' In these words our Lord clearly declares both on what condition, and in what degree or manner, we may look to be forgiven of God. All our trespasses and sins are forgiven us *if* we forgive, and *as* we forgive, others. This is a point of the utmost importance. And our blessed Lord is so jealous lest at any time we should let it slip out of our thoughts, that He not only inserts it in the body of His prayer, but presently after repeats it twice over. 'If,' saith He, 'ye forgive men their trespasses, your heavenly Father will also forgive you: but if ye forgive not men their trespasses, neither

will your Father forgive your trespasses' (verses 14, 15). Secondly, God forgives us *as* we forgive others. So that if any malice or bitterness, if any taint of unkindness or anger remains, if we do not clearly, fully, and from the heart, forgive all men their trespasses, we so far cut short the forgiveness of our own: God cannot clearly and fully forgive us: He may show us some degree of mercy; but we will not suffer Him to blot out all our sins, and forgive all our iniquities.

In the meantime, while we do not from our hearts forgive our neighbour his trespasses, what manner of prayer are we offering to God whenever we utter these words? We are indeed setting God at open defiance; we are daring Him to do His worst. 'Forgive us our trespasses, as we forgive them that trespass against us!' That is, in plain terms, 'Do not Thou forgive us at all; we desire no favour at Thy hands. We pray that Thou wilt keep our sins in remembrance, and that Thy wrath may abide upon us.' But can you seriously offer such a prayer to God? And hath He not yet cast you quick into hell? O tempt Him no longer! Now, even now, by His grace, forgive as you would be forgiven! Now have compassion on thy fellow servant, as God hath had, and will have, pity on thee!

15. 'And lead us not into temptation, but deliver us from evil'—'And lead us not into temptation.' The word translated *temptation* means trial of any kind. And so the English word temptation, was formerly taken in an indifferent sense; although now it is usually understood of solicitation to sin. St. James uses the word in both these senses: first, in its general, then in its restrained, acceptation. He takes it in the former sense when he saith, 'Blessed is the man that endureth temptation: for when he is tried,' or approved of God, 'he shall receive the crown of life' (Jas. i. 12). He immediately adds, taking the word in the latter sense, 'Let no man say when he is tempted, I am tempted of God: for God cannot be tempted with evil, neither tempteth He any man: but every man is tempted, when he is *drawn away* of his own lust,' or *desire*, εξελκομενος—drawn out of God, in whom alone he is safe—'*and enticed*'; caught as a fish with a bait. Then it is, when he is thus *drawn away and enticed,* that he properly enters into temptation. Then temptation covers him as a cloud; it overspreads his whole soul. Then how hardly shall he escape out of the snare! Therefore we beseech God 'not

to lead us into temptation, that is (seeing God tempteth no man), not to suffer us to be led into it. 'But deliver us from evil.' Rather, *'from the evil one,'* απο του πονηρου. Ο πονηρος is unquestionably *the wicked one,* emphatically so called, the prince and god of this world, who works with mighty power in the children of disobedience. But all those who are the children of God by faith are delivered out of his hands. He may fight against them; and so he will. But he cannot conquer, unless they betray their own souls. He may torment for a time, but he cannot destroy; for God is on their side, who will not fail, in the end, to 'avenge His own elect, that cry unto Him day and night.' Lord, when we are tempted, suffer us not to enter into temptation! Do Thou make a way for us to escape, that the wicked one touch us not!

16. The conclusion of this divine prayer, commonly called 'the doxology,' is a solemn thanksgiving, a compendious acknowledgement of the attributes and works of God. 'For Thine is the kingdom,'—the sovereign right of all things that are, or ever were created; yea, Thy kingdom is an everlasting kingdom, and Thy dominion endureth throughout all ages. 'The power,'—the executive power whereby Thou governest all things in Thy everlasting kingdom, whereby Thou doest whatsoever pleaseth Thee, in all places of Thy dominion. 'And the glory,'—the praise due from every creature, for Thy power, and the mightiness of Thy kingdom, and for all Thy wondrous works which Thou workest from everlasting, and shalt do, world without end, 'for ever and ever. Amen!' So be it!

I believe it will not be unacceptable to the serious reader to subjoin

A PARAPHRASE ON THE LORD'S PRAYER

1 FATHER of all! whose powerful voice
   Called forth this universal frame;
 Whose mercies over all rejoice,
   Through endless ages still the same.
 Thou, by Thy word, upholdest all;
   Thy bounteous love to all is showed:
 Thou hear'st Thy every creature's call,
   And fillest every mouth with good.

2 In heaven Thou reign'st, enthroned in light,
   Nature's expanse beneath Thee spread;

Earth, air, and sea, before Thy sight,
　　And hell's deep gloom, are open laid.
Wisdom, and might, and love, are Thine;
　　Prostrate before Thy face we fall,
Confess Thine attributes divine,
　　And hail Thee Sovereign Lord of all!

3 Thee, Sovereign Lord, let all confess,
　　That moves in earth, or air, or sky,
Revere Thy power, Thy goodness bless,
　　Tremble before Thy piercing eye.
All ye who owe to Him your birth,
　　In praise your every hour employ:
Jehovah reigns! Be glad, O Earth!
　　And shout, ye morning stars, for joy!

4 Son of Thy Sire's eternal love,
　　Take to Thyself Thy mighty power;
Let all earth's sons Thy mercy prove,
　　Let all Thy bleeding grace adore.
The triumphs of Thy love display:
　　In every heart reign Thou alone;
Till all Thy foes confess Thy sway,
　　And glory ends what grace begun.

5 Spirit of grace, and health, and power,
　　Fountain of light and love below;
Abroad Thine healing influence shower,
　　O'er all the nations let it flow.
Inflame our hearts with perfect love;
　　In us the work of faith fulfil;
So not heaven's host shall swifter move,
　　Than we on earth to do Thy will.

6 Father,'tis Thine each day to yield
　　Thy children's wants a fresh supply:
Thou cloth'st the lilies of the field,
　　And hearest the young ravens cry.
On Thee we cast our care; we live
　　Through Thee, who know'st our every need.
O feed us with Thy grace, and give
　　Our souls this day the living bread!

7 Eternal, spotless Lamb of God,
　　Before the world's foundation slain,
Sprinkle us ever with Thy blood;
　　O cleanse, and keep us ever clean!
To every soul (all praise to Thee!)

Our bowels of compassion move;
And all mankind by this may see
God is in us; for God is love.

8 Giver and Lord of life, whose power
    And guardian came for all are free,
To Thee, in fierce temptation's hour,
    From sin and Satan let us flee.
Thine, Lord, we are, and ours Thou art;
    In us be all Thy goodness showed;
Renew, enlarge, and fill our heart
    With peace, and joy, and heaven, and God.

9 Blessing and honour, praise and love,
    Co-equal, co-eternal Three,
In earth below, in heaven above,
    By all Thy works be paid to Thee.
Thrice Holy! Thine the Kingdom is,
    The power omnipotent is Thine;
And when created nature dies,
    Thy never-ceasing glories shine.

SERMON XXII

UPON OUR LORD'S SERMON ON THE MOUNT

DISCOURSE VII

The only fast prescribed in the law is that on the Great Day of Atonement, on the tenth day of the seventh month. After the return from the Captivity other fasts were instituted in commemoration of events connected with the siege and taking of Jerusalem on the seventeenth day of the fourth month (Tammuz), the ninth of the fifth month (Ab), the third of the seventh month (Tisri), and the tenth of the tenth month (lebet). Special fasts were frequently proclaimed; and the practice of private fasting became more and more common. The Pharisees fasted every week on Mondays and Thursdays, and doubtless many of the more pious amongst the people followed their example. Hence our Lord, assuming that His hearers would fast as a part of their normal religious life, gives the directions here set out, as a warning against ostentation in fasting, and the practice of it with a view of securing a reputation for piety. Though He and His disciples would certainly keep the fast of the Day of Atonement, it is Plain from Matt. ix 14 that they did not observe the weekly fasts; and our Lord left no injunctions to His Church as to this means of grace. The Jewish Christians naturally took over into their new faith their old habit of fasting, and used it both privately and on certain special occasions. In the *Didache* we find bi-weekly fasts prescribed on Wednesdays and Fridays, instead of the days on which 'the hypocrites' fast, i.e. Mondays and Thursdays; but this would apply only to Jewish Christians. In the fourth century we find the forty days' fast of Lent generally established. During the fifth century the Rogation fast on the three days before Ascension Day was instituted in the Western Church; and also the Ember Days or fasts of the four seasons, on the Wednesdays, Fridays, and Saturdays after the First Sunday in Lent, Pentecost, Holy Cross Day (September 14), and St. Lucy's Day (December 13). Peculiar to the Western Church were also the single-day fasts on the vigil before sixteen festivals and saints' days (set out at the beginning of the Book of Common Prayer). The Oxford Methodists made a point of observing all the fasts of the Church, including the Wednesdays as well as the Fridays of every week; and this Wesley kept up rigidly during his residence in Georgia. After his return many of his society resolved on August 17, 1739, to observe all Fridays as fast-days; and in the Rules of the Society (1743), which still stand good, members are required to evidence their desire of salvation by 'fasting or abstinence.' In the *Large*

Minutes (1763) Mr. Wesley says under the head of fasting, 'God led us to this at Oxford. And He led all of you to it, when you first set out. How often do you fast now? Every Friday? In what degree?' In the *Form of Discipline* of 1797 this is enlarged upon: 'Do you fast every Friday? The neglect of this is sufficient to account for our feebleness and faintness of spirit. We are continually grieving the Holy Spirit by the habitual neglect of a plain duty I Let us amend from this hour. . . . Begin next Friday, and avow this duty wherever you go.' It is also directed that 'A general fast shall be held in all our Societies, the first Friday after New Year's Day, after Lady Day, after Midsummer Day, and after Michaelmas Day.' This rule was reaffirmed by the Conference of 1900 (see also *Minutes*, 1920, p. 28). How far it is effectively observed in England I cannot say; it is certainly not observed in Australia.

I think it may be safely said that the tendency in Methodism has been to leave the time and measure of fasting to the conscience of the individual. Neither our Lord nor His Apostles left any explicit directions on this head; and we are not bound by the traditional practice of the early and mediaeval Churches, nor indeed by Wesley's own views, which were largely the result of his early High-Church training. On the other hand, the revival of fasting would make for a more robust and less self-indulgent type of character amongst us; and it is to be hoped that the study of this very sane and wise sermon may influence some of us to make experiment of this means of grace

Moreover when ye fast be not as the hypocrites, of a sad countenance: for they disfigure their faces, that they may appear unto men to fast. Verily I say unto you, They have their reward.
But thou, when thou fastest, anoint thine head, and wash thy face,
That thou appear not unto men to fast, but unto thy Father which is in secret: and thy Father, which seeth in secret, shall reward thee openly.—MATT vi. 16-18.

1. It has been the endeavour of Satan, from the beginning of the world, to put asunder what God hath joined together; to separate inward from outward religion; to set one of these at variance with the other. And herein he has met with no small success among those who were 'ignorant of his devices.'

Many, in all ages, having a zeal for God, but not according to knowledge, have been strictly attached to the 'righteousness of the law,' the performance of outward duties, but in the meantime wholly regardless of inward righteousness, 'the righteousness which is of God by faith.' And many have run into the opposite extreme, disregarding all outward duties, perhaps even 'speaking evil of the law, and judging the law,' so far as it enjoins the performance of them.

2. It is by this very device of Satan, that faith and works have been so often set at variance with each other. And many who had a real zeal for God have, for a time, fallen into the snare on either hand. Some have magnified faith to the utter exclusion of good works, not only from being the cause of our justification (for we know that a man is justified freely by the redemption which is in Jesus), but from being the necessary fruit of it, yea, from having any place in the religion of Jesus Christ. Others, eager to avoid this dangerous mistake, have run as much too far the contrary way; and either maintained that good works were the cause, at least the previous condition, of justification—or spoken of them as if they were all in all, the whole religion of Jesus Christ.

3. In the same manner have the end and the means of religion been set at variance with each other. Some well-meaning men have seemed to place all religion in attending the prayers of the Church, in receiving the Lord's supper, in hearing sermons, and reading books of piety; neglecting, meantime, the end of all these, the love of God and their neighbour. And this very thing has confirmed others in the neglect, if not contempt, of the ordinances of God—so wretchedly abused, to undermine and overthrow the very end they were designed to establish.

4. But of all the means of grace there is scarce any concerning which men have run into greater extremes, than that of which our Lord speaks in the above-mentioned words; I mean religious fasting. How have some exalted this beyond all Scripture and reason; and others utterly disregarded it—as it were, revenging themselves by undervaluing as much as the former had overvalued it! Those have spoken of it as if it were all in all; if not the end itself, yet infallibly connected with it: these, as if it were just nothing; as if it were a fruitless labour, which had no relation at all thereto. Whereas it is certain the truth lies between them both. It is not all, nor yet is it nothing. It is not the end, but it is a precious means thereto; a means which God Himself has ordained, and in which therefore, when it is duly used, He will surely give us His blessing.

In order to set this in the clearest light, I shall endeavour to show, first, what is the nature of fasting, and what the several sorts and degrees thereof; secondly, what are the reasons, grounds, and ends of it: thirdly, how we may answer the most plausible objections against it: and, fourthly, in what manner it should be performed.

I. 1. I shall endeavour to show, first, what is the nature of fasting, and what the several sorts and degrees thereof. As to the nature of it, all the inspired writers, both in the Old Testament and the New, take the word, to *fast,* in one single sense, for not to eat, to abstain from food. This is so clear, that it would be labour lost to quote the words of David. Nehemiah, Isaiah, and the prophets which followed, or of our Lord and His apostles; all agreeing in this, that to fast is, not to eat for a time prescribed.

2. To this, other circumstances were usually joined by them of old, which had no necessary connexion with it. Such were, the neglect of their apparel; the laying aside those ornaments which they were accustomed to wear; the putting on mourning; the strewing ashes upon their head; or wearing sackcloth next their skin. But we find little mention made in the New Testament of any of these indifferent circumstances. Nor does it appear that any stress was laid upon them by the Christians of the purer ages; however some penitents might voluntarily use them, as outward signs of inward humiliation. Much less did the Apostles, or the Christians contemporary with them, beat or tear their own flesh: such discipline as this was not unbecoming the priests or worshippers of Baal. The gods of the Heathens were but devils; and it was doubtless acceptable to their devil-god, when his priests (1 Kings xviii. 28) 'cried aloud, and cut themselves after their manner, till the blood gushed out upon them'; but it cannot be pleasing to Him, nor become His followers, who 'came not to destroy men's lives, but to save them.'

3. As to the degrees or measures of fasting, we have instances of some who have fasted several days together. So Moses, Elijah, and our blessed Lord, being endued with supernatural strength for that purpose, are recorded to have fasted, without intermission, 'forty days and forty nights.' But the time of fasting, more frequently mentioned in Scripture, is one day, from morning till evening. And this was the fast commonly observed among the ancient Christians. But besides these, they had also their half-fasts (*semi-jejunia,* as Tertullian styles them) on the fourth and sixth days of the week (Wednesday and

Friday), throughout the year; on which they took no sustenance till three in the afternoon, the time when they returned from the public service.

4. Nearly related to this, is what our Church seems peculiarly to mean by the term *abstinence*; which may be used when we cannot fast entirely, by reason of sickness or bodily weakness. This is the eating little; the abstaining in part; the taking a smaller quantity of food than usual. I do not remember any scriptural instance of this. But neither can I condemn it; for the Scripture does not. It may have its use, and receive a blessing from God.

5. The lowest kind of fasting, if it can be called by that name, is the abstaining from pleasant food. Of this, we have several instances in Scripture, besides that of Daniel and his brethren, who, from a peculiar consideration, namely, that they might 'not defile themselves with the portion of the king's meat, nor with the wine which he drank' (a daily provision of which the king had appointed for them), requested and obtained, of the prince of the eunuchs, pulse to eat, and water to drink (Dan. i. 8, &c.). Perhaps from a mistaken imitation of this might spring the very ancient custom of abstaining from flesh and wine during such times as were set apart for fasting and abstinence,—if it did not rather arise from a supposition that these were the most pleasant food, and a belief that it was proper to use what was least pleasing at those times of solemn approach to God.

6. In the Jewish Church there were some stated fasts. Such was the fast of the seventh month, appointed by God Himself to be observed by all Israel under the severest penalty. 'The Lord spake unto Moses, saying, On the tenth day of this seventh month there shall be a day of atonement: and ye shall afflict your souls, . . . to make an atonement for you before the Lord your God. For whatsoever soul it be that shall not be afflicted in that same day, he shall be cut off from among his people' (Lev. xxiii. 26, &c.). In after-ages, several other stated fasts were added to these. So mention is made, by the Prophet Zechariah, of the fast, not only' of the seventh, but also of the fourth, of the fifth, and of the tenth month' (viii. 19).

In the ancient Christian Church there were likewise stated fasts, and those both annual and weekly. Of the former sort was that before Easter; observed by some for eight-and-forty hours;

by others, for an entire week; by many, for two weeks; taking no sustenance till the evening of each day: of the latter, those of the fourth and sixth days of the week, observed (as Epiphanius writes, remarking it as an undeniable fact) εν ολη τη οικουμενη—*in the whole habitable earth;* at least in every place where any Christians made their abode. The annual fasts in our Church are, 'the forty days of Lent, the Ember days at the four seasons, the Rogation days, and the Vigils or Eves of several solemn festivals; the weekly, all Fridays in the year, except Christmas-day.'

But beside those which were fixed, in every nation fearing God there have always been occasional fasts, appointed from time to time, as the particular circumstances and occasions of each required. So when 'the children of Moab, and the children of Ammon, came against Jehoshaphat to battle, Jehoshaphat set himself to seek the Lord, and proclaimed a fast throughout all Judah' (2 Chron. xx. 1, 3). And so, 'in the fifth year of Jehoiakim the son of Josiah, in the ninth month,' when they were afraid of the king of Babylon, the princes of 'Judah proclaimed a fast before the Lord, to all the people in Jerusalem' (Jer. xxxvi. 9).

And, in like manner, particular persons, who take heed unto their ways, and desire to walk humbly and closely with God, will find frequent occasion for private seasons of thus afflicting their souls before their Father which is in secret. And it is to this kind of fasting that the directions here given do chiefly and primarily refer.

II. 1. I proceed to show, in the second place, what are the grounds, the reasons, and ends of fasting.

And, first, men who are under strong emotions of mind, who are affected with any vehement passion, such as sorrow or fear, are often swallowed up therein, and even forget to eat their bread. At such seasons they have little regard for food, not even what is needful to sustain nature, much less for any delicacy or variety; being taken up with quite different thoughts. Thus when Saul said, 'I am sore distressed; for the Philistines make war against me, and God is departed from me'; it is recorded, 'He had eaten no bread all the day, nor all the night' (1 Sam. xxviii. 15, 20). Thus those who were in the ship with St. Paul, 'when no small tempest lay upon them, and all hope that they should be saved was taken away,' 'continued fasting, having taken nothing,' no regular meal, for fourteen days together' (Acts xxvii. 33). And thus David, and all the men that were with him, when they heard that the people were fled from the battle, and that many of the people were fallen and dead, and Saul and Jonathan his son were dead also, 'mourned, and wept, and fasted until even, for Saul and Jonathan, and for the house of Israel' (2 Sam. i. 12).

Nay, many times they whose minds are deeply engaged are impatient of any interruption, and even loathe their needful food, as diverting their thoughts from what they desire should engross their whole attention: even as Saul, when, on the occasion mentioned before, he had 'fallen all along upon the earth, and there was no strength in him,' yet said, 'I will not eat,' till 'his servants together with the woman, compelled him.'

2. Here, then, is the natural ground of fasting. One who is under deep affliction, overwhelmed with sorrow for sin, and a strong apprehension of the wrath of God, would, without any rule, without knowing or considering whether it were a command of God or not, 'forget to eat his bread,' abstain not only from pleasant but even from needful food; like St. Paul, who, after he was led into Damascus, 'was three days without sight, and did neither eat nor drink' (Acts ix. 9).

Yea, when the storm rose high, 'when an horrible dread overwhelmed' one who had [long] been without God in the world, his soul would 'loathe all manner of meat'; it would be unpleasing and irksome to him; he would be impatient of anything that should interrupt his ceaseless cry, 'Lord, save! or I perish.'

How strongly is this expressed by our Church in the first part of the Homily on Fasting!—'When men feel in themselves the heavy burden of sin, see damnation to be the reward of it, and behold, with the eye of their mind, the horror of hell, they tremble, they quake, and are inwardly touched with sorrowfulness of heart, and cannot but accuse themselves, and open their grief unto Almighty God, and call unto Him for mercy. This being done seriously, their mind is so occupied (taken up), partly with sorrow and heaviness, partly with an earnest desire to be delivered from this danger of hell and damnation, that all desire of meat and drink is laid apart, and loathsomeness (or loathing) of all worldly things and pleasure cometh in place. So that nothing then liketh them more than to weep, to lament, to mourn, and both with words and behaviour of body to show themselves weary of life.'

3. Another reason or ground of fasting is this: many of those who now fear God are deeply sensible how often they have sinned against Him, by the abuse of these lawful things. They know how much they have sinned by excess of food; how long they have transgressed the holy law of God, with regard to temperance, if not sobriety too; how they have indulged their sensual appetites, perhaps to the impairing even their bodily health, certainly to the no small hurt of their soul. For hereby they continually fed and increased that sprightly folly, that airiness of mind, that levity of temper, that gay inattention to things of the deepest concern, that giddiness and carelessness of spirit, which were no other than drunkenness of soul, which stupefied all their noblest faculties, no less than excess of wine or strong drink. To remove, therefore, the effect, they remove the cause: they keep at a distance from all excess. They abstain, as far as is possible, from what had wellnigh plunged them in everlasting perdition. They often wholly refrain; always take care to be sparing and temperate in all things.

4. They likewise well remember how fullness of bread increased not only carelessness and levity of spirit, but also foolish and unholy desires, yea, unclean and vile affections. And this experience puts beyond all doubt. Even a genteel, regular sensuality is continually sensualizing the soul, and sinking it into a level with the beasts that perish. It cannot be expressed what an effect a variety and delicacy of food have on the mind as well as the body; making it just ripe for every pleasure of sense, as soon as opportunity shall invite. Therefore, on this ground also, every wise man will refrain his soul, and keep it low; will wean it more and more from all those indulgences of the inferior appetites, which naturally tend to chain it down to earth, and to pollute as well as debase it. Here is another perpetual reason for fasting; to remove the food of lust and sensuality, to withdraw the incentives of foolish and hurtful desires, of vile and vain affections.

5. Perhaps we need not altogether omit (although I know not if we should do well to lay any great stress upon it) another

reason for fasting, which some good men have largely insisted on; namely, the punishing themselves for having abused the good gifts of God, by sometimes wholly refraining from them; thus exercising a kind of holy revenge upon themselves, for their past folly and ingratitude, in turning the things which should have been for their health into an occasion of falling. They suppose David to have had an eye to this, when he said, 'I wept and chastened,' or punished, 'my soul with fasting'; and St. Paul, when he mentions 'what revenge' godly sorrow occasioned in the Corinthians.

6. A fifth and more weighty reason for fasting is, that it is an help to prayer; particularly when we set apart larger portions of time for private prayer. Then especially it is that God is often pleased to lift up the souls of His servants above all the things of earth, and sometimes to rap them up, as it were, into the third heavens. And it is chiefly, as it is an help to prayer, that it has so frequently been found a means, in the hand of God, of confirming and increasing, not one virtue, not chastity only (as some have idly imagined, without any ground either from Scripture, reason, or experience), but also seriousness of spirit, earnestness, sensibility and tenderness of conscience, deadness to the world, and consequently the love of God, and every holy and heavenly affection.

7. Not that there is any natural or necessary connexion between fasting, and the blessings God conveys thereby. But He will have mercy *as* He will have mercy; He will convey whatsoever seemeth Him good by whatsoever means He is pleased to appoint. And He hath, in all ages, appointed this to be a means of averting His wrath, and obtaining whatever blessings we, from time to time, stand in need of.

How powerful a means this is to avert the wrath of God, we may learn from the remarkable instance of Ahab. 'There was none like him who did sell himself'—wholly give himself up, like a slave bought with money—'to work wickedness.' Yet, when he 'rent his clothes, and put sackcloth upon his flesh, and fasted, and went softly, the word of the Lord came to Elijah, saying, Seest thou how Ahab humbleth himself before Me? Because he humbleth himself before Me, I will not bring the evil in his days.'

It was for this end, to avert the wrath of God, that Daniel sought God 'with fasting, and sackcloth, and ashes.' This appears from the whole tenor of his prayer, particularly from the solemn conclusion of it: 'O Lord, according to all Thy righteousness,' or mercies, 'let Thy anger be turned away from Thy holy mountain. . . . Hear the prayer of Thy servant, and cause Thy face to shine upon Thy sanctuary that is desolate. . . . O Lord, hear; O Lord, forgive; O Lord, hearken and do, for Thine own sake' (Dan. ix. 3, 16, &c.).

8. But it is not only from the people of God that we learn, when His anger is moved, to seek Him by fasting and prayer; but even from the Heathens. When Jonah had declared, 'Yet forty days, and Nineveh shall be overthrown,' the people of Nineveh 'proclaimed a fast, and put on sackcloth, from the greatest of them unto the least. For the king of Nineveh arose from his throne, and laid his robe from him, and covered him with sackcloth, and sat in ashes. And he caused it to be proclaimed and published through Nineveh. Let neither man nor beast, herd nor flock, taste anything: let them not feed, nor drink water' (not that the beasts had sinned, or could repent; but that, by their example, man might be admonished, considering that, for his sin, the anger of God was hanging over all creatures): 'who can tell if God will turn and repent, and turn away from His fierce anger, that we perish not?' And their labour was not in vain. The fierce anger of God was turned away from them. 'God saw their works' (the fruits of that repentance and faith which He had wrought in them by His prophet); 'and God repented of the evil, that He had said He would do unto them; and He did it not' (Jonah iii. 4, &c.).

9. And it is a means not only of turning away the wrath of God, but also of obtaining whatever blessings we stand in need of. So, when the other tribes were smitten before the Benjamites, 'all the children of Israel went up unto the house of God, and wept, and fasted that day until even'; and then the Lord said, 'Go up' again; 'for to-morrow I will deliver them into thine hand' (Judges xx. 26, &c.). So Samuel gathered all Israel together, when they were in bondage to the Philistines, 'and they fasted on that day' before the Lord: and when 'the Philistines drew near to battle against Israel, the Lord thundered' upon them 'with a great thunder, and discomfited them; and they were smitten before Israel' (1 Sam. vii. 6). So Ezra: 'I proclaimed a fast at the river Ahava, that we might afflict ourselves before our God, to

seek of Him a right way for us, and for our little ones; and He was entreated of us' (viii. 21). So Nehemiah: 'I fasted and prayed before the God of heaven, and said, Prosper, I pray Thee, Thy servant this day, and grant him mercy in the sight of this man': and God granted him mercy in the sight of the king (i. 4-11).

10. In like manner, the Apostles always joined fasting with prayer when they desired the blessing of God on any important undertaking. Thus we read (Acts xiii.), 'There were in the church that was at Antioch certain prophets and teachers: as they ministered to the Lord, and fasted,' doubtless for direction in this very affair, 'the Holy Ghost said. Separate Me Barnabas and Saul for the work whereunto I have called them. And when they had' a second time 'fasted and prayed, and laid their hands on them, they sent them away' (verses 1-3).

Thus also Paul and Barnabas themselves, as we read in the following chapter, when they 'returned again to Lystra. Iconium, and Antioch, confirming the souls of the disciples, and when they had ordained them elders in every church, and had prayed with fasting, commended them to the Lord' (Acts xiv. 23).

Yea, that blessings are to be obtained in the use of this means, which are not otherwise attainable, our Lord expressly declares in His answer to His disciples, asking, 'Why could not we cast him out? Jesus said unto them, Because of your unbelief: for verily I say unto you, If ye have faith as a grain of mustard-seed, ye shall say unto this mountain, Remove hence to yonder place; and it shall-remove; and nothing shall be impossible unto you. Howbeit this kind' of devils 'goeth not out but by prayer and fasting' (Matt. xvii. 19, &c.),—these being the appointed means of attaining that faith whereby the very devils are subject unto you.

11. These were the appointed means: for it was not merely by the light of reason, or of natural conscience, as it is called, that the people of God have been, in all ages, directed to use fasting as a means to these ends; but they have been, from time to time, taught it of God Himself, by clear and open revelations of His will. Such is that remarkable one by the Prophet Joel: 'Therefore saith the Lord, Turn ye to Me with all your heart, and with fasting, and with weeping, and with mourning; . . . who knoweth if He will return and repent, and leave a blessing behind Him? Blow the trumpet in Zion, sanctify a fast, call a

solemn assembly; . . . then will the Lord be jealous for His land, and pity His people. Yea, I will send you corn, and wine, and oil; . . . I will no more make you a reproach among the heathen' (Joel ii. 12, &c.).

Nor are they only temporal blessings which God directs His people to expect in the use of these means. For, at the same time that He promised to those who should seek Him with fasting, and weeping, and mourning, 'I will restore to you the years which the locust hath eaten, the canker-worm, and the caterpillar, and the palmer-worm, My great army,' He subjoins, 'So shall ye eat and be satisfied, and praise the name of the Lord your God. . . . Ye shall also know that I am in the midst of Israel, and that I am the Lord your God.' And then immediately follows the great gospel promise: 'I will pour out My Spirit upon all flesh; and your sons and your daughters shall prophesy, your old men shall dream dreams, and your young men shall see visions: and also upon the servants and upon the handmaids in those days will I pour out My Spirit.'

12. Now whatsoever reasons there were to quicken those of old, in the zealous and constant discharge of this duty, they are of equal force still to quicken us. But above all these, we have a peculiar reason for being 'in fastings often'; namely, the command of Him by whose name we are called. He does not, indeed, in this place expressly enjoin either fasting, giving of alms, or prayer; but His directions *how* to fast, to give alms, and to pray, are of the same force with such injunctions. For the commanding us to do anything *thus*, is an unquestionable command to do that thing; seeing it is impossible to perform it *thus,* if it be not performed at all. Consequently, the saying, 'Give alms, pray, fast,' *in such a manner,* is a clear command to perform all those duties; as well as to perform them in that *manner* which shall in no wise lose its reward.

And this is a still farther motive and encouragement to the performance of this duty; even the promise which our Lord has graciously annexed to the due discharge of it: 'Thy Father, which seeth in secret, shall reward thee openly.' Such are the plain grounds, reasons, and ends of fasting; such our encouragement to persevere therein, notwithstanding abundance of objections which men, wiser than their Lord, have been continually raising against it.

III. 1. The most plausible of these I come now to consider. And, first, it has been frequently said, 'Let a Christian fast from sin, and not from food: this is what God requires at his hands.' So He does; but He requires the other also. Therefore this ought to be done, and that not left undone.

View your argument in its full dimensions; and you will easily judge of the strength of it:—

If a Christian ought to abstain from sin, then he ought not to abstain from food:

But a Christian ought to abstain from sin:

Therefore he ought not to abstain from food.

That a Christian ought to abstain from sin, is most true; but how does it follow from hence that he ought not to abstain from food? Yea, let him do both the one and the other. Let him, by the grace of God, always abstain from sin; and let him often abstain from food, for such reasons and ends as experience and Scripture plainly show to be answered thereby.

2. 'But is it not better' (as it has, secondly, been objected) 'to abstain from pride and vanity, from foolish and hurtful desires, from peevishness, and anger, and discontent, than from food?' Without question, it is. But here again we have need to remind you of our Lord's words: 'These things ought ye to have done, and not to leave the other undone.' And, indeed, the latter is only in order to the former; it is a means to that great end. We abstain from food with this view,—that, by the grace of God conveyed into our souls through this outward means in conjunction with all the other channels of His grace which He hath appointed, we may be enabled to abstain from every passion and temper which is not pleasing in His sight. We refrain from the one, that, being endued with power from on high, we may be able to refrain from the other. So that your argument proves just the contrary to what you designed. It proves that we ought to fast. For if we ought to abstain from evil tempers and desires, then we ought thus to abstain from food; since these little instances of self-denial are the ways God hath chose, wherein to bestow that great salvation.

3. 'But we do not find it so in fact' (this is a third objection): 'we have fasted much and often; but what did it avail? We were not a whit better; we found no blessing therein. Nay, we have found it an hindrance rather than an help. Instead of preventing anger,

for instance, or fretfulness, it has been a means of increasing them to such a height, that we could neither bear others nor ourselves.' This may very possibly be the case. It is possible either to fast or pray in such a manner as to make you much worse than before; more unhappy, and more unholy. Yet the fault does not lie in the means itself, but in the manner of using it. Use it still, but use it in a different manner. Do what God commands *as* He commands it; and then, doubtless, His promise shall not fail: His blessing shall be withheld no longer; but, when thou fastest in secret, 'He that seeth in secret shall reward thee openly.'

4. 'But is it not mere superstition' (so it has been, fourthly, objected), 'to imagine that God regards such little things as these?' If you say it is, you condemn all the generations of God's children. But will you say, These were all weak, superstitious men? Can you be so hardy as to affirm this, both of Moses and Joshua, of Samuel and David, of Jehoshaphat, Ezra, Nehemiah, and all the prophets? yea, of a greater than all,—the Son of God Himself? It is certain, both our Master, and all these His servants, did imagine that fasting is not a little thing, and that He who is higher than the highest doth regard it. Of the same judgement, it is plain, were all His Apostles 'after they were filled with the Holy Ghost and with wisdom.' When they had the 'unction of the Holy One teaching them all things' they still approved themselves the ministers of God, 'by fastings,' as well as 'by the armour of righteousness on the right hand and on the left.' After 'the bridegroom was taken from them, then did they fast in those days.' Nor would they attempt anything (as we have seen above) wherein the glory of God was nearly concerned such as the sending forth labourers into the harvest, without solemn fasting as well as prayer.

5. 'But if fasting be indeed of so great importance, and attended with such a blessing, is it not best,' say some, fifthly, 'to fast always? not to do it now and then, but to keep a continual fast? to use as much abstinence, at all times, as our bodily strength will bear?' Let none be discouraged from doing this. By all means use as little and plain food, exercise as much self-denial herein, at all times, as your bodily strength will bear. And this may conduce, by the blessing of God, to several of the great ends above mentioned. It may be a considerable help, not only to chastity, but also to heavenly-mindedness; to the

weaning your affections from things below, and setting them on things above. But this is not fasting, scriptural fasting; it is never termed so in all the Bible. It, in some measure, answers some of the ends thereof; but still it is another thing. Practise it by all means; but not so as thereby to set aside a command of God, and an instituted means of averting His judgements, and obtaining the blessings of His children.

6. Use continually then as much abstinence as you please; which, taken thus, is no other than Christian temperance; but this need not at all interfere with your observing solemn times of fasting and prayer. For instance: your habitual abstinence or temperance would not prevent your fasting in secret, if you were suddenly overwhelmed with huge sorrow and remorse, and with horrible fear and dismay. Such a situation of mind would almost constrain you to fast: you would loathe your daily food; you would scarce endure even to take such supplies as were needful for the body, till God 'lifted you up out of the horrible pit, and set your feet upon a rock, and ordered your goings.' The same would be the case if you were in agony of desire, vehemently wrestling with God for His blessing. You would need none to instruct you not to eat bread till you had obtained the request of your lips.

7. Again: had you been at Nineveh when it was proclaimed throughout the city, 'Let neither man nor beast, herd nor flock, taste anything; let them not feed or drink water, but let them cry mightily unto God'; would your continual fast have been any reason for not bearing part in that general humiliation? Doubtless it would not. You would have been as much concerned as any other not to taste food on that day.

No more would abstinence, or the observing a continual fast, have excused any of the children of Israel from fasting on the tenth day of the seventh month, the great annual day of atonement. There was no exception for these in that solemn decree, 'Whatsoever soul it be, that shall not be afflicted,' shall not fast, 'in that day, he shall be cut off from among his people.'

Lastly, had you been with the brethren in Antioch, at the time when they fasted and prayed, before the sending forth of Barnabas and Saul, can you possibly imagine that your temperance or abstinence would have been a sufficient cause for not joining therein? Without doubt, if you had not, you would soon have been cut off from the Christian community. You would have deservedly been cast out from among them, as bringing confusion into the church of God.

IV. 1. I am, in the last place, to show, in what manner we are to fast, that it may be an acceptable service unto the Lord. And, first, let it be done unto the Lord, with our eye singly fixed on Him. Let our intention herein be this, and this alone, to glorify our Father which is in heaven; to express our sorrow and shame for our manifold transgressions of His holy law; to wait for an increase of purifying grace, drawing our affections to things above; to add seriousness and earnestness to our prayers; to avert the wrath of God; and to obtain all the great and precious promises which He hath made to us in Jesus Christ.

Let us beware of mocking God, of turning our fast, as well as our prayers, into an abomination unto the Lord, by the mixture of any temporal view, particularly by seeking the praise of men. Against this our blessed Lord more peculiarly guards us in the words of the text. 'Moreover, when ye fast, be ye not as the hypocrites'—such were too many who were called the people of God; 'of a sad countenance'; sour, affectedly sad, putting their looks into a peculiar form. 'For they disfigure their faces,' not only by unnatural distortions, but also by covering them with dust and ashes; 'that they may appear unto men to fast'; this is their chief, if not only, design. 'Verily I say unto you, they have their reward'; even the admiration and praise of men. 'But thou, when thou fastest, anoint thy head and wash thy face': do as thou art accustomed to do at other times; 'that thou appear not unto men to fast': let this be no part of thy intention; if they know it without any design of thine, it matters not, thou art neither the better nor the worse; 'but unto thy Father which is in secret: and thy Father, which seeth in secret, shall reward thee openly.'

2. But, if we desire this reward, let us beware, secondly, of fancying we *merit* anything of God by our fasting. We cannot be too often warned of this; inasmuch as a desire to 'establish our own righteousness,' to procure salvation of debt and not of grace, is so deeply rooted in all our hearts. Fasting is only a way which God hath ordained, wherein we wait for His unmerited mercy; and wherein, without any desert of ours, He hath promised freely to give us His blessing.

3. Not that we are to imagine, the performing the bare outward act will receive any blessing from God. 'Is it such a fast that I have chosen saith the Lord; a day for a man to afflict his soul? is it to bow down his head as a bulrush, and to spread sackcloth and ashes under him?' Are these outward acts, however strictly performed, all that is meant by a man's 'afflicting his soul'? 'Wilt thou call this a fast, and an acceptable day to the Lord?' No, surely: if it be a mere external service, it is all but lost labour. Such a performance may possibly afflict the body; but, as to the soul, it profiteth nothing.

4. Yea, the body may sometimes be afflicted too much, so as to be unfit for the works of our calling. This also we are diligently to guard against; for we ought to preserve our health, as a good gift of God. Therefore care is to be taken, whenever we fast, to proportion the fast to our strength. For we may not offer God murder for sacrifice, or destroy our bodies to help our souls.

But at these solemn seasons, we may, even in great weakness of body, avoid that other extreme, for which God condemns those who of old expostulated with Him for not accepting their fasts. 'Wherefore have we fasted, say they, and Thou seest not? . . . Behold, in the day of your fast you find pleasure, saith the Lord.' If we cannot wholly abstain from food, we may, at least, abstain from pleasant food; and then we shall not seek His face in vain.

5. But let us take care to afflict our souls as well as our bodies. Let every season, either of public or private fasting, be a season of exercising all those holy affections which are implied in a broken and contrite heart. Let it be a season of devout mourning, of godly sorrow for sin; such a sorrow as that of the Corinthians, concerning which the Apostle saith, 'I rejoice, not that ye were made sorry, but that ye sorrowed to repentance. For ye were made sorry after a godly manner, that ye might receive damage by us in nothing. For godly sorrow,' η κατα Θεον λυπη—the sorrow which is according to God, which is a precious gift of His Spirit, lifting the soul to God from whom it flows—'worketh repentance to salvation, not to be repented of.' Yea, and let our sorrowing after a godly sort work in us the same inward and outward *repentance* the same entire change of heart, renewed after the image of God, in righteousness and true holiness; and the same change of life, till we are holy as He is

holy, in all manner of conversation. Let it work in us the same *carefulness* to be found in Him, without spot and blameless; the same *clearing of ourselves,* by our lives rather than words, by our abstaining from all appearance of evil; the same *indignation,* vehement abhorrence of every sin; the same *fear* of our own deceitful hearts; the same *desire* to be in all things conformed to the holy and acceptable will of God; the same *zeal* for whatever may be a means of His glory, and of our growth in the knowledge of our Lord Jesus Christ; and the same *revenge* against Satan and all his works, against all filthiness both of flesh and spirit (2 Cor. vii. 9, &c.).

6. And with fasting let us always join fervent prayer, pouring out our whole souls before God, confessing our sins with all their aggravations, humbling ourselves under His mighty hand, laying open before Him all our wants, all our guiltiness and helplessness. This is a season for enlarging our prayers, both in behalf of ourselves and of our brethren. Let us now bewail the sins of our people; and cry aloud for the city of our God, that the Lord may build up Zion and cause His face to shine on her desolations. Thus, we may observe, the men of God, in ancient times, always joined prayer and fasting together; thus the Apostles, in all the instances cited above; and thus our Lord joins them in the discourse before us.

7. It remains only, in order to our observing such a fast as is acceptable to the Lord, that we add alms thereto; works of mercy, after our power, both to the bodies and souls of men: 'With such sacrifices' also 'God is well pleased.' Thus the angel declares to Cornelius, fasting and praying in his house, 'Thy prayers and thine alms are come up for a memorial before God' (Acts x. 4, &c.). And thus God Himself expressly and largely declares: 'Is not this the fast that I have chosen? to loose the bands of wickedness, to undo the heavy burdens, and to let the oppressed go free, and that ye break every yoke? Is it not to deal thy bread to the hungry, and that thou bring the poor that are cast out to thy house? when thou seest the naked, that thou cover him; and that thou hide not thyself from thine own flesh? Then shall thy light break forth as the morning, and thine health shall spring forth speedily: and thy righteousness shall go before thee; the glory of the Lord shall be thy reward. Then shalt thou call, and the Lord shall answer: thou shalt cry, and He shall

say, Here I am. . . . If,' when thou fastest, 'thou draw out thy soul to the hungry, and satisfy the afflicted soul; then shall thy light rise in obscurity, and thy darkness be as the noon-day. And the Lord shall guide thee continually, and satisfy thy soul in drought, and make fat thy bones: and thou shalt be like a watered garden, and like a spring of water, whose waters fail not' (Isa. lviii. 6, &c.).

SERMON XXIII

UPON OUR LORD'S SERMON ON THE MOUNT

DISCOURSE VIII

This sermon was begun on Thursday, January 29, 1736, whilst Wesley was on his voyage to Georgia, in the midst of a violent thunderstorm, and was finished in the course of the next few days (*Journal*, Standard Edition, i. 144). It is based on chaps. iv and vi of Law's *Serious Call*, from which it has some long quotations. I find in the sermon-register that Wesley preached from verse 20 at the Foundery on November 9, 1760; and from verse 22 at Epworth on August 2, and at the Foundery on November 11 of the next year. He returned to the same subject towards the close of his life in the sermons on The Single Eye (No. CXVIII) written at Bristol on September 25, 1789, and on Worldly Folly (No. CXIX), written at Balham on February 29, 1790. In the first of these he refers both to Jeremy Taylor's *Holy Living* and to Law's *Serious Call,* which he characterizes as 'a treatise which will hardly be excelled, if it be equalled, in the English tongue, either for beauty of expression or for justness and depth of thought.' It is good to find that his quarrel with Law had not blotted from his memory the blessing he had received from his works in the earlier stages of his religious development. Sermons XLIV (The Use of Money) and LI (The Good Steward) should be read along with this discourse, as representing Wesley's more mature thoughts on the right attitude of the Christian towards worldly wealth.

Neither Wesley nor Law quite realized the direct bearing of the saying about the single eye on the earlier verses of the passage. They both take the phrase to indicate purity of intention, the fixing of the eye of the soul entirely upon God. But in Jewish usage an evil eye means specifically niggardliness, and a good or sound eye liberality. Thus Deut. xv. 9: 'Beware lest . . . thine eye be evil against thy poor brother and thou give him nought; Prov. xxiii. 6: 'Eat not thou the bread of him that hath an evil eye . . . for, Eat and drink, saith he to thee; but his heart is not with thee'; Prov. xxviii. 22: 'He that hath an evil eye hasteth after riches'; Prov. xxii. 9: 'He that hath a good eye shall be blessed; for he giveth of his bread to the poor'; Ecclus. xiv. 10: 'An evil eye is grudging of bread, and he is miserly at his table.' A good or sound eye is therefore an eye that looks generously upon the poor; and the phrase 'Let thine eye be single' is in direct antithesis to the hoarding-up of treasures upon earth. The eye is thought of as the channel through which light comes into the body; if it is απλους i.e. healthy, the light comes in freely; but if it is diseased, the light is obstructed. So if a man is generous, the light of God comes into his soul; he knows God through sympathy with God's own goodness; but if he is mean and miserly, he shuts God out of his heart, and he becomes ever darker and darker in his spiritual conceptions. One feels sorry to interfere with an interpretation which has been so common, and which has given to the phrase 'a single eye' such a well-understood meaning in devotional literature; but truth must prevail.

In regard to verses 19 and 20, two things must be observed: First, that we have here an example of the common Hebrew idiom of exaggerated antithesis. When two things are to be compared, instead of saying 'This is preferable to that,' Hebrew rhetoric says, 'That is bad and this is good'; or if two courses of action are in question, instead of saying, 'Do this rather than that,' it says, 'Do not do that, but do this.' Thus Jeremiah (vii. 22) says, 'I spake not unto your fathers, nor commanded them in the day that I brought them out of the land of Egypt, concerning burnt offerings or sacrifices; but this thing I commanded them, saying, Hearken unto my voice, and I will be your God,' i.e. obedience is better than sacrifice (cf. Isa. i. 10-17). In Luke xiv. 26 our Lord says, 'If any man cometh unto Me, and hateth not his own father and mother . . . he cannot be My disciple'; in Matt. x. 37 the saying is given without the rhetorical figure, 'He that loveth father or mother more than Me is not worthy of Me.' So in Rom. ix. 13: 'Jacob I loved, but Esau I hated.' In Luke xiv. 12 our Lord says, 'When thou makest a dinner or a supper, call not thy friends, nor thy brethren, . . . but bid the poor, the maimed, the lame, the blind.' This is not a prohibition of friendly mutual entertainments, but means that it is better to entertain the poor than to make feasts for one's friends. Matt. x. 20: 'It is not ye who speak, but the Spirit of your Father which speaketh in you.' So here we have not an absolute prohibition of saving money; the meaning is that it is better to lay up treasure in heaven by giving to the poor than to hoard money for oneself.

Second, the profound difference between the economic conditions of our Lord's time and those under which we live must not be forgotten. In those days practically the only way in which the peasants in our Lord's congregation could save money or jewellery was by burying it in the ground, like the unprofitable servant in the parable, where it would be liable to be corroded and spoilt; or by concealing it in their houses, where it might easily be stolen. There was no method by which money could be at once saved for the owner's future use, and meantime employed in productive service. Nowadays, through savings banks and building societies and insurance companies, a poor man can invest his savings, so that they will be available for himself and his family in time of sickness or old age, and in the meantime will become part of the working capital of the community and be used in productive activities. And his money will do far more good in that way than if he gave the few shillings of his monthly savings to the poor directly. Similarly, the man

who is making large profits in his business benefits the poor far more by
increasing his business, and so finding employment for them, than by
indiscriminate charity. There will always be plenty of opportunity for
generous giving to the sick and the aged and the unfortunate as well;
but the best use of wealth is to employ it in finding remunerative work
for those who want it. The motive is everything. What our Lord does
positively forbid is the engaging in business solely for the sake of
making money for oneself, and the spending of our profits in selfish
and extravagant indulgences, or hoarding them for the sake of
ultimately possessing a great fortune.

*Lay not up for yourselves treasures upon earth, where moth and rust doth
    corrupt, and where thieves break through and steal:*
*But lay up for yourselves treasures in heaven, where neither moth nor rust doth
    corrupt, and where thieves do not break through nor steal:*
For where your treasure is, there will your heart be also.
*The light of the body is the eye: if therefore thine eye be single thy whole body shall
    be full of light.*
*But if thine eye be evil, thy whole body shall be full of darkness. If therefore the light
    that is in thee be darkness, how great is that darkness!*—MATT. vi. 19-23.

1. From those which are commonly termed religious actions,
and which are real branches of true religion, where they spring
from a pure and holy intention, and are performed in a manner
suitable thereto, our Lord proceeds to the actions of common
life; and shows that the same purity of intention is as
indispensably required in our ordinary business, as in giving
alms, or fasting, or prayer.

And without question, the same purity of intention, 'which
makes our alms and devotions acceptable, must also make our
labour or employment a proper offering to God. If a man
pursues his business, that he may raise himself to a state of figure
and riches in the world, he is no longer serving God in his
employment, and has no more title to a reward from God, than
he who gives alms that he may be seen, or prays that he may be
heard, of men. For vain and earthly designs are no more
allowable in our employments, than in our alms and devotions.
They are not only evil when they mix with our good works,' with
our religious actions, 'but they have the same evil nature when
they enter into the common business of our employments. If it
were allowable to pursue them in our worldly employments, it
would be allowable to pursue them in our devotions. But as our
alms and devotions are not an acceptable service but when they

proceed from a pure intention, so our common employment cannot be reckoned a service to Him but when it is performed with the same piety of heart.'

2. This our blessed Lord declares in the liveliest manner, in those strong and comprehensive words, which He explains, enforces, and enlarges upon, throughout this whole chapter: 'The light of the body is the eye: if therefore thine eye be single, thy whole body shall be full of light. But if thine eye be evil, thy whole body shall be full of darkness.' The eye is the intention: what the eye is to the body, the intention is to the soul. As the one guides all the motions of the body, so does the other those of the soul. This eye of the soul is then said to be single, when it looks at one thing only; when we have no other design, but to 'know God, and Jesus Christ whom He hath sent'—to know Him with suitable affections, loving Him as He hath loved us; to please God in all things; to serve God (as we love Him) with all our heart, and mind, and soul, and strength; and to enjoy God in all, and above all things, in time and in eternity.

3. 'If thine eye be' thus 'single,' thus fixed on God, 'thy whole body shall be full of light.' 'Thy whole body': —all that is guided by the intention, as the body is by the eye: all thou art; all thou doest; thy desires, tempers, affections; thy thoughts, and words, and actions. The whole of these 'shall be full of light'; full of true, divine knowledge. This is the first thing we may here understand by light. 'In His light thou shalt see light.' 'He which of old commanded light to shine out of darkness, shall shine in thy heart': He shall enlighten the eyes of thy understanding with the knowledge of the glory of God. His Spirit shall reveal unto thee the deep things of God. The inspiration of the Holy One shall give thee understanding, and cause thee to know wisdom secretly. Yea, the anointing which thou receivest of Him 'shall abide in thee, and teach thee of all things.'

How does experience confirm this! Even after God hath opened the eyes of our understanding, if we seek or desire anything else than God, how soon is our foolish heart darkened! Then clouds again rest upon our souls. Doubts and fears again overwhelm us. We are tossed to and fro, and know not what to do, or which is the path wherein we should go. But when we desire and seek nothing but God, clouds and doubts vanish away. We who 'were sometimes darkness are now light in the

Lord.' The night now shineth as the day; and we find 'the path of the upright is light.' God showeth us the path wherein we should go, and maketh plain the way before our face.

4. The second thing which we may here understand by light, is holiness. While thou seekest God in all things, thou shalt find Him in all—the fountain of all holiness continually filling thee with His own likeness, with justice, mercy, and truth. While thou lookest unto Jesus, and Him alone, thou shalt be filled with the mind that was in Him. Thy soul shall be renewed day by day, after the image of Him that created it. If the eye of thy mind be not removed from Him, if thou endurest 'seeing Him that is invisible,' and seeking nothing else in heaven or earth, then as thou beholdest the glory of the Lord, thou shalt be transformed 'into the same image, from glory to glory, by the Spirit of the Lord.'

And it is also matter of daily experience, that 'by grace we are' thus 'saved through faith.' It is by faith that the eye of the mind is opened, to see the light of the glorious love of God: and as long as it is steadily fixed thereon, on God in Christ, reconciling the world unto Himself, we are more and more filled with the love of God and man; with meekness, gentleness, long-suffering; with all the fruits of holiness which are through Christ Jesus, to the glory of God the Father.

5. This light which fills him who has a single eye implies, thirdly, happiness, as well as holiness. Surely 'light is sweet, and a pleasant thing it is to see the sun.' But how much more, to see the Sun of Righteousness continually shining upon the soul! And if there be any consolation in Christ, if any comfort of love, if any peace that passeth all understanding, if any rejoicing in hope of the glory of God, they all belong to him whose eye is single. Thus is his 'whole body full of light.' He walketh in the light as God is in the light, rejoicing evermore, praying without ceasing, and in everything giving thanks; enjoying whatever is the will of God concerning him in Christ Jesus.

6. 'But if thine eye be evil, thy whole body shall be full of darkness.' 'If thine eye be evil': we see there is no medium between a single and an evil eye. If the eye be not single, then it is evil. If the intention, in whatever we do, be not singly to God, if we seek anything else, then our mind and conscience are defiled.

Our eye therefore is evil, if, in anything we do, we aim at any other end than God; if we have any view, but to know and to love God, to please and serve Him in all things; if we have any other design than to enjoy God, to be happy in Him both now and for ever.

7. If thine eye be not singly fixed on God, 'thy whole body shall be full of darkness.' The veil shall still remain on thy heart. Thy mind shall be more and more blinded by 'the god of this world,' 'lest the light of the glorious gospel of Christ should shine upon thee.' Thou wilt be full of ignorance and error touching the things of God, not being able to receive or discern them. And even when thou hast some desire to serve God, thou wilt be full of uncertainty as to the manner of serving Him; finding doubts and difficulties on every side, and not seeing any way to escape.

Yea, if thine eye be not single, if thou seek any of the things of earth, thou shalt be full of ungodliness and unrighteousness; thy desires, tempers, affections, being all out of course; being all dark, and vile, and vain. And thy conversation will be evil, as well as thy heart; not 'seasoned with salt,' or 'meet to minister grace unto the hearers'; but idle, unprofitable, corrupt, grievous to the Holy Spirit of God.

8. Both destruction and unhappiness are in thy ways; 'for the way of peace hast thou not known.' There is no peace, no settled, solid peace, for them that know not God. There is no true nor lasting content for any who do not seek Him with their whole heart. While thou aimest at any of the things that perish, 'all that cometh is vanity'; yea, not only vanity, but 'vexation of spirit'; and that both in the pursuit and the enjoyment also. Thou walkest indeed in a vain shadow, and disquietest thyself in vain. Thou walkest in darkness that may be felt. Sleep on; but thou canst not take thy rest. The dreams of life can give pain; and that thou knowest: but ease they cannot give. There is no rest in this world or the world to come, but only in God, the centre of spirits.

'If the light which is in thee be darkness, how great is that darkness!' If the intention, which ought to enlighten the whole soul, to fill it with knowledge, and love, and peace, and which in fact does, so long as it is single, as long as it aims at God alone,—if this be darkness; if it aim at anything beside God, and consequently cover the soul with darkness instead of light, with ignorance and error, with sin and misery; O how great is that darkness! It is the very smoke which ascends out of the bottomless pit! It is the essential night which reigns in the lowest deep, in the land of the shadow of death!

9. Therefore, 'lay not up for yourselves treasures upon earth, where moth and rust doth corrupt, and where thieves break through and steal.' If you do, it is plain your eye is evil; it is not singly fixed on God.

With regard to most of the commandments of God, whether relating to the heart or life, the Heathens of Africa or America stand much on a level with those that are called Christians. The Christians observe them (a few only being excepted) very near as much as the Heathens. For instance: the generality of the natives of England, commonly called Christians, are as sober and as temperate as the generality of the Heathens near the Cape of Good Hope. And so the Dutch or French Christians are as humble and as chaste as the Choctaw or Cherokee Indians. It is not easy to say, when we compare the bulk of the nations in Europe with those in America, whether the superiority lies on the one side or the other. At least, the American has not much the advantage. But we cannot affirm this with regard to the command now before us. Here the Heathen has far the pre-eminence. He desires and seeks nothing more than plain food to eat, and plain raiment to put on; and he seeks this only from day to day: he reserves, he lays up nothing; unless it be as much corn at one season of the year as he will need before that season returns. This command, therefore, the Heathens, though they know it not, do constantly and punctually observe. They 'lay up for themselves no treasures upon earth'; no stores of purple or fine linen, of gold or silver, which either 'moth or rust may corrupt, or thieves break through and steal.' But how do the Christians observe what they profess to receive as a command of the most high God? Not at all; not in any degree; no more than if no such command had ever been given to man. Even the good Christians, as they are accounted by others as well as themselves, pay no manner of regard thereto. It might as well be still hid in its original Greek, for any notice they take of it. In what Christian city do you find one man of five hundred, who makes the least scruple of laying up just as much treasure as he can—of increasing his goods just as far as he is able? There are, indeed, those who would not do this unjustly: there are many who will neither rob nor steal; and some who will not defraud their neighbour; nay, who will not gain either by his ignorance or necessity. But this is quite another point. Even these do not scruple the thing, but the manner of it. They do not scruple the 'laying up treasures upon earth'; but the laying them up by dishonesty. They do not start at disobeying Christ, but at a breach of heathen morality. So that even these honest men do no more obey this command than a highwayman or a house-breaker. Nay, they never designed to obey it. From their youth up, it never entered into their thoughts. They were bred up by their Christian parents, masters, and friends, without any instruction at all concerning it; unless it were this,—to break it as soon and as much as they could, and to continue breaking it to their lives' end.

10. There is no one instance of spiritual infatuation in the world which is more amazing than this. Most of these very men read, or hear the Bible read—many of them every Lord's day. They have read or heard these words an hundred times, and yet never suspect that they are themselves condemned thereby, any more than by those which forbid parents to offer up their sons or daughters unto Moloch. O that God would speak to these miserable self-deceivers with His own voice, His mighty voice; that they may at last awake out of the snare of the devil, and the scales may fall from their eyes!

11. Do you ask what it is to 'lay up treasures on earth'? It will be needful to examine this thoroughly. And let us, first, observe what is not forbidden in this command, that we may then clearly discern what is.

We are not forbidden in this command, first, to 'provide things honest in the sight of all men,' to provide wherewith we may render unto all their due, whatsoever they can justly demand of us. So far from it, that we are taught of God to 'owe no man anything.' We ought, therefore, to use all diligence in our calling, in order to owe no man anything; this being no other than a plain law of common justice, which our Lord came 'not to destroy, but to fulfil.'

Neither, secondly, does He here forbid the providing for ourselves such things as are needful for the body; a sufficiency of plain, wholesome food to eat, and clean raiment to put on. Yea, it is our duty, so far as God puts it into our power, to provide these things also; to the end we may eat our own bread, and be burdensome to no man.

Nor yet are we forbidden, thirdly, to provide for our children, and for those of our own household. This also it is our duty to do, even upon principles of heathen morality. Every man ought to provide the plain necessaries of life, both for his own wife and children; and to put them into a capacity of providing these for themselves, when he is gone hence and is no more seen. I say, of providing *these*; the plain necessaries of life; not delicacies; not superfluities;—and that by their diligent labour; for it is no man's duty to furnish them, any more than himself, with the means either of luxury or idleness. But if any man provide not thus far for his own children (as well as for the widows of his own house, of whom primarily St. Paul is speaking in those well-known words to Timothy), he hath practically 'denied the faith, and is worse than an infidel,' or Heathen.

Lastly. We are not forbidden, in these words, to lay up, from time to time, what is needful for the carrying on our worldly business, in such a measure and degree as is sufficient to answer the foregoing purposes,—in such a measure as, first, to owe no man anything; secondly, to procure for ourselves the necessaries of life; and, thirdly, to furnish those of our own house with them while we live, and with the means of procuring them when we are gone to God.

12. We may now clearly discern (unless we are unwilling to discern it) what that is which is forbidden here. It is, the designedly procuring more of this world's goods than will answer the foregoing purposes. The labouring after a larger measure of worldly substance, a larger increase of gold and silver—the laying up any more than these ends require—is what is here expressly and absolutely forbidden. If the words have any meaning at all, it must be this; for they are capable of no other. Consequently, whoever he is that, owing no man anything, and having food and raiment for himself and his household, together with a sufficiency to carry on his worldly business, so far as answers these reasonable purposes; whosoever, I say, being already in these circumstances, seeks a still larger portion on earth; he lives in an open, habitual denial of the Lord that bought him. 'He hath' practically 'denied the faith, and is worse than' an African or American 'infidel.'

13. Hear ye this, all ye that dwell in the world, and love the world wherein ye dwell! Ye may be 'highly esteemed of men'; but ye are 'an abomination in the sight of God'! How long shall your souls cleave to the dust? How long will ye load yourselves with thick clay? When will ye awake and see, that the open, speculative Heathens are nearer the kingdom of heaven than you? When will ye be persuaded to choose the better part; that which cannot be taken away from you? When will ye seek only to 'lay up treasures in heaven; renouncing, dreading, abhorring all other? If you aim at 'laying up treasures on earth,' you are not barely losing your time, and spending your strength for that which is not bread; for what is the fruit if you succeed? You have murdered your own soul! You have extinguished the last spark of spiritual life therein! Now indeed, in the midst of life, you are in death! You are a living man, but a dead Christian! 'For where your treasure is, there will your heart be also.' Your heart is sunk into the dust; your soul cleaveth to the ground. Your affections are set, not on things above, but on things of the earth; on poor husks, that may poison, but cannot satisfy, an everlasting spirit, made for God. Your love, your joy, your desire, are all placed on the things which perish in the using. You have thrown away the treasure in heaven. God and Christ are lost! You have gained riches and hell-fire!

14. O 'how hardly shall they that have riches enter into the kingdom of God!' When our Lord's disciples were astonished at His speaking thus, He was so far from retracting it, that He repeated the same important truth in stronger terms than before. 'It is easier for a camel to go through the eye of a needle, than for a rich man to enter into the kingdom of God.' How hard is it for them, whose every word is applauded, not to be wise in their own eyes! How hard for them not to think themselves better than the poor, base, uneducated herd of men! How hard not to seek happiness in their riches, or in things dependent upon them; in gratifying the desire of the flesh, the desire of the eye, or the pride of life! O ye rich, how can ye escape the damnation of hell? Only with God all things are possible!

15. And even if you do not succeed, what is the fruit of your endeavouring to lay up treasures on earth? 'They that will be rich,' οι βουλομενοι πλουτειν, they that *desire*, that *endeavour* after it, whether they succeed or no, 'fall into temptation and a

snare'—a gin, a trap of the devil; 'and into many foolish and hurtful lusts'—επιθυμιας ανοητους, *desires,* with which *reason hath nothing to do*; such as properly belong not to rational and immortal beings, but only to the brute beasts, which have no understanding; 'which drown men in destruction and perdition,' in present and eternal misery. Let us but open our eyes, and we may daily see the melancholy proofs of this—men who, desiring, resolving to be rich, coveting after money, the root of all evil, have already pierced themselves through with many sorrows, and anticipated the hell to which they are going!

The cautiousness with which the Apostle here speaks is highly observable. He does not affirm this absolutely of the rich: for a man may possibly be rich, without any fault of his, by an overruling Providence, preventing his own choice; but he affirms it of οι βουλομενοι πλουτειν, *those who desire* or seek *to be rich.* Riches, dangerous as they are, do not always 'drown men in destruction and perdition'; but the *desire of riches* does. Those who calmly desire, and deliberately seek to attain them, whether they do, in fact, gain the world or no, do infallibly lose their own souls. These are they that sell Him who bought them with His blood, for a few pieces of gold or silver. These enter into a covenant with death and hell; and their covenant shall stand: for they are daily making themselves meet to partake of their inheritance with the devil and his angels.

16. O who shall warn this generation of vipers to flee from the wrath to come! Not those who lie at their gate, or cringe at their feet, desiring to be fed with the crumbs that fall from their tables. Not those who court their favour, or fear their frown; none of those who mind earthly things. But if there be a Christian upon earth, if there be a man who hath overcome the world, who desires nothing but God, and fears none but Him that is able to destroy both body and soul in hell; 'thou. O man of God, speak, and spare not; lift up thy voice like a trumpet.' Cry aloud, and show these honourable sinners the desperate condition wherein they stand! It may be, one in a thousand may have ears to hear; may arise and shake himself from the dust; may break loose from these chains that bind him to the earth, and at length lay up treasurcs in heaven.

17. And if it should be, that one of these by the mighty power of God awoke and asked, 'What must I do to be saved?' the

answer, according to the oracles of God, is clear, full, and express. God doth not say to thee, 'Sell all that thou hast.' Indeed, He who seeth the hearts of men saw it needful to enjoin this in one peculiar case, that of the young rich ruler. But He never laid it down for a general rule to all rich men, in all succeeding generations. His general direction is, first, 'Be not high-minded.' God seeth not as man seeth. He esteems thee not for thy riches, for thy grandeur or equipage, for any qualification or accomplishment which is directly or indirectly owing to thy wealth, which can be bought or pro cured thereby. All these are with Him as dung and dross: let them be so with thee also. Beware thou think not thyself to be one jot wiser or better for all these things. Weigh thyself in another balance: estimate thyself only by the measure of faith and love which God hath given thee. If thou hast more of the knowledge and love of God than he, thou art on this account, and no other, wiser and better, more valuable and honourable, than him who is with the dogs of thy flock. But if thou hast not this treasure, thou art more foolish, more vile, more truly contemptible, I will not say than the lowest servant under thy roof, but than the beggar laid at thy gate full of sores.

18. Secondly. 'Trust not in uncertain riches.' Trust not in them for help: and trust not in them for happiness.

First. Trust not in them for help. Thou art miserably mistaken, if thou lookest for this in gold or silver. These are no more able to set thee *above the world,* than to set thee above the devil. Know that both the world, and the prince of this world, laugh at all such preparations against them. These will little avail in the day of trouble; even if they remain in the trying hour. But it is not certain that they will; for how oft do they 'make themselves wings and fly away'! But if not, what support will they afford, even in the ordinary troubles of life? The desire of thy eyes, the wife of thy youth, thy son, thine only son, or the friend which was as thy own soul, is taken away at a stroke. Will thy riches reanimate the breathless clay, or call back its late inhabitant? Will they secure thee from sickness, diseases, pain? Do these visit the poor only? Nay, he that feeds thy flocks, or tills thy ground, has less sickness and pain than thou. He is more rarely visited by these unwelcome guests; and if they come there at all, they are more easily driven away from the little cot, than

from 'the cloud-topt palaces.' And during the time that thy body
is chastened with pain, or consumes away with pining sickness,
how do thy treasures help thee? Let the poor Heathen answer,—

> *Ut lippum pictae tabulae fomenta podagrum,*
> *Auriculas citharae collecta sorde dolentes.*

19. But there is at hand a greater trouble than all these. Thou
art to die! Thou art to sink into dust; to return to the ground
from which thou wast taken; to mix with common clay. Thy
body is to go to the earth as it was, while thy spirit returns to God
that gave it. And the time draws on: the years slide away with a
swift though silent pace. Perhaps your day is far spent: the noon
of life is past, and the evening shadows begin to rest upon you.
You feel in yourself sure approaching decay. The springs of life
wear away apace. Now what help is there in your riches? Do they
sweeten death? Do they endear that solemn hour? Quite the
reverse. 'O death, how bitter art thou to a man that liveth at rest
in his possessions!' How unacceptable to him is that awful
sentence, 'This night shall thy soul be required of thee'! Or will
they prevent the unwelcome stroke, or protract the dreadful
hour? Can they deliver your soul, that it should not see death?
Can they restore the years that are past? Can they add to your
appointed time a month, a day, an hour, a moment? Or will the
good things you have chosen for your portion here follow you
over the great gulf? Not so: naked came you into this world;
naked must you return.

> *Linquenda tellus et domus, et placens*
> *Uxor; neque harum, quas colis, arborum,*
> *Te, praeter invisam cupressum,*
> *Ulla brevem dominum sequetur!*

Surely, were not these truths too plain to be observed, because
they are too plain to be denied, no man that is to die could
possibly trust for help in uncertain riches.

20. And trust not in them for happiness: for here also they will
be found 'deceitful upon the weights.' Indeed this every
reasonable man may infer from what has been observed already.
For if neither thousands of gold and silver, nor any of the
advantages or pleasures purchased thereby, can prevent our

being miserable, it evidently follows, they cannot make us happy. What happiness can they afford to him who in the midst of all, is constrained to cry out,

> To my new courts sad thought does still repair,
> And round my gilded roofs hangs hovering care?

Indeed experience is here so full, strong, and undeniable, that it makes all other arguments needless. Appeal we therefore to fact. Are the rich and great the only happy men? And is each of them more or less happy in proportion to his measure of riches? Are they happy at all? I had wellnigh said, they are of all men most miserable! Rich man, for once speak the truth from thy heart! Speak, both for thyself and for thy brethren!

> Amidst our plenty something still,—
> To me, to thee, to him is wanting!
> That cruel something. unpossessed,
> Corrodes and leavens all the rest

Yea, and so it will, till thy wearisome days of vanity are shut up in the night of death.

Surely, then, to trust in riches for happiness is the greatest folly of all that are under the sun! Are you not convinced of this? Is it possible you should still expect to find happiness in money, or all it can procure? What! can silver and gold, and eating and drinking, and horses and servants and glittering apparel, and diversions and pleasures (as they are called) make thee happy? They can as soon make thee immortal!

21. These are all dead show. Regard them not. Trust thou in the living God; so shalt thou be safe under the shadow of the Almighty; His faithfulness and truth shall be thy shield and buckler. He is a very present help in time of trouble; such an help as can never fail. Then shalt thou say, if all thy other friends die, 'The Lord liveth, and blessed be my strong Helper!' He shall remember thee when thou liest sick upon thy bed; when vain is the help of man. When all the things of the earth can give no support, He will 'make all thy bed in thy sickness,' He will sweeten thy pain: the consolations of God shall cause thee to clap thy hands in the flames. And even when this house of earth is wellnigh shaken down, when it is just ready to drop into the dust,

He will teach thee to say, 'O death! where is thy sting? O grave! where is thy victory? Thanks be unto God which giveth' me 'the victory, through' my 'Lord Jesus Christ.'

O trust in Him for happiness as well as for help. All the springs of happiness are in Him. Trust 'in Him who giveth us all things richly to enjoy,' παρεχοντι ημιν πλουσιως παντα εις απολαυσιν—who, of His own rich and free mercy, holds them out to us, as in His own hand, that, receiving them as His gifts, and as pledges of His love, we may enjoy all that we possess. It is His love gives a relish to all we taste—puts life and sweetness into all; while every creature leads us up to the great Creator, and all earth is a scale to heaven. He transfuses the joys that are at His own right hand into all He bestows on His thankful children; who, having fellowship with the Father and His Son Jesus Christ, enjoys Him in all, and above all.

22. Thirdly. Seek not to increase in goods. 'Lay not up for' thyself 'treasures upon earth.' This is a flat, positive command; full as clear as, 'Thou shalt not commit adultery.' How then is it possible for a rich man to grow richer, without denying the Lord that bought him? Yea how can any man who has already the necessaries of life, gain or aim at more, and be guiltless?. 'Lay not up,' saith our Lord, 'treasures upon earth.' If, in spite of this, you do and will lay up money or goods which 'moth or rust may corrupt, or thieves break through and steal'; if you will add house to house, or field to field,—why do you call yourself a Christian? You do not obey Jesus Christ. You do not design it. Why do you name yourself by His name? 'Why call ye Me, Lord, Lord,' saith He Himself, 'and do not the things which I say?'

23. If you ask, 'But what must we do with our goods, seeing we have more than we have occasion to use, if we must not lay them up? Must we throw them away?' I answer. If you threw them into the sea, if you were to cast them into the fire and consume them, they would be better bestowed than they are now. You cannot find so mischievous a manner of throwing them away, as either the laying them up for your posterity, or the laying them out upon yourselves in folly and superfluity. Of all possible methods of throwing them away, these two are the very worst; the most opposite to the gospel of Christ, and the most pernicious to your own soul.

How pernicious to your own soul the latter of these is, has been excellently shown by a late writer:—

'If we waste our money, we are not only guilty of wasting a talent which God has given us, but we do ourselves this farther harm, we turn this useful talent into a powerful means of corrupting ourselves; because so far as it is spent wrong, so far it is spent in the support of some wrong temper, in gratifying some vain and unreasonable desires, which, as Christians, we are obliged to renounce.

'As wit and fine parts cannot be only trifled away but will expose those that have them to greater follies; so money cannot be only trifled away, but, if it is not used according to reason and religion, will make people live a more silly and extravagant life, than they would have done without it: if, therefore, you do not spend your money in doing good to others, you must spend it to the hurt of yourself. You act like one that refuses the cordial to his sick friend, which he cannot drink himself without inflaming his blood. For this is the case of superfluous money: if you give it to those that want it, it is a cordial; if you spend it upon yourself, in something that you do not want, it only inflames and disorders your mind.

'In using riches where they have no real use, nor we any real want, we only use them to our great hurt, in creating unreasonable desires, in nourishing ill tempers, in indulging foolish passions, and supporting a vain turn of mind. For high eating and drinking, fine clothes and fine houses, state and equipage, gay pleasures and diversions, do all of them naturally hurt and disorder our heart. They are the food and nourishment of all the folly and weakness of our nature. They are all of them the support of something that ought not to be supported. They are contrary to that sobriety and piety of heart which relishes divine things. They are so many weights upon our mind, that make us less able and less inclined to raise our thoughts and affections to things above.

'So that money thus spent is not merely wasted or lost, but it is spent to bad purposes and miserable effects; to the corruption and disorder of our hearts; to the making us unable to follow the sublime doctrines of the gospel. It is but like keeping money from the poor to buy poison for ourselves.'

24. Equally inexcusable are those who lay up what they do not need for any reasonable purposes:—

'If a man had hands, and eyes, and feet, that he could give to those that wanted them; if he should lock them up in a chest, instead of giving them to his brethern that were blind and lame, should we not justly reckon him an inhuman wretch? If he should rather choose to amuse himself with hoarding them up, than entitle himself to an eternal reward, by giving them to those that wanted eyes and hands, might we not justly reckon him mad?

'Now, money has very much the nature of eyes and feet. If therefore we lock it up in chests, while the poor and distressed want it for their necessary uses, we are not far from the cruelty of him that chooses rather to hoard up the hands and eyes, than to give them to those that want them. If we choose to lay it up, rather than to entitle ourselves to an eternal reward by disposing of our money well, we are guilty of his madness that rather chooses to lock up eyes and hands than to make himself for ever blessed by giving them to those that want them.'

25. May not this be another reason why rich men shall so hardly enter into the kingdom of heaven? A vast majority of them are under a curse, under the peculiar curse of God; inasmuch as, in the general tenor of their lives, they are not only robbing God, continually embezzling and wasting their Lord's goods, and, by that very means, corrupting their own souls, but also robbing the poor, the hungry, the naked; wronging the widow and the fatherless; and making themselves accountable for all the want, affliction, and distress which they may but do not remove. Yea, doth not the blood of all those who perish for want of what they either lay up, or lay out needlessly, cry against them from the earth? O what account will they give to Him who is ready to judge both the quick and the dead!

26. The true way of employing what you do not want yourselves, you may, fourthly, learn from those words of our Lord, which are the counterpart of what went before: 'Lay up for yourselves treasures in heaven; where neither moth nor rust doth corrupt, and where thieves do not break through and steal.' Put out whatever thou canst spare, upon better security than this world can afford. Lay up thy treasures in the bank of heaven; and God shall restore them in that day. 'He that hath

pity upon the poor lendeth unto the Lord: and look, what he layeth out, it shall be paid him again.' 'Place that,' saith He, 'unto My account. Howbeit, thou owest Me thine own self besides!'

Give to the poor with a single eye, with an upright heart, and write, 'So much given to God.' For 'inasmuch as ye did it unto one of the least of these My brethren, ye have done it unto Me.'

This is the part of a 'faithful and wise steward'; not to sell either his houses or lands, or principal stock, be it more or less, unless some peculiar circumstance should require it; and not to desire or endeavour to increase it, any more than to squander it away in vanity; but to employ it wholly to those wise and reasonable purposes for which his Lord has lodged it in his hands. The wise steward, after having provided his own household with what is needful for life and godliness, makes himself friends with all that remains, from time to time, of the 'mammon of unrighteousness; that when he fails, they may receive him into everlasting habitations'—that whensoever his earthly tabernacle is dissolved, they who were before carried into Abraham's bosom, after having eaten his bread, and worn the fleece of his flock, and praised God for the consolation, may welcome him into paradise, and into 'the house of God, eternal in the heavens.'

27. We 'charge' you, therefore, 'who are rich in this world,' as having authority from our great Lord and Master αγαθοεργειν—to be *habitually doing good,* to live in a course of good works. 'Be ye merciful, as your Father which is in heaven is merciful'; who doeth good, and ceaseth not. 'Be ye merciful'— how far? After your power; with all the ability which God giveth. Make this your only measure of doing good; not any beggarly maxims or customs of the world. We 'charge you to be rich in good works'; as you have much, to give plenteously. 'Freely ye have received, freely give'; so as to lay up no treasure but in heaven. Be ye 'ready to distribute' to every one, according to his necessity. Disperse abroad; give to the poor; deal your bread to the hungry. Cover the naked with a garment; entertain the stranger; carry or send relief to them that are in prison, Heal the sick; not by miracle, but through the blessing of God upon your seasonable support. Let the blessing of him that was ready to perish, through pining want, come upon thee. Defend the

oppressed, plead the cause of the fatherless, and make the widow's heart sing for joy.

28. We exhort you, in the name of the Lord Jesus Christ, to be 'willing to communicate'; κοινωνικους ειναι; to be of the same spirit (though not in the same outward state) with those believers of ancient times, who remained steadfast, εν τη κοινωνια, in that blessed and holy *fellowship,* wherein 'none said that anything was his own, but they had all things common.' Be a steward, a faithful and wise steward, of God and of the poor; differing from them in these two circumstances only,—that your wants are first supplied, out of the portion of your Lord's goods which remains in your hands; and, that you have the blessedness of giving. Thus 'lay up for yourselves a good foundation,' not in the world which now is, but rather 'for the time to come, that ye may lay hold on eternal life.' The great foundation indeed of all the blessings of God, whether temporal or eternal, is the Lord Jesus Christ. His righteousness and blood, what He hath done, and what He hath suffered for us. And 'other foundation,' in this sense, 'can no man lay'; no, not an apostle; no, not an angel from heaven. But through His merits, whatever we do in His name is a foundation for a good reward, in the day when 'every man shall receive his own reward, according to his own labour.' Therefore 'labour' thou, 'not for the meat that perisheth, but for that which endureth unto everlasting life.' Therefore 'whatsoever thy hand' now 'findeth to do, do it with thy might.' Therefore let

> No fair occasion pass unheeded by;
> Snatching the golden moments as they fly,
> Thou by few fleeting years ensure eternity!

'By patient continuance in well-doing, seek' thou 'for glory, and honour, and immortality.' In a constant, zealous performance of all good works, wait thou for that happy hour when the King shall say, 'I was an hungered, and ye gave me meat: I was thirsty, and ye gave Me drink: I was a stranger, and ye took Me in: naked, and ye clothed Me: I was sick, and ye visited Me: I was in prison, and ye came unto Me. . . . Come, ye blessed of My Father, receive the kingdom prepared for you from the foundation of the world!'

SERMON XXIV

UPON OUR LORD'S SERMON ON THE MOUNT

DISCOURSE IX

The first sermon preached by Wesley after his ordination was from a part of this text (verse 33). The service was held on September 26 1725, at the church at South Leigh (see above, p. 263). The present discourse follows much the same lines as this first sermon; and some of the sentences therein are repeated here. But it is much more fully elaborated, especially in the sections on the meaning of God's righteousness. The MS. of this sermon has been preserved, and is in the Colman Collection; a facsimile was issued by the Wesleyan Methodist Book-Room in 1903. Matt. vi. 24 occurs as the text of a sermon on September 12, 1756, at Bishop Bonner's Chapel, an old palace of the Bishops of London not far from the Children's Home in Bonner Road, London; at the Foundery during September of the same year; at Bandon in Ireland on July 12, 1758; at Manchester on April 23, 1759; at Bath on November 3, 1760; and first at Bristol and then at Kingswood on September 21, 1761. This was no doubt based on sections i to 13 of this discourse.

No man can serve two masters: for either he will hate the one, and love the other; or else he will hold to the one, and despise the other. Ye cannot serve God and mammon.

Therefore I say unto you, Take no thought for your life, what ye shall eat, or what ye shall drink; nor yet for your body, what ye shall put on. Is not the life more than meat, and the body than raiment?

Behold the fowls of the air: for they sow not, neither do they reap, nor gather into barns; yet your heavenly Father feedeth them. Are ye not much better than they?

Which of you by taking thought can add one cubit unto his stature?

And why take ye thought for raiment? Consider the lilies of the field, how they grow; they toil not, neither do they spin:

And yet I say unto you, That even Solomon in all his glory was not arrayed like one of these.

Wherefore, if God so clothe the grass of the field, which to-day is, and tomorrow is cast into the oven, shall He not much more clothe you, O ye of little faith?

Therefore take no thought, saying. What shall we eat? or What shall we drink? or, Wherewithal shall we be clothed?

(For after all these things do the Gentiles seek:) for your heavenly Father knoweth that ye have need of all these things.

But seek ye first the kingdom of God, and his righteousness; and all these things
*   shall be added unto you.*
Take therefore no thought for the morrow: for the morrow shall take thought for
*   the things of itself. Sufficient unto the day is the evil thereof.*—MATT. vi.
*   24-34.*

1. It is recorded of the nations whom the King of Assyria, after
he had carried Israel away into captivity, placed in the cities of
Samaria, that 'they feared the Lord, and served their own gods.'
'These nations,' saith the inspired writer, 'feared the Lord';
performed an outward service to Him (a plain proof that they
had a fear of God, though not according to knowledge); 'and
served their graven images, both their children, and their
children's children: as did their fathers, so do they unto this day'
(2 Kings xvii. 33, &c.).

How nearly does the practice of most modern Christians
resemble this of the ancient Heathens! 'They fear the Lord';
they also perform an outward service to Him, and hereby show
they have some fear of God; but they likewise 'serve their own
gods.' There are those who 'teach them,' as there were who
taught the Assyrians, 'the manner of the God of the land'; the
God whose name the country bears to this day, and who was
once worshipped there with an holy worship: 'Howbeit,' they do
not serve Him alone; they do not fear Him enough for this: but
'every nation maketh gods of their own: every nation in the cities
wherein they dwell.' 'These nations fear the Lord'; they have not
laid aside the outward form of worshipping Him; but 'they serve
their graven images,' silver and gold, the work of men's hands:
money, pleasure, and praise, the gods of this world, more than
divide their service with the God of Israel. This is the manner
both of 'their children and their children's children: as did their
fathers, so do they unto this day.'

2. But although, speaking in a loose way, after the common
manner of men, those poor Heathens were said to 'fear the
Lord,' yet we may observe the Holy Ghost immediately adds,
speaking according to the truth and real nature of things, 'They
fear not the Lord, neither do after the law and the
commandment which the Lord commanded the children of
Jacob; with whom the Lord made a covenant, and charged
them, saying, Ye shall not fear other gods, nor serve them; but

the Lord your God ye shall fear; and He shall deliver you out of the hand of your enemies.'

The same judgement is passed by the unerring Spirit of God, and indeed by all, the eyes of whose understanding He hath opened to discern the things of God, upon these poor Christians, commonly so called. If we speak according to the truth and real nature of things, 'they fear not the Lord, neither do they serve Him.' For they do not 'after the covenant the Lord hath made with them, neither after the law and commandment which He hath commanded them, saying, Thou shalt worship the Lord thy God, and Him only shalt thou serve,' 'They serve other gods unto this day.' And 'no man can serve two masters.'

3. How vain is it for any man to aim at this,—to attempt the serving of two masters! Is it not easy to foresee what must be the unavoidable consequence of such an attempt? 'Either he will hate the one and love the other; or else he will hold to the one, and despise the other.' The two parts of this sentence, although separately proposed, are to be understood in connexion with each other; for the latter part is a consequence of the former. He will naturally hold to him whom he loves. He will so cleave to him, as to perform to him a willing, faithful, and diligent service. And, in the meantime, he will so far at least despise the master he hates as to have little regard to his commands, and to obey them, if at all, in a slight and careless manner. Therefore, whatsoever the wise men of the world may suppose, 'ye cannot serve God and mammon.'

4. Mammon was the name of one of the heathen gods, who was supposed to preside over riches. It is here understood of riches themselves; gold and silver; or in general, money; and, by a common figure of speech, of all that may be purchased thereby; such as ease, honour, and sensual pleasure.

But what are we here to understand by serving God, and what by serving mammon?   We cannot serve God, unless we *believe* in Him. This is the only true foundation of serving Him. Therefore, the believing in God, as 'reconciling the world to Himself through Christ Jesus,' the believing in Him, as a loving, pardoning God, is the first great branch of His service.

And thus to believe in God implies, to trust in Him as our strength, without whom we can do nothing, who every moment endues us with power from on high, without which it is

impossible to please Him; as our help, our only help in time of
trouble, who compasseth us about with songs of deliverance; as
our shield, our defender, and the lifter up of our head above all
our enemies that are round about us.

It implies, to trust in God as our happiness; as the centre of
spirits; the only rest of our souls; the only good who is adequate
to all our capacities, and sufficient to satisfy all the desires He
hath given us.

It implies (what is nearly allied to the other), to trust in God as
our end; to have an eye to Him in all things; to use all things only
as means of enjoying Him: wheresoever we are, or whatsoever
we do, to see Him that is invisible, looking on us well pleased,
and to refer all things to Him in Christ Jesus.

5. Thus to believe, is the first thing we are to understand by
serving God. The second is, to *love* Him.

Now to love God, in the manner the Scripture describes, in the
manner God Himself requires of us, and by requiring engages
to work in us, is to love Him as the ONE GOD; that is, 'with all
our heart, and with all our soul, and with all our mind, and with
all our strength,'—it is to desire God alone for His own sake; and
nothing else, but with reference to Him,—to rejoice in God,—to
delight in the Lord; not only to seek, but find, happiness in Him;
to enjoy God as the chiefest among ten thousand; to rest in Him,
as our God and our all: in a word, to have such a possession of
God as makes us always happy.

6. A third thing we are to understand by serving God is, to
resemble or *imitate* Him.

So the ancient Father: *Optimus Dei cultus, imitari quem colis*: 'It is
the best worship or service of God, to imitate Him you worship.'

We here speak of imitating or resembling Him in the spirit of
our minds: for here the true Christian imitation of God begins.
'God is a Spirit'; and they that imitate or resemble Him must do it
'in spirit and in truth.'

Now God is love: therefore, they who resemble Him in the
spirit of their minds are transformed into the same image. They
are merciful even as He is merciful. Their soul is all love. They
are kind, benevolent, compassionate, tenderhearted; and that
not only to the good and gentle, but also to the froward. Yea,
they are, like Him, loving unto every man, and their mercy
extends to all His works.

7. One thing more we are to understand by serving God, and that is, the *obeying* Him; the glorifying Him with our bodies, as well as with our spirits; the keeping His outward commandments; the zealously doing whatever He hath enjoined; the carefully avoiding whatever He hath forbidden; the performing all the ordinary actions of life with a single eye and a pure heart, offering them all in holy, fervent love, as sacrifices to God through Jesus Christ.

8. Let us consider now, what we are to understand, on the other hand, by serving mammon. And, first, it implies, the *trusting* in riches, in money, or the things purchasable thereby, as our strength, the means whereby we shall perform whatever cause we have in hand; the trusting in them as our help, by which we look to be comforted in, or delivered out of trouble.

It implies, the trusting in the world for happiness; the supposing that 'a man's life,' the comfort of his life, 'consisteth in the abundance of the things which he possesseth'; the looking for rest in the things that are seen; for content in outward plenty; the expecting that satisfaction in the things of the world, which can never be found out of God.

And if we do this, we cannot but make the world our end; the ultimate end, if not of all, at least of many, of our undertakings, many of our actions and designs; in which we shall aim only at an increase of wealth, at the obtaining pleasure or praise, at the gaining a larger measure of temporal things, without any reference to things eternal.

9. The serving mammon implies, secondly, *loving* the world; desiring it for its own sake; the placing our joy in the things thereof, and setting our hearts upon them; the seeking (what indeed it is impossible we should find) our happiness therein; the resting, with the whole weight of our souls, upon the staff of this broken reed; although daily experience shows it cannot support, but will only 'enter into our hand and pierce it.'

10. To *resemble,* to be *conformed* to, the world, is a third thing we are to understand by serving mammon; to have not only designs, but desires, tempers affections, suitable to those of the world; to be of an earthly, sensual mind, chained down to the things of earth; to be self-willed, inordinate lovers of ourselves, to think highly of our own attainments; to desire and delight in the praise of men; to fear, shun and abhor reproach; to be

impatient of reproof, easy to be provoked, and swift to return evil for evil.

11. To serve mammon is lastly, to *obey* the world, by outwardly conforming to its maxims and customs; to walk as other men walk, in the common road, in the broad, smooth, beaten path: to be in the fashion; to follow a multitude; to do like the rest of our neighbours: that is, to do the will of the flesh and the mind, to gratify our appetites and inclinations; to sacrifice to ourselves; aim at our own ease and pleasure, in the general course both of our words and actions.

Now what can be more undeniably clear than that we cannot thus serve God and mammon?

12. Does not every man see, that he cannot *comfortably* serve both? that to trim between God and the world is the sure way to be disappointed in both, and to have no rest either in one or the other? How uncomfortable a condition must he be in, who, having the fear but not the love of God—who, serving Him, but not with all his heart—has only the toils and not the joys of religion! He has religion enough to make him miserable, but not enough to make him happy: his religion will not let him enjoy the world; and the world will not let him enjoy God. So that, by halting between both, he loses both, and has no peace either in God or the world.

13. Does not every man see, that he cannot serve both *consistently* with himself? What more glaring inconsistency can be conceived, than must continually appear in his whole behaviour, who is endeavouring to obey both these masters,—striving to 'serve God and mammon'? He is indeed 'a sinner that goeth two ways'; one step forward and another backward. He is continually building up with one hand, and pulling down with the other. He loves sin, and he hates it: he is always seeking, and yet always fleeing from, God. He Would, and he would not. He is not the same man for one day; no, not for an hour together. He is a motley mixture of all sorts of contrarieties; a heap of contradictions jumbled in one. O be consistent with thyself one way or the other! Turn to the right hand or to the left. If mammon be God, serve thou him; if the Lord, then serve Him. But never think of serving either at all, unless it be with thy whole heart.

14. Does not every reasonable, every thinking man see, that he

cannot *possibly* serve God and mammon? because there is the most absolute contrariety, the most irreconcilable enmity, between them. The contrariety between the most opposite things on earth, between fire and water, darkness and light, vanishes into nothing, when compared to the contrariety between God and mammon. So that, in whatsoever respect you serve the one, you necessarily renounce the other. Do you believe in God through Christ? Do you trust in Him as your strength, your help, your shield, and your exceeding great reward?—as your happiness, your end in all, above all things? Then you cannot trust in riches. It is absolutely impossible you should, so long as you have this faith in God. Do you thus trust in riches? Then you have denied the faith. You do not trust in the living God. Do you love God? Do you seek and find happiness in Him? Then you cannot love the world, neither the things of the world. You are crucified to the world, and the world crucified to you. Do you love the world? Are your affections set on things beneath? Do you seek happiness in earthly things? Then it is impossible you should love God. Then the love of the Father is not in you. Do you resemble God? Are you merciful, as your Father is merciful? Are you transformed, by the renewal of your mind, into the image of Him that created you? Then you cannot be conformed to the present world. You have renounced all its affections and lusts. Are you conformed to the world? Does your soul still bear the image of the earthly? Then you are not renewed in the spirit of your mind. You do not bear the image of the heavenly. Do you obey God? Are you zealous to do His will on earth as the angels do in heaven? Then it is impossible you should obey mammon. Then you set the world at open defiance. You trample its customs and maxims under foot, and will neither follow nor be led by them. Do you follow the world? Do you live like other men? Do you please men? Do you please yourself? Then you cannot be a servant of God. You are of your master and father, the devil.

15. Therefore, 'thou shalt worship the Lord thy God, and Him only shalt thou serve.' Thou shalt lay aside all thoughts of obeying two masters of serving God and mammon. Thou shalt propose to thyself no end no help no happiness, but God. Thou shalt seek nothing in earth or heaven but Him: thou shalt aim at nothing, but to know, to love, and enjoy Him. And because this is

all your business below, the only view you can reasonably have, the one design you are to pursue in all things,—'Therefore I say unto you' (as our Lord continues His discourse), 'Take no thought for your life, what ye shall eat, or what ye shall drink; nor yet for your body, what ye shall put on': a deep and weighty direction, which it imports us well to consider, and thoroughly to understand.

16. Our Lord does not here require, that we should be utterly without thought, even touching the concerns of this life. A giddy, careless temper is at the farthest remove from the whole religion of Jesus Christ. Neither does He require us to be 'slothful in business,' to be slack and dilatory therein. This, likewise, is contrary to the whole spirit and genius of His religion. A Christian abhors sloth as much as drunkenness; and flees from idleness as he does from adultery. He well knows, that there is one kind of thought and care with which God is well pleased; which is absolutely needful for the due performance of those outward works unto which the providence of God has called him.

It is the will of God, that every man should labour to eat his own bread; yea, and that every man should provide for his own, for them of his own household. It is likewise His will, that we should 'owe no man anything, but provide things honest in the sight of all men.' But this cannot be done without taking some thought, without having some care upon our minds; yea often not without long and serious thought, not without much and earnest care. Consequently this care, to provide for ourselves and our household, this thought how to render to all their dues, our blessed Lord does not condemn. Yea, it is good and acceptable in the sight of God our Saviour.

It is good and acceptable to God, that we should so take thought concerning whatever we have in hand, as to have a clear comprehension of what we are about to do, and to plan our business before we enter upon it. And it is right that we should carefully consider, from time to time, what steps we are to take therein; as well as that we should prepare all things beforehand, for the carrying it on in the most effectual manner. This care, termed by some, 'the care of the head,' it was by no means our Lord's design to condemn.

17. What He here condemns is, the care of the heart; the

anxious, uneasy care; the care that hath torment: all such care as does hurt, either to the soul or body. What He forbids is, that care which, sad experience shows, wastes the blood and drinks up the spirits; which anticipates all the misery it fears, and comes to torment us before the time. He forbids only that care which poisons the blessings of to-day, by fear of what may be to-morrow; which cannot enjoy the present plenty, through apprehensions of future want. This care is not only a sore disease, a grievous sickness of soul, but also a heinous offence against God, a sin of the deepest dye. It is an high affront to the gracious Governor and wise Disposer of all things; necessarily implying, that the great Judge does not do right; that He does not order all things well. It plainly implies, that He is wanting, either in wisdom, if He does not know what things we stand in need of; or in goodness, if He does not provide those things for all who put their trust in Him. Beware, therefore, that you take not thought in this sense: be ye anxiously careful for nothing. Take no uneasy thought: this is a plain, sure rule. Uneasy care is unlawful care. With a single eye to God, do all that in you lies to provide things honest in the sight of all men: and then give up all into better hands; leave the whole event to God.

18. 'Take no thought' of this kind, no uneasy thought, even 'for your life, what ye shall eat, or what ye shall drink; nor yet for your body, what ye shall put on. Is not the life more than meat, and the body than raiment?' If then God gave you life, the greater gift, will He not give you food to sustain it? If He hath given you the body, how can ye doubt but He will give you raiment to cover it? more especially, if you give yourselves up to Him, and serve Him with your whole heart. 'Behold,' see before your eyes, 'the fowls of the air: for they sow not, neither do they reap, nor gather into barns'; and yet they lack nothing; 'yet your heavenly Father feedeth them. Are ye not much better than they?' Ye that are creatures capable of God are ye not of more account in the eyes of God? of a higher rank in the scale of beings? 'And which of you, by taking thought, can add one cubit to his stature?' What profit have you then from this anxious thought? It is every way fruitless and unavailing.

'And why take ye thought for raiment?' Have ye not a daily reproof wherever you turn your eyes? 'Consider the lilies of the field, how they grow; they toil not, neither do they spin; and yet

I say unto you, that even Solomon in all his glory was not arrayed like one of these. Wherefore, if God so clothe the grass of the field, which to-day is, and to-morrow is cast into the oven' (is cut down, burned up, and seen no more), 'shall He not much more clothe you, O ye of little faith?' you, whom He made to endure for ever and ever, to be pictures of His own eternity! Ye are indeed of little faith; otherwise ye could not doubt of His love and care; no, not for a moment.

19. 'Therefore take no thought, saying, What shall we eat,' if we lay up no treasure upon earth? 'What shall we drink,' if we serve God with all our strength, if our eye be singly fixed on Him? 'Wherewithal shall we be clothed,' if we are not conformed to the world, if we disoblige those by whom we might be profited? 'For after all these things do the Gentiles seek'—the Heathens who know not God. But ye are sensible 'your heavenly Father knoweth that ye have need of all these things.' And He hath pointed out to you an infallible way of being constantly supplied therewith: 'Seek ye first the kingdom of God, and His righteousness; and all these things shall be added unto you.'

20. 'Seek ye first the kingdom of God': before ye give place to any other thought or care, let it be your concern that the God and Father of our Lord Jesus Christ (who 'gave His only-begotten Son,' to the end that, believing in Him, 'ye might not perish, but have everlasting life') may reign in your heart, may manifest Himself in your soul, and dwell and rule there; that He may 'cast down every high thing which exalteth itself against the knowledge of God, and bring into captivity every thought to the obedience of Christ.' Let God have the sole dominion over you: let Him reign without a rival: let Him possess all your heart, and rule alone. Let Him be your one desire, your joy, your love; so that all that is within you may continually cry out, 'The Lord God omnipotent reigneth.'

'Seek the kingdom of God, and His righteousness.' Righteousness is the fruit of God's reigning in the heart. And what is righteousness, but love?—the love of God and of all mankind, flowing from faith in Jesus Christ, and producing humbleness of mind, meekness, gentleness, long-suffering, patience, deadness to the world; and every right disposition of heart, toward God and toward man. And by these it produces all holy actions, whatsoever are lovely or of good report; whatsoever works of faith and labour of love are acceptable to God, and profitable to man.

'His righteousness': this is all His righteousness still: it is His own free gift to us, for the sake of Jesus Christ the righteous, through whom alone it is purchased for us: and it is His work: it is He alone that worketh it in us, by the inspiration of the Holy Spirit.

21. Perhaps the well observing this may give light to some other scriptures, which we have not always so clearly understood. St. Paul, speaking in his Epistle to the Romans concerning the unbelieving Jews, saith, 'They, being ignorant of God's righteousness, and going about to establish their own righteousness, have not submitted themselves unto the righteousness of God.' I believe this may be one sense of the words: they were 'ignorant of God's righteousness,' not only of the righteousness of Christ, imputed to every believer, whereby all his sins are blotted out, and he is reconciled to the favour of God; but (which seems here to be more immediately understood) they were ignorant of that inward righteousness, of that holiness of heart, which is with the utmost propriety termed 'God's righteousness,' as being both His own free gift through Christ, and His own work by His almighty Spirit. And because they were 'ignorant' of this, they 'went about to establish their own righteousness.' They laboured to establish that outside righteousness which might very properly be termed their own. For neither was it wrought by the Spirit of God, nor was it owned or accepted of Him. They might work this themselves, by their own natural strength; and when they had done, it was a stink in His nostrils. And yet, trusting in this, they would 'not submit themselves unto the righteousness of God.' Yea, they hardened themselves against that faith whereby alone it was possible to attain it. 'For Christ is the end of the law for righteousness to every one that believeth.' Christ, when He said, 'It is finished!' put an end to the law,—to the law of external rites and ceremonies, that He might bring a better righteousness through His blood, by that one oblation of Himself once offered, even the image of God, into the inmost soul of every one that believeth.

22. Nearly related to these are those words of the Apostle, in his Epistle to the Philippians: 'I count all things but dung, that I

may win Christ'; an entrance into His everlasting kingdom; 'and be found in Him,' believing in Him, 'not having mine own righteousness, which is of the law, but that which is through the faith of Christ, the righteousness which is of God by faith.' 'Not having my own righteousness, which is of the law'; a barely external righteousness, the outside religion I formerly had, when I hoped to be accepted of God because I was, 'touching the righteousness which is of the law, blameless'; 'but that which is through the faith of Christ, the righteousness which is of God by faith; that holiness of heart, that renewal of the soul in all its desires, tempers, and affections, 'which is of God' (it is the work of God,—and not of man), 'by faith'; through the faith of Christ, through the revelation of Jesus Christ in us, and by faith in His blood; whereby alone we obtain the remission of our sins, and an inheritance among those that are sanctified.

23. 'Seek ye first' this 'kingdom of God' in your hearts; this righteousness, which is the gift and work of God, the image of God renewed in your souls; 'and all these things shall be added unto you'; all things needful for the body; such a measure of all as God sees most for the advancement of His kingdom. These shall be added—they shall be thrown in, over and above. In seeking the peace and the love of God, you shall not only find what you more immediately seek, even the kingdom that cannot be moved; but also what you seek not—not at all for its own sake, but only in reference to the other. You shall find, in your way to the kingdom, all outward things, so far as they are expedient for you. This care God hath taken upon Himself: cast you all your care upon Him. He knoweth your wants; and whatsoever is lacking He will not fail to supply.

24. 'Therefore take no thought for the morrow.' Not only, take ye no thought how to lay up treasures on earth, how to increase in worldly substance; take no thought how to procure more food than you can eat, or more raiment than you can put on, or more money than is required from day to day, for the plain, reasonable purposes of life;—but take no uneasy thought, even concerning those things which are absolutely needful for the body. Do not trouble yourself now, with thinking what you shall do at a season which is yet afar off. Perhaps that season will never come; or it will be no concern of yours before then you will have passed through all the waves, and be landed in eternity. All

those distant views do not belong to you, who are but a creature of a day. Nay, what have you to do with the morrow, more strictly speaking? Why should you perplex yourself without need? God provides for you to-day what is needful to sustain the life which He hath given you. It is enough: give yourself up into His hands. If you live another day, He will provide for that also.

25. Above all, do not make the care of future things a pretence for neglecting present duty. This is the most fatal way of 'taking thought for the morrow.' And how common is it among men! Many, if we exhort them to keep a conscience void of offence, to abstain from what they are convinced is evil, do not scruple to reply, 'How then must we live? Must we not take care of ourselves and of our families?' And this they imagine to be a sufficient reason for continuing in known, wilful sin. They say, and perhaps think, they would serve God now, were it not that they should, by-and-by, lose their bread. They would prepare for eternity; but they are afraid of wanting the necessaries of life. So they serve the devil for a morsel of bread; they rush into hell for fear of want; they throw away their poor souls, lest they should, some time or other, fall short of what is needful for their bodies!

It is not strange that they who thus take the matter out of God's hand should be so often disappointed of the very things they seek; that, while they throw away heaven to secure the things of earth, they lose the one, but do not gain the other. The jealous God, in the wise course of His providence, frequently suffers this. So that they who will not cast their care on God, who, taking thought for temporal things, have little concern for things eternal, lose the very portion which they have chosen. There is a visible blast on all their undertakings; whatsoever they do, it doth not prosper; insomuch, that after they have forsaken God for the world, they lose what they sought, as well as what they sought not: they fall short of the kingdom of God, and His righteousness: nor yet are other things added unto them.

26. There is another way of 'taking thought for the morrow,' which is equally forbidden in these words. It is possible to take thought in a wrong manner, even with regard to spiritual things; to be so careful about what may be by and-by as to neglect what is now required at our hands. How insensibly do we slide into this, if we are not continually watching unto prayer! How easily we

are carried away, in a kind of waking dream, projecting distant schemes, and drawing fine scenes in our own imagination! We think, what good we will do when we are in such a place, or when such a time is come! How useful we will be, how plenteous in good works, when we are easier in our circumstances! How earnestly we will serve God, when once such an hindrance is out of the way!

Or perhaps you are now in heaviness of soul: God, as it were, hides His face from you. You see little of the light of His countenance: you cannot taste His redeeming love. In such a temper of mind, how natural is it to say, 'O how I will praise God, when the light of His countenance shall be again lifted up upon my soul! How will I exhort others to praise Him, when His love is again shed abroad in my heart! Then I will do thus and thus: I will speak for God in all places: I will not be ashamed of the gospel of Christ. Then I will redeem the time: I will use to the uttermost every talent I have received.' Do not believe thyself. Thou wilt not do it then, unless thou doest it now. 'He that is faithful in that which is little,' of whatsoever kind it be, whether it be worldly substance or the fear or love of God, 'will be faithful in that which is much.' But if thou now hidest one talent in the earth, thou wilt then hide five: that is, if ever they are given; but there is small reason to expect they ever will. Indeed, 'unto him that hath,' that is, uses what he hath, 'shall be given, and he shall have more abundantly. But from him that hath not,' that is, uses not the grace which he hath already received, whether in a larger or smaller degree, 'shall be taken away even that which he hath.'

27. And take no thought for the temptations of tomorrow. This also is a dangerous snare. Think not, 'When such a temptation comes, what shall I do? how shall I stand? I feel I have not power to resist: I am not able to conquer that enemy.' Most true: you have not now the power which you do not now stand in need of. You are not able at this time to conquer that enemy; and at this time he does not assault you. With the grace you have now, you could not withstand the temptations which you have not. But when the temptation comes, the grace will come. In greater trials you will have greater strength. When sufferings abound, the consolations of God will, in the same proportion, abound also. So that, in every situation, the grace of

God will be sufficient for you. He doth not suffer you 'to be tempted' today 'above that ye are able to bear'; and 'in every temptation He will make a way to escape.' 'As thy days, so thy strength shall be.'

28. 'Let the morrow,' therefore, 'take thought for the things of itself'; that is, when the morrow comes, then think of it. Live thou to-day. Be it thy earnest care to improve the present hour. This is your own; and it is your all. The past is as nothing, as though it had never been. The future is nothing to you: it is not yours; perhaps it never will be. There is no depending on what is yet to come; for you 'know not what a day may bring forth.' Therefore live to-day: lose not an hour: use this moment: for it is your portion. 'Who knoweth the things which have been before him, or which shall be after him under the sun?' The generations that were from the beginning of the world, where are they now? Fled away: forgotten. They were; they lived their day; they were shook off the earth, as leaves off their trees: they mouldered away into common dust! Another and another race succeeded; then they 'followed the generation of their fathers, and shall never more see the light.' Now is thy turn upon the earth. 'Rejoice, O young man, in the days of thy youth!' Enjoy the very, very now, by enjoying Him 'whose years fail not.' Now let thine eye be singly fixed on Him in 'whom is no variableness neither shadow of turning'! Now give Him thy heart; now stay thyself on Him; now be thou holy, as He is holy! Now lay hold on the blessed opportunity of doing His acceptable and perfect will! Now rejoice to 'suffer the loss of all things,' so thou mayest 'win Christ.'

29. Gladly suffer to-day, for His name's sake, whatsoever He permits this day to come upon thee. But look not at the sufferings of to-morrow. 'Sufficient unto the day is the evil therof.' Evil it is, speaking after the manner of men; whether it be reproach or want, pain or sickness; but in the language of God, all is blessing; it is a precious balm prepared by the wisdom of God, and variously dispensed among His children, according to the various sicknesses of their souls. And He gives in one day sufficient for that day; proportioned to the want and strength of the patient. If, therefore, thou snatchest to-day what belongs to the morrow; if thou addest this to what is given thee already, it will be more than thou canst bear: this is the way, not to heal, but

to destroy thy own soul. Take, therefore, just as much as He gives thee to-day: to-day, do and suffer His will! To-day, give up thyself, thy body, soul, and spirit to God, through Christ Jesus; desiring nothing, but that God may be glorified in all thou art, all thou doest, all thou sufferest; seeking nothing, but to know God, and His Son Jesus Christ, through the eternal Spirit; pursuing nothing, but to love Him, to serve Him, and to enjoy Him at this hour, and to all eternity!

Now unto 'God the Father, who hath made me and all the world'; unto 'God the Son, who hath redeemed me and all mankind'; unto 'God the Holy Ghost, who sanctifieth me and all the elect people of God'; be honour and praise, majesty and dominion, for ever and ever! Amen.

SERMON XXV

UPON OUR LORD'S SERMON ON THE MOUNT

DISCOURSE X

I find record of this sermon, or rather a sermon on verse 7 ('Ask, and it shall be given you') being preached on June 2, 1742, at Mrs. Holmes's. Smith House, Lightcliffe, near Halifax, the first home of Methodism in that district (see photograph in Standard Edition of *Journal*, iii. 297); in the church at Wroot on June 13 of the same year; and at Morvah on April 12, 1744. From the text Matt. vii. 7 Wesley preached at Taddington in May 1747; at Lewisham on September 29, 1747; at Garth on February 19, 1748; and at Snowsfields in September 1761.

The original connexion of this passage is not easy to determine. The first section on judging follows in St. Luke's version immediately on Matt. v. 48, and is an example of the mercifulness which is there commended. The section on prayer occurs in a different context in Luke xi 9-13. The Golden Rule in St. Luke's version follows Matt. v. 42, where it seems more natural. Probably St. Matthew placed it here as the conclusion of the sermon, what follows being of the nature of an epilogue. Wesley's suggestion that our Lord now 'proceeds to point out the main hindrances of this religion' is not at all convincing. Votaw's idea is better, that the first section deals with the conduct of members of the kingdom towards their fellow men; and that the second is really extraneous to the present discourse.

Judge not, that ye be not judged.

For with what judgement ye judge ye shall be judged: and with what ' measure ye mete, it shall be measured to you again.

And why beholdest thou the mote that is in thy brother's eye, but considerest not the beam that is in thine own eye?

Or how wilt thou say to thy brother, Let me Pull out the mote out of time eye ; and, behold, a beam is in thine own eye?

Thou hypocrite, first cast out the beam out of thine own eye; and then shall thou see clearly to cast out the mote out of thy brother's eye.

Give not that which is holy unto the dogs, neither cast ye your pearls before swine, lest they trample them under their feet and turn again and rend you.

Ask, and it shall be given you; seek, and ye shall find; knock, and it shall be opened unto you:

For every one that asketh receiveth; and he that seeketh findeth; and to him that knocketh it shall be opened.

Or what man is there of you, whom if his son ask bread, will he give him a stone?

Or if he ask a fish, will he give him a serpent?

*If ye then, being evil, know how to give good gifts unto your children, how much
   more shall your Father which is in heaven give good things to them that ask
   Him?*

*Therefore all things whatsoever ye would that men should do to you, do ye even so
   to them: for this is the law and the prophets.*—MATT. vii. 1-12.

1. Our blessed Lord, having now finished His main design, having first delivered the sum of true religion, carefully guarded against those glosses of men whereby they would make the Word of God of none effect; and having next laid down rules touching that right intention which we are to preserve in all outward actions; now proceeds to point out the main hindrances of this religion, and concludes all with a suitable application.

2. In the fifth chapter, our great Teacher has fully described inward religion in its various branches. He has there laid before us those dispositions of soul which constitute real Christianity; the tempers contained in that 'holiness, without which no man shall see the Lord'; the affections which, when flowing from their proper fountain, from a living faith in God through Christ Jesus, are intrinsically and essentially good and acceptable to God. In the sixth He hath shown how all our actions, likewise, even those that are indifferent in their own nature, may be made holy and good and acceptable to God, by a pure and holy intention. Whatever is done without this, He declares, is of no value with God: whereas, whatever outward works are thus consecrated to God are, in His sight, of great price.

3. In the former part of this chapter, He points out the most common and most fatal hindrances of this holiness: in the latter, He exhorts us by various motives, to break through all, and secure that prize of our high calling.

4. The first hindrance He cautions us against is judging. 'Judge not, that ye be not judged.' Judge not others that ye be not judged of the Lord; that ye bring not vengeance on your own heads. 'For with what judgement ye judge, ye shall be judged; and with what measure ye mete, it shall be measured to you again': a plain and equitable rule, whereby God permits you to determine for yourselves, in what manner he shall deal with you in the judgement of the great day.

5. There is no station of life, nor any period of time, from the hour of our first repenting and believing the gospel, till we are

made perfect in love, wherein this caution is not needful for every child of God. For occasions of judging can never be wanting; and the temptations to it are innumerable; many whereof are so artfully disguised, that we fall into the sin before we suspect any danger. And unspeakable are the mischiefs produced hereby,—always to him that judges another, thus wounding his own soul, and exposing himself to the righteous judgement of God; and frequently to those who are judged, whose hands hang down, who are weakened and hindered in their course, if not wholly turned out of the way, and caused to [draw] back even to perdition. Yea, how often, when this 'root of bitterness springs up, are many defiled thereby'; by reason whereof the way of truth itself is evil spoken of, and that worthy name blasphemed whereby we are called!

6. Yet it does not appear that our Lord designed this caution only, or chiefly, for the children of God; but rather for the children of the world, for the men who know not God. These cannot but hear of those who are not of the world; who follow after the religion above described; who endeavour to be humble, serious, gentle, merciful, and pure in heart; who earnestly desire such measures of these holy tempers as they have not yet attained, and wait for them in doing all good to all men, and patiently suffering evil. Whoever go but thus far, cannot be hid, no more than a 'city set upon a hill.' And why do not those who 'see their good works, glorify their Father which is in heaven?' What excuse have they for not treading in their steps—for not imitating their example, and being followers of them, as they are also of Christ? Why, in order to provide an excuse for themselves, they condemn those whom they ought to imitate. They spend their time in finding out their neighbours' faults, instead of amending their own. They are so busied about others going out of the way, that themselves never come into it at all; at least, never get forward; never go beyond a poor dead form of godliness, without the power.

7. It is to these more especially that our Lord says, 'Why beholdest thou the mote that is in thy brother's eye'—the infirmities, the mistakes, the imprudence, the weakness of the children of God—'but considerest not the beam that is in thine own eye?' Thou considerest not the damnable impenitence, the satanic pride, the accursed self-will, the idolatrous love of the

world, which are in thyself and which make thy whole life an
abomination to the Lord. Above all, with what supine
carelessness and indifference art thou dancing over the mouth
of hell! And 'how then,' with what grace, with what decency or
modesty, 'wilt thou say to thy brother, Let me pull out the mote
out of thine eye': the excess of zeal for God, the extreme of
self-denial, the too great disengagement from worldly cares and
employments, the desire to be day and night in prayer, or
hearing the words of eternal life? 'And, behold, a beam is in
thine own eye!' Not a mote, like one of these.—'Thou hypocrite!'
who pretendest to care for others, and hast no care for thy own
soul; who makest a show of zeal for the cause of God, when in
truth thou neither lovest nor fearest Him! 'First cast out the
beam out of thine own eye': cast out the beam of impenitence!
Know thyself! See and feel thyself a sinner! Feel that thy inward
parts are very wickedness, that thou art altogether corrupt and
abominable, and that the wrath of God abideth on thee! Cast out
the beam of pride; abhor thyself; sink down as in dust and ashes;
be more and more little, and mean, and base, and vile in thine
own eyes! Cast out the beam of self-will! Learn what that
meaneth, 'If any man will come after Me, let him renounce
himself.' Deny thyself, and take up thy cross daily. Let thy whole
soul cry out, 'I came down from heaven'—for so thou didst, thou
neverdying spirit, whether thou knowest it or no—'not to do my
own will, but the will of Him that sent me.' Cast out the beam of
love of the world. Love not the world, neither the things of the
world. Be thou crucified unto the world, and the world crucified
unto thee. Only *use the world, but enjoy* God. Seek all thy happiness
in Him! Above all, cast out the grand beam, that supine
carelessness and indifference! Deeply consider that 'one thing is
needful'; the one thing which thoy hast scarce ever thought of.
Know and feel, that thou art a poor, vile, guilty worm, quivering
over the great gulf! What art thou? A sinner born to die; a leaf
driven before the wind; a vapour ready to vanish away; just
appearing, and then scattered into air, to be no more seen! See
this! 'And then shalt thou see clearly to cast out the mote out of
thy brother's eye.' Then, if thou hast leisure from the concerns
of thy own soul, thou shalt know how to correct thy brother also.

8. But what is properly the meaning of this word, 'Judge not'?

What is the judging which is here forbidden? It is not the same as evil-speaking, although it is frequently joined therewith. Evil-speaking is the relating anything that is evil concerning an absent person; whereas judging may indifferently refer either to the absent or the present. Neither does it necessarily imply the speaking at all, but only the thinking evil of another. Not that all kind of thinking evil of others is that judging which our Lord condemns. If I see one commit robbery or murder, or hear him blaspheme the name of God, I cannot refrain from thinking ill of the robber or murderer. Yet this is not evil judging: there is no sin in this, nor anything contrary to tender affection.

9. The thinking of another in a manner that is contrary to love, is that judging which is here condemned; and this may be of various kinds. For, first we may think another to blame when he is not. We may lay to his charge (at least in our own mind) the things of which he is not guilty; the words which he has never spoke, or the actions which he has never done. Or we may think his manner of acting was wrong, although in reality it was not. And even where nothing can justly be blamed, either in the thing itself, or in the manner of doing it, we may suppose his intention was not good, and so condemn him on that ground; at the same time that He who searches the heart sees his simplicity and godly sincerity.

10. But we may not only fall into the sin of judging, by condemning the innocent; but also, secondly, by condemning the guilty in a higher degree than he deserves. This species of judging is likewise an offence against justice, as well as mercy; and yet such an offence as nothing can secure us from but the strongest and tenderest affection. Without this, we readily suppose one who is acknowledged to be in fault, to be more in fault than he really is. We undervalue whatever good is found in him. Nay, we are not easily induced to believe that anything good can remain in him in whom we have found anything that is evil.

11. All this shows a manifest want of that love which ου λογιζεται κακον—*thinketh no evil*; evil; which never draws an unjust or unkind conclusion from any premises whatsoever. Love will not infer from a person's falling once into an act of open sin, that he is accustomed so to do; that he is habitually guilty of it: and if he was habitually guilty once, love does not

conclude he is so still; much less, that if he is now guilty of this, therefore he is guilty of other sins also. These evil reasonings all pertain to that sinful judging which our Lord here guards us against; and which we are in the highest degree concerned to avoid, if we love either God or our own souls.

12. But supposing we do not condemn the innocent, neither the guilty any farther than they deserve; still we may not be altogether clear of the snare: for there is a third sort of sinful judging, which is the condemning any person at all where there is not sufficient evidence. And be the facts we suppose ever so true, yet that does not acquit us. For they ought not to have been supposed, but proved; and till they were, we ought to have formed no judgement. I say, 'till they were'; for neither are we excused, although the facts admit of ever so strong a proof, unless that proof be produced before we pass sentence, and compared with the evidence on the other side. Nor can we be excused, if ever we pass a full sentence before the accused has spoken for himself. Even a Jew might teach us this, as a mere lesson of justice, abstracted from mercy and brotherly love: 'Doth our law,' says Nicodemus, 'judge any man, before it hear him, and know what he doeth?' (John vii. 51). Yea, a Heathen could reply, when the chief of the Jewish nation desired to have judgement against his prisoner, 'It is not the manner of the Romans' to judge 'any man, before he that is accused have the accusers face to face, and have licence to answer for himself concerning the crime laid against him.'

13. Indeed we could not easily fall into sinful judging, were we only to observe that rule which another of those heathen Romans affirms to have been the measure of his own practice. 'I am so far,' says he, 'from lightly believing every man's or any man's evidence against another, that I do not easily or immediately believe a man's evidence against himself. I always allow him second thoughts, and many times counsel too.' Go, thou who art called a Christian, and do likewise: lest the Heathen rise and condemn thee in that day!

14. But how rarely should we condemn or judge one another, at least how soon would that evil be remedied, were we to walk by that clear and express rule which our Lord Himself has taught us!—'If thy brother shall trespass against thee,' or if thou hear or believe that he hath, 'go and tell him of his fault between thee

and him alone.' This is the first step thou art to take. 'But if he will not hear, take with thee one or two more, that in the mouth of two or three witnesses every word may be established.' This is the second step. 'If he neglect to hear them, tell it unto the church'; either to the overseers thereof, or to the whole congregation. Thou hast then done thy part. Then think of it no more, but commend the whole to God.

15. But supposing thou hast by the grace of God 'cast the beam out of thine own eye,' and dost now clearly see 'the mote' or the beam 'which is in thy brother's eye,' yet beware thou dost not receive hurt thyself by endeavouring to help him. Still 'give not that which is holy unto dogs.' Do not lightly account any to be of this number; but if it evidently appear that they deserve the title, then 'cast ye not your pearls before swine.' Beware of that zeal which is not according to knowledge. For this is another great hindrance in their way who would be 'perfect as their heavenly Father is perfect.' They who desire this cannot but desire that all mankind should partake of the common blessing. And when we ourselves first partake of the heavenly gift, the divine 'evidence of things not seen,' we wonder that all mankind do not see the things which we see so plainly; and make no doubt at all but we shall open the eyes of all we have any intercourse with. Hence we are for attacking all we meet without delay, and constraining them to see, whether they will or no; and by the ill success of this intemperate zeal we often suffer in our own souls. To prevent this spending our strength in vain, our Lord adds this needful caution (needful to all, but more especially to those who are now warm in their first love), 'Give not that which is holy unto the dogs, neither cast ye your pearls before swine, lest they trample them under their feet, and turn again and rend you.'

16. 'Give not that which is holy unto the dogs.' Beware of thinking that any deserve this appellation, till there is full and incontestable proof, such as you can no longer resist. But when it is clearly and indisputably proved, that they are unholy and wicked men, not only strangers to but enemies to God, to all righteousness and true holiness; 'give not that which is holy,' το αγιον—'the holy thing,' emphatically so called, unto these. The holy, the peculiar doctrines of the gospel—such as were hid from the ages and generations of old, and are now made known to us, only by the revelation of Jesus Christ, and by the

inspiration of His Holy Spirit—are not to be prostituted unto these men, who know not if there be any Holy Ghost. Not indeed that the ambassadors of Christ can refrain from declaring them in the great congregation, wherein some of these may probably be: we must speak, whether men will hear or whether they will forbear; but this is not the case with private Christians. They do not bear that awful character; nor are they under any manner of obligation to force these great and glorious truths on them who contradict and blaspheme, who have a rooted enmity against them. Nay, they ought not so to do, but rather to lead them as they are able to bear. Do not begin a discourse with these upon remission of sins, and the gift of the Holy Ghost; but talk with them in their own manner, and upon their own principles. With the rational, honourable, and unjust Epicure, reason of 'righteousness, temperance, and judgement to come.' This is the most probable way to make Felix tremble. Reserve higher subjects for men of higher attainments.

17. Neither 'cast your pearls before swine.' Be very unwilling to pass this judgement on any man; but if the fact be plain and undeniable, if it is clear beyond all dispute, if the swine do not endeavour to disguise themselves, but rather glory in their shame, making no pretence to purity, either of heart or life, but working all uncleanness with greediness; then cast not ye your pearls before them. Talk not to them of the mysteries of the kingdom; of the things which eye hath not seen, nor ear heard; which, of consequence, as they have no other inlets of knowledge, no spiritual senses, it cannot enter into their hearts to conceive. Tell not them of the exceeding great and precious promises which God hath given us in the Son of His love. What conception can they have of being made partakers of the divine nature, who do not even desire to escape the corruption that is in the world through lust? Just as much knowledge as swine have of pearls, and as much relish as the have for them, so much relish have they for the deep things of God, so much knowledge of the mysteries of the gospel, who are immersed in the mire of this world, in worldly pleasures, desires, and cares. O cast not those pearls before these, 'lest they trample them under their feet!'—lest they utterly despise what they cannot understand, and speak evil of the things which they know not. Nay, it is probable, this would not be the only inconvenience which would

follow: it would not be strange, if they were, according to their
nature, to 'turn again and rend you'; if they were to return you
evil for good, cursing for blessing, and hatred for your good will.
Such is the enmity of the carnal mind against God, and all the
things of God. Such is the treatment you are to expect from
these, if you offer them the unpardonable affront of endeavouring to save their souls from death, to pluck them as brands
out of the burning.

18. And yet you need not utterly despair even of these, who,
for the present, 'turn again and rend you.' For if all your
arguments and persuasives fail, there is yet another remedy left,
and one that is frequently found effectual, when no other
method avails; this is prayer. Therefore, whatever you desire or
want, either for others or for your own soul, 'ask, and it shall be
given you; seek, and ye shall find; knock, and it shall be opened
unto you.' The neglect of this is a third grand hindrance of
holiness. Still we 'have not, because we ask not.' O how meek and
gentle, how lowly in heart, how full of love both to God and men,
might ye have been at this day, if you had only asked; if you had
continued instant in prayer! Therefore, now, at least,' ask, and it
shall be given unto you' 'Ask,' that ye may thoroughly
experience, and perfectly practise, the whole of that religion
which our Lord has here so beautifully described. It shall then
be given you to be holy as He is holy, both in heart and in all
manner of conversation. 'Seek,' in the way He hath ordained, in
searching the Scriptures, in hearing His word, in meditating
thereon, in fasting, in partaking of the Supper of the Lord; and
surely ye shall find: ye shall find that pearl of great price, that
faith which overcometh the world, that peace which the world
cannot give, that love which is the earnest of your inheritance.
'Knock'; continue in prayer, and in every other way of the Lord:
be not weary or faint in your mind: press on to the mark: take no
denial; let Him not go until He bless you. 'And the door' of
mercy, of holiness, of heaven, 'shall be opened unto you.'

19. It is in compassion to the hardness of our heart, so
unready to believe the goodness of God, that our Lord is pleased
to enlarge upon this head, and to repeat and confirm what He
hath spoken. 'For every one,' saith He, 'that asketh, receiveth';
so that none need come short of the blessing; 'and he that
seeketh,' even every one that seeketh, 'findeth' the love and the

image of God; 'and to him that knocketh,' to every one that knocketh, the gate of righteousness shall be opened. So that here is no room for any to be discouraged, as though they might ask, or seek, or knock in vain. Only remember always to pray, to seek, to knock, and not to faint. And then the promise standeth sure. It is firm as the pillars of heaven,—yea, more firm; for heaven and earth shall pass away; but His word shall not pass away.

20. To cut off every pretence for unbelief, our blessed Lord, in the following verses, illustrates yet farther what He had said, by an appeal to what passes in our own breasts: 'What man,' saith He, 'is there of you, whom if his son ask bread, will give him a stone?' Will even natural affection permit you to refuse the reasonable request of one you love? 'Or if he ask a fish, will he give him a serpent?' Will he give him hurtful instead of profitable things? So that even from what you feel and do yourselves, you may receive the fullest assurance, as, on the one hand, that no ill effect can possibly attend your asking, so, on the other, that it will be attended with that good effect, a full supply of all your wants. For 'if ye, being evil, know how to give good gifts unto your children, how much more shall your Father which is in heaven,' who is pure, unmixed, essential goodness, 'give good things to them that ask Him?' or (as He expresses it on another occasion),' give the Holy Ghost to them that ask Him?' In Him are included all good things: all wisdom, peace, joy, love; the whole treasures of holiness and happiness; all that God hath prepared for them that love Him.

21. But that your prayer may have its full weight with God, see that ye be in charity with all men. For, otherwise, it is more likely to bring a curse than a blessing on your own head; nor can you expect to receive any blessing from God while you have not charity towards your neighbour. Therefore, let this hindrance be removed without delay. Confirm your love towards one another, and towards all men. And love them not in word only, but in deed and in truth. 'Therefore, all things whatsoever ye would that men should do to you, do ye even so to them; for this is the law and the prophets.'

22. This is that royal law, that golden rule of mercy, as well as justice, which even the heathen Emperor caused to be written over the gate of his palace; a rule which many believe to be

naturally engraved on the mind of every one that comes into the world. And thus much is certain, that it commends itself, as soon as heard, to every man's conscience and understanding; insomuch that no man can knowingly offend against it, without carrying his condemnation in his own breast.

23. 'This is the law and the prophets.' Whatsoever is written in that law which God of old revealed to mankind, and whatsoever precepts God has given by His holy prophets which have been since the world began, they are all summed up in these few words, they are all contained in this short direction. And this, rightly understood, comprises the whole of that religion which our Lord came to establish upon earth.

24. It may be understood either in a positive or negative sense. If understood in a negative sense, the meaning is, 'Whatever ye would not that men should do to you, do not ye unto them.' Here is a plain rule, always ready at hand, always easy to be applied. In all cases relating to your neighbour, make his case your own. Suppose the circumstances to be changed, and yourself to be just as he is now; and then beware that you indulge no temper or thought, that no word pass out of your lips, that you take no step, which you should have condemned in him, upon such a change of circumstances. If understood in a direct and positive sense, the plain meaning of it is, 'Whatsoever you could reasonably desire of him, supposing yourself to be in his circumstances, that do, to the uttermost of your power, to every child of man.'

25. To apply this in one or two obvious instances: it is clear to every man's own conscience, we would not that others should judge us, should causelessly or lightly think evil of us; much less would we that any should speak evil of us —should publish our real faults or infirmities. Apply this to yourself. Do not unto another what you would not he should do unto you; and you will never more judge your neighbour, never causelessly or lightly think evil of any one; much less will you speak evil; you will never mention even the real fault of an absent person, unless so far as you are convinced it is absolutely needful for the good of other souls.

26. Again: we would that all men should love and esteem us, and behave towards us according to justice, mercy, and truth. And we may reasonably desire, that they should do us all the good they can do, without injuring themselves; yea, that in

outward things (according to the known rule), their superfluities should give way to our conveniences; their conveniences, to our necessities; and their necessities, to our extremities. Now, then, let us walk by the same rule: let us do unto all as we would they should do to us. Let us love and honour all men. Let justice, mercy, and truth govern all our minds and actions. Let our superfluities give way to our neighbour's conveniences (and who then will have any superfluities left?); our conveniences, to our neighbour's necessities; our necessities, to his extremities.

27. This is pure and genuine morality. This do, and thou shalt live. 'As many as walk by this rule, peace be to them and mercy'; for they are 'the Israel of God.' But then, be it observed, none can walk by this rule (nor ever did from the beginning of the world), none can love his neighbour as himself, unless he first love God. And none can love God, unless he believe in Christ; unless he have redemption through His blood, and the Spirit of God bearing witness with his spirit that he is a child of God. Faith, therefore, is still the root of all, of present as well as future salvation. Still we must say to every sinner, 'Believe in the Lord Jesus Christ, and thou shalt be saved': thou shalt be saved now, that thou mayest be saved for ever; saved on earth, that thou mayest be saved in heaven. Believe in Him, and thy faith will work by love. Thou wilt love the Lord thy God, because He hath loved thee: thou wilt love thy neighbour as thyself: and then it will be thy glory and joy, to exert and increase this love; not barely by abstaining from what is contrary thereto, from every unkind thought, word, and action, but by showing all that kindness to every man which thou wouldest he should show unto thee.

SERMON XXVI

UPON OUR LORD'S SERMON ON THE MOUNT

DISCOURSE XI

Here begins the epilogue to the Sermon. The better reading is, 'Enter ye in by the narrow gate; for wide and broad is the way that leadeth to destruction, and many are they that enter in thereby. How narrow is the gate and contracted the way that leadeth unto life, and how few are they that find it!' It is advisable to replace 'strait' by 'narrow,' for the former word is very liable to be confused with 'straight'; as indeed it is by John Bunyan in the *Pilgrim's Progress,* where he describes the narrow way as being 'as straight as a rule can make-it.' The thought of the two ways is found in Jer. xxi. 8: 'Behold, I set before you the way of life and the way of death.' Indeed, the figure is common both in Hebrew and early Christian literature. Here our Lord is thinking of the narrow gate of an Eastern city; which the people pass through from within to a narrow path which 'leads away' from the city to the place whither they are going. The gate is thus the entrance to the way of life, like the wicket-gate in the *Pilgrim's Progress*; and the city is the 'City of Destruction.' A similar saying is found in a different context in Luke xiii. 24; but there the gate, or rather door, is the door of heaven, and the reference is eschatological. Many will try to get into heaven in vain at the last day—quite a different idea.

Enter ye in at the strait gate: for wide is the gate, and broad is the way, that leadeth to destruction, and many there be which go in thereat:
Because strait is the gate, and narrow is the way, which leadeth unto life, and few there be that find it.—MATT. vii. 13, 14.

1. Our Lord, having warned us of the dangers which easily beset us at our first entrance upon real religion, the hindrances which naturally arise from within, from the wickedness of our own hearts; now proceeds to apprise us of the hindrances from without, particularly ill example and ill advice. By one or the other of these, thousands, who once ran well, have drawn back unto perdition—yea, many of those who were not novices in religion, who had made some progress in righteousness. His caution, therefore, against these He presses upon us with all possible earnestness, and repeats again and again, in variety of

expressions, lest by any means we should let it slip. Thus, effectually to guard us against the former, 'Enter ye in,' saith He, 'at the strait gate: for wide is the gate, and broad is the way, that leadeth to destruction, and many there be which go in thereat: because strait is the gate, and narrow is the way, which leadeth unto life, and few there be that find it': to secure us from the latter, 'Beware,' saith He, 'of false prophets.' We shall, at present, consider the former only.

2. 'Enter ye in,' saith our blessed Lord, 'at the strait gate: for wide is the gate, and broad is the way, that leadeth to destruction, and many there be which go in thereat: because strait is the gate, and narrow is the way, which leadeth unto life, and few there be that find it.'

3. In these words we may observe, first, the inseparable properties of the way to hell: 'Wide is the gate, broad the way, that leadeth to destruction, and many there be that go in thereat': secondly, the inseparable properties of the way to heaven: 'Strait is that gate, and few there be that find it': thirdly, a serious exhortation grounded thereon, 'Enter ye in at the strait gate.'

I. 1. We may observe, first, the inseparable properties of the way to hell: 'wide is the gate, and broad is the way, that leadeth to destruction, and many there be which go in thereat.'

2. Wide indeed is the gate, and broad the way, that leadeth to destruction! For sin is the gate of hell, and wickedness the way to destruction. And how wide a gate is that of sin! How broad is the way of wickedness! The 'commandment' of God 'is exceeding broad'; as extending not only to all our actions, but to every word which goeth out of our lips, yea, every thought that rises in our heart. And sin is equally broad with the commandment, seeing any breach of the commandment is sin. Yea, rather, it is a thousand times broader; since there is only one way of keeping the commandment; for we do not properly keep it, unless both the thing done, the manner of doing it, and all the other circumstances, are right: but there are a thousand ways of breaking every commandment; so that this gate is wide indeed.

3. To consider this a little more particularly: how wide do those parent-sins extend, from which all the rest derive their being; that carnal mind which is enmity against God, pride of

heart, self-will, and love of the world! Can we fix any bounds to them? Do they not diffuse themselves through all our thoughts, and mingle with all our tempers? Are they not the leaven which leavens, more or less, the whole mass of our affections? May we not, on a close and faithful examination of ourselves, perceive these roots of bitterness continually springing up, infecting all our words, and tainting all our actions? And how innumerable an offspring do they bring forth, in every age and nation! Even enough to cover the whole earth with darkness and cruel habitations.

4. O who is able to reckon up their accursed fruits; to count all the sins, whether against God or our neighbour not which imagination might paint, but which may be matter of daily melancholy experience! Nor need we range over all the earth to find them. Survey any one kingdom, any single country, or city, or town; and how plenteous is this harvest! And let it not be one of those which are still overspread with Mahometan or Pagan darkness; but of those which name the name of Christ, which profess to see the light of His glorious gospel. Go no farther than the kingdom to which we belong, the city wherein we are now. We call ourselves Christians; yea, and that of the purest sort: we are Protestants; Reformed Christians! But, alas! who shall carry on the reformation of our opinions into our hearts and lives? Is there not a cause? For how innumerable are our sins; and those of the deepest dye! Do not the grossest abominations, of every kind abound among us from day to day? Do not sins of every sort cover the land, as the waters cover the sea? Who can count them? Rather go and count the drops of rain, or the sands on the sea-shore. So 'wide is the gate,' so 'broad is the way, that leadeth to destruction'!

5. 'And many there be who go in at' that gate; many who walk in that way; almost as many as go in at the gate of death as sink into the chambers of the grave. For it cannot be denied (though neither can we acknowledge it but with shame and sorrow of heart), that even in this, which is called a Christian country, the generality of every age and sex, of every profession and employment, of every rank and degree, high and low, rich and poor, are walking in the way of destruction. The far greater part of the inhabitants of this city, to this day, live in sin; in some palpable, habitual, known transgression of the law they profess

to observe; yea, in some outward transgression, some gross, visible kind of ungodliness or unrighteousness, some open violation of their duty, either to God or man. These then, none can deny, are all in the way that leadeth to destruction. Add to these, those who have a name indeed that they live, but were never yet alive to God; those that outwardly appear fair to men, but are inwardly full of all uncleanness; full of pride or vanity, of anger or revenge, of ambition or covetousness; lovers of themselves, lovers of the world, lovers of pleasure, more than lovers of God. These, indeed, may be highly esteemed of men; but they are an abomination to the Lord. And how greatly will these saints of the world swell the number of the children of hell! Yea, add all, whatever they be in other respects, whether they have more or less of the form of godliness, who, 'being ignorant of God's righteousness and seeking to establish their own righteousness' as the ground of their reconciliation to God and acceptance with Him, of consequence have not 'submitted themselves unto the righteousness which is of God' by faith. Now, all these things joined together in one, how terribly true is our Lord's assertion, 'Wide is the gate, and broad is the way, that leadeth to destruction, and many there be which go in thereat!'

6. Nor does this only concern the vulgar herd—the poor, base, stupid part of mankind. Men of eminence in the world, men who have many fields and yoke of oxen, do not desire to be excused from this. On the contrary,' many wise men after the flesh,' according to the human methods of judging, 'many mighty,' in power, in courage, in riches, many 'noble, are called'; called into the broad way, by the world, the flesh, and the devil; and they are not disobedient to that calling. Yea, the higher they are raised in fortune and power, the deeper do they sink into wickedness. The more blessings they have received from God, the more sins do they commit; using their honour or riches, their learning or wisdom, not as means of working out their salvation, but rather of excelling in vice, and so ensuring their own destruction.

II. 1. And the very reason why many of these go on so securely in the broad way, is, because it is broad; not considering that this is the inseparable property of the way to destruction. 'Many there be,' saith our Lord, 'which go in thereat'; for the very reason why they should flee from it; even 'because strait is the gate, and narrow the way, that leadeth unto life, and few there be that find it.'

2. This is an inseparable property of the way to heaven. So narrow is the way that leadeth unto life—unto life ever lasting—so strait the gate, that nothing unclean, nothing unholy can enter. No sinner can pass through that gate, until he is saved from all his sins. Not only from his outward sins, from his evil 'conversation received by tradition from his fathers.' It will not suffice, that he hath 'ceased to do evil,' and 'learned to do well'; he must not only be saved from all sinful actions, and from all evil and useless discourse; but inwardly changed, thoroughly renewed in the spirit of his mind: otherwise he cannot pass through the gate of life, he cannot enter into glory.

3. For, 'narrow is the way that leadeth unto life'; the way of universal holiness. Narrow indeed is the way of poverty of spirit; the way of holy mourning; the way of meekness; and that of hungering and thirsting after righteousness. Narrow is the way of mercifulness; of love unfeigned; the way of purity of heart; of doing good unto all men; and of gladly suffering evil, all manner of evil, for righteousness' sake.

4. 'And few there be that find it.' Alas! how few find even the way of heathen honesty! How few are there that do nothing to another which they would not another should do unto them! How few that are clear before God, from acts either of injustice or unkindness! How few that do not 'offend with their tongue'! that speak nothing unkind, nothing untrue! What a small proportion of mankind are innocent even of outward trans-gressions! And how much smaller a proportion have their hearts right before God,—clean and holy in His sight! Where are they, whom His allsearching eye discerns to be truly humble; to abhor themselves in dust and ashes in the presence of God their Saviour; to be deeply and steadily serious, feeling their wants, and 'passing the time of their sojourning with fear'; truly meek and gentle, never 'overcome of evil, but overcoming evil with good'; thoroughly athirst for God, and continually panting after a renewal in His likeness? How thinly are they scattered over the earth whose souls are enlarged in love to all mankind; and who love God with all their strength, who have given Him their hearts, and desire nothing else in earth or heaven! How few are

those lovers of God and man, that spend their whole strength in doing good unto all men; and are ready to suffer all things, yea, death itself, to save one soul from eternal death!

5. But while so few are found in the way of life, and so many in the way of destruction, there is great danger lest the torrent of example should bear us away with them. Even a single example, if it be always in our sight, is apt to make much impression upon us; especially when it has nature on its side, when it falls in with our own inclinations. How great then must be the force of so numerous examples, continually before our eyes; and all conspiring, together with our own hearts, to carry us down the stream of nature! How difficult must it be to stem the tide, and to keep 'ourselves unspotted in the world'!

6. What heightens the difficulty still more is, that they are not the rude and senseless part of mankind, at least not these alone, who set us the example, who throng the downward way; but the polite, the well-bred, the genteel, the wise, the men who understand the world, the men of knowledge of deep and various learning, the rational, the eloquent! These are all, or nearly all, against us. And how shall we stand against these? Do not their tongues drop manna and have they not learned all the arts of soft persuasion?—and of reasoning too? for these are versed in all controversies, and strife of words. It is therefore a small thing with them to prove that the way is *right,* because it is *broad*; that he who follows a multitude cannot do evil, but only he who will not follow them; that your way must be wrong, because it is *narrow,* and because there are so few that find it. These will make it clear to a demonstration, that evil is good, and good is evil; that the way of holiness is the way of destruction, and the way of the world the only way to heaven.

7. O how can unlearned and ignorant men maintain their cause against such opponents! And yet these are not all with whom they must contend, however unequal to the task: for there are many mighty, and noble, and powerful men, as well as wise, in the road that leadeth to destruction; and these have a shorter way of confuting, than that of reason and argument. They usually apply, not to the understanding, but to the fears, of any that oppose them,—a method that seldom fails of success, even where argument profits nothing, as lying level to the capacities of all men; for all can fear, whether they can reason or

no. And all who have not a firm trust in God, a sure reliance both on His power and love, cannot but fear to give any disgust to those who have the power of the world in their hands. What wonder therefore, if the example of these is a law to all who know not God?

8. Many rich are likewise in the broad way. And these apply to the hopes of men, and to all their foolish desires, as strongly and effectually as the mighty and noble to their fears. So that hardly can you hold on in the way of the kingdom, unless you are dead to all below, unless you are crucified to the world, and the world crucified to you, unless you desire nothing more but God.

9. For how dark, how uncomfortable, how forbidding, is the prospect on the opposite side! A strait gate; a narrow way! and few finding that gate; few walking in the way! Besides, even those few are not wise men, not men of learning or eloquence. They are not able to reason either strongly or clearly: they cannot propose an argument to any advantage. They know not how to prove what they profess to believe; or to explain even what they say they experience. Surely such advocates as these will never recommend, but rather discredit, the cause they have espoused.

10. Add to this, that they are not noble, not honourable men: if they were, you might bear with their folly. They are men of no interest, no authority, of no account in the world. They are mean and base; low in life; and such as have no power, if they had the will, to hurt you. Therefore there is nothing at all to be feared from them; and there is nothing at all to hope: for the greater part of them may say, 'Silver and gold have I none'; at least a very moderate share. Nay, some of them have scarce food to eat, or raiment to put on. For this reason, as well as because their ways are not like those of other men, they are everywhere spoken against are despised, have their names cast out as evil, are variously persecuted, and treated as the filth and offscouring of the world. So that both your fears, your hopes, and all your desires (except those which you have immediately from God) yea, all your natural passions, continually incline you to return into the broad way.

III. 1. Therefore it is, that our Lord so earnestly exhorts, 'Enter ye in at the strait gate.' Or (as the same exhortation is

elsewhere expressed), 'Strive to enter in':Αγωνιζεσθε εισε-
λθειν—'strive as in an agony': 'For many,' saith our Lord, 'shall
seek to enter in,' indolently strive, 'and shall not be able.'

2. It is true, He intimates what may seem another reason for
this, for their not being able to enter in, in the words which
immediately follow these. For after He had said, 'Many, I say
unto you, will seek to enter in, and shall not be able,' He subjoins,
'When once the master of the house is risen up, and hath shut to
the door, and ye begin to stand without,' αρξησθε εξω
εσταναι—rather, ye *stand without*: for αρξησθε seems to be only
an elegant expletive—'and to knock at the door, saying, Lord,
Lord, open unto us; He shall answer and say unto you, I know
you not: depart from Me, all ye workers of iniquity' (Luke xiii.
24, &c.).

3. It may appear, upon a transient view of these words, that
their delaying to seek at all, rather than their manner of seeking,
was the reason why they were not able to enter in. But it comes,
in effect, to the same thing. They were, therefore, commanded
to depart, because they had been 'workers of iniquity'; because
they had walked in the broad road; in other words, because they
had not agonized to 'enter in at the strait gate.' Probably they did
seek, before the door was shut; but that did not suffice: and they
did *strive*, after the door was shut; but then it was too late.

4. Therefore strive ye now, in this your day, to 'enter in at the
strait gate.' And in order thereto, settle it in your heart, and let it
be ever uppermost in your thoughts, that if you are in a broad
way, you are in the way that leadeth to destruction. If many go
with you, as sure as God is true, both they and you are going to
hell! If you are walking as the generality of men walk, you are
walking to the bottomless pit! Are many wise, many rich, many
mighty, or noble, travelling with you in the same way? By this
token, without going any farther, you know it does not lead to
life. Here is a short, a plain, an infallible rule, before you enter
into particulars. In whatever profession you are engaged, you
must be singular, or be damned! The way to hell has nothing
singular in it; but the way to heaven is singularity all over. If you
move but one step towards God, you are not as other men are.
But regard not this. It is far better to stand alone, than to fall into
the pit. Run, then, with patience the race which is set before
thee, though thy companions therein are but few. They will not

always be so. Yet a little while, and thou wilt' come to an innumerable company of angels, to the general assembly and church of the first-born, and to the spirits of just men made perfect.'

5. Now, then, 'strive to enter in at the strait gate,' being penetrated with the deepest sense of the inexpressible danger your soul is in, so long as you are in a broad way,—so long as you are void of poverty of spirit and all that inward religion which the many, the rich, the wise, account madness. 'Strive to enter in'; being pierced with sorrow and shame for having so long run on with the unthinking crowd, utterly neglecting, if not despising, that 'holiness without which no man can see the Lord.' Strive as in an agony of holy fear, lest 'a promise being made you of entering into His rest,' even that 'rest which remaineth for the people of God,' you should nevertheless 'come short of it.' Strive, in all the fervour of desire, with 'groanings which cannot be uttered.' Strive by prayer without ceasing; at all times, in all places, lifting up your heart to God and giving Him no rest, till you 'awake up after His likeness,' and are 'satisfied' with it.

6. To conclude. 'Strive to enter in at the strait gate,' not only by this agony of soul, of conviction, of sorrow, of shame, of desire, of fear, of unceasing prayer; but likewise by ordering thy conversation aright, by walking with all thy strength in all the ways of God, the way of innocence, of piety, and of mercy. Abstain from all appearance of evil; do all possible good to all men; deny thyself thy own will, in all things, and take up thy cross daily. Be ready to cut off thy right hand, to pluck out thy right eye and cast it from thee; to suffer the loss of goods, friends, health, all things on earth, so thou mayest enter into the kingdom of heaven.

SERMON XXVII

UPON OUR LORD'S SERMON ON THE MOUNT

DISCOURSE XII

On Sunday, January 30, 1743, Wesley walked over from Windsor to Egham, a town on the Thames, opposite to Staines, some four or five miles from Windsor, 'where Mr.—— preached one of the most miserable sermons I ever heard; stuffed so full of dull, senseless, improbable lies of those he complimented with the title of "false prophets." I preached at one, and endeavoured to rescue the poor text (Matt. vii. 15) out of so bad hands.' I suppose Mr.—— had been abusing the Methodist preachers. On March 13, 1757, Wesley preached from verse 16 at Snowsfields, but was feeling unwell; and to his great joy, John Fletcher, who had that day been ordained at Whitehall, came to his help, and took the Communion service along with him at West Street. He preached from verse 20 at the Chapel (i.e. West Street) on August 23, 1761.

It is clear from the passage in the great eschatological discourse (Matt. xxiv. 24) that our Lord had definite prevision of the 'false Christs and false prophets' who would trouble the Church after His ascension; but it seems strange that He should refer to them so early as this. Probably these verses are an editorial insertion taken from a later discourse; but appropriate here because these false Prophets would dissuade men from entering in at the 'narrow gate,' and lead them along 'the broad road.'

The main object of Wesley's sermon is to give his people directions as to their hearing and receiving the Communion from ministers of the Church of England who were manifestly ungodly men, or who taught doctrines opposed to those advocated by Wesley. It is of course well known that Wesley never meant his people to separate from the Church of England. In the *Minutes* of 1766 he denies that the Methodists are Dissenters; the Methodist services, he says, were in a sense public worship, but not such as supersedes the Church service. If they were they would be essentially defective. For they seldom had the four grand parts of public prayer: deprecation, petition, intercession, and thanksgiving. Neither were they, even on the Lord's Day, concluded with the Lord's Supper. He concludes, 'I advise, therefore, all the Methodists in England and Ireland, who have been brought up in the Church, constantly to attend the service of the Church at least, every Lord's day.' In *Minutes,* 1769, he says, 'Let us keep to the Church. They that leave the Church leave the Methodists. . . . Let every

402

preacher go [to church] always on Sunday morning, and, when he can, in the afternoon.' But in 1784 he ordained Coke and Asbury as Superintendents and Whatcoat and Vasey as Elders for America, with power to administer the Sacraments and hold full services, for which he prepared a 'liturgy little differing from that of the Church of England'; soon after, he did the same thing for Scotland. The question could not but be raised, whether the same power ought not to be given to the Methodist preachers in England; and in 1786 he yielded so far as to allow his preachers to hold service in church hours (1) when the minister is a notoriously wicked man; (2) when he preaches Arian, or any equally pernicious, doctrine; (3) when there are not churches in the town sufficient to contain half the people; (4) when there is no church at all within two or three miles (*Minutes*, 1786). In *Minutes*, 1788, the assistants have discretion given them to read the Prayer-Book in the preaching-houses on Sunday mornings, where the Society acquiesce in it, but not on the Sundays when the sacrament is administered in the parish church; and the people are to be 'strenuously exhorted to attend the sacrament in the parish church on those Sundays.' In a letter dated January 9, 1782, in answer to an appeal from five Methodists at Baildon, near Bradford, he allows that 'if the minister began either to preach the absolute decrees, or to rail at and ridicule Christian perfection, they should quietly and silently go out of the church; yet attend it again the next opportunity.' The Conference of 1793 was beyond question right when it affirmed: 'Our venerable father, who is gone to his great reward, lived and died a member and friend of the Church of England. His attachment to it was so strong and so unshaken, that nothing but irresistible necessity induced him to deviate from it in any degree.' The Conference felt that a similar irresistible necessity now faced it; and it decided that the Lord's Supper might be administered by the preachers where the whole Society was unanimous for it, 'and will not be contented without it.'

This sermon was separately published in 1758 as *A Caution against False Prophets, particularly Recommended to the People called Methodists.*

Beware of false prophets, which come to you in sheep's clothing, but inwardly they are ravening wolves.
Ye shall know them by their fruits. Do men gather grapes of thorns or figs of thistles?
Even so every good tree bringeth forth good fruit; but a corrupt tree bringeth forth evil fruit.
A good tree cannot bring forth evil fruit; neither can a corrupt tree bring forth good fruit.
Every tree that bringeth not forth good fruit is hewn down and cast into the fire.
Wherefore by their fruits ye shall know them.—MATT. vii. 15-20.

1. It is scarce possible to express or conceive what multitudes of souls run on to destruction, because they would not be

persuaded to walk in a *narrow* way, even though it were the way to everlasting salvation. And the same thing we may still observe daily. Such is the folly and madness of mankind, that thousands of men still rush on in the way to hell, only because it is a *broad* way. They walk in it themselves, because others do: because so many perish, they will add to the number. Such is the amazing influence of example over the weak, miserable children of men! It continually peoples the regions of death, and drowns numberless souls in everlasting perdition.

2. To warn mankind of this, to guard as many as possible against this spreading contagion, God has commanded His watchmen to cry aloud, and show the people the danger they are in. For this end He has sent His servants, the prophets, in their succeeding generations, to point out the narrow path, and exhort all men not to be conformed to this world. But what, if the watchmen themselves fall into the snare against which they should warn others? What, if 'the prophets prophesy deceit'? if they cause the 'people to err from the way'? What shall be done, if they point out, as the way to eternal life, what is in truth the way to eternal death; and exhort others to walk, as they do themselves, in the broad, not the narrow way?

3. Is this an unheard-of, is it an uncommon thing? Nay, God knoweth it is not. The instances of it are almost innumerable. We may find them in every age and nation. But how terrible is this—when the ambassadors of God turn agents for the devil!—when they who are commissioned to teach men the way to heaven do in fact teach them the way to hell! These are like the locusts of Egypt, 'which eat up the residue that had escaped, that had remained after the hail.' They devour even the residue of men that had escaped, that were not destroyed by ill example. It is not, therefore, without cause, that our wise and gracious Master so solemnly cautions us against them: 'Beware,' saith He, 'of false prophets, which come to you in sheep's clothing, but inwardly they are ravening wolves.'

4. A caution this of the utmost importance. That it may the more effectually sink into our hearts, let us inquire, first, who these false prophets are: secondly, what appearance they put on: and, thirdly, how we may know what they really are, notwithstanding their fair appearance.

I. 1. We are, first, to inquire who these false prophets are. And this it is needful to do the more diligently, because these very men have so laboured to 'wrest this scripture to their own,' though not only their own, 'destruction.' In order, therefore, to cut off all dispute, I shall raise no dust (as the manner of some is), neither use any loose, rhetorical exclamations, to deceive the hearts of the simple; but speak rough, plain truths, such as none can deny who has either understanding or modesty left, and such truths as have the closest connexion with the whole tenor of the preceding discourse: whereas too many have interpreted these words without any regard to all that went before; as if they bore no manner of relation to the sermon in the close of which they stand.

2. By *prophets* here (as in many other passages of Scripture, particularly in the New Testament) are meant, not those who foretell things to come, but those who speak in the name of God; those men who profess to be sent of God, to teach others the way to heaven.

Those are *false* prophets, who teach a false way to heaven, a way which does not lead thither; or (which comes in the end to the same point), who do not teach the true.

3. Every broad way is infallibly a false one. Therefore this is one plain, sure rule: 'They who teach men to walk in a broad way, a way that many walk in, are false prophets.'

Again: the true way to heaven is a narrow way. Therefore this is another plain, sure rule: 'They who do not teach men to walk in a narrow way, to be singular, are false prophets.'

4. To be more particular: the only true way to heaven is that pointed out in the preceding sermon. Therefore they are false prophets who do not teach men to walk in this way.

Now the way to heaven pointed out in the preceding sermon is the way of lowliness, mourning, meekness and holy desire, love of God and of our neighbour, doing good, and suffering evil for Christ's sake. They are, therefore, false prophets, who teach, as the way to heaven any other way than this.

5. It matters not what they call that other way. They may call it faith; or good works; or faith and works; or repentance; or repentance, faith, and new obedience. All these are good words: but if, under these, or any other terms whatever, they teach men any way distinct from this, they are properly false prophets.

6. How much more do they fall under that condemnation, who speak evil of this good way; but above all, they who teach the directly opposite way, the way of pride, of levity, of passion, of worldly desires, of loving pleasure more than God, of unkindness to our neighbour, of unconcern for good works, and suffering no evil, no persecution, for righteousness' sake!

7. If it be asked, 'Why, who ever did teach this, or who does teach it, as the way to heaven?' I answer, Ten thousand wise and honourable men; even all those, of whatever denomination, who encourage the proud, the trifler, the passionate, the lover of the world, the man of pleasure, the unjust or unkind, the easy, careless, harmless, useless creature, the man who suffers no reproach for righteousness' sake, to imagine he is in the way to heaven. These are false prophets in the highest sense of the word. These are traitors both to God and man. These are no other than the first-born of Satan; the eldest sons of Apollyon, the destroyer. These are far above the rank of ordinary cut-throats; for they murder the souls of men. They are continually peopling the realms of night; and whenever they follow the poor souls whom they have destroyed, 'hell shall be moved from beneath to meet them at their coming.'

II. 1. But do they come now in their own shape? By no means. If it were so, they could not destroy. You would take the alarm, and flee for your life. Therefore they put on a quite contrary appearance (which was the second thing to be considered): 'they come to you in sheep's clothing, although inwardly they are ravening wolves.'

2. 'They come to you in sheep's clothing'; that is, with an appearance of harmlessness. They come in the most mild, inoffensive manner, without any mark or token of enmity. Who can imagine that these quiet creatures would do any hurt to any one? Perhaps they may not be so zealous and active in doing good as one would wish they were. However, you see no reason to suspect that they have even the desire to do any harm. But this is not all.

3. They come, secondly, with an appearance of usefulness. Indeed to this, to do good, they are particularly called. They are set apart for this very thing. They are particularly commissioned to watch over your soul, and to train you up to eternal life. It is

their whole business, to 'go about doing good, and healing those that are oppressed of the devil.' And you have always been accustomed to look upon them in this light, as messengers of God, sent to bring you a blessing.

4. They come, thirdly, with an appearance of religion. All they do is for conscience' sake! They assure you, it is out of mere zeal for God, that they are making God a liar. It is out of pure concern for religion, that they would destroy it, root and branch. All they speak is only from a love of truth, and a fear lest it should suffer; and, it may be, from a regard for the Church, and a desire to defend her from all her enemies.

5. Above all, they come with an appearance of love. They take all these pains only for *your* good. They should not trouble themselves about you, but that they have a kindness for you. They will make large professions of their goodwill, of their concern for the danger you are in and of their earnest desire to preserve you from error, from being entangled in new and mischievous doctrines. They should be very sorry to see one who *means* so well, hurried into any extreme, perplexed with strange and unintelligible notions, or deluded into enthusiasm. Therefore it is that they advise you to keep still in the plain middle way; and to beware of 'being righteous over-much,"lest you should 'destroy yourself.'

III. 1. But how may we know what they really are, notwithstanding their fair appearance? This was the third thing into which it was proposed to inquire. Our blessed Lord saw how needful it was for all men to know false prophets, however disguised. He saw, likewise, how unable most men were to deduce a truth through a long train of consequences. He therefore gives us a short and plain rule, easy to be understood by men of the meanest capacities, and easy to be applied upon all occasions: 'Ye shall know them by their fruits.'

2. Upon all occasions you may easily apply this rule. In order to know whether any who speak in the name of God are false or true prophets, it is easy to observe, first, What are the fruits of their doctrine as to themselves? What effect has it had upon their lives? Are they holy and unblamable in all things? What effect has it had upon their hearts? Does it appear by the general tenor of their conversation, that their tempers are holy,

heavenly, divine? that the mind is in them which was in Christ Jesus? that they are meek, lowly, patient, lovers of God and man, and zealous of good works?

3. You may easily observe, secondly, what are the fruits of their doctrine as to those that hear them—in many, at least, though not in all; for the Apostles themselves did not convert all that heard them. Have these the mind that was in Christ? And do they walk as He also walked? And was it by hearing these men that they began so to do? Were they inwardly and outwardly wicked till they heard them? If so, it is a manifest proof that those are true prophets, teachers sent of God. But if it is not so, if they do not effectually teach either themselves or others to love and serve God, it is a manifest proof that they are false prophets: that God hath not sent them.

4. An hard saying this! How few can bear it? This our Lord was sensible of, and therefore condescends to prove it at large, by several clear and convincing arguments. 'Do men,' says He, 'gather grapes of thorns, or figs of thistles?' (verse 16). Do you expect that these evil men should bring forth good fruit? As well might you expect that thorns should bring forth grapes, or that figs should grow upon thistles! 'Every good tree bringeth forth good fruit; but a corrupt tree bringeth forth evil fruit' (verse 17). Every true prophet, every teacher whom I have sent, bringeth forth the good fruit of holiness. But a false prophet, a teacher whom I have not sent, brings forth only sin and wickedness. 'A good tree cannot bring forth evil fruit, neither can a corrupt tree bring forth good fruit.' A true prophet, a teacher sent from God, does not bring forth good fruit sometimes only, but always; not accidentally, but by a kind of necessity. In like manner, a false prophet, one whom God hath not sent, does not bring forth evil fruit accidentally, or sometimes only, but always, and of necessity. 'Every tree that bringeth not forth good fruit is hewn down, and cast into the fire' (verse 19). Such infallibly will be the lot of those prophets who bring not forth good fruit, who do not save souls from sin, who do not bring sinners to repentance. 'Wherefore,' let this stand as an eternal rule, 'By their fruits ye shall know them' (verse 20). They who, in fact, bring the proud, passionate, unmerciful, lovers of the world, to be lowly, gentle, lovers of God and man,—they are true prophets; they are sent from God, who therefore confirms their word. On the other

hand, they whose hearers, if unrighteous before, remain unrighteous still, or, at least, void of any righteousness which 'exceeds the righteousness of the Scribes and Pharisees,'—they are false prophets; they are not sent of God; therefore their word falls to the ground: and, without a miracle of grace, they and their hearers together will fall into the bottomless pit!

5. O 'beware of these false prophets'! For though they 'come in sheep's clothing, yet inwardly they are ravening wolves.' They only destroy and devour the flock—they tear them in pieces, if there is none to help them. They will not, cannot, lead you in the way to heaven. How should they, when they know it not themselves? O beware they do not turn you out of the way, and cause you to 'lose what you have wrought'!

6. But perhaps you will ask, 'If there is such danger in hearing them, ought I to hear them at all?' It is a weighty question, such as deserves the deepest consideration, and ought not to be answered but upon the calmest thought, the most deliberate reflection. For many years I have been almost afraid to speak at all concerning it; being unable to determine one way or the other, or to give any judgement upon it. Many reasons there are which readily occur, and incline me to say, 'Hear them not.' And yet what our Lord speaks concerning the false prophets of His own times seems to imply the contrary: 'Then spake Jesus unto the multitude, and to His disciples, saying, The Scribes and the Pharisees sit in Moses' seat'—are the ordinary, stated teachers in your Church: 'all, therefore, whatsoever they bid you observe, that observe and do. But do not ye after their works; for they say, and do not.' Now, that these were false prophets in the highest sense, our Lord hath shown during the whole course of His ministry; as indeed He does in those very words, 'They say, and do not.' Therefore, by their fruits His disciples could not but know them, seeing they were open to the view of all men. Accordingly, He warns them again and again, to beware of these false prophets. And yet He does not forbid them to hear even these: nay, He, in effect, commands them so to do, in those words, 'All, therefore, whatsoever they bid you observe, that observe and do': for unless they heard them, they could not know, much less observe, whatsoever they bade them do. Here, then, our Lord Himself gives a plain direction, both to His

Apostles and the whole multitude, in some circumstances, to
hear even false prophets, known and acknowledged so to be.

7. But perhaps it will be said, 'He only directed to hear them
when they read the Scripture to the congregation.' I answer, At
the same time that they thus read the Scripture, they generally
expounded it too. And here is no kind of intimation that they
were to hear the one, and not the other also. Nay, the very terms,
'All things whatsoever they bid you observe,' exclude any such
limitation.

8. Again: unto them, unto false prophets, undeniably such, is
frequently committed (O grief to speak! for surely these things
ought not so to be) the administration of the sacrament also. To
direct men, therefore, not to hear them, would be, in effect, to
cut them off from the ordinances of God. But this we dare not
do; considering the validity of the ordinance doth not depend
on the goodness of him that administers, but on the faithfulness
of Him that ordained it, who will and doth meet us in His
appointed ways. Therefore, on this account, likewise, I scruple
to say, 'Hear not even the false prophets.' Even by these who are
under a curse themselves, God can and doth give us His blessing.
For the bread which they break, we have experimentally known
to be 'the communion of the body of Christ'; and the cup which
God blessed, even by their unhallowed lips, was to us the
communion of the blood of Christ.

9. All, therefore, which I can say is this: In any particular case,
wait upon God by humble and earnest prayer, and then act
according to the best light you have: act according to what you
are persuaded, upon the whole, will be most for your spiritual
advantage. Take great care that you do not judge rashly; that
you do not lightly think any to be false prophets: and when you
have full proof, see that no anger or contempt have any place in
your heart. After this, in the presence and in the fear of God,
determine for yourself. I can only say, if by experience you find
that the hearing them hurts your soul, then hear them not; then
quietly refrain, and hear those that profit you. If, on the other
hand, you find it does not hurt your soul, you then may hear
them still. Only, 'take heed how you hear': beware of them and
of their doctrine. Hear with fear and trembling, lest you should
be deceived, and given up, like them, to a strong delusion. As
they continually mingle truth and lies, how easily may you take

in both together! Hear with fervent and continual prayer to Him who alone teacheth man wisdom. And see that you bring whatever you hear 'to the law and to the testimony.' Receive nothing untried, nothing till it is weighed in the balance of the sanctuary: believe nothing they say, unless it is clearly confirmed by [plain] passages of holy writ. Wholly reject whatsoever differs therefrom, whatever is not confirmed thereby. And, in particular, reject, with the utmost abhorrence, whatsoever is described as the way of salvation, that is either different from, or short of, the way our Lord has marked out in the foregoing discourse.

10. I cannot conclude without addressing a few plain words to those of whom we have now been speaking. O ye false prophets! O ye dry bones! hear ye, for once, the word of the Lord! How long will ye lie in the name of God, saying, 'God hath spoken!' and God hath not spoken by you? How long will ye pervert the right ways of the Lord, putting darkness for light, and light for darkness? How long will ye teach the way of death, and call it the way of life? How long will ye deliver to Satan the souls whom ye profess to bring unto God?

11. 'Woe unto you, ye blind leaders of the blind; for ye shut the kingdom of heaven against men. Ye neither go in yourselves, neither suffer ye them that are entering to go in.' Them that would 'strive to enter in at the strait gate,' ye call back into the broad way. Them that have scarce gone one step in the ways of God, you devilishly caution against going too far. Them that just begin to 'hunger and thirst after righteousness,' you warn not to 'be righteous overmuch.' Thus you cause them to stumble at the very threshold; yea, to fall and rise no more. O wherefore do ye this? What profit is there in their blood, when they go down to the pit? Miserable profit to you! 'They shall perish in their iniquity; but their blood will God require at your hands!'

12. Where are your eyes? Where is your understanding? Have ye deceived others, till you have deceived yourselves also? Who hath required this at your hands, to teach a way which ye never knew? Are you 'given up to' so 'strong a delusion,' that ye not only teach but 'believe a lie'? And can you possibly believe that God hath sent you? that ye are His messengers? Nay, if the Lord had sent you, the work of the Lord would prosper in your hand. As the Lord liveth, if ye were messengers of God, He would

'confirm the word of His messengers.' But the work of the Lord doth not prosper in your hand: you bring no sinners to repentance. The Lord doth not confirm your word; for you save no souls from death.

13. How can you possibly evade the force of our Lord's words—so full, so strong, so express? How can ye evade knowing yourselves by your fruits—evil fruits of evil trees? And how should it be otherwise? 'Do men gather grapes of thorns, or figs of thistles?' Take this to yourselves, ye to whom it belongs! O ye barren trees, why cumber ye the ground? 'Every good tree bringeth forth good fruit.' See ye not, that here is no exception? Take knowledge, then, ye are not good trees; for ye do not bring forth good fruit. 'But a corrupt tree bringeth forth evil fruit'; and so have ye done from the beginning. Your speaking, as from God, has only confirmed them that heard you in the tempers, if not works, of the devil. O take warning of Him in whose name ye speak, before the sentence He hath pronounced take place: 'Every tree which bringeth not forth good fruit is hewn down and cast into the fire.'

14. My dear brethren, harden not your hearts! You have too long shut your eyes against the light. Open them now before it is too late; before you are cast into outer darkness! Let not any temporal consideration weigh with you; for eternity is at stake. Ye have run before ye were sent. O go no farther! Do not persist to damn yourselves and them that hear you! You have no fruit of your labours. And why is this? Even because the Lord is not with you. But can you go this warfare at your own cost? It cannot be. Then humble yourselves before Him. Cry unto Him out of the dust, that He may first quicken *thy* soul; give *thee* the faith that worketh by love; that is lowly and meek, pure and merciful, zealous of good works, rejoicing in tribulation, in reproach, in distress, in persecution for righteousness' sake! So shall 'the Spirit of glory and of Christ rest upon thee,' and it shall appear that God hath sent thee. So shalt thou indeed 'do the work of an Evangelist, and make full proof of thy ministry.' So shall the word of God in thy mouth be 'an hammer that breaketh the rocks in pieces'! It shall then be known by thy fruits that thou art a prophet of the Lord, even by the children whom God hath given thee. And having 'turned many to righteousness,' thou shalt 'shine as the stars for ever and ever!'

SERMON XXVIII

UPON OUR LORD'S SERMON ON THE MOUNT

DISCOURSE XIII

This sermon is recorded as having been preached at Bexley some time during January 1753. In *Journal*, Sunday, July 20, 1766, it is recorded: 'After preaching at eight, I went to St. Saviour-gate Church [in York]. Towards the close of the prayers the rector sent the sexton to tell me the pulpit was at my service. I preached on the conclusion of the Gospel for the day, "Not every one that saith unto Me, Lord, Lord," &c. I did not see one person laugh or smile, though we had an elegant congregation.' In an article on 'Methodism in York,' by Daniel M'Allum, in the *Methodist Magazine*, July 1827, he says: 'At that time the Rev. Mr. Cordeux was incumbent of the living of St. Saviour's; and he warned his congregation against hearing "that vagabond Wesley preach." Mr. Wesley came to the city on a Saturday, preached in Peaseholme Green Chapel, and again on the Sunday morning; in the forenoon of that day he went to St. Saviour's Church, dressed in his canonicals. The clergyman in the course of reading the prayers saw a stranger cleric, and sent an officer to invite him to take the pulpit. He accepted the invitation, and took his text from the Gospel of the day, Matt. vii. 21. After service the vicar asked the clerk if he knew who the stranger was. "Sir," said he, "he is the vagabond Wesley, of whom you warned us." "Aye indeed," was the reply, "we are trapped; but never mind, we had a good sermon." The Dean heard of the affair, and threatened to lay a complaint before the Archbishop. Mr. Cordeux, afraid of the consequences, took an early opportunity, when some occasion brought him into the presence of his Grace, to tell him that he had allowed Mr. Wesley to occupy his pulpit. "And you did right," said the prelate. The matter of the complaint was never more heard of; and Mr. Cordeux was so far from repenting of what he had done, that some years afterwards he made a second offer of his pulpit, and Mr. Wesley preached upon the eight Beatitudes. An aged disciple, who still remains, and who was present on this occasion, says that Mr. Wesley took occasion to remark on the words "Blessed are they who are persecuted for righteousness' sake, for theirs is the kingdom of heaven"—"Perhaps no man in England knows more of what this means than I do." ' This second sermon, as appears from the *Journal*, was preached in the morning of Sunday, May 7, 1786.

Verses 21-3 are connected with the previous paragraph about false teachers, who are warned that even successful ministration in Christ's name will not admit them at last to heaven if they have not practised the righteousness set forth in the sermon as the sole condition of entrance. The final verses are the appropriate conclusion of the whole discourse.

The last sentence of I. 1, 'Reader, if God hath ever blessed my word to thy soul, pray that He may be merciful to me a sinner,' is obviously an addition to the sermon as preached, when Wesley prepared it for publication. What a human, genuine appeal it is! Here is no autocratic, self-satisfied ecclesiastic, but a diffident soul, conscious of its own failures and mistakes, and crying out for sympathy and love.

Not every one that saith unto Me, Lord, Lord, shall enter into the kingdom of heaven; but he that doeth the will of My Father which is in heaven.

Many will say to Me in that day, Lord, Lord, have we not prophesied in Thy name? and in Thy name have cast out devils? and in Thy name done many wonderful works?

And then will I profess unto them, I never knew you: depart from Me, ye that work iniquity.

Therefore whosoever heareth these sayings of Mine, and doeth them, I will liken him unto a wise man, which built his house upon a rock:

And the rain descended, and the floods came, and the winds blew, and beat upon that house; and it fell not: for it was founded upon a rock.

And every one that heareth these sayings of Mine, and doeth them not, shall be likened unto a foolish man, which built his house upon the sand:

And the rain descended, and the floods came, and the winds blew, and beat upon that house; and it fell: and great was the fall of it.—MATT. vii. 21-27.

1. Our Divine Teacher, having declared the whole counsel of God with regard to the way of salvation, and observed the chief hindrances of those who desire to walk therein, now closes the whole with these weighty words; thereby, as it were, setting His seal to His prophecy, and impressing His whole authority on what He had delivered, that it might stand firm to all generations.

2. For thus saith the Lord, that none may ever conceive there is any other way than this, 'Not every one that saith unto Me, Lord, Lord, shall enter into the kingdom of heaven, but he that doeth the will of My Father which is in heaven. Many will say to Me in that day, Lord, Lord, have we not prophesied in Thy name? and in Thy name have cast out devils? and in Thy name done many wonderful works? And then will I profess unto them, I never knew you: depart from Me, ye that work iniquity. Therefore, every one that heareth these sayings of Mine and doeth them not, shall be likened unto a foolish man, which built his house upon the sand: and the rain descended, and the floods

came, and the winds blew, and beat upon that house; and it fell: and great was the fall of it.'

3. I design, in the following discourse, first, to consider the case of him who thus builds his house upon the sand: secondly, to show the wisdom of him who builds upon a rock: and, thirdly, to conclude with a practical application.

I. 1. And, first, I am to consider the case of him who builds his house upon the sand. It is concerning him our Lord saith, 'Not every one that saith unto Me, Lord, Lord, shall enter into the kingdom of heaven.' And this is a decree which cannot pass; which standeth fast for ever and ever. It therefore imports us in the highest degree, thoroughly to understand the force of these words. Now, what are we to understand by that expression, 'That saith unto Me, Lord, Lord'? It undoubtedly means, *that thinks of going to heaven by any other way than that which I have now described.* It therefore implies (to begin at the lowest point) all good words, all verbal religion. It includes whatever creeds we may rehearse, whatever professions of faith we make, whatever number of prayers we may repeat, whatever thanksgivings we read or say to God. We may speak good of His name, and declare His lovingkindness to the children of men. We may be talking of all His mighty acts, and telling of His salvation from day to day. By comparing spiritual things with spiritual, we may show the meaning of the oracles of God. We may explain the mysteries of His kingdom, which have been hid from the beginning of the world. We may speak with the tongue of angels, rather than men, concerning the deep things of God. We may proclaim to sinners, 'Behold the Lamb of God, who taketh away the sin of the world!' Yea, we may do this with such a measure of the power of God, and such demonstration of His Spirit, as to save many souls from death, and hide a multitude of sins. And yet it is very possible, all this may be no more than saying, 'Lord, Lord.' After I have thus successfully preached to others, still I myself may be a castaway. I may, in the hand of God, snatch many souls from hell, and yet drop into it when I have done. I may bring many others to the kingdom of heaven, and yet myself never enter there. Reader, if God hath ever blessed my word to *thy* soul, pray that He may be merciful to *me* a sinner!

2. The saying, 'Lord, Lord,' may, secondly, imply the doing no

harm. We may abstain from every presumptuous sin, from
every kind of outward wickedness. We may refrain from all
those ways of acting or speaking which are forbidden in holy
writ. We may be able to say to all those among whom we live,
'Which of you convinceth me of sin?' We may have a conscience
void of any external offence, towards God and towards man. We
may be clear of all uncleanness, ungodliness, and unrighteousness, as to the outward act; or (as the Apostle testifies concerning
himself), 'touching the righteousness of the law,' that is, outward
righteousness, 'blameless.' But yet we are not hereby justified.
Still this is no more than saying, 'Lord, Lord'; and if we go no
farther than this, we shall never' enter into the kingdom of
heaven.'

3. The saying, 'Lord, Lord,' may imply, thirdly, many of what
are usually styled good works. A man may attend the supper of
the Lord, may hear abundance of excellent sermons, and omit
no opportunity of partaking all the other ordinances of God. I
may do good to my neighbour, deal my bread to the hungry, and
cover the naked with a garment. I may be so zealous of good
works as even to 'give all my goods to feed the poor.' Yea, and I
may do all this with a desire to please God, and a real belief that I
do please Him thereby (which is undeniably the case of those our
Lord introduces, saying unto Him, 'Lord, Lord'); and still I may
have no part in the glory which shall be revealed.

4. If any man marvels at this, let him acknowledge he is a
stranger to the whole religion of Jesus Christ; and, in particular,
to that perfect portraiture thereof which He has set before us in
this discourse. For how far short is all this of that righteousness
and true holiness which He has described therein! How widely
distant from that inward kingdom of heaven which is now
opened in the believing soul!—which is first sown in the heart as
a grain of mustard-seed, but afterwards putteth forth great
branches, on which grow all the fruits of righteousness, every
good temper, and word, and work.

5. Yet as clearly as He had declared this, as frequently as He
had repeated, that none who have not this kingdom of God
within them shall enter into the kingdom of heaven; our Lord
well knew, that many would not receive this saying, and
therefore confirms it yet again: 'Many' (saith He: not one; not a
few only; it is not a rare or an uncommon case) 'shall say unto Me

in that day,' not only, We have said many prayers; We have spoken Thy praise; We have refrained from evil; We have exercised ourselves in doing good,—but, what is abundantly more than this, 'We have prophesied in Thy name; in Thy name have we cast out devils; in Thy name done many wonderful works.' 'We have prophesied,'—we have declared Thy will to mankind; we have showed sinners the way to peace and glory. And we have done this 'in Thy name,' according to the truth of Thy gospel; yea, and by Thy authority, who didst confirm the word with the Holy Ghost sent down from heaven. For in or by Thy name, by the power of Thy Word and of Thy Spirit, 'have we cast out devils'; out of the souls which they had long claimed as their own, and whereof they had full and quiet possession. 'And in Thy name,' by Thy power, not our own, 'have we done many wonderful works'; insomuch that 'even the dead heard the voice of the Son of God' speaking by us, and lived. 'And then will I profess' even 'unto them, I never knew you'; no, not then, when you were 'casting out devils in My name'; even then I did not know you as My own; for your heart was not right toward God. Ye were not yourselves meek and lowly; ye were not lovers of God, and of all mankind; ye were not renewed in the image of God; ye were not holy as I am holy. 'Depart from Me, ye' who, notwithstanding all this, are 'workers of iniquity';—ἀνομια: ye are transgressors of My law, My law of holy and perfect love.

6. It is to put this beyond all possibility of contradiction, that our Lord confirms it by that apposite comparison: 'Every one,' saith He, 'who heareth these sayings of Mine, and doeth them not, shall be likened unto a foolish man, which built his house upon the sand. And the rain descended, and the floods came, and the winds blew, and beat upon that house'—as they will surely do, sooner or later, upon every soul of man; even the floods of outward affliction, or inward temptation; the storms of pride, anger, fear, or desire— 'and it fell: and great was the fall of it'; so that it perished for ever and ever. Such must be the portion of all who rest in anything short of that religion which is above described. And the greater will their fall be, because they heard those sayings, and' yet 'did them not.'

II. 1. I am, secondly, to show the wisdom of him that doeth them, that buildeth his house upon a rock. He indeed is wise,

'who doeth the will of My Father which is in heaven.' He is truly
wise, whose 'righteousness exceeds the righteousness of the
Scribes and Pharisees.' He is poor in spirit; knowing himself
even as also he is known. He sees and feels all his sin, and all his
guilt, till it is washed away by the atoning blood. He is conscious
of his lost estate, of the wrath of God abiding on him, and of his
utter inability to help himself, till he is filled with peace and joy in
the Holy Ghost. He is meek and gentle, patient toward all men,
never 'returning evil for evil, or railing for railing, but
contrariwise blessing,' till he overcomes evil with good. His soul
is athirst for nothing on earth, but only for God, the living God.
He has bowels of love for all mankind, and is ready to lay down
his life for his enemies. He loves the Lord his God with all his
heart, and with all his mind, and soul, and strength. He alone
shall enter into the kingdom of heaven, who, in this spirit, doeth
good unto all men; and who, being for this cause despised and
rejected of men, being hated, reproached, and persecuted,
rejoices and is 'exceeding glad,' knowing in whom he hath
believed, and being assured these light, momentary afflictions
will 'work out for him an eternal weight of glory.'

2. How truly wise is this man! He knows himself: an
everlasting spirit, which came forth from God, and was sent
down into an house of clay, not to do his own will, but the will of
Him that sent him. He knows the world: the place in which he is
to pass a few days or years, not as an inhabitant, but as a stranger
and sojourner, in his way to the everlasting habitations; and
accordingly he uses the world as not abusing it, and as knowing
the fashion of it passes away. He knows God: his Father and his
Friend, the parent of all good, the centre of the spirits of all
flesh, the sole happiness of all intelligent beings. He sees, clearer
than the light of the noon-day sun, that this is the end of man, to
glorify Him who made him for Himself, and to love and enjoy
Him for ever. And with equal clearness he sees the means to that
end, to the enjoyment of God in glory; even now to know, to
love, to imitate God, and to believe in Jesus Christ whom He
hath sent.

3. He is a wise man, even in God's account; for 'he buildeth his
house upon a rock'; upon the Rock of Ages, the everlasting
Rock, the Lord Jesus Christ. Fitly is He so called: for He
changeth not: He is 'the same yesterday, and to-day, and for

ever.' To Him both the men of God of old, and the Apostle citing
His words, bear witness: 'Thou, Lord, in the beginning hast laid
the foundation of the earth; and the heavens are the works of
Thine hands. They shall perish; but Thou remainest: and they
all shall wax old as doth a garment; and as a vesture shalt Thou
fold them up, and they shall be changed: but Thou art the same,
and Thy years shall not fail' (Heb. i. 10-12). Wise, therefore, is
the man who buildeth on Him; who layeth Him for his only
foundation; who builds only upon His blood and righteousness,
upon what He hath done and suffered for us. On this
corner-stone he fixes his faith, and rests the whole weight of his
soul upon it. He is taught of God to say, 'Lord, I have sinned! I
deserve the nethermost hell; but I am justified freely by Thy
grace, through the redemption that is in Jesus Christ; and the
life I now live, I live by faith in Him, who loved me, and gave
Himself for me. The life I now live; namely, a divine, heavenly
life; a life which is hid with Christ in God. I now live, even in the
flesh, a life of love; of pure love both to God and man; a life of
holiness and happiness; praising God, and doing all things to
His glory.'

4. Yet, let not such an one think that he shall not see war any
more; that he is now out of the reach of temptation. It still
remains for God to prove the grace He hath given: he shall be
tried as gold in the fire. He shall be tempted not less than they
who know not God: perhaps abundantly more; for Satan will not
fail to try to the uttermost those whom he is not able to destroy.
Accordingly, 'the rain' will impetuously descend; only at such
times and in such manner as seems good, not to the prince of the
power of the air, but to Him 'whose kingdom ruleth over all.'
'The floods,' or torrents, will come; they will lift up their waves
and rage horribly. But to them also, the Lord that sitteth above
the water-floods, that remaineth a King for ever, will say,
'Hitherto shall ye come, and no farther: here shall your proud
waves be stayed.' 'The winds will blow, and beat upon that
house,' as though they would tear it up from the foundation: but
they cannot prevail: it falleth not; for it is founded upon a rock.
He buildeth on Christ by faith and love; therefore, he shall not
be cast down. He 'shall not fear though the earth be moved, and
though the hills be carried into the midst of the sea.' 'Though the
waters thereof rage and swell, and the mountains shake at the

tempest of the same'; still he 'dwelleth under the defence of the Most High, and is safe under the shadow of the Almighty.'

III. 1. How nearly then does it concern every child of man, practically to apply these things to himself; diligently to examine on what foundation he builds, whether on a rock or on the sand! How deeply are *you* concerned to inquire, 'What is the foundation of *my* hope? Whereon do I build my expectation of entering into the kingdom of heaven? Is it not built on the sand? upon my *orthodoxy*, or right opinions, which, by a gross abuse of words, I have called *faith*? upon my having a set of notions, supposed more rational or scriptural than [many] others have?' Alas! what madness is this! Surely this is building on the sand, or, rather, on the froth of the sea! Say, I am convinced of this: 'Am I not, again, building my hope on what is equally unable to support it? Perhaps on my belonging to 'so excellent a Church; reformed after the true Scripture model; blessed with the purest doctrine, the most primitive Liturgy, the most apostolical form of government!"' These are, doubtless, so many reasons for praising God, as they may be so many helps to holiness; but they are not holiness itself: and if they are separate from it, they will profit me nothing; nay, they will leave me the more without excuse, and exposed to the greater damnation. Therefore, if I build my hope upon this foundation, I am still building upon the sand.

2. You cannot, you dare not, rest here. Upon what next will you build your hope of salvation?--upon your innocence? upon your doing no harm? your not wronging or hurting any one? Well; allow this plea to be true. You are just in all your dealings; you are a downright honest man; you pay every man his own; you neither cheat nor extort; you act fairly with all mankind; and you have a conscience towards God; you do not live in any known sin. Thus far is well: but still it is not the thing. You may go thus far, and yet never come to heaven. When all this harmlessness flows from a right principle, it is the *least part* of the religion of Christ. But in you it does not flow from a right principle, and therefore is no part at all of religion. So that in grounding your hope of salvation on this, you are still building upon the sand.

3. Do you go farther yet? Do you add to the doing no harm,

the attending all the ordinances of God? Do you, at all opportunities, partake of the Lord's supper? use public and private prayer? fast often? hear and search the Scriptures, and meditate thereon? These things, likewise, ought you to have done, from the time you first set your face towards heaven. Yet these things also are nothing, being alone. They are nothing without 'the weightier matters of the law.' And those you have forgotten; at least, you experience them not: faith, mercy, and the love of God; holiness of heart; heaven opened in the soul. Still, therefore, you build upon the sand.

4. Over and above all this, are you zealous of good works? Do you, as you have time, do good to all men? Do you feed the hungry, and clothe the naked, and visit the fatherless and widow in their affliction? Do you visit those that are sick? relieve them that are in prison? Is any a stranger, and you take him in? Friend, come up higher! Do you 'prophesy' in the 'name' of Christ? Do you preach the truth as it is in Jesus? And does the influence of His Spirit attend your word, and make it the power of God unto salvation? Does He enable you to bring sinners from darkness to light, from the power of Satan unto God? Then go and learn what thou hast so often taught, 'By grace are ye saved through faith'; 'Not by works of righteousness which we have done, but of His own mercy He saveth us.' Learn to hang naked upon the cross of Christ, counting all thou hast done but dung and dross! Apply to Him just in the spirit of the dying thief, of the harlot with her seven devils! else thou art still on the sand; and, after saving others, thou wilt lose thy own soul.

5. Lord, increase my faith, if I now believe! else, give me faith, though but as a grain of mustard-seed!——But 'what doth it profit, if a man say he hath faith, and have not works Can' that 'faith save him'? O no! That faith which hath not works, which doth not produce both inward and outward holiness, which does not stamp the whole image of God on the heart, and purify us as He is pure; that faith which does not produce the whole of the religion described in the foregoing chapters, is not the faith of the gospel, not the Christian faith, not the faith which leads to glory. O beware of this, above all other snares of the devil,——of resting on unholy, unsaving faith! If thou layest stress on this, thou art lost for ever: thou still buildest thy house upon the sand.

When 'the rain descends, and the floods come,' it will surely fall, 'and great will be the fall of it.'

6. Now, therefore, build thou upon a rock. By the grace of God know thyself. Know and feel that thou wast shapen in wickedness, and in sin did thy mother conceive thee; and that thou thyself hast been heaping sin upon sin, ever since thou couldest discern good from evil. Own thyself guilty of eternal death; and renounce all hope of ever being able to save thyself. Be it all thy hope, to be washed in His blood, and purified by His Spirit, 'who Himself bore' all 'thy sins in His own body upon the tree.' And if thou knowest He hath taken away thy sins, so much the more abase thyself before Him, in a continual sense of thy total dependence on Him for every good thought, and word, and work, and of thy utter inability to all good unless He 'water thee every moment.'

7. Now weep for your sins, and mourn after God, till He turns your heaviness into joy. And even then weep with them that weep; and for them that weep not for themselves. Mourn for the sins and miseries of mankind; and see but just before your eyes, the immense ocean of eternity, without a bottom or a shore, which has already swallowed up millions of millions of men, and is gaping to devour them that yet remain! See here, the house of God eternal in the heavens! there, hell and destruction without a covering!—and thence learn the importance of every moment, which just appears and is gone for ever!

8. Now add to your seriousness, meekness of wisdom. Hold an even scale as to all your passions, but in particular, as to anger, sorrow, and fear. Calmly acquiesce in whatsoever is the will of God. Learn in every state wherein you are, therewith to be content. Be mild to the good: be gentle toward all men; but especially toward the evil and the unthankful. Beware, not only of outward expressions of anger, such as calling thy brother, *Raca,* or *Thou fool*; but of every inward emotion contrary to love, though it go no farther than the heart. Be angry at sin, as an affront offered to the Majesty of heaven; but love the sinner still: like our Lord, who 'looked round about upon the Pharisees with anger, being grieved for the hardness of their hearts.' He was grieved at the sinners, angry at the sin. Thus be thou 'angry, and sin not'!

9. Now do thou hunger and thirst, not for 'the meat that

perisheth, but for that which endureth unto everlasting life.'
Trample under foot the world, and the things of the world; all
these riches, honours, pleasures. What is the world to thee? Let
the dead bury their dead; but follow thou after the image of
God. And beware of quenching that blessed thirst, if it is already
excited in thy soul, by what is vulgarly called religion; a poor,
dull farce, a religion of form, of outside show, which leaves the
heart still cleaving to the dust, as earthly and sensual as ever. Let
nothing satisfy thee but the power of godliness, but a religion
that is spirit and life; the dwelling in God and God in thee; the
being an inhabitant of eternity; the entering in by the blood of
sprinkling 'within the veil,' and 'sitting in heavenly places with
Christ Jesus'!

10. Now, seeing thou canst do all things through Christ
strengthening thee, be merciful as thy Father in heaven is
merciful! Love thy neighbour as thyself! Love friends and
enemies as thy own soul: and let thy love be long-suffering and
patient towards all men. Let it be kind, soft, benign; inspiring
thee with the most amiable sweetness, and the most fervent and
tender affection. Let it rejoice in the truth wheresoever it is
found; the truth that is after godliness. Enjoy whatsoever brings
glory to God, and promotes peace and good-will among men. In
love, cover all things: of the dead and the absent speaking
nothing but good; believe all things which may any way tend to
clear your neighbour's character; hope all things in his favour;
and endure all things, triumphing over all opposition: for true
love never faileth, in time or in eternity.

11. Now be thou pure in heart; purified through faith from
every unholy affection; 'cleansing thyself from all filthiness of
flesh and spirit, and perfecting holiness in the fear of God.'
Being, through the power of His grace, purified from pride, by
deep poverty of spirit; from anger, from every unkind or
turbulent passion, by meekness and mercifulness; from every
desire but to please and enjoy God, by hunger and thirst after
righteousness; now love the Lord thy God with all thy heart, and
with all thy strength!

12. In a word: let thy religion be the religion of the heart. Let it
lie deep in thy inmost soul. Be thou little, and base, and mean,
and vile (beyond what words can express) in thy own eyes;
amazed and humbled to the dust by the love of God which is in

Christ Jesus. Be serious. Let the whole stream of thy thoughts, words, and actions flow from the deepest conviction that thou standest on the edge of the great gulf, thou and all the children of men, just ready to drop in, either into everlasting glory or everlasting burnings! Let thy soul be filled with mildness, gentleness, patience, long-suffering towards all men; at the same time that all which is in thee is athirst for God, the living God, longing to awake up after His likeness and to be satisfied with it! Be thou a lover of God and of all mankind! In this spirit do and suffer all things! Thus show thy faith by thy works; thus 'do the will of thy Father which is in heaven'! And, as sure as thou now walkest with God on earth, thou shalt also reign with Him in glory!

SERMON XXIX

THE ORIGINAL, NATURE, PROPERTY, AND USE OF THE LAW

This and the two following sermons are part of Wesley's polemic against the Antinomianism which made such havoc in his Societies in the forties. See introduction to Sermons XII and XLIX. The chief exponents of the doctrine of the imputed righteousness of Christ, and the freedom of the believer from the law, were Count Zinzendorf and his Moravian followers, Molther and Spangenberg; the Rev. William Cudworth, who was at this time connected with Whitefield, but afterwards became minister of the Independent Chapel in Margaret Street, London, and (under Cudworth's influence) the Rev. James Hervey. Their doctrinal views were capable of an interpretation which was in harmony with holiness of life, although they maintained that this holiness was imputed and not inherent; and Wesley himself admits in the conclusion of the *Second Dialogue between an Antinomian and his Friend,* and in Sermon XLIX, that the controversy between himself and them was to some extent at least 'a strife about words.' But to preach to unlettered and ignorant Christians that they were 'free from the law' inevitably led to the most monstrous practical abuses; and some of them claimed even freedom to take the property of others and to commit adultery, to say nothing of other sins, such as gluttony, drunkenness, idleness, and the like. It was this tendency of the Moravian doctrines that provoked the righteous indignation of Wesley, and infused his pamphlets and sermons against them with a white-hot passion which sometimes degenerated into personal abuse. Thus at the end of the *First Dialogue between an Antinomian and his Friend,* he says: 'What does all this come to at the last? A mere, empty 'strife of words.' All that is really uncommon in your doctrine is a heap of broad absurdities, in most of which you grossly contradict yourselves, as well as Scripture and common sense. In the meantime, you boast and vapour, as if "ye were the men, and wisdom should die with you." I pray God to "humble you, and prove you, and show you what is in your hearts"!' He was especially incensed against Cudworth, of whom he says in his *Journal,* April 27, 1759, 'He is as incapable as a brute beast of being convinced even in the smallest point.' Cudworth was not behindhand in strong language; he avowed that he abhorred Wesley 'as much as he did the Pope, and ten times more than he did the devil.' Happily these sermons are free from any abuse of this sort, and deal with the question in dispute in a judicial temper, and with sound and convincing logic.

In studying them, it would be well for the reader to peruse the two Dialogues already mentioned. The first was published early in 1745; the tenets of the Antinomian are given in the exact language used by Zinzendorf in the well-known Latin dialogue with Wesley, transcribed in the *Journal*, 1 September 3, 1741, and by other Moravian writers. 'The words,' Wesley says in a footnote, 'are transcribed from late authors. I am not willing to name them.' This pamphlet was at once answered by Cudworth in a *Dialogue between a Preacher of Inherent Righteousness and a Preacher of God's Righteousness,* and Wesley responded in the *Second Dialogue,* also published in 1745, in which Cudworth is quoted throughout by name. At the Conference of this year at Bristol, it was asked, 'What can we do to stop the progress of Antinomianism?' and the answer was, 'Write one or two more dialogues': the *Second Dialogue* was the result. These three sermons were apparently written either at Kingswood in November or at his friend Charles Greenwood's at Stoke Newington, in December 1749 (*Journal,* October 30 and December 11, 1749). Mr. Greenwood was one of the first trustees of Wesley's New Chapel in City Road; his house was still standing in 1915, and a photograph of it may be seen in the Standard Edition of the *Journal,* vi. 393. They were evidently intended rather for publication than preaching; and I have not found any record of any one of them being actually delivered; though no doubt the substance of them was given in the study of Rom. vii. with the Bands in Bristol on Tuesday, November 18, 1740, and of Romans iii. at Short's Gardens, London, on November 24 of the same year. They were first published in Vol. III of the Sermons, 1750; and the next year they appeared separately from the rest of the volume in pamphlet form.

Wherefore the law is holy, and the commandment holy, and just, and good.—ROM. vii. 12.

1. Perhaps there are few subjects within the whole compass of religion so little understood as this. The reader of this Epistle is usually told, by 'the law' St. Paul means the Jewish law; and so, apprehending himself to have no concern therewith, passes on without farther thought about it. Indeed some are not satisfied with this account; but observing the Epistle is directed to the Romans, thence infer that the Apostle in the beginning of this chapter alludes to the old Roman law. But as they have no more concern with this, than with the ceremonial law of Moses, so they spend not much thought on what they suppose is occasionally mentioned barely to illustrate another thing.

2. But a careful observer of the Apostle's discourse will not be content with these light explications of it. And the more he weighs the words, the more convinced he will be, that St. Paul, by

'the law' mentioned in this chapter, does not mean either the ancient law of Rome, or the ceremonial law of Moses. This will clearly appear to all who attentively consider the tenor of his discourse. He begins the chapter, 'Know ye not, brethren (for I speak to them that know the law),' to them who have been instructed therein from their youth, 'that the law hath dominion over a man as long as he liveth?' (What! the law of Rome only, or the ceremonial law? No, surely; but the moral law.) 'For,' to give a plain instance, 'the woman which hath an husband is bound by the' moral 'law to her husband so long as he liveth; but if the husband be dead, she is loosed from the law of her husband. So then if, while her husband liveth, she be married to another man, she shall be called an adulteress: but if her husband be dead, she is free from that law: so that she is no adulteress, though she be married to another man.' From this particular instance the Apostle proceeds to draw that general conclusion: 'Wherefore, my brethren,' by a plain parity of reason, 'ye also are become dead to the law,' the whole Mosaic institution, 'by the body of Christ,' offered for you, and bringing you under a new dispensation: 'That ye should' without any blame 'be married to another, even to Him who is raised from the dead'; and hath thereby given proof of His authority to make the change; 'that we should bring forth fruit unto God.' And this we can do now, whereas before we could not: 'for when we were in the flesh'—under the power of the flesh, that is, of corrupt nature, which was necessarily the case till we knew the power of Christ's resurrection, 'the motions of sins, which were by the law'—which were shown and inflamed by the Mosaic law, not conquered, 'did work in our members'—broke out various ways, 'to bring forth fruit unto death.' 'But now we are delivered from the law'; from that whole moral, as well as ceremonial economy; 'that being dead whereby we were held'—that entire institution being now as it were dead, and having no more authority over us than the husband, when dead, hath over his wife: 'That we should serve Him'—who died for us and rose again, 'in newness of spirit'—in a new spiritual dispensation; 'and not in the oldness of the letter' —with a bare outward service, according to the letter of the Mosaic institution (verses 1-6).

3. The Apostle, having gone thus far in proving that the Christian had set aside the Jewish dispensation, and that the

moral law itself, though it could never pass away, yet stood on a different foundation from what it did before,—now stops to propose and answer an objection: 'What shall we say then? Is the law sin? So some might infer from a misapprehension of those words, 'the motions of sins, which were by the law.' 'God forbid!' saith the Apostle, that we should say so. Nay, the law is an irreconcilable enemy to sin; searching it out, wherever it is. 'I had not known sin, but by the law: for I had not known lust,' evil desire, to be sin, 'except the law had said, Thou shalt not covet' (verse 7). After opening this farther, in the four following verses, he subjoins this general conclusion, with regard more especially to the moral law, from which the preceding instance was taken: 'Wherefore the law is holy, and the commandment holy, and just, and good.'

4. In order to explain and enforce these deep words, so little regarded, because so little understood, I shall endeavour to show, first, the original of this law; secondly, the nature thereof; thirdly, the properties—that it is holy, and just, and good; and, fourthly, the uses of it.

I. 1. I shall, first, endeavour to show the original of the moral law, often called 'the law,' by way of eminence. Now this is not, as some may have possibly imagined, of so late an institution as the time of Moses. Noah declared it to men long before that time and Enoch before him. But we may trace its original higher still, even beyond the foundation of the world: to that period, unknown indeed to men, but doubtless enrolled in the annals of eternity, when 'the morning stars' first 'sang together,' being newly called into existence. It pleased the great Creator to make these, His first-born sons, intelligent beings, that they might know Him that created them. For this end He endued them with understanding to discern truth from falsehood, good from evil; and, as a necessary result of this, with liberty, a capacity of choosing the one and refusing the other. By this they were, likewise, enabled to offer Him a free and willing service; a service rewardable in itself, as well as most acceptable to their gracious Master.

2. To employ all the faculties which He had given them, particularly their understanding and liberty, He gave them a law, a complete model of all truth, so far as is intelligible to a

finite being; and of all good, so far as angelic minds were capable of embracing it. It was also the design of their beneficent Governor herein to make way for a continual increase of their happiness; seeing every instance of obedience to that law would both add to the perfection of their nature, and entitle them to an higher reward, which the righteous Judge would give in its season.

3. In like manner, when God, in His appointed time, had created a new order of intelligent beings, when He had raised man from the dust of the earth, breathed into him the breath of life, and caused him to become a living soul, endued with power to choose good or evil; he gave to this free, intelligent creature the same law as to His first-born children,—not wrote, indeed, upon tables of stone, or any corruptible substance, but engraven on his heart by the finger of God; wrote in the inmost spirit both of men and of angels; to the intent it might never be far off, never hard to be understood, but always at hand, and always shining with clear light, even as the sun in the midst of heaven.

4. Such was the original of the law of God. With regard to man, it was coeval with his nature; but with regard to the elder sons of God, it shone in its full splendour 'or ever the mountains were brought forth, or the earth and the round world were made.' But it was not long before man rebelled against God, and, by breaking this glorious law, wellnigh effaced it out of his heart; the eyes of his understanding being darkened in the same measure as his soul was 'alienated from the life of God.' And yet God did not despise the work of His own hands; but, being reconciled to man through the Son of His love, He, in some measure, re-inscribed the law on the heart of His dark, sinful creature. 'He' again 'showed thee, O man, what is good,' although not as in the beginning, 'even to do justly, and to love mercy, and to walk humbly with thy God.'

5. And this He showed, not only to our first parents, but likewise to all their posterity, by 'that true light which enlightens every man that cometh into the world.' But, notwithstanding this light, all flesh had, in process of time, 'corrupted their way before Him'; till He chose out of mankind a peculiar people, to whom He gave a more perfect knowledge of His law; and the heads of this, because they were slow of understanding, He

wrote on two tables of stone, which He commanded the fathers to teach their children, through all succeeding generations.

6. And thus it is, that the law of God is now made known to them that know not God. They hear, with the hearing of the ear, the things that were written aforetime for our instruction. But this does not suffice: they cannot, by this means, comprehend the height, and depth, and length, and breadth thereof. God alone can reveal this by His Spirit. And so He does to all that truly believe, in consequence of that gracious promise made to all the Israel of God: 'Behold, the days come, saith the Lord, that I will make a new covenant with the house of Israel. And this shall be the covenant that I will make; I will put My law in their inward parts, and write it in their hearts; and I will be their God, and they shall be My people' (Jer. xxxi. 31, &c.).

II. 1. The nature of that law which was originally given to angels in heaven and man in paradise, and which God has so mercifully promised to write afresh in the hearts of all true believers, was the second thing I proposed to show. In order to which, I would first observe, that although the 'law' and the 'commandment' are sometimes differently taken (the commandment meaning but a part of the law), yet in the text they are used as equivalent terms, implying one and the same thing. But we cannot understand here, either by one or the other, the ceremonial law. It it not the ceremonial law, whereof the Apostle says, in the words above recited, 'I had not known sin, but by the law': this is too plain to need a proof. Neither is it the ceremonial law which saith, in the words immediately subjoined, 'Thou shalt not covet.' Therefore the ceremonial law has no place in the present question.

2. Neither can we understand by 'the law' mentioned in the text the Mosaic dispensation. It is true, the word is sometimes so understood; as when the Apostle says, speaking to the Galatians (iii. 17), 'The covenant that was confirmed before'; namely, with Abraham, the father of the faithful, 'the law,' that is, the Mosaic dispensation, 'which was four hundred and thirty years after, cannot disannul.' But it cannot be so understood in the text; for the Apostle never bestows so high commendations as these upon that imperfect and shadowy dispensation. He nowhere affirms the Mosaic to be a spiritual law; or, that it is holy, and just, and

good. Neither is it true, that God will write that law in the hearts of those whose iniquities He remembers no more. It remains, that 'the law,' eminently so termed; is no other than the moral law.

3. Now, this law is an incorruptible picture of the High and Holy ONE that inhabiteth eternity. It is He whom, in His essence, no man hath seen, or can see, made visible to men and angels. It is the face of God unveiled; God manifested to His creatures as they are able to bear it; manifested to give, and not to destroy, life—that they may see God and live. It is the heart of God disclosed to man. Yea, in some sense, we may apply to this law what the Apostle says of His Son: it is απαυγασμα της δοξης, και χαρακτηρ της υποστασεως αυτου—*the streaming forth or out-beaming of His glory, the express image of His person.*

4. 'If virtue,' said the ancient Heathen, 'could assume such a shape as that we could behold her with our eyes, what wonderful love would she excite in us!' If virtue could do this! It is done already. The law of God is all virtues in one, in such a shape as to be beheld with open face by all those whose eyes God hath enlightened. What is the law but divine virtue and wisdom assuming a visible form? What is it but the original ideas of truth and good, which were lodged in the uncreated mind from eternity, now drawn forth and clothed with such a vehicle as to appear even to human understanding.

5. If we survey the law of God in another point of view, it is supreme, unchangeable reason; it is unalterable rectitude; it is the everlasting fitness of all things that are or ever were created. I am sensible, what a shortness, and even impropriety, there is, in these and all other human expressions, when we endeavour by these faint pictures to shadow out the deep things of God. Nevertheless, we have no better, indeed no other way, during this our infant state of existence. As we now 'know' but 'in part,' so we are constrained to 'prophesy,' that is, speak of the things of God, 'in part' also. 'We cannot order our speech by reason of darkness,' while we are in this house of clay. While I am 'a child,' I must 'speak as a child': but I shall soon 'put away childish things'; for 'when that which is perfect is come, that which is in part shall be done away.'

6. But to return. The law of God (speaking after the manner of men) is a copy of the eternal mind, a transcript of the divine

nature; yea, it is the fairest offspring of the everlasting Father, the brightest efflux of His essential wisdom, the visible beauty of the Most High. It is the delight and wonder of cherubim and seraphim, and all the company of heaven and the glory and joy of every wise believer, every well-instructed child of God upon earth.

III. 1. Such is the nature of the ever-blessed law of God. I am, in the third place, to show the properties of it:—not all; for that would exceed the wisdom of an angel; but those only which are mentioned in the text. These are three: it is holy, just, and good. And, first, the law is holy.

2. In this expression the Apostle does not appear to speak of its effects, but rather of its nature: as St. James, speaking of the same thing under another name, says, 'The wisdom from above' (which is no other than this law, written in our heart) 'is first pure' (iii. 17); αγνη,—*chaste, spotless;* eternally and essentially holy. And, consequently, when it is transcribed into the life, as well as the soul, it is (as the same Apostle terms it, i. 27) θρησκεια καθαρα και αμιαντος,—*pure religion and undefiled*; or, the pure, clean, unpolluted worship of God.

3. It is, indeed, in the highest degree, pure, chaste, clean, holy. Otherwise it could not be the immediate offspring, and much less the express resemblance, of God, who is essential holiness. It is pure from all sin, clean and unspotted from any touch of evil. It is a chaste virgin, incapable of any defilement, of any mixture with that which is unclean or unholy. It has no fellowship with sin of any kind: for 'what communion hath light with darkness?' As sin is, in its very nature, enmity to God, so His law is enmity to sin.

4. Therefore it is that the Apostle rejects with such abhorrence that blasphemous supposition, that the law of God is either sin itself, or the cause of sin. God forbid that we should suppose it is the cause of sin, because it is the discoverer of it; because it detects the hidden things of darkness, and drags them out into open day. It is true, by this means (as the Apostle observes, Rom. vii. 13), 'sin appears to be sin.' All its disguises are torn away, and it appears in its native deformity. It is true likewise, that 'sin, by the commandment, becomes exceeding sinful': being now committed against light and knowledge, being stripped even of

the poor plea of ignorance, it loses its excuse, as well as disguise, and becomes far more odious both to God and man. Yea, and it is true, that 'sin worketh death by that which is good'; which in itself is pure and holy. When it is dragged out to light, it rages the more: when it is restrained, it bursts out with greater violence. Thus the Apostle (speaking in the person of one who was convinced of sin, but not yet delivered from it), 'Sin, taking occasion by the commandment' detecting and endeavouring to restrain it, disdained the restraint, and so much the more 'wrought in me all manner of concupiscence' (verse 8); all manner of foolish and hurtful desire, which that commandment sought to restrain. Thus, 'when the commandment came, sin revived' (verse 9); it fretted and raged the more. But this is no stain on the commandment. Though it is abused, it cannot be defiled. This only proves that 'the heart of man is desperately wicked.' But 'the law' of God 'is holy' still.

5. And it is, secondly, just. It renders to all their due. It prescribes exactly what is right, precisely what ought to be done, said, or thought, both with regard to the Author of our being, with regard to ourselves, and with regard to every creature which He has made. It is adapted, in all respects, to the nature of things, of the whole universe, and every individual. It is suited to all the circumstances of each, and to all their mutual relations, whether such as have existed from the beginning, or such as commenced in any following period. It is exactly agreeable to the fitnesses of things, whether essential or accidental. It clashes with none of these in any degree; nor is ever unconnected with them. If the word be taken in that sense, there is nothing arbitrary in the law of God. Although still the whole and every part thereof is totally dependent upon His will; so that, 'Thy will be done,' is the supreme, universal law both in earth and heaven.

6. 'But is the will of God the cause of His law? Is His will the original of right and wrong? Is a thing *therefore* right, because God wills it? or does He will it because it is right?'

I fear this celebrated question is more curious than useful. And perhaps in the manner it is usually treated of, it does not so well consist with the regard that is due from a creature to the Creator and Governor of all things. It is hardly decent for man to call the supreme God to give an account to him. Nevertheless,

with awe and reverence we may speak a little. The Lord pardon
us if we speak amiss!

7. It seems, then, that the whole difficulty arises from
considering God's will as distinct from God: otherwise it
vanishes away. For none can doubt but God is the cause of the
law of God. But the will of God is God Himself. It is God
considered as willing thus or thus. Consequently, to say that the
will of God, or that God Himself, is the cause of the law, is one
and the same thing.

8. Again: If the law, the immutable rule of right and wrong,
depends upon the nature and fitnesses of things, and on their
essential relations to each other (I do not say, their eternal
relations; because the eternal relation of things existing in time,
is little less than a contradiction); if, I say, this depends on the
nature and relations of things, then it must depend on God, or
the will of God; because those things themselves, with all their
relations, are the works of His hands. By His will, 'for His
pleasure' alone, they all 'are and were created.'

9. And yet it may be granted (which is probably all that a
considerate person would contend for), that in every particular
case, God wills this or this (suppose, that men should honour
their parents), because it is right, agreeable to the fitness of
things, to the relation wherein they stand.

10. The law, then, is right and just concerning all things. And
it is good as well as just. This we may easily infer from the
fountain whence it flowed. For what was this, but the goodness
of God? What but goodness alone inclined Him to impart that
divine copy of Himself to the holy angels? To what else can we
impute His bestowing upon man the same transcript of His own
nature? And what but tender love constrained Him afresh to
manifest His will to fallen man—either to Adam, or any of his
seed, who like him were 'come short of the glory of God'? Was it
not mere love that moved Him to publish His law after the
understandings of men were darkened? and to send His
prophets to declare that law to the blind, thoughtless children of
men? Doubtless His goodness it was which raised up Enoch and
Noah to be preachers of righteousness; which caused Abraham,
His friend, and Isaac, and Jacob, to bear witness to His truth. It
was His goodness alone, which, when 'darkness had covered the
earth, and thick darkness the people,' gave a written law to

Moses, and, through Him, to the nation whom He had chosen. It was love which explained these living oracles by David and all the prophets that followed; until, when the fullness of time was come, He sent His only-begotten Son, 'not to destroy the law, but to fulfil,' confirm every jot and tittle thereof; till, having wrote it in the hearts of all His children, and put all His enemies under His feet, 'He shall deliver up' His mediatorial 'kingdom to the Father, that God may be all in all.'

11. And this law, which the goodness of God gave at first, and has preserved through all ages, is, like the fountain from whence it springs, full of goodness and benignity: it is mild and kind; it is, as the Psalmist expresses it, 'sweeter than honey and the honey-comb.' It is winning and amiable. It includes 'whatsoever things are lovely or of good report. If there be any virtue, if there be any praise' before God and His holy angels, they are all comprised in this; wherein are hid all the treasures of the divine wisdom, and knowledge, and love.

12. And it is good in its effects, as well as in its nature. As the tree is, so are its fruits. The fruits of the law of God written in the heart are 'righteousness, and peace, and assurance for ever.' Or rather, the law itself is righteousness, filling the soul with a peace which passeth all understanding, and causing us to rejoice evermore, in the testimony of a good conscience toward God. It is not so properly a pledge, as 'an earnest, of our inheritance,' being a part of the purchased possession. It is God made manifest in our flesh, and bringing with Him eternal life; assuring us by that pure and perfect love, that we are 'sealed unto the day of redemption'; that He will 'spare us as a man spareth his own son that serveth him,' 'in that day when He maketh up His jewels'; and that there remaineth for us 'a crown of glory which fadeth not away.'

IV. 1. It remains only to show, in the fourth and last place, the uses of the law. And the first use of it, without question, is, to convince the world of sin. This is, indeed, the peculiar work of the Holy Ghost; who can work it without any means at all, or by whatever means it pleaseth Him, however insufficient in themselves, or even improper, to produce such an effect. And, accordingly, some there are whose hearts have been broken in pieces in a moment, either in sickness or in health, without any visible cause, or any outward means whatever; and others (one in an age) have been awakened to a sense of the 'wrath of God abiding on them,' by hearing that 'God was in Christ, reconciling the world unto Himself.' But it is the ordinary method of the Spirit of God to convict sinners by the law. It is this which, being set home on the conscience, generally breaketh the rocks in pieces. It is more especially this part of the word of God which is ζων και ενεργης,—*quick and powerful,* full of life and energy, 'and sharper than any two-edged sword.' This, in the hand of God and of those whom He hath sent, pierces through all the folds of a deceitful heart, and 'divides asunder even the soul and the spirit'; yea, as it were, the very 'joints and marrow.' By this is the sinner discovered to himself. All his fig-leaves are torn away, and he sees that he is 'wretched, and poor, and miserable, and blind, and naked.' The law flashes conviction on every side. He feels himself a mere sinner. He has nothing to pay. His 'mouth is stopped,' and he stands 'guilty before God.'

2. To slay the sinner is, then, the first use of the law; to destroy the life and strength wherein he trusts, and convince him that he is dead while he liveth; not only under the sentence of death, but actually dead unto God, void of all spiritual life, 'dead in trespasses and sins.' The second use of it is, to bring him unto life, unto Christ, that he may live. It is true, in performing both these offices, it acts the part of a severe schoolmaster. It drives us by force, rather than draws us by love. And yet love is the spring of all. It is the spirit of love which, by this painful means, tears away our confidence in the flesh, which leaves us no broken reed whereon to trust, and so constrains the sinner, stripped of all, to cry out in the bitterness of his soul, or groan in the depth of his heart,

> I give up every plea beside,—
> Lord, I am damn'd; but Thou hast died.

3. The third use of the law is, to keep us alive. It is the grand means whereby the blessed Spirit prepares the believer for larger communications of the life of God.

I am afraid this great and important truth is little understood, not only by the world, but even by many whom God hath taken out of the world, who are real children of God by faith. Many of these lay it down as an unquestioned truth, that when we come to Christ, we have done with the law; and that, in this sense, 'Christ is the end of the law to every one that believeth.' 'The end of the law': so He is, 'for righteousness,' for justification, 'to every one that believeth.' Herein the law is at an end. It justifies none, but only brings them to Christ; who is also, in another respect, the end or scope of the law—the point at which it continually aims. But when it has brought us to Him, it has yet a farther office, namely, to keep us with Him. For it is continually exciting all believers, the more they see of its height, and depth, and length, and breadth, to exhort one another so much the more,—

> Closer and closer let us cleave
> To His beloved embrace;
> Expect His fullness to receive,
> And grace to answer grace.

4. Allowing then, that every believer has done with the law, as it means the Jewish ceremonial law, or the entire Mosaic dispensation (for these Christ hath taken out of the way); yea, allowing we have done with the moral law, as a means of procuring our justification (for we are 'justified freely by His grace, through the redemption that is in Jesus'); yet, in another sense, we have not done with this law: for it is still of unspeakable use, first, in convincing us of the sin that yet remains both in our hearts and lives, and thereby keeping us close to Christ, that His blood may cleanse us every moment; secondly, in deriving strength from our Head into His living members, whereby He empowers them to do what His law commands; and, thirdly, in confirming our hope of whatsoever it commands and we have not yet attained,—of receiving grace upon grace, till we are in actual possession of the fullness of His promises.

5. How clearly does this agree with the experience of every true believer! While he cries out, 'O what love have I unto Thy law! all the day long is my study in it'; he sees daily, in that divine mirror, more and more of his own sinfulness. He sees more and more clearly, that he is still a sinner in all things—that neither his heart nor his ways are right before God; and that every moment sends him to Christ. This shows him the meaning of what is written, 'Thou shalt make a plate of pure gold, and grave upon it, 'HOLINESS TO THE LORD. And it shall be upon Aaron's forehead'

(the type of our great High-Priest), 'that Aaron may bear the iniquity of the holy things, which the children of Israel shall hallow in all their holy gifts' (so far are our prayers or holy things from atoning for the rest of our sin); 'and it shall be always upon his forehead, that they may be accepted before the Lord' (Exod. xxviii. 36, 38).

6. To explain this by a single instance: the law says, 'Thou shalt not kill'; and hereby (as our Lord teaches), forbids not only outward acts, but every unkind word or thought. Now, the more I look into this perfect law, the more I feel how far I come short of it; and the more I feel this, the more I feel my need of His blood to atone for all my sin, and of His Spirit to purify my heart, and make me 'perfect and entire, lacking nothing.'

7. Therefore I cannot spare the law one moment, no more than I can spare Christ; seeing I now want it as much to keep me to Christ, as I ever wanted it to bring me to Him. Otherwise, this 'evil heart of unbelief' would immediately depart from the living God.' Indeed each is continually sending me to the other—the law to Christ, and Christ to the law. On the one hand, the height and depth of the law constrain me to fly to the love of God in Christ; on the other, the love of God in Christ endears the law to me 'above gold or precious stones'; seeing I know every part of it is a gracious promise which my Lord will fulfil in its season.

8. Who art thou then, O man, that 'judgest the law, and speakest evil of the law?'—that rankest it with sin, Satan, and death, and sendest them all to hell together? The Apostle James esteemed judging or 'speaking evil of the law' so enormous a piece of wickedness, that he knew not how to aggravate the guilt of judging our brethren more, than by showing it included this. 'So now,' says he, 'thou art not a doer of the law, but a judge!' A judge of that which God hath ordained to judge thee! So thou hast set up thyself in the judgement-seat of Christ, and cast down the rule whereby He will judge the world! O take knowledge what advantage Satan hath gained over thee; and, for the time to come, never think or speak lightly of, much less dress up as a scarecrow, this blessed instrument of the grace of God. Yea, love and value it for the sake of Him from whom it came, and of Him to whom it leads. Let it be thy glory and joy, next to the cross of Christ. Declare its praise, and make it honourable before all men.

9. And if thou art thoroughly convinced that it is the offspring of God, that it is the copy of all His inimitable perfections, and that it is 'holy, and just, and good,' but especially to them that believe; then, instead of casting it away as a polluted thing, see that thou cleave to it more and more. Never let the law of mercy and truth, of love to God and man, of lowliness, meekness, and purity, forsake thee. 'Bind it about thy neck; write it on the table of thy heart.' Keep close to the law, if thou wilt keep close to Christ; hold it fast; let it not go. Let this continually lead thee to the atoning blood, continually confirm thy hope, till all the 'righteousness of the law is fulfilled in thee,' and thou art 'filled with all the fullness of God.'

10. And if thy Lord hath already fulfilled His word, if He hath already 'written His law in thy heart,' then 'stand fast in the liberty wherewith Christ hath made thee free.' Thou art not only made free from Jewish ceremonies, from the guilt of sin, and the fear of hell (these are so far from being the whole, that they are the least and lowest part of Christian liberty); but, what is infinitely more, from the power of sin, from serving the devil, from offending God. O stand fast in this liberty: in comparison of which, all the rest is not even worthy to be named! Stand fast in loving God with all thy heart, and serving Him with all thy strength! This is perfect freedom; thus to keep His law, and to walk in all His commandments blameless. 'Be not entangled again with the yoke of bondage.' I do not mean of Jewish bondage; nor yet of bondage to the fear of hell: these, I trust, are far from thee. But beware of being entangled again with the yoke of sin, of any inward or outward transgression of the law. Abhor sin far more than death or hell; abhor sin itself, far more than the punishment of it. Beware of the bondage of pride, of desire, of anger; of every evil temper, or word, or work. 'Look unto Jesus'; and in order thereto, look more and more into the perfect law, 'the law of liberty'; and 'continue therein'; so shalt thou daily 'grow in grace, and in the knowledge of our Lord Jesus Christ.'

SERMON XXX

THE LAW ESTABLISHED THROUGH FAITH

DISCOURSE I

See introduction to previous sermon.

Do we then make void the law through faith? God forbid: yea, we establish the law.—ROM. iii. 31.

1. St. Paul, having in the beginning of this Epistle laid down his general proposition, namely, that 'the gospel of Christ is the power of God unto salvation to every one that believeth'—the powerful means whereby God makes every believer a partaker of present and eternal salvation—goes on to show that there is no other way under heaven whereby men can be saved. He speaks particularly of salvation from the guilt of sin, which he commonly terms justification. And that all men stood in need of this, that none could plead their own innocence, he proves at large by various arguments, addressed to the Jews as well as the Heathens. Hence he infers (in the 19th verse of this chapter), 'that every mouth,' whether of Jew or Heathen, must be 'stopped' from excusing or justifying himself, 'and all the world become guilty before God.' 'Therefore,' saith he, by his own obedience, 'by the works of the law, shall no flesh be justified in His sight.' 'But now the righteousness of God without the law'—without our previous obedience thereto—'is manifested'; even 'the righteousness of God which is by faith of Jesus Christ unto all and upon all that believe.' 'For there is no difference'—as to their need of justification, or the manner wherein they attain it—'for all have sinned, and come short of the glory of God'; the glorious image of God wherein they were created: and all (who attain) 'are justified freely by His grace through the redemption that is in Jesus Christ; whom God hath set forth to be a propitiation through faith in His blood: that He might be just, and yet the justifier of him which believeth in Jesus'—that

without any impeachment to His justice, He might show him mercy for the sake of that propitiation. 'Therefore we conclude' (which was the grand position he had undertaken to establish), 'that a man is justified by faith, without the works of the law' (verses 20-28).

2. It was easy to foresee an objection which might be made, and which has in fact been made in all ages; namely, that to say we are justified without the works of the law, is to abolish the law. The Apostle, without entering into a formal dispute, simply denies the charge. 'Do we then,' says he, 'make void the law through faith? God forbid! yea, we establish the law.'

3. The strange imagination of some, that St. Paul, when he says, 'A man is justified without the works of the law,' means only the ceremonial law, is abundantly confuted by these very words. For did St. Paul establish the ceremonial law? It is evident he did not. He did make void that law through faith, and openly avowed his doing so. It was the moral law only of which he might truly say, We do not make void, but establish this through faith.

4. But all men are not herein of his mind. Many there are who will not agree to this. Many in all ages of the Church, even among those who bore the name of Christians, have contended, that 'the faith once delivered to the saints' was designed to make void the whole law. They would no more spare the moral than the ceremonial law, but were for 'hewing,' as it were, both 'in pieces before the Lord'; vehemently maintaining,' If you establish any law, Christ shall profit you nothing; Christ is become of no effect to you; ye are fallen from grace.'

5. But is the zeal of these men according to knowledge? Have they observed the connexion between the law and faith? and that, considering the close connexion between them, to destroy one is indeed to destroy both—that, to abolish the moral law, is, in truth, to abolish faith and the law together? as leaving no proper means, either of bringing us to faith, or of stirring up that gift of God in our soul.

6. It therefore behoves all who desire either to come to Christ, or to walk in Him whom they have received, to take heed how they 'make void the law through faith'; to secure us effectually against which, let us inquire, first, Which are the most usual ways of making 'void the law through faith'? And, secondly, how we may follow the Apostle, and by faith 'establish the law.'

I. 1. Let us, first, inquire, Which are the most usual ways of making void the law through faith? Now the way for a preacher to make it all void at a stroke, is, not to preach it at all. This is just the same thing as to blot it out of the oracles of God. More especially, when it is done with design; when it is made a rule, not to preach the law: and the very phrase, 'a preacher of the law,' is used as a term of reproach, as though it meant little less than an enemy to the gospel.

2. All this proceeds from the deepest ignorance of the nature, properties, and use of the law; and proves, that those who act thus, either know not Christ—are utter strangers to living faith—or, at least, that they are but babes in Christ and, as such, 'unskilled in the word of righteousness.'

3. Their grand plea is this: that preaching the gospel, that is, according to their judgement, the speaking of nothing but the sufferings and merits of Christ, answers all the ends of the law. But this we utterly deny. It does not answer the very first end of the law, namely, the convincing men of sin; the awakening those who are still asleep on the brink of hell. There may have been here and there an exempt case. One in a thousand may have been awakened by the gospel: but this is no general rule: the ordinary method of God is, to convict sinners by the law, and that only. The gospel is not the means which God hath ordained, or which our Lord Himself used, for this end. We have no authority in Scripture for applying it thus, nor any ground to think it will prove effectual. Nor have we any more ground to expect this, from the nature of the thing. 'They that be whole,' as our Lord Himself observes, 'need not a physician, but they that are sick.' It is absurd, therefore, to offer a physician to them that are whole or that at least imagine themselves so to be. You are first to convince them that they are sick; otherwise they will not thank you for your labour. It is equally absurd to offer Christ to them whose heart is whole, having never yet been broken. It is, in the proper sense, 'casting pearls before swine.' Doubtless 'they will trample them under foot'; and it is no more than you have reason to expect, if they also 'turn again and rend you.'

4. 'But although there is no command in Scripture to offer Christ to the careless sinner, yet are there not scriptural precedents for it?' I think not: I know not any. I believe you cannot produce one, either from the four Evangelists, or the

Acts of the Apostles. Neither can you prove this to have been the practice of any of the Apostles, from any passage in all their writings.

5. 'Nay, does not the Apostle Paul say, in his former Epistle to the Corinthians, "We preach Christ crucified"? (i. 23); and in his latter, "We preach not ourselves, but Christ Jesus the Lord"?' (iv. 5).

We consent to rest the cause on this issue; to tread in his steps, to follow his example. Only preach you just as Paul preached, and the dispute is at an end.

For although we are certain he preached Christ in as perfect a manner as the very chief of the Apostles, yet who preached the law more than St. Paul? Therefore he did not think the gospel answered the same end.

6. The very first sermon of St. Paul's which is recorded, concludes in these words: 'By Him all that believe are justified from all things, from which ye could not be justified by the law of Moses. Beware, therefore, lest that come upon you, which is spoken of in the prophets; Behold, ye despisers, and wonder, and perish: for I work a work in your days, a work which you will in no wise believe, though a man declare it unto you' (Acts xiii. 39, &c.). Now, it is manifest all this is preaching the law, in the sense wherein you understand the term; even although great part of, if not all, his hearers were either Jews or religious proselytes (verse 43), and, therefore, probably many of them, in some degree at least, convinced of sin already. He first reminds them, that they could not be justified by the law of Moses, but only by faith in Christ; and then severely threatens them with the judgements of God, which is, in the strongest sense, preaching the law.

7. In his next discourse, that to the Heathens at Lystra (xiv. 15, &c.), we do not find so much as the name of Christ: the whole purport of it is, that they should 'turn from those vain idols unto the living God.' Now confess the truth. Do not you think, if you had been there, you could have preached much better than he? I should not wonder if you thought too that his *preaching so ill* occasioned his being *so ill treated;* and that his being *stoned* was a just judgement upon him for not *preaching Christ!*

8. To the jailor indeed, when 'he sprang in, and came trembling, and fell down before Paul and Silas, and said. Sirs,

what must I do to be saved?' he immediately said 'Believe on the Lord Jesus Christ' (Acts xvi. 29 &c.); and in the case of one so deeply convinced of sin who would not have said the same? But to the men of Athens you find him speaking in a quite different manner; reproving their superstition, ignorance, and idolatry; and strongly moving them to repent, from the consideration of a future judgement, and of the resurrection from the dead (xvii. 24-31). Likewise when Felix sent for Paul, on purpose that he might 'hear him concerning the faith in Christ'; instead of preaching Christ in *your* sense (which would probably have caused the Governor either to mock or to contradict and blaspheme), 'he reasoned of righteousness, temperance, and judgement to come,' till Felix (hardened as he was) 'trembled' (xxiv. 24, 25). Go thou, and tread in his steps. Preach Christ to the careless sinner, by reasoning 'of righteousness, temperance, and judgement to come'!

9. If you say, 'But he preached Christ in a different manner in his Epistles': I answer, (1) He did not there preach at all; not in that sense wherein we speak: for preaching, in our present question means speaking before a congregation. But waiving this, I answer, (2) His Epistles are directed, not to unbelievers such as those we are now speaking of, but 'to the saints of God,' in Rome, Corinth, Philippi, and other places. Now, unquestionably, he would speak more of Christ to these, than to those who were without God in the world. And yet, (3) Every one of these is full of the law, even the Epistles to the Romans and the Galatians, in both of which he does what you term 'preaching the law,' and that to believers, as well as unbelievers.

10. From hence it is plain, you know not what it is to preach Christ, in the sense of the Apostle. For doubtless St. Paul judged himself to be preaching Christ, both to Felix, and at Antioch, Lystra, and Athens: from whose example every thinking man must infer, that not only the declaring the love of Christ to sinners, but also the declaring that He will come from heaven in flaming fire, is, in the Apostle's sense, preaching Christ; yea, in the full scriptural meaning of the word. To preach Christ, is to preach what He hath revealed, either in the Old or New Testament; so that you are then as really preaching Christ, when you are saying, 'The wicked shall be turned into hell, and all the

people that forget God,' as when you are saying, 'Behold the Lamb of God, which taketh away the sin of the world!'

11. Consider this well: that to preach Christ, is to preach all things that Christ hath spoken—all His promises; all His threatenings and commands; all that is written in His book; and then you will know how to preach Christ without making void the law.

12. 'But does not the greatest blessing attend those discourses wherein we peculiarly preach the merits and sufferings of Christ?'

Probably when we preach to a congregation of mourners, or of believers, these will be attended with the greatest blessing; because such discourses are peculiarly suited to their state. At least, these will usually convey the most comfort. But this is not always the greatest blessing. I may sometimes receive a far greater by a discourse that cuts me to the heart, and humbles me to the dust. Neither should I receive that comfort, if I were to preach or to hear no discourses but on the sufferings of Christ. These, by constant repetition, would lose their force, and grow more and more flat and dead, till at length they would become a dull round of words, without any spirit, or life, or virtue. So that thus to preach Christ must, in process of time, make void the gospel, as well as the law.

II. 1. A second way of making void the law through faith is, the teaching that faith supersedes the necessity of holiness. This divides itself into a thousand smaller paths, and many there are that walk therein. Indeed there are few that wholly escape it; few who are convinced, we are saved by faith, but are sooner or later, more or less, drawn aside into this by-way.

2. All those are drawn into this by-way who, if it be not their settled judgement that faith in Christ entirely sets aside the necessity of keeping His law; yet suppose, either, (1) That holiness is less necessary now than it was before Christ came; or, (2) That a less degree of it is necessary; or, (3) That it is less necessary to believers than to others. Yea, and so are all those who, although their judgement be right in the general, yet think they may take more liberty in particular cases than they could have done before they believed. Indeed, the using the term *liberty,* in such a manner, for liberty from obedience or holiness,

shows at once that their judgement is perverted, and that they are guilty of what they imagined to be far from them; namely of making void the law through faith, by supposing faith to supersede holiness.

3. The first plea of those who teach this expressly is, that we are now under the covenant of grace, not works; and therefore we are no longer under the necessity of performing the works of the law.

And who ever was under the covenant of works? None but Adam before the fall. He was fully and properly under that covenant, which required perfect, universal obedience, as the one condition of acceptance, and left no place for pardon, upon the very least transgression. But no man else was ever under this, neither Jew nor Gentile; neither before Christ nor since. All his sons were and are under the covenant of grace. The manner of their acceptance is this: the free grace of God, through the merits of Christ, gives pardon to them that believe; that believe with such a faith as, working by love, produces all obedience and holiness.

4. The case is not, therefore, as you suppose, that men were *once* more obliged to obey God, or to work the works of His law, than they are *now*. This is a supposition you cannot make good. But we should have been obliged, if we had been under the covenant of works, to have done those works antecedent to our acceptance. Whereas now all good works, though as necessary as ever, are not antecedent to our acceptance, but consequent upon it. Therefore the nature of the covenant of grace gives you no ground, no encouragement at all, to set aside any instance or degree of obedience; any part or measure of holiness.

5. 'But are we not justified by faith, without the works of the law?' Undoubtedly we are; without the works either of the ceremonial or the moral law. And would to God all men were convinced of this! It would prevent innumerable evils; Antinomianism in particular: for, generally speaking, they are the Pharisees who make the Antinomians. Running into an extreme so palpably contrary to Scripture, they occasion others to run into the opposite one. These, seeking to be justified by works, affright those from allowing any place for them.

6. But the truth lies between both. We are, doubtless, justified by faith. This is the corner-stone of the whole Christian building. We are justified without the works of the law, as any

previous condition of justification; but they are an immediate fruit of that faith whereby we are justified. So that if good works do not follow our faith, even all inward and outward holiness, it is plain our faith is nothing worth; we are yet in our sins. Therefore, that we are justified by faith, even by faith without works, is no ground for making void the law through faith; or for imagining that faith is a dispensation from any kind or degree of holiness.

7. 'Nay, but does not St. Paul expressly say, "Unto him that worketh not, but believeth on Him that justifieth the ungodly, his faith is counted for righteousness"? And does it not follow from hence, that faith is to a believer in the room, in the place, of righteousness? But if faith is in the room of righteousness or holiness, what need is there of this too?'

This, it must be acknowledged, comes home to the point, and is, indeed, the main pillar of Antinomianism. And yet it needs not a long or laboured answer. We allow, (1) That God justifies the ungodly; him that, till that hour, is totally ungodly—full of all evil, void of all good: (2) That He justifies the ungodly that worketh not; that, till that moment, worketh no good work—neither can he; for an evil tree cannot bring forth good fruit: (3) That He justifies him by faith alone, without any goodness or righteousness preceding: and, (4) That faith is then counted to him for righteousness; namely, for preceding righteousness; that is, God, through the merits of Christ, accepts him that believes, as if he had aready fulfilled all righteousness. But what is all this to your point? The Apostle does not say, either here or elsewhere, that this faith is counted to him for *subsequent righteousness.* He does teach that there is no righteousness *before* faith; but where does he teach that there is none *after it?* He does assert, holiness cannot Precede justification; but not, that it need not *follow* it. St. Paul, therefore, gives you no colour for making void the law, by teaching that faith supersedes the necessity of holiness.

III. 1. There is yet another way of making void the law through faith, which is more common than either of the former: and that is, the doing it practically; the making it void in *fact,* though not in *principle*; the *living* as if faith was designed to excuse us from holiness.

How earnestly does the Apostle guard us against this, in those well-known words: 'What then? shall we sin, because we are not under the law, but under grace? God forbid' (Rom. vi. 15): a caution which it is needful thoroughly to consider, because it is of the last importance.

2. The being 'under the law,' may here mean, (1) The being obliged to observe the ceremonial law: (2) The being obliged to conform to the whole Mosaic institution: (3) The being obliged to keep the whole moral law, as the condition of our acceptance with God: and, (4) The being under the wrath and curse of God; under sentence of eternal death; under a sense of guilt and condemnation, full of horror and slavish fear.

3. Now although a believer is 'not without law to God, but under the law to Christ,' yet from the moment he believes, he is not 'under the law,' in any of the preceding senses. On the contrary, he is 'under grace,' under a more benign, gracious dispensation. As he is no longer under the ceremonial law, nor under the Mosaic institution; as he is not obliged to keep even the moral law, as the condition of his acceptance; so he is delivered from the wrath and the curse of God, from all sense of guilt and condemnation, and from all that horror and fear of death and hell whereby he was all his life before subject to bondage. And he now performs (which while 'under the law' he could not do) a willing and universal obedience. He obeys not from the motive of slavish fear, but on a nobler principle; namely, the grace of God ruling in his heart, and causing all his works to be wrought in love.

4. What then? Shall this evangelical principle of action be less powerful than the legal? Shall we be less obedient to God from filial love than we were from servile fear?

It is well if this is not a common case; if this practical Antinomianism, this unobserved way of making void the law through faith, has not infected thousands of believers.

Has it not infected you? Examine yourself honestly and closely. Do you not do now what you durst not have done when you was 'under the law,' or (as we commonly call it) under conviction? For instance: you durst not then indulge yourself in food: you took just what was needful, and that of the cheapest kind. Do you not allow yourself more latitude now? Do you not indulge yourself a *little* more than you did? O beware lest you 'sin because you are not under the law, but under grace.'

5. When you was under conviction, you durst not indulge the lust of the eye in any degree. You would not do anything, great or small, merely to gratify your curiosity. You regarded only cleanliness and necessity, or at most very moderate convenience, either in furniture or apparel; superfluity and finery of whatever kind, as well as fashionable elegance, were both a terror and an abomination to you.

Are they so still? Is your conscience as tender now in these things as it was then? Do you still follow the same rule both in furniture and apparel, trampling all finery, all superfluity, everything useless, everything merely ornamental, however fashionable, under foot? Rather, have you not resumed what you had once laid aside, and what you could not then use without wounding your conscience? And have you not learned to say, 'O, I am not so scrupulous now'? I would to God you were! Then you would not *sin* thus; 'because you are not under the law, but under grace!'

6. You was once scrupulous too of commending any to their face; and still more, of suffering any to commend you. It was a stab to your heart; you could not bear it; you sought the honour that cometh of God only. You could not endure such conversation; nor any conversation which was not good to the use of edifying. All idle talk, all trifling discourse, you abhorred; you hated as well as feared it; being deeply sensible of the value of time, of every precious, fleeting moment. In like manner, you dreaded and abhorred idle expense; valuing your money only less than your time, and trembling lest you should be found an unfaithful steward, even of the mammon of unrighteousness.

Do you now look upon praise as deadly poison, which you can neither give nor receive but at the peril of your soul? Do you still dread and abhor all conversation which does not tend to the use of edifying; and labour to improve every moment, that it may not pass without leaving you better than it found you? Are not you less careful as to the expense both of money and time? Cannot you now lay out either, as you could not have done once? Alas! how has that 'which should have been for your health, proved to you an occasion of falling'! How have you 'sinned because you was not under the law, but under grace'!

7. God forbid you should any longer continue thus to 'turn the grace of God into lasciviousness'! O remember how clear and strong a conviction you once had concerning all these things! And, at the same time, you was fully satisfied from whom that conviction came. The world told you, you was in a delusion; but you knew it was the voice of God. In these things you was not too scrupulous then; but you are not now scrupulous enough. God kept you longer in that painful school, that you might learn those great lessons the more perfectly. And have you forgot them already? O recollect them before it is too late! Have you suffered so many things in vain? I trust it is not yet in vain. Now use the conviction without the pain! Practise the lesson without the rod! Let not the mercy of God weigh less with you now, than His fiery indignation did before. Is love a less powerful motive than fear? If not, let it be an invariable rule, 'I will do nothing now I am "under grace," which I durst not have done when "under the law." '

8. I cannot conclude this head without exhorting you to examine yourself, likewise, touching sins of omission. Are you as clear of these, now you 'are under grace,' as you was when 'under the law'? How diligent was you then in hearing the Word of God! Did you neglect any opportunity? Did you not attend thereon day and night? Would a small hindrance have kept you away? a little business? a visitant? a slight indisposition? a soft bed? a dark or cold morning? Did not you then fast often; or use abstinence to the uttermost of your power? Was not you much in prayer (cold and heavy as you was), while you was hanging over the mouth of hell? Did you not speak and not spare even for an unknown God? Did you not boldly plead His cause, reprove sinners, and avow the truth before an adulterous generation? And are you now a believer in Christ? Have you the faith that overcometh the world? What! and are you less zealous for your Master now, than you was when you knew Him not? less diligent in fasting, in prayer, in hearing His word, in calling sinners to God? O repent! See and feel your grievous loss! Remember from whence you are fallen! Bewail your unfaithfulness! Now be zealous and do the first works; lest, if you continue to 'make void the law through faith,' God cut you off, and appoint you your portion with the unbelievers.

SERMON XXXI

THE LAW ESTABLISHED THROUGH FAITH

DISCOURSE II

See introduction to Sermon XXIX.

*Do we then make void the law through faith? God forbid: yea, we establish the
law.*—ROM. iii.31.

1. It has been shown in the preceding discourse, which are the
most usual ways of making void the law through faith; namely,
first, the not preaching it at all; which effectually makes it all
void at a stroke; and this under colour of preaching Christ and
magnifying the gospel, though it be, in truth, destroying both
the one and the other;—secondly, the teaching (whether
directly or indirectly), that faith supersedes the necessity of
holiness; that this is less necessary now, or a less degree of it
necessary, than before Christ came; that it is less necessary to us,
because we believe, than otherwise it would have been; or, that
Christian liberty is a liberty from any kind or degree of holiness
(so perverting those great truths, that we are now under the
covenant of grace, and not of works that a man is justified by
faith, without the works of the law; and that 'to him that worketh
not, but believeth his faith is counted for righteousness');—or,
thirdly, the doing this practically; the making void the law in
practice though not in principle; the living or acting as if faith
was designed to excuse us from holiness; the allowing ourselves
in sin, 'because we are not under the law, but under grace.' It
remains to inquire how we may follow a better pattern, how we
may be able to say, with the Apostle, 'Do we then make void the
law through faith? God forbid: yea we establish the law.'

2. We do not, indeed, establish the old ceremonial law: we
know that is abolished for ever. Much less do we establish the
whole Mosaic dispensation: this we know our Lord has nailed to
His cross. Nor yet do we so establish the moral law (which it is to

451

be feared too many do), as if the fulfilling it, the keeping all the commandments, were the condition of our justification: if it were so, surely 'in His sight should no man living be justified.' But all this being allowed, we still, in the Apostle's sense, 'establish the law,' the moral law.

I. 1. We establish the law, first by our doctrine; by endeavouring to preach it in its whole extent, to explain and enforce every part of it, in the same manner as our great Teacher did while upon earth. We establish it by following St. Peter's advice: 'If any man speak, let him speak as the oracles of God'; as the holy men of old, moved by the Holy Ghost, spoke and wrote for our instruction; and as the Apostles of our blessed Lord, by the direction of the same Spirit. We establish it whenever we speak in His name, by keeping back nothing from them that hear; by declaring to them, without any limitation or reserve, the whole counsel of God. And in order the more effectually to establish it, we use herein great plainness of speech. 'We are not as many that *corrupt* the word of God': καπηλευοντες (as artful men their bad wine); we do not *cauponize, mix, adulterate,* or *soften* it, to make it suit the taste of the hearers: 'but as of sincerity, but as of God, in the sight of God, speak we in Christ'; as having no other aim, than 'by manifestation of the truth to commend ourselves to every man's conscience in the sight of God.'

2. We then by our doctrine, establish the law, when we thus openly declare it to all men; and that in the fullness wherein it is delivered by our blessed Lord and His Apostles; when we publish it in the height, and depth, and length, and breadth thereof. We then establish the law, when we declare every part of it, every commandment contained therein, not only in its full, literal sense, but likewise in its spiritual meaning; not only with regard to the outward actions, which it either forbids or enjoins but also with respect to the inward principle, to the thoughts, desires, and intents of the heart.

3. And indeed this we do the more diligently, not only because it is of the deepest importance,—inasmuch as all the fruit, every word and work, must be only evil continually, if the tree be evil, if the dispositions and tempers of the heart be not right before God,—but likewise, because as important as these things are,

they are little considered or understood—so little, that we may truly say of the law too, when taken in its full spiritual meaning, it is 'a mystery which was hid from ages and generations since the world began.' It was utterly hid from the heathen world. They, with all their boasted wisdom, neither found out God, nor the law of God; not in the letter, much less in the spirit of it. 'Their foolish hearts were' more and more 'darkened'; while 'professing themselves wise, they became fools.' And it was almost equally hid, as to its spiritual meaning, from the bulk of the jewish nation. Even these, who were so ready to declare concerning others, 'This people that knoweth not the law are cursed,' pronounced their own sentence therein, as being under the same curse, the same dreadful ignorance. Witness our Lord's continual reproof of the wisest among them for their gross misinterpretations of it. Witness the supposition almost universally received among them, that they needed only to make clean the outside of the cup; that the paying tithe of mint, anise, and cummin—outward exactness—would atone for inward unholiness, for the total neglect both of justice and mercy, of faith and the love of God. Yea so absolutely was the spiritual meaning of the law hidden from the wisest of them, that one of their most eminent Rabbis comments thus on those words of the Psalmist, 'If I incline unto iniquity with my heart, the Lord will not hear me': 'That is,' saith he, 'if it be only in my heart, if I do not commit outward wickedness, the Lord will not regard it; He will not punish me, unless I proceed to the outward act'!

4. But, alas! the law of God, as to its inward, spiritual meaning, is not hid from the Jews or Heathens only, but even from what is called the Christian world; at least, from a vast majority of them. The spiritual sense of the commandments of God is still a mystery to these also. Nor is this observable only in those lands which are overspread with Romish darkness and ignorance: but this is too sure that the far greater part even of those who are called *Reformed Christians* are utter strangers at this day to the law of Christ, in the purity and spirituality of it.

5. Hence it is that to this day 'the Scribes and Pharisees,' the men who have the form but not the power of religion, and who are generally wise in their own eyes, and righteous in their own conceits,— 'hearing these things, are offended'; are deeply offended, when we speak of the religion of the heart; and

particularly when we show, that, without this, were we to 'give all our goods to feed the poor,' it would profit us nothing. But offended they must be; for we cannot but speak the truth as it is in Jesus. It is our part, whether they will hear, or whether they will forbear to deliver our own soul. All that is written in the book of God we are to declare, not as pleasing men, but the Lord. We are to declare, not only all the promises, but all the threatenings too, which we find therein. At the same time that we proclaim all the blessings and privileges which God hath prepared for His children, we are likewise to 'teach all the things whatsoever He hath commanded.' And we know that all these have their use; either for the awakening those that sleep, the instructing the ignorant, the comforting the feeble-minded, or the building up and perfecting of the saints. We know that 'all Scripture, given by inspiration of God is profitable,' either 'for doctrine,' or 'for reproof'; either 'for correction, or for instruction in righteousness'; and that 'the man of God,' in the process of the work of God in his soul, has need of every part thereof, that he may at length 'be perfect, throughly furnished unto all good works.'

6. It is our part thus to preach Christ, by preaching all things whatsoever He hath revealed. We may indeed, without blame, yea, and with a peculiar blessing from God, declare the love of our Lord Jesus Christ; we may speak, in a more especial manner, of the' Lord our Righteousness'; we may expatiate upon the grace of God in Christ, 'reconciling the world unto Himself'; we may, at proper opportunities, dwell upon His praise, as 'bearing the iniquities of us all, as wounded for our transgressions, and bruised for our iniquities, that by His stripes we might be healed': but still we should not preach Christ according to His word, if we were wholly to confine ourselves to this; we are not ourselves clear before God, unless we proclaim Him in all His offices. To preach Christ, as a workman that needeth not to be ashamed, is to preach Him, not only as our great High-Priest, 'taken from among men, and ordained for men, in things pertaining to God'—as such 'reconciling us to God by His blood,' and 'ever living to make intercession for us';—but likewise as the Prophet of the Lord, 'who of God is made unto us wisdom'; who, by His Word and His Spirit, is with us always, 'guiding us into all truth';—yea, and as remaining a King for ever; as giving laws to

all whom He has bought with His blood; as restoring those to the image of God, whom He had first reinstated in His favour; as reigning in all believing hearts until He has 'subdued all things to Himself,'—until He hath utterly cast out all sin, and brought in everlasting righteousness.

II. 1. We establish the law, secondly, when we so preach faith in Christ as not to supersede, but produce, holiness; to produce all manner of holiness, negative and positive, of the heart and of the life.

In order to this, we continually declare (what should be frequently and deeply considered by all who would not 'make void the law through faith'), that faith itself, even Christian faith, the faith of God's elect, the faith of the operation of God, still is only the handmaid of love. As glorious and honourable as it is, it is not the end of the commandment. God hath given this honour to love alone: love is the end of all the commandments of God. Love is the end, the sole end, of every dispensation of God, from the beginning of the world to the consummation of all things. And it will endure when heaven and earth flee away; for 'love' alone 'never faileth.' Faith will totally fail; it will be swallowed up in sight, in the everlasting vision of God. But even then, love,—

> Its nature and its office still the same,
> Lasting its lamp, and unconsumed its flame,
> In deathless triumph shall for ever live,
> And endless good diffuse, and endless praise receive.

2. Very excellent things are spoken of faith; and whosoever is a partaker thereof may well say with the Apostle, 'Thanks be to God for His unspeakable gift.' Yet still it loses all its excellence when brought into a comparison with love. What St. Paul observes concerning the superior glory of the gospel, above that of the law, may, with great propriety, be spoken of the superior glory of love, above that of faith: 'Even that which was made glorious hath no glory, in this respect, by reason of the glory that excelleth. For if that which is done away is glorious, much more doth that which remaineth exceed in glory.' Yea, all the glory of faith, before it is done away, arises hence, that it ministers to love: it is the great temporary means which God has ordained to promote that eternal end.

3. Let those who magnify faith beyond all proportion, so as to swallow up all things else, and who so totally misapprehend the nature of it as to imagine it stands in the place of love, consider farther, that as love will exist after faith, so it did exist long before it. The angels who, from the moment of their creation, beheld the face of their Father that is in heaven, had no occasion for faith, in its general notion, as it is the evidence of things not seen. Neither had they need of faith, in its more particular acceptation, faith in the blood of Jesus: for He took not upon Him the nature of angels; but only the seed of Abraham. There was, therefore, no place before the foundation of the world for faith, either in the general or particular sense. But there was for love. Love existed from eternity, in God, the great ocean of love. Love had a place in all the children of God, from the moment of their creation: they received at once, from their gracious Creator, to exist and to love.

4. Nor is it certain (as ingeniously and plausibly as many have descanted upon this), that faith, even in the general sense of the word, had any place in paradise. It is highly probable, from that short and uncircumstantial account which we have in holy writ, that Adam, before he rebelled against God, walked with Him by sight, and not by faith.

> For then his reason's eye was strong and clear,
> And (as an eagle can behold the sun)
> Might have beheld his Maker's face as near
> As th' intellectual angels could have done.

He was then able to talk with Him face to face, whose face we cannot now see and live; and consequently had no need of that faith, whose office it is to supply the want of sight.

5. On the other hand, it is absolutely certain, faith, in its particular sense, had then no place. For in that sense, it necessarily pre-supposes sin, and the wrath of God declared against the sinner; without which there is no need of an atonement for sin, in order to the sinner's reconciliation with God. Consequently, as there was no need of an atonement before the fall, so there was no place for faith in that atonement; man being then pure from every stain of sin; holy as God is holy. But love even then filled his heart; it reigned in him without a rival, and it was only when love was lost by sin, that faith was

added, not for its own sake, nor with any design that it should exist any longer than until it had answered the end for which it was ordained,—namely, to restore man to the love from which he was fallen. At the fall, therefore, was added this evidence of things unseen, which before was utterly needless; this confidence in redeeming love, which could not possibly have any place till the promise was made, that 'the Seed of the woman should bruise the serpent's head.'

6. Faith, then, was originally designed of God to reestablish the law of love. Therefore, in speaking thus, we are not undervaluing it, or robbing it of its due praise; but, on the contrary, showing its real worth, exalting it in its just proportion, and giving it that very place which the wisdom of God assigned it from the beginning. It is the grand means of restoring that holy love wherein man was originally created. It follows, that although faith is of no value in itself (as neither is any other means whatsoever), yet as it leads to that end, the establishing anew the law of love in our hearts; and as, in the present state of things, it is the only means under heaven for effecting it; it is on that account an unspeakable blessing to man, and of unspeakable value before God.

III. 1. And this naturally brings us to observe, thirdly, the most important way of establishing the law; namely, the establishing it in our own hearts and lives. Indeed, without this, what would all the rest avail? We might establish it by our doctrine; we might preach it in its whole extent; might explain and enforce every part of it; we might open it in its most spiritual meaning, and declare the mysteries of the kingdom; we might preach Christ in all His offices, and faith in Christ as opening all the treasures of His love; and yet all this time, if the law we preached were not established in our hearts, we should be of no more account before God, than 'sounding brass, or tinkling cymbals'; all our preaching would be so far from profiting ourselves, that it would only increase our damnation.

2. This is, therefore, the main point to be considered,—How may we establish the law in our own hearts, so that it may have its full influence on our lives? And this can only be done by faith.

Faith alone it is which effectually answers this end, as we learn from daily experience. For so long as we walk by faith, not by sight, we go swiftly on in the way of holiness. While we steadily look, not at the things which are seen, but at those which are not seen, we are more and more crucified to the world, and the world crucified to us. Let but the eye of the soul be constantly fixed, not on the things which are temporal, but on those which are eternal, and our affections are more and more loosened from earth, and fixed on things above. So that faith, in general, is the most direct and effectual means of promoting all righteousness and true holiness; of establishing the holy and spiritual law in the hearts of them that believe.

3. And by faith, taken in its more particular meaning, for a confidence in a pardoning God, we establish His law in our own hearts, in a still more effectual manner. For there is no motive which so powerfully inclines us to love God, as the sense of the love of God in Christ. Nothing enables us like a piercing conviction of this to give our hearts to Him who was given for us. And from this principle of grateful love to God arises love to our brother also. Neither can we avoid loving our neighbour, if we truly believe the love wherewith God hath loved us. Now this love to man, grounded on faith, and love to God, 'worketh no ill to' our 'neighbour'; consequently, it is, as the Apostle observes, 'the fulfilling of the' whole negative 'law.' 'For this, Thou shalt not commit adultery: Thou shalt not kill: Thou shalt not steal: Thou shalt not bear false witness: Thou shalt not covet: and if there be any other commandment, it is briefly comprehended in this saying. Thou shalt love thy neighbour as thyself.' Neither is love content with barely working no evil to our neighbour. It continually incites us to do good, as we have time and opportunity; to do good, in every possible kind, and in every possible degree, to all men. It is, therefore, the fulfilling of the positive, likewise, as well as of the negative, law of God.

4. Nor does faith fulfil either the negative or positive law as to the external part only; but it works inwardly by love, to the purifying of the heart, the cleansing of it from all vile affections. Every one that hath this faith in himself 'purifieth himself even as He is pure,'—purifieth himself from every earthly, sensual desire; from all vile and inordinate affections; yea, from the whole of that carnal mind which is enmity against God. At the

same time, if it have its perfect work, it fills him with all goodness, righteousness, and truth. It brings all heaven into his soul; and causes him to walk in the light, even as God is in the light.

5. Let us thus endeavour to establish the law in ourselves; not sinning 'because we are under grace,' but rather using all the power we receive thereby, 'to fulfil all righteousness.' Calling to mind what light we received from God while His Spirit was convincing us of sin, let us beware we do not put out that light; what we had then attained let us hold fast. Let nothing induce us to build again what we have destroyed; to resume anything, small or great, which we then clearly saw was not for the glory of God, or the profit of our own soul; or to neglect anything, small or great, which we could not then neglect, without a check from our own conscience. To increase and perfect the light which we had before, let us now add the light of faith. Confirm we the former gift of God, by a deeper sense of whatever He had then shown us; by a greater tenderness of conscience, and a more exquisite sensibility of sin. Walking now with joy, and not with fear, in a dear, steady sight of things eternal, we shall look on pleasure, wealth, praise, all the things of earth, as on bubbles upon the water; counting nothing important, nothing desirable, nothing worth a deliberate thought, but only what is 'within the veil,' where Jesus' sitteth at the right hand of God.'

6. Can *you* say, 'Thou art merciful to my unrighteousness; my sins Thou rememberest no more'? Then, for the time to come, see that you fly from sin, as from the face of a serpent! For how exceeding sinful does it appear to you now! How heinous above all expression! On the other hand, in how amiable a light do you now see the holy and perfect will of God! Now, therefore, labour that it may be fulfilled, both in you, by you, and upon you! Now watch and pray, that you may sin no more, that you may see and shun the least transgression of His law! You see the motes which you could not see before, when the sun shines into a dark place. In like manner, you see the sins which you could not see before, now the Sun of Righteousness shines in your heart. Now then do all diligence to walk, in every respect, according to the light you have received! Now be zealous to receive more light daily, more of the knowledge and love of God, more of the Spirit of Christ, more of His life, and of the power of His resurrection! Now use

all the knowledge, and love, and life, and power you have already attained; so shall you continually go on from faith to faith; so shall you daily increase in holy love, till faith is swallowed up in sight, and the law of love is established to all eternity!

SERMON XXXII

THE NATURE OF ENTHUSIASM

This sermon was first published in Vol. III of the Sermons in 1750, and at least three editions in separate form were published during Wesley's lifetime. The whole chapter was the subject of a series of expositions at the Foundery in December 1740, and at Bristol (or Kingswood?) the previous May. This verse is set down as the text at the Chapel (West Street) on Christmas Day 1752, and at London (presumably the Foundery) the next day. In its present form it was probably one of those prepared for publication in November and December 1749. See introduction to Sermon XXIX. Its purpose was to answer the charge of 'Enthusiasm' which had been constantly made against Wesley and the Methodists since 1739. On October 14, 1739, the Rev. Charles Wheatley, preaching at St. Paul's Cathedral, described the Methodists as 'rapturous enthusiasts, preaching up unaccountable sensations, violent emotions, and sudden changes; boasting of immediate inspirations, and laying a blasphemous claim to greater miracles than ever were wrought even by Christ Himself.' The same year Dr. Joseph Trapp preached four sermons in different London churches against 'the doctrines and practices of certain modern enthusiasts,' and published them. The Rev. Josiah Tucker accused Whitefield of 'blasphemous and enthusiastic notions'; and Bishop Gibson, in his Pastoral Charge of August 1, arraigns the Methodists as enthusiasts on nine counts, to wit: their claim to extraordinary communications from God; to a special mission; to divine inspiration; to divine power in their preaching; to the gift of the Holy Ghost; to prophecy; to be the equals of the apostles and even of Christ; to be the preachers of a new gospel; and to use extraordinary methods of teaching. Pamphlet followed pamphlet, some more scurrilous and abusive than others, but all concurring in the charge of Enthusiasm. The *Scots Magazine* and the *Weekly Miscellany* were prominent in the baiting of the 'crack-brained enthusiasts.'

Passing over a host of minor assailants, we come in 1744 to the Rev. Thomas Church's *Remarks on Mr. Wesley's Last Journal*, a calm and reasonable criticism; he was, as Wesley himself said in 1777, 'a gentleman, a scholar, and a Christian; and as such he both spoke and wrote'; and he answered him in the same spirit. Church's definition of Enthusiasm is worth quoting: 'Enthusiasm is a false persuasion of an extraordinary divine assistance, which leads men on to such conduct as

461

is only to be justified by the supposition of such assistance. An enthusiast is then sincere, but mistaken. His intentions are good, but his actions most abominable.' He proceeds to detail the marks of Enthusiasm, namely, the following one's own warm imagination rather than the Word of God; the resting on ecstasies; hence liability to error; superiority to reason and argument; treating his opponents as men who are fighting against God; trusting in dreams; talking like an inspired person and applying Scripture phrases to oneself without regard to their original meaning. Wesley says, 'You have drawn, sir (in the main) a true picture of an enthusiast. But it is no more like me than I am like a centaur'; and he proceeds to answer the points in order. Church concludes with two 'grand instances' of Wesley's enthusiasm: (1) his having recourse to casting lots or opening the Bible at random, as recorded some eight times in his *Journal*; which Wesley justifies by saying that he never did this until after full consideration it seemed impossible to decide the question; he then left the decision, not, as Church said, 'to chance,' but to the Lord in whose hand is 'the whole disposal thereof.' (2) His record in the *Journal* of several cases of the cure of sick persons through prayer; and of other remarkable providential interpositions. Wesley's answer is, 'I do not know that God hath anyway precluded Himself from thus exerting His sovereign power, from working miracles in any kind or degree, in any age, to the end of the world.' Wesley's two answers to Church were published in 1745 and 1746.

Finally came Bishop Lavington's *Enthusiasm of Methodists and Papists Compared,* a feeble and abusive attack, which Wesley answered in 1750 and 1751 in two 'Letters to the Author.' This sermon is thus part of a controversy which had been going on for over ten years. With great skill Wesley not only answers the charges against himself, but carries the war into the enemies' camp by affirming that they are the real enthusiasts, because they imagine themselves to be Christians when they are not; they are thus 'mere madmen, mere enthusiasts all!'

This reiterated charge of Enthusiasm was ultimately based upon the teaching of Wesley in regard to the direct witness of the Spirit, and the consequent possibility of personal fellowship with God. The doctrine was no doubt open to abuse, and the extravagant pretensions to which it led in the case of many uneducated men, who laid claim to divine inspiration for all that they said or did gave some colour to the objections and criticisms of its opponents. See introduction to Sermon X.

As to the word itself, it is, in spite of Wesley's opinion in paragraph 6, derived from the participial form of a supposititious verb ενθειοθια, from εν and Θεος, meaning to be possessed or inspired by the Deity. The suggestion that it has something to do with εν θυσια, in sacrifice, is quite impossible. The adjective ενθεος, inspired, occurs in the Greek tragedians; but it was Plato who made the word 'enthusiasm' current coin. By it he meant a direct intuition of the divine through the indwelling of God in the soul; and he distinguished four types of enthusiast—the Seer or Prophet, the Mystic or Saint, the Poet, and the Philosopher. It first appeared in English at the beginning of the seventeenth century, and was originally used in the Platonic sense; we find it employed to describe the divine influence on the priestess at Delphi, the Sibyls, and the Bacchanals; and the divine 'frenzy' of the poet and the musician. But through the decline of spiritual religion after the Restoration, and the almost universal triumph of materialism and cold correctness in the early eighteenth century, it was inevitable that any one who claimed any sort of spiritual communion with God should be looked upon as an impostor or a madman; and so the word became degraded to mean a fancied or fraudulent inspiration. Thus Shaftesbury in *Charac.* section 7 (1711) says: 'Inspiration is a real feeling of the Divine Presence, and Enthusiasm is a false one.' Locke says: 'Enthusiasm is founded neither in reason nor divine revelation, but rises from the conceits of a warmed or over-weening brain.' It is in this sense exclusively that both Wesley and his opponents use the word. With the spiritual revival, of which Wesley on the religious, and Wordsworth on the literary side, were the leaders, the word recovered from the blight that had fallen on it; and from the opening of the nineteenth century it stands for 'rapturous intensity of feeling in favour of a person, principle, cause, &c.; passionate eagerness in any pursuit, proceeding from an intense conviction of the worthiness of the object' (*N. E. Dict.*). Even as early as 1771, John Fletcher, in his *Fourth Check,* defines 'the true enthusiasts' as 'those who are really inspired by the grace and love of God.' There is now a tendency to use enthusiast, enthusiastic, and enthusiastically in a good sense; and to retain enthusiastical for the eighteenth-century sense, as equivalent to fanatical.

And Festus said with a loud voice, Paul, thou art beside thyself.—ACTS xxvi. 24.

I. And so say all the world, the men who know not God, of all that are of Paul's religion: of every one who is so a follower of him, as he was of Christ. It is true, there is a sort of religion, nay, and it is called Christianity too, which may be practised without any such imputation, which is generally allowed to be consistent with common sense,—that is, a religion of form, a round of outward duties, performed in a decent, regular manner. You may add orthodoxy thereto, a system of right opinions, yea, and some quantity of heathen morality; and yet not many will pronounce, that 'much religion hath made you mad.' But if you aim at the religion of the heart, if you talk of 'righteousness, and peace, and joy in the Holy Ghost,' then it will not be long before your sentence is passed, 'Thou art beside thyself.'

2. And it is no compliment which the men of the world pay you herein. They, for once, mean what they say. They not only affirm, but cordially believe, that every man is beside himself, who says, 'the love of God is shed abroad in' his 'heart by the Holy Ghost given unto him'; and that God has enabled him to rejoice in Christ 'with joy unspeakable and full of glory.' If a man is indeed alive to God, and dead to all things here below; if he continually sees Him that is invisible, and accordingly walks by faith, and not by sight; then they account it a clear case: beyond all dispute 'much religion hath made him mad.'

3. It is easy to observe, that the determinate thing which the world accounts madness is, that utter contempt of all temporal things, and steady pursuit of things eternal; that divine conviction of things not seen; that rejoicing in the favour of God; that happy, holy love of God; and that testimony of His Spirit with our spirit, that we are the children of God,—that is, in truth, the whole spirit, and life, and power of the religion of Jesus Christ.

4. They will, however, allow, in other respects, the man acts and talks like one in his senses. In other things, he is a reasonable man; it is in these instances only his head is touched. It is therefore acknowledged, that the madness under which he labours is of a particular kind; and accordingly they are accustomed to distinguish it by a particular name, 'enthusiasm.'

5. A term this, which is exceeding frequently used, which is scarce ever out of some men's mouths; and yet it is exceeding rarely understood, even by those who use it most. It may be, therefore, not unacceptable to serious men, to all who desire to understand what they speak or hear, if I endeavour to explain the meaning of this term—to show what enthusiasm is. It may be an encouragement to those who are unjustly charged therewith; and may possibly be of use to some who are justly charged with it; at least to others who might be so, were they not cautioned against it.

6. As to the word itself, it is generally allowed to be of Greek extraction. But whence the Greek word, ενθουσιασμος, is derived, none has yet been able to show. Some have endeavoured to derive it from εν Θεω—*in God*; because all enthusiasm has reference to Him. But this is quite forced; there being small resemblance between the word derived, and those

they strive to derive it from. Others would derive it from εν θυσια—*in sacrifice*; because many of the enthusiasts of old were affected in the most violent manner during the time of sacrifice. Perhaps it is a fictitious word, invented from the noise which some of those made who were so affected.

7. It is not improbable, that one reason why this uncouth word has been retained in so many languages was, because men were not better agreed concerning the meaning than concerning the derivation of it. They therefore adopted the Greek word, because they did not understand it: they did not translate it into their own tongues, because they knew not how to translate it; it having been always a word of a loose, uncertain sense, to which no determinate meaning was affixed.

8. It is not, therefore, at all surprising, that it is so variously taken at this day; different persons understanding it in different senses, quite inconsistent with each other. Some take it in a good sense, for a divine impulse or impression, superior to all the natural faculties, and suspending, for the time, either in whole or in part, both the reason and the outward senses. In this meaning of the word, both the Prophets of old, and the Apostles, were proper enthusiasts; being, at divers times, so filled with the Spirit, and so influenced by Him who dwelt in their hearts, that the exercise of their own reason, their senses, and all their natural faculties, being suspended, they were wholly actuated by the power of God, and 'spake' only 'as they were moved by the Holy Ghost.'

9. Others take the word in an indifferent sense, such as is neither morally good nor evil: thus they speak of the enthusiasm of the poets; of Homer and Virgil in particular. And this a late eminent writer extends so far as to assert, there is no man excellent in his profession, whatsoever it be, who has not in his temper a strong tincture of enthusiasm. By 'enthusiasm' these appear to understand, an uncommon vigour of thought; a peculiar fervour of spirit, a vivacity and strength not to be found in common men; elevating the soul to greater and higher things than cool reason could have attained.

10. But neither of these is the sense wherein the word 'enthusiasm' is most usually understood. The generality of men, if no farther agreed, at least agree thus far concerning it, that it is something evil: and this is plainly the sentiment of all those who

call the religion of the heart 'enthusiasm.' Accordingly, I shall take it in the following pages, as an evil; a misfortune, if not a fault.

11. As to the nature of enthusiasm, it is undoubtedly a disorder of the mind, and such a disorder as greatly hinders the exercise of reason. Nay, sometimes it wholly sets it aside: it not only dims but shuts the eyes of the understanding. It may, therefore, well be accounted a species of madness; of madness rather than of folly: seeing a fool is properly one who draws wrong conclusions from right premises; whereas a madman draws right conclusions, but from wrong premises. And so does an enthusiast. Suppose his premises true, and his conclusions would necessarily follow. But here lies his mistake: his premises are false. He imagines himself to be what he is not: and therefore, setting out wrong, the farther he goes, the more he wanders out of the way.

12. Every enthusiast, then, is properly a madman. Yet his is not an ordinary, but a religious, madness. By 'religious,' I do not mean, that it is any part of religion: quite the reverse. Religion is the spirit of a sound mind; and, consequently, stands in direct opposition to madness of every kind. But I mean, it has religion for its object; it is conversant about religion. And so the enthusiast is generally talking of religion, of God, or of the things of God; but talking in such a manner that every reasonable Christian may discern the disorder of his mind. Enthusiasm in general may then be described in some such manner as this: a religious madness arising from some falsely imagined influence or inspiration of God; at least, from imputing something to God which ought not to be imputed to Him, or expecting something from God which ought not to be expected from Him.

13. There are innumerable sorts of enthusiasm. Those which are most common, and for that reason most dangerous. I shall endeavour to reduce under a few general heads, that they may be more easily understood and avoided.

The first sort of enthusiasm which I shall mention, is that of those who imagine they have the grace which they have not. Thus some imagine, when it is not so, that they have redemption through Christ, 'even the forgiveness of sins.' These are usually such as 'have no root in themselves'; no deep repentance, or thorough conviction. 'Therefore they receive the word with joy.' And 'because they have no deepness of earth,' no deep work in their heart, therefore the seed 'immediately springs up.' There is immediately a superficial change, which, together with that light joy, striking in with the pride of their unbroken heart, and with their inordinate self-love, easily persuades them they have already 'tasted the good word of God, and the powers of the world to come.'

14. This is properly an instance of the first sort of enthusiasm: it is a kind of madness, arising from the imagination that they have that grace which, in truth, they have not: so that they only deceive their own souls. Madness it may be justly termed: for the reasonings of these poor men are right, were their premises good; but as those are a mere creature of their own imagination, so all that is built on them falls to the ground. The foundation of all their reveries is this: they imagine themselves to have faith in Christ. If they had this, they would be 'kings and priests to God'; possessed of 'a kingdom which cannot be moved': but they have it not; consequently, all their following behaviour is as wide of truth and soberness as that of the ordinary madman, who, fancying himself an earthly king, speaks and acts in that character.

15. There are many other enthusiasts of this sort. Such, for instance, is the fiery zealot for religion; or, more properly, for the opinions and modes of worship which he dignifies with that name. This man, also, strongly imagines himself to be a believer in Jesus; yea, that he is a champion for the faith which was once delivered to the saints. Accordingly, all his conduct is formed upon that vain imagination. And allowing his supposition to be just, he would have some tolerable plea for his behaviour; whereas now it is evidently the effect of a distempered brain, as well as of a distempered heart.

16. But the most common of all the enthusiasts of this kind are those who imagine themselves Christians, and are not. These abound, not only in all parts of our land, but in most parts of the habitable earth. That they are not Christians, is clear and undeniable, if we believe the oracles of God. For Christians are holy; these are unholy: Christians love God; these love the world: Christians are humble; these are proud: Christians are gentle; these are passionate: Christians have the mind which was

in Christ; these are at the utmost distance from it. Consequently, they are no more Christians, than they are archangels. Yet they imagine themselves so to be; and they can give several reasons for it: for they have been *called* so ever since they can remember; they were *christened* many years ago; they embrace the *Christian opinions*, vulgarly termed the Christian or catholic faith; they use the *Christian modes of worship*, as their fathers did before them; they live what is called a good *Christian life*, as the rest of their neighbours do. And who shall presume to think or say that these men are not Christians?—though without one grain of true faith in Christ, or of real, inward holiness; without ever having tasted the love of God, or been 'made partakers of the Holy Ghost!'

17. Ah poor self-deceivers! Christians ye are not. But you are enthusiasts in a high degree. Physicians, heal yourselves! But first know your disease: your whole life is enthusiasm; as being all suitable to the imagination, that you have received that grace of God which you have not. In consequence of this grand mistake, you blunder on, day by day, speaking and acting under a character which does in no wise belong to you. Hence arises that palpable, glaring inconsistency that runs through your whole behaviour; which is an awkward mixture of real Heathenism and imaginary Christianity. Yet still, as you have so vast a majority on your side, you will always carry it by mere dint of numbers, 'that you are the only men in your senses, and all are lunatics who are not as you are.' But this alters not the nature of things. In the sight of God, and His holy angels, yea, and all the children of God upon earth, you are mere madmen, mere enthusiasts all! Are you not? Are you not 'walking in a vain shadow,' a shadow of religion, a shadow of happiness? Are you not still 'disquieting yourselves in vain' with misfortunes as imaginary as your happiness or religion? Do you not fancy yourselves great or good—very knowing and very wise? How long? Perhaps till death brings you back to your senses, to bewail your folly for ever and ever!

18. A second sort of enthusiasm is that of those who imagine they have such gifts from God as they have not. Thus some have imagined themselves to be endued with a power of working miracles, of healing the sick by a word or a touch, of restoring sight to the blind: yea, even of raising the dead—a notorious instance of which is still fresh in our own history. Others have

undertaken to prophesy, to foretell things to come, and that with the utmost certainty and exactness. But a little time usually convinces these enthusiasts. When plain facts run counter to their predictions, experience performs what reason could not, and sinks them down into their senses.

19. To the same class belong those who, in preaching or prayer, imagine themselves to be so influenced by the Spirit of God, as, in fact, they are not. I am sensible, indeed, that without Him we can do nothing, more especially in our public ministry; that all our preaching is utterly vain, unless it be attended with His power; and all our prayer, unless His Spirit therein help our infirmities. I know, if we do not both preach and pray by the Spirit, it is all but lost labour; seeing the help that is done upon earth He doeth it Himself, who worketh all in all. But this does not affect the case before us. Though there is a real influence of the Spirit of God, there is also an imaginary one: and many there are who mistake the one for the other. Many suppose themselves to be under that influence, when they are not, when it is far from them. And many others suppose they are more under that influence than they really are. Of this number, I fear, are all they who imagine that God dictates the very words they speak; and that, consequently, it is impossible they should speak anything amiss, either as to the matter or manner of it. It is well known how many enthusiasts of this sort also have appeared during the present century; some of whom speak in a far more authoritative manner than either St. Paul or any of the Apostles.

20. The same sort of enthusiasm, though in a lower degree, is frequently found in men of a private character. They may likewise imagine themselves to be influenced or directed by the Spirit when they are not. I allow, 'if any man have not the Spirit of Christ, he is none of His'; and that if ever we either think, speak, or act aright, it is through the assistance of that blessed Spirit. But how many impute things to Him, or expect things from Him, without any rational or scriptural ground! Such are they who imagine, they either do or shall receive *particular directions* from God, not only in points of importance, but in things of no moment; in the most trifling circumstances of life. Whereas in these cases God has given us our own reason for a guide; though never excluding the secret assistance of His Spirit.

21. To this kind of enthusiasm they are peculiarly exposed, who expect to be directed of God, either in spiritual things or in common life, in what is justly called an *extraordinary* manner: I mean, by visions or dreams, by strong impressions or sudden impulses on the mind. I do not deny, that God has, of old times, manifested His will in this manner; or, that He can do so now: nay, I believe He does, in some very rare instances. But how frequently do men mistake herein! How are they misled by pride, and a warm imagination, to ascribe such impulses or impressions, dreams or visions, to God, as are utterly unworthy of Him! Now this is all pure enthusiasm; all as wide of religion, as it is of truth and soberness.

22. Perhaps some may ask, 'Ought we not then to inquire what is the will of God in all things? And ought not His will to be the rule of our practice?' Unquestionably it ought. But how is a sober Christian to make this inquiry? to know what is the will of God? Not by waiting for supernatural dreams; not by expecting God to reveal it in visions; not by looking for any *particular impressions* or sudden impulses on his mind: no; but by consulting the oracles of God. 'To the law and to the testimony!' This is the general method of knowing what is' the holy and acceptable will of God.'

23. 'But how shall I know what is the will of God, in such and such a particular case? The thing proposed is, in itself, of an indifferent nature, and so left undetermined in Scripture.' I answer, the Scripture itself gives you a general rule, applicable to all particular cases: 'The will of God is our sanctification.' It is His will that we should be inwardly and outwardly holy; that we should be good, and do good, in every kind and in the highest degree whereof we are capable. Thus far we tread upon firm ground. This is as clear as the shining of the sun. In order, therefore, to know what is the will of God in a particular case, we have only to apply this general rule.

24. Suppose, for instance, it were proposed to a reasonable man to marry, or to enter into a new business: in order to know whether this is the will of God, being assured, 'It is the will of God concerning me, that I should be as holy and do as much good as I can,' he has only to inquire, 'In which of these states can I be most holy, and do the most good?' And this is to be determined, partly by reason, and partly by experience.

Experience tells him what advantages he has in his present state, either for being or doing good; and reason is to show, what he certainly or probably will have in the state proposed. By comparing these, he is to judge which of the two may most conduce to his being and doing good: and as far as he knows this, so far he is certain what is the will of God.

25. Meantime, the assistance of His Spirit is supposed, during the whole process of the inquiry. Indeed it is not easy to say, in how many ways that assistance is conveyed. He may bring many circumstances to our remembrance; may place others in a stronger and clearer light; may insensibly open our mind to receive conviction, and fix that conviction upon our heart. And to a concurrence of many circumstances of this kind, in favour of what is acceptable in His sight, He may superadd such an unutterable peace of mind, and so uncommon a measure of His love, as will leave us no possibility of doubting, that this, even this, is His will concerning us.

26. This is the plain, scriptural, rational way to know what is the will of God in a particular case. But considering how seldom this way is taken, and what a flood of enthusiasm must needs break in on those who endeavour to know the will of God by unscriptural, irrational ways; it were to be wished that the expression itself were far more sparingly used. The using it, as some do, on the most trivial occasions, is a plain breach of the third commandment. It is a gross way of taking the name of God in vain, and betrays great irreverence toward Him. Would it not be far better, then, to use other expressions, which are not liable to such objections? For example: instead of saying, on any particular occasion, 'I want to know what is the will of God'; would it not be better to say, 'I want to know what will be most for my improvement; and what will make me most useful?' This way of speaking is clear and unexceptionable: it is putting the matter on a plain, scriptural issue, and that without any danger of enthusiasm.

27. A third very common sort of enthusiasm (if it does not coincide with the former) is that of those who think to attain the end without using the means, by the immediate power of God. If, indeed, those means were providentially withheld, they would not fall under this charge. God can, and sometimes does, in cases of this nature, exert His own immediate power. But they

who expect this when they have those means, and will not use them, are proper enthusiasts. Such are they who expect to understand the holy Scriptures, without reading them, and meditating thereon; yea, without using all such helps as are in their power, and may probably conduce to that end. Such are they who designedly speak in the public assembly without any premeditation. I say 'designedly'; because there may be such circumstances as, at some times, make it unavoidable. But whoever despises that great means of speaking profitably is so far an enthusiast.

28. It may be expected that I should mention what some have accounted a fourth sort of enthusiasm, namely, the imagining those things to be owing to the providence of God which are not owing thereto. But I doubt: I know not what things they are which are not owing to the providence of God; in ordering, or at least in governing, of which, this is not either directly or remotely concerned. I except nothing but sin; and even in the sins of others, I see the providence of God to me. I do not say His *general* providence; for this I take to be a sounding word, which means just nothing. And if there be a *particular* providence, it must extend to all persons and all things. So our Lord understood it, or He could never have said, 'Even the hairs of your head are all numbered'; and, 'Not a sparrow falleth to the ground without' the will of 'your Father' which is in heaven. But if it be so, if God preside *universis tanquam singulis, et singulis tanquam universis*; 'over the whole universe as over every single person, and over every single person as over the whole universe'; what is it (except only our own sins) which we are not to ascribe to the providence of God? So that I cannot apprehend there is any room here for the charge of enthusiasm.

29. If it be said, the charge lies here: 'When you impute *this* to Providence, you imagine yourself the peculiar favourite of heaven': I answer, you have forgot some of the last words I spoke: *Praesidet universis tanquam singulis*; 'His providence is over all men in the universe, as much as over any single person.' Do you not see that he who, believing this, imputes anything which befalls him to Providence, does not therein make himself any more the favourite of heaven, than he supposes every man under heaven to be? Therefore you have no pretence, upon this ground, to charge him with enthusiasm.

30. Against every sort of this it behoves us to guard with the utmost diligence; considering the dreadful effects it has so often produced, and which, indeed, naturally result from it. Its immediate offspring is pride; it continually increases this source from whence it flows; and hereby it alienates us more and more from the favour and from the life of God. It dries up the very springs of faith and love, of righteousness and true holiness; seeing all these flow from grace: but 'God resisteth the proud, and giveth grace' only 'to the humble.'

31. Together with pride there will naturally arise an unadvisable and unconvincible spirit. So that into whatever error or fault the enthusiast falls, there is small hope of his recovery. For reason will have little weight with him (as has been frequently and justly observed) who imagines he is led by an higher guide,—by the immediate wisdom of God. And as he grows in pride, so he must grow in unadvisableness and in stubbornness also. He must be less and less capable of being convinced, less susceptible of persuasion; more and more attached to his own judgement and his own will, till he is altogether fixed and immovable.

32. Being thus fortified both against the grace of God, and against all advice and help from man, he is wholly left to the guidance of his own heart, and of the king of the children of pride. No marvel, then, that he is daily more rooted and grounded in contempt of all mankind, in furious anger, in every unkind disposition, in every earthly and devilish temper. Neither can we wonder at the terrible outward effects which have flowed from such dispositions in all ages; even all manner of wickedness, all the works of darkness, committed by those who call themselves Christians, while they wrought with greediness such things as were hardly named even among the Heathens.

Such is the nature, such the dreadful effects, of that manyheaded monster, Enthusiasm! From the consideration of which we may now draw some plain inferences, with regard to our own practice.

33. And, first, if enthusiasm be a term, though so frequently used, yet so rarely understood, take you care not to talk of you know not what; not to use the word till you understand it. As in all other points, so likewise in this, learn to think before you

speak. First know the meaning of this hard word; and then use it, if need require.

34. But if so few, even among men of education and learning, much more among the common sort of men, understand this dark, ambiguous word, or have any fixed notion of what it means; then, secondly, beware of judging or calling any man an enthusiast, upon common report. This is by no means a sufficient ground for giving any name of reproach to any man; least of all is it a sufficient ground for so black a term of reproach as this. The more evil it contains, the more cautious you should be how you apply it to any one; to bring so heavy an accusation, without full proof, being neither consistent with justice nor mercy.

35. But if enthusiasm be so great an evil, beware you are not entangled therewith yourself. Watch and pray, that you fall not into the temptation. It easily besets those who fear or love God. O beware you do not think of yourself more highly than you ought to think. Do not imagine you have attained that grace of God which you have not attained. You may have much joy; you may have a measure of love; and yet not have living faith. Cry unto God, that He would not suffer you, blind as you are, to go out of the way; that you may never fancy yourself a believer in Christ, till Christ is revealed in you, and till His Spirit witnesses with your spirit that you are a child of God.

36. Beware you are not a fiery, persecuting enthusiast. Do not imagine that God has called you (just contrary to the spirit of Him you style your Master) to destroy men's lives, and not to save them. Never dream of forcing men into the ways of God. Think yourself, and let think. Use no constraint in matters of religion. Even those who are farthest out of the way never compel to come in by any other means than reason, truth, and love.

37. Beware you do not run with the common herd of enthusiasts, fancying you are a Christian when you are not. Presume not to assume that venerable name, unless you have a clear, scriptural title thereto; unless you have the mind which was in Christ, and walk as He also walked.

38. Beware you do not fall into the second sort of enthusiasm,—fancying you have those gifts from God which you have not. Trust not in visions or dreams; in sudden

impressions, or strong impulses of any kind. Remember, it is not by these you are to know what is the will of God on any particular occasion; but by applying the plain Scripture rule, with the help of experience and reason, and the ordinary assistance of the Spirit of God. Do not lightly take the name of God in your mouth; do not talk of the will of God on every trifling occasion: but let your words, as well as your actions, be all tempered with reverence and godly fear.

39. Beware, lastly, of imagining you shall obtain the end without using the means conducive to it. God can give the end without any means at all; but you have no reason to think He will. Therefore constantly and carefully use all those means which He has appointed to be the ordinary channels of His grace. Use every means which either reason or Scripture recommends, as conducive (through the free love of God in Christ) either to the obtaining or increasing any of the gifts of God. Thus expect a daily growth in that pure and holy religion which the world always did, and always will, call 'enthusiasm'; but which, to all who are saved from real enthusiasm, from merely nominal Christianity, is 'the wisdom of God, and the power of God'; the glorious image of the Most High; 'righteousness and peace'; a 'fountain of living water, springing up into everlasting life'!

SERMON XXXIII

A CAUTION AGAINST BIGOTRY

I have not found any record of the preaching of this sermon. It was apparently written for publication in the third volume of the Sermons (1750). It is a remarkable exhibition of breadth of view and readiness to cooperate with all sincere and earnest Christians, especially when it is remembered that Wesley was by birth and training a High Anglican, and that at this time he was being attacked and vilified on all hands by members both of his own Church and of the various dissenting bodies. When there are so many indications of a desire for closer union amongst the Churches of Christ as are happily manifesting themselves to-day, this and the following sermon ought to be republished and widely circulated.

And John answered Him, saying, Master, we saw one casting out devils in Thy name, and he followeth not us: and we forbad him, because he followeth not us. But Jesus said, Forbid him not.—MARK ix. 38, 39.

1. In the preceding verses we read, that after the twelve had been disputing 'which of them should be the greatest. Jesus took a little child, and set him in the midst of them, and taking him in His arms, said unto them, 'Whosoever shall receive one of these little children in My name, receiveth Me; and whosoever receiveth Me, receiveth not Me' only, 'but Him that sent Me.' Then 'John answered,' that is, said, with reference to what our Lord had spoken just before, 'Master, we saw one casting out devils in Thy name, and we forbad him, because he followeth not us.' As if he had said, 'Ought we to have received him? In receiving him, should we have received Thee? Ought we not rather to have forbidden him? Did not we do well therein?' 'But Jesus said, Forbid him not.'

2. The same passage is recited by St. Luke, and almost in the same words. But it may be asked, 'What is this to us, seeing no man now *casts out devils*? Has not the power of doing this been withdrawn from the Church, for twelve or fourteen hundred

years? How then are *we* concerned in the case here proposed, or in our Lord's decision of it?'

3. Perhaps more nearly than is commonly imagined; the case proposed being no uncommon case. That we may reap our full advantage from it, I design to show, first, in what sense men may, and do, now cast out devils; secondly, what we may understand by, 'He followeth not us.' I shall, thirdly, explain our Lord's direction, 'Forbid him not'; and conclude with an inference from the whole.

I. 1. I am, in the first place, to show, in what sense men may, and do, now cast out devils.

In order to have the clearest view of this, we should remember, that (according to the scriptural account) as God dwells and works in the children of light, so the devil dwells and works in the children of darkness. As the Holy Spirit possesses the souls of good men, so the evil spirit possesses the souls of the wicked. Hence it is that the Apostle terms him 'the god of this world'; from the uncontrolled power he has over worldly men. Hence our blessed Lord styles him 'the prince of this world'; so absolute is his dominion over it. And hence St. John: 'We know that we are of God, and' all who are not of God, 'the whole world,' εν τω πονηρω κειται,—not *lieth in wickedness,* but *'lieth in the wicked one'*; lives and moves in him, as they who are not of the world do in God.

2. For the devil is not to be considered only as 'a roaring lion, going about seeking whom he may devour'; nor barely as a subtle enemy, who cometh unawares upon poor souls, and 'leads them captive at his will'; but as he who dwelleth in them, and walketh in them; who ruleth the darkness or wickedness of this world (of worldly men and all their dark designs and actions), by keeping possession of their hearts, setting up his throne there, and bringing every thought into obedience to himself. Thus the 'strong one armed keepeth his house'; and if this 'unclean spirit' sometimes 'go out of a man,' yet he often returns with 'seven spirits worse than himself, and they enter in and dwell there.' Nor can he be idle in his dwelling. He is continually 'working in' these 'children of disobedience.' He works in them with power, with mighty energy, transforming them into his own likeness,

effacing all the remains of the image of God, and preparing them for every evil word and work.

3. It is, therefore, an unquestionable truth, that the god and prince of this world still possesses all who know not God. Only the manner wherein he possesses them now differs from that wherein he did it of old time. *Then* he frequently tormented their bodies as well as souls, and that openly, without any disguise: *now* he torments their souls only (unless in some rare cases), and that as covertly as possible. The reason of this difference is plain: it was then his aim to drive mankind into superstition; therefore, he wrought as openly as he could. But it is his aim to drive us into infidelity; therefore, he works as privately as he can: for the more secret he is, the more he prevails.

4. Yet, if we may credit historians, there are countries, even now, where he works as openly as aforetime. 'But why in savage and barbarous countries only? Why not in Italy, France, or England?' For a very plain reason: he knows his men; and he knows what he has to do with each. To Laplanders he appears barefaced; because he is to fix them in superstition and gross idolatry. But with you he is pursuing a different point. He is to make you idolize yourselves; to make you wiser in your own eyes than God Himself, than all the oracles of God. Now, in order to this, he must not appear in his own shape: that would frustrate his design. No: he uses all his art to make you deny his being, till he has you safe in his own place.

5. He reigns, therefore, although in a different way, yet as absolute in one land as in the other. He has the gay Italian infidel in his teeth, as sure as the wild Tartar. But he is fast asleep in the mouth of the lion, who is too wise to wake him out of sleep. So he only plays with him for the present, and when he pleases, swallows him up!

The god of this world holds his English worshippers full as fast as those in Lapland. But it is not his business to affright them, lest they should fly to the God of heaven. The prince of darkness, therefore, does not appear, while he rules over these his willing subjects. The conqueror holds his captives so much the safer, because they imagine themselves at liberty. Thus 'the strong one armed keepeth his house, and his goods are in peace'; neither the Deist nor nominal Christian suspects he is there: so he and they are perfectly at peace with each other.

6. All this while he works with energy in them. He blinds the eyes of their understanding, so that the light of the glorious gospel of Christ cannot shine upon them. He chains their souls down to earth and hell, with the chains of their own vile affections. He binds them down to the earth, by love of the world, love of money, of pleasure, of praise. And by pride, envy, anger, hate, revenge, he causes their souls to draw nigh unto hell; acting the more secure and uncontrolled, because they know not that he acts at all.

7. But how easily may we know the cause from its effects! These are sometimes gross and palpable. So they were in the most refined of the heathen nations. Go no farther than the admired, the virtuous Romans; and you will find these, when at the height of their learning and glory, 'filled with all unrighteousness, fornication, wickedness, covetousness, maliciousness; full of envy, murder, debate, deceit, malignity; whisperers, backbiters, despiteful, proud, boasters, disobedient to parents, covenant-breakers, without natural affection, implacable, unmerciful.'

8. The strongest parts of this description are confirmed by one whom some may think a more unexceptionable witness. I mean, their brother Heathen, Dion Cassius; who observes, that, before Caesar's return from Gaul, not only gluttony and lewdness of every kind were open and barefaced; not only falsehood, injustice, and unmercifulness abounded, in public courts, as well as private families; but the most outrageous robberies, rapine, and murders were so frequent in all parts of Rome, that few men went out of doors without making their wills, as not knowing if they should return alive!

9. As gross and palpable are the works of the devil armong many (if not all) the modern Heathens. The natural religion of the Creeks, Cherokees, Chickasaws, and all other Indians bordering on our southern settlements (not of a few single men, but of entire nations), is to torture all their prisoners from morning till night, till at length they roast them to death; and upon the slightest undesigned provocation, to come behind and shoot any of their own countrymen! Yea, it is a common thing among them, for the son, if he thinks his father lives too long, to

knock out his brains; and for a mother, if she is tired of her children, to fasten stones about their necks, and throw three or four of them into the river, one after another!

10. It were to be wished, that none but Heathens had practised such gross, palpable works of the devil. But we dare not say so. Even in cruelty and bloodshed, how little have the Christians come behind them! And not the Spaniards or Portuguese alone, butchering thousands in South America: not the Dutch only in the East Indies, or the French in North America, following the Spaniards step by step: our own countrymen, too, have wantoned in blood, and exterminated whole nations; plainly proving thereby what spirit it is that dwells and works in the children of disobedience.

11. These monsters might almost make us overlook the works of the devil that are wrought in our own country. But, alas! we cannot open our eyes even here, without seeing them on every side. Is it a small proof of his power, that common swearers, drunkards, whoremongers, adulterers, thieves, robbers, sodo-mites, murderers, are still found in every part of our land? How triumphant does the prince of this world reign in all these children of disobedience?

12. He less openly, but no less effectually, works in dissemblers, tale-bearers, liars, slanderers; in oppressors and extortioners; in the perjured, the seller of his friend, his honour, his conscience, his country. And yet these may talk of religion or conscience still; of honour, virtue, and public spirit! But they can no more deceive Satan than they can God. He likewise knows those that are his: and a great multitude they are, out of every nation and people, of whom he has full possession at this day.

13. If you consider this, you cannot but see in what sense men may now also cast out devils: yea, and every minister of Christ does cast them out, if his Lord's work prosper in his hand.

By the power of God attending his word, he brings these sinners to repentance; an entire inward as well as outward change, from all evil to all good. And this is, in a sound sense, to cast out devils, out of the souls wherein they had hitherto dwelt. The strong one can no longer keep his house. A stronger than he is come upon him, and hath cast him out, and taken possession for himself, and made it an habitation of God through His Spirit. Here, then, the energy of Satan ends, and the Son of God 'destroys the works of the devil.' The understanding of the sinner is now enlightened, and his heart sweetly drawn to God. His desires are refined, his affections purified; and being filled with the Holy Ghost, he grows in grace till he is not only holy in heart, but in all manner of conversation.

14. All this is indeed the work of God. It is God alone who can cast out Satan. But He is generally pleased to do this by man, as an instrument in His hand: who is then said to cast out devils in His name, by His power and authority. And He sends whom He will send upon this great work; but usually such as man would never have thought of: for 'His ways are not as our ways, neither His thoughts as our thoughts.' Accordingly He chooses the weak to confound the mighty; the foolish to confound the wise; for this plain reason, that He may secure the glory to Himself; that 'no flesh may glory in His sight.'

II. 1. But shall we not forbid one who thus 'casteth out devils,' if 'he followeth not us'? This, it seems, was both the judgement and practice of the Apostle, till he referred the case to his Master. 'We forbad him,' saith he, 'because he followeth not us!' which he supposed to be a very sufficient reason. What we may understand by this expression, 'He followeth not us,' is the next point to be considered.

The lowest circumstance we can understand thereby, is, He has no outward connexion with us. We do not labour in conjunction with each other. He is not our fellow-helper in the gospel. And indeed whensoever our Lord is pleased to send many labourers into His harvest, they cannot all act in subordination to, or connexion with, each other. Nay, they cannot all have personal acquaintance with, nor be so much as known to, one another. Many there will necessarily be, in different parts of the harvest, so far from having any mutual intercourse, that they will be as absolute strangers to each other, as if they had lived in different ages. And concerning any of these whom we know not, we may doubtless say, 'He followeth not us.'

2. A second meaning of this expression may be, He is not of our party. It has long been matter of melancholy consideration to all who pray for the peace of Jerusalem, that so many several parties are still subsisting among those who are all styled

Christians. This has been particularly observable in our own countrymen, who have been continually dividing from each other, upon points of no moment, and many times such as religion had no concern in. The most trifling circumstances have given rise to different parties, which have continued for many generations; and each of these would be ready to object to one who was on the other side, 'He followeth not us.'

3. That expression may mean, thirdly, He differs from us in our religious opinions. There was a time when all Christians were of one mind, as well as of one heart; such great grace was upon them all, when they were first filled with the Holy Ghost! But how short a space did this blessing continue! How soon was that unanimity lost! and difference of opinion sprang up again, even in the Church of Christ,—and that not in nominal but in real Christians; nay, in the very chief of them, the Apostles themselves! Nor does it appear that the difference which then began was ever entirely removed. We do not find that even those pillars in the temple of God, so long as they remained upon earth, were ever brought to think alike, to be of one mind, particularly with regard to the ceremonial law. It is therefore no way surprising, that infinite varieties of opinion should now be found in the Christian Church. A very probable consequence of this is, that whenever we see any 'casting out devils,' he will be one that, in this sense, 'followeth not us'—that is not of our opinion. It is scarce to be imagined he will be of our mind in all points, even of religion. He may very probably think in a different manner from us, even on several subjects of importance; such as the nature and use of the moral law, the eternal decrees of God, the sufficiency and efficacy of His grace, and the perseverance of His children.

4. He may differ from us, fourthly, not only in opinion, but likewise in some point of practice. He may not approve of that manner of worshipping God which is practised in our congregation; and may judge that to be more profitable for his soul which took its rise from Calvin or Martin Luther. He may have many objections to that Liturgy which we approve of beyond all others; many doubts concerning that form of church government which we esteem both apostolical and scriptural. Perhaps he may go farther from us yet: he may, from a principle of conscience, refrain from several of those which we believe to

be the ordinances of Christ. Or, if we both agree that they are ordained of God, there may still remain a difference between us, either as to the manner of administering those ordinances, or the persons to whom they should be administered. Now the unavoidable consequence of any of these differences will be, that he who thus differs from us must separate himself, with regard to those points, from our society. In this respect, therefore, 'he followeth not us': he is not (as we phrase it) 'of our Church.'

5. But in a far stronger sense 'he followeth not us,' who is not only of a different Church, but of such a Church as we account to be in many respects anti-scriptural and anti-Christian,—a Church which we believe to be utterly false and erroneous in her doctrines, as well as very dangerously wrong in her practice; guilty of gross superstition as well as idolatry,—a Church that has added many articles to the faith which was once delivered to the saints; that has dropped one whole commandment of God, and made void several of the rest by her traditions; and that, pretending the highest veneration for, and strictest conformity to, the ancient Church, has nevertheless brought in numberless innovations, without any warrant either from antiquity or Scripture. Now, most certainly, 'he followeth not us,' who stands at so great a distance from us.

6. And yet there may be a still wider difference than this. He who differs from us in judgement or practice, may possibly stand at a greater distance from us in affection than in judgement. And this indeed is a very natural and a very common effect of the other. The differences which begin in points of opinion seldom terminate there. They generally spread into the affections, and then separate chief friends. Nor are any animosities so deep and irreconcilable as those that spring from disagreement in religion. For this cause the bitterest enemies of a man are those of his own household. For this the father rises against his own children, and the children against the father; and perhaps persecute each other even to the death, thinking all the time they are doing God service. It is therefore nothing more than we may expect, if those who differ from us, either in religious opinions or practice, soon contract a sharpness, yea, bitterness towards us; if they are more and more prejudiced against us, till they conceive as ill an opinion of our persons as of

our principles. An almost necessary consequence of this will be, they will speak in the same manner as they think of us. They will set themselves in opposition to us, and, as far as they are able, hinder our work; seeing it does not appear to them to be the work of God, but either of man or of the devil. He that thinks, speaks, and acts in such a manner as this, in the highest sense, 'followeth not us.'

7. I do not indeed conceive, that the person of whom the Apostle speaks in the text (although we have no particular account of him, either in the context, or in any other part of holy writ) went so far as this. We have no ground to suppose that there was any material difference between him and the Apostles; much less that he had any prejudice either against them or their Master. It seems we may gather thus much from our Lord's own words, which immediately follow the text: 'There is no man which shall do a miracle in My name, that can lightly speak evil of Me.' But I purposely put the case in the strongest light, adding all the circumstances which can well be conceived; that, being forewarned of the temptation in its full strength, we may in no case yield to it, and fight against God.

III. 1. Suppose, then, a man have no intercourse with us, suppose he be not of our party, suppose he separate from our Church, yea, and widely differ from us, both in judgement, practice, and affection; yet if we see even this man 'casting out devils,' Jesus saith, 'Forbid him not.' This important direction of our Lord I am, in the third place, to explain.

2. If we see this man casting out devils: But it is well if, in such a case, we would believe even what we saw with our eyes, if we did not give the lie to our own senses. He must be little acquainted with human nature who does not immediately perceive how extremely unready we should be to believe that any man does cast out devils who 'followeth not us' in all or most of the senses above recited: I had almost said, in any of them; seeing we may easily learn even from what passes in our own breasts, how unwilling men are to allow anything good in those who do not in all things agree with themselves.

3. 'But what is a sufficient, reasonable proof, that a man does (in the sense above) cast out devils?' The answer is easy. Is there full proof, (1) That a person before us was a gross, open sinner?

(2) That he is not so now? that he has broke off his sins, and lives a Christian life? And (3) That this change was wrought by his hearing this man preach? If these three points be plain and undeniable, then you have sufficient, reasonable proof, such as you cannot resist without wilful sin, that this man casts out devils.

4. Then 'forbid him not.' Beware how you attempt to hinder him, either by your authority, or arguments, or persuasions. Do not in any wise strive to prevent his using all the power which God has given him. If you have *authority* with him, do not use that authority to stop the work of God. Do not furnish him with *reasons* why he ought not any more to speak in the name of Jesus. Satan will not fail to supply him with these, if you do not second him therein. *Persuade* him not to depart from the work. If he should give place to the devil and you, many souls might perish in their iniquity, but their blood would God require at *your* hands.

5. 'But what, if he be only a layman, who casts out devils! Ought I not to forbid him then?'

Is the fact allowed? Is there reasonable proof that this man has or does cast out devils? If there is, forbid him not; no, not at the peril of your soul. Shall not God work by whom He will work? No man can do these works unless God is with him; unless God hath sent him for this very thing. But if God hath sent him, will you call him back? Will you forbid him to go?

6. 'But I do not know that he is sent of God.' 'Now herein is a marvellous thing' (may any of the seals of his mission say, any whom he hath brought from Satan to God), 'that ye know not whence this man is, and, behold, he hath opened mine eyes! If this man were not of God, he could do nothing.' If you doubt the fact, send for the parents of the man: send for his brethren, friends, acquaintance. But if you cannot doubt this, if you must needs acknowledge 'that a notable miracle hath been wrought'; then with what conscience, with what face, can you charge him whom God hath sent, 'not to speak any more in His name'?

7. I allow, that it is highly expedient, whoever preaches in His name should have an outward as well as an inward call; but that it is *absolutely necessary,* I deny.

'Nay, is not the Scripture express? "No man taketh this honour unto himself, but he that is called of God, as was Aaron" '(Heb. v. 4).

Numberless times has this text been quoted on the occasion, as containing the very strength of the cause; but surely never was so unhappy a quotation. For, first, Aaron was not called to preach at all: he was called 'to offer gifts and sacrifice for sin.' That was his peculiar employment. Secondly, these men do not offer sacrifice at all, but only preach; which Aaron did not. Therefore it is not possible to find one text in all the Bible which is more wide of the point than this.

8. 'But what was the practice of the apostolic age?' You may easily see in the Acts of the Apostles. In the eighth chapter we read, 'There was a great persecution against the church which was at Jerusalem; and they were all scattered abroad throughout the regions of Judea and Samaria, except the Apostles' (verse 1). 'Therefore they that were scattered abroad went everywhere preaching the word' (verse 4). Now, were all these outwardly called to preach? No man in his senses can think so. Here, then, is an undeniable proof, what was the practice of the apostolic age. Here you see not one, but a multitude of lay preachers, men that were only sent of God.

9. Indeed, so far is the practice of the apostolic age from inclining us to think it was *unlawful* for a man to preach before he was ordained, that we have reason to think it was then accounted *necessary*. Certainly the practice and the direction of the Apostle Paul was, to *prove* a man before he was ordained at all. 'Let these' (the deacons), says he, 'first be proved; then let them use the office of a deacon' (1 Tim. iii. 10). *Proved,* how? By setting them to construe a sentence of Greek, and asking them a few commonplace questions? O amazing proof of a minister of Christ! Nay; but by making a clear, open trial (as is still done by most of the Protestant Churches of Europe), not only whether their lives be holy and unblameable, but whether they have such gifts as are absolutely and indispensably necessary in order to edify the Church of Christ.

10. But what if a man has these, and has brought sinners to repentance, and yet the Bishop will not ordain him? Then the Bishop does forbid him to cast out devils. But I dare not forbid him; I have published my reasons to all the world. Yet it is still insisted, I ought to do it. You who insist upon it answer those reasons. I know not that any have done this yet, or even made an attempt of doing it. Only some have spoken of them as very weak

and trifling: and this was prudent enough; for it is far easier to despise, at least seem to despise, an argument, than to answer it. Yet till this is done I must say, when I have reasonable proof that any man does cast out devils, whatever others do, I dare not forbid him, lest I be found even to fight against God.

11. And whosoever thou art that fearest God, 'forbid him not,' either directly or indirectly. There are many ways of doing this. You indirectly forbid him, if you either wholly deny, or despise and make little account of, the work which God has wrought by his hands. You indirectly forbid him, when you discourage him in his work, by drawing him into disputes concerning it, by raising objections against it, or frightening him with consequences which very possibly will never be. You forbid him when you show any unkindness toward him either in language or behaviour; and much more when you speak of him to others either in an unkind or a contemptuous manner; when you endeavour to represent him to any, either in an odious or a despicable light. You are forbidding him all the time you are speaking evil of him, or making no account of his labours. O forbid him not in any of these ways; nor by forbidding others to hear him,—by discouraging sinners from hearing that word which is able to save their souls!

12. Yea, if you would observe our Lords direction in its full meaning and extent, then remember His word: 'He that is not for us is against us; and he that gathereth not with Me scattereth': he that gathereth not men into the kingdom of God, assuredly scatters them from it. For there can be no neuter in this war. Every one is either on God's side, or on Satan's. Are you on God's side? Then you will not only not forbid any man that casts out devils, but you will labour, to the uttermost of your power, to forward him in the work. You will readily acknowledge the work of God, and confess the greatness of it. You will remove all difficulties and objections, as far as may be, out of his way. You will strengthen his hands by speaking honourably of him before all men, and avowing the things which you have seen and heard. You will encourage others to attend upon his word, to hear him whom God hath sent. And you will omit no actual proof of tender love, which God gives you an opportunity of showing him.

IV. 1. If we willingly fail in any of these points, if we either directly or indirectly forbid him, 'because he followeth not us,' then we are bigots. This is the inference I draw from what has been said. But the term 'bigotry,' I fear, as frequently as it is used, is almost as little understood as 'enthusiasm.' It is too strong an attachment to, or fondness for, our own party, opinion, church, and religion. Therefore he is a bigot who is so fond of any of these, so strongly attached to them, as to forbid any who casts out devils because he differs from himself in any or all these particulars.

2. Do *you* beware of this. Take care (1) That you do not convict yourself of bigotry, by your unreadiness to believe that any man does cast out devils, who differs from you. And if you are clear thus far, if you acknowledge the fact, then examine yourself, (2) Am I not convicted of bigotry in this, in forbidding him directly or indirectly? Do I not directly forbid him on this ground, because he is not of my party, because he does not fall in with my opinions, or because he does not worship God according to that scheme of religion which I have received from my fathers?

3. Examine yourself, Do I not indirectly at least forbid him, on any of these grounds? Am I not sorry that God should thus own and bless a man that holds such erroneous opinions? Do I not discourage him, because he is not of my Church, by disputing with him concerning it, by raising objections, and by perplexing his mind with distant consequences? Do I show no anger, contempt, or unkindness of any sort, either in my words or actions? Do I not mention behind his back, his (real or supposed) faults—his defects or infirmities? Do not I hinder sinners from hearing his word? If you do any of these things, you are a bigot to this day.

4. 'Search me, O Lord, and prove me. Try out my reins and my heart! Look well if there be any way of' bigotry 'in me, and lead me in the way everlasting.' In order to examine ourselves thoroughly, let the case be proposed in the strongest manner. What, if I were to see a Papist, an Arian, a Socinian, casting out devils? If I did, I could not forbid even him, without convicting myself of bigotry. Yea, if it could be supposed that I should see a jew, a Deist, or a Turk, doing the same, were I to forbid him either directly or indirectly, I should be no better than a bigot still.

5. O stand clear of this! But be not content with not forbidding any that casts out devils. It is well to go thus far; but do not stop here. If you will avoid all bigotry, go on. In every instance of this kind, whatever the instrument be, acknowledge the finger of God. And not only acknowledge, but rejoice in His work, and praise His name with thanksgiving. Encourage whomsoever God is pleased to employ, to give himself wholly up thereto. Speak well of him wheresoever you are; defend his character and his mission. Enlarge, as far as you can, his sphere of action; show him all kindness in word and deed; and cease not to cry to God in his behalf, that he may save both himself and them that hear him.

6. I need add but one caution: Think not the bigotry of another is any excuse for your own. It is not impossible, that one who casts out devils himself, may yet forbid you so to do. You may observe, this is the very case mentioned in the text. The Apostles forbade another to do what they did themselves. But beware of retorting. It is not your part to return evil for evil. Another's not observing the direction of our Lord, is no reason why you should neglect it. Nay, but let him have all the bigotry to himself. If he forbid *you* do not you forbid *him*. Rather labour, and watch, and pray the more, to confirm your love toward him. If he speak all manner of evil of you, speak all manner of good (that is true) of *him*. Imitate herein that glorious saying of a great man (O that he had always breathed the same spirit!), 'Let Luther call me a hundred devils; I will still reverence him as a messenger of God.'

SERMON XXXIV

CATHOLIC SPIRIT

This sermon was first published in Vol. III of the Sermons, 1750. Wesley preached it at Newcastle on September 8, 1749, and at Bristol on November 3 of the same year; he doubtless revised it for the press in December at Stoke Newington along with the rest; see introduction to Sermon XXIX. It was republished separately by H. Cock in 1755, with a hymn appended by Charles Wesley on Catholic Love. This hymn was greatly beloved by Dean Stanley.

I

Weary of all this wordy strife,
　These notions, forms, and modes, and names,
To Thee, the Way, the Truth, the Life,
　Whose love my simple heart inflames,
Divinely taught, at last I fly
　With Thee and Thine to live and die.

II

Forth from the midst or *Babel* brought,
　Parties and sects I cast behind;
Inlarged my heart, and free my thought,
　Where'er the latent truth I find,
The latent truth with joy to own,
And bow to Jesus' name alone.

III

Redeem'd by Thine almighty grace,
　I taste my glorious liberty,
With open arms the world embrace,
　But *cleave* to those who cleave to Thee;
But only in Thy saints *delight*,
Who walk with God in purest white.

IV

One with the little flock I rest,
　The members sound who hold the Head;
The chosen few, with pardon blest,

And by the anointing Spirit led
Into the mind that was in Thee,
Into the depths of Deity.

V

My brethren, friends, and kinsmen these,
   Who do my heavenly Father's will,
Who *aim* at perfect holiness,
   And all Thy counsels to fulfil,
Athirst to be whatever Thou art,
And love their God with all their heart.

VI

For these, howe'er in flesh disjoin'd,
   Where'er dispersed o'er earth abroad,
Unfeigned, unbounded love I find,
   And constant as the life of God;
Fountain of life, from thence it sprung,
As pure, as even, and as strong.

VII

Join'd to the hidden church unknown
   In this sure bond of perfectness,
Obscurely safe, I dwell alone,
   And glory in the uniting grace,
To me, to each believer given,
To all Thy saints in earth and heaven.

                               C. W.

   The text is purely a motto; Jehu is not only discarded, like 'poor Agrippa' in the 'Almost Christian,' but is stigmatized as 'a mixed character'; and Wesley expressly states (par. 12) that in examining the meaning of the question, he does not try to discover what Jehu implied in it, but what a follower of Christ should understand thereby. When Wesley sent a copy of the sermon to the Rev. Mr. Clark, of Hollymount, that gentleman's criticism, 'Your propositions and observations have no more foundation in the text than in the first chapter of Genesis,' was entirely justified. Jehu had waded through slaughter to a throne; he had murdered two kings and one hundred and twelve princes, and had given Queen Jezebel to the dogs to eat; he was now on his way to destroy by a ruthless massacre the priests and worshippers of Baal, not for religious but for political reasons for they would probably have resisted the murderer of their patrons. Ahab and Jezebel. On the road he met the stern fanatic Jehonadab, who, in his passionate revolt against the prevailing Baal-worship and luxury of the times, had led his Kenites into the solitudes of the wilderness, and bound them with a vow to live always in tents away from a corrupt civilization, and to abstain altogether from wine and strong drink. Jehu recognized in him a valuable ally in his crusade, though his motive was altogether different; and asking, 'Are you with me in this business?' on receiving his vehement answer, 'I am, I am!' he dragged him up into his own chariot. (Not the last time that a crafty politician has given countenance to his proceedings by gaining the alliance of a fanatical religionist.) All this has little enough to do with the Catholic Spirit; but Wesley did not mind. The question and answer divorced from its context suited his purpose, and so he took it for the text of this, one of the noblest sermons he ever preached.

It was on the broad, catholic lines here drawn that he had founded his Societies. The only condition laid down for admission to them was that the candidate should have 'a desire to flee from the wrath to come, to be saved from his sins.' In the *Plain Account* (1748) he says, 'Orthodoxy, or right opinions, is, at best, but a very slender part of religion, if it can be allowed to be any part of it at all'; and forty years later, in the sermon on the Ministerial Office (No CXV) he concludes: 'We, by the grace of God, hold on our way; being ourselves still members of the Church of England, as we were from the beginning, but receiving all that love God in every Church, as our brother, and sister, and mother. And in order to their union with us, we require no unity in opinions, or in modes of worship, but barely that they "fear God and work righteousness" as was observed. Now, this is utterly a new thing, unheard of in any other Christian community. In what Church or congregation beside, throughout the Christian world, can members be admitted upon these terms, without any other conditions? Point any such out, whoever can; I know none in Europe, Asia, Africa, or America! This is the glory of the Methodists, and of them alone! They are themselves no particular sect or party; but they receive those, of all parties, who endeavour "to do justly, and love mercy, and walk humbly with their God.' " See also the *Journal*, May 18, 1788,' I do not know any other religious society . . . wherein such liberty of conscience is now allowed, or has been allowed, since the age of the Apostles. Here is our glorying; and a glorying peculiar to us. What society shares it with us?'

And when he was departed thence, he lighted on Jehonadab the son of Rechab
coming to meet him: and he saluted him and said to him, Is thine heart right,
as my heart is with thy heart? And Jehonadab answered, It is. If it be, give
me thine hand.—2 KINGS X. 15.

1. It is allowed even by those who do not pay this great debt, that love is due to all mankind; the royal law, 'Thou shalt, love thy neighbour as thyself,' carrying its own evidence to all that hear it: and that, not according to the miserable construction put upon it by the zealots of old times, 'Thou shalt love thy

neighbour,' thy relation, acquaintance, friend, 'and hate thine enemy': not so; 'I say unto you,' saith our Lord, 'Love your enemies, bless them that curse you, do good to them that hate you, and pray for them that despitefully use you, and persecute you; that ye may be the children,' may appear so to all mankind, 'of your Father which is in heaven; who maketh His sun to rise on the evil and on the good, and sendeth rain on the just and on the unjust.'

2. But it is sure, there is a peculiar love which we owe to those that love God. So David: 'All my delight is upon the saints that are in the earth, and upon such as excel in virtue.' And so a greater than he: 'A new commandment I give unto you, That ye love one another; as I have loved you, that ye also love one another. By this shall all men know that ye are My disciples, if ye have love one to another' (John xiii. 34, 35). This is that love on which the Apostle John so frequently and strongly insists: 'This,' saith he, 'is the message that ye heard from the beginning, that we should love one another' (1 John iii. 11). 'Hereby perceive we the love of God, because He laid down His life for us: and we ought,' if love should call us thereto, 'to lay down our lives for the brethren' (verse 16). And again: 'Beloved, let us love one another: for love is of God. He that loveth not, knoweth not God; for God is love' (iv. 7, 8). 'Not that we loved God, but that He loved us, and sent His Son to be the propitiation for our sins. Beloved, if God so loved us, we ought also to love one another' (verses 10, 11).

3. All men approve of this; but do all men practise it? Daily experience shows the contrary. Where are even the Christians who 'love one another as He hath given us commandment'? How many hindrances lie in the way! The two grand, general hindrances are, first, that they cannot all think alike; and, in consequence of this, secondly, they cannot all walk alike; but in several smaller points their practice must differ in proportion to the difference of their sentiments.

4. But although a difference in opinions or modes of worship may prevent an entire external union, yet need it prevent our union in affection? Though we cannot think alike, may we not love alike? May we not be of one heart, though we are not of one opinion? Without all doubt, we may. Herein all the children of God may unite, notwithstanding these smaller differences.

These remaining as they are, they may forward one another in love and in good works.

5. Surely in this respect the example of Jehu himself, as mixed a character as he was of, is well worthy both the attention and imitation of every serious Christian. 'And when he was departed thence, he lighted on Jehonadab the son of Rechab coming to meet him: and he saluted him, and said to him, Is thine heart right, as my heart is with thy heart? And Jehonadab answered, It is. If it be, give me thine hand.'

The text naturally divides itself into two parts:—First, a question proposed by Jehu to Jehonadab: 'Is thine heart right, as my heart is with thy heart?' Secondly, an offer made on Jehonadab's answering, 'It is': 'If it be, give me thine hand.'

I. 1. And, first, let us consider the question proposed by Jehu to Jehonadab, 'Is thine heart right, as my heart is with thy heart?'

The very first thing we may observe in these words, is, that here is no inquiry concerning Jehonadab's opinions. And yet it is certain, he held some which were very uncommon, indeed quite peculiar to himself; and some which had a close influence upon his practice; on which, likewise, he laid so great a stress, as to entail them upon his children's children, to their latest posterity. This is evident from the account given by Jeremiah, many years after his death: 'I took Jaazaniah and his brethren, and all his sons, and the whole house of the Rechabites, . . . and set before them pots full of wine, and cups, and said unto them, Drink ye wine. But they said, We will drink no wine for Jonadab,' or Jehonadab, 'the son of Rechab, our father' (it would be less ambiguous, if the words were placed thus: 'Jehonadab our father, the son of Rechab'; out of love and reverence to whom, he probably desired his descendants might be called by his name), 'commanded us, saying, Ye shall drink no wine, neither ye, nor your sons for ever. Neither shall ye build house, nor sow seed, nor plant vineyard, nor have any: but all your days ye shall dwell in tents. . . . And we have obeyed, and done according to all that Jonadab our father commanded us' (Jer. xxxv. 3-10).

2. And yet Jehu (although it seems to have been his manner, both in things secular and religious, to *drive furiously*) does not concern himself at all with any of these things, but lets Jehonadab abound in his own sense. And neither of them

appears to have given the other the least disturbance touching the opinions which he maintained.

3. It is very possible, that many good men now also may entertain peculiar opinions; and some of them may be as singular herein as even Jehonadab was. And it is certain, so long as we know but *in part,* that all men will not see all things alike. It is an unavoidable consequence of the present weakness and shortness of human understanding, that several men will be of several minds in religion as well as in common life. So it has been from the beginning of the world, and so it will be 'till the restitution of all things.'

4. Nay, farther: although every man necessarily believes that every particular opinion which he holds is true (for to believe any opinion is not true, is the same thing as not to hold it); yet can no man be assured that all his own opinions, taken together, are true. Nay, every thinking man is assured they are not; seeing *humanum est errare et nescire:* 'to be ignorant of many things, and to mistake in some, is the necessary condition of humanity.' This, therefore, he is sensible, is his own case. He knows, in the general, that he himself is mistaken; although in what particulars he mistakes, he does not, perhaps he cannot, know.

5. I say, 'perhaps he cannot know'; for who can tell how far invincible ignorance may extend? or (that comes to the same thing) invincible prejudice?—which is often so fixed in tender minds, that it is afterwards impossible to tear up what has taken so deep a root. And who can say, unless he knew every circumstance attending it, how far any mistake is culpable? seeing all guilt must suppose some concurrence of the will; of which He only can judge who searcheth the heart.

6. Every wise man, therefore, will allow others the same liberty of thinking which he desires they should allow him; and will no more insist on their embracing his opinions, than he would have them to insist on his embracing theirs. He bears with those who differ from him, and only asks him with whom he desires to unite in love that single question, 'Is thy heart right, as my heart is with thy heart?'

7. We may, secondly, observe, that here is no inquiry made concerning Jehonadab's mode of worship; although it is highly probable there was, in this respect also, a very wide difference between them. For we may well believe Jehonadab, as well as all

his posterity, worshipped God at Jerusalem: whereas Jehu did not: he had more regard to state-policy than religion. And, therefore, although he slew the worshippers of Baal, and 'destroyed Baal out of Israel'; yet from the convenient sin of Jeroboam, the worship of 'the golden calves,' he 'departed not' (2 Kings x. 29).

8. But even among men of an upright heart, men who desire to 'have a conscience void of offence,' it must needs be, that, as long as there are various opinions, there will be various ways of worshipping God; seeing a variety of opinions necessarily implies a variety of practice. And as, in all ages, men have differed in nothing more than in their opinions concerning the Supreme Being, so in nothing have they more differed from each other, than in the manner of worshipping Him. Had this been only in the heathen world, it would not have been at all surprising: for we know, these 'by' their 'wisdom knew not God'; nor, therefore, could they know how to worship Him. But is it not strange, that even in the Christian world, although they all agree in the general, 'God is a Spirit; and they that worship Him must worship Him in spirit and in truth'; yet the particular modes of worshipping God are almost as various as among the Heathens?

9. And how shall we choose among so much variety? No man can choose for, or prescribe to, another. But every one must follow the dictates of his own conscience, in simplicity and godly sincerity. He must be fully persuaded in his own mind; and then act according to the best light he has. Nor has any creature power to constrain another to walk by his own rule. God has given no right to any of the children of men thus to lord it over the conscience of his brethren; but every man must judge for himself, as every man must give an account of himself to God.

10. Although, therefore, every follower of Christ is obliged, by the very nature of the Christian institution, to be a member of some particular congregation or other, some Church, as it is usually termed (which implies a particular manner of worshipping God; for 'two cannot walk together unless they be agreed.'); yet none can be obliged by any power on earth but that of his own conscience, to prefer this or that congregation to another, this or that particular manner of worship. I know it is commonly supposed that the place of our birth fixes the Church to which

we ought to belong; that one, for instance, who is born in England, ought to be a member of that which is styled the Church of England; and consequently, to worship God in the particular manner which is prescribed by that Church. I was once a zealous maintainer of this; but I find many reasons to abate of this zeal. I fear it is attended with such difficulties as no reasonable man can get over. Not the least of which is, that if this rule had took place, there could have been no Reformation from Popery; seeing it entirely destroys the right of private judgement, on which that whole Reformation stands.

11. I dare not, therefore, presume to impose my mode of worship on any other. I believe it is truly primitive and apostolical: but my belief is no rule for another. I ask not, therefore, of him with whom I would unite in love, Are you of my church, of my congregation? Do you receive the same form of church government, and allow the same church officers, with me? Do you join in the same form of prayer wherein I worship God? I inquire not, Do you receive the supper of the Lord in the same posture and manner that I do? nor whether, in the administration of baptism, you agree with me in admitting sureties for the baptized; in the manner of administering it; or the age of those to whom it should be administered. Nay, I ask not of you (as clear as I am in my own mind), whether you allow baptism and the Lord's supper at all. Let all these things stand by: we will talk of them, if need be, at a more convenient season; my only question at present is this, 'Is thine heart right, as my heart is with thy heart?'

12. But what is properly implied in the question? I do not mean, What did Jehu imply therein? But, What should a follower of Christ understand thereby, when he proposes it to any of his brethren?

The first thing implied is this: Is thy heart right with God? Dost thou believe His being, and His perfections? His eternity, immensity, wisdom, power? His justice, mercy, and truth? Dost thou believe that He now 'upholdeth all things by the word of His power'? and that He governs even the most minute, even the most noxious, to His own glory, and the good of them that love Him? Hast thou a divine evidence, a supernatural conviction, of the things of God? Dost thou 'walk by faith, not by sight'? looking not at temporal things, but things eternal?

13. Dost thou believe in the Lord Jesus Christ, 'God over all, blessed for ever'? Is He revealed in thy soul? Dost thou know Jesus Christ and Him crucified? Does He dwell in thee, and thou in Him? Is He formed in thy heart by faith? Having absolutely disclaimed all thy own works, thy own righteousness, hast thou 'submitted thyself unto the righteousness of God,' which is by faith in Christ Jesus? Art thou 'found in Him, not having thy own righteousness, but the righteousness which is by faith'? And art thou, through Him, 'fighting the good fight of faith, and laying hold of eternal life'?

14. Is thy faith ενεργουμενη δι αγαπης—*filled with the energy of love*? Dost thou love God (I do not say 'above all things,' for it is both an unscriptural and an ambiguous expression, but) 'with all thy heart, and with all thy mind and with all thy soul, and with all thy strength'? Dost thou seek all thy happiness in Him alone? And dost thou find what thou seekest? Does thy soul continually 'magnify the Lord, and thy spirit rejoice in God thy Saviour'? Having learned 'in everything to give thanks,' dost thou find 'it is a joyful and a pleasant thing to be thankful'? Is God the centre of thy soul, the sum of all thy desires? Art thou accordingly laying up thy treasure in heaven, and counting all things else dung and dross? Hath the love of God cast the love of the world out of thy soul? Then thou art 'crucified to the world'; thou art dead to all below; and thy 'life is hid with Christ in God.'

15. Art thou employed in doing, 'not thy own will, but the will of Him that sent thee'—of Him that sent thee down to sojourn here awhile, to spend a few days in a strange land, till, having finished the work He hath given thee to do, thou return to thy Father's house? Is it thy meat and drink 'to do the will of thy Father which is in heaven'? Is thine eye single in all things? always fixed on Him? always looking unto Jesus? Dost thou point at Him in whatsoever thou doest? in all thy labour, thy business, thy conversation? aiming only at the glory of God in all; 'whatsoever thou doest, either in word or deed, doing it all in the name of the Lord Jesus; giving thanks unto God, even the Father, through Him'?

16. Does the love of God constrain thee to serve Him with fear, to 'rejoice unto Him with reverence'? Art thou more afraid of displeasing God, than either of death or hell? Is nothing so terrible to thee as the thought of offending the eyes of His glory?

Upon this ground, dost thou 'hate all evil ways,' every transgression of His holy and perfect law; and herein 'exercise thyself, to have a conscience void of offence toward God, and toward man'?

17. Is thy heart right toward thy neighbour? Dost thou love, as thyself, all mankind, without exception? 'If you love those only that love you, what thank have ye?' Do you 'love your enemies'? Is your soul full of good-will, of tender affection, toward them? Do you love even the enemies of God, the unthankful and unholy? Do your bowels yearn over them? Could you 'wish yourself' temporally 'accursed' for their sake? And do you show this by 'blessing them that curse you, and praying for those that despitefully use you, and persecute you'?

18. Do you show your love by your works? While you have time, as you have opportunity, do you in fact 'do good to all men,' neighbours or strangers, friends or enemies, good or bad? Do you do them all the good you can; endeavouring to supply all their wants; assisting them both in body and soul, to the uttermost of your power?—If thou art thus minded, may every Christian say, yea, if thou art but sincerely desirous of it, and following on till thou attain, then 'thy heart is right, as my heart is with thy heart.'

II. 1. 'If it be, give me thy hand.' I do not mean, 'Be of my opinion.' You need not: I do not expect or desire it. Neither do I mean, 'I will be of your opinion.' I cannot: it does not depend on my choice: I can no more think, than I can see or hear, as I will. Keep you your opinion; I mine; and that as steadily as ever. You need not even endeavour to come over to me, or bring me over to you. I do not desire you to dispute those points, or to hear or speak one word concerning them. Let all opinions alone on one side and the other: only 'give me thine hand.'

2. I do not mean, 'Embrace my modes of worship'; or, 'I will embrace yours.' This also is a thing which does not depend either on your choice or mine. We must both act as each is fully persuaded in his own mind. Hold you fast that which you believe is most acceptable to God, and I will do the same. I believe the Episcopal form of church government to be scriptural and apostolical. If you think the Presbyterian or Independent is better, think so still, and act accordingly. I believe infants ought

to be baptized; and that this may be done either by dipping or sprinkling. If you are otherwise persuaded, be so still, and follow your own persuasion. It appears to me, that forms of prayer are of excellent use, particularly in the great congregation. If you judge extemporary prayer to be of more use, act suitably to your own judgement. My sentiment is, that I ought not to forbid water, wherein persons may be baptized; and that I ought to eat bread and drink wine, as a memorial of my dying Master: however, if you are not convinced of this, act according to the light you have. I have no desire to dispute with you one moment upon any of the preceding heads. Let all these smaller points stand aside. Let them never come into sight. 'If thine heart is as my heart,' if thou lovest God and all mankind, I ask no more: 'give me thine hand.'

3. I mean, first, love me: and that not only as thou lovest all mankind; not only as thou lovest thine enemies, or the enemies of God, those that hate thee, that 'despitefully use thee, and persecute thee'; not only as a stranger, as one of whom thou knowest neither good nor evil,—I am not satisfied with this,—no; 'if thine heart be right, as mine with thy heart,' then love me with a very tender affection, as a friend that is closer than a brother; as a brother in Christ, a fellow citizen of the New Jerusalem, a fellow soldier engaged in the same warfare, under the same Captain of our salvation. Love me as a companion in the kingdom and patience of Jesus, and a joint heir of His glory.

4. Love me (but in a higher degree than thou dost the bulk of mankind) with the love that is *long-suffering and kind*; that is patient,—if I am ignorant or out of the way, bearing and not increasing my burden; and is tender, soft, and compassionate still; that *envieth not,* if at any time it please God to prosper me in His work even more than thee. Love me with the love that is *not provoked,* either at my follies or infirmities; or even at my acting (if it should sometimes so appear to thee) not according to the will of God. Love me so as to *think no evil* of me; to put away all jealousy and evil-surmising. Love me with the love that *covereth all things*; that never reveals either my faults or infirmities,—that believeth all things; is always willing to think the best, to put the fairest construction on all my words and actions,—that *hopeth all things*; either that the thing related was never done; or not done with such circumstances as are related; or, at least, that it was

done with a good intention, or in a sudden stress of temptation. And hope to the end, that whatever is amiss will, by the grace of God, be corrected; and whatever is wanting, supplied, through the riches of His mercy in Christ Jesus.

5. I mean, secondly, commend me to God in all thy prayers; wrestle with Him in my behalf, that He would speedily correct what He sees amiss, and supply what is wanting in me. In thy nearest access to the throne of grace, beg of Him who is then very present with thee, that my heart may be more as thy heart, more right both toward God and toward man; that I may have a fuller conviction of things not seen, and a stronger view of the love of God in Christ Jesus; may more steadily walk by faith, not by sight; and more earnestly grasp eternal life. Pray that the love of God and of all mankind may be more largely poured into my heart; that I may be more fervent and active in doing the will of my Father which is in heaven; more zealous of good works, and more careful to abstain from all appearance of evil.

6. I mean, thirdly, provoke me to love and to good works. Second thy prayer, as thou hast opportunity, by speaking to me, in love, whatsoever thou believest to be for my soul's health. Quicken me in the work which God has given me to do, and instruct me how to do it more perfectly. Yea, 'smite me friendly, and reprove me,' whereinsoever I appear to thee to be doing rather my own will, than the will of Him that sent me. O speak and spare not, whatever thou believest may conduce, either to the amending my faults, the strengthening my weakness, the building me up in love, or the making me more fit, in any kind, for the Master's use.

7. I mean, lastly, love me not in word only, but in deed and in truth. So far as in conscience thou canst (retaining still thy own opinions, and thy own manner of worshipping God), join with me in the work of God; and let us go on hand in hand. And thus far, it is certain, thou mayest go. Speak honourably, wherever thou art, of the work of God, by whomsoever He works, and kindly of His messengers. And, if it be in thy power, not only sympathize with them when they are in any difficulty or distress, but give them a cheerful and effectual assistance, that they may glorify God on thy behalf.

8. Two things should be observed with regard to what has been spoken under this last head: the one, that whatsoever love,

whatsoever offices of love, whatsoever spiritual or temporal
assistance, I claim from him whose heart is right, as my heart is
with his, the same I am ready, by the grace of God, according to
my measure, to give him: the other, that I have not made this
claim in behalf of myself only, but of all whose heart is right
toward God and man, that we may all love one another as Christ
hath loved us.

III. 1. One inference we may make from what has been said.
We may learn from hence, what is a catholic spirit.

There is scarce any expression which has been more grossly
misunderstood, and more dangerously misapplied, than this:
but it will be easy for any who calmly consider the preceding
observations, to correct any such misapprehensions of it, and to
prevent any such misapplication.

For, from hence we may learn, first, that a catholic spirit is not
speculative latitudinarianism. It is not an indifference to all
opinions: this is the spawn of hell, not the offspring of heaven.
This unsettledness of thought, this being 'driven to and fro, and
tossed about with every wind of doctrine,' is a great curse, not a
blessing; an irreconcilable enemy, not a friend, to true
catholicism. A man of a truly catholic spirit has not now his
religion to seek. He is fixed as the sun in his judgement
concerning the main branches of Christian doctrine. It is true,
he is always ready to hear and weigh whatsoever can be offered
against his principles; but as this does not show any wavering in
his own mind, so neither does it occasion any. He does not halt
between two opinions, nor vainly endeavour to blend them into
one. Observe this, you who know not what spirit ye are of: who
call yourselves men of a catholic spirit, only because you are of a
muddy understanding; because your mind is all in a mist;
because you have no settled, consistent principles, but are for
jumbling all opinions together. Be convinced, that you have
quite missed your way; you know not where you are. You think
you are got into the very spirit of Christ; when, in truth, you are
nearer the spirit of Antichrist. Go, first, and learn the first
elements of the gospel of Christ, and then shall you learn to be of
a truly catholic spirit.

2. From what has been said, we may learn, secondly, that a
catholic spirit is not any kind of *practical* latitudinarianism. It is

not indifference as to public worship, or as to the outward manner of performing it. This, likewise, would not be a blessing, but a curse. Far from being an help thereto, it would, so long as it remained, be an unspeakable hindrance to the worshipping of God in spirit and in truth. But the man of a truly catholic spirit, having weighed all things in the balance of the sanctuary, has no doubt, no scruple at all, concerning that particular mode of worship wherein he joins. He is clearly convinced, that *this* manner of worshipping God is both scriptural and rational. He knows none in the world which is more scriptural, none which is more rational. Therefore, without rambling hither and thither, he cleaves close thereto, and praises God for the opportunity of so doing.

3. Hence we may, thirdly, learn, that a catholic spirit is not indifference to all congregations. This is another sort of latitudinarianism, no less absurd and unscriptural than the former. But it is far from a man of a truly catholic spirit. He is fixed in his congregation as well as his principles. He is united to one, not only in spirit, but by all the outward ties of Christian fellowship. There he partakes of all the ordinances of God. There he receives the supper of the Lord. There he pours out his soul in public prayer, and joins in public praise and thanksgiving. There he rejoices to hear the word of reconciliation, the gospel of the grace of God. With these his nearest, his best-beloved brethren, on solemn occasions, he seeks God by fasting. These particularly he watches over in love, as they do over his soul; admonishing, exhorting, comforting, reproving, and every way building up each other in the faith. These he regards as his own household; and therefore, according to the ability God has given him, naturally cares for them, and provides that they may have all the things that are needful for life and godliness.

4. But while he is steadily fixed in his religious principles, in what he believes to be the truth as it is in Jesus; while he firmly adheres to that worship of God which he judges to be most acceptable in His sight; and while he is united by the tenderest and closest ties to one particular congregation,—his heart is enlarged toward all mankind, those he knows and those he does not; he embraces with strong and cordial affection neighbours and strangers, friends and enemies. This is catholic or universal

love. And he that has this is of a catholic spirit. For love alone gives the title to this character: catholic love is a catholic spirit.

5. If, then, we take this word in the strictest sense, a man of a catholic spirit is one who, in the manner above-mentioned, gives his hand to all whose hearts are right with his heart: one who knows how to value, and praise God for, all the advantages he enjoys, with regard to the knowledge of the things of God, the true scriptural manner of worshipping Him, and, above all, his union with a congregation fearing God and working righteousness: one who, retaining these blessings with the strictest care, keeping them as the apple of his eye, at the same time loves—as friends, as brethren in the Lord, as members of Christ and children of God, as joint partakers now of the present kingdom of God, and fellow heirs of His eternal kingdom—all, of whatever opinion or worship, or congregation, who believe in the Lord Jesus Christ; who love God and man; who, rejoicing to please, and fearing to offend God, are careful to abstain from evil, and zealous of good works. He is the man of a truly catholic spirit, who bears all these continually upon his heart; who, having an unspeakable tenderness for their persons, and longing for their welfare, does not cease to commend them to God in prayer, as well as to plead their cause before men; who speaks comfortably to them, and labours, by all his words, to strengthen their hands in God. He assists them to the uttermost of his power in all things, spiritual and temporal. He is ready 'to spend and be spent for them'; yea, to lay down his life for their sake.

6. Thou, O man of God, think on these things! If thou art already in this way, go on. If thou hast heretofore mistook the path, bless God who hath brought thee back! And now run the race which is set before thee, in the royal way of universal love. Take heed, lest thou be either wavering in thy judgement, or straitened in thy bowels: but keep an even pace, rooted in the faith once delivered to the saints, and grounded in love, in true catholic love, till thou art swallowed up in love for ever and ever!

SERMON XXXV

CHRISTIAN PERFECTION

This sermon was first published in 1741, with Charles Wesley's hymn appended. In *A Plain Account of Christian Perfection*, 1,. Wesley says: 'I think it was in the latter end of the year 1740 that I had a conversation with Dr. Gibson, then Bishop of London, at Whitehall. He asked me what I meant by perfection. I told him without any disguise or reserve. When I ceased speaking, he said, "Mr. Wesley, if this be all you mean, publish it to all the world. If any one then can confute what you say, he may have free leave." I answered, "My Lord, I will"; and accordingly wrote and published the sermon on Christian Perfection.' It is curious that there is no reference to this interview in the *Journal*; but on Sunday, January 4, 1741, Wesley preached from Phil. iii. 13, 14 at Bristol; and again at Kingswood on March 22. Phil. iii. was the subject of his expositions to the Bands in London during the first week in April. A second edition of the sermon appeared in 1743, published by Gooding of Newcastle, no doubt during Wesley's visit there in March.

A Plain Account of Christian Perfection as believed and taught by the Rev. Mr. John Wesley from the year 1725 to the year 1765 was published in 1766. In the fourth edition the title is altered to 'from the year 1725 to the year 1777.' In it he traces the steps by which he was led to embrace this doctrine, and names and gives large extracts from the various works in which he advocated it. He finds the origin of it in Jeremy Taylor's *Holy Living and Dying,* which he read in 1725; Thomas a Kempis in 1726; and 'a year or two after' Law's *Christian Perfection and Serious Call* convinced him more than ever of the necessity of being wholly devoted to God. His study of the Bible confirmed what he had learnt from these writers, and in the sermon on the Circumcision of the Heart (No. XIII), preached before the University in 1733, he declared the possibility and duty of perfection; and he says that this is the view he still holds 'without any material addition or diminution.' He goes on to quote from the *Hymns and Sacred Poems* (1739), *The Character of a Methodist* (1742), this sermon (1741) the preface to the second volume of *Hymns* (1741), and the *Hymns and Sacred Poems* (1742), the *Minutes* of 1744, 1745, 1746, and 1747, Charles Wesley's *Hymns and Sacred Poems* (1749 and 1752), *Thoughts on Christian Perfection,* appended to the fourth volume of the Sermons (1760), *Farther Thoughts on Christian Perfection* (1763), *Cautions and Directions to the Greatest Professors* (1762), and a brief review of the whole subject, written in 1764, and printed in full. He sums it up from three points of view as (1) Purity of intention, dedicating all the life to God; (2) All the mind which was in Christ, enabling us to walk as Christ walked; the renewal of the heart in the whole image of God; (3) Loving God with all our heart, and our neighbour as ourselves; in other words, Full Consecration, Entire Sanctification, Perfect Love. On January 27, 1767, he wrote a page of 'Brief Thoughts on Christian Perfection,' which he published in his collected *Works,* 1771. The student should also read Sermon LXXVI, on Heb. vi. 1.

In spite of his assertion that his views had not changed in any material point from 1725 to 1765, he certainly modified them as time went on. In the earlier sermons, e.g. The Almost Christian, Circumcision of the Heart, The Witness of our own Spirit, he teaches that the justified believer is entirely freed from sin at his conversion. But this he corrects in the sermons on Sin in Believers and The Repentance of Believers (1767), in which he maintains that, though the believer is saved from outward sin, yet inward sin, the carnal mind, still remains and wars against the spirit. 'We may by the spirit mortify the deeds of the body; yet . . . by all the grace which is given at justification we cannot extirpate them. Most sure we cannot, till it shall please our Lord to speak the second time "Be clean"; and then only the leprosy is cleansed. Then only the evil root, the carnal mind, is destroyed; and inbred sin subsists no more' (Sermon XLVII, i. 20). So in *Farther Thoughts,* Q. 15, he says of the entirely sanctified man, 'One commends me. Here is a temptation to pride. But instantly my soul is humbled before God, and I feel no pride. A man strikes me. Here is a temptation to anger. But my heart overflows with love. And I feel no anger at all. A woman solicits me. Here is a temptation to lust. But in the instant I shrink back; and I feel no desire or lust at all.' The justified man feels pride, or anger, or lust; but by the grace of God he does not yield to them; the entirely sanctified man does not feel them at all. Wesley was profoundly right when he taught that the only way by which such a result could be achieved was the complete domination of the love of God in the heart. Both he and many of his followers have been brought into some confusion of view by the idea that the carnal mind is something in man which can be removed, like an aching tooth or a cancerous growth; or a sort of stain or defilement which can be washed away, like an inkblot, or a patch of filth on the body. Now the carnal mind is not a *thing* at all. It is really the absence of a sufficient inhibition upon the desires of the flesh and the mind. Recent psychological investigations have shown that the strongest instincts can be completely inhibited by a dominating emotion, so that they are not even felt. The sense of loyalty and devotion to duty will do it; many of our boys who have been at the front in the late war have told me that though beforehand they were horribly afraid, yet when the time came to 'go over the top' all fear vanished, and the only thought present to their minds was the exhilarating sense of a duty to be done. Fear can utterly annihilate all other feelings; so can hate; so can anger. I remember when I was a child dashing my hand through a glass window to strike a little playmate in a fit of rage, without the slightest fear of the consequences; and I bear the scar of the cut to this day. Professor James instances a mother rushing into the street in her night-gown in front of a motor-car to save her child's life; in the passion of mother-love she felt neither shame nor fear. Now, of all such inhibitions, love is the strongest; and of all loves, the love of God. The destruction of the carnal mind thus means its total inhibition by the love of God ruling in the heart; it is what has well been called 'the expulsive power of a higher affection.' In the overwhelming sense of the love of God no other feeling can as much as rise into consciousness. And Wesley was right in saying that this effect is often instantaneous. Professor James gives definite and well-authenticated cases of instantaneous deliverance from resentment, from fear, from the craving for drink and tobacco, even from sexual desire, by the domination of the divine love. And in many of the cases he quotes the desire never returned, even after the immediate excitement had passed away. One of the foulest-mouthed men in a Yorkshire village in my old circuit got converted. The next Sunday I met him in the class; and he told us that the day after his conversion, he had slipped on the ice and struck his head on the edge of a step, and to his amazement, as he put it, 'when I got up, I wasn't swearing.' Of course one experience of this complete exaltation above even the rising of desire does not guarantee its continuance; one of the wisest things Wesley ever said on the subject is at the end of the *Minutes* of 1770: 'Does not talking of a justified or a sanctified *state* tend to mislead men? almost naturally leading them to trust in what was done in one moment? Whereas, we are every hour and every moment pleasing or displeasing to God, according to our works; according to the whole of our inward tempers, and our outward behaviour.' Still, the tendency is for the experience to become more and more habitual, until it is practically continuous.

At first Wesley was disposed to think that, once attained, the experience could never be lost, and that it included the assurance of final perseverance; but he changed his view on this point and declared in *Thoughts* (1767) 'I do not include an impossibility of falling from it, either in part or in whole.'

Admitting the possibility in the perfect Christian of infirmity and mistake he was willing to give up the phrase 'sinless perfection,' though he saw no real objection to it, as mistakes and infirmities are not properly sins. He believed that it was to be obtained by faith; and if by faith, it might be now. But he also believed that that act of faith must be preceded by a gradual work of grace, through which faith became perfected. Faith can only be strengthened by exercise; and only a strong faith can grasp the fullness of the promises. As to the time at which the blessing is received, he says in 1767, 'I believe this instant generally is the instant of death, the moment before the soul leaves the body. But I believe it may be ten, twenty, or forty years before.' He never professed himself to have received it. Logically, he could see no reason why the ideal could not be at any time realized, provided a man had the requisite faith; but he came more and more to see that it was an ideal, to which the believer approximates ever more closely, though it may be impossible to say that he has absolutely attained it. It would have saved him a good deal of trouble if he had seen clearly that the Scripture sets up an ideal, both for the justified and the entirely sanctified believer, which is not at all less valuable because it is an ideal. Geometry loses none of its value because there never was *in rerum natura* a perfectly straight line or an absolutely true circle.

I strongly recommend all students of this subject to read my old chief—the Rev. Benjamin Hellier's—essay on 'The Scriptural Doctrine of Holiness,' and his address on 'The Preaching of Holiness,' both contained in his *Life* by his son and daughter. I know nothing so sane and stimulating; and it was my great privilege to hear from his own lips the arguments there set forth, and to see his doctrine daily illustrated in his life.

Not as though I had already attained, either were already Perfect.—PHIL. iii. 12.

I. There is scarce any expression in holy writ, which has given more offence than this. The word *perfect* is what many cannot bear. The very sound of it is an abomination to them; and whosoever *preaches perfection* (as the phrase is), that is, asserts that it is attainable in this life, runs great hazard of being accounted by them worse than a heathen man or a publican.

2. And hence, some have advised, wholly to lay aside the use of those expressions, 'because they have given so great offence.' But are they not found in the oracles of God? If so, by what authority can any messenger of God lay them aside, even though all men should be offended? We have not so learned Christ; neither may we thus give place to the devil. Whatsoever God hath spoken, that will we speak, whether men will hear, or whether they will forbear; knowing, that then alone can any minister of Christ be 'pure from the blood of all men,' when he hath 'not shunned to declare unto them all the counsel of God.'

3. We may not, therefore, lay these expressions aside, seeing they are the words of God and not of man. But we may and ought to explain the meaning of them; that those who are sincere of heart may not err to the right hand or left, from the mark of the prize of their high calling. And this is the more needful to be done, because, in the verse already repeated, the Apostle speaks of himself as not perfect: 'Not,' saith he, 'as though I were already perfect.' And yet immediately after, in the fifteenth verse, he speaks of himself, yea, and many others,

as perfect: 'Let us,' saith he, 'as many as be perfect, be thus minded.'

4. In order, therefore, to remove the difficulty arising from this seeming contradiction, as well as to give light to them who are pressing forward to the mark, and that those who are lame be not turned out of the way, I shall endeavour to show,—

> I. IN WHAT SENSE CHRISTIANS ARE NOT; AND,
> II. IN WHAT SENSE THEY ARE, PERFECT.

I. 1. In the first place, I shall endeavour to show, in what sense Christians are *not perfect*. And both from experience and Scripture it appears, first, that they are not perfect in knowledge: they are not so perfect in this life as to be free from ignorance. They know, it may be, in common with other men, many things relating to the present world; and they know, with regard to the world to come, the general truths which God hath revealed. They know likewise (what the natural man receiveth not; for these things are spiritually discerned) 'what manner of love' it is, wherewith 'the Father' hath loved them, 'that they should be called the sons of God.' They know the mighty working of His Spirit in their hearts; and the wisdom of His providence, directing all their paths and causing all things to work together for their good. Yea, they know in every circumstance of life what the Lord requireth of them, and how to keep a conscience void of offence both toward God and toward man.

2. But innumerable are the things which they know not. Touching the Almighty Himself, they cannot search Him out to perfection. 'Lo, these are but a part of His ways; but the thunder of His power, who can understand?' They cannot understand, I will not say, how 'there are Three that bear record in heaven, the Father, the Son, and the Holy Spirit, and these Three are One'; or how the eternal Son of God 'took upon Himself the form of a servant';—but not any one attribute, not any one circumstance, of the divine nature. Neither is it for them to know the times and seasons when God will work His great works upon the earth; no, not even those which He hath in part revealed by His servants and prophets since the world began. Much less do they know when God, having 'accomplished the number of His elect, will

hasten His kingdom'; when 'the heavens shall pass away with a great noise, and the elements shall melt with fervent heat.'

3. They know not the reasons even of many of His present dispensations with the sons of men; but are constrained to rest here: Though 'clouds and darkness are round about Him, righteousness and judgement are the habitation of His seat.' Yea, often with regard to His dealings with themselves, doth their Lord say unto them, 'What I do, thou knowest not now; but thou shalt know hereafter.' And how little do they know of what is ever before them, of even the visible works of His hands!—how 'He spreadeth the north over the empty place, and hangeth the earth upon nothing'; how He unites all the parts of this vast machine by a secret chain, which cannot be broken. So great is the ignorance, so very little the knowledge, of even the best of men!

4. No one, then, is so perfect in this life, as to be free from ignorance. Nor, secondly, from mistake; which indeed is almost an unavoidable consequence of it; seeing those who 'know but in part' are ever liable to err touching the things which they know not. It is true, the children of God do not mistake as to the things essential to salvation: they do not 'put darkness for light, or light for darkness'; neither 'seek death in the error of their life.' For they are 'taught of God'; and the way which He teaches them, the way of holiness, is so plain, that 'the wayfaring man, though a fool, need not err therein.' But in things unessential to salvation they do err, and that frequently. The best and wisest of men are frequently mistaken even with regard to facts; believing those things not to have been which really were, or those to have been done which were not. Or, suppose they are not mistaken as to the fact itself, they may be with regard to its circumstances; believing them, or many of them, to have been quite different from what, in truth, they were. And hence cannot but arise many farther mistakes. Hence they may believe either past or present actions which were or are evil, to be good; and such as were or are good, to be evil. Hence also they may judge not according to truth with regard to the characters of men; and that, not only by supposing good men to be better, or wicked men to be worse, than they are; but by believing them to have been or to be good men, who were or are very wicked; or

perhaps those to have been or to be wicked men, who were or are holy and unreprovable.

5. Nay, with regard to the holy Scriptures themselves, as careful as they are to avoid it, the best of men are liable to mistake, and do mistake day by day; especially with respect to those parts thereof which less immediately relate to practice. Hence, even the children of God are not agreed as to the interpretation of many places in holy writ; nor is their difference of opinion any proof that they are not the children of God, on either side; but it is a proof that we are no more to expect any living man to be infallible, than to be omniscient.

6. If it be objected to what has been observed under this and the preceding head, that St. John, speaking to his brethren in the faith, says, 'Ye have an unction from the Holy One, and ye know all things' (1 John ii. 20); the answer is plain: 'Ye know all things that are needful for your souls' health.' That the Apostle never designed to extend this farther, that he could not speak it in an absolute sense, is clear, first, from hence: that otherwise he would describe the disciple as 'above his Master'; seeing Christ Himself, as man, knew not all things. 'Of that hour,' saith He, 'knoweth no man: no, not the Son, but the Father only.' It is clear, secondly, from the Apostle's own words that follow, 'These things have I written unto you concerning them that deceive you'; as well as from his frequently repeated caution, 'Let no man deceive you'; which had been altogether needless, had not those very persons who had that unction from the Holy One been liable, not to ignorance only, but to mistake also.

7. Even Christians, therefore, are not *so* perfect as to be free either from ignorance or error: we may, thirdly, add, nor from infirmities. Only let us take care to understand this word aright: only let us not give that soft title to known sins, as the manner of some is. So, one man tells us, 'Every man has his infirmity, and mine is drunkenness'; another has the infirmity of uncleanness; another, that of taking God's holy name in vain; and yet another has the infirmity of calling his brother, 'Thou fool' or returning 'railing for railing.' It is plain that all you who thus speak, if ye repent not, shall, with your infirmities go quick into hell! But I mean hereby, not only those which are properly termed *bodily infirmities,* but all those inward or outward imperfections which are not of a moral nature. Such are the weakness or slowness of

understanding, dullness or confusedness of apprehension, incoherency of thought irregular quickness or heaviness of imagination. Such (to mention no more of this kind) is the want of a ready or retentive memory. Such, in another kind, are those which are commonly, in some measure, consequent upon these; namely, slowness of speech, impropriety of language, ungracefulness of pronunciation; to which one might add a thousand nameless defects, either in conversation or behaviour. These are the infirmities which are found in the best of men, in a larger or smaller proportion. And from these none can hope to be perfectly freed, till the spirit returns to God that gave it.

8. Nor can we expect, till then, to be wholly free from temptation. Such perfection belongeth not to this life. It is true, there are those who, being given up to work all uncleanness with greediness, scarce perceive the temptations which they resist not; and so seem to be without temptation. There are also many whom the wise enemy of souls seeing to be fast asleep in the dead form of godliness, will not tempt to gross sin, lest they should awake before they drop into everlasting burnings. I know there are also children of God who, being now justified freely, having found redemption in the blood of Christ, for the present feel no temptation. God hath said to their enemies, 'Touch not Mine anointed, and do My children no harm.' And for this season, it may be for weeks or months. He causeth them to ride on high places, He beareth them as on eagles' wings, above all the fiery darts of the wicked one. But this state will not last always; as we may learn from that single consideration, that the Son of God Himself, in the days of His flesh, was tempted even to the end of His life. Therefore, so let his servant expect to be; for 'it is enough that he be as his Master.'

9. Christian perfection, therefore, does not imply (as some men seem to have imagined) an exemption either from ignorance, or mistake, or infirmities, or temptations. Indeed, it is only another term for holiness. They are two names for the same thing. Thus, every one that is holy is, in the Scripture sense, perfect. Yet we may, lastly, observe, that neither in this respect is there any absolute perfection on earth. There is no *perfection of degrees*, as it is termed; none which does not admit of a continual increase. So that how much soever any man has attained, or in how high a degree soever he is perfect, he hath

still need to 'grow in grace,' and daily to advance in the knowledge and love of God his Saviour.

II. 1. In what sense, then, are Christians perfect? This is what I shall endeavour, in the second place, to show. But it should be premised, that there are several stages in Christian life, as in natural; some of the children of God being but new-born babes, others having attained to more maturity. And accordingly St. John in his First Epistle (ii. 12, &c.), applies himself severally to those he terms 'little children,' those he styles 'young men,' and those whom he entitles 'fathers.' 'I write unto you, little children,' saith the Apostle, 'because your sins are forgiven you': because thus far you have attained; being 'justified freely,' you 'have peace with God through Jesus Christ.' 'I write unto you, young men, because ye have overcome the wicked one': or (as he afterwards addeth), 'because ye are strong, and the word of God abideth in you.' Ye have quenched the fiery darts of the wicked one, the doubts and fears wherewith he disturbed your first peace; and the witness of God, that your sins are forgiven, now abideth in your heart. 'I write unto you, fathers, because ye have known Him that is from the beginning.' Ye have known both the Father, and the Son, and the Spirit of Christ, in your inmost soul. Ye are 'perfect men,' being grown up to 'the measure of the stature of the fullness of Christ.'

2. It is of these chiefly I speak in the latter part of this discourse; for these only are perfect Christians. But even babes in Christ are in such a sense perfect, or born of God (an expression taken also in divers senses), as, first, not to commit sin. If any doubt of this privilege of the sons of God, the question is not to be decided by abstract reasonings, which may be drawn out into an endless length, and leave the point just as it was before. Neither is it to be determined by the experience of this or that particular person. Many may suppose they do not commit sin, when they do; but this proves nothing either way. To the law and to the testimony we appeal. 'Let God be true, and every man a liar.' By His Word will we abide, and that alone. Hereby we ought to be judged.

3. Now, the Word of God plainly declares, that even those who are justified, who are born again in the lowest sense, 'do not continue in sin'; that they cannot 'live any longer therein' (Rom.

vi. 12); that they are 'planted together in the likeness of the death' of Christ (verse 5); that their 'old man is crucified with Him,' the body of sin being destroyed, so that henceforth they do not serve sin; that, being dead with Christ, they are free from sin (verses 6, 7); that they are 'dead unto sin, and alive unto God' (verse 11); that 'sin hath no more dominion over them,' who are 'not under the law, but under grace'; but that these, 'being free from sin are become the servants of righteousness' (verses 14, 18).

4. The very least which can be implied in these words, is, that the persons spoken of therein, namely, all real Christians, or believers in Christ, are made free from outward sin. And the same freedom, which St. Paul here expresses in such variety of phrases, St. Peter expresses in that one (1 Pet. iv. 1, 2): 'He that hath suffered in the flesh hath ceased from sin; that he no longer should live to the desires of men, but to the will of God.' For this *ceasing from sin,* if it be interpreted in the lowest sense, as regarding only the outward behaviour, must denote the ceasing from the outward act, from any outward transgression of the law.

5. But most express are the well-known words of St. John, in the third chapter of his First Epistle, verse 8, &c.: 'He that committeth sin is of the devil; for the devil sinneth from the beginning. For this purpose the Son of God was manifested, that He might destroy the works of the devil. Whosoever is born of God doth not commit sin; for His seed remaineth in him: and he cannot sin, because he is born of God.' And those in the fifth (verse 18): 'We know that whosoever is born of God sinneth not; but he that is begotten of God keepeth himself, and that wicked one toucheth him not.'

6. Indeed it is said, this means only, He sinneth not *wilfully*; or he doth not commit sin *habitually*; or, *not as other men do*; or, *not as He did before*. But by whom is this said? by St. John? No: there is no such word in the text; nor in the whole chapter; nor in all his Epistle; nor in any part of his writings whatsoever. Why, then, the best way to answer a bold assertion is, simply to deny it. And if any man can prove it from the Word of God, let him bring forth his strong reasons.

7. And a sort of reason there is, which has been frequently brought to support these strange assertions, drawn from the

examples recorded in the Word of God: 'What!' say they, 'did
not Abraham himself commit sin prevaricating, and denying his
wife? Did not Moses commit sin, when he provoked God at the
waters of strife? Nay, to produce one for all, did not even David,
"the man after God's own heart," commit sin, in the matter of
Uriah the Hittite; even murder and adultery?' It is most sure he
did. All this is true. But what is it you would infer from hence? It
may be granted, first, that David, in the general course of his life,
was one of the holiest men among the Jews; and, secondly, that
the holiest men among the Jews did sometimes commit sin. But
if you would hence infer, that all Christians do and must commit
sin as long as they live, this consequence we utterly deny: it will
never follow from those premises.

8. Those who argue thus seem never to have considered that
declaration of our Lord (Matt. xi. 11): 'Verily I say unto you,
Among them that are born of women there hath not risen a
greater than John the Baptist: notwithstanding he that is least in
the kingdom of heaven is greater than he.' I fear, indeed, there
are some who have imagined 'the kingdom of heaven,' here, to
mean the kingdom of glory; as if the Son of God had just
discovered to us, that the least glorified saint in heaven is greater
than any man upon earth! To mention this is sufficiently to
refute it. There can, therefore, no doubt be made, but 'the
kingdom of heaven,' here (as in the following verse, where it is
said to be taken by force), or, 'the kingdom of God,' as St. Luke
expresses it, is that kingdom of God on earth whereunto all true
believers in Christ, all real Christians, belong. In these words,
then, our Lord declares two things: First, that before His coming
in the flesh, among all the children of men there had not been
one greater than John the Baptist; whence it evidently follows,
that neither Abraham, David, nor any Jew, was greater than
John. Our Lord, secondly, declares, that he which is least in the
kingdom of God (in that kingdom which He came to set up on
earth, and which the violent now began to take by force) is
greater than he, not a greater prophet, as some have interpreted
the word; for this is palpably false in fact; but greater in the
grace of God, and the knowledge of our Lord Jesus Christ.
Therefore we cannot measure the privileges of real Christians
by those formerly given to the Jews. Their 'ministration' (or
dispensation), we allow, 'was glorious'; but ours 'exceeds in

glory.' So that whosoever would bring down the Christian dispensation to the Jewish standard, whosoever gleans up the examples of weakness, recorded in the law and the prophets, and thence infers that they who have 'put on Christ' are endued with no greater strength, doth greatly err, neither 'knowing the Scriptures, nor the power of God.'

9. 'But are there not assertions in Scripture which prove the same thing, if it cannot be inferred from those examples? Does not the Scripture say expressly, "Even a just man sinneth seven times a day"?' I answer, No; the Scripture says no such thing. There is no such text in all the Bible. That which seems to be intended is the sixteenth verse of the twenty-fourth chapter of the Proverbs; the words of which are these: 'A just man falleth seven times, and riseth up again.' But this is quite another thing. For, first, the words 'a day' are not in the text. So that if a just man fall seven times in his life, it is as much as is affirmed here. Secondly, here is no mention of *falling into sin* at all: what is here mentioned is, *falling into temporal affliction*. This plainly appears from the verse before, the words of which are these: 'Lay not wait, O wicked man, against the dwelling of the righteous; spoil not his resting-place.' It follows, 'For a just man falleth seven times, and riseth up again: but the wicked shall fall into mischief.' As if he had said, 'God will deliver him out of his trouble; but when thou fallest, there shall be none to deliver thee.'

10. 'But, however, in other places,' continue the objectors, 'Solomon does assert plainly, "There is no man that sinneth not" (1 Kings viii. 46; 2 Chron. vi. 36); yea, "There is not a just man upon earth, that doeth good, and sinneth not"' (Eccles. vii. 20). I answer, Without doubt, thus it was in the days of Solomon. Yea, thus it was from Adam to Moses, from Moses to Solomon, and from Solomon to Christ. There was then no man that sinned not. Even from the day that sin entered into the world, there was not a just man upon earth that did good and sinned not, until the Son of God was manifested to take away our sins. It is unquestionably true, that 'the heir, as long as he is a child, differeth nothing from a servant.' And that even so they (all the holy men of old, who were under the Jewish dispensation) were, during that infant state of the Church, 'in bondage under the elements of the world.' 'But when the fullness of the time was

come, God sent forth His Son, made under the law, to redeem them that were under the law, that they might receive the adoption of sons,'that they might receive that 'grace which is now made manifest by the appearing of our Saviour Jesus Christ; who hath abolished death, and brought life and immortality to light through the gospel' (2 Tim. i. 10). Now, therefore, they 'are no more servants but sons.' So that, whatsoever was the case of those under the law we may safely affirm with St. John that since the gospel was given, 'he that is born of God sinneth not.'

11. It is of great importance to observe, and that more carefully than is commonly done, the wide difference there is between the Jewish and the Christian dispensation; and that ground of it which the same Apostle assigns in the seventh chapter of his Gospel (verses 38, &c.). After he had there related those words of our blessed Lord, 'He that believeth on Me, as the Scripture hath said, out of his belly shall flow rivers of living water,' he immediately subjoins, 'This spake He of the Spirit—ου εμελλον λαμβανειν οι πιστευοντες εις αυτου— *which they who should believe on Him were afterwards to receive.* For the Holy Ghost was not yet given; because that Jesus was not yet glorified.' Now, the Apostle cannot mean here (as some have taught), that the miracle-working power of the Holy Ghost was not yet given. For this was given: our Lord had given it to all His Apostles, when He first sent them forth to preach the gospel. He then gave them power over unclean spirits to cast them out; power to heal the sick; yea, to raise the dead. But the Holy Ghost was not yet given in His sanctifying graces, as He was after Jesus was glorified. It was then when 'He ascended up on high, and led captivity captive,' that He 'received' those 'gifts for men, yea, even for the rebellious, that the Lord God might dwell among them.' And when the day of Pentecost was fully come, then first it was, that they who 'waited for the promise of the Father' were made more than conquerors over sin by the Holy Ghost given unto them.

12. That this great salvation from sin was not given till Jesus was glorified, St. Peter also plainly testifies; where, speaking of his brethren in the flesh, as now 'receiving the end of their faith, the salvation of their souls,' he adds (1 Pet. i. 9, 10, &c.), 'Of which salvation the prophets have inquired and searched

diligently, who prophesied of the grace,' that is, the gracious dispensation, 'that should come unto you: searching what, or what manner of time the Spirit of Christ which was in them did signify, when it testified beforehand the sufferings of Christ, and the glory,' the glorious salvation, 'that should follow. Unto whom it was revealed, that not unto themselves, but unto us they did minister the things, which are now reported unto you by them that have preached the gospel unto you with the Holy Ghost sent down from heaven'; namely, at the day of Pentecost, and so unto all generations, into the hearts of all true believers. On this ground, even 'the grace which was brought unto them by the revelation of Jesus Christ,' the Apostle might well build that strong exhortation, 'Wherefore girding up the loins of your mind, . . . as He which hath called you is holy, so be ye holy in all manner of conversation.'

13. Those who have duly considered these things must allow, that the privileges of Christians are in no wise to be measured by what the Old Testament records concerning those who were under the Jewish dispensation; seeing the fullness of time is now come, the Holy Ghost is now given, the great salvation of God is brought unto men by the revelation of Jesus Christ. The kingdom of heaven is now set up on earth; concerning which the Spirit of God declared of old (so far is David from being the pattern or standard of Christian perfection), 'He that is feeble among them at that day shall be as David; and the house of David shall be as God, as the angel of the Lord before them' (Zech. xii. 8).

14. If, therefore, you would prove that the Apostle's words, 'He that is born of God sinneth not,' are not to be understood according to their plain, natural, obvious meaning, it is from the New Testament you are to bring your proofs, else you will fight as one that beateth the air. And the first of these which is usually brought is taken from the examples recorded in the New Testament. 'The Apostles themselves,' it is said, 'committed sin; nay, the greatest of them, Peter and Paul: St. Paul by his sharp contention with Barnabas; and St. Peter, by his dissimulation at Antioch.' Well, suppose both Peter and Paul did then commit sin; what is it you would infer from hence? that all the other Apostles committed sin sometimes? There is no shadow of proof in this. Or would you thence infer, that all the other Christians of

the apostolic age committed sin? Worse and worse: this is such an inference as, one would imagine, a man in his senses could never have thought of. Or will you argue thus: 'If two of the Apostles did once commit sin, then all other Christians, in all ages, do and will commit sin as long as they live'? Alas, my brother! a child of common understanding would be ashamed of such reasoning as this. Least of all can you with any colour of argument infer, that any man must commit sin at all. No; God forbid we should thus speak! No necessity of sinning was laid upon them. The grace of God was surely sufficient for them. And it is sufficient for us at this day. With the temptation which fell on them, there was a way to escape; as there is to every soul of man in every temptation. So that whosoever is tempted to any sin, need not yield; for no man is tempted above that he is able to bear.

15. 'But St. Paul besought the Lord thrice, and yet he could not escape from his temptation.' Let us consider his own words literally translated: 'There was given to me a thorn in the flesh, an angel' or messenger 'of Satan, to buffet me. Touching this I besought the Lord thrice, that it,' or he, 'might depart from me. And He said unto me. My grace is sufficient for thee: for My strength is made perfect in weakness. Most gladly therefore will I rather glory in' these 'my weaknesses, that the strength of Christ may rest upon me. Therefore I take pleasure in weaknesses; . . . for when I am weak, then am I strong.'

16. As this scripture is one of the strongholds of the patrons of sin, it may be proper to weigh it thoroughly. Let it he observed, then, first, it does by no means appear that this thorn, whatsoever it was, occasioned St. Paul to commit sin; much less laid him under any necessity of doing so. Therefore, from hence it can never be proved that any Christian must commit sin. Secondly, the Ancient Fathers inform us, it was bodily pain,—a violent headache, saith Tertullian (*De Pudic.*); to which both Chrysostom and St. Jerome agree. St. Cyprian expresses it, a little more generally, in those terms, 'Many and grievous torments of the flesh and of the body.' Thirdly, to this exactly agree the Apostle's own words: 'A thorn in the flesh, to smite, beat, or buffet me.' 'My strength is made perfect in weakness'; which same word occurs no less than four times in these two verses only. But, fourthly, whatsoever it was, it could not be

either inward or outward sin. It could no more be inward stirrings, than outward expressions, of pride, anger, or lust. This is manifest, beyond all possible exception, from the words that immediately follow: 'Most gladly will I glory in' these 'my weaknesses, that the strength of Christ may rest upon me.' What! did he glory in pride, in anger, in lust? Was it through these *weaknesses* that the strength of Christ rested upon him? He goes on: 'Therefore, I take pleasure in weaknesses; for when I am weak, then am I strong'; that is, when I am weak *in body,* then am I strong *in spirit.* But will any man dare to say, 'When I am weak by pride or lust, then am I strong in spirit'? I call you all to record this day, who find the strength of Christ resting upon you, can you glory in anger, or pride, or lust? Can you take pleasure in these infirmities? Do these weaknesses make you strong? Would you not leap into hell, were it possible, to escape them? Even by yourselves, then, judge, whether the Apostle could glory and take pleasure in them. Let it be, lastly, observed, that this thorn was given to St. Paul above fourteen years before he wrote this Epistle; which itself was wrote several years before he finished his course. So that he had, after this, a long course to run, many battles to fight, many victories to gain, and great increase to receive in all the gifts of God, and the knowledge of Jesus Christ. Therefore, from any spiritual weakness (if such had been) which he at that time felt, we could by no means infer that he was never made strong; that Paul the aged, the father in Christ, still laboured under the same weaknesses: that he was in no higher state till the day of his death. From all which it appears, that this instance of St. Paul is quite foreign to the question, and does in no wise clash with the assertion of St. John, 'He that is born of God sinneth not.'

17. 'But does not St. James directly contradict this? His words are, 'In many things we offend all' (iii. 2): and is not offending the same as committing sin?' In this place. I allow it is : I allow the persons here spoken of did commit sin; yea, that they all committed many sins. But who are the persons here spoken of? Why, those many masters or teachers, whom God had not sent (probably the same vain men who taught that faith without works, which is so sharply reproved in the preceding chapter); not the Apostle himself, nor any real Christian. That in the word *we* (used by a figure of speech common in all other, as well as the

inspired, writings) the Apostle could not possibly include himself or any other true believer, appears evidently, first, from the same word in the ninth verse: 'Therewith,' saith he, 'bless we God, and therewith curse we men. Out of the same mouth proceedeth blessing and cursing.' True, but not out of the mouth of the Apostle, nor of any one who is in Christ a new creature. Secondly, from the verse immediately preceding the text, and manifestly connected with it: 'My brethren, be not many masters' (or teachers), 'knowing that we shall receive the greater condemnation.' 'For in many things we offend all.' *We!* Who? Not the Apostles, nor true believers; but they who knew they should *receive the greater condemnation*, because of those many offences. But this could not be spoke of the Apostle himself, or of any who trod in his steps; seeing 'there is no condemnation to them who walk not after the flesh, but after the Spirit.' Nay, thirdly, the very verse itself proves, that, 'We offend all,' cannot be spoken either of all men, or of all Christians: for in it there immediately follows the mention of a man who *offends not*, as the we first mentioned did; from whom, therefore, he is professedly contradistinguished, and pronounced *a perfect man*.

18. So clearly does St. James explain himself, and fix the meaning of his own words. Yet, lest any one should still remain in doubt, St. John, writing many years after St. James, puts the matter entirely out of dispute by the express declarations above recited. But here a fresh difficulty may arise: how shall we reconcile St. John with himself? In one place he declares, 'Whosoever is born of God doth not commit sin'; and again, 'We know that he which is born of God sinneth not'; and yet in another, he saith, 'If we say that we have no sin, we deceive ourselves, and the truth is not in us'; and again, 'If we say that we have not sinned, we make Him a liar, and His word is not in us.'

19. As great a difficulty as this may at first appear, it vanishes away, if we observe, first, that the tenth verse fixes the sense of the eighth: 'If we say we have no sin,' in the former, being explained by, 'If we say we have not sinned,' in the latter verse. Secondly, that the point under present consideration is not whether we *have or have not sinned heretofore*; and neither of these verses asserts that we *do sin, or commit sin now*. Thirdly, that the ninth verse explains both the eighth and tenth: 'If we confess our sins, He is faithful and just to forgive us our sins, and to

cleanse us from all unrighteousness': as if he had said, 'I have before affirmed, "The blood of Jesus Christ cleanseth us from all sin"; but let no man say, I need it not; I have no sin to be cleansed from. If we say that we have no sin, that we have not sinned, we deceive ourselves, and make God a liar: but "if we confess our sins, He is faithful and just," not only "to forgive our sins," but also "to cleanse us from all unrighteousness"; that we may "go and sin no more." '

20. St. John, therefore, is well consistent with himself, as well as with the other holy writers; as will yet more evidently appear, if we place all his assertions touching this matter in one view; he declares, first, the blood of Jesus Christ cleanseth us from all sin. Secondly, no man can say, I have not sinned. I have no sin to be cleansed from. Thirdly, but God is ready both to forgive our past sins, and to save us from them for the time to come. Fourthly, 'These things write I unto you,' saith the Apostle, 'that you may not sin. But if any man' should 'sin,' or *have sinned* (as the word might be rendered), he need not continue in sin; seeing 'we have an Advocate with the Father, Jesus Christ the righteous.' Thus far all is clear. But lest any doubt should remain in a point of so vast importance, the Apostle resumes this subject in the third chapter, and largely explains his own meaning: 'Little children,' saith he, 'let no man deceive you': (as though I had given any encouragement to those that continue in sin): he that doeth righteousness is righteous, even as He is righteous. He that committeth sin is of the devil; for the devil sinneth from the beginning. For this purpose the Son of God was manifested, that He might destroy the works of the devil. Whosoever is born of God doth not commit sin; for His seed remaineth in him: and he cannot sin, because he is born of God. In this the children of God are manifest, and the children of the devil' (verses 7-10). Here the point, which till then might possibly have admitted of some doubt in weak minds, is purposely settled by the last of the inspired writers, and decided in the clearest manner. In conformity, therefore, both to the doctrine of St. John, and to the whole tenor of the New Testament, we fix this conclusion,—*a Christian is so far perfect, as not to commit sin.*

21. This is the glorious privilege of every Christian; yea, though he be but a babe in Christ. But it is only of those who *are strong* in the Lord, 'and have overcome the wicked one,' or rather

of those who 'have known Him that is from the beginning,' that it can be affirmed they are in such a sense perfect, as, secondly, to be freed from evil thoughts and evil tempers. First, from evil or sinful thoughts. But here let it be observed, that thoughts concerning evil are not always evil thoughts; that a thought concerning sin, and a sinful thought, are widely different. A man, for instance, may think of a murder which another has—committed; and yet this is no evil or sinful thought. So our blessed Lord Himself doubtless thought of, or understood, the thing spoken by the devil, when he said, 'All these things will I give Thee, if Thou wilt fall down and worship me.' Yet had He no evil or sinful thought; nor indeed was capable of having any. And even hence it follows, that neither have real Christians; for 'every one that is perfect is as his Master' (Luke vi. 40). Therefore, if He was free from evil or sinful thoughts, so are they likewise.

22. And, indeed, whence should evil thoughts proceed, in the servant who is as his Master? 'Out of the heart of man' (if at all) 'proceed evil thoughts' (Mark vii. 21). If, therefore, his heart be no longer evil, then evil thoughts can no longer proceed out of it. If the tree were corrupt, so would be the fruit: but the tree is good; the fruit, therefore, is good also (Matt. xii. 33); our Lord Himself bearing witness, 'Every good tree bringeth forth good fruit. A good tree cannot bring forth evil fruit, 'as' a corrupt tree cannot bring forth good fruit' (Matt. vii. 17, 18).

23. The same happy privilege of real Christians, St. Paul asserts from his own experience. 'The weapons of our warfare,' saith he, 'are not carnal, but mighty through God to the pulling down of strongholds; casting down imaginations' (or *reasonings* rather, for so the word λογισμους signifies; all the reasonings of pride and unbelief against the declarations, promises, or gifts of God), 'and every high thing that exalteth itself against the knowledge of God, and bringing into captivity every thought to the obedience of Christ' (2 Cor. x. 4, &c.).

24. And as Christians indeed are freed from evil thoughts, so are they, secondly, from evil tempers. This is evident from the above-mentioned declaration of our Lord Himself: 'The disciple is not above his Master: but every one that is perfect shall be as his Master.' He had been delivering, just before, some of

the sublimest doctrines of Christianity, and some of the most grievous to flesh and blood. 'I say unto you, Love your enemies, do good to them which hate you; . . , and unto him that smiteth thee on the one cheek, offer also the other.' Now these He well knew the world would not receive; and therefore immediately adds, 'Can the blind lead the blind? will they not both fall into the ditch?' As if He had said, 'Do not confer with flesh and blood, touching these things—with men void of spiritual discernment, the eyes of whose understanding God hath not opened—lest they and you perish together.' In the next verse He removes the two grand objections with which these wise fools meet us at every turn: 'These things are too grievous to be borne'; or, 'They are too high to be attained,'—saying, ' "The disciple is not above his Master"; therefore, if I have suffered, be content to tread in My steps. And doubt ye not then, but I will fulfil My word: "For every one that is perfect shall be as his Master." ' But his Master was free from all sinful tempers. So, therefore, is His disciple, even every real Christian.

25. Every one of these can say with St. Paul, 'I am crucified with Christ: nevertheless I live; yet not I, but Christ liveth in me,'—words that manifestly describe a deliverance from inward as well as from outward sin. This is expressed both negatively, *I live not* (my evil nature, the body of sin, is destroyed); and positively, *Christ liveth in me;* and, therefore, all that is holy, and just, and good. Indeed, both these, *Christ liveth in me,* and *I live not,* are inseparably connected; for 'what communion hath light with darkness, or Christ with Belial?'

26. He, therefore, who liveth in true believers hath 'purified their hearts by faith'; insomuch that every one that hath Christ in him, the hope of glory, 'purifieth himself, even as He is pure' (1 John iii. 3). He is purified from pride; for Christ was lowly of heart. He is pure from self-will or desire; for Christ desired only to do the will of His Father, and to finish His work. And he is pure from anger, in the common sense of the word; for Christ was meek and gentle, patient and long-suffering. I say, in the common sense of the word; for all anger is not evil. We read of our Lord Himself (Mark iii. 5), that He once looked round with anger.' But with what kind of anger? The next word shows, συλλυοπουμενος, 'being,' at the same time 'grieved for the

hardness of their hearts.' So then He was angry at the sin, and in the same moment grieved for the sinners; angry or displeased at the offence, but sorry for the offenders. With anger, yea, hatred. He looked upon the thing; with grief and love upon the persons. Go, thou that art perfect, and do likewise. Be thus angry, and thou sinnest not; feeling a displacency at every offence against God, but only love and tender compassion to the offender.

27. Thus doth Jesus 'save His people from their sins'; and not only from outward sins, but also from the sins of their hearts; from evil thoughts, and from evil tempers. 'True,' say some, 'we shall thus be saved from our sins; but not till death; not in this world.' But how are we to reconcile this with the express words of St. John?—'Herein is our love made perfect, that we may have boldness in the day of judgement: because as He is, so are we in this world.' The Apostle here, beyond all contradiction, speaks of himself and other living Christians, of whom (as though he had foreseen this very evasion, and set himself to overturn it from the foundation) he flatly affirms, that not only at or after death, but *in this world,* they are as their Master (1 John iv. 17).

28. Exactly agreeable to this are his words in the first chapter of this Epistle (verse 5, &c.), 'God is light, and in Him is no darkness at all. If we walk in the light, . . . we have fellowship one with another, and the blood of Jesus Christ His Son cleanseth us from all sin.' And again: 'If we confess our sins, He is faithful and just to forgive us our sins, and to cleanse us from all unrighteousness.' Now, it is evident, the Apostle here also speaks of a deliverance wrought *in this world.* For he saith not, The blood of Christ will cleanse at the hour of death, or in the day of judgement; but, it 'cleanseth,' at the time present, 'us,' living Christians, 'from all sin.' And it is equally evident, that if *any* sin remain, we are not cleansed from *all sin;* if *any* unrighteousness remain in the soul, it is not cleansed from *all* unrighteousness. Neither let any sinner against his own soul say, that this relates to justification only, or the cleansing us from the guilt of sin; first, because this is confounding together what the Apostle clearly distinguishes, who mentions first, *to forgive us our sins,* and then *to cleanse us from all unrighteousness.* Secondly, because this is asserting justification by works, in the strongest

sense possible; it is making all inward as well as outward holiness necessarily previous to justification. For if the cleansing here spoken of is no other than the cleansing us from the guilt of sin, then we are not cleansed from guilt, that is, are not justified, unless on condition of 'walking in the light, as He is in the light.' It remains, then, that Christians are saved in this world from all sin, from all unrighteousness; that they are now in such a sense perfect, as not to commit sin, and to be freed from evil thoughts and evil tempers.

29. Thus hath the Lord fulfilled the things He spake by His holy prophets which have been since the world began,—by Moses in particular, saying (Deut. xxx. 6), I 'will circumcise thine heart and the heart of thy seed, to love the Lord thy God with all thy heart, and with all thy soul'; by David, crying out, 'Create in me a clean heart, and renew a right spirit within me'; and most remarkably by Ezekiel, in those words, 'Then will I sprinkle clean water upon you, and ye shall be clean from all your filthiness, and from all your idols, will I cleanse you. A new heart also will I give you, and a new spirit will I put within you; . . . and cause you to walk in My statutes, and ye shall keep My judgements, and do them. . . . Ye shall be My people, and I will be your God. I will also save you from all your uncleannesses. . . . Thus saith the Lord God: In the day that I shall have cleansed you from all your iniquities, . . . the Heathen shall know that I the Lord build the ruined places; . . . I the Lord have spoken it, and I will do it' (Ezek. xxxvi. 25, &c.).

30. 'Having therefore these promises, dearly beloved,' both in the law and in the prophets, and having the prophetic word confirmed unto us in the gospel, by our blessed Lord and His Apostles; 'let us cleanse ourselves from all filthiness of flesh and spirit, perfecting holiness in the fear of God.' 'Let us fear, lest' so many 'promises being made us of entering into His rest,' which he that hath entered into has ceased from his own works, 'any of us should come short of it.' 'This one thing let us do, forgetting those things which are behind, and reaching forth unto those things which are before, let us press toward the mark for the prize of the high calling of God in Christ Jesus'; crying unto Him day and night, till we also are 'delivered from the bondage of corruption, into the glorious liberty of the sons of God'!

THE PROMISE OF SANCTIFICATION

(Ezek. xxxvi. 25, &c.)

BY THE REV. CHARLES WESLEY

1 God of all power, and truth, and grace,
    which shall from age to age endure;
Whose word, when heaven and earth shall pass,
    Remains, and stands for ever sure.

2 Calmly to Thee my soul looks up,
    And waits Thy promises to prove;
The object of my steadfast hope,
    The seal of Thine eternal love.

3 That I Thy mercy may proclaim,
    That all mankind Thy truth may see,
Hallow Thy great and glorious name,
    And perfect holiness in me.

4 Chose from the world if now I stand,
    Adorn'd in righteousness divine;
If, brought unto the promised land,
    I justly call the Saviour mine;

5 Perform the work Thou hast begun,
    My inmost soul to Thee convert:
Love me, for ever love Thine own,
    And sprinkle with Thy blood my heart.

6 Thy sanctifying Spirit pour,
    To quench my thirst and wash me clean:
Now, Father, let the gracious shower
    Descend, and make me pure from sin.

7 Purge me from every sinful blot;
    My idols all be cast aside;
Cleanse me from every evil thought,
    From all the filth of self and pride.

8 Give me a new, a perfect heart,
    From doubt, and fear, and sorrow free;
The mind which was in Christ impart,
    And let my spirit cleave to Thee.

9 O take this heart of stone away!
    (Thy rule it doth not, cannot own;)

In me no longer let it stay:
O take away this heart of stone!

10 The hatred of my carnal mind
Out of my flesh at once remove;
Give me a tender heart, resign'd,
And pure, and fill'd with faith and love.

11 Within me Thy good Spirit place,
Spirit of health, and love, and power;
Plant in me Thy victorious grace,
And sin shall never enter more.

12 Cause me to walk in Christ my way,
And I Thy statutes shall fulfil;
In every point Thy law obey,
And perfectly perform Thy will.

13 Hast Thou not said, who canst not lie,
That I Thy law shall keep and do?
Lord, I believe, though men deny:
They all are false; but Thou art true.

14 O that I now, from sin released,
Thy word might to the utmost prove!
Enter into the promised rest,
The Canaan of Thy perfect love!

15 There let me ever, ever dwell;
Be Thou my God, and I will be
Thy servant! O set to Thy seal!
Give me eternal life in Thee.

16 From all remaining filth within
Let me in Thee salvation have:
From actual and from inbred sin,
My ransom'd soul persist to save.

17 Wash out my old original stain;
Tell me no more it cannot be,
Demons or men! The Lamb was slain,
His blood was all pour'd out for me!

18 Sprinkle it, Jesus on my heart:
One drop of Thy all-cleansing blood
Shall make my sinfulness depart,
And fill me with the life of God.

19 Father, supply my every need;
      Sustain the life Thyself hast given;
    Call for the corn, the living bread,
      The manna that comes down from heaven.

20 The gracious fruits of righteousness,
      Thy blessings' unexhausted store,
    In me abundantly increase;
      Nor let me ever hunger more.

21 Let me no more, in deep complaint,
      'My leanness, O my leanness!' cry;
    Alone consumed with pining want,
      Of all my Father's children I!

22 The painful thirst, the fond desire,
      Thy joyous presence shall remove;
    While my full soul doth still require
      The whole eternity of love.

23 Holy, and true, and righteous Lord,
      I wait to prove Thy perfect will!
    Be mindful of Thy gracious word,
      And stamp me with Thy Spirit's seal.

24 Thy faithful mercies let me find,
      In which Thou causest me to trust;
    Give me Thy meek and lowly mind,
      And lay my spirit in the dust.

25 Show me how foul my heart hath been,
      When all renew'd by grace I am;
    When Thou hast emptied me of sin,
      Show me the fullness of my shame.

26 Open my faith's interior eye,
      Display Thy glory from above;
    And all I am shall sink and die,
      Lost in astonishment and love.

27 Confound, o'erpower me, with Thy grace;
      I would be by myself abhorr'd;
    (All might, all majesty, all praise,
      All glory be to Christ my Lord!)

28 Now let me gain perfection's height!
      Now let me into nothing fall!
    Be less than nothing in my sight,
      And feel that Christ is all in all!

SERMON XXXVI

WANDERING THOUGHTS

This sermon has had a curious history. It was not included in Vol. III of the sermons published in 1750 by W. Strahan; but it first appeared in an undated edition of the volume published by William Pine of Bristol, and it was retained in the same place in the edition of the *WORKS* of 1771, and in the eight-volume edition of the Sermons of 1787-8, which did not include the other sermons added to the first four volumes in the 1771 edition. It has been legally decided that it is one of the Standard Sermons (see below, p. 340). The date of the volume in which it first appeared can be pretty closely determined from three independent considerations: (1) In paragraph 4 two lines are quoted from a hymn of Charles Wesley's, first published in *Hymns of Intercession* in 1758. (2) It is recorded to have been preached twice and twice only in the Sermon Register, on November 30, 1760, at Spitalfields, and on January 1, 1761, at West Street. Just in the same way Sermon XXXIV, on The Catholic Spirit, was preached twice, in September and November 1749, before being published in 1750. It looks as if Wesley wanted to try the sermon over a time or two before making his final revision for the press. This would make the date of publication 1761. (3) William Pine, a Bristol Methodist, began publishing for Wesley in 1760. The fourth volume of the sermons was published in that year in two editions, though they are not numbered as first and second: the first impression was published by J. Grabham, the second by J. Grabham and W. Pine in Wine Street, as if Pine had joined Grabham during the year; and in 1761 Pine's name alone appears as the publisher of the tenth extract from the *Journal*. From that time until 1775 he did all Wesley's Bristol publishing, but then they quarrelled on account of Pine's strong and, as Wesley thought, disloyal sympathy with the Americans. Hence 1761 would be about the earliest date possible for the undated edition of Vol. III of the Sermons.

There is no record in Green's *Bibliogpaphy* of any separate edition of this sermon; but the Wesleyan Conference Office Library possesses five eighteenth-century editions (the first of which is dated 1762), and we have in our Queen's College Library one published by Story in 1808.

Its object is clear. One of the charges made against Wesley just at this time was that he made 'the way to heaven much more narrow and difficult than either Jesus Christ or His Apostles have made it . . ., requiring such degrees of perfection as are not in the power of human nature, in its present state of infirmity, to attain to' (Clark's *Montanus Redivivus*, 1760). In the sermon on Christian Perfection, and in many others, he taught that entirely sanctified Christians are 'freed from evil thoughts'; and though he is careful to explain that no thought is evil until it is welcomed and entertained, the phrase might well lead a man of tender conscience to doubt as to his entire salvation, if any thoughts of evil ever came into his mind. Here Wesley shows that a large class of what he calls 'wandering thoughts' are not sinful, and need not cause the believer any concern or self-condemnation; a most salutary lesson.

In *Minutes*, 1766, it is directed that this sermon should be 'carefully dispersed' by the assistants.

Bringing into captivity every thought to the obedience of Christ.—2 COR. x. 5.

1. But will God so 'bring every thought into captivity to the obedience of Christ,' that no wandering thought will find a place in the mind, even while we remain in the body? So some have vehemently maintained; yea, have affirmed that none are perfected in love unless they are so far perfected in understanding, that all wandering thoughts are done away; unless not only every affection and temper be holy and just and good, but every individual thought which arises in the mind be wise and regular.

2. This is a question of no small importance. For how many of those who fear God, yea, and love Him, perhaps with all their heart, have been greatly distressed on this account! How many, by not understanding it right, have not only been distressed, but greatly hurt in their souls; cast into unprofitable, yea mischievous reasonings, such as slackened their motion towards God, and weakened them in running the race set before them! Nay, many, through misapprehensions of this very thing, have cast away the precious gift of God. They have been induced, first to doubt of, and then to deny, the work God had wrought in their souls; and hereby have grieved the Spirit of God, till He withdrew and left them in utter darkness!

3. How is it then, that amidst the abundance of books which have been lately published almost on all subjects we should have none upon wandering thoughts? at least none that will at all satisfy a calm and serious mind? In order to do this in some degree, I purpose to inquire,—

I. WHAT ARE THE SEVERAL SORTS OF WANDERING
    THOUGHTS?
II. WHAT ARE THE GENERAL OCCASIONS OF THEM?
III. WHICH OF THEM ARE SINFUL AND WHICH NOT?
IV. WHICH OF THEM WE MAY EXPECT AND PRAY TO BE
    DELIVERED FROM?

I. 1. I purpose to inquire, first, What are the several sorts of
wandering thoughts? The particular sorts are innumerable; but,
in general, they are of two sorts: thoughts that wander from
God; and thoughts that wander from the particular point we
have in hand.

2. With regard to the former, all our thoughts are naturally of
this kind: for they are continually wandering from God: we
think nothing about Him: God is not in all our thoughts: we are,
one and all, as the Apostle observes 'without God in the world.'
We think of what we love; but we do not love God; therefore, we
think not of Him. Or, if we are now and then constrained to
think of Him for a time, yet, as we have no pleasure therein, nay,
rather, as these thoughts are not only insipid, but distasteful and
irksome to us, we drive them out as soon as we can, and return to
what we love to think of. So that the world and the things of the
world—what we shall eat, what we shall drink, what we shall put
on; what we shall see, what we shall hear, what we shall gain; how
we shall please our senses or our imagination—takes up all our
time, and engrosses all our thought. So long, therefore, as we
love the world; that is, so long as we are in our natural state; all
our thoughts, from morning to evening, and from evening to
morning, are no other than wandering thoughts.

3. But many times we are not only 'without God in the world,'
but also fighting against Him; as there is in every man by nature
a 'carnal mind which is enmity against God': no wonder,
therefore, that men abound with unbelieving thoughts; either
saying in their hearts, 'There is no God,' or questioning, if not
denying, His power or wisdom, His mercy or justice, or holiness.
No wonder that they so often doubt of His providence, at least,
of its extending to all events; or that, even though they allow it,
they still entertain murmuring or repining thoughts. Nearly
related to these, and frequently connected with them, are proud
and vain imaginations. Again: sometimes they are taken up with
angry, malicious, or revengeful thoughts; at other times, with

airy scenes of pleasure, whether of sense or imagination; whereby the earthy, sensual mind becomes more earthy and sensual still. Now by all these they make flat war with God: these are wandering thoughts of the highest kind.

4. Widely different from these are the other sort of wandering thoughts; in which the heart does not wander from God but the understanding wanders from the particular point it had then in view. For instance: I sit down to consider those words in the verse preceding the text: 'The weapons of our warfare are not carnal, but mighty through God.' I think, 'This ought to be the case with all that are called Christians. But how far is it otherwise! Look round into almost every part of what is termed 'the Christian world.' What manner of weapons are these using? In what kind of warfare are they engaged,

> While men, like friends, each other tear,
> In all the hellish rage or war?

See how *these* Christians love one another! Wherein are they preferable to Turks and Pagans? What abomination can be found among Mahometans or Heathens which is not found among Christians also?' And thus my mind runs of, before I am aware, from one circumstance to another. Now, all these are, in some sense, wandering thoughts: for although they do not wander from God, much less fight against Him, yet they do wander from the particular point I had in view.

II. Such is the nature, such are the sorts (to speak rather usefully, than philosophically) of wandering thoughts. But what are the general occasions of them? This we are, in the second place, to consider.

1. And it is easy to observe, that the occasions of the former sort of thoughts, which oppose or wander from God, are, in general, sinful tempers. For instance: why is not God in all the thoughts, in any of the thoughts, of a natural man? For a plain reason: be he rich or poor, learned or unlearned, he is an Atheist (though not vulgarly so called); he neither knows nor loves God. Why are his thoughts continually wandering after the world? Because he is an idolater. He does not indeed worship an image, or bow down to the stock of a tree; yet is he sunk into equally

damnable idolatry: he loves, that is, worships, the world. He seeks happiness in the things that are seen, in the pleasures that perish in the using. Why is it that his thoughts are perpetually wandering from the very end of his being, the knowledge of God in Christ? Because he is an unbeliever; because he has no faith; or, at least, no more than a devil. So all these wandering thoughts easily and naturally spring from that evil root of unbelief.

2. The case is the same in other instances: pride, anger, revenge, vanity, lust, covetousness—every one of them occasions thoughts suitable to its own nature. And so does every sinful temper of which the human mind is capable. The particulars it is hardly possible, nor is it needful, to enumerate: it suffices to observe, that as many evil tempers as find a place in any soul, so many ways that soul will depart from God, by the worst kind of wandering thoughts.

3. The occasions of the latter kind of wandering thoughts are exceeding various. Multitudes of them are occasioned by the natural union between the soul and body. How immediately and how deeply is the understanding affected by a diseased body! Let but the blood move irregularly in the brain, and all regular thinking is at an end. Raging madness ensues; and then farewell to all evenness of thought. Yea, let only the spirits be hurried or agitated to a certain degree, and a temporary madness, a delirium, prevents all settled thought. And is not the same irregularity of thought, in a measure, occasioned by every nervous disorder? So does 'the corruptible body press down the soul, and cause it to muse about many things.'

4. But does it only cause this in the time of sickness or preternatural disorder? Nay, but more or less, at all times, even in a state of perfect health. Let a man be ever so healthy, he will be more or less delirious every four-and-twenty hours. For does he not sleep? And while he sleeps, is he not liable to dream? And who then is master of his own thoughts, or able to preserve the order and consistency of them? Who can then keep them fixed to any one point, or prevent their wandering from pole to pole?

5. But suppose we are awake, are we always so awake that we can steadily govern our thoughts? Are we not unavoidably exposed to contrary extremes, by the very nature of this machine, the body? Sometimes we are too heavy, too dull and

languid, to pursue any chain of thought. Sometimes, on the other hand, we are too lively. The imagination, without leave, starts to and fro, and carries us away hither and thither, whether we will or no; and all this from the merely natural motion of the spirits, or vibration of the nerves.

6. Farther: How many wanderings of thought may arise from those various associations of our ideas which are made entirely without our knowledge, and independently on our choice! How these connexions are formed, we cannot tell; but they are formed in a thousand different manners. Nor is it in the power of the wisest or holiest of men to break those associations, or prevent what is the necessary consequence of them, and matter of daily observation. Let the fire but touch one end of the train, and it immediately runs on to the other.

7. Once more: Let us fix our attention as studiously as we are able on any subject, yet let either pleasure or pain arise especially if it be intense, and it will demand our immediate attention, and attach our thought to itself. It will interrupt the steadiest contemplation, and divert the mind from its favourite subject.

8. These occasions of wandering thoughts lie within, are wrought into our very nature. But they will likewise naturally and necessarily arise from the various impulse of outward objects. Whatever strikes upon the organ of sense, the eye or ear, will raise a perception in the mind. And, accordingly, whatever we see or hear will break in upon our former train of thought. Every man, therefore, that does anything in our sight, or speaks anything in our hearing, occasions our mind to wander, more or less, from the point it was thinking of before.

9. And there is no question but those evil spirits who are continually seeking whom they may devour make use of all the foregoing occasions to hurry and distract our minds. Sometimes by one, sometimes by another of these means, they will harass and perplex us, and, so far as God permits, interrupt our thoughts, particularly when they are engaged on the best subjects. Nor is this at all strange: they well understand the very springs of thought; and know on which of the bodily organs the imagination, the understanding, and every other faculty of the mind more immediately depends. And hereby they know how, by affecting those organs, to affect the operations dependent on them. Add to this, that they can inject a thousand thoughts,

without any of the preceding means; it being as natural for spirit to act upon spirit, as for matter to act upon matter. These things being considered, we cannot [wonder] that our thought so often wanders from any point which we have in view.

III. 1. What kind of wandering thoughts are sinful, and what not, is the third thing to be inquired into. And, first, all those thoughts which wander from God, which leave Him no room in our minds, are undoubtedly sinful. For all these imply practical Atheism; and by these we are without God in the world. And so much more are all those which are contrary to God, which imply opposition or enmity to Him. Such are all murmuring, discontented thoughts, which say, in effect, 'We will not have Thee to rule over us'; all unbelieving thoughts, whether with regard to His being, His attributes, or His providence. I mean, His particular providence over all things, as well as all persons, in the universe; that without which 'not a sparrow falls to the ground,' by which 'the hairs of our head are all numbered'; for as to a general providence (vulgarly so called), contradistinguished from a particular, it is only a decent, well-sounding word, which means just nothing.

2. Again: All thoughts which spring from sinful tempers are undoubtedly sinful. Such, for instance, are those that spring from a revengeful temper, from pride, or lust, or vanity. 'An evil tree cannot bring forth good fruit': therefore, if the tree be evil, so must the fruit be also.

3. And so must those be which either produce or feed any sinful temper; those which either give rise to pride or vanity, to anger or love of the world, or confirm and increase these or any other unholy temper, passion, or affection. For not only whatever flows from evil is evil; but also whatever leads to it; whatever tends to alienate the soul from God, and to make or keep it earthly, sensual, and devilish.

4. Hence, even those thoughts which are occasioned by weakness or disease, by the natural mechanism of the body, or by the laws of vital union, however innocent they may be in themselves, do nevertheless become sinful, when they either produce or cherish and increase in us any sinful temper; suppose the desire of the flesh, the desire of the eye, or the pride of life. In like manner, the wandering thoughts, which are

occasioned by the words or actions of other men, if they cause or feed any wrong disposition, then commence sinful. And the same we may observe of those which are suggested or injected by the devil. When they minister to any earthly or devilish temper (which they do, whenever we give place to them, and thereby make them our own), then they are equally sinful with the tempers to which they minister.

5. But, abstracting from these cases, wandering thoughts, in the latter sense of the word, that is, thoughts wherein our understanding wanders from the point it has in view, are no more sinful than the motion of the blood in our veins, or of the spirits in our brain. If they arise from an infirm consititution, or from some accidental weakness or distemper, they are as innocent as it is to have a weak constitution or a distempered body. And surely no one doubts but a bad state of nerves, a fever of any kind, and either a transient or a lasting delirium, may consist with perfect innocence. And if they should arise in a soul which is united to an healthful body, either from the natural union between the body and soul, or from any of ten thousand changes which may occur in those organs of the body that minister to thought,—in any of these cases they are as perfectly innocent as the causes from which they spring. And so they are when they spring from the casual, involuntary associations of our ideas.

6. If our thoughts wander from the point we had in view, by means of other men variously affecting our senses, they are equally innocent still: for it is no more a sin to understand what I see and hear, and in many cases cannot help seeing, hearing, and understanding, than it is to have eyes and ears. 'But if the devil injects wandering thoughts, are not those thoughts evil?' They are troublesome, and in that sense evil; but are not sinful. I do not know that he spoke to our Lord with an audible voice; perhaps he spoke to His heart only, when he said, 'All these things will I give Thee, if Thou wilt fall down and worship me.' But whether he spoke inwardly or outwardly, our Lord doubtless understood what he said. He had therefore a thought correspondent to those words. But was it a sinful thought? We know it was not. In Him was no sin, either in action, or word, or thought. Nor is there any sin in a thousand thoughts of the same kind, which Satan may inject into any of our Lord's followers.

7. It follows, that none of these wandering thoughts (whatever unwary persons have affirmed, thereby grieving whom the Lord had not grieved) are inconsistent with perfect love. Indeed, if they were, then not only sharp pain, but sleep itself, would be inconsistent with it. Sharp pain; for whenever this supervenes, whatever we were before thinking of, it will interrupt our thinking, and of course draw our thoughts into another channel. Yea, and sleep itself; as it is a state of insensibility and stupidity; and such as is generally mixed with thoughts wandering over the earth, loose, wild, and incoherent. Yet certainly these are consistent with perfect love: so then are all wandering thoughts of this kind.

IV. 1. From what has been observed, it is easy to give a clear answer to the last question, What kind of wandering thoughts we may expect and pray to be delivered from.

From the former sort of wandering thoughts—those wherein the heart wanders from God; from all that are contrary to His will, or that leave us without God in the world—every one that is perfected in love is unquestionably delivered. This deliverance, therefore, we may expect; this we may, we ought to pray for. Wandering thoughts of this kind imply unbelief, if not enmity against God; but both of these He will destroy, will bring utterly to an end. And indeed, from all sinful wandering thoughts we shall be absolutely delivered. All that are perfected in love are delivered from these; else they were not saved from sin. Men and devils will tempt them all manner of ways; but they cannot prevail over them.

2. With regard to the latter sort of wandering thoughts, the case is widely different. Till the cause is removed, we cannot in reason expect the effect should cease. But the causes or occasions of these will remain as long as we remain in the body. So long, therefore, we have all reason to believe the effects will remain also.

3. To be more particular: Suppose a soul, however holy, to dwell in a distempered body; suppose the brain be so thoroughly disordered, as that raging madness follows; will not all the thoughts be wild and unconnected as long as that disorder continues? Suppose a fever occasions that temporary madness which we term 'a delirium'; can there be any just connexion of

thought till that delirium is removed? Yea, suppose what is called 'a nervous disorder' to rise to so high a degree as to occasion at least a partial madness; will there not be a thousand wandering thoughts? And must not these irregular thoughts continue as long as the disorder which occasions them?

4. Will not the case be the same with regard to those thoughts that necessarily arise from violent pain? They will more or less continue, while that pain continues, by the inviolable order of nature. This order, likewise, will obtain, where the thoughts are disturbed, broken, or interrupted, by any defect of the apprehension, judgement, or imagination, flowing from the natural constitution of the body. And how many interruptions may spring from the unaccountable and involuntary association of our ideas! Now, all these are directly or indirectly caused by the corruptible body pressing down the mind. Nor, therefore, can we expect them to be removed till 'this corruptible shall put on incorruption.'

5. And then only, when we lie down in the dust, shall we be delivered from those wandering thoughts which are occasioned by what we see and hear, among those by whom we are now surrounded. To avoid these, we must go out of the world: for as long as we remain therein, as long as there are men and women round about us, and we have eyes to see, and ears to hear, the things which we daily see and hear will certainly affect our mind, and will more or less break in upon and interrupt our preceding thoughts.

6. And as long as evil spirits roam to and fro in a miserable, disordered world, so long they will assault (whether they can prevail or no) every inhabitant of flesh and blood. They will trouble even those whom they cannot destroy: they will attack, if they cannot conquer. And from these attacks of our restless, unwearied enemies, we must not look for an entire deliverance, till we are lodged 'where the wicked cease from troubling, and where the weary are at rest.'

7. To sum up the whole: To expect deliverance from those wandering thoughts which are occasioned by evil spirits is to expect that the devil should die or fall asleep, or, at least, should no more go about as a roaring lion. To expect deliverance from those which are occasioned by other men is to expect either that men should cease from the earth, or that we should be absolutely

secluded from them, and have no intercourse with them; or that having eyes we should not see, neither hear with our ears, but be as senseless as stocks or stones. And to pray for deliverance from those which are occasioned by the body is, in effect, to pray that we may leave the body: otherwise it is praying for impossibilities and absurdities; praying that God would reconcile contradictions, by continuing our union with a corruptible body without the natural, necessary consequences of that union. It is as if we should pray to be angels and men, mortal and immortal, at the same time. Nay!—but when that which is immortal is come, mortality is done away.

8. Rather let us pray, both with the spirit and with the understanding, that all these things may work together for our good; that we may suffer all the infirmities of our nature, all the interruptions of men, all the assaults and suggestions of evil spirits, and in all be 'more than conquerors.' Let us pray, that we may be delivered from all sin; that both root and branch may be destroyed; that we may be 'cleansed from all pollution of flesh and spirit,' from every evil temper, and word, and work; that we may 'love the Lord our God with all our heart, with all our mind, with all our soul, and with all our strength'; that all the fruit of the Spirit may be found in us—not only love, joy, peace, but also 'long-suffering, gentleness, goodness, fidelity, meekness, temperance.' Pray that all these things may flourish and abound, may increase in you more and more, till an abundant entrance be ministered unto you, into the everlasting kingdom of our Lord Jesus Christ!

SERMON XXXVII

SATAN'S DEVICES

This sermon, like the last, was intended to guard the preaching of entire sanctification from certain misunderstandings and dangers which had arisen in the Societies. It was apparently written for publication; I find no record of its having been actually preached. It is based on the *Minutes* of June 17, 1747, the relevant portions of which will be the best introduction to it.

Q. 2. What do we allow them (i.e. the brethren who differ from us with regard to entire sanctification)?

A. We grant, 1. That many of those who have died in the faith yea, the greater part of those we have known, were not sanctified throughout . . . till a little before death;

2. That the term sanctified is continually applied by St. Paul to all that were justified.

3. That by this term alone he rarely (if ever) means saved from all sin;

4. That consequently it is not proper to use it in this sense, without adding the word 'wholly.' 'entirely.' or the like;

5. That the inspired writers almost continually speak of or to those who were justified; but very rarely, either of or to those who were wholly sanctified;

6. That, consequently, it behoves us to speak in public almost continually of the state of justification; but more rarely . . . concerning entire sanctification.

Q. 16. Does not the harshly preaching perfection tend to bring believers into a kind of bondage or slavish fear?

A. It does. Therefore we should always place it in the most amiable light, so that it may excite only hope, joy, and desire.

Q. 17. Why may we not continue in the joy of faith even till we are made perfect?

A. Why indeed? Since holy grief does not quench this joy. . . .

Q. 18. Do we not discourage believers from rejoicing evermore?

A. We ought not so to do. Let them all their life long rejoice unto God, so it be with reverence. And even if lightness or pride should mix with their joy, let us not strike at the joy itself . . . but at that lightness or pride.

Q. 19. Ought we to be anxiously careful about perfection? Lest we should die before we have attained?

A. In no wise. We ought to be thus careful for nothing, neither spiritual nor temporal.

Q. 20. But ought we not to be troubled, on account of the sinful nature which still remains in us?

A. It is good for us to have a deep sense of this, and to be much ashamed before the Lord. But this should only incite us the more earnestly tu turn unto Christ every moment. . . . And therefore, when the sense of our sin most abounds, the sense of His love should much more abound.

Q. 22. Is not the teaching believers to be continually poring upon their inbred sin the ready way to make them forget that they were purged from their former sins?

A. We find by experience it is; or to make them undervalue, and account it a little thing; whereas indeed (though there are still greater gifts behind) this is inexpressibly great and glorious.

We are not ignorant of his devices.—2 COR. ii. 11.

1. The devices whereby the subtle god of this world labours to destroy the children of God—or at least to torment whom he cannot destroy, to perplex and hinder them in running the race which is set before them—are numberless as the stars of heaven, or the sand upon the sea-shore. But it is of one of them only that I now propose to speak (although exerted in various ways), whereby he endeavours to divide the gospel against itself, and by one part of it to overthrow the other.

2. The inward kingdom of heaven, which is set up in the hearts of all that repent and believe the gospel, is no other than 'righteousness, and peace, and joy in the Holy Ghost.' Every babe in Christ knows we are made partakers of these, the very hour that we believe in Jesus. But these are only the first-fruits of His Spirit; the harvest is not yet. Although these blessings are inconceivably great, yet we trust to see greater than these. We trust to love the Lord our God, not only as we do now, with a weak, though sincere affection, but 'with all our heart, with all our mind, with all our soul, and with all our strength.' We look for power to 'rejoice evermore, to pray without ceasing, and in everything to give thanks'; knowing, 'this is the will of God in Christ Jesus concerning us.'

3. We expect to be 'made perfect in love'; in that which casts out all painful fear, and all desire but that of glorifying Him we love, and of loving and serving Him more and more. We look for such an increase in the experimental knowledge and love of God

our Saviour, as will enable us always 'to walk in the light as He is in the light.' We believe the whole mind will be in us 'which was also in Christ Jesus'; that we shall love every man so as to be ready to lay down our life for his sake; so as, by this love, to be freed from anger, and pride, and from every unkind affection. We expect to be 'cleansed from all our idols,' 'from all filthiness,' whether 'of flesh or spirit'; to be 'saved from all our uncleannesses,' inward or outward; to be purified 'as He is pure.'

4. We trust in His promise who cannot lie, that the time will surely come, when, in every word and work, we shall do His blessed will on earth, as it is done in heaven; when all our conversation shall be seasoned with salt, all meet to minister grace to the hearers; when, whether we eat or drink, or whatever we do, it shall be done to the glory of God; when all our words and deeds shall be 'in the name of the Lord Jesus, giving thanks unto God, even the Father, through Him.'

5. Now this is the grand device of Satan, to destroy the first work of God in the soul, or at least to hinder its increase, by our expectation of that greater work. It is therefore my present design, first, to point out the several ways whereby he endeavours this: and, secondly, to observe how we may retort these fiery darts of the wicked one: how we may rise the higher, by what he intends for an occasion of our falling.

I. 1. I am, first, to point out the several ways whereby Satan endeavours to destroy the first work of God in the soul, or at least to hinder its increase, by our expectation of that greater work. And, 1. He endeavours to damp our joy in the Lord, by the consideration of our own vileness, sinfulness, unworthiness; added to this, that there must be a far greater change than is yet, or we cannot see the Lord. If we knew we must remain as we are, even to the day of our death, we might possibly draw a kind of comfort, poor as it was, from that necessity. But as we know we need not remain in this state, as we are assured there is a greater change to come, and that unless sin be all done away in this life, we cannot see God in glory, that subtle adversary often damps the joy we should otherwise feel in what we have already attained, by a perverse representation of what we have not attained, and the absolute necessity of attaining it. So that we cannot rejoice in what we have, because there is more which we have not. We cannot rightly taste the goodness of God, who hath done so great things for us, because there are so much greater things which, as yet, He hath not done. Likewise, the deeper conviction God works in us of our present unholiness, and the more vehement desire we feel in our heart of the entire holiness He hath promised, the more are we tempted to think lightly of the present gifts of God, and to undervalue what we have already received, because of what we have not received.

2. If he can prevail thus far, if he can damp our joy, he will soon attack our peace also. He will suggest, 'Are you fit to see God? He is of purer eyes than to behold iniquity. How, then, can you flatter yourself, so as to imagine He beholds you with approbation? God is holy: you are unholy. What communion hath light with darkness? How is it possible that you, unclean as you are, should be in a state of acceptance with God? You see indeed the mark, the prize of your high calling; but do you not see it is afar off? How can you presume, then, to think that all your sins are already blotted out? How can this be, until you are brought nearer to God, until you bear more resemblance to Him?' Thus will he endeavour not only to shake your peace, but even to overturn the very foundation of it; to bring you back, by insensible degrees, to the point from whence you set out first, even to seek for justification by works, or by your own righteousness,—to make something in you the ground of your acceptance, or, at least, necessarily previous to it.

3. Or, if we hold fast, 'Other foundation can no man lay than that which is laid, even Jesus Christ'; and, 'I am justified freely by God's grace, through the redemption which is in Jesus'; yet he will not cease to urge, 'But the tree is known by its fruits: and have you the fruits of justification? Is that mind in you which was in Christ Jesus? Are you dead unto sin, and alive unto righteousness? Are you made conformable to the death of Christ, and do you know the power of His resurrection?' And then, comparing the small fruits we feel in our souls with the fullness of the promises, we shall be ready to conclude, 'Surely God hath not said that my sins are forgiven me! Surely I have not received the remission of my sins; for what lot have I among them that are sanctified?'

4. More especially in the time of sickness and pain he will press

this with all his might: 'Is it not the word of Him that cannot lie, 'Without holiness no man shall see the Lord'? But you are not holy; you know it well; you know holiness is the full image of God; and how far is this above, out of your sight? You cannot attain unto it. Therefore, all your labour has been in vain. All these things you have suffered in vain. You have spent your strength for nought. You are yet in your sins, and must therefore perish at the last.' And thus, if your eye be not steadily fixed on Him who hath borne all your sins, he will bring you again under that 'fear of death,' whereby you was so long 'subject unto bondage,' and, by this means, impair, if not wholly destroy, your peace, as well as joy in the Lord.

5. But his masterpiece of subtilty is still behind. Not content to strike at your peace and joy, he will carry his attempts farther yet: he will level his assault against your righteousness also. He will endeavour to shake, yea, if it be possible, to destroy, the holiness you have already received, by your very expectation of receiving more, of attaining all the image of God.

6. The manner wherein he attempts this may partly appear from what has been already observed. For, first, by striking at our joy in the Lord, he strikes likewise at our holiness: seeing joy in the Holy Ghost is a precious means of promoting every holy temper; a choice instrument of God, whereby He carries on much of His work in a believing soul. And it is a considerable help, not only to inward, but also to outward, holiness. It strengthens our hands to go on in the work of faith, and in the labour of love; manfully to 'fight the good fight of faith, and to lay hold on eternal life.' It is peculiarly designed of God to be a balance both against inward and outward sufferings; to 'lift up the hands that hang down, and confirm the feeble knees.' Consequently, whatever damps our joy in the Lord, proportionably obstructs our holiness. And therefore, so far as Satan shakes our joy, he hinders our holiness also.

7. The same effect will ensue, if he can, by any means, either destroy or shake our peace. For the peace of God is another precious means of advancing the image of God in us. There is scarce a greater help to holiness than this, a continual tranquillity of spirit, the evenness of a mind stayed upon God, a calm repose in the blood of Jesus. And without this, it is scarce possible to 'grow in grace,' and in the vital 'knowledge of our

Lord Jesus Christ.' For all fear (unless the tender, filial fear)
freezes and benumbs the soul. It binds up all the springs of
spiritual life, and stops all motion of the heart toward God. And
doubt, as it were, bemires the soul, so that it sticks fast in the deep
clay. Therefore, in the same proportion as either of these
prevail, our growth in holiness is hindered.

8. At the same time that our wise adversary endeavours to
make our conviction of the necessity of perfect love an occasion
of shaking our peace by doubts and fears, he endeavours to
weaken, if not destroy, our faith. Indeed these are inseparably
connected, so that they must stand or fall together. So long as
faith subsists, we remain in peace; our heart stands fast, while it
believes in the Lord. But if we let go our faith, our filial
confidence in a loving, pardoning God, our peace is at an end,
the very foundation on which it stood being overthrown. And
this is the only foundation of holiness, as well as of peace;
consequently, whatever strikes at this, strikes at the very root of
all holiness: for without this faith, without an abiding sense that
Christ loved me, and gave Himself for me, without a continuing
conviction that God for Christ's sake is merciful to me a sinner, it
is impossible that I should love God: 'We love Him, because He
first loved us'; and in proportion to the strength and clearness of
our conviction that He hath loved us, and accepted us in His
Son. And unless we love God, it is not possible that we should
love our neighbour as ourselves; nor, consequently, that we
should have any right affections, either toward God, or toward
man. It evidently follows, that whatever weakens our faith,
must, in the same degree, obstruct our holiness: and this is not
only the most effectual, but also the most compendious way of
destroying all holiness; seeing it does not affect any one
Christian temper, any single grace or fruit of the Spirit, but, so
far as it succeeds, tears up the very root of the whole work of
God.

9. No marvel, therefore, that the ruler of the darkness of this
world should here put forth all his strength. And so we find by
experience. For it is far easier to conceive, than it is to express,
the unspeakable violence wherewith this temptation is frequently urged on them who hunger and thirst after righteousness. When they see, in a strong and clear light, on the one hand
the desperate wickedness of their own hearts, on the other hand

the unspotted holiness to which they are called in Christ Jesus; on the one hand the depth of their own corruption, of their total alienation from God, on the other the height of the glory of God, that image of the Holy One, wherein they are to be renewed; there is, many times, no spirit left in them; they could almost cry out, 'With God this is impossible!' They are ready to give up both faith and hope; to cast away that very confidence, whereby they are to overcome all things, through Christ strengthening them; whereby, 'after they have done the will of God,' they are to 'receive the promise.'

10. And if they 'hold fast the beginning of their confidence steadfast unto the end,' they shall undoubtedly receive the promise of God, reaching through both time and eternity. But here is another snare laid for our feet: while we earnestly pant for that part of the promise which is to be accomplished here, 'for the glorious liberty of the children of God,' we may be led unawares from the consideration of the glory which shall hereafter be revealed. Our eye may be insensibly turned aside from that crown which the righteous Judge hath promised to give at that day 'to all that love His appearing'; and we may be drawn away from the view of that incorruptible inheritance which is reserved in heaven for us. But this also would be a loss to our souls, and an obstruction to our holiness. For to walk in the continual sight of our goal, is a needful help in our running the race that is set before us. This it was, the having 'respect unto the recompence of the reward,' which, of old time, encouraged Moses, rather 'to suffer affliction with the people of God, than to enjoy the pleasures of sin for a season; esteeming the reproach of Christ greater riches than the treasures of Egypt.' Nay, it is expressly said of a greater than he, that, 'for the joy that was set before Him, He endured the cross, and despised the shame,' till He 'sat down at the right hand of the throne of God.' Whence we may easily infer, how much more needful for us is the view of that joy set before us, that we may endure whatever cross the wisdom of God lays upon us, and press on through holiness to glory.

11. But while we are reaching to this, as well as to that glorious liberty which is preparatory to it, we may be in danger of falling into another snare of the devil, wherein he labours to entangle the children of God. We may take too much thought for

to-morrow, so as to neglect the improvement of to-day. We may so expect perfect love, as not to use that which is already shed abroad in our hearts. There have not been wanting instances of those who have greatly suffered hereby. They were so taken up with what they were to receive hereafter, as utterly to neglect what they had already received. In expectation of having five talents more, they buried their one talent in the earth. At least, they did not improve it as they might have done to the glory of God, and the good of their own souls.

12. Thus does the subtle adversary of God and man endeavour to make void the counsel of God, by dividing the gospel against itself, and making one part of it overthrow the other; while the first work of God in the soul is destroyed by the expectation of His perfect work. We have seen several of the ways wherein he attempts this, by cutting off, as it were, the springs of holiness. But this he likewise does more directly, by making that blessed hope an occasion of unholy tempers.

13. Thus, whenever our heart is eagerly athirst for all the great and precious promises; when we pant after the fullness of God, as the hart after the water-brook; when our soul breaketh out in fervent desire, 'Why are His chariot-wheels so long a-coming?'—he will not neglect the opportunity of tempting us to murmur against God. He will use all his wisdom, and all his strength, if haply, in an unguarded hour, we may be influenced to repine at our Lord for thus delaying His coming. At least, he will labour to excite some degree of fretfulness or impatience; and, perhaps, of envy at those whom we believe to have already attained the prize of our high calling. He well knows, that, by giving way to any of these tempers, we are pulling down the very thing we would build up. By *thus* following after perfect holiness, we become more unholy than before. Yea, there is great danger that our last state should be worse than the first; like them of whom the Apostle speaks in those dreadful words, 'It had been better for them not to have known the way of righteousness, than, after they have known it, to turn from the holy commandment delivered to them.'

14. And from hence he hopes to reap another advantage, even to bring up an evil report of the good way. He is sensible, how few are able to distinguish (and too many are not willing so to do) between the accidental abuse, and the natural tendency,

of a doctrine. These, therefore, will he continually blend together, with regard to the doctrine of Christian perfection; in order to prejudice the minds of unwary men against the glorious promises of God. And how frequently, how generally. I had almost said how universally, has he prevailed herein! For who is there that observes any of these accidental ill effects of this doctrine, and does not immediately conclude, this is its natural tendency; and does not readily cry out, 'See, these are the fruits (meaning the natural, necessary fruits) of such doctrine?' Not so: they are fruits which may accidentally spring from the abuse of a great and precious truth: but the abuse of this, or any other scriptural doctrine, does by no means destroy its use. Neither can the unfaithfulness of man, perverting his right way, make the promise of God of no effect. No: let God be true, and every man a liar. The word of the Lord, it shall stand. 'Faithful is He that hath promised: He also will do it.' Let us not then be 'removed from the hope of the gospel.' Rather let us observe, which was the second thing proposed, how we may retort these fiery darts of the wicked one; how we may rise the higher by what he intends for an occasion of our falling.

II. 1. And, first, does Satan endeavour to damp your joy in the Lord, by the consideration of your sinfulness; added to this, that without entire, universal holiness, no man can see the Lord? You may cast back this dart upon his own head, while, through the grace of God, the more you feel of your own vileness, the more you rejoice in confident hope, that all this shall be done away. While you hold fast this hope, every evil temper you feel, though you hate it with a perfect hatred, may be a means, not of lessening your humble joy, but rather of increasing it. 'This and this,' may you say, 'shall likewise perish from the presence of the Lord. Like as the wax melteth at the fire, so shall this melt away before His face.' By this means, the greater that change is which remains to be wrought in your soul, the more may you triumph in the Lord, and rejoice in the God of your salvation, who hath done so great things for you already, and will do so much greater things than these.

2. Secondly: the more vehemently he assaults your peace with that suggestion; 'God is holy; you are unholy; you are immensely distant from that holiness without which you cannot see God:

how then can you be in the favour of God? How can you fancy you are justified?'—take the more earnest heed to hold fast that, 'Not by works of righteousness which I have done, I am found in Him; I am accepted in the Beloved, not having my own righteousness (as the cause, either in whole or in part, of our justification before God), but that which is by faith in Christ, the righteousness which is of God by faith.' O bind this about your neck: write it upon the table of thy heart. Wear it as a bracelet upon thy arm, as frontlets between thine eyes: 'I am justified freely by His grace, through the redemption that is in Jesus Christ.' Value and esteem, more and more, that precious truth, 'By grace we are saved through faith.' Admire, more and more, the free grace of God, in so loving the world as to give 'His only begotten Son, that whosoever believeth on Him, might not perish, but have everlasting life.' So shall the sense of the sinfulness you feel, on the one hand, and of the holiness you expect, on the other, both contribute to establish your peace, and to make it flow as a river. So shall that peace flow on with an even stream, in spite of all those mountains of ungodliness, which shall become a plain in the day when the Lord cometh to take full possession of your heart. Neither will sickness, or pain, or the approach of death occasion any doubt or fear. You know a day, an hour, a moment, with God, is as a thousand years. He cannot be straitened for time wherein to work whatever remains to be done in your soul. And God's time is always the best time. Therefore be thou careful for nothing: only make thy requests known unto Him, and that, not with doubt or fear, but thanksgiving; as being previously assured, He cannot withhold from thee any manner of thing that is good.

3. Thirdly: the more you are tempted to give up your shield, to cast away your faith, your confidence in His love, so much the more take heed that you hold fast that whereunto you have attained; so much the more labour to stir up the gift of God which is in you. Never let that slip, 'I have "an Advocate with the Father, Jesus Christ the righteous"; and, "The life I now live, I live by faith in the Son of God, who loved me, and gave Himself for me" ' Be this thy glory, and crown of rejoicing; and see that no one take thy crown. Hold that fast: 'I know that my Redeemer liveth, and shall stand at the latter day upon the earth': and, 'I now "have redemption in His blood, even the forgiveness of

sins." ' Thus, being filled with all peace and joy in believing, press on, in the peace and joy of faith, to the renewal of thy whole soul in the image of Him that created thee! Meanwhile, cry continually to God, that thou mayest see that prize of thy high calling, not as Satan represents it, in a horrid, dreadful shape, but in its genuine, native beauty; not as something that must be, or thou wilt go to hell, but as what may be, to lead thee to heaven. Look upon it as the most desirable gift which is in all the stores of the rich mercies of God. Beholding it in this true point of light, thou wilt hunger after it more and more; thy whole soul will be athirst for God, and for this glorious conformity to His likeness; and, having received a good hope of this, and strong consolation through grace, thou wilt no more be weary or faint in thy mind, but wilt follow on till thou attainest.

4. In the same power of faith, press on to glory. Indeed, this is the same prospect still. God hath joined from the beginning, pardon, holiness, heaven. And why should man put them asunder? O beware of this! Let not one link of the golden chain be broken. 'God for Christ's sake hath forgiven me. He is now renewing me in His own image. Shortly He will make me meet for Himself, and take me to stand before His face. I, whom He hath justified through the blood of His Son, being thoroughly sanctified by His Spirit, shall quickly ascend to the 'New Jerusalem, the city of the living God.' Yet a little while and I shall 'come to the general assembly and church of the first-born, and to God the Judge of all, and to Jesus the Mediator of the new covenant.' How soon will these shadows flee away, and the day of eternity dawn upon me! How soon shall I drink of 'the river of the water of life, going out of the throne of God and of the Lamb! There all His servants shall praise Him, and shall see His face, and His name shall be upon their foreheads. And no night shall be there; and they have no need of a candle, or the light of the sun. For the Lord God enlighteneth them, and they shall reign for ever and ever." '

5. And if you thus 'taste of the good word, and of the powers of the world to come,' you will not murmur against God, because you are not yet 'meet for the inheritance of the saints in light.' Instead of repining at your not being wholly delivered, you will praise God for thus far delivering you. You will magnify God for what He hath done, and take it as an earnest of what He will do.

You will not fret against Him, because you are not yet renewed, but bless Him because you shall be; and because 'now is your salvation' from all sin 'nearer than when you' first 'believed.' Instead of uselessly tormenting yourself because the time is not fully come, you will calmly and quietly wait for it, knowing that it 'will come, and will not tarry.' You may therefore the more cheerfully endure, as yet, the burden of sin that still remains in you, because it will not always remain. Yet a little while, and it shall be clean gone. Only 'tarry thou the Lord's leisure': be strong, and 'He shall comfort thy heart'; and put thou thy trust in the Lord!

6. And if you see any who appear (so far as man can judge, but God alone searcheth the hearts) to be already partakers of their hope, already 'made perfect in love'; far from envying the grace of God in them, let it rejoice and comfort your heart. Glorify God for their sake! 'If one member is honoured,' shall not 'all the members rejoice with it'? Instead of jealousy or evil surmising concerning them, praise God for the consolation! Rejoice in having a fresh proof of the faithfulness of God, in fulfilling all His promises; and stir yourself up the more to 'apprehend that for which you are also apprehended of Christ Jesus'!

7. In order to this, redeem the time. Improve the present moment. Buy up every opportunity of growing in grace, or of doing good. Let not the thought of receiving more grace to-morrow, make you negligent of to-day. You have one talent now: if you expect five more, so much the rather improve that you have. And the more you expect to receive hereafter, the more labour for God now. Sufficient for the day is the grace thereof. God is now pouring His benefits upon you: now approve yourself a faithful steward of the present grace of God. Whatever may be to-morrow, give all diligence to-day to 'add to your faith courage, temperance, patience, brotherly kindness,' and the fear of God, till you attain that pure and perfect love! Let these things be now 'in you, and abound'! Be not now slothful or unfruitful: 'so shall an entrance be ministered unto you into the everlasting kingdom of our Lord Jesus Christ'!

8. Lastly: if in time past you have abused this blessed hope of being holy as He is holy, yet do not therefore cast it away. Let the abuse cease, the use remain. Use it now to the more abundant glory of God, and profit of your own soul. In steadfast faith, in

calm tranquillity of spirit, in full assurance of hope, rejoicing evermore for what God hath done, press ye on unto perfection! Daily growing in the knowledge of our Lord Jesus Christ, and going on from strength to strength, in resignation, in patience, in humble thankfulness for what ye have attained, and for what ye shall, run the race set before you, 'looking unto Jesus,' till, through perfect love, ye enter into His glory!

SERMON XXXVIII

ORIGINAL SIN

This sermon was first published in 1759 by Grabham of Bristol as a twopenny pamphlet; and it was placed first in the fourth volume of the Sermons in 1760. Its origin is to be found in the publication by Dr. John Taylor in 1740 of a treatise entitled *The Scripture Doctrine of Original Sin Proposed to Free and Candid Examination*, Dr. Taylor was a learned Presbyterian minister, but with pronounced leanings to Socinianism. He was pastor of a church in Norwich, and the famous Octagon Chapel was built for him there in 1756 at a cost of over £5,000. Wesley saw it in 1757, and thought it 'the most elegant one in Europe'; he describes (*Journal*, November 23) its mahogany and brass fittings, and adds, with a touch of unworthy sarcasm, 'How can it be thought that the old, coarse gospel should find admission here?' Dr. Taylor was also the first President of the Presbyterian Theological College at Warrington, and held that position until his death in 1761. He denied the divinity of our Lord, though he thought Him 'a person of consummate virtue' (Sermon CV, 101. Wesley was at Shackerley, six miles beyond Bolton, in Lancashire, in August 1748, and found in his congregation 'many disciples of Dr. Taylor, laughing at original sin, and consequently at the whole frame of scriptural Christianity.' Again, on April 10, 1751, he rode 'to Shackerley. Being now in the very midst of Mr. Taylor's disciples, I enlarged much more than I am accustomed to do on the doctrine of Original Sin; and determined, if God should give me a few years' life, publicly to answer his new gospel.' He carried out his intention in the early part of 1757, and published his answer as *The Doctrine of Original Sin; According to Scripture, Reason, and Experience*; a treatise in four parts, rearranged in seven parts in the Words, 1771. Taylor's standpoint was frankly Pelagian. He did not believe that man came into the world with a sinful nature; nor did he accept any federal relationship between Adam and his descendants. He granted that men were degenerate, but held that they still had power to do their duty if they chose. Wesley respected his character and learning, and prayed for his conversion to the truth; and in a letter to Sir Harry Trelawney he says, 'I have reason to believe he was convinced of his mistake before he died, but to acknowledge this publicly was too hard a task for him.' The only record of his having seen Dr. Taylor is in *Journal*, August 10, 1760; he was meeting the Society at Cork, when 'a person hugely daubed with gold thrust violently in. By his appearance I should have judged him to be some nobleman. But I was afterwards informed it was Dr. Taylor.'

This sermon was little more than a summary of Part I of the treatise. Wesley attached great importance to it, and in *Minutes,* 1766, he asks: 'Q. Have the sermons on Wandering Thoughts, In-being Sin. The Lord our Righteousness, and The Scripture Way of Salvation, been carefully dispersed? A. No. Let each Assistant do it now.' The sermon on In-being Sin is this one. (The use of in-being as an adjective is not recorded in the N. E. Dict.) The first record of its being preached is on February 1, 1758, at the Chapel (i.e. West Street); it occurs six times more in 1758, and seven times in 1759, the last date being June 10. Two of the entries are significantly at Norwich. Dr. Taylor's city.

In spite of its title, the sermon deals rather with the universality of sin than with its origin. In section 4 it is stated in St. Paul's language that 'by one man's disobedience all men were constituted sinners'; that 'in Adam all die'; and that consequently all men are by nature children of wrath, dead in trespasses and sins; but there is no discussion of the nature of the Fall, or of the interpretation of the account of it in Genesis. For a discussion of this question, see introduction to Sermon V. The most important qualification of the doctrine of total depravity, by which alone it is saved from being a palpable misrepresentation of the facts, is the recognition that to every man is given a measure of the grace of the Holy Spirit, by which he is moved and helped to do right and to seek after God. As we have seen, Wesley fully accepted this doctrine of Prevenient Grace; but in this sermon he barely refers to it in i. 4, and so his account of the natural condition of mankind is felt to be unreal. This is more obvious still in the first part of the treatise on Original Sin, in which all the vices of humanity are combined in a lurid picture without the admission of a single redeeming feature. How utterly misleading, for example, is a description of the moral condition of the old Greek and Roman world which has not a word to say of the legislation of Lycurgus, the philosophy of Socrates and Plato, the teaching of the great Tragedians, the heroism of Leonidas, the honour of Regulus, the ethics of Cato and Marcus Antoninus and Epictetus, or the patriotism of Brutus! The whole thing gives us the impression of an advocate, who piles up and exaggerates everything that can be said for his side of the case, and ignores all the facts that are against him. Dr. Pope (*Theology,* ii. 63) says: 'The absolute corruption of the roots of our nature is a Manichaean error . . . contradicted by the whole doctrine of original sin as taught in Scripture. Apart from Christ, and in hard theory, the ruin of man is complete. But man has never been in such a far country as not to hear the appeal of the Father.' Quite so; and Wesley sets forth here that 'hard theory' and treats it as if it expressed the actual fact. If it were not for the grace of God, man would be the monster of evil that he describes; but the grace of God cannot be thus eliminated. The moral condition of man is the product of three factors: his own fallen nature, the God-created environment in which he lives and which on the whole makes for righteousness, and the constant immanent activity of the Holy Spirit; and no account of it which leaves out the second and third factors can be anything but a caricature. If Wesley had said, 'This is what man would be apart from the divine influences exerted by his environment and by the Holy Spirit,' he might have justified his position; but he does not say so. What he does try to convey is that anterior to, and apart from, the revelation of God's pardoning love in Jesus Christ, man is absolutely and hopelessly under the control of evil; and this is not true. The student should read the chapter on 'Man and Redemption' in Dr. Scott Lidgett's *Christian Religion*; especially section ii. 2 and 3, from which I quote the following sentences: 'The frequent phrase that this is a ruined world is overstrained, in the same way as the doctrine of sin is overstrained when it is represented that total depravity means that human nature, as we know it, has become completely worthless through sin. . . . The extremer statements upon this subject find their biblical support by over-emphasizing certain passages of St. Paul's writings in separation from their context and from the whole of his thought' (which is Wesley's easily besetting error in exegesis). Again: 'In concrete reality, the worthlessness of the flesh does not exclude the underlying presence of the Spirit, not merely along the frontiers of human life, but actually invading its territory. . . . The Christian doctrine never sees man as totally apart from God except for such abstract purposes as are illustrated by the writings of St. Paul.'

At the same time Wesley's main argument is not affected by his exaggerated and one-sided statements. Sin, however restrained by the grace of the Spirit, is universal, and cries out for redemption. 'We are all wicked,' says Seneca (*De Ira*, lii. 26); 'what one man blames in another, each will find in his own bosom. We being ourselves wicked, live among the wicked.' Kant wrote a treatise *On the Radical Evil of Human Nature*. Aristotle (*Nic. Ethics*, iii. 1) says: 'We are more naturally disposed [towards things that are wrong] and more easily carried away to excess, than to propriety of conduct.' Hume (*On the Passions*, vi.) says: 'We naturally desire what is forbid, and often take a pleasure in performing actions merely because they are unlawful.' Comte (*Phil. Positive*, vi. 5) says: 'We must regret that even in the best natures the social affections are so overborne by the personal, as rarely to command conduct in a direct way.' Even Herbert Spencer (*Data of Ethics*, xv.) admits: 'Considered from the evolution point of view, the acts of men during the transition which has been, is still, and long will be, in progress, must, in most cases, be of the kind here classed as least wrong,' i.e. not right absolutely, but only less wrong than they might conceivably be. The general testimony of philosophers, poets, historians, satirists, is that Sin is the universal fact.

And God saw that the wickedness of man was great in the earth, and that every imagination of the thoughts of his heart was only evil continually.—GEN. vi. 5.

1. How widely different is this from the fair pictures of human nature which men have drawn in all ages! The writings of many of the ancients abound with gay descriptions of the dignity of man; whom some of them paint as having all virtue and happiness in his composition, or, at least, entirely in his power, without being beholden to any other being: yea, as self-sufficient, able to live on his own stock, and little inferior to God Himself.

2. Nor have Heathens alone, men who are guided in their researches by little more than the dim light of reason, but many likewise of them that bear the name of Christ, and to whom are entrusted the oracles of God, spoken as magnificently concerning the nature of man, as if it were all innocence and perfection. Accounts of this kind have particularly abounded in the present century: and perhaps in no part of the world more than in our own country. Here not a few persons of strong understanding, as well as extensive learning, have employed their utmost abilities to show, what they termed, 'the fair side of human nature.' And it must be acknowledged, that, if their accounts of him be just, man is still but 'a little lower than the angels'; or, as the words may be more literally rendered, 'a little less than God.'

3. Is it any wonder, that these accounts are very readily received by the generality of men? For who is not easily persuaded to think favourably of himself? Accordingly, writers of this kind are most universally read, admired, applauded. And innumerable are the converts they have made, not only in the gay but the learned world. So that it is now quite unfashionable to talk otherwise, to say anything to the disparagement of human nature; which is generally allowed, notwithstanding a few infirmities, to be very innocent, and wise, and virtuous!

4. But, in the meantime, what must we do with our Bibles?—for they will never agree with this. These accounts, however pleasing to flesh and blood, are utterly irreconcilable with the scriptural. The Scripture avers, that 'by one man's disobedience all men were constituted sinners'; that 'in Adam all died,' spiritually died, lost the life and the image of God; that fallen, sinful Adam then 'begat a son in his own likeness'—nor was it possible he should beget him in any other; for 'who can bring a clean thing out of an unclean?'—that consequently we, as well as other men, were by nature 'dead in trespasses and sins,'

'without hope, without God in the world,' and, therefore, 'children of wrath'; that every man may say, 'I was shapen in wickedness, and in sin did my mother conceive me'; that 'there is no difference,' in that 'all have sinned and come short of the glory of God,' of that glorious image of God wherein man was originally created. And hence, when' the Lord looked down from heaven upon the children of men, He saw they were all gone out of the way; they were altogether become abominable, there was none righteous, no, not one, 'none that truly sought after God: just agreeable this to what is declared by the Holy Ghost in the words above recited, 'God saw,' when He looked down from heaven before, 'that the wickedness of man was great in the earth'; so great, that 'every imagination of the thoughts of his heart was only evil continually.' This is God's account of man: from which I shall take occasion, first, to show what men were before the flood: secondly, to inquire, whether they are not the same now: and, thirdly, to add some inferences.

I. 1. I am, first, by opening the words of the text, to show what men were before the flood. And we may fully depend on the account here given: for God saw it, and He cannot be deceived. He 'saw that the wickedness of man was great':—not of this or that man; not of a few men only; not barely of the greater part, but of man in general; of men universally. The word includes the whole human race, every partaker of human nature. And it is not easy for us to compute their numbers, to tell how many thousands and millions they were. The earth then retained much of its primaeval beauty and original fruitfulness. The face of the globe was not rent and torn as it is now; and spring and summer went hand in hand. It is therefore probable, it afforded sustenance for far more inhabitants than it is now capable of sustaining; and these must be immensely multiplied, while men begat sons and daughters for seven or eight hundred years together. Yet among all this inconceivable number, only 'Noah found favour with God.' He alone (perhaps including part of his household) was an exception from the universal wickedness, which, by the just judgement of God, in a short time after brought on universal destruction. All the rest were partakers in the same guilt, as they were in the same punishment.

2. 'God saw all the imaginations of the thoughts of his

heart'—of his soul, his inward man, the spirit within him, the principle of all his inward and outward motions. He 'saw all the imaginations'—it is not possible to find a word of a more extensive signification. It includes whatever is formed, made, fabricated within; all that is or passes in the soul; every inclination, affection, passion, appetite; every temper, design, thought. It must of consequence include every word and action, as naturally flowing from these fountains, and being either good or evil according to the fountain from which they severally flow.

3. Now God saw that all this, the whole thereof, was evil—contrary to moral rectitude; contrary to the nature of God, which necessarily includes all good; contrary to the divine will, the eternal standard of good and evil; contrary to the pure, holy image of God, wherein man was originally created, and wherein he stood when God, surveying the works of His hands, saw them all to be very good; contrary to justice, mercy, and truth, and to the essential relations which each man bore to his Creator and his fellow creatures.

4. But was there not good mingled with the evil? Was there not light intermixed with the darkness? No, none at all: 'God saw that the whole imagination of the heart of man was only evil.' It cannot indeed be denied, but many of them, perhaps all, had good motions put into their hearts; for the Spirit of God did then also 'strive with man,' if haply he might repent, more especially during that gracious reprieve, the hundred and twenty years, while the ark was preparing. But still 'in his flesh dwelt no good thing'; all his nature was purely evil: it was wholly consistent with itself, and unmixed with anything of an opposite nature.

5. However, it may still be matter of inquiry, 'Was there no intermission of this evil? Were there no lucid intervals, wherein something good might be found in the heart of man?' We are not here to consider, what the grace of God might occasionally work in his soul; and, abstracted from this, we have no reason to believe there was any intermission of that evil. For God, who 'saw the whole imagination of the thoughts of his heart to be *only* evil,' saw likewise, that it was always the same, that it 'was only evil *continually*'; every year, every day, every hour, every moment. He never deviated into good.

II. Such is the authentic account of the whole race of mankind which He who knoweth what is in man, who searcheth the heart and trieth the reins hath left upon record for our instruction. Such were all men before God brought the flood upon the earth. We are, secondly, to inquire, whether they are the same now.

1. And this is certain, the Scripture gives us no reason to think any otherwise of them. On the contrary, all the above-cited passages of Scripture refer to those who lived after the flood. It was above a thousand years after, that God declared by David concerning the children of men, 'They are all gone out of the way' of truth and holiness; 'there is none righteous, no, not one.' And to this bear all the prophets witness, in their several generations. So Isaiah, concerning God's peculiar people (and certainly the Heathens were in no better condition), 'The whole head is sick, and the whole heart faint. From the sole of the foot even unto the head there is no soundness in it; but wounds, and bruises, and putrefying sores.' The same account is given by all the Apostles yea by the whole tenor of the oracles of God. From all these we learn, concerning man in his natural state, unassisted by the grace of God, that 'every imagination of the thoughts of his heart is' still 'evil, only evil,' and that 'continually.'

2. And this account of the present state of man is confirmed by daily experience. It is true, the natural man discerns it not: and this is not to be wondered at. So long as a man born blind continues so, he is scarce sensible of his want: much less, could we suppose a place where all were born without sight, would they be sensible of the want of it. In like manner, so long as men remain in their natural blindness of understanding, they are not sensible of their spiritual wants, and of this in particular. But as soon as God opens the eyes of their understanding, they see the state they were in before; they are then deeply convinced, that 'every man living,' themselves especially, are, by nature, 'altogether vanity'; that is, folly and ignorance sin and wickedness.

3. We see when God opens our eyes, that we were before αθεοι εν τω κοσμω—*without God,* or rather, *Atheists in the world.* We had by nature, no knowledge of God no acquaintance with Him. It is true, as soon as we came to the use of reason, we learned 'the invisible things of God, even His eternal power and Godhead, from the things that are made.' From the things that

are seen we inferred the existence of an eternal, powerful Being, that is not seen. But still, although we acknowledged His being, we had no acquaintance with Him. As we know there is an Emperor of China, whom yet we do not know; so we knew there was a King of all the earth, yet we knew Him not. Indeed we could not by any of our natural faculties. By none of these could we attain the knowledge of God. We could no more perceive Him by our natural understanding, than we could see Him with our eyes. For 'no one knoweth the Father but the Son, and he to whom the Son willeth to reveal Him. And no one knoweth the Son but the Father, and he to whom the Father revealeth Him.'

4. We read of an ancient king who, being desirous to know what was the *natural language* of men, in order to bring the matter to a certain issue, made the following experiment: he ordered two infants, as soon as they were born, to be conveyed to a place prepared for them, where they were brought up without any instruction at all, and without ever hearing a human voice. And what was the event? Why, that when they were at length brought out of their confinement, they spake no language at all; they uttered only inarticulate sounds, like those of other animals. Were two infants in like manner to be brought up from the womb without being instructed in any religion, there is little room to doubt but (unless the grace of God interposed) the event would be just the same. They would have no religion at all: they would have no more knowledge of God than the beasts of the field, than the wild ass's colt. Such is natural religion, abstracted from traditional, and from the influences of God's Spirit.

5. And having no knowledge, we can have no love of God: we cannot love Him we know not. Most men *talk* indeed of loving God, and perhaps imagine they do; at least, few will acknowledge they do not love Him: but the fact is too plain to be denied. No man loves God by nature, any more than he does a stone, or the earth he treads upon. What we love we delight in: but no man has naturally any delight in God. In our natural state we cannot conceive how any one should delight in Him. We take no pleasure in Him at all; He is utterly tasteless to us. To love God! it is far above, out of our sight. We cannot, naturally, attain unto it.

6. We have by nature, not only no love, but no fear of God. It is

allowed, indeed, that most men have, sooner or later, a kind of senseless, irrational fear, properly called 'superstition'; though the blundering Epicureans gave it the name of 'religion.' Yet even this is not natural, but acquired; chiefly by conversation or from example. By nature 'God is not in all our thoughts': we leave Him to manage His own affairs, to sit quietly, as we imagine, in heaven, and leave us on earth to manage ours; so that we have no more of the fear of God before our eyes, than of the love of God in our hearts.

7. Thus are all men 'Atheists in the world.' But Atheism itself does not screen us from idolatry. In his natural state, every man born into the world is a rank idolater. Perhaps, indeed, we may not be such in the vulgar sense of the word. We do not, like the idolatrous Heathens, worship molten or graven images. We do not bow down to the stock of a tree, to the work of our own hands. We do not pray to the angels or saints in heaven, any more than to the saints that are upon the earth. But what then? We have set up our idols in our hearts; and to these we bow down, and worship them: we worship ourselves, when we pay that honour to ourselves which is due to God only. Therefore, all pride is idolatry; it is ascribing to ourselves what is due to God alone. And although pride was not made for man, yet where is the man that is born without it? But hereby we rob God of His inalienable right, and idolatrously usurp His glory.

8. But pride is not the only sort of idolatry which we are all by nature guilty of. Satan has stamped his own image on our heart in self-will also. 'I will,' said he, before he was cast out of heaven, 'I will sit upon the sides of the north': I will do my own will and pleasure, independently on that of my Creator. The same does every man born into the world say and that in a thousand instances; nay, and avow it too, without ever blushing upon the account, without either fear or shame. Ask the man, 'Why did you do this?' He answers, 'Because I had a mind to it.' What is this but, 'Because it was my will'; that is, in effect, because the devil and I are agreed; because Satan and I govern our actions by one and the same principle. The will of God, meantime, is not in his thoughts, is not considered in the least degree; although it be the supreme rule of every intelligent creature, whether in heaven or earth, resulting from the essential, unalterable relation which all creatures bear to their Creator.

9. So far we bear the image of the devil, and tread in his steps. But at the next step we leave Satan behind; we run into an idolatry whereof he is not guilty: I mean, love of the world; which is now as natural to every man, as to love his own will. What is more natural to us than to seek happiness in the creature, instead of the Creator—to seek that satisfaction in the works of His hands, which can be found in God only? What more natural than 'the desire of the flesh'? that is, of the pleasure of sense in every kind? Men indeed talk magnificently of despising these low pleasures, particularly men of learning and education. They affect to sit loose to the gratification of those appetites wherein they stand on a level with the beasts that perish. But it is mere affectation! for every man is conscious to himself, that in this respect he is, by nature, a very beast. Sensual appetites, even those of the lowest kind, have, more or less, the dominion over him. They lead him captive; they drag him to and from in spite of his boasted reason. The man, with all his good breeding, and other accomplishments, has no pre-eminence over the goat: nay, it is much to be doubted, whether the beast has not the pre-eminence over him. Certainly he has, it was that said, 'How can ye believe who receive honour one of another, and seek not the honour which cometh of God only?' But if this be really so, if it be impossible to believe, and consequently to please God, so long as we receive or seek honour one of another, and seek not the honour which cometh of God only; then in what a condition are all mankind! the Christians as well as Heathens! since they all seek honour one of another! since it is as natural for them so to do, themselves being the judges, as it is to see the light which strikes upon their eye, or to hear the sound which enters their ear; yea, since they account it a sign of a virtuous mind, to seek the praise of men, and of a vicious one to be content with the honour that cometh of God only!

III. 1. I proceed to draw a few inferences from what has been said. And, first, from hence we may learn one grand fundamental difference between Christianity, considered as a system of doctrines, and the most refined Heathenism. Many of the ancient Heathens have largely described the vices of particular men. They have spoken much against their covetousness, or cruelty; their luxury, or prodigality. Some have dared to say, that 'no man is born without vices of one kind or another.' But still, as none of them were apprised of the fall of man, so none of them knew of his total corruption. They knew not that all men were empty of all good, and filled with all manner of evil. They were wholly ignorant of the entire depravation of the whole human nature, of every man born into the world, in every faculty of his soul, not so much by those particular vices which reign in particular persons, as by the general flood of Atheism and idolatry, of pride, selfwill, and love of the world. This, therefore, is the first grand distinguishing point between Heathenism and Christianity. The one acknowledges that many men are infected with many vices, and even born with a proneness to them; but supposes withal, that in some the natural good much over-balances the evil: the other declares that all men are 'conceived in sin,' and 'shapen in wickedness'—that hence there is in every man a 'carnal mind, which is enmity against God; which is not, cannot be, subject to' His 'law'; and which so infects the whole soul, that 'there dwelleth in' him, 'in his flesh,' in his natural state, 'no good thing'; but 'every imagination of the thoughts of his heart is evil,' only evil, and that 'continually.'

2. Hence we may, secondly, learn, that all who deny this, call it 'original sin,' or by any other title, are but heathens still, in the fundamental point which differences Heathenism from Christianity. They may, indeed, allow, that men have many vices; that some are born with us; and that consequently, we are not born altogether so wise or so virtuous as we should be; there being few that will roundly affirm, 'We are born with as much propensity to good as to evil, and that every man is, by nature, as virtuous and wise as Adam was at his creation.' But here is the *shibboleth*: Is man by nature filled with all manner of evil? Is he void of all good? Is he wholly fallen? Is his soul totally corrupted? Or to come back to the text, is 'every imagination of the thoughts of his heart only evil continually'? Allow this, and you are so far a Christian. Deny it, and you are but an Heathen still.

3. We may learn from hence, in the third place, what is the proper nature of religion, of the religion of Jesus Christ. It is Θεραπεια Ψυχης—God's method of *healing a soul* which is thus

diseased. Hereby the great Physician of souls applies medicines to heal this sickness; to restore human nature, totally corrupted in all its faculties. God heals all our Atheism by the knowledge of Himself, and of Jesus Christ whom He hath sent; by giving us faith, a divine evidence and conviction of God, and the things of God—in particular, of this important truth, 'Christ loved *me*, and gave Himself for *me*.' By repentance and lowliness of heart, the deadly disease of pride is healed; that of self-will by resignation, a meek and thankful submission to the will of God; and for the love of the world in all its branches, the love of God is the sovereign remedy. Now, this is properly religion, 'faith' thus 'working by love': working the genuine meek humility, entire deadness to the world, with a loving, thankful acquiescence in, and conformity to, the whole will and word of God.

4. Indeed, if man were not thus fallen, there would be no need of all this. There would be no occasion for this work in the heart, this renewal in the spirit of our mind. The superfluity of godliness would then be a more proper expression than the 'superfluity of naughtiness.' For an outside religion, without any godliness at all, would suffice to all rational intents and purposes. It does, accordingly, suffice, in the judgement of those who deny this corruption of our nature. They make very little more of religion than the famous Mr. Hobbes did of reason. According to him, reason is only 'a well-ordered train of words': according to them, religion is only a well-ordered train of words and actions. And they speak consistently with themselves; for if the inside be not full of wickedness, if this be clean already, what remains, but to 'cleanse the outside of the cup'? Outward reformation, if their supposition be just, is indeed the one thing needful.

5. But ye have not so learned the oracles of God. Ye know that He who seeth what is in man gives a far different account both of nature and grace, of our fall and our recovery. Ye know that the great end of religion is, to renew our hearts in the image of God, to repair that total loss of righteousness and true holiness which we sustained by the sin of our first parents. Ye know that all religion which does not answer this end, all that stops short of this, the renewal of our soul in the image of God, after the likeness of Him that created it, is no other than a poor farce, and a mere mockery of God, to the destruction of our own soul. O

beware of all those teachers of lies, who would palm this upon you for Christianity! Regard them not, although they should come unto you with all the deceivableness of unrighteousness; with all smoothness of language, all decency, yea, beauty and elegance of expression, all professions of earnest good-will to you, and reverence for the holy Scriptures. Keep to the plain, old faith, 'once delivered to the saints,' and delivered by the Spirit of God to our hearts. Know your disease! Know your cure! Ye were born in sin: therefore, 'ye must be born again,' born of God. By nature ye are wholly corrupted: by grace ye shall be wholly renewed. In Adam ye all died: in the second Adam, in Christ, ye all are made alive. 'You that were dead in sins hath He quickened': He hath already given you a principle of life, even faith in Him who loved you and gave Himself for you! Now, 'go on from faith to faith,' until your whole sickness be healed, and all that 'mind be in you which was also in Christ Jesus'!

SERMON XXXIX

THE NEW BIRTH

The first mention I find of this text is on May 29, 1743, the day of the opening of the West Street Chapel. After preaching there in the morning on 'the gospel for the day, part of the third chapter of St. John,' which includes this verse, Wesley 'preached at the Great Gardens' (in Whitechapel)' at five, to an immense congregation, on "Ye must be born again." ' The Great Gardens lay to the north of Whitechapel Road, about 200 yards east of St. Mary's Church; the position is still marked by Great Garden Street. In the Sermon Register (1747-61) this text occurs once in December 1749, once in 1750, once in 1751, three times in 1753, three times in 1755, eleven in 1756, four in 1757, fourteen in 1758, twelve in 1759, three times in 1760, and not at all in 1761. In 1759 on three occasions Gen. vi. 5 (Original Sin) was the morning subject, and this sermon immediately followed in the afternoon or evening, which throws light on the relative position of these sermons in the volume of 1760. The reason for the New Birth is, as division I shows, the Fall of Man.

Sermons XIV and XV, which deal with the same subject, were published in Vol. II of the Sermons in 1748; and it seems likely that this sermon took their place, and became more and more a favourite with the preacher, until it too was printed in the fourth volume in 1760. It contains no new doctrine; but the distinction between justification, regeneration, and sanctification is drawn with a firmer hand; the necessity for the New Birth is traced back to the Fall; the analogy between physical and spiritual birth, already indicated in Sermon XV, i, is more fully worked out; and the statement in Sermon XIV, 1, that the privileges of the New Birth 'are ordinarily annexed to baptism' is carefully guarded from any possible misunderstanding.

Ye must be born again.—JOHN iii. 7.

1. If any doctrines within the whole compass of Christianity may be properly termed 'fundamental,' they are doubtless these two,—the doctrine of justification, and that of the new birth: the former relating to that great work which God does *for us,* in forgiving our sins; the latter, to the great work which God does *in us,* in renewing our fallen nature. In order of time, neither of

these is before the other; in the moment we are justified by the grace of God, through the redemption that is in Jesus, we are also 'born of the Spirit'; but in order of *thinking*, as it is termed, justification precedes the new birth. We first conceive His wrath to be turned away, and then His Spirit to work in our hearts.

2. How great importance then must it be of, to every child of man, thoroughly to understand these fundamental doctrines! From a full conviction of this, many excellent men have wrote very largely concerning justification, explaining every point relating thereto, and opening the scriptures which treat upon it. Many likewise have wrote on the new birth: and some of them largely enough; but yet not so clearly as might have been desired, nor so deeply and accurately; having either given a dark, abstruse account of it, or a slight and superficial one. Therefore a full, and at the same time a clear, account of the new birth seems to be wanting still; such as may enable us to give a satisfactory answer to these three questions: first, why must we be born again—what is the foundation of this doctrine of the new birth? secondly, How must we be born again—what is the nature of the new birth? and, thirdly, Wherefore must we be born again—to what end is it necessary? These questions, by the assistance of God, I shall briefly and plainly answer; and then subjoin a few inferences which will naturally follow.

I. 1. And, first, Why must we be born again? What is the foundation of this doctrine? The foundation of it lies near as deep as the creation of the world; in the scriptural account whereof we read, 'And God,' the three-one God, 'said, Let us make man in our image, after our likeness. So God created man in His own image, in the image of God created He him' (Gen. i. 26, 27):—not barely in his *natural image,* a picture of His own immortality; a spiritual being, endued with understanding freedom of will, and various affections; nor merely in his *political image,* the governor of this lower world, having 'dominion over the fishes of the sea, and over all the earth: but chiefly in his *moral image*; which, according to the Apostle, is 'righteousness and true holiness' (Eph. iv. 24). In this image of God was man made. 'God is love'; accordingly, man at his creation was full of love; which was the sole principle of all his tempers, thoughts, words, and actions. God is full of justice, mercy, and truth; so was man as he came from the hands of his Creator. God is spotless purity; and so man was in the beginning pure from every sinful blot; otherwise God could not have pronounced him, as well as all the other works of His hands, 'very good' (Gen. i. 31). This he could not have been, had he not been pure from sin, and filled with righteousness and true holiness. For there is no medium: if we suppose an intelligent creature not to love God, not to be righteous and holy, we necessarily suppose him not to be good at all; much less to be 'very good.'

2. But, although man was made in the image of God, yet he was not made immutable. This would have been inconsistent with that state of trial in which God was pleased to place him. He was therefore created able to stand, and yet liable to fall. And this God Himself apprised him of, and gave him a solemn warning against it. Nevertheless, man did not abide in honour: he fell from his high estate. He 'ate of the tree whereof the Lord had commanded him, Thou shalt not eat thereof.' By this wilful act of disobedience to his Creator, this flat rebellion against his Sovereign, he openly declared that he would no longer have God to rule over him, that he would be governed by his own will, and not the will of Him that created him; and that he would not seek his happiness in God, but in the world, in the works of his hands. Now, God had told him before, 'In the day that thou eatest' of that fruit, 'thou shalt surely die.' And the word of the Lord cannot be broken. Accordingly, in that day he did die: he died to God—the most dreadful of all deaths. He lost the life of God: he was separated from Him, in union with whom his spiritual life consisted. The body dies when it is separated from the soul, the soul, when it is separated from God. But this separation from God, Adam sustained in the day, the hour, he ate of the forbidden fruit. And of this he gave immediate proof, presently showing by his behaviour, that the love of God was extinguished in his soul, which was now 'alienated from the life of God.' Instead of this, he was now under the power of servile fear, so that he fled from the presence of the Lord. Yea, so little did he retain even of the knowledge of Him who filleth heaven and earth, that he endeavoured to 'hide himself from the Lord God among the trees of the garden' (Gen. iii. 8); so had he lost both the knowledge and the love of God, without which the image of God could not subsist. Of this, therefore, he was

deprived at the same time, and became unholy as well as unhappy. In the room of this, he had sunk into pride and self-will, the very image of the devil; and into sensual appetites and desires, the image of the beasts that perish.

3. If it be said, 'Nay, but that threatening, "In the day that thou eatest thereof, thou shalt surely die," refers to temporal death, and that alone, to the death of the body only'; the answer is plain; to affirm this is flatly and palpably to make God a liar; to aver that the God of truth positively affirmed a thing contrary to truth. For it is evident Adam did not *die* in this sense, 'in the day that he ate thereof.' He lived, in the sense opposite to this death, above nine hundred years after. So that this cannot possibly be understood of the death of the body, without impeaching the veracity of God. It must therefore be understood of spiritual death, the loss of the life and image of God.

4. And in Adam all died, all human kind, all the children of men who were then in Adam's loins. The natural consequence of this is, that every one descended from him comes into the world spiritually dead, dead to God, wholly dead in sin; entirely void of the life of God; void of the image of God, of all that righteousness and holiness wherein Adam was created. Instead of this, every man born into the world now bears the image of the devil, in pride and self-will; the image of the beast, in sensual appetites and desires. This, then, is the foundation of the new birth,—the entire corruption of our nature. Hence it is, that, being born in sin, we must be 'born again.' Hence every one that is born of a woman must be born of the Spirit of God.

II. 1. But how must a man be born again? What is the nature of the new birth? This is the second question. And a question it is of the highest moment that can be conceived. We ought not, therefore, in so weighty a concern, to be content with a slight inquiry; but to examine it with all possible care, and to ponder it in our hearts, till we fully understand this important point, and clearly see how we are to be born again.

2. Not that we are to expect any minute, philosophical account of the manner how this is done. Our Lord sufficiently guards us against any such expectation, by the words immediately following the text; wherein He reminds Nicodemus of as indisputable a fact as any in the whole compass of nature, which,

notwithstanding, the wisest man under the sun is not able fully to explain. 'The wind bloweth where it listeth,'—not by thy power or wisdom; 'and thou hearest the sound thereof,'—thou art absolutely assured, beyond all doubt, that it doth blow; 'but thou canst not tell whence it cometh, nor whither it goeth,'—the precise manner how it begins and ends, rises and falls, no man can tell. 'So is every one that is born of the Spirit': thou mayest be as absolutely assured of the fact, as of the blowing of the wind; but the precise manner how it is done, how the Holy Spirit works this in the soul, neither thou nor the wisest of the children of men is able to explain.

3. However, it suffices for every rational and Christian purpose, that, without descending into curious, critical inquiries, we can give a plain scriptural account of the nature of the new birth. This will satisfy every reasonable man, who desires only the salvation of his soul. The expression, 'being born again,' was not first used by our Lord in His conversation with Nicodemus: it was well known before that time, and was in common use among the Jews when our Saviour appeared among them. When an adult Heathen was convinced that the Jewish religion was of God, and desired to join therein, it was the custom to baptize him first before he was admitted to circumcision. And when he was baptized, he was said to be born again; by which they meant, that he who was before a child of the devil was now adopted into the family of God, and accounted one of His children. This expression, therefore, which Nicodemus, being 'a teacher in Israel,' ought to have understood well, our Lord uses in conversing with him; only in a stronger sense than he was accustomed to. And this might be the reason of his asking, 'How can these things be?' They cannot be literally: a man cannot 'enter a second time into his mother's womb, and be born': but they may, spiritually: a man may be born from above, born of God, born of the Spirit, in a manner which bears a very near analogy to the natural birth.

4. Before a child is born into the world he has eyes, but sees not; he has ears, but does not hear. He has a very imperfect use of any other sense. He has no knowledge of any of the things of the world, or any natural understanding. To that manner of existence which he then has, we do not even give the name of life. It is then only when a man is born, that we say he begins to

live. For as soon as he is born, he begins to see the light, and the various objects with which he is encompassed. His ears are then opened, and he hears the sounds which successively strike upon them. At the same time, all the other organs of sense begin to be exercised upon their proper objects. He likewise breathes, and lives in a manner wholly different from what he did before. How exactly doth the parallel hold in all these instances! While a man is in a mere natural state, before he is born of God, he has, in a spiritual sense, eyes and sees not; a thick impenetrable veil lies upon them: he has ears, but hears not; he is utterly deaf to what he is most of all concerned to hear. His other spiritual senses are all locked up: he is in the same condition as if he had them not. Hence he has no knowledge of God; no intercourse with Him; he is not at all acquainted with Him. He has no true knowledge of the things of God, either of spiritual or eternal things; therefore, though he is a living man, he is a dead Christian. But as soon as he is born of God, there is a total change in all these particulars. The "eyes of his understanding are opened' (such is the language of the great Apostle); and, He who of old 'commanded light to shine out of darkness shining on his heart, he sees the light of the glory of God,' His glorious love, 'in the face of Jesus Christ.' His ears being opened he is now capable of hearing the inward voice of God saying 'Be of good cheer; thy sins are forgiven thee'; 'Go and sin no more.' This is the purport of what God speaks to his heart; although perhaps not in these very words. He is now ready to hear whatsoever 'He that teacheth man knowledge' is pleased, from time to time, to reveal to him. He 'feels in his heart,' to use the language of our Church, 'the mighty working of the Spirit of God'; not in a gross, carnal sense, as the men of the world stupidly and wilfully misunderstand the expression; though they have been told again and again, we mean thereby neither more nor less than this: he feels, is inwardly sensible of, the graces which the Spirit of God works in his heart. He feels, he is conscious of, a 'peace which passeth all understanding.' He many times feels such a joy in God as is 'unspeakable, and full of glory.' He feels 'the love of God shed abroad in his heart by the Holy Ghost which is given unto him'; and all his spiritual senses are then exercised to discern spiritual good and evil. By the use of these, he is daily increasing in the knowledge of God, of Jesus Christ whom He hath sent, and of all the things pertaining to His inward kingdom. And now he may be properly said to live: God having quickened him by His Spirit, he is alive to God through Jesus Christ. He lives a life which the world knoweth not of, a 'life which is hid with Christ in God.' God is continually breathing, as it were, upon the soul; and his soul is breathing unto God. Grace is descending into his heart; and prayer and praise ascending to heaven: and by this intercourse between God and man, this fellowship with the Father and the Son, as by a kind of spiritual respiration, the life of God in the soul is sustained; and the child of God grows up, till he comes to the 'full measure of the stature of Christ.'

5. From hence it manifestly appears, what is the nature of the new birth. It is that great change which God works in the soul when He brings it into life; when He raises it from the death of sin to the life of righteousness. It is the change wrought in the whole soul by the almighty Spirit of God when it is 'created anew in Christ Jesus'; when it is 'renewed after the image of God in righteousness and true holiness'; when the love of the world is changed into the love of God; pride into humility; passion into meekness; hatred, envy, malice, into a sincere, tender, disinterested love for all mankind. In a word, it is that change whereby the earthly, sensual, devilish mind is turned into the 'mind which was in Christ Jesus.' This is the nature of the new birth: 'so is every one that is born of the Spirit.'

III. 1. It is not difficult for any who has considered these things, to see the necessity of the new birth, and to answer the third question, Wherefore, to what end, is it necessary that we should be born again? It is very easily discerned, that this is necessary, first, in order to holiness. For what is holiness according to the oracles of God? Not a bare external religion, a round of outward duties, how many soever they be, and how exactly soever performed. No: gospel holiness is no less than the image of God stamped upon the heart; it is no other than the whole mind which was in Christ Jesus; it consists of all heavenly affections and tempers mingled together in one. It implies such a continual, thankful love to Him who hath not withheld from us His Son, His only Son, as makes it natural, and in a manner necessary to us, to love every child of man; as fills us 'with bowels of mercies, kindness, gentleness, long-suffering.' It is such a love of God as teaches us to be blameless in all manner of conversation; as enables us to present our souls and bodies, all we are and all we have, all our thoughts, words, and actions, a continual sacrifice to God, acceptable through Christ Jesus. Now, this holiness can have no existence till we are renewed in the image of our mind. It cannot commence in the soul till that change be wrought; till, by the power of the Highest overshadowing us, we are 'brought from darkness to light, from the power of Satan unto God'; that is, till we are born again; which, therefore, is absolutely necessary in order to holiness.

2. But 'without holiness no man shall see the Lord,' shall see the face of God in glory. Of consequence, the new birth is absolutely necessary in order to eternal salvation. Men may indeed flatter themselves (so desperately wicked and so deceitful is the heart of man!) that they may live in their sins till they come to the last gasp, and yet afterwards live with God; and thousands do really believe, that they have found a broad way which leadeth not to destruction. 'What danger,' say they, 'can a woman be in that is so *harmless* and so *virtuous?* What fear is there that so *honest* a man, one of so strict *morality,* should miss of heaven; especially, if, over and above all this, they constantly attend on church and sacrament?' One of these will ask with all assurance, 'What! shall not I do as well as my neighbours?' Yes, as well as your unholy neighbours; as well as your neighbours that die in their sins! For you will all drop into the pit together, into the nethermost hell! You will all lie together in the lake of fire; 'the lake of fire burning with brimstone.' Then at length, you will see (but God grant you may see it before!) the necessity of holiness in order to glory; and, consequently, of the new birth, since none can be holy, except he be born again.

3. For the same reason, except he be born again, none can be happy even in this world. For it is not possible, in the nature of things, that a man should be happy who is not holy. Even the poor, ungodly poet could tell us, *Nemo malus felix*: 'No wicked man is happy.' The reason is plain: all unholy tempers are uneasy tempers: not only malice, hatred, envy, jealousy, revenge, create a present hell in the breast; but even the softer passions, if not kept within due bounds, give a thousand times more pain than pleasure. Even 'hope,' when 'deferred' (and how often must this be the case!) 'maketh the heart sick': and every

desire which is not according to the will of God is liable to 'pierce' us 'through with many sorrows': and all those general sources of sin—pride, self-will, and idolatry—are, in the same proportion as they prevail, general sources of misery. Therefore, as long as these reign in any soul, happiness has no place there. But they must reign till the bent of our nature is changed, that is, till we are born again; consequently, the new birth is absolutely necessary in order to happiness in this world, as well as in the world to come.

IV. I proposed in the last place to subjoin a few inferences, which naturally follow from the preceding observations.

1. And first it follows, that baptism is not the new birth: they are not one and the same thing. Many indeed seem to imagine that they are just the same; at least, they speak as if they thought so; but I do not know that this opinion is publicly avowed by any denomination of Christians whatever. Certainly it is not by any within these kingdoms, whether of the established Church, or dissenting from it. The judgement of the latter is clearly declared in their large Catechism: Q. 'What are the parts of a sacrament? A. The parts of a sacrament are two: the one an outward and sensible sign; the other, an inward and spiritual grace, thereby signified. Q. What is baptism? A. Baptism is a sacrament, wherein Christ hath ordained the washing with water, to be a sign and seal of regeneration by His Spirit.' Here it is manifest, baptism, the sign, is spoken of as distinct from regeneration, the thing signified.

In the Church Catechism likewise, the judgement of our Church is declared with the utmost clearness: Q. 'What meanest thou by this word, sacrament? A. I mean an outward and visible sign of an inward and spiritual grace. Q. What is the outward part or form in baptism? A. Water, wherein the person is baptized, in the name of the Father, Son, and Holy Ghost. Q. What is the inward part, or thing signified? A. A death unto sin, and a new birth unto righteousness.' Nothing, therefore, is plainer, than that, according to the Church of England, baptism is not the new birth.

But indeed the reason of the thing is so clear and evident, as not to need any other authority. For what can be more plain, than that the one is an external, the other an internal, work; that the one is a visible, the other an invisible thing, and therefore wholly different from each other?—the one being an act of man, purifying the body; the other a change wrought by God in the soul: so that the former is just as distinguishable from the latter, as the soul from the body, or water from the Holy Ghost.

2. From the preceding reflections we may, secondly, observe, that as the new birth is not the same thing with baptism, so it does not always accompany baptism: they do not constantly go together. A man may possibly be 'born of water,' and yet not be 'born of the Spirit.' There may sometimes be the outward sign, where there is not the inward grace. I do not now speak with regard to infants: it is certain our Church supposes that all who are baptized in their infancy are at the same time born again; and it is allowed that the whole Office for the Baptism of Infants proceeds upon this supposition. Nor is it an objection of any weight against this, that we cannot comprehend how this work can be wrought in infants. For neither can we comprehend how it is wrought in a person of riper years. But whatever be the case with infants, it is sure all of riper years who are baptized are not at the same time born again. 'The tree is known by its fruits.' And hereby it appears too plain to be denied, that divers of those who were children of the devil before they were baptized continue the same after baptism; 'for the works of their father they do': they continue servants of sin, without any pretence either to inward or outward holiness.

3. A third inference which we may draw from what has been observed, is, that the new-birth is not the same with sanctification. This is indeed taken for granted by many; particularly by an eminent writer, in his late treatise on the nature and grounds of Christian Regeneration. To waive several other weighty objections which might be made to that tract, this is a palpable one: it all along speaks of regeneration as a progressive work, carried on in the soul by slow degrees, from the time of our first turning to God. This is undeniably true of sanctification; but of regeneration, the new birth, it is not true. This is a part of sanctification, not the whole; it is the gate to it, the entrance into it. When we are born again, then our sanctification, our inward and outward holiness begins; and thenceforward we are gradually to 'grow up in Him who is our Head.' This expression of the Apostle admirably illustrates the difference between one

and the other, and farther points out the exact analogy there is between natural and spiritual things. A child is born of a woman in a moment, or at least in a very short time: afterward he gradually and slowly grows, till he attains to the stature of a man. In like manner, a child is born of God in a short time, if not in a moment. But it is by slow degrees that he afterward grows up to the measure of the full stature of Christ. The same relation, therefore, which there is between our natural birth and our growth, there is also between our new birth and our sanctification.

4. One point more we may learn from the preceding observations. But it is a point of so great importance, as may excuse the considering it the more carefully, and prosecuting it at some length. What must one who loves the souls of men, and is grieved that any of them should perish, say to one whom he sees living in Sabbath-breaking, drunkenness, or any other wilful sin? What can he say, if the foregoing observations are true, but 'You must be born again'? 'No,' says a zealous man, 'that cannot be: how can you talk so uncharitably to the man? Has he not been baptized already? He cannot be born again now.' Can he not be born again? Do you affirm this? Then he cannot be saved. Though he be as old as Nicodemus was, yet 'except he be born again, he cannot see the kingdom of God.' Therefore in saying, 'He cannot be born again,' you in effect deliver him over to damnation. And where lies the uncharitableness now? on my side, or on yours? I say, he may be born again, and so become an heir of salvation. You say, 'He cannot be born again:' and if so, he must inevitably perish! So you utterly block up his way to salvation, and send him to hell, out of mere charity!

But perhaps the sinner himself, to whom in real charity we say, 'You must be born again,' has been taught to say, 'I defy your new doctrine: I need not be born again; I was born again when I was baptized. What! would you have me deny my baptism?' I answer, first, there is nothing under heaven which can excuse a lie; otherwise I should say to an open sinner, 'If you have been baptized, do not own it. For how highly does this aggravate your guilt! How will it increase your damnation! Was you devoted to God at eight days old, and have you been all these years devoting yourself to the devil? Was you, even before you had the use of reason, consecrated to God the Father, the Son, and the Holy Ghost? And have you, ever since you had the use of it, been flying in the face of God, and consecrating yourself to Satan? Does the abomination of desolation—the love of the world, pride, anger, lust, foolish desire, and a whole train of vile affections—stand where it ought not? Have you set up all these accursed things in that soul which was once a temple of the Holy Ghost; set apart for an 'habitation of God, through the Spirit'; yea, solemnly given up to Him? And do you glory in this, that you once belonged to God? O be ashamed! blush! hide yourself in the earth! Never boast more of what ought to fill you with confusion, to make you ashamed before God and man'! I answer, secondly, you have already denied your baptism; and that in the most effectual manner. You have denied it a thousand and a thousand times; and you do so still, day by day. For in your baptism you renounced the devil and all his works. Whenever, therefore, you give place to him again, whenever you do any of the works of the devil, then you deny your baptism. Therefore you deny it by every wilful sin; by every act of uncleanness, drunkenness, or revenge; by every obscene or profane word; by every oath that comes out of your mouth. Every time you profane the day of the Lord, you thereby deny your baptism; yea, every time you do anything to another which you would not he should do to you. I answer, thirdly, be you baptized or unbaptized, you must be born again; otherwise it is not possible you should be inwardly holy; and without inward as well as outward holiness, you cannot be happy, even in this world, much less in the world to come. Do you say, 'Nay, but I do no harm to any man; I am honest and just in all my dealings; I do not curse, or take the Lord's name in vain; I do not profane the Lord's day; I am no drunkard; I do not slander my neighbour, nor live in any wilful sin'? If this be so, it were much to be wished that all men went as far as you do. But you must go farther yet, or you cannot be saved: still 'you must be born again.' Do you add, 'I do go farther yet; for I not only do no harm, but do all the good I can'? I doubt that fact: I fear you have had a thousand opportunities of doing good which you have suffered to pass by unimproved, and for which therefore you are accountable to God. But if you had improved them all, if you really had done all the good you possibly could to all men, yet this does not at all alter the case; still 'you must be born again.' Without this nothing will do any good to your poor, sinful, polluted soul. 'Nay, but I constantly attend all the ordinances of God: I keep to my church and sacrament.' It is well you do; but all this will not keep you from hell, except you be born again. Go to church twice a day; go to the Lord's table every week; say ever so many prayers in private; hear ever so many good sermons; read ever so many good books; still 'you must be born again': none of these things will stand in the place of the new birth; no, nor anything under heaven. Let this, therefore, if you have not already experienced this inward work of God, be your continual prayer: 'Lord, add this to all Thy blessings,—let me be born again! Deny whatever Thou pleasest, but deny not this; let me be 'born from above!' Take away whatsoever seemeth Thee good—reputation, fortune, friends, health—only give me this, to be born of the Spirit, to be received among the children of God! Let me be born, "not of corruptible seed, but incorruptible, by the word of God, which liveth and abideth for ever"; and then let me daily "grow in grace, and in the knowledge of our Lord and Saviour Jesus Christ"!'

SERMON XL

THE WILDERNESS STATE

On March 28, 1740, the *Journal* records: 'From these words, "Then was Jesus led by the Spirit into the wilderness to be tempted of the devil," I took occasion to describe that wilderness state, that state of doubts, and fears, and strong temptations, which so many go through, though in different degrees, after they have received remission of sins.' The first note of John xvi. 22 as a text is in the Sermon Register for March 1, 1751, at Westminster; the sermon was repeated at Snowsfields on May 25, and at West Street on May 30. It is mentioned five times more in 1751, twenty-one times in 1752, four times in 1753, once in 1754, once in 1755, and once in 1756. It seems then to have been laid aside, until it was published in Vol. IV of the Sermons in 1760. It was in part a criticism of Law's *Spirit of Prayer,* which was published in 1749 and in a second edition in 1752.

The best introduction to the sermon is Wesley's account of his own experience in his *Journal* for January 4, 1739, more than six months after his conversion. 'My friends affirm I am mad, because I said I was not a Christian a year ago. I affirm I am not a Chnstian now. Indeed, what I might have been I know not, had I been faithful to the grace then given, when, expecting nothing less, I received such a sense of the forgiveness of my sins as till then I never knew. But that I am not a Christian at this day I as assuredly know as that Jesus is the Christ.' He goes on to say that he has not any love of God—'I do not love either the Father or the Son'; that he still loves the world, and takes more pleasure in it than in God; that he has no abiding joy in the Holy Ghost; and that he has not the peace of God. He concludes, 'I have not the fruits of the Spirit of Christ. Though I have constantly used all the means of grace for twenty years. I am not a Christian.' He records many similar cases in his *Journal* of periods of deep depression following on conversion. What he did not recognize is that this is the result of the working of a psychological law, that it is impossible to have a high wave of emotional excitement without a correspondingly deep trough of subsequent depression. 'Nervous energy, when directed vigorously in a certain way, completely expends itself, and must then have a period of recuperation' (Starbuck, *Psychology of Religion,* p. 357). Starbuck found that in 93 per cent. of women and 77 per cent. of men there was a lapse after conversion into inactivity and indifference, or storm and stress, or doubt; though it was only in 5 and 7 per cent. respectively of these cases that the relapse was permanent. Where the conversion had been of the instantaneous type, the relapses were more frequent by 10 per cent.; as indeed one would expect. The relapse may be attended or preceded by conscious neglect of duty or commission of sin; or it may be purely a state of nervous depression: these two conditions Wesley distinguishes as darkness and heaviness respectively, and deals with them separately in this and the following sermon. It is doubtful how far it would be possible to discriminate exactly between the two conditions in all cases; but broadly, Wesley's distinction is sound, and his practical directions are both scriptural and sensible.

The analogy between the early history of Israel and the development of the Christian life struck many of the old commentators. The bondage in Egypt corresponds to the natural life before conversion, the crossing of the Red Sea to baptism and conversion, the wanderings in the wilderness to the period of doubt and conflict following conversion, and the entrance into the Promised Land to the attainment of perfect love and stability. For example, Samuel Mather, in *Types of the Old Testament* (2nd ed. 1705), p. 158, says: 'The marching through the wilderness was typical of the wilderness of an unregenerate condition'; and it prefigures 'troubles, difficulties, temptations, in the way to heaven.' Burrough, in *Holy Courage,* makes the same application of the story.

Ye now have sorrow: but I will see you again, and your heart shall rejoice, and your joy no man taketh from you.—JOHN xvi. 22.

1. After God had wrought a great deliverance for Israel, by bringing them out of the house of bondage, they did not immediately enter into the land which He had promised to their fathers; but 'wandered out of the way in the wilderness,' and were variously tempted and distressed. In like manner, after God has delivered them that fear Him from the bondage of sin and Satan, after they are 'justified freely by His grace, through the redemption that is in Jesus,' yet not many of them immediately enter into 'the rest which remaineth for the people of God.' The greater part of them wander, more or less, out of the good way into which He hath brought them. They come, as it were, into a 'waste and howling desert,' where they are variously tempted and tormented: and this, some, in allusion to the case of the Israelites, have termed 'a wilderness state.'

2. Certain it is, that the condition wherein these are has a right to the tenderest compassion. They labour under an evil and sore disease; though one that is not commonly understood; and for this very reason it is the more difficult for them to find a remedy.

Being in darkness themselves, they cannot be supposed to understand the nature of their own disorder; and few of their brethren, nay, perhaps, of their teachers, know either what their sickness is, or how to heal it. So much the more need there is to inquire, first, what is the nature of this disease? secondly, what is the cause? and, thirdly, what is the cure of it?

I. 1. And, first, what is the nature of this disease, into which so many fall after they have believed? Wherein does it properly consist? and what are the genuine symptoms of it? It properly consists in the loss of that faith which God once wrought in their heart. They that are *in the wilderness* have not now that divine 'evidence,' that satisfactory conviction, 'of things not seen,' which they once enjoyed. They have not now that inward demonstration of the Spirit which before enabled each of them to say, 'The life I live, I live by faith in the Son of God, who loved me, and gave Himself for me.' The light of heaven does not now 'shine in their hearts' neither do they 'see Him that is invisible'; but darkness is again on the face of their souls, and blindness on the eyes of their understanding. The Spirit no longer 'witnesses with their spirits, that they are the children of God': neither does He continue as the Spirit of adoption, 'crying' in their hearts, 'Abba, Father.' They have not now a sure trust in His love, and a liberty of approaching Him with holy boldness. 'Though He slay me, yet will I trust in Him,' is no more the language of their heart; but they are shorn of their strength, and become weak and feeble-minded, even as other men.

2. Hence, secondly, proceeds the loss of love; which cannot but rise or fall, at the same time, and in the same proportion, with true, living faith. Accordingly, they that are deprived of their faith, are deprived of the love of God also. They cannot now say, 'Lord, Thou knowest all things. Thou knowest that I love Thee.' They are not now happy in God, as every one is that truly loves Him. They do not delight in Him as in time past, and 'smell the odour of His ointments.' Once, all their 'desire was unto Him, and to the remembrance of His name'; but now even their desires are cold and dead, if not utterly extinguished. And as their love of God is waxed cold, so is also their love of their neighbour. They have not now that zeal for the souls of men, that longing after their welfare, that fervent, restless, active

desire of their being reconciled to God. They do not feel those 'bowels of mercies' for the sheep that are lost, that tender 'compassion for the ignorant, and them that are out of the way.' Once they were 'gentle toward all men, meekly instructing such as opposed the truth; and, 'if any was overtaken in a fault, restoring such an one in the spirit of meekness': but, after a suspense, perhaps of many days, anger begins to regain its power; yea, peevishness and impatience thrust sore at them that they may fall; and it is well if they are not sometimes driven, even to 'render evil for evil, and railing for railing.'

3. In consequence of the loss of faith and love, follows, thirdly, loss of joy in the Holy Ghost. For if the loving consciousness of pardon be no more, the joy resulting therefrom cannot remain. If the Spirit does not witness with our spirit that we are the children of God, the joy that flowed from the inward witness must also be at an end. And, in like manner, they who once 'rejoiced with joy unspeakable,' 'in hope of the glory of God,' now they are deprived of that 'hope full of immortality,' are deprived of the joy it occasioned; as also of that which resulted from a consciousness of 'the love of God,' then 'shed abroad in their hearts.' For the cause being removed so is the effect; the fountain being dammed up, those living waters spring no more to refresh the thirsty soul.

4. With loss of faith and love and joy, there is also joined, fourthly, the loss of that 'peace which' once passed 'all understanding.' That sweet tranquillity of mind, that composure of spirit, is gone. Painful doubt returns; doubt, whether we ever did, and perhaps whether we ever shall, believe. We begin to doubt, whether we ever did find in our hearts the real testimony of the Spirit; whether we did not rather deceive our own souls, and mistake the voice of nature for the voice of God; nay, and perhaps, whether we shall ever hear His voice, and find favour in His sight. And these doubts are again joined with servile fear, with that fear which hath torment. We fear the wrath of God, even as before we believed: we fear, lest we should be cast out of His presence; and thence sink again into that fear of death, from which we were before wholly delivered.

5. But even this is not all; for loss of peace is accompanied with loss of power. We know every one who has peace with God, through Jesus Christ, has power over all sin. But whenever he

loses the peace of God, he loses also the power over sin. While that peace remained, power also remained, even over the besetting sin, whether it were the sin of his nature, of his constitution, [the sin] of his education, or his profession; yea, and over those evil tempers and desires which, till then, he could not conquer. Sin had then no more dominion over him; but he hath now no more dominion over sin. He may struggle, indeed, but he cannot overcome; the crown is fallen from his head. His enemies again prevail over him, and, more or less, bring him into bondage. The glory is departed from him, even the kingdom of God which was in his heart. He is dispossessed of righteousness, as well as of peace and joy in the Holy Ghost.

II. 1. Such is the nature of what many have termed, and not improperly, 'the wilderness state.' But the nature of it may be more fully understood by inquiring, secondly, What are the causes of it? These, indeed, are various. But I dare not rank among these the bare, arbitrary, sovereign will of God. He 'rejoiceth in the prosperity of His servants: He delighteth not to afflict or grieve the children of men.' His invariable will is our sanctification, attended with 'peace and joy in the Holy Ghost.' These are His own free gifts; and we are assured 'the gifts of God are,' on His part, 'without repentance.' He never repenteth of what He hath given, or desires to withdraw them from us. Therefore He never *deserts* us, as some speak: it is we only that *desert* Him.

(i.) 2. The most usual cause of inward darkness is sin, of one kind or another. This it is which generally occasions what is often a complication of sin and misery. And, first, sin of commission. This may frequently be observed to darken the soul in a moment; especially if it be a known, a wilful, or presumptuous sin. If, for instance, a person, who is now walking in the clear light of God's countenance should be any way prevailed on to commit a single act of drunkenness, or uncleanness, it would be no wonder if in that very hour he fell into utter darkness. It is true, there have been some very rare cases, wherein God has prevented this, by an extraordinary display of His pardoning mercy, almost in the very instant. But in general, such an abuse of the goodness of God, so gross an insult on His love, occasions an immediate estrangement from God, and a 'darkness that may be felt.'

3. But it may be hoped this case is not very frequent; that there are not many who so despise the riches of His goodness as, while they walk in His light, so grossly and presumptuously to rebel against Him. That light is much more frequently lost by giving way to sins of omission. This, indeed, does not immediately quench the Spirit, but gradually and slowly. The former may be compared to pouring water upon a fire; the latter, to withdrawing the fuel from it. And many times will that loving Spirit reprove our neglect, before He departs from us. Many are the inward checks, the secret notices, He gives, before His influences are withdrawn. So that only a train of omissions, wilfully persisted in, can bring us into utter darkness.

4. Perhaps no sin of omission more frequently occasions this than the neglect of private prayer; the want whereof cannot be supplied by any other ordinance whatever. Nothing can be more plain, than that the life of God in the soul does not continue, much less increase, unless we use all opportunities of communion with God, and pouring out our hearts before Him. If, therefore, we are negligent of this, if we suffer business, company, or any avocation whatever, to prevent these secret exercises of the soul (or, which comes to the same thing, to make us hurry them over in a slight and careless manner), that life will surely decay. And if we long or frequently intermit them, it will gradually die away.

5. Another sin of omission, which frequently brings the soul of a believer into darkness, is the neglect of what was so strongly enjoined, even under the Jewish dispensation: 'Thou shalt, in any wise, rebuke thy neighbour, and not suffer sin upon him: thou shalt not hate thy brother in thy heart.' Now, if we do hate our brother in our heart, if we do not rebuke him when we see him in a fault, but suffer sin upon him, this will soon bring leanness into our own soul; seeing hereby we are partakers of his sin. By neglecting to reprove our neighbour we make his sin our own: we become accountable for it to God: we saw his danger, and gave him no warning so, 'if he perish in his iniquity,' God may justly require 'his blood at our hands.' No wonder then, if by thus grieving the Spirit, we lose the light of His countenance.

6. A third cause of our losing this is, the giving way to some

kind of inward sin. For example: we know, every one that is 'proud in heart is an abomination to the Lord'; and that, although this pride of heart should not appear in the outward conversation. Now, how easily may a soul filled with peace and joy fall into this snare of the devil! How natural is it for him to imagine that he has more grace, more wisdom or strength, than he really has! to 'think more highly of himself than he ought to think'! How natural to glory in something he has received, as if he had not received it! But seeing God continually 'resisteth the proud, and giveth grace' only 'to the humble,' this must certainly obscure, if not wholly destroy, the light which before shone on his heart.

7. The same effect may be produced by giving place to anger, whatever the provocation or occasion be; yea, though it were coloured over with the name of 'zeal for the truth,' or 'for the glory of God.' Indeed, all zeal which is any other than the flame of love is 'earthly, animal, and devilish.' It is the flame of wrath: it is flat, sinful anger, neither better nor worse. And nothing is a greater enemy to the mild, gentle love of God than this: they never did, they never can, subsist together in one breast. In the same proportion as this prevails, love and joy in the Holy Ghost decrease. This is particularly observable in the case of *offence*; I mean, anger at any of our brethren, at any of those who are united with us either by civil or religious ties. If we give way to the spirit of offence but one hour, we lose the sweet influences of the Holy Spirit; so that, instead of amending them, we destroy ourselves, and become an easy prey to any enemy that assaults us.

8. But suppose we are aware of this snare of the devil, we may be attacked from another quarter. When fierceness and anger are asleep, and love alone is waking, we may be no less endangered by desire, which equally tends to darken the soul. This is the sure effect of any foolish desire, any vain or inordinate affection. If we set our affection on things of the earth, on any person or thing under the sun; if we desire anything but God, and what tends to God; if we seek happiness in any creature; the jealous God will surely contend with us, for He can admit of no rival. And if we will not hear His warning voice, and return unto Him with our whole soul, if we continue to grieve Him with our idols, and running after other gods, we

shall soon be cold, barren, and dry; and the god of this world will blind and darken our hearts.

9. But this he frequently does, even when we do not give way to any positive sin. It is enough, it gives him sufficient advantage, if we do not 'stir up the gift of God which is in us'; if we do not agonize continually 'to enter in at the strait gate'; if we do not earnestly 'strive for the mastery,' and 'take the kingdom of heaven by violence.' There needs no more than not to fight, and we are sure to be conquered. Let us only be careless or 'faint in our mind,' let us be easy and indolent, and our natural darkness will soon return, and overspread our soul. It is enough, therefore, if we give way to spiritual sloth; this will effectually darken the soul: it will as surely destroy the light of God, if not so swiftly, as murder or adultery.

10. But it is well to be observed, that the cause of our darkness (whatsoever it be, whether omission or commission, whether inward or outward sin) is not always nigh at hand. Sometimes the sin which occasioned the present distress may lie at a considerable distance. It might be committed days, or weeks, or months before. And that God now withdraws His light and peace on account of what was done so long ago, is not (as one might at first imagine) an instance of His severity, but rather a proof of His long-suffering and tender mercy. He waited all this time, if haply we would see, acknowledge, and correct what was amiss; and, in default of this, He at length shows His displeasure, if thus, at last He may bring us to repentance.

(ii.) 1. Another general cause of this darkness is *ignorance*; which is likewise of various kinds. If men know not the Scriptures, if they imagine there are passages either in the Old or New Testament which assert, that all believers, without exception, must sometimes be in darkness; this ignorance will naturally bring upon them the darkness which they expect. And how common a case has this been among us! How few are there that do not expect it! And no wonder, seeing they are taught to expect it; seeing their guides lead them into this way. Not only the mystic writers of the Romish Church, but many of the most spiritual and experimental in our own (very few of the last century excepted), lay it down with all assurance, as a plain, unquestionable scripture doctrine, and cite many texts to prove it.

2. Ignorance also of the work of God in the soul frequently occasions this darkness. Men imagine (because so they have been taught, particularly by writers of the Romish communion, whose plausible assertions too many Protestants have received without due examination) that they are not always to walk in luminous faith that this is only a *lower dispensation*; that as they rise higher, they are to leave those *sensible comforts*, and to live by *naked faith* (naked, indeed, if it be stripped both of love, and peace, and joy in the Holy Ghost!); that a state of light and joy is good, but a state of darkness and dryness is better; that it is by these alone we can be purified from pride, love of the world, and inordinate self-love; and that, therefore, we ought neither to expect nor desire to walk in the light always. Hence it is (though other reasons may concur), that the main body of pious men in the Romish Church generally walk in a dark uncomfortable way, and if ever they receive soon lose the light of God.

(iii.) 1. A third general cause of this darkness is *temptation*. When the candle of the Lord first shines on our head, temptation frequently flees away, and totally disappears. All is calm within, perhaps without too, while God makes our enemies to be at peace with us. It is then very natural to suppose that we shall not see war any more. And there are instances wherein this calm has continued, not only for weeks, but for months or years. But commonly it is otherwise: in a short time 'the winds blow, the rains descend, and the floods arise' anew. They who know not either the Son or the Father, and consequently hate His children, when God slackens the bridle which is in their teeth, will show that hatred in various instances. As of old, 'he that was born after the flesh persecuted him that was born after the Spirit, even so it is now'; the same cause still producing the same effect. The evil which yet remains in the heart will then also move afresh; anger, and many other roots of bitterness, will endeavour to spring up. At the same time, Satan will not be wanting to cast in his fiery darts; and the soul will have to wrestle, not only with the world, not only 'with flesh and blood, but with principalities and powers, with the rulers of the darkness of this world, with wicked spirits in high places.' Now, when so various assaults are made at once, and perhaps with the utmost violence, it is not strange if it should occasion, not only heaviness, but even darkness in a weak believer,—more especially, if he was not watching; if these assaults are made in an hour when he looked not for them; if he expected nothing less, but had fondly told himself 'the day of evil would return no more.'

2. The force of those temptations which arise from within will be exceedingly heightened if we before thought too highly of ourselves, as if we had been cleansed from all sin. And how naturally do we imagine this during the warmth of our first love! How ready are we to believe that God has 'fulfilled in us the' whole 'work of faith with power'; that because we *feel* no sin, we *have* none in us; but the soul is all love! And well may a sharp attack from an enemy whom we supposed to be not only conquered but slain, throw us into much heaviness of soul; yea, sometimes, into utter darkness: particularly when we *reason* with this enemy, instead of instantly calling upon God, and casting ourselves upon Him, by simple faith, who 'alone knoweth how to deliver' His 'out of temptation.'

III. These are the usual causes of this second darkness. Inquire we, thirdly, what is the cure of it?

1. To suppose that this is one and the same in all cases, is a great and fatal mistake; and yet extremely common, even among many who pass for experienced Christians, yea, perhaps, take upon them to be teachers in Israel, to be the guides of other souls. Accordingly, they know and use but one medicine, whatever be the cause of the distemper. They begin immediately to apply the promises; to *preach the gospel,* as they call it. To give comfort, is the single point at which they aim; in order to which they say many soft and tender things, concerning the love of God to poor, helpless sinners, and the efficacy of the blood of Christ. Now this is *quackery* indeed, and that of the worst sort, as it tends, if not to kill men's bodies, yet, without the peculiar mercy of God, 'to destroy both their bodies and souls in hell.' It is hard to speak of these 'daubers with untempered mortar,' these promise-mongers, as they deserve. They well deserve the title, which has been ignorantly given to others: they are *spiritual mountebanks.* They do, in effect, make 'the blood of the covenant an unholy thing.' They vilely prostitute the promises of God, by thus applying them to all without distinction. Whereas, indeed, the cure of spiritual, as of bodily, diseases must be as various as

are the causes of them. The first thing, therefore, is, to find out the cause; and this will naturally point out the cure.

2. For instance: is it sin which occasions darkness? What sin? Is it outward sin of any kind? Does your conscience accuse you of committing any sin, whereby you grieve the Holy Spirit of God? Is it on this account that He is departed from you, and that joy and peace are departed with Him? And how can you expect they should return, till you put away the accursed thing? 'Let the wicked forsake his way'; 'cleanse your hands, ye sinners'; 'put away the evil of your doings'; so shall your 'light break out of obscurity'; the Lord will return and 'abundantly pardon.'

3. If, upon the closest search, you can find no sin of commission which causes the cloud upon your soul, inquire next, if there be not some sin of omission which separates between God and you. Do you 'not suffer sin upon your brother'? Do you reprove them that sin in your sight? Do you walk in all the ordinances of God? in public, family, private prayer? If not, if you habitually neglect any one of these known duties, how can you expect that the light of His countenance should continue to shine upon you? Make haste to 'strengthen the things that remain'; then your soul shall live. 'Today, if ye will hear His voice,' by His grace supply what is lacking. When you hear a voice behind you saying, 'This is the way, walk thou in it,' harden not your heart; be no more 'disobedient to the heavenly calling.' Till the sin, whether of omission or commission, be removed, all comfort is false and deceitful. It is only skinning the wound over, which still festers and rankles beneath. Look for no peace within, till you are at peace with God; which cannot be without 'fruits meet for repentance.'

4. But perhaps you are not conscious of even any sin of omission which impairs your peace and joy in the Holy Ghost. Is there not, then, some inward sin, which, as a root of bitterness, springs up in your heart to trouble you? Is not your dryness and barrenness of soul occasioned by your heart's 'departing from the living God'? Has not 'the foot of pride come against' you? Have you not thought of yourself 'more highly than you ought to think'? Have you not, in any respect, 'sacrificed to your own net, and burned incense to your own drag'? Have you not ascribed your success in any undertaking to your own courage, or strength, or wisdom? Have you not boasted of something 'you

have received, as though you had not received it'? Have you not gloried in anything, 'save in the cross of our Lord Jesus Christ'? Have you not sought after or desired the praise of men? Have you not taken pleasure in it? If so, you see the way you are to take. If you have fallen by pride, 'humble yourself under the mighty hand of God, and He will exalt you in due time.' Have you not forced Him to depart from you, by giving place to anger? Have you not 'fretted yourself because of the ungodly'? or 'been envious against the evil-doers'? Have you not been offended at any of your brethren, looking at their (real or imagined) sin, so as to sin yourself against the great law of love, by estranging your heart from them? Then look unto the Lord, that you may renew your strength; that all this sharpness and coldness may be done away; that love, and peace, and joy may return together, and you may be invariably kind to each other, and 'tender-hearted, forgiving one another, even as God for Christ's sake hath forgiven you.' Have not you given way to any foolish desire? to any kind or degree of inordinate affection? How then can the love of God have place in your heart, till you put away your idols? 'Be not deceived: God is not mocked': He will not dwell in a divided heart. As long, therefore, as you cherish Delilah in your bosom, He has no place there. It is vain to hope for a recovery of His light, till you pluck out the right eye, and cast it from you. O let there be no longer delay! Cry to Him, that He may enable you so to do! Bewail your own impotence and helplessness; and, the Lord being your helper, enter in at the strait gate: take the kingdom of heaven by violence! Cast out every idol from His sanctuary, and the glory of the Lord shall soon appear.

5. Perhaps it is this very thing, the want of striving, spiritual sloth, which keeps your soul in darkness. You dwell at ease in the land; there is no war in your coasts; and so you are quiet and unconcerned. You go on in the same even track of outward duties, and are content there to abide. And do you wonder, meantime, that your soul is dead? O stir yourself up before the Lord! Arise, and shake yourself from the dust; wrestle with God for the mighty blessing; pour out your soul unto God in prayer, and continue therein with all perseverance! Watch! Awake out of sleep; and keep awake!—otherwise there is nothing to be

expected, but that you will be alienated more and more from the light and life of God.

6. If, upon the fullest and most impartial examination of yourself, you cannot discern that you at present give way either to spiritual sloth, or any other inward or outward sin, then call to mind the time that is past. Consider your former tempers, words, and actions. Have these been right before the Lord? 'Commune with Him in your chamber, and be still'; and desire of Him to try the ground of your heart, and bring to your remembrance whatever has at any time offended the eyes of His glory. If the guilt of any unrepented sin remain on your soul, it cannot be but you will remain in darkness, till, having been renewed by repentance, you are again washed by faith in 'the fountain opened for sin and uncleanness.'

7. Entirely different will be the manner of the cure, if the cause of the disease be not sin, but ignorance. It may be ignorance of the meaning of Scripture; perhaps occasioned by ignorant commentators—ignorant, at least, in this respect, however knowing and learned they may be in other particulars. And, in this case, that ignorance must be removed before we can remove the darkness arising from it. We must show the true meaning of those texts which have been misunderstood. My design does not permit me to consider all the passages of Scripture which have been pressed into this service. I shall just mention two or three, which are frequently brought to prove, that all believers must, sooner or later, 'walk in darkness.'

8. One of these is Isa. l. 10: 'Who is among you that feareth the Lord, that obeyeth the voice of His servant, that walketh in darkness, and hath no light? let him trust in the name of the Lord, and stay upon his God.' But how does it appear, either from the text or context, that the person here spoken of ever had light? One who is convinced of sin 'feareth the Lord, and obeyeth the voice of His servant.' And him we should advise, though he was still dark of soul, and had never seen the light of God's countenance, yet to 'trust in the name of the Lord, and stay upon his God.' This text, therefore, proves nothing less than that a believer in Christ 'must sometimes *walk in darkness.*'

9. Another text which has been supposed to speak the same doctrine is Hos. ii. 14: 'I will allure her, and bring her into the wilderness, and speak comfortably unto her.' Hence it has been

inferred, that God will bring every believer *into the wilderness,* into a state of deadness and darkness. But it is certain, the text speaks no such thing; for it does not appear that it speaks of particular believers at all: it manifestly refers to the Jewish nation; and, perhaps, to that only. But if it be applicable to particular persons, the plain meaning of it is this: I will draw him by love; I will next convince him of sin; and then comfort him by My pardoning mercy.

10. A third scripture, from whence the same inference has been drawn, is that above recited, 'Ye now have sorrow: but I will see you again, and your heart shall rejoice, and your joy no man taketh from you.' This has been supposed to imply, that God would, after a time, withdraw Himself from all believers; and that they could not, till after they had thus sorrowed, have the joy which no man could take from them. But the whole context shows, that our Lord is here speaking personally to the Apostles, and no others; and that He is speaking concerning those particular events, His own death and resurrection. 'A little while,' says He, 'and ye shall not see Me,' namely, whilst I am in the grave: 'and again, a little while, and ye shall see Me'; when I am risen from the dead. 'Ye will weep and lament, and the world will rejoice: but your sorrow shall be turned into joy.' 'Ye now have sorrow,' because I am about to be taken from your head; 'but I will see you again,' after My resurrection, 'and your heart shall rejoice; and your joy,' which I will then give you, 'no man taketh from you.' All this we know was literally fulfilled in the particular case of the Apostles. But no inference can be drawn from hence with regard to God's dealings with believers in general.

11. A fourth text (to mention no more), which has been frequently cited in proof of the same doctrine, is 1 Pet. iv. 12: 'Beloved think it not strange concerning the fiery trial which is to try you.' But this is full as foreign to the point as the preceding. The text, literally rendered, runs thus: 'Beloved, wonder not at the burning which is among you, which is for your trial.' Now, however this may be accommodated to inward trials, in a secondary sense; yet, primarily, it doubtless refers to martyr-dom, and the sufferings connected with it. Neither, therefore, is this text anything at all to the purpose for which it is cited. And

we may challenge all men to bring one text, either from the Old or New Testament, which is any more to the purpose than this.

12. 'But is not darkness much more profitable for the soul than light? Is not the work of God in the heart most swiftly and effectually carried on during a state of inward suffering? Is not a believer more swiftly and thoroughly purified by sorrow, than by joy?—by anguish, and pain, and distress, and spiritual martyrdoms, than by continual peace?' So the Mystics teach; so it is written in their books; but not in the oracles of God. The Scripture nowhere says that the absence of God best perfects His work in the heart! Rather, His presence, and a clear communion with the Father and the Son: a strong consciousness of this will do more in an hour, than His absence in an age. Joy in the Holy Ghost will far more effectually purify the soul, than the want of that joy; and the peace of God is the best means of refining the soul from the dross of earthly affections. Away then with the idle conceit, that the kingdom of God is divided against itself; that the peace of God and joy in the Holy Ghost, are obstructive of righteousness; and that we are saved, not by faith, but by unbelief; not by hope but by despair!

13. So long as men dream thus they may well 'walk in darkness': nor can the effect cease, till the cause is removed. But yet we must not imagine it will immediately cease, even when the cause is no more. When either ignorance or sin has caused darkness, one or the other may be removed, and yet the light which was obstructed thereby may not immediately return. As it is the free gift of God, He may restore it, sooner or later, as it pleases Him. In the case of sin, we cannot reasonably expect that it should immediately return. The sin began before the punishment, which may, therefore, justly remain after the sin is at an end. And even in the natural course of things, though a wound cannot be healed while the dart is sticking in the flesh; yet neither is it healed as soon as that is drawn out, but soreness and pain may remain long after.

14. Lastly. If darkness be occasioned by manifold and heavy and unexpected temptations, the best way of removing and preventing this is, to teach believers always to expect temptation, seeing they dwell in an evil world, among wicked, subtle, malicious spirits, and have an heart capable of all evil. Convince them that the whole work of sanctification is not, as they

imagined, wrought at once; that when they first believe they are but as new-born babes, who are gradually to grow up, and may expect many storms before they come to the full stature of Christ. Above all, let them be instructed, when the storm is upon them, not to reason with the devil, but to pray; to pour out their souls before God, and show Him of their trouble. And these are the persons unto whom, chiefly, we are to apply the great and precious promises; not to the ignorant, till the ignorance is removed, much less to the impenitent sinner. To these we may largely and affectionately declare the loving-kindness of God our Saviour, and, expatiate upon His tender mercies which have been ever of old. Here we may dwell upon the faithfulness of God, whose 'word is tried to the uttermost'; and upon the virtue of that blood which was shed for us, to 'cleanse us from all sin': and God will then bear witness to His word, and bring their souls out of trouble. He will say, 'Arise, shine; for thy light is come, and the glory of the Lord is risen upon thee.' Yea, and that light, if thou walk humbly and closely with God, will 'shine more and more unto the perfect day.'

SERMON XLI

HEAVINESS THROUGH
MANIFOLD TEMPTATIONS

Judging by the Sermon Register, this sermon was first preached at Epworth on June 9, 1755; it was repeated on August 2 at West Street. It occurs twice in 1756, and three times in 1757. It was evidently written after the preceding sermon, and was intended to supplement its teaching. In Sermon XL Wesley had ascribed the darkness which he there speaks of entirely to sin of some kind; but he had come to see that believers may be subject to depression without any consciousness of having brought it about by sin, and so he now distinguishes between darkness, which is always the result of sin, and heaviness, which does not presuppose any such backsliding of heart from God. The sermon was first published in Vol. IV of the Sermons in 1760.

Now for a season, if need be, Ye are in heaviness through manifold temptations.—1 PET. i. 6.

1. In the preceding discourse I have particularly spoken of that darkness of mind into which those are often observed to fall who once walked in the light of God's countenance. Nearly related to this is the heaviness of soul which is still more common, even among believers. Indeed, almost all the children of God experience this, in an higher or lower degree. And so great is the resemblance between one and the other, that they are frequently confounded together; and we are apt to say, indifferently, 'Such an one is in darkness,' or, 'Such an one is in heaviness'; as if they were equivalent terms, one of which implied no more than the other. But they are far, very far, from it. Darkness is one thing; heaviness is another. There is a difference, yea, a wide and essential difference, between the former and the latter. And such a difference it is, as all the children of God are deeply concerned to understand: otherwise, nothing will be more easy than for them to slide out of heaviness into darkness. In order to prevent this, I will endeavour to show,—

I.   WHAT MANNER OF PERSONS THOSE WERE TO WHOM
     THE APOSTLE SAYS, 'YE ARE IN HEAVINESS':
II. WHAT KIND OF HEAVINESS THEY WERE IN:
III. WHAT WERE THE CAUSES: AND,
IV. WHAT WERE THE ENDS OF IT. I SHALL CONCLUDE
     WITH SOME INFERENCES.

I. 1. I am, in the first place, to show what manner of persons those were to whom the Apostle says, 'Ye are in heaviness.' And, first, it is beyond all dispute, that they were believers at the time the Apostle thus addressed them: for so he expressly says (verse 5), 'Ye who are kept by the power of God through faith unto salvation.' Again (verse 7), he mentions 'the trial of their faith, much more precious than that of gold which perisheth.' And yet again (verse 9), he speaks of their 'receiving the end of their faith, the salvation of their souls.' At the same time, therefore, that they were 'in heaviness,' they were possessed of living faith. Their heaviness did not destroy their faith: they still 'endured, as seeing Him that is invisible.'

2. Neither did their heaviness destroy their peace; the 'peace which passeth all understanding'; which is inseparable from true, living faith. This we may easily gather from the second verse, wherein the Apostle prays, not that grace and *peace* may be *given* them, but only that it may 'be *multiplied* unto' them; that the blessing which they already enjoyed might be more abundantly bestowed upon them.

3. The persons to whom the Apostle here speaks were also full of a living hope. For thus he speaks (verse 3), 'Blessed be the God and Father of our Lord Jesus Christ, who according to His abundant mercy hath begotten us again'—me and you, all of us who are 'sanctified by the Spirit,' and enjoy the 'sprinkling of the blood of Jesus Christ'—'unto a living hope, unto an inheritance, 'that is, unto a living hope of an inheritance, 'incorruptible, undefiled, and that fadeth not away.' So that, notwithstanding their heaviness, they still retained an hope full of immortality.

4. And they still 'rejoiced in hope of the glory of God.' They were filled with joy in the Holy Ghost. So (verse 8), the Apostle having just mentioned the final 'revelation of Jesus Christ' (namely, when He cometh to judge the world), immediately adds, 'In whom, though now ye see Him not,' not with your bodily eyes, 'yet believing, ye rejoice with joy unspeakable and

full of glory.' Their heaviness, therefore, was not only consistent with living hope, but also with joy unspeakable: at the same time they were thus heavy, they nevertheless rejoiced with joy full of glory.

5. In the midst of their heaviness they likewise still enjoyed the love of God, which had been shed abroad in their hearts; 'whom,' says the Apostle, 'having not seen, ye love.' Though ye have not seen Him face to face; yet, knowing Him by faith, ye have obeyed His word, 'My son, give Me thy heart.' He is your God, and your love, the desire of your eyes, and your 'exceeding great reward.' Ye have sought and found happiness in Him: ye 'delight in the Lord,' and He hath given you your 'hearts' desire.'

6. Once more: though they were heavy, yet were they holy; they retained the same power over sin. They were still 'kept' from this, 'by the power of God'; they were 'obedient children, not fashioned according to their former desires'; but 'as He that had called them is holy,' so were they 'holy in all manner of conversation.' Knowing they were 'redeemed by the precious blood of Christ, as a lamb without spot, and without blemish,' they had, through the faith and hope, which they had in God, 'purified their souls by the Spirit.' So that, upon the whole, their heaviness well consisted with faith, with hope, with love of God and man, with the peace of God, with joy in the Holy Ghost, with inward and outward holiness. It did no way impair, much less destroy, any part of the work of God in their hearts. It did not at all interfere with that 'sanctification of the Spirit' which is the root of all true obedience; neither with the happiness which must needs result from grace and peace reigning in the heart.

II. 1. Hence we may easily learn what kind of heaviness they were in,—the second thing which I shall endeavour to show. The word, in the original, is λυπηθεντες—*made sorry, grieved*: from λυπη—*grief,* or *sorrow.* This is the constant, literal meaning of the word: and, this being observed, there is no ambiguity in the expression, nor any difficulty in understanding it. The persons spoken of here were *grieved*: the heaviness they were in was neither more nor less than *sorrow,* or *grief,*—a passion which every child of man is well acquainted with.

2. It is probable our translators rendered it *heaviness* (though a less common word) to denote two things: first, the degree, and

next, the continuance, of it. It does indeed seem, that it is not a slight or inconsiderable degree of grief which is here spoken of; but such as makes a strong impression upon, and sinks deep into the soul. Neither does this appear to be a transient sorrow, such as passes away in an hour; but rather, such as having taken fast hold of the heart, is not presently shaken off, but continues for some time, as a settled temper rather than a passion, even in them that have a living faith in Christ, and the genuine love of God in their hearts.

3. Even in these, this heaviness may sometimes be so deep, as to overshadow the whole soul; to give a colour, as it were, to all the affections; such as will appear in the whole behaviour. It may likewise have an influence over the body: particularly in those that are either of a naturally weak constitution, or weakened by some accidental disorder, especially of the nervous kind. In many cases, we find 'the corruptible body presses down the soul': in this, the soul rather presses down the body, and weakness it more and more. Nay, I will not say that deep and lasting sorrow of heart may not sometimes weaken a strong constitution, and lay the foundation of such bodily disorders as are not easily removed: and yet, all this may consist with a measure of that faith which still worketh by love.

4. This may well be termed a 'fiery trial'; and though it is not the same with that the Apostle speaks of in the fourth chapter, yet many of the expressions there used concerning outward sufferings may be accommodated to this inward affliction. They cannot, indeed with any propriety, be applied to them that are in darkness. These do not, cannot rejoice; neither is it true that 'the spirit of glory and of God resteth upon' them. But He frequently doth on those that are in heaviness; so that, though sorrowful, yet are they always rejoicing.

III. 1. But to proceed to the third point: what are the causes of such sorrow or heaviness in a true believer? The Apostle tells us clearly: 'Ye are in heaviness,' says he, 'through manifold temptations'; ποικίλοις—*manifold,* not only many in number, but of many kinds. They may be varied and diversified a thousand ways, by the change or addition of numberless circumstances. And this very diversity and variety make it more difficult to guard against them. Among these we may rank all bodily disorders; particularly acute diseases, and violent pain of every kind, whether affecting the whole body, or the smallest part of it. It is true, some who have enjoyed uninterrupted health, and have felt none of these, may make light of them, and wonder that sickness, or pain of body, should bring heaviness upon the mind. And perhaps one in a thousand is of so peculiar a constitution as not to feel pain like other men. So hath it pleased God to show His almighty power, by producing some of these prodigies of nature, who have seemed not to regard pain at all, though of the severest kind; if that contempt of pain was not owing partly to the force of education, partly to a preternatural cause—to the power either of good or evil spirits, who raised those men above the state of mere nature. But, abstracting from these particular cases, it is, in general, a just observation, that

> Pain is perfect misery, and extreme
> Quite overturns all patience.

And even where this is prevented by the grace of God, where men do 'possess their souls in patience,' it may, nevertheless, occasion much inward heaviness: the soul sympathizing with the body.

2. All diseases of long continuance, though less painful, are apt to produce the same effect. When God appoints over us consumption, or the chilling and burning ague, if it be not speedily removed, it will not only 'consume the eyes,' but 'cause sorrow of heart.' This is eminently the case with regard to all those which are termed *nervous disorders*. And faith does not overturn the course of nature: natural causes still produce natural effects. Faith no more hinders the *sinking of the spirits* (as it is called) in an hysteric illness, than the rising of the pulse in a fever.

3. Again: when 'calamity cometh as a whirlwind, and poverty as an armed man'; is this a little temptation? Is it strange if it occasion sorrow and heaviness? Although this also may appear but a small thing to those that stand at a distance, or who look, and 'pass by on the other side'; yet it is otherwise to them that feel it. 'Having food and raiment' (indeed the latter word, σκεπασματα, implies *lodging* as well as *apparel*), we may, if the

love of God is in our hearts, 'be therewith content.' But what shall they do who have none of these? who, as it were, 'embrace the rock for a shelter'? who have only the earth to lie upon, and only the sky to cover them? who have not a dry, or warm, much less a clean, abode for themseves and their little ones? no, nor clothing to keep themselves, or those they love next themselves, from pinching cold, either by day or night? I laugh at the stupid Heathen crying out,

> *Nil habet infelix paupertas durius in se,*
> *Quam quod ridiculos homines facit!*

Has poverty nothing worse in it than this, that it *makes men liable to be laughed at*? It is a sign this idle poet talked by rote of the things which he knew not. Is not want of food something worse than this? God pronounced it as a curse upon man, that he should earn it 'by the sweat of his brow.' But how many are there in this Christian country, that toil, and labour, and sweat, and have it not at last, but struggle with weariness and hunger together? Is it not worse for one, after a hard day's labour, to come back to a poor, cold, dirty, uncomfortable lodging, and to find there not even the food which is needful to repair his wasted strength? You that live at ease in the earth, that want nothing but eyes to see, ears to hear, and hearts to understand how well God hath dealt with you, is it not worse to seek bread day by day, and find none? perhaps to find the comfort also of five or six children crying for what he has not to give! Were it not that he is restrained by an unseen hand, would he not soon 'curse God and die'? O want of bread! want of bread! Who can tell what this means, unless he hath felt it himself? I am astonished it occasions no more than heaviness even in them that believe.

4. Perhaps, next to this, we may place the death of those who were near and dear unto us; of a tender parent and one not much declined into the vale of years; of a beloved child, just rising into life, and clasping about our heart; of a friend that was as our own soul—next the grace of God, the last, best gift of Heaven. And a thousand circumstances may enhance the distress. Perhaps the child, the friend, died in our embrace!— Perhaps, was snatched away when we looked not for it!

flourishing, cut down like a flower. In all these cases, we not only may, but ought to, be affected: it is the design of God that we should. He would not have us stocks and stones. He would have our affections regulated, not extinguished.

Therefore, 'nature unreproved may drop a tear.' There may be sorrow without sin.

5. A still deeper sorrow we may feel for those who are dead while they live; on account of the unkindness, ingratitude, apostasy, of those who were united to us in the closest ties. Who can express what a lover of souls may feel for a friend, a brother, dead to God? for an husband, a wife, a parent, a child rushing into sin, as an horse into the battle; and, in spite of all arguments and persuasions, hasting to work out his own damnation. And this anguish of spirit may be heightened to an inconceivable degree, by the consideration, that he who is now posting to destruction once ran well in the way of life. Whatever he was in time past serves now to no other purpose than to make our reflections on what he is more piercing and afflictive.

6. In all these circumstances, we may be assured, our great adversary will not be wanting to improve his opportunity. He, who is always 'walking about, seeking whom he may devour,' will then, especially, use all his power, all his skill, if haply he may gain any advantage over the soul that is already cast down. He will not be sparing of his fiery darts, such as are most likely to find an entrance, and to fix most deeply in the heart, by their suitableness to the temptation that assaults it. He will labour to inject unbelieving, or blasphemous, or repining thoughts. He will suggest that God does not regard, does not govern, the earth; or, at least, that He does not govern it aright, not by the rules of justice and mercy. He will endeavour to stir up the heart against God, to renew our natural enmity against Him. And if we attempt to fight him with his own weapons, if we begin to reason with him, more and more heaviness will undoubtedly ensue, if not utter darkness.

7. It has been frequently supposed, that there is another cause, if not of darkness, at least, of heaviness; namely, God's withdrawing Himself from the soul, because it is His sovereign will. Certainly He will do this, if we grieve His Holy Spirit, either by outward or inward sin; either by doing evil, or neglecting to do good; by giving way either to pride or anger, to spiritual

sloth, to foolish desire, or inordinate affection. But that He ever withdraws Himself *because He will,* merely because it is His good pleasure, I absolutely deny. There is no text in all the Bible which gives any colour for such a supposition. Nay, it is a supposition, contrary, not only to many particular texts, but to the whole tenor of Scripture. It is repugnant to the very nature of God: it is utterly beneath His majesty and wisdom (as an eminent writer strongly expresses it), 'to play at bo-peep with His creatures.' It is inconsistent both with His justice and mercy, and with the sound experience of all His children.

8. One more cause of heaviness is mentioned by many of those who are termed 'mystic authors.' And the notion has crept in, I know not how, even among plain people who have no acquaintance with them. I cannot better explain this, than in the words of a late writer, who relates this as her own experience: 'I continued so happy in my Beloved, that, although I should have been forced to live a vagabond in a desert, I should have found no difficulty in it. This state had not lasted long, when, in effect, I found myself led into a desert. I found myself in a forlorn condition, altogether poor, wretched, and miserable. The proper source of this grief is, the knowledge of ourselves; by which we find that there is an extreme unlikeness between God and us. We see ourselves most opposite to Him; and that our inmost soul is entirely corrupted, depraved, and full of all kind of evil and malignity, of the world and the flesh, and all sorts of abominations.'—From hence it has been inferred, that the knowledge of ourselves, without which we should perish everlastingly, must, even after we have attained justifying faith, occasion the deepest heaviness.

9. But upon this I would observe, (1) In the preceding paragraph, this writer says, 'Hearing I had not a true faith in Christ, I offered myself up to God, and immediately felt His love.' It may be so; and yet it does not appear that this was justification. It is more probable, it was no more than what are usually termed, the 'drawings of the Father.' And if so, the heaviness and darkness which followed was no other than conviction of sin; which, in the nature of things, must precede that faith whereby we are justified. (2) Suppose she was justified almost the same moment she was convinced of wanting faith, there was then no time for that gradually-increasing self-

knowledge which uses to precede justification; in this case, therefore, it came after, and was probably the more severe, the less it was expected. (3) It is allowed there will be a far deeper, a far clearer and fuller knowledge of our inbred sin, of our total corruption by nature, after justification, than ever there was before it. But this need not occasion darkness of soul: I will not say, that it must bring us into heaviness. Were it so, the Apostle would not have used that expression, *if need be*; for there would be an absolute, indispensable need of it, for all that would know themselves; that is, in effect, for all that would know the perfect love of God, and be thereby 'made meet to be partakers of the inheritance of the saints in light.' But this is by no means the case. On the contrary, God may increase the knowledge of ourselves to any degree, and increase, in the same proportion, the knowledge of Himself, and the experience of His love. And in this case there would be no 'desert,' no 'misery,' no 'forlorn condition'; but love, and peace, and joy, gradually springing up into everlasting life.

IV. 1. For what ends, then (which was the fourth thing to be considered), does God permit heaviness to befall so many of His children? The Apostle gives us a plain and direct answer to this important question: 'that the trial of their faith, which is much more precious than gold that perisheth, though it be tried by fire, may be found unto praise, and honour, and glory, at the revelation of Jesus Christ' (verse 7). There may be an allusion to this, in that well-known passage of the fourth chapter (although it primarily relates to quite another thing, as has been already observed): 'Think it not strange concerning the fiery trial which is to try you: but rejoice that ye are partakers of the sufferings of Christ; that, when His glory shall be revealed, ye may likewise rejoice with exceeding great joy' (verse 12, &c.).

2. Hence we learn, that the first and great end of God's permitting the temptations which bring heaviness on His children, is the trial of their faith, which is tried by these, even as gold by the fire. Now we know, gold tried in the fire is purified thereby; is separated from its dross. And so is faith in the fire of temptation; the more it is tried, the more it is purified; yea, and not only purified, but also strengthened, confirmed, increased abundantly, by so many more proofs of the wisdom and power,

the love and faithfulness of God. This, then—to increase our faith—is one gracious end of God's permitting those manifold temptations.

3. They serve to try, to purify, to confirm, and increase that living hope also, whereunto 'the God and Father of our Lord Jesus Christ hath begotten us again of His abundant mercy.' Indeed our hope cannot but increase in the same proportion with our faith. On this foundation it stands: believing in His name, living by faith in the Son of God, we hope for, we have a confident expectation of, the glory which shall be revealed; and, consequently, whatever strengthens our faith, increases our hope also. At the same time it increases our joy in the Lord, which cannot but attend an hope full of immortality. In this view the Apostle exhorts believers in the other chapter: 'Rejoice that ye are partakers of the sufferings of Christ.' On this very account, 'happy are you: for the Spirit of glory and of God resteth upon you': and hereby ye are enabled, even in the midst of sufferings, to 'rejoice with joy unspeakable and full of glory.'

4. They rejoice the more, because the trials which increase their faith and hope increase their love also; both their gratitude to God for all His mercies, and their good-will to all mankind. Accordingly, the more deeply sensible they are of the loving-kindness of God their Saviour, the more is their heart inflamed with love to Him who 'first loved us.' The clearer and stronger evidence they have of the glory that shall be revealed, the more do they love Him who hath purchased it for them, and 'given them the earnest' thereof 'in their hearts.' And this, the increase of their love, is another end of the temptations permitted to come upon them.

5. Yet another is, their advance in holiness; holiness of heart, and holiness of conversation,—the latter naturally resulting from the former; for a good tree will bring forth good fruit. And all inward holiness is the immediate fruit of the faith that worketh by love. By this the blessed Spirit purifies the heart from pride, self-will, passion; from love of the world, from foolish and hurtful desires, from vile and vain affections. Beside that, sanctified afflictions have, through the grace of God, an immediate and direct tendency to holiness. Through the operation of His Spirit, they humble, more and more, and abase the soul before God. They calm and meeken our turbulent

spirit, tame the fierceness of our nature, soften our obstinacy and self-will, crucify us to the world, and bring us to expect all our strength from, and to seek all our happiness in, God.

6. And all these terminate in that great end, that our faith, hope, love, and holiness 'may be found,' if it doth not yet appear, 'unto praise' from God Himself, 'and honour' from men and angels, 'and glory,' assigned by the great Judge to all that have endured unto the end. And this will be assigned in that awful day to every man, 'according to his works'; according to the work which God had wrought in his heart, and the outward works which he has wrought for God; and likewise according to what he had suffered: so that all these trials are unspeakable gain. So many ways do these 'light afflictions, which are but for a moment, work out for us a far more exceeding and eternal weight of glory!'

7. Add to this the advantage which others may receive by seeing our behaviour under affliction. We find by experience, example frequently makes a deeper impression upon us than precept. And what examples have a stronger influence, not only on those who are partakers of like precious faith, but even on them who have not known God, than that of a soul calm and serene in the midst of storms; sorrowful, yet always rejoicing; meekly accepting whatever is the will of God, however grievous it may be to nature; saying, in sickness and pain, 'The cup which my Father hath given me, shall I not drink it?'—in loss or want, 'The Lord gave; the Lord hath taken away; blessed be the name of the Lord!'

V. 1. I am to conclude with some inferences. And, first, how wide is the difference between darkness of soul, and heaviness; which, nevertheless, are so generally confounded with each other, even by experienced Christians! Darkness, or the wilderness state, implies a total loss of joy in the Holy Ghost: heaviness does not; in the midst of this we may 'rejoice with joy unspeakable.' They that are in darkness have lost the peace of God: they that are in heaviness have not; so far from it, that at the very time 'peace,' as well as 'grace,' may 'be multiplied' unto them. In the former, the love of God is waxed cold, if it be not utterly extinguished; in the latter, it retains its full force, or, rather, increases daily. In these, faith itself, if not totally lost, is, however, grievously decayed: their evidence and conviction of things not seen, particularly of the pardoning love of God, is not so clear or strong as in time past; and their trust in Him is proportionably weakened: those, though they see Him not, yet have a clear, unshaken confidence in God, and an abiding evidence of that love whereby all their sins are blotted out. So that as long as we can distinguish faith from unbelief, hope from despair, peace from war, the love of God from the love of the world, we may infallibly distinguish heaviness from darkness!

2. We may learn from hence, secondly, that there may be need of heaviness, but there can be no need of darkness. There may be need of our being in 'heaviness for a season,' in order to the ends above recited; at least, in this sense, as it is a natural result of those 'manifold temptations,' which are needful to try and increase our faith, to confirm and enlarge our hope, to purify our heart from all unholy tempers, and to perfect us I love. And, by consequence, they are needful in order to brighten our crown, and add to our eternal weight of glory. But we cannot say, that darkness is needful in order to any of these ends. It is no way conducive to them: the loss of faith, hope, love, is surely neither conducive to holiness, nor to the increase of that reward in heaven which will bein proportion to our holiness on earth.

3. From the Apostle's manner of speaking we may gather, thirdly, that even heaviness is not *always* needful. 'Now, for a season, if need be': so it is not needful for *all persons*;. nor for any person at *all times*. God is able, He has both power and wisdom, to work, when He pleases, the same work of grace in any soul by other means. And in some instances He does so; He causes those whom it pleaseth Him to go on from strength to strength, even till they 'perfect holiness in His fear,' with scarce any heaviness at all; as having an absolute power over the heart of man, and moving all the springs of it at His pleasure. But these cases are rare: God generally sees good to try 'acceptable men in the furnace of affliction.' So that manifold temptations, and heaviness, more or less, are usually the portion of His dearest children.

4. We ought, therefore, lastly, to watch and pray, and use our utmost endeavours to avoid falling into darkness. But we need not be solicitous how to avoid, so much as how to improve by, heaviness. Our great care should be, so to behave ourselves

under it, so to wait upon the Lord therein, that it may fully answer all the design of His love, in permitting it to come upon us; that it may be a means of increasing our faith, of confirming our hope, of perfecting us in all holiness. Whenever it comes, let us have an eye to those gracious ends for which it is permitted, and use all diligence that we may not make void the counsel of God against ourselves. Let us earnestly work together with Him, by the grace which He is continually giving us, in 'purifying ourselves from all pollution, both of flesh and spirit,' and daily growing in the grace of our Lord Jesus Christ, till we are received into His everlasting kingdom!

SERMON XLII

SELF-DENIAL

In *Journal,* February 20, 1738, Wesley writes: 'I returned to London. On Tuesday (the 21st) I preached at Great St. Helen's on "If any man will come after Me, let him deny himself, and take up his cross daily, and follow Me." ' He preached again at St. Helen's on April 23 and May 9. On Sunday, January 17, 1790, he records: 'In the afternoon I preached in Great St. Helen's to a large congregation. It is, I believe, fifty years since I preached there before. What has God wrought since that time!' This venerable church, with its curious double nave, stands on the east side of Bishopsgate Street Within, in Great St. Helen's Place. It was founded in 1212, and was one of the few London churches that escaped the Great Fire. Sir John Crosby, the builder of Crosby House, and Sir Thomas Gresham, the founder of the Royal Exchange, are buried there. The name of William Shakespeare stands nineteenth in a list of the inhabitants of the parish of St. Helen's as the owner of property of the value of £5, probably the furniture of his lodging.

The sermon was thus first written in Wesley's pre-conversion period, probably at Savannah; but the references in I. 1 to the 'smooth Moravian' and in iii. 2 to the Latin conversation with Count Zinzendorf in 1741 indicate that it was revised after that time, and most likely after the final breach with the Moravians in 1745. In the *Journal* for August 16, 1744, he gives in full a letter on self-denial which he had just received, probably from the Rev. Henry Piers, Vicar of Bexley; and on February 17, 1745, another from W. B. (possibly William Briggs, one of his first Book Stewards) on the same subject. He was therefore thinking seriously about this question in 1744-5, and I should be inclined to date the revision of the sermon at this time, especially as it does not occur at all in the Sermon Register 1747-61. His view of its importance remained the same to the end; in March 1790 he attributes the want of increase in the Society at Bristol 'to nothing but want of self-denial.'

The exegesis of the text is on conventional lines, and its primary meaning is ignored. As the context shows, our Lord had just predicted His own death; and what He means is that every one who desires to be His disciple must renounce himself, and be prepared to die on the cross with Him, if necessary. The criminal to be executed was compelled to carry the cross, or at least the cross-beam of it, to the place where he was to suffer; hence 'to take up the cross daily' means to be ready any day for a shameful death for Christ's sake. The phrase has been whittled down till it is used for the smallest instances of self-denial, and it may be said that the less is included in the greater; but we ought not to forget the full force of it, as our Lord here uses it. The word 'self-denial' has been similarly weakened; a man will say that he has denied himself when he has merely given up smoking! To deny oneself is to renounce reputation and life for Christ's sake—nothing less.

And He said to them all, If any man will come after Me, let him deny himself, and take up his cross daily, and follow Me.—LUKE ix. 23.

1. It has been frequently imagined, that the direction here given related chiefly, if not wholly, to the Apostles; at least to the Christians of the first ages, or those in a state of persecution. But this is a grievous mistake: for although our blessed Lord is here directing His discourse more immediately to His Apostles, and those other disciples who attended Him in the days of His flesh: yet, in them He speaks to us, and to all mankind, without any exception or limitation. The very reason of the thing puts it beyond dispute, that the duty which is here enjoined is not peculiar to them, or to the Christians of the early ages. It no more regards any particular order of men, or particular time, than any particular country. No: it is of the most universal nature, respecting all times, and all persons, yea, and all things; not meats and drinks only, and things pertaining to the senses. The meaning is, 'If any man,' of whatever rank, station, circumstances, in any nation, in any age of the world, 'will' effectually 'come after Me, let him deny himself' in all things; let him 'take up his cross,' of whatever kind; yea, and that 'daily; and follow Me.'

2. The *denying* ourselves, and the *taking up our cross,* in the full extent of the expression, is not a thing of small concern: it is not expedient only, as are some of the circumstantials of religion; but it is absolutely, indispensably necessary, either to our becoming or continuing His disciples. It is absolutely necessary, in the very nature of the thing, to our coming after Him, and following Him; insomuch that, as far as we do not practise it, we are not His disciples. If we do not continually deny ourselves, we do not learn of Him, but of other masters. If we do not take up our cross daily, we do not come after Him, but after the world, or the prince of the world, or our own fleshly mind. If we are not walking in the way of the cross, we are not following Him; we are

not treading in His steps; but going back from, or at least wide of, Him.

3. It is for this reason, that so many ministers of Christ, in almost every age and nation, particularly since the Reformation of the Church from the innovations and corruptions gradually crept into it, have wrote and spoke so largely on this important duty, both in their public discourses and private exhortations. This induced them to disperse abroad many tracts upon the subject; and some in our own nation. They knew, both from the oracles of God and from the testimony of their own experience, how impossible it was not t deny our Master, unless we will deny ourselves; and how vainly we attempt to follow Him that was crucified, unless we take up our own cross daily.

4. But may not this very consideration make it reasonable to inquire, If so much has been said and wrote on the subject already, what need is there to say or write any more? I answer, there are no inconsiderable numbers, even of people fearing God, who have not had the opportunity either of hearing what has been spoke, or reading what has been wrote, upon it. And, perhaps, if they had read much of what has been written, they would not have been much profited. Many who have wrote (some of them large volumes), do by no means appear to have understood the subject. Either they had imperfect views of the very nature of it (and then they could never explain it to others), or they were unacquainted with the due extent of it; they did not see how exceeding broad this command is; or they were not sensible of the absolute, the indispensable necessity of it. Others speak of it in so dark, so perplexed, so intricate, so mystical a manner, as if they designed rather to conceal it from the vulgar, than to explain it to common readers. Others speak admirably well, with great clearness and strength, on the necessity of self-denial; but then they deal in generals only, without coming to particular instances, and so are of little use to the bulk of mankind, to den of ordinary capacity and education. And if some of them do descend to particulars, it is to those particulars only which do not affect the generality of men, since they seldom, if ever, occur in common life; such as the enduring imprisonment, or tortures—the giving up, in a literal sense, their houses or lands, their husbands or wives, children or life itself; to none of which we are called, nor are likely to be, unless

God should permit times of public persecution to return. In the meantime, I know of no writer in the English tongue who has described the nature of self-denial in plain and intelligible terms, such as lie level with common understandings, and applied it to those little particulars which daily occur in common life. A discourse of this kind is wanted still; and it is wanted the more, because in every stage of the spiritual life, although there is a variety of particular hindrances of our attaining grace or growing therein, yet are all resolvable into these general ones,—either we do not deny ourselves, or we do not take up our cross.

In order to supply this defect in some degree, I shall endeavour to show, first, what it is for a man to deny himself, and what to take up his cross; and, secondly, that if a man be not fully Christ's disciple, it is always owing to the want of this.

I. 1. I shall, first, endeavour to show, what it is for a man to 'deny himself, and take up his cross daily.' This is a point which is, of all others, most necessary to be considered and thoroughly understood, even on this account, that it is, of all others, most opposed by numerous and powerful enemies. All our nature must certainly rise up against this, even in its own defence; the world, consequently, the men who take nature, not grace, for their guide, abhor the very sound of it. And the great enemy of our souls, well knowing its importance, cannot but move every stone against it. But this is not all: even those who have in some measure shaken off the yoke of the devil, who have experienced, especially of late years, a real work of grace in their hearts, yet are no friends to this grand doctrine of Christianity, though it is so peculiarly insisted on by their Master. Some of them are as deeply and totally ignorant concerning it, as if there was not one word about it in the Bible. Others are farther off still, having unawares imbibed strong prejudices against it. These they have received partly from outside Christians, men of a fair speech and behaviour, who want nothing of godliness but the power, nothing of religion but the spirit; and partly from those who did once, if they do not now, 'taste of the powers of the world to come.' But are there any of these who do not both practise self-denial themselves, and recommend it to others? You are little acquainted with mankind, if you doubt of this. There are whole bodies of men who only do not declare war against it. To go no farther than London: look upon the whole body of Predestinarians, who by the free mercy of God have lately been called out of the darkness of nature into the light of faith. Are they patterns of self-denial? How few of them even profess to practise it at all! How few of them recommend it themselves, or are pleased with them that do! Rather, do they not continually represent it in the most odious colours, as if it were seeking 'salvation by works,' or seeking 'to establish our own righteousness'? And how readily do Antinomians of all kinds, from the smooth Moravian, to the boisterous, foul-mouthed Ranter, join the cry, with their silly, unmeaning cant of *legality*, and *preaching the law*! Therefore you are in constant danger of being wheedled, hectored, or ridiculed out of this important gospel doctrine, either by false teachers, or false brethren (more or less beguiled from the simplicity of the gospel), if you are not deeply grounded therein. Let fervent prayer, then, go before, accompany, and follow what you are now about to read, that it may be written in your heart by the finger of God, so as never to be erased.

2. But what is self-denial? Wherein are we to deny ourselves? And whence does the necessity of this arise? answer, the will of God is the supreme, unalterable rule for every intelligent creature; equally binding every angel in heaven, and every man upon earth. Nor can it be otherwise: this is the natural, necessary result of the relation between creatures and their Creator. But if the will of God be our one rule of action in everything, great and small, it follows, by undeniable consequence, that we are not to do our own will in anything. Here, therefore, we see at once the nature, with the ground and reason, of self-denial. We see the nature of self-denial: it is the denying or refusing to follow our own will, from a conviction that the will of God is the only rule of action to us. And we see the reason thereof, because we are creatures; because 'it is He that hath made us, and not we ourselves.'

3. This reason for self-denial must hold, even with regard to the angels of God in heaven; and with regard to man, innocent and holy, as he came out of the hands of his Creator. But a farther reason for it arises from the condition wherein all men are since the fall. We are all now 'shapen in wickedness, and in

sin did our mother conceive us.' Our nature is altogether corrupt in every power and faculty. And our will, depraved equally with the rest, is wholly bent to indulge our natural corruption. On the other hand, it is the will of God that we resist and counteract that corruption, not at some times or in some things only, but at all times and in all things. Here, therefore, is a farther ground for constant and universal self-denial.

4. To illustrate this a little further; the will of God is a path leading straight to God. The will of man, which once ran parallel with it, is now another path, not only different from it, but, in our present state, directly contrary to it: it leads from God. If, therefore, we walk in the one, we must necessarily quit the other. We cannot walk in both. Indeed, a man *of faint heart and feeble hands may go in two ways,* one after the other. But he cannot walk in two ways at the same time: he cannot, at one and the same time, follow his own will, and follow the will of God: he must choose the one or the other; denying God's will, to follow his own; or denying himself, to follow the will of God.

5. Now, it is undoubtedly pleasing, for the time, to follow our own will, by indulging, in any instance that offers, the corruption of our nature: but by following it in anything, we so far strengthen the perverseness of our will; and by indulging it we continually increase the corruption of our nature. So by the food which is agreeable to the palate, we often increase a bodily disease: it gratifies the taste, but it inflames the disorder; it brings pleasure, but it also brings death.

6. On the whole, then, to deny ourselves, is to deny our own will, where it does not fall in with the will of God; and that however pleasing it may be. It is, to deny ourselves any pleasure which does not spring from, and lead to, God; that is, in effect, to refuse going out of our way, though into a pleasant, flowery path; to refuse what we know to be deadly poison, though agreeable to the taste.

7. And every-one that would follow Christ, that would be His real disciple, must not only deny himself, but take up his cross also. A cross is anything contrary to our will, anything displeasing to our nature. So that taking up our cross goes a little farther than denying ourselves; it rises a little higher, and is a more difficult task to flesh and blood; it being more easy to forgo pleasure, than to endure pain.

8. Now, in running 'the race that is set before us,' according to the will of God, there is often a cross lying in the way; that is, something which is not only not joyous, but grievous; something which is contrary to our will, which is displeasing to our nature. What, then, is to be done? The choice is plain: either we must take up our cross, or we must turn aside from the way of God, 'from the holy commandment delivered to us'; if we do not stop altogether, or turn back to everlasting perdition!

9. In order to the healing of that corruption, that evil disease, which every man brings with him into the world, it is often needful to pluck out, as it were, a right eye, to cut off a right hand,—so painful is either the thing itself which must be done, or the only means of doing it; the parting, suppose, with a foolish desire, with an inordinate affection; or a separation from the object of it, without which it can never be extinguished. In the former kind, the tearing away such a desire or affection, when it is deeply rooted in the soul, is often like the piercing of a sword, yea, like 'the dividing asunder of the soul and spirit, the joints and marrow.' The Lord then sits upon the soul as a refiner's fire, to burn up all the dross thereof. And this is a cross indeed; it is essentially painful; it must be so, in the very nature of the thing. The soul cannot be thus torn asunder it cannot pass through the fire, without pain.

10. In the latter kind, the means to heal a sin-sick soul, to cure a foolish desire, an inordinate affection, are often painful, not in the nature of the thing but from the nature of the disease. So when our Lord said to the rich young man, 'Go, sell that thou hast, and give to the poor' (as well knowing, this was the only means of healing his covetousness), the very thought of it gave him so much pain that he went away sorrowful'; choosing rather to part with his hope of heaven, than his possessions on earth. This was a burden he could not consent to lift, a cross he would not take up. And in the one kind or the other every follower of Christ will surely have need. to 'take up his cross daily.'

11. The 'taking up' differs a little from 'bearing his cross.' We are then properly said to 'bear our cross,' when we endure what is laid upon us without our choice, with meekness and resignation. Whereas, we do not properly 'take up our cross,' but when we voluntarily suffer what it is in our power to avoid; when we willingly embrace the will of God, though contrary to our

own; when we choose what is painful, because it is the will of our wise and gracious Creator.

12. And thus it behoves every disciple of Christ to take up, as well as to bear, his cross. Indeed, in one sense, it is not *his* alone; it is common to him, and many others; seeing there is no temptation befalls any man, ει μη ανθρωπινος,—'but such as is common to men': such as is incident and adapted to their common nature and situation in the present world. But, in another sense, as it is considered with all its circumstances, it is his; peculiar to himself; it is prepared of God for him; it is given by God to him, as a token of His love. And if he receives it as such, and, after using such means to remove the pressure as Christian wisdom directs, lies as clay in the potter's hand; it is disposed and ordered by God for his good, both with regard to the quality of it, and in respect to its quantity and degree, its duration, and every other circumstance.

13. In all this, we may easily conceive our blessed Lord to act as the Physician of our souls, not merely 'for His own pleasure, but for our profit, that we may be partakers of His holiness.' If, in searching our wounds, He puts us to pain, it is only in order to heal them. He cuts away what is putrefied or unsound, in order to preserve the sound part. And if we freely choose the loss of a limb, rather than the whole body should perish; how much more should we choose, figuratively, to cut off a right hand, rather than the whole soul should be cast into hell!

14. We see plainly, then, both the nature and ground of taking up our cross. It does not imply the *disciplining ourselves* (as some speak); the literally tearing our own flesh; the wearing hair-cloth, or iron girdles, or anything else that would impair our bodily health (although we know not what allowance God may make for those who act thus through involuntary ignorance); but the embracing the will of God, though contrary to our own; the choosing wholesome, though bitter, medicines; the freely accepting temporary pain, of whatever kind, and in whatever degree, when it is either essentially or accidentally necessary to eternal pleasure.

II. 1. I am, secondly, to show, that it is always owing to the want either of self-denial, or taking up his cross, that any man does not thoroughly follow Him, is not fully a disciple of Christ.

It is true, this may be partly owing, in some cases, to the want of the means of grace: of hearing the true word of God spoken with power; of the sacraments, or of Christian fellowship. But where none of these is wanting, the great hindrance of our receiving or growing in the grace of God is always the want of denying ourselves, or taking up our cross.

2. A few instances will make this plain. A man hears the word which is able to save his soul: he is well pleased with what he hears, acknowledges the truth, and is a little affected by it; yet he remains 'dead in trespasses and sins,' senseless and unawakened. Why is this? Because he will not part with his bosom sin, though he now knows it is an abomination to the Lord. He came to hear, full of lust and unholy desires; and he will not part with them. Therefore no deep impression is made upon him, but his foolish heart is still hardened: that is, he is still senseless and unawakened, because he will not deny himself.

3. Suppose he begins to awake out of sleep, and his eyes are a little opened, why are they so quickly closed again? Why does he again sink into the sleep of death? Because he again yields to his bosom sin; he drinks again of the pleasing poison. Therefore it is impossible that any lasting impression should be made upon his heart; that is, he relapses into his fatal insensibility, because he will not deny himself.

4. But this is not the case with all. We have many instances of those who when once awakened sleep no more. The impressions once received do not wear away: they are not only deep, but lasting. And yet, many of these have not found what they seek: they mourn, and yet are not comforted. Now, why is this? It is because they do not 'bring forth fruits meet for repentance'; because they do not, according to the grace they have received, 'cease from evil, and do good.' They do not cease from the easily besetting sin, the sin of their constitution, of their education, or of their profession; or they omit doing the good they may, and know they ought to do, because of some disagreeable circumstances attending it: that is, they do not attain faith, because they will not 'deny themselves,' or 'take up their cross.'

5. But this man did receive 'the heavenly gift'; he did 'taste of the powers of the world to come'; he saw 'the light of the glory of God in the face of Jesus Christ'; the 'peace which passeth all understanding' did rule his heart and mind; and 'the love of

God was shed abroad' therein, 'by the Holy Ghost which was given unto him.' Yet he is now weak as another man; he again relishes the things of earth, and has more taste for the things which are seen than for those which are not seen; the eye of his understanding is closed again, so that he cannot 'see Him that is invisible'; his love is waxed cold, and the peace of God no longer rules in his heart. And no marvel; for he has again given place to the devil, and grieved the Holy Spirit of God. He has turned again unto folly, to some pleasing sin, if not in outward act, yet in heart. He has given place to pride, or anger or desire, to self-will or stubbornness. Or he did not stir up the gift of God which was in him; he gave way to spiritual sloth, and would not be at the pains of 'praying always, and watching there unto with all perseverance': that is, he made shipwreck of the faith, for want of self-denial, and taking up his cross daily.

6. But perhaps he has not made shipwreck of the faith: he has still a measure of the Spirit of adoption, which continues to witness with his spirit that he is a child of God. However, he is not 'going on to perfection'; he is not, as once, hungering and thirsting after righteousness, panting after the whole image and full enjoyment of God, as the hart after the waterbrook. Rather he is weary and faint in his mind, and, as it were, hovering between life and death. And why is he thus, but because he hath forgotten the word of God, 'By works is faith made perfect'? He does not use all diligence in working the works of God. He does not 'continue instant in prayer,' private as well as public; in communicating, hearing, meditation, fasting, and religious conference. If he does not wholly neglect some of these means, at least he does not use them all with his might. Or he is not zealous of works of charity, as well as works of piety. He is not merciful after his power, with the full ability which God giveth. He does not fervently serve the Lord by doing good to men, in every kind and in every degree he can, to their souls as well as their bodies. And why does he not continue in prayer? Because in times of dryness it is pain and grief unto him. He does not continue in hearing at all opportunities, because sleep is sweet; or it is cold, or dark, or rainy. But why does he not continue in works of mercy? Because he cannot feed the hungry, or clothe the naked, unless he retrench the expense of his own apparel, or use cheaper and less pleasing food. Beside which, the visiting the

sick, or those that are in prison, is attended with many disagreeable circumstances. And so are most works of spiritual mercy; reproof in particular. He *would* reprove his neighbour; but sometimes shame, sometimes fear, comes between; for he may expose himself, not only to ridicule, but to heavier inconveniences too. Upon these and the like considerations he omits one or more, if not all, works of mercy and piety. Therefore, his faith is not made perfect, neither can he grow in grace; namely, because he will not deny himself, and take up his daily cross.

7. It manifestly follows, that it is always owing to the want either of self-denial, or taking up his cross, that a man does not thoroughly follow his Lord, that he is not fully a disciple of Christ. It is owing to this, that he who is dead in sin does not awake, though the trumpet be blown; that he who begins to awake out of sleep, yet has no deep or lasting conviction; that he who is deeply and lastingly convinced of sin does not attain remission of sins; that some who have received this heavenly gift retain it not, but make shipwreck of the faith; and that others, if they do not draw back to perdition, yet are weary and faint in their mind, and do not reach the mark of the prize of the high calling of God in Christ Jesus.

III. 1. How easily may we learn hence, that they know neither the Scripture nor the power of God, who directly or indirectly, in public or in private, oppose the doctrine of self-denial and the daily cross! How totally ignorant are these men of an hundred particular texts, as well as of the general tenor of the whole oracles of God! And how entirely unacquainted must they be with true, genuine, Christian experience—of the manner wherein the Holy Spirit ever did, and does at this day, work in the souls of men! They may talk, indeed, very loudly and confidently (a natural fruit of ignorance), as though they were the only men who understood either the Word of God, or the experience of His children; but their words are, in every sense, *vain words*; they are weighed in the balance, and found wanting.

2. We may learn from hence, secondly, the real cause why not only many particular persons, but even bodies of men, who were once burning and shining lights, have now lost both their light and heat. If they did not hate and oppose, they at least lightly

esteemed, this precious gospel doctrine. 'If they did not boldly say, '*Abnegationem omnem proculcamus, internecioni damus*'; 'We trample all self-denial under foot, we devote it to destruction'; yet they neither valued it according to its high importance, nor took any pains in practising it. '*Hanc mystici docent,*' said that great, bad man;' the *mystic* writers teach self-denial.' No; the *inspired* writers! 'And God teaches it to every soul who is willing to hear His voice!

3. We may learn from hence, thirdly, that it is not enough for a minister of the gospel not to oppose the doctrine of self-denial, to say nothing concerning it. Nay, he cannot satisfy his duty by saying a little in favour of it. If he would, indeed, be pure from the blood of all men, he must speak of it frequently and largely; he must inculcate the necessity of it in the clearest and strongest manner; he must press it with his might, on all persons, at all times, and in all places; laying—'line upon line, line upon line, precept upon precept, precept upon precept'; so shall he have a conscience void of offence; so shall he save his own soul and those that hear him.

4. Lastly: see that you apply this, every one of you, to your own soul. Meditate upon it when you are in secret: ponder it in your heart! Take care not only to understand it thoroughly, but to remember it to your lives' end! Cry unto the Strong for strength, that you may no sooner understand, than enter upon the practice of it! Delay not the time, but practise it immediately, from this very hour! Practise it universally on every one of the thousand occasions which occur in all circumstances of life! Practise it daily, without intermission, from the hour you first set your hand to the plough, and enduring therein to the end, till your spirit returns to God!

SERMON XLIII

THE CURE OF EVIL-SPEAKING

The first notice of this sermon is on February 5, 1752, when it was preached at Bristol. It was obviously suggested by the same outbreak of ill-natured gossip which led on January 29 to the signing of the following document by John and Charles Wesley and eleven of their preachers (see facsimile in Standard edition of *Journal,* iv. 9).

'It is agreed by us whose names are under-written:

1. That we will not listen, or willingly inquire after any ill concerning each other.

2. That, if we do hear any ill of each other, we will not be forward to believe it.

3. That, as soon as possible, we will communicate what we hear by speaking or writing to the person concerned.

4. That, till we have done this, we will not write or speak a syllable of it to any other person whatever.

5. That neither will we mention it, after we have done this, to any other person.

6. That we will not make any exception to any of these rules, unless we think ourselves absolutely obliged in conscience so to do.'

The sermon was preached six times more in 1752, once in 1753, and once in 1758. It was first published in Vol. IV of the sermons in 1760. Sermon LXV, on The Duty of Reproving our Neighbour, should be read and compared with it. It is an eminently practical and sensible discourse, and it would be well if its directions were faithfully observed. The Class-meeting system, which brings the members into such close and confidential relations with one another, is peculiarly liable to the danger of thoughtless or malicious gossip.

If thy brother shall trespass against thee, go and tell him his fault between thee and him alone: if he shall hear thee, thou hast gained thy brother.

But if he will not hear thee, then take with thee one or two more, that in the mouth of two or three witnesses every word may be established.

And if he shall neglect to hear them, tell it unto the church: but if he neglect to hear the church, let him be unto thee as an heathen man and a publican.—MATT. xviii. 15-17.

1. 'Speak evil of no man,' says the great Apostle: as plain a command as, 'Thou shalt do no murder.' But who, even among

Christians, regards this command? Yea, how few are there that so much as understand it! What is evil-speaking? It is not, as some suppose, the same with lying or slandering. All a man says may be as true as the Bible; and yet the saying of it is evil-speaking. For evil-speaking is neither more nor less than speaking evil of an absent person; relating something evil, which was really done or said by one that is not present when it is related. Suppose, having seen a man drunk, or heard him curse or swear, I tell this when he is absent; it is evil-speaking. In our language this is also, by an extremely proper name, termed 'backbiting.' Nor is there any material difference between this and what we usually style 'tale-bearing.' If the tale be delivered in a soft and quiet manner (perhaps with expressions of good-will to the person, and of hope that things may not be quite so bad), then we call it 'whispering.' But in whatever manner it be done, the thing is the same; the same in substance, if not in circumstance. Still it is evil-speaking; still this command, 'Speak evil of no man,' is trampled under foot; if we relate to another the fault of a third person, when he is not present to answer for himself.

2. And how extremely common is this sin, among all orders and degrees of men! How do high and low, rich and poor, wise and foolish, learned and unlearned, run into it continually! Persons who differ from each other in all things else, nevertheless agree in this. How few are there that can testify before God, 'I am clear in this matter; I have always set a watch before my mouth, and kept the door of my lips'! What conversation do you hear, of any considerable length, whereof evil-speaking is not one ingredient? and that even among persons who, in the general, have the fear of God before their eyes, and do really desire to have a conscience void of offence toward God and toward man.

3. And the very commonness of this sin makes it difficult to be avoided. As we are encompassed with it on every side, so, if we are not deeply sensible of the danger, and continually guarding against it, we are liable to be carried away by the torrent. In this instance, almost the whole of mankind is, as it were, in a conspiracy against us. And their example steals upon us, we know not how; so that we insensibly slide into the imitation of it. Besides, it is recommended from within, as well as from without.

There is scarce any wrong temper in the mind of man, which may not be occasionally gratified by it, and consequently incline us to it. It gratifies our pride, to relate those faults of others whereof we think ourselves not to be guilty. Anger, resentment, and all unkind tempers, are indulged by speaking against those with whom we are displeased; and, in many cases, by reciting the sins of their neighbours, men indulge their own foolish and hurtful desires.

4. Evil-speaking is the more difficult to be avoided, because it frequently attacks us in disguise. We speak thus out of a noble, generous (it is well if we do not say), holy indignation, against these vile creatures! We commit sin from mere hatred of sin! We serve the devil out of pure zeal for God! It is merely in order to punish the wicked that we run into this wickedness. 'So do the passions' (as one speaks), 'all justify themselves,' and palm sin upon us under the veil of holiness!

5. But is there no way to avoid the snare? Unquestionably there is. Our blessed Lord has marked out a plain way for His followers, in the words above recited. None, who warily and steadily walk in this path, will ever fall into evil-speaking. This rule is either an infallible preventive, or a certain cure of it. In the preceding verses, our Lord had said, 'Woe to the world, because of offences,'—unspeakable misery will arise in the world from this baleful fountain (*offences* are all things whereby any one is turned out of, or hindered in, the ways of God): 'For it must be that offences come,'—such is the nature of things; such the wickedness, folly, and weakness of mankind: 'but woe to that man,'—miserable is that man, 'by whom the offence cometh.' 'Wherefore, if thy hand, thy foot, thine eye, cause thee to offend,'—if the most dear enjoyment, the most beloved and useful person, turn thee out of or hinder thee in the way, 'pluck it out,'—cut them off, and cast them from thee. But how can we avoid giving offence to some, and being offended at others? especially suppose they are quite in the wrong, and we see it with our own eyes? Our Lord here teaches us how: He lays down a sure method of avoiding offences and evil-speaking together. 'If thy brother shall trespass against thee, go and tell him of his fault between thee and him alone: if he shall hear thee, thou hast gained thy brother. But if he will not hear thee, then take with thee one or two more, that in the mouth of two or three witnesses

every word may be established. And if he shall neglect to hear
them, tell it unto the church: but if he neglect to hear the church,
let him be unto thee as an heathen man and a publican.'

I. 1. First. 'If thy brother shall sin against thee, go and tell
him of his fault between thee and him alone.' The most literal
way of following this first rule, where it is practicable, is the best:
therefore, if thou seest with thine own eyes a brother, a fellow
Christian, commit undeniable sin, or hearest it with thine own
ears, so that it is impossible for thee to doubt the fact, then thy
part is plain: take the very first opportunity of going to him; and,
if thou canst have access, 'tell him of his fault between thee and
him alone.' Indeed, great care is to be taken that this is done in a
right spirit, and in a right manner. The success of a reproof
greatly depends on the spirit wherein it is given. Be not,
therefore, wanting in earnest prayer to God, that it may be given
in a lowly spirit; with a deep, piercing conviction, that it is God
alone who maketh thee to differ; and that if any good be done by
what is now spoken, God doeth it Himself. Pray that He would
guard thy heart, enlighten thy mind, and direct thy tongue to
such words as He may please to bless. See that thou speak in a
meek as well as a lowly spirit; for the 'wrath of man worketh not
the righteousness of God.' If he be 'overtaken in a fault,' he can
no otherwise be restored, than 'in the spirit of meekness.' If he
opposes the truth, yet he cannot be brought to the knowledge
thereof, but by gentleness. Still speak in a spirit of tender love,
'which many waters cannot quench.' If love is not conquered, it
conquers all things. Who can tell the force of love?

> Love can bow down the stubborn neck,
>   The stone to flesh convert;
> Soften, and melt, and pierce, and break
>   An adamantine heart.

Confirm, then, your love toward him, and you will thereby 'heap
coals of fire upon his head.'

2. But see that the manner also wherein you speak be
according to the gospel of Christ. Avoid everything in look,
gesture, word, and tone of voice, that savours of pride or
self-sufficiency. Studiously avoid everything magisterial or
dogmatical, everything that looks like arrogance or assuming.

Beware of the most distant approach to disdain, overbearing, or contempt. With equal care avoid all appearance of anger; and though you use great plainness of speech, yet let there be no reproach, no railing accusation, no token of any warmth but that of love. Above all, let there be no shadow of hate or ill-will, no bitterness or sourness of expression; but use the air and language of sweetness as well as gentleness, that all may appear to flow from love in the heart. And yet this sweetness need not hinder your speaking in the most serious and solemn manner; as far as may be, in the very words of the oracles of God (for there are none like them), and as under the eye of Him who is coming to judge the quick and dead.

3. If you have not an opportunity of speaking to him in person, or cannot have access, you may do it by a messenger; by a common friend, in whose prudence, as well as uprightness, you can thoroughly confide. Such a person, speaking in your name, and in the spirit and manner above described, may answer the same end, and, in a good degree, supply your lack of service. Only beware you do not feign the want of opportunity, in order to shun the cross; neither take it for granted that you cannot have access, without ever making the trial. Whenever you can speak in your own person, it is far better. But you should rather do it by another, than not at all: this way is better than none.

4. But what, if you can neither speak yourself, nor find such a messenger as you can confide in? If this be really the case, it then only remains to write. And there may be some circumstances which make this the most advisable way of speaking. One of these circumstances is, when the person with whom we have to do is of so warm and impetuous a temper as does not easily bear reproof, especially from an equal or inferior. But it may be so introduced and softened in writing as to make it far more tolerable. Besides, many will read the very same words, which they could not bear to hear. It does not give so violent a shock to their pride, nor so sensibly touch their honour. And suppose it makes little impression at first, they will, perhaps give it a second reading, and, upon farther consideration, lay to heart what before they disregarded. If you add your name, this is nearly the same thing as going to him, and speaking in person. And this

should always be done, unless it be rendered improper by some very particular reason.

5. It should be well observed, not only that this is a step which our Lord absolutely commands us to take, but that He commands us to take this step first, before we attempt any other. No alternative is allowed, no choice of anything else: this is the way; walk thou in it. It is true, He enjoins us, if need require, to take two other steps; but they are to be taken successively after this step, and neither of them before it: much less are we to take any other step, either before or beside this. To do anything else, or not to do this, is, therefore, equally inexcusable.

6. Do not think to excuse yourself for taking an entirely different step, by saying, 'Why, I did not speak to any one, till I was so burdened that I could not refrain.' You was burdened! It was no wonder you should, unless your conscience was seared; for you was under the guilt of sin, of disobeying a plain commandment of God! You ought immediately to have gone, and told 'your brother of his fault between you and him alone.' If you did not, how should you be other than burdened (unless your heart was utterly hardened), while you was trampling the command of God under foot, and 'hating your brother in your heart'? And what a way you have found to unburden yourself! God reproves you for a sin of omission, for not telling your brother of his fault; and you comfort yourself under His reproof by a sin of commission, by telling your brother's fault to another person! Ease bought by sin is a dear purchase! I trust in God, you will have no ease, but will be burdened so much the more, till you 'go to your brother and tell him,' and no one else.

7. I know but of one exception to this rule: there may be a peculiar case, wherein it is necessary to accuse the guilty, though absent, in order to preserve the innocent. For instance: you are acquainted with the design which a man has against the property or life of his neighbour. Now, the case may be so circumstanced, that there is no other way of hindering that design from taking effect, but the making it known, without delay, to him against whom it is laid. In this case, therefore, this rule is set aside, as is that of the Apostle, 'Speak evil of no man': and it is lawful, yea, it is our bounden duty, to speak evil of an absent person, in order to prevent his doing evil to others and himself at the same time. But remember, meanwhile, that all evil-speaking is, in its own

nature, deadly poison. Therefore if you are sometimes constrained to use it as a medicine, yet use it with fear and trembling; seeing it is so dangerous a medicine, that nothing but absolute necessity can excuse your using it at all. Accordingly, use it as seldom as possible; never but when there is such a necessity: and even then use as little of it as is possible; only so much as is necessary for the end proposed. At all other times, 'go and tell him of his fault between thee and him alone.'

II. 1. But what, 'if he will not hear'? if he repay evil for good? if he be enraged rather than convinced? What, if he hear to no purpose, and go on still in the evil of his way? We must expect this will frequently be the case; the mildest and tenderest reproof will have no effect; but the blessing we wished for another will return into our own bosom. And what are we to do then? Our Lord has given us a clear and full direction. Then 'take with thee one or two more': this is the second step. Take one or two whom you know to be of a loving spirit, lovers of God and of their neighbour. See, likewise, that they be of a lowly spirit, and 'clothed with humility.' Let them also be such as are meek and gentle, patient and long-suffering; not apt to 'return evil for evil, or railing for railing, but contrariwise blessing.' Let them be men of understanding, such as are endued with wisdom from above; and men unbiassed, free from partiality, free from prejudice of any kind. Care should likewise be taken, that both the persons and their characters be well known to him: and let those that are acceptable to him be chosen preferable to any others.

2. Love will dictate the manner wherein they should proceed, according to the nature of the case. Nor can any one particular manner be prescribed for all cases. But perhaps, in general, one might advise, before they enter upon the thing itself, let them mildly and affectionately declare that they have no anger or prejudice toward him, and that it is merely from a principle of good-will that they now come, or at all concern themselves with his affairs. To make this the more apparent, they might then calmly attend to your repetition of your former conversation with him, and to what he said in his own defence, before they attempted to determine anything. After this they would be better able to judge in what manner to proceed, 'that by the

mouth of two or three witnesses every word might be established'; that whatever you have said may have its full force by the additional weight of their authority.

3. In order to this, may they not, (1) Briefly repeat what you spoke, and what he answered? (2) Enlarge upon, open, and confirm the reasons which you had given? (3) Give weight to your reproof, showing how just, how kind, and how seasonable it was? And, lastly, enforce the advices and persuasions which you had annexed to it? And these may likewise hereafter, if need should require, bear witness of what was spoken.

4. With regard to this, as well as the preceding rule, we may observe, that our Lord gives us no choice, leaves us no alternative, but expressly commands us to do this, and nothing else in the place of it. He likewise directs us when to do this; neither sooner nor later; namely, *after* we have taken the first, and *before* we have taken the third step. It is then only that we are authorized to relate the evil another has done, to those whom we desire to bear a part with us in this great instance of brotherly love. But let us have a care how we relate it to any other person, till both these steps have been taken. If we neglect to take these, or if we take any others, what wonder if we are burdened stiil? For we are sinners against God, and against our neighbour; and how fairly soever we may colour it, yet, if we have any conscience, our sin will find us out, and bring a burden upon our soul.

III. 1. That we may be thoroughly instructed in this weighty affair, our Lord has given us a still farther direction: 'If he will not hear them,' then, and not till then, 'tell it to the church.' This is the third step. All the question is, how this word, 'the church,' is here to be understood. But the very nature of the thing will determine this beyond all reasonable doubt. You cannot tell it to the national Church, the whole body of men termed 'the Church of England.' Neither would it answer any Christian end if you could: this, therefore, is not the meaning of the word. Neither can you tell it to that whole body of people in England with whom you have a more immediate connexion. Nor, indeed, would this answer any good end: the word, therefore, is not to be understood thus. It would not answer any valuable end to tell the faults of every particular member to the church (if you would so term it), the congregation or society, united together in London. It remains that you tell it to the elder or elders of the church, to those who are overseers of that flock of Christ to which you both belong, who watch over yours and his soul, 'as they that must give account.' And this should be done, if it conveniently can, in the presence of the person concerned, and, though plainly, yet with all the tenderness and love which the nature of the thing will admit. It properly belongs to their office, to determine concerning the behaviour of those under their care, and to rebuke, according to the demerit of the offence, 'with all authority.' When, therefore, you have done this, you have done all which the Word of God, or the law of love, requireth of you: you are not now partaker of his sin: but if he perish, his blood is on his own head.

2. Here, also, let it be observed, that this, and no other, is the third step which we are to take; and that we are to take it in its order after the other two; not before the second, much less the first, unless in some very particular circumstance. Indeed, in one case, the second step may coincide with this: they may be, in a manner, one and the same. The elder or elders of the church may be so connected with the offending brother, that they may set aside the necessity, and supply the place, of the one or two witnesses; so that it may suffice to tell it to them, after you have told it to your brother, 'between you and him alone.'

3. When you have done this, you have delivered your own soul. 'If he will not hear the church,' if he persist in his sin, 'let him be to thee as an heathen man and a publican.' You are under no obligation to think of him any more; only when you commend him to God in prayer. You need not speak of him any more, but leave him to his own Master. Indeed, you still owe to him, as to all other Heathens, earnest, tender good-will. You owe him courtesy, and, as occasion offers, all the offices of humanity. But have no friendship, no familiarity with him; no other intercourse than with an open Heathen.

4. But if this be the rule by which Christians walk, which is the land where the Christians live? A few you may possibly find scattered up and down, who make a conscience of observing it. But how very few! How thinly scattered upon the face of the earth! And where is there any body of men that universally walk thereby? Can we find them in Europe? or, to go no farther, in

Great Britain or Ireland? I fear not: I fear we may search these kingdoms throughout, and yet search in vain. Alas for the Christian world! Alas for Protestants, for Reformed Christians! Oh, 'who will rise up with me against the wicked?' 'Who will take God's part' against the evil-speakers? Art thou the man? By the grace of God, wilt thou be one who art not carried away by the torrent? Art thou fully determined, God being thy helper, from this very hour to set a watch a continual 'watch, before thy mouth, and keep the door of thy lips'? From this hour wilt thou walk by this rule 'Speaking evil of no man'? If thou seest thy brother do evil, wilt thou 'tell him of his fault between thee and him alone'? afterwards, 'take one or two' witnesses, and then only 'tell it to the church'? If this be the full purpose of thy heart, then learn one lesson well, 'Hear evil of no man.' If there were no hearers, there would be no speakers, of evil. And is not (according to the vulgar proverb) the receiver as bad as the thief? If, then, any begin to speak evil in thy hearing, check him immediately. Refuse to hear the voice of the charmer, charm he never so sweetly; let him use ever so soft a manner, so mild an accent, ever so many professions of good-will for him whom he is stabbing in the dark, whom he smiteth under the fifth rib! Resolutely refuse to hear, though the whisperer complain of being 'burdened till he speak.' *Burdened*! thou fool! dost thou travail with thy cursed secret, as a woman travaileth with child? Go, then, and be delivered of thy burden in the way the Lord hath ordained! First, 'go and tell thy brother of his fault between thee and him alone': next, 'take with thee one or two' common friends, and tell him in their presence: if neither of these steps take effect, then 'tell it to the church.' But, at the peril of thy soul, tell it to no one else, either before or after, unless in that one exempt case, when it is absolutely needful to preserve the innocent! Why shouldest thou burden another as well as thyself, by making him partaker of thy sin?

5. Oh that all you who bear the reproach of Christ, who are in derision called Methodists, would set an example to the Christian world, so called, at least in this one instance! Put ye away evil-speaking, tale-bearing, whispering: let none of them proceed out of your mouth! See that you 'speak evil of no man'; of the absent, nothing but good. If ye must be distinguished, whether ye will or no, let this be the distinguishing mark of a

Methodist: 'He censures no man behind his back: by this fruit ye may know him.' What a blessed effect of this self-denial should we quickly feel in our hearts! How would our 'peace flow as a river,' when we thus 'followed peace with all men'! How would the love of God abound in our own souls, while we thus confirmed our love to our brethren! And what an effect would it have on all that were united together in the name of the Lord Jesus! How would brotherly love continually increase, when this grand hindrance of it was removed! All the members of Christ's mystical body would then naturally care for each other. 'If one member suffered, all would suffer with it'; 'if one was honoured, all would rejoice with it'; and every one would love his brother 'with a pure heart fervently.' Nor is this all: but what an effect might this have, even on the wild unthinking world! How soon would they descry in us, what they could not find among all the thousands of their brethren, and cry (as Julian the apostate to his heathen courtiers), 'See how these Christians love one another!' By this chiefly would God convince the world, and prepare them also for His kingdom; as we may easily learn from those remarkable words in our Lord's last, solemn prayer: 'I pray for them who shall believe in Me, that they may be one, as Thou, Father, art in Me, and I in Thee, . . . that the world may believe that Thou hast sent Me.' The Lord hasten the time! The Lord enable us thus to love one another, not only 'in word and in tongue, but in deed and in truth,' even as Christ hath loved us!

SERMON XLIV

THE USE OF MONEY

At the beginning of 1744 London was thrown into a state of almost panic alarm by the news that the Young Pretender had arrived in France, and that he was making preparations to invade England. On February 15 the King communicated the intelligence to the Houses of Parliament, and a general fast-day was proclaimed for Friday the 17th. Wesley says, 'We observed Friday the 17th as a day of solemn fasting and prayer. In the afternoon, many being met together,' (presumably at the Foundery), 'I exhorted them now, while they had opportunity, to make to themselves "friends of the mammon of unrighteousness"; to deal their bread to the hungry, to clothe the naked, and not to hide themselves from their own flesh. And God opened their hearts, so that they contributed near fifty pounds, which I began laying out the very next hour in linen, woollen, and shoes for those whom I knew to be diligent and yet in want.' Ten days later a second collection was made of about thirty pounds; astonishingly generous gifts, for they would be worth altogether at least £300 as money goes now; and the London Society was almost entirely made up of poor people. It may be worth while to remember that this was the year of the first Methodist Conference, and of Wesley's last University Sermon (No. IV on Scriptural Christianity).

The text is mentioned in the Sermon Register once in 1748, seven times in the latter part of 1750, five times in 1751, six times in 1752, and twice in 1753. It occurs once again in 1757, and the sermon was first published in Vol. IV of the Sermons in 1760. The substance of its teaching will be found in Sermon XXIII; and in the later Sermons LXXXVII, CVIII, and CXXVI. In Sermon LXXXVII, which was written in Wesley's seventy-eighth year, i.e. in 1780, he says, 'I do not remember that in three-score years I have heard one sermon preached upon this subject. . . . I have myself frequently touched upon it in preaching, and twice in what I have published to the world; once in explaining our Lord's Sermon on the Mount, and once in the discourse on The Mammon of Unrighteousness; but I have never yet either published or preached any sermon expressly upon the subject'—i.e. the danger of riches. In Sermon CVIII he speaks of himself as 'stumbling upon the dark mountains,' and says, 'I would fain leave one word with you before I go hence'; and Sermon CXXVI is dated September 21, 1790. Similar teaching is found in Sermon LXVIII, 16, and CXVI, 8.

632

The famous 'three plain rules'—Gain all you can, Save all you can, Give all you can—are repeated in all the later sermons, and in many other places; and if they were universally practised, they would prove themselves the best preventive and remedy of the distrust and hatred of the capitalists by the working classes

In the *Minutes* for 1766 it is lamented that 'many Methodists grow rich, and thereby lovers of the present world'; and it is suggested that the sermons in the fourth volume should be publicly read everywhere, as supplying them with remedies suited to the disease. As years went on, Wesley became more and more concerned about this matter. In Sermon LXVIII, 16, he says, 'I have not known threescore rich persons, perhaps not half the number, during three-score years, who, as far as I can judge, were not less holy than they would have been had they been poor.' In Sermon CXVI, 9, he breaks out, 'O that God would enable me once more, before I go hence and am no more seen, to lift up my voice like a trumpet to those who gain and save all they can, but do not give all they can. . . . I am distressed. I know not what to do. . . . The Methodists grow more and more self-indulgent, because they grow rich. And it is an observation which admits of few exceptions, that nine in ten of these decreased in grace in the same proportion as they increased in wealth.' In Sermon CXXVI, 16, he appeals with touching pathos to the rich Methodists. 'After having served you between sixty and seventy years with dim eyes, shaking hands, and tottering feet, I give you one more advice before I sink into the dust. . . . I am pained for you who are rich in this world. Do you give all you can? . . . I pray consider, what are you the better for what you leave behind you? What does it signify, whether you leave behind you ten thousand pounds, or ten thousand shoes and boots? O leave nothing behind you! Send all you have before you into a better world! Lend it, lend it all unto the Lord, and it shall be paid you again. Is there any danger that *His* truth should fail?'

And Wesley practised what he preached. In Sermon LXXXVII, ii. 6, he says, 'Permit me to speak as freely of myself as I would of another man. I gain all I can (namely, by writing) without hurting either soul or body. I save all I can, not willingly wasting anything, not a sheet of paper, not a cup of water. I do not lay out anything, not a shilling, unless as a sacrifice to God. Yet by giving all I can, I am effectually secured from laying up treasure upon earth. . . . I cannot help leaving my books behind me, whenever God calls me hence; but in every other respect my own hands will be my executors.' At the end of Sermon CXVI, written in 1789, he says, 'I call God to record upon my soul that I advise no more than I practise. I do, blessed be God, gain, and save, and give all I can.' On August 1, 1790, he writes in his Diary, 'As my sight fails me much, I do not purpose to keep any more accounts. It suffices that I gain all I can, I save all I can, and I give all I can, that is, all I have.—J. W.' His challenge that, if he left more than £10 in his will, any one could call him a thief and a liar, was redeemed; apart from his book-concern, he only left the loose money in his clothes and bureau, and £6 for the poor men who should carry his body to the grave. During the latter part of his life he gave away from the profits of his books about £1,000 a year; and he is computed to have bestowed in charity not less than £30,000 during his lifetime.

I say unto you, Make to yourselves friends of the mammon of unrighteousness;
that, when ye fail, they may receive you into everlasting habitations.—LUKE xvi. 9.

1. Our Lord, having finished the beautiful parable of the Prodigal Son, which He had particularly addressed to those who murmured at His receiving publicans and sinners, adds another relation of a different kind, addressed rather to the children of God. 'He said unto His disciples'—not so much to the Scribes and Pharisees, to whom He had been speaking before—'There was a certain rich man, who had a steward, and he was accused to him of wasting his goods. And calling him, he said, Give an account of thy stewardship, for thou canst be no longer steward' (verses 1, 2). After reciting the method which the bad steward used to provide against the day of necessity, our Saviour adds, 'His lord commended the unjust steward'; namely, in this respect, that he used timely precaution; and subjoins this weighty reflection, 'The children of this world are wiser in their generation than the children of light' (verse 8): those who seek no other portion than this world 'are wiser' (not absolutely; for they are, one and all, the veriest fools, the most egregious madmen under heaven; but, 'in their generation;,' in their own way; they are more consistent with themselves; they are truer to their acknowledged principles; they more steadily pursue their end) 'than the children of light,'—than they who see 'the light of the glory of God in the face of Jesus Christ.' Then follow the words above recited: 'And I'—the only-begotten Son of God, the Creator, Lord, and possessor of heaven and earth, and all that is therein; the Judge of all, to whom ye are to 'give an account of your stewardship,' when ye 'can be no longer stewards'; 'I say unto you'—learn in this respect, even of the unjust steward—'make yourselves friends,' by wise, timely precaution, 'of the mammon of unrighteousness.' 'Mammon' means riches, or money. It is termed 'the mammon of unrighteousness,' because of the unrighteous manner wherein it is frequently procured, and wherein even that which was honestly procured is generally

employed. 'Make yourselves friends' of this, by doing all possible good, particularly to the children of God; 'that, when ye fail'—when ye return to dust, when ye have no more place under the sun—those of them who are gone before 'may receive you,' may welcome you, into 'everlasting habitations.'

2. An excellent branch of Christian wisdom is here inculcated by our Lord on all His followers, namely, the right use of money,—a subject largely spoken of, after their manner, by men of the world; but not sufficiently considered by those whom God hath chosen out of the world. These, generally, do not consider, as the importance of the subject requires, the use of this excellent talent. Neither do they understand how to employ it to the greatest advantage; the introduction of which into the world is one admirable instance of the wise and gracious providence of God. It has, indeed, been the manner of poets, orators, and philosophers, in almost all ages and nations, to rail at this, as the grand corrupter of the world, the bane of virtue, the pest of human society. Hence, nothing so commonly heard, as

> *Ferrum, ferroque nocentius aurum:*
> (And gold, more mischievous than keenest steel.)

Hence the lamentable complaint,

> *Effodiuntur opes, irritamenta malorum.*
> (Wealth is dug up, incentive to all ill.)

Nay, one celebrated writer gravely exhorts his countrymen, in order to banish all vice at once, to 'throw all their money in to the sea':

> *In mare proximum,*
> *Summi materiem mali!*

But is not all this mere empty rant? Is there any solid reason therein? By no means. For, let the world be as corrupt as it will, is gold or silver to blame? 'The love of money,' we know, 'is the root of all evil'; but not the thing itself. The fault does not lie in the money, but in them that use it. It may be used ill: and what may not? But it may likewise be used well: it is full as applicable to the best, as to the worst uses. It is of unspeakable service to all civilized nations, in all the common affairs of life: it is a most compendious instrument of transacting all manner of business and (if we use it according to Christian wisdom) of doing all manner of good. It is true, were man in a state of innocence, or were all men 'filled with the Holy Ghost,' so that, like the infant church at Jerusalem, 'no man counted anything he had his own,' but 'distribution was made to every one as he had need,' the use of it would be superseded; as we cannot conceive there is anything of the kind among the inhabitants of heaven. But, in the present state of mankind, it is an excellent gift of God, answering the noblest ends. In the hands of His children, it is food for the hungry, drink for the thirsty, raiment for the naked: it gives to the traveller and the stranger where to lay his head. By it we may supply the place of an husband to the widow, and of a father to the fatherless. We may be a defence for the oppressed, a means of health to the sick, of ease to them that are in pain; it may be as eyes to the blind, as feet to the lame; yea, a lifter up from the gates of death.

3. It is, therefore, of the highest concern, that all who fear God know how to employ this valuable talent; that they be instructed how it may answer these glorious ends, and in the highest degree. And, perhaps, all the instructions which are necessary for this may be reduced to three plain rules, by the exact observance whereof we may approve ourselves faithful stewards of 'the mammon of unrighteousness.'

I. 1. The first of these is (he that heareth, let him understand!) 'Gain all you can.' Here we may speak like the children of the world: we meet them on their own ground. And it is our bounden duty to do this: we ought to gain all we can gain, without buying gold too dear, without paying more for it than it is worth. But this it is certain we ought not to do; we ought not to gain money at the expense of life, nor (which is in effect the same thing) at the expense of our health. Therefore, no gain whatsoever should induce us to enter into, or to continue in, any employ, which is of such a kind, or is attended with so hard or so long labour, as to impair our constitution. Neither should we begin or continue in any business which necessarily deprives us of proper seasons for food and sleep, in such a proportion as our nature requires. Indeed, there is a great difference here. Some employments are absolutely and totally unhealthy; as those which imply the dealing much with arsenic, or other equally hurtful minerals, or the breathing an air tainted with streams of melting lead, which must at length destroy the firmest constitution. Others may not be absolutely unhealthy, but only to persons of a weak constitution. Such are those which require many hours to be spent in writing; especially if a person write sitting, and lean upon his stomach, or remain long in an uneasy posture. But whatever it is which reason or experience shows to be destructive of health or strength, that we may not submit to; seeing 'the life is more' valuable 'than meat, and the body than raiment': and, if we are already engaged in such an employ, we should exchange it, as soon as possible, for some which, if it lessen our gain, will, however, not lessen our health.

2. We are, secondly, to gain all we can without hurting our mind, any more than our body. For neither may we hurt this: we must preserve, at all events, the spirit of an healthful mind. Therefore, we may not engage or continue in any sinful trade; any that is contrary to the law of God, or of our country. Such are all that necessarily imply our robbing or defrauding the king of his lawful customs. For it is, at least, as sinful to defraud the king of his right, as to rob our fellow subjects: and the king has full as much right to his customs as we have to our houses and apparel. Other businesses there are which, however innocent in themselves, cannot be followed with innocence now; at least not in England; such, for instance, as will not afford a competent maintenance without cheating or lying, or conformity to some custom which is not consistent with a good conscience: these, likewise, are sacredly to be avoided, whatever gain they may be attended with, provided we follow the custom of the trade; for to gain money, we must not lose our souls. There are yet others which many pursue with perfect innocence, without hurting either their body or mind; and yet, perhaps, you cannot: either they may entangle you in that company which would destroy your soul; and by repeated experiments it may appear that you cannot separate the one from the other; or there may be an idiosyncrasy—a peculiarity in your constitution of soul (as there is in the bodily constitution of many), by reason whereof that employment is deadly to you, which another may safely follow. So I am convinced, from many experiments, I could not study, to any degree of perfection, either mathematics, arithmetic, or

algebra, without being a Deist, if not an Atheist: and yet others may study them all their lives without sustaining any inconvenience. None, therefore, can here determine for another; but every man must judge for himself, and abstain from whatever he in particular finds to be hurtful to his soul.

3. We are, thirdly, to gain all we can, without hurting our neighbour. But this we may not, cannot do, if we love our neighbour as ourselves. We cannot, if we love every one as ourselves, hurt any one *in his substance.* We cannot devour the increase of his lands, and perhaps the lands and houses themselves, by gaming, by overgrown bills (whether on account of physic, or law, or anything else), or by requiring or taking such interest as even the laws of our country forbid. Hereby all pawnbroking is excluded: seeing, whatever good we might do thereby, all unprejudiced men see with grief to be abundantly overbalanced by the evil. And if it were otherwise, yet we are not allowed to 'do evil that good may come.' We cannot, consistent with brotherly love, sell our goods below the market price; we cannot study to ruin our neighbour's trade, in order to advance our own; much less can we entice away, or receive, any of his servants or workmen whom he has need of. None can gain by swallowing up his neighbour's substance, without gaining the damnation of hell!

4. Neither may we gain by hurting our neighbour *in his body.* Therefore we may not sell anything which tends to impair health. Such is, eminently, all that liquid fire, commonly called drams, or spirituous liquors. It is true, these may have a place in medicine; they may be of use in some bodily disorders; although there would rarely be occasion for them, were it not for the unskilfulness of the practitioner. Therefore, such as prepare and sell then only for this end may keep their conscience clear. But who are they? Who prepare them only for this end? Do you know ten such distillers in England? Then excuse these. But all who sell them in the common way, to any that will buy, are poisoners general. They murder His Majesty's subjects by wholesale, neither does their eye pity or spare. They drive them to hell, like sheep. And what is their gain? Is it not the blood of these men? Who then would envy their large estates and sumptuous palaces? A curse is in the midst of them: the curse of God cleaves to the stones, the timber, the furniture of them! The

curse of God is in their gardens, their walks, their groves; a fire
that burns to the nethermost hell! Blood, blood is there: the
foundation, the floor, the walls, the roof, are stained with blood!
And canst thou hope, O thou man of blood, though thou art
'clothed in scarlet and fine linen, and farest sumptuously every
day'; canst thou hope to deliver down thy *fields of blood* to the
third generation? Not so; for there is a God in heaven:
therefore, thy name shall soon be rooted out. Like as those
whom thou hast destroyed, body and soul, 'thy memorial shall
perish with thee!'

5. And are not they partakers of the same guilt, though in a
lower degree, whether surgeons, apothecaries, or physicians,
who play with the lives or health of men, to enlarge their own
gain? who purposely lengthen the pain or disease, which they
are able to remove speedily? who protract the cure of their
patient's body, in order to plunder his substance? Can any man
be clear before God, who does not shorten every disorder 'as
much as he can,' and remove all sickness and pain 'as soon as he
can'? He cannot: for nothing can be more clear, than that he
does not ['love his neighbour as himself'; than that he does not]*
'do unto others, as he would they should do unto himself.'

6. This is dear-bought gain. And so is whatever is procured by
hurting our neighbour *in his soul*; by ministering suppose, either
directly or indirectly, to his unchastity or intemperance; which
certainly none can do who has any fear of God, or any real desire
of pleasing Him. It nearly concerns all those to consider this,
who have anything to do with taverns, victualling-houses,
opera-houses, play-houses, or any other places of public,
fashionable diversion. If these profit the souls of men, you are
clear; your employment is good, and your gain innocent; but if
they are either sinful in themselves, or natural inlets to sin of
various kinds, then, it is to be feared, you have a sad account to
make. O beware, lest God say in that day, 'These have perished
in their iniquity, but their blood do I require at thy hands!'

7. These cautions and restrictions being observed, it is the
bounden duty of all who are engaged in worldly business to
observe that first and great rule of Christian wisdom, with
respect to money, 'Gain all you can.' Gain all you can by honest

---

*The words in brackets are omitted from the 1787 and 1825 editions.

industry. Use all possible diligence in your calling. Lose no time. If you understand yourself, and your relation to God and man, you know you have none to spare. If you understand your particular calling, as you ought, you will have no time that hangs upon your hands. Every business will afford some employment sufficient for every day and every hour. That wherein you are placed, if you follow it in earnest, will leave you no leisure for silly, unprofitable diversions. You have always something better to do, something that will profit you, more or less. And 'whatsoever thy hand findeth to do, do it with thy might.' Do it as soon as possible: no delay! No putting off from day to day, or from hour to hour! Never leave anything till tomorrow, which you can do to-day. And do it as well as possible. Do not sleep or yawn over it: put your whole strength to the work. Spare no pains. Let nothing be done by halves, or in a slight and careless manner. Let nothing in your business be left undone, if it can be done by labour or patience.

8. Gain all you can, by common sense, by using in your business all the understanding which God has given you. It is amazing to observe, how few do this; how men run on in the same dull track with their forefathers. But whatever they do who know not God, this is no rule for you. It is a shame for a Christian not to improve upon *them* in whatever he takes in hand. You should be continually learning, from the experience of others, or from your own experience, reading, and reflection, to do everything you have to do better to-day than you did yesterday. And see that you practise whatever you learn, that you may make the best of all that is in your hands.

II. 1. Having gained all you can, by honest wisdom, and unwearied diligence, the second rule of Christian prudence is, 'Save all you can.' Do not throw the precious talent into the sea: leave that folly to heathen philosophers. Do not throw it away in idle expenses, which is just the same as throwing it into the sea. Expend no part of it merely to gratify the desire of the flesh, the desire of the eye, or the pride of life.

2. Do not waste any part of so precious a talent, merely in gratifying the desires of the flesh; in procuring the pleasures of sense, of whatever kind; particularly, in enlarging the pleasure of tasting. I do not mean, avoid gluttony and drunkenness only:

an honest Heathen would condemn these. But there is a regular, reputable kind of sensuality, an elegant epicurism, which does not immediately disorder the stomach, nor (sensibly at least) impair the understanding; and yet (to mention no other effects of it now) it cannot be maintained without considerable expense. Cut off all this expense! Despise delicacy and variety, and be content with what plain nature requires.

3. Do not waste any part of so precious a talent, merely in gratifying the desire of the eye, by superfluous or expensive apparel, or by needless ornaments. Waste no part of it in curiously adorning your houses; in superfluous or expensive furniture; in costly pictures, painting, gilding, books; in elegant rather than useful gardens. Let your neighbours, who know nothing better, do this: 'let the dead bury their dead.' But 'what is that to thee?' says our Lord: 'follow thou Me.' Are you willing? Then you are able so to do!

4. Lay out nothing to gratify the pride of life, to gain the admiration or praise of men. This motive of expense is frequently interwoven with one or both of the former. Men are expensive in diet, or apparel, or furniture, not barely to please their appetite, or to gratify their eye, or their imagination, but their vanity too. 'So long as thou doest well unto thyself, men will speak good of thee.' So long as thou art 'clothed in purple and fine linen, and farest sumptuously every day,' no doubt many will applaud thy elegance of taste, thy generosity and hospitality. But do not buy their applause so dear. Rather be content with the honour that cometh from God.

5. Who would expend anything in gratifying these desires, if he considered, that to gratify them is to increase them? Nothing can be more certain than this: daily experience shows, the more they are indulged, they increase the more. Whenever, therefore, you expend anything to please your taste or other senses, you pay so much for sensuality. When you lay out money to please your eye, you give so much for an increase of curiosity—for a stronger attachment to these pleasures which perish in the using. While you are purchasing anything which men use to applaud, you are purchasing more vanity. Had you not then enough of vanity, sensuality, curiosity, before? Was there need of any addition? And would you pay for it too? What

manner of wisdom is this? Would not the literally throwing your
money into the sea be a less mischievous folly?

6. And why should you throw away money upon your
children, any more than upon yourself, in delicate food, in gay
or costly apparel, in superfluities of any kind? Why should you
purchase for them more pride or lust, more vanity, or foolish
and hurtful desires? They do not want any more; they have
enough already; nature has made ample provision for them:
why should you be at farther expense to increase their
temptations and snares, and to pierce them through with many
sorrows?

7. Do not leave it to them to throw away. If you have good
reason to believe they would waste what is now in your
possession, in gratifying, and thereby increasing the desire of
the flesh, the desire of the eye, or the pride of life; at the peril of
theirs and your own soul, do not set these traps in their way. Do
not offer your sons or your daughters unto Belial, any more
than unto Moloch. Have pity upon them, and remove out of
their way what you may easily foresee would increase their sins,
and consequently plunge them deeper into everlasting perdition! How amazing, then, is the infatuation of those parents who
think they can never leave their children enough! What! cannot
you leave them enough of arrows, firebrands, and death? not
enough of foolish and hurtful desires? not enough of pride, lust,
ambition, vanity? not enough of everlasting burnings? Poor
wretch! thou fearest where no fear is. Surely both thou and they,
when ye are lifting up your eyes in hell, will have enough both of
'the worm that never dieth,' and of 'the fire that never shall be
quenched'!

8. 'What then would you do, if you was in my case? if you had
a considerable fortune to leave?' Whether I *would* do it or no, I
know what I *ought* to do: this will admit of no reasonable
question. If I had one child, elder or younger, who knew the
value of money, one who, I believed would put it to the true use,
I should think it my absolute, indispensable duty to leave that
child the bulk of my fortune; and to the rest just so much as
would enable them to live in the manner they had been
accustomed to do. 'But what, if all your children were equally
ignorant of the true use of money?' I ought then (hard saying!
who can hear it?) to give each what would keep him above want;

and to bestow all the rest in such a manner as I judged would be most for the glory of God.

III. 1. But let not any man imagine that he has done anything, barely by going thus far, by 'gaining and saving all he can,' if he were to stop here. All this is nothing, if a man go not forward, if he does not point all this at a farther end. Nor, indeed, can a man properly be said to save anything, if he only lays it up. You may as well throw you money into the sea, as bury it in the earth. And you may as well bury it in the earth, as in your chest, or in the Bank of England. Not to use, is effectually to throw it away. If, therefore, you would indeed 'make yourselves friends of the mammon of unrighteousness,' add the third rule to the two preceding. Having, first, gained all you can, and, secondly, saved all you can, then 'give all you can.'

2. In order to see the ground and reason of this, consider, when the Possessor of heaven and earth brought you into being, and placed you in this world, He placed you here, not as a proprietor, but a steward: as such He entrusted you, for a season, with goods of various kinds; but the sole property of these still rests in Him, nor can ever be alienated from Him. As you yourself are not your own, but His, such is, likewise, all that you enjoy. Such is your soul and your body, not your own, but God's. And so is your substance in particular. And He has told you, in the most clear and express terms, how you are to employ it for Him, in such a manner, that it may be all an holy sacrifice, acceptable through Christ Jesus. And this light, easy service, He hath promised to reward with an eternal weight of glory.

3. The directions which God has given us, touching the use of our worldly substance, may be comprised in the following particulars. If you desire to be a faithful and a wise steward, out of that portion of your Lord's goods which He has for the present lodged in your hands, but with the right of resuming whenever it pleases Him, first, provide things needful for yourself; food to eat, raiment to put on, whatever nature moderately requires for preserving the body in health and strength. Secondly, provide these for your wife, your children, your servants, or any others who pertain to your household. If, when this is done, there be an overplus left, then 'do good to them that are of the household of faith.'

If there be an overplus still, 'as you have opportunity, do good unto all men.' In so doing, you give all you can; nay, in a sound sense, all you have: for all that is laid out in this manner is really given to God. You 'render unto God the things that are God's,' not only by what you give to the poor, but also by that which you expend in providing things needful for yourself and your household.

4. If, then, a doubt should at any time arise in your mind concerning what you are going to expend, either on yourself or any part of your family, you have an easy way to remove it. Calmly and seriously inquire, '(1) In expending this, am I acting according to my character? Am I acting herein, not as a proprietor, but as a steward of my Lord's goods? (2) Am I doing this in obedience to His Word? In what scripture does He require me so to do? (3) Can I offer up this action, this expense, as a sacrifice to God through Jesus Christ? (4) Have I reason to believe, that for this very work I shall have a reward at the resurrection of the just?' You will seldom need anything more to remove any doubt which arises on this head; but, by this four-fold consideration, you will receive clear light as to the way wherein you should go.

5. If any doubt still remain, you may farther examine yourself by prayer, according to those heads of inquiry. Try whether you can say to the Searcher of hearts, your conscience not condemning you, 'Lord, Thou seest I am going to expend this sum on that food, apparel, furniture. And Thou knowest, I act therein with a single eye, as a steward of Thy goods, expending this portion of them thus, in pursuance of the design Thou hadst in entrusting me with them. Thou knowest I do this in obedience to Thy Word, as Thou commandest, and because Thou commandest it. Let this, I beseech Thee, be an holy sacrifice, acceptable through Jesus Christ! And give me a witness in myself, that for this labour of love I shall have a recompense when Thou rewardest every man according to his works.' Now, if your conscience bear you witness in the Holy Ghost, that this prayer is well-pleasing to God, then have you no reason to doubt but that expense is right and good, and such as will never make you ashamed.

6. You see, then, what it is to 'make yourselves friends of the mammon of unrighteousness,' and by what means you may

procure, 'that when ye fail, they may receive you into everlasting habitations.' You see the nature and extent of truly Christian prudence, so far as it relates to the use of that great talent, money. Gain all you can, without hurting either yourself or your neighbour, in soul or body, by applying hereto with uninter-mitted diligence, and with all the understanding which God has given you;—save all you can, by cutting off every expense which serves only to indulge foolish desire; to gratify either the desire of the flesh, the desire of the eye, or the pride of life; waste nothing, living or dying, on sin or folly, whether for yourself or your children;—and then give all you can, or, in other words, give all you have to God. Do not stint yourself, like a Jew rather than a Christian, to this or that proportion. Render unto God, not a tenth, not a third, not half, but all that is God's, be it more or less; by employing all on yourself, your household, the household of faith, and all mankind, in such a manner, that you may give a good account of your stewardship, when ye can be no longer stewards; in such a manner as the oracles of God direct, both by general and particular precepts; in such a manner, that whatever ye do may be 'a sacrifice of a sweet-smelling savour to God' and that every act may be rewarded in that day, when the Lord cometh with all His saints.

7. Brethren, can we be either wise or faithful stewards unless we thus manage our Lord's goods? We cannot, as not only the oracles of God, but our own conscience, beareth witness. Then why should we delay? Why should we confer any longer with flesh and blood or men of the world? Our kingdom, our wisdom, is not of this world: heathen custom is nothing to us. We follow no men any farther than they are followers of Christ. Hear ye Him: yea to-day, while it is called to-day, hear and obey His voice! At this hour, and from this hour, do His will: fulfil His word, in this and in all things! I entreat you in the name of the Lord Jesus, act up to the dignity of your calling! No more sloth! Whatsoever your hand findeth to do, do it with your might! No more waste! Cut off every expense which fashion, caprice, or flesh and blood demand! No more covetousness! But employ whatever God has entrusted you with, in doing good, all possible good, in every possible kind and degree, to the household of faith, to all men! This is no small part of 'the wisdom of the just.' Give all ye have, as well as all ye are, a spiritual sacrifice to Him

who withheld not from you His Son, His only Son: so 'laying up in store for yourselves a good foundation against the time to come, that ye may attain eternal life'!

Here end the sermons in Vol. IV of the original edition. In the edition of the *Works* in 1771, Sermons LI, LII, and LIII were added; but they are not amongst the Standard Sermons. See General Introduction on The Standards of Methodist Doctrine (above, i. 13)

SERMON XLV

THE WITNESS OF THE SPIRIT

DISCOURSE II

This sermon was written at Newry on April 4, 1767, and published separately by Pine of Bristol in the same year. It appeared in the *Works* of 1771 as No. XI of the sermons; but it is not contained in the edition of the sermons of 1787–8. Its purpose was (1) to show that Wesley had not changed his views on this subject since the publication of the previous sermon in 1746; ii. 3: 'After twenty years' further consideration I see no cause to retract any part of this'; (2) to confirm the doctrine by the experience of the multitudes who had been converted through the preaching of the Methodists during these years; (3) to answer some of the objections which had been raised against it. I find no record of its having been preached; it is rather a treatise than a sermon.

Some of the most important attacks on Wesley's teaching between 1746 and 1767 were as follows:

The Enthusiam of Methodists and Papists Compared, published by Bishop Lavington of Exeter in 1749; with a third part in 1751.

A Serious Address to the Rev. Mr. John Wesley in relation to the principal doctrine advanced and maintained by him and his assistants, by John Parkhurst. This doctrine is that of the witness of the Spirit. This was published in 1753.

Original Letters between the Rev. Mr. John Wesley and Mr. Richard Tompson respecting the doctrine of Assurance, published in 1760, but written in 1755–6.

An Apology for the Clergy, published in 1755.

A Dissertation on Enthusiasm, by Thomas Green, Vicar of Wymeswould, published in 1755.

The History of Modern Enthusiam, by the Rev. Theophilus Evans, published 1756.

The Use and Extent of Reason in Matters of Religion, by Thomas Griffith, 1756.

Methodism Displayed and Enthusiam Detected, 1757.

Various pamphlets by the Rev. Dr. Free, 1758-9.

Methodism Examined, by the Rev. John Downes, 1759.

A Friendly and Compassionate Address to Methodists, by Alexander Jephson, 1760.

Principles and Practices of the Methodists, Considered, by the Rev. John Green, Dean of Lincoln, 1760.

Montanus Redivivus, by the Rev. James Clark, 1760.

Sermons by Dr. Hitchcock and the Rev. John Allen, 1761.

Caution against Religious Delusion, by William Rackhouse, 1763.

Four Charges to the Clergy, by Thomas Rutherforth, 1763

The Doctrine of Grace, by Warburton, Bishop of Gloucester, 1763.

Besides these there were numberless pamphlets, letters to the papers, ribald poems and plays, almost all of them ridiculing the claim of the Methodists to supernatural light and inspiration. Such objections as have any show of reason Wesley deals with in the fourth section of this sermon; but a large part of these alleged criticisms and refutations of his teaching is mere vulgar abuse and wilful misunderstanding.

Dr. Beet says, in the *London Quarterly Review* for January 1921:

Wesley's first sermon on the Witness of the Spirit, written apparently about A.D. 1747, is unsatisfactory. It does not notice that Paul's own cry, Abba, Father, which he has just asserted to be prompted by the Spirit of God, is itself a twofold witness that the writer and his readers are children of God. Nor does he notice the light shed on this testimony by the word *witness*, in Acts xv. 8: 'God bare them witness, by giving them the Holy Spirit, even as to us.' He does not even mention the all-important parallel in Gal. iv. 6, 7, which throws great light on Rom. viii. 15, 16.

The second sermon gives us John Wesley's mature thought, twenty years later. In it, Gal. iv. 6, 7 is quoted or mentioned three times; and Rom. viii. 16 is viewed in its relation to the preceding verses. But that this human cry, prompted by the Spirit of God, is the double and decisive testimony of two witnesses that Paul and his readers are in very truth children of God is not clearly stated. In these sermons, the writer has also misunderstood the Witness of our own spirit. But in Sermon XI, for which the writer appropriately takes another text, this last important topic is profitably discussed.

The above defects need not surprise us. Very few men are equally effective in action and as leaders of thought. But John Wesley, the father o the Methodist Revival, has rendered immense service to English theology by calling conspicuous attention to important elements, previously overlooked, in Christ's message to men. The real embodiiment of Methodist theology is the Methodist Hymn-Book, and especially Charles Wesley's hymns. Thus the active labour of one brother found a needful supplement in the other's quiet thought. This last has permanent embodiment in the most useful form possible, in the hymns which appeal to the intelligence and the heart of all who read the English language.

The Spirit itself beareth witness with our spirit that we are the children of God.—ROM. viii. 16.

I. 1. None who believe the Scriptures to be the Word of God can doubt the importance of such a truth as this—a truth revealed therein, not once only, not obscurely, not incidentally; but frequently, and that in express terms; but solemnly and of set purpose, as denoting one of the peculiar privileges of the children of God.

2. And it is the more necessary to explain and defend this truth, because there is a danger on the right hand and on the left. If we deny it, there is a danger lest our religion degenerate into mere formality; lest, having 'a form of godliness,' we

neglect, if not 'deny, the power of it.' If we allow it, but do not understand what we allow, we are liable to run into all the wildness of enthusiasm. It is therefore needful, in the highest degree, to guard those who fear God from both these dangers, by a scriptural and rational illustration and confirmation of this momentous truth.

3. It may seem, something of this kind is the more needful because so little has been wrote on the subject with any clearness; unless some discourses on the wrong side of the question, which explain it quite away. And it cannot be doubted, but these were occasioned, at least in a great measure, by the crude, unscriptural, irrational explication of others, who 'knew not what they spake, nor whereof they affirmed.'

4. It more nearly concerns the Methodists, so called, clearly to understand, explain, and defend this doctrine; because it is one grand part of the testimony which God has given them to bear to all mankind. It is by His peculiar blessing upon them in searching the Scriptures, confirmed by the experience of His children, that this great evangelical truth has been recovered, which had been for many years wellnigh lost and forgotten.

II. 1. But what is the witness of the Spirit? The original word, μαρτυρια, may be rendered either (as it is in several places) *the witness*, or less ambiguously, *the testimony* or *the record*: so it is rendered in our translation (1 John v. 11), 'This is the record,' the testimony, the sum of what God testifies in all the inspired writings, 'that God hath given unto us eternal life, and this life is in His Son.' The testimony now under consideration is given by the Spirit of God to and with our spirit: He is the Person testifying. What He testifies to us is, 'that we are the children of God.' The immediate result of this testimony is, 'the fruit of the Spirit'; namely, 'love, joy, peace, long-suffering, gentleness, goodness'; and without these, the testimony itself cannot continue. For it is inevitably destroyed, not only by the commission of any outward sin, or the omission of known duty, but by giving way to any inward sin; in a word, by whatever grieves the Holy Spirit of God.

2. I observed many years ago, 'It is hard to find words in the language of men, to explain the deep things of God. Indeed, there are none that will adequately express what the Spirit of

God works in His children. But perhaps one might say (desiring any who are taught of God, to correct, soften, or strengthen the expression), by the testimony of the Spirit, I mean, an inward impression on the soul, whereby the Spirit of God immediately and directly witnesses to my spirit, that I am a child of God; that Jesus Christ hath loved me, and given Himself for me; that all my sins are blotted out, and I, even I, am reconciled to God.'

3. After twenty years' further consideration, I see no cause to retract any part of this. Neither do I conceive how any of these expressions may be altered, so as to make them more intelligible. I can only add, that if any of the children of God will point out any other expressions which are more clear, or more agreeable to the Word of God, I will readily lay these aside.

4. Meantime let it be observed, I do not mean hereby, that the Spirit of God testifies this by any outward voice; no, nor always by an inward voice, although He may do this sometimes. Neither do I suppose, that He always applies to the heart (though He often may) one or more texts of Scripture. But He so works upon the soul by His immediate influence, and by a strong, though inexplicable operation, that the stormy wind and troubled waves subside, and there is a sweet calm; the heart resting as in the arms of Jesus, and the sinner being clearly satisfied that God is reconciled, that all his 'iniquities are forgiven, and his sins covered.'

5. Now what is the matter of dispute concerning this? Not whether there be a witness or testimony of the Spirit. Not whether the Spirit does testify with our spirit that we are the children of God. None can deny this, without flatly contradicting the Scriptures, and charging a lie upon the God of truth. Therefore, that there is a testimony of the Spirit is acknowledged by all parties.

6. Neither is it questioned, whether there is an indirect witness, or testimony, that we are the children of God. This is nearly, if not exactly, the same with the testimony of a good conscience towards God; and is the result of reason, or reflection of what we feel in our own souls. Strictly speaking, it is a conclusion drawn partly from the Word of God, and partly from our own experience. The Word of God says, every one who has the fruit of the Spirit is a child of God; experience, or inward consciousness, tells me, that I have the fruit of the Spirit; and

hence I rationally conclude, 'Therefore I am a child of God.' This is likewise allowed on all hands, and so is no matter of controversy.

7. Nor do we assert, that there can be any real testimony of the Spirit without the fruit of the Spirit. We assert, on the contrary, that the fruit of the Spirit immediately springs from this testimony; not always indeed in the same degree, even when the testimony is first given; and much less afterwards. Neither joy nor peace is always at one stay; no, nor love; as neither is the testimony itself always equally strong and clear.

8. But the point in question is, whether there be any *direct* testimony of the Spirit at all; whether there be any other testimony of the Spirit, than that which arises from a consciousness of the fruit.

III. 1. I believe there is; because that is the plain, natural meaning of the text, 'The Spirit itself beareth witness with our spirit, that we are the children of God.' It is manifest, here are two witnesses mentioned, who together testify the same thing; the Spirit of God, and our own spirit. The late Bishop of London, in his sermon on this text, seems astonished that any one can doubt of this, which appears upon the very face of the words. Now, 'The testimony of our own spirit,' says the Bishop, 'is one, which is the consciousness of our own sincerity'; or, to express the same thing a little more clearly, the consciousness of the fruit of the Spirit. When our spirit is conscious of this, of love, joy, peace, long-suffering, gentleness, goodness it easily infers from these premisses, that we are the children of God.

2. It is true, that great man supposes the other witness to be, 'the consciousness of our own good works.' This, he affirms, is the testimony of God's Spirit. But this is included in the testimony of our own spirit; yea, and in sincerity, even according to the common sense of the word. So the Apostle, 'Our rejoicing is this, the testimony of our conscience, that in simplicity and godly sincerity we have had our conversation in the world'; where, it is plain, sincerity refers to our words and actions at least as much as to our inward dispositions. So that this is not another witness, but the very same that he mentioned before; the consciousness of our good works being only one branch of the consciousness of our sincerity. Consequently here is only one

witness still. If, therefore, the text speaks of two witnesses, one of these is not the consciousness of our good works, neither of our sincerity; all this being manifestly contained in the testimony of our spirit.

3. What then is the other witness? This might easily be learned, if the text itself were not sufficiently clear, from the verse immediately preceding: 'Ye have received, not the spirit of bondage, but the spirit of adoption, whereby we cry, Abba, Father.' It follows, 'The Spirit itself beareth witness with our spirit, that we are the children of God.'

4. This is farther explained by the parallel text (Gal. iv. 6), 'Because ye are sons, God hath sent forth the Spirit of His Son into your hearts, crying, Abba, Father.' Is not this something *immediate* and *direct*, not the result of reflection or argumentation? Does not this Spirit cry, 'Abba, Father,' in our hearts, the moment it is given, antecedently to any reflection upon our sincerity; yea, to any reasoning whatsoever? And is not this the plain, natural sense of the words, which strikes any one as soon as he hears them? All these texts then, in their most obvious meaning, describe a direct testimony of the Spirit.

5. That the testimony of the Spirit of God must, in the very nature of things, be antecedent to the testimony of our own spirit, may appear from this single consideration: we must be holy in heart and life before we can be conscious that we are so. But we must love God before we can be holy at all, this being the root of all holiness. Now, we cannot love God, till we know He loves us: 'We love Him, because He first loved us'; and we cannot know His love to us, till His Spirit witnesses it to our spirit. Till then we cannot believe it; we cannot say, 'The life which I now live, I live by faith in the Son of God, who loved me, and gave Himself for me.'

> Then, only then we feel
> Our interest in His blood,
> And cry, with joy unspeakable,
> Thou art my Lord, my God!

Since, therefore, the testimony of His Spirit must precede the love of God, and all holiness, of consequence it must precede our consciousness thereof.

6. And here properly comes in, to confirm this scriptural

doctrine, the experience of the children of God; the experience not of two or three, not of a few, but of a great multitude which no man can number. It has been confirmed both in this and in all ages, by 'a cloud' of living and dying 'witnesses.' It is confirmed by *your* experience and *mine*. The Spirit itself bore witness to my spirit, that I was a child of God, gave me an evidence hereof; and I immediately cried, 'Abba, Father!' And this I did (and so did you) before I 'reflected on, or was conscious of, any fruit of the Spirit. It was from this testimony received, that love, joy, peace, and the whole fruit of the Spirit flowed. First, I heard,

> Thy sins are forgiven! Accepted thou art!—
> I listen'd, and heaven sprung up in my heart.

7. But this is confirmed, not only by the experience of the children of God—thousands of whom can declare that they never did know themselves to be in the favour of God till it was dirrectly witnessed to them by His Spirit—but by all those who are convinced of sin, who feel the wrath of God abiding on them. These cannot be satisfied with anything less than a direct testimony from His Spirit—that He is 'merciful to their unrighteousness, and remembers their sins and iniquities no more.' Tell any of these, 'You are to know you are a child, by reflecting on what He has wrought in you, on your love, joy, and peace'; and will he not immediately reply, 'By all this I know I am a child of the devil? I have no more love to God than the devil has; my carnal mind is enmity against God. I have no joy in the Holy Ghost; my soul is sorrowful even unto death. I have no peace; my heart is a troubled sea; I am all storm and tempest.' And which way can these souls possibly be comforted, but by a divine testimony (not that they are good, or sincere, or conformable to the Scripture in heart and life, but) that God *justifieth the ungodly?*—him that, till the moment he is justified, is all ungodly, void of all true holiness; 'him that worketh not,' that worketh nothing that is truly good, till he is conscious that he is accepted, not for any 'works of righteousness which he hath done,' but by the mere, free mercy of God; wholly and solely for what the Son of God hath done and suffered for him. And can it be any otherwise, if 'a man is justified by faith, without the works of the law'? If so, what inward or outward goodness can he be

conscious of antecedent to his justification? Nay, is not the having nothing to pay, that is, the being conscious that 'there dwelleth in us no good thing,' neither inward nor outward goodness, essentially, indispensably necessary, before we can be 'justified freely, through the redemption that is in Jesus Christ'? Was ever any man justified since his coming into the world, or can any man ever be justified, till he is brought to that point,—

> I give up every plea beside,—
> Lord, I am damn'd; but Thou hast died?

8. Every one, therefore, who denies the existence of such a testimony, does in effect deny justification by faith. It follows, that either he never experienced this, either he never was justified, or that he has forgotten, as St. Peter speaks, του καθαρισμου των παλαι αυτου αμαρτιων, *the purification from his former sins*; the experience he then had himself; the manner wherein God wrought in his own soul, when his former sins were blotted out.

9. And the experience even of the children of the world here confirms that of the children of God. Many of these have a desire to please God: some of them take much pains to please Him: but do they not, one and all, count it the highest absurdity for any to talk of *knowing* his sins are forgiven? Which of *them* even pretends to any such thing? And yet many of them are conscious of their own sincerity. Many of them undoubtedly have, in a degree, the testimony of their own spirit, a consciousness of their own uprightness. But this brings them no consciousness that they are forgiven; no knowledge that they are the children of God. Yea, the more sincere they are, the more uneasy they generally are, for want of knowing it; plainly showing that this cannot be known in a satisfactory manner, by the bare testimony of our own spirit, without God's directly testifying that we are His children.

IV. But abundance of objections have been made to this; the chief of which it may be well to consider.

1. It is objected, first, 'Experience is not sufficient to prove a doctrine which is not founded on Scripture.' This is undoubtedly true; and it is an important truth: but it does not affect the

present question; for it has been shown, that this doctrine is founded on Scripture: therefore experience is properly alleged to confirm it.

2. 'But madmen, French prophets, and enthusiasts of every kind, have imagined they experienced this witness.' They have so; and perhaps not a few of them did, although they did not retain it long: but if they did not, this is no proof at all that others have not experienced it; as a madman's imagining himself a king, does not prove that there are no *real* kings.

'Nay, many who pleaded strongly for this, have utterly decried the Bible.' Perhaps so; but this was no necessary consequence: thousands plead for it who have the highest esteem for the Bible.

'Yea, but many have fatally deceived themselves hereby, and got above all conviction.' And yet a scriptural doctrine is no worse, though men abuse it to their own destruction.

3. 'But I lay it down as an undoubted truth, the fruit of the Spirit is the witness of the Spirit.' Not undoubted; thousands doubt of, yea, flatly deny it: but let that pass. 'If this witness be sufficient, there is no need of any other. But it is sufficient, unless in one of these cases: 1. The *total absence* of the fruit of the Spirit.' And this is the case, when the direct witness is first given. 2. 'The *not perceiving it*. But to contend for it in this case, is to contend for being in the favour of God, and not knowing it.' True; not knowing it at that time any otherwise than by the testimony which is given for that end. And this we do contend for; we contend that the direct witness may shine clear, even while the indirect one is under a cloud.

4. It is objected, secondly, "The design of the witness contended for is, to prove that the profession we make is genuine. But it does not prove this.' I answer, the proving this is not the design of it. It is antecedent to our making any profession at all, but that of being lost, undone, guilty, helpless sinners. It is designed to assure those to whom it is given, that they are children of God; that they are 'justified freely by His grace, through the redemption that is in Jesus Christ.' And this does not suppose that their preceding thoughts, words, and actions, are conformable to the rule of Scripture; it supposes quite the reverse; namely, that they are sinners all over; sinners both in heart and life. Were it otherwise, God would *justify the*

godly; and *their own works* would be counted to them for righteousness. And I cannot but fear that a supposition of our being justified by works is at the root of all these objections; for, whoever cordially believes that God *imputes* to all that are justified *righteousness without works,* will find no difficulty in allowing the witness of His Spirit, preceding the fruit of it.

5. It is objected, thirdly, 'One Evangelist says, "Your heavenly Father will give the Holy Spirit to them that ask Him." The other Evangelist calls the same thing "good gifts"; abundantly demonstrating that the Spirit's way of bearing witness is by giving good gifts.' Nay, here is nothing at all about *bearing witness,* either in the one text or the other. Therefore till this demonstration is better demonstrated, I let it stand as it is.

6. It is objected, fourthly, 'The Scripture says, "The tree is known by its fruits. Prove all things. Try the spirits. Examine yourselves." ' Most true. Therefore, let every man who believes he 'hath the witness in himself,' try whether it be of God: if the fruit follow, it is; otherwise it is not. For certainly 'the tree is known by its fruit': hereby we *prove* if it be 'of God.' 'But the direct witness is never referred to in the book of God.' Not as standing alone; not as a single witness; but as connected with the other; as giving a *joint testimony*; testifying *with our spirit,* that we are children of God. And who is able to prove, that it is not *thus* referred to in this very scripture? 'Examine yourselves whether ye be in the faith; prove your own selves. Know ye not your own selves, that Jesus Christ is in you?' It is by no means clear, that they did not know this by a *direct* as well as a *remote* witness. How is it proved, that they did not know it, first, by an inward consciousness; and then, by love, joy, and peace?'

7. 'But the testimony arising from the internal and external change is constantly referred to in the Bible.' It is so: and we constantly refer thereto, to confirm the testimony of the Spirit.

'Nay, all the marks *you* have given, whereby to distinguish the operations of God's Spirit from delusion, refer to the change wrought in us and upon us.' This, likewise, is undoubtedly true.

8. It is objected, fifthly, that 'the direct witness of the Spirit does not secure us from the greatest delusion. And is that a witness fit to be trusted, whose testimony cannot be depended on? that is forced to fly to something else, to prove what it asserts?' I answer: To secure us from all delusion, God gives us

two witnesses that we are His children. And this they testify conjointly. Therefore, 'what God hath joined together, let not man put asunder.' And while they are joined, we cannot be deluded: their testimony can be depended on. They are fit to be trusted in the highest degree, and need nothing else to prove what they assert.

'Nay, the direct witness only asserts, but does not prove anything.' By two witnesses shall every word be established. And when the Spirit witnesses with our spirit, as God designs it to do, then it fully proves that we are children of God.

9. It is objected, sixthly, 'You own the change wrought is a sufficient testimony, unless in the case of severe trials, such as that of our Saviour upon the cross; but none of us can be tried in that manner.' But you or I may be tried in such a manner, and so may any other child of God, that it will be impossible for us to keep our filial confidence in God without the direct witness of His Spirit.

10. It is objected, lastly, 'The greatest contenders for it are some of the proudest and most uncharitable of men.' Perhaps some of the *hottest* contenders for it are both proud and uncharitable; but many of the *firmest* contenders for it are eminently meek and lowly in heart; and, indeed, in all other respects also,

True followers of their lamb-like Lord.

The preceding objections are the most considerable that I have heard, and I believe contain the strength of the cause. Yet I apprehend whoever calmly and impartially considers those objections and the answers together, will easily see that they do not destroy, no, nor weaken, the evidence of that great truth, that the Spirit of God does *directly,* as well as *indirectly,* testify that we are children of God.

V. 1. The sum of all is this: the testimony of the Spirit is an inward impression on the souls of believers, whereby the Spirit of God directly testifies to their spirit, that they are children of God. And it is not questioned, whether there is a testimony of the Spirit; but whether there is any *direct* testimony; whether there is any other than that which arises from a consciousness of the fruit of the Spirit. We believe there is; because this is the plain natural meaning of the text, illustrated both by the preceding words, and by the parallel passage in the Epistle to the Galatians; because, in the nature of the thing, the testimony must precede the fruit which springs from it; and because this plain meaning of the Word of God is confirmed by the experience of innumerable children of God; yea, and by the experience of all who are convinced of sin, who can never rest till they have a direct witness; and even of the children of the world, who, not having the witness in themselves, one and all declare, none can *know* his sins forgiven.

2. And whereas it is objected, that experience is not sufficient to prove a doctrine unsupported by Scripture; that madmen and enthusiasts of every kind have imagined such a witness; that the design of that witness is to prove our profession genuine, which design it does not answer; that the Scripture says, 'The tree is known by its fruit,' 'examine yourselves, prove your own selves,' and, meantime, the direct witness is never referred to in all the book of God; that it does not secure us from the greatest delusions; and, lastly, that the change wrought in us is a sufficient testimony, unless in such trials as Christ alone suffered,—we answer, 1. Experience is sufficient to *confirm* a doctrine which is grounded on Scripture. 2. Though many fancy they experience what they do not, this is no prejudice to real experience. 3. The design of that witness is, to assure us we are children of God; and this design it does answer. 4. The true witness of the Spirit is known by its fruit, 'love, peace, joy'; not indeed preceding, but following it. 5. It cannot be proved, that the direct as well as the indirect witness is not referred to in that very text, 'Know ye not your own selves, that Jesus Christ is in you?' 6. The Spirit of God, witnessing with our spirit, does secure us from all delusion: and, lastly, we are all liable to trials, wherein the testimony of our own spirit is not sufficient; wherein nothing less than the direct testimony of God's Spirit can assure us that we are His children.

3. Two inferences may be drawn from the whole: the first, Let none ever presume to rest in any supposed testimony of the Spirit, which is separate from the fruit of it. If the Spirit of God does really testify that we are the children of God, the immediate consequence will be the fruit of the Spirit, even 'love, joy, peace,

long-suffering, gentleness, goodness, fidelity, meekness, temperance.' And however this fruit may be clouded for a while, during the time of strong temptation, so that it does not appear to the tempted person, while Satan is sifting him as wheat; yet the substantial part of it remains, even under the thickest cloud. It is true, joy in the Holy Ghost may be withdrawn, during the hour of trial; yea, the soul may be 'exceeding sorrowful,' while 'the hour and power of darkness' continue; but even this is generally restored with increase, till we rejoice 'with joy unspeakable and full of glory.'

4. The second inference is, Let none rest in any supposed fruit of the Spirit without the witness. There may be foretastes of joy, of peace, of love, and those not delusive, but really from God, long before we have the witness in ourselves; before the Spirit of God witnesses with our spirits that we have 'redemption in the blood of Jesus, even the forgiveness of sins.' Yea, there may be a [degree] of longsuffering, of gentleness, of fidelity, meekness, temperance (not a shadow thereof, but a real degree, by the preventing grace of God), before we 'are accepted in the Beloved,' and, consequently, before we have a testimony of our acceptance: but it is by no means advisable to rest here; it is at the peril of our souls if we do. If we are wise, we shall be continually crying to God, until His Spirit cry in our heart, 'Abba, Father!' This is the privilege of all the children of God, and without this we can never be assured that we are His children. Without this we cannot retain a steady peace, nor avoid perplexing doubts and fears. But when we have once received this Spirit of adoption, this 'peace, which passeth all understanding,' and which expels all painful doubt and fear, will 'keep our hearts and minds in Christ Jesus.' And when this has brought forth its genuine fruit, all inward and outward holiness, it is undoubtedly the will of Him that calleth us, to give us always what He has once given: so that there is no need that we should ever more be deprived of either the testimony of God's Spirit or the testimony of our own, the consciousness of our walking in all righteousness and true holiness.

NEWRY, *April* 4, 1767.

SERMON XLVI

ON SIN IN BELIEVERS

The *Journal* for March 28, 1763, says: 'I retired to Lewisham, and
wrote the sermon on Sin in Believers in order to remove a mistake
which some were labouring to propagate—that there is no sin in any
that are justified.' He went, no doubt, to the house of his friend
Ebenezer Blackwell at Lewisham, now one of the metropolitan
boroughs, but then a pleasant country village, south of Deptford and
Greenwich, and about five miles in a direct line south-east of St. Paul's.
Blackwell was a partner in Martin's Lombard Street Bank, and was a
faithful friend to Wesley from the beginning of his evangelistic working
1739, until his own death on April 21, 1782. Here Wesley was nursed
during his serious illness in 1754; and he records in his *Journal* for
August 24, 1782, a visit to his widow: 'We took one more walk,' he says,
'round the garden and meadow which he took so much pains to
improve. Upwards of forty years this has been my place of retirement
when I could spare two or three days from London.' A view of the
house will be found in the Standard edition of the *Journal*, v. 157. The
sermon was published as a twopenny pamphlet at the Foundery in
1763.

Wesley had a previous sermon on the same text which he preached
on February 5, 1738, at St. John the Evangelist, Millbank, Westminster;
at St. Ann's, Manchester, on March 19 following, and at Whitam
(Wytham, near Oxford) on the next Sunday. It is also recorded as
delivered at the Foundery at six o'clock in the morning of Sunday, May
3, 1741, and at 3.45 on the following Tuesday at 'the dancing-room' at
Deptford. The text is found occasionally in the sermon list, the last
entry being February 2, 1760. It was appropriately chosen for a New
Year's Day sermon at Bristol in 1758, and at Norwich in 1760. He
describes it (*Journal*, May 3, 1741) as 'the scriptural account of one who
is in Christ a new creature, from whom old things are passed away, and
in whom all things are become new.' But in spite of Mr. Curnock's note
in *Journal*, i. 436, I do not believe that this older sermon had anything in
common with the one written at Lewisham, except the text. The
description just quoted does not fit the Lewisham sermon, and sections
iv. 4-13 are definitely stated in a footnote to be an answer to an article in
the *Christian Magazine*, obviously of that year. The two quotations from
hymns are from the *Hymns and Sacred Poems*, of 1739, so could not be in
the 1738 sermon. The next sermon is also a new sermon on an old text,

Mark i. 15, but it has nothing in common with Sermon VII on The Way to the Kingdom.

This sermon is most valuable as a corrective to the conclusion which might fairly be drawn from some of the earlier sermons, that after conversion, the believer is entirely free from sin; and that the existence of sinful desires in him is proof that he has not exercised saving faith in Christ.

If any man be in Christ, he is a new creature.—2 COR. v. 17.

I. 1. Is there then sin in him that is in Christ? Does sin *remain* in one that believes in Him? Is there any sin in them that are born of God or are they wholly delivered from it? Let no one imagine this to be a question of mere curiosity; or that it is of little importance whether it be determined one way or the other. Rather it is a point of the utmost moment to every serious Christian; the resolving of which very nearly concerns both his present and eternal happiness.

2. And yet I do not know that ever it was controverted in the primitive Church. Indeed there was no room for disputing concerning it, as all Christians were agreed. And so far as I have ever observed, the whole body of ancient Christians, who have left us anything in writing, declare with one voice, that even believers in Christ, till they are 'strong in the Lord and in the power of His might,' have need to 'wrestle with flesh and blood,' with an evil nature, as well as 'with principalities and powers.'

3. And herein our own Church (as indeed in most points) exactly copies after the primitive; declaring in her Ninth Article, 'Original sin is the corruption of the nature of every man, whereby man is in his own nature inclined to evil, so that the flesh lusteth contrary to the Spirit. And this infection of nature doth remain, yea, in them that are regenerated whereby the lust of the flesh called in Greek φρονημα σαρκος, is not subject to the law of God. And although there is no condemnation for them that believe, yet this lust hath of itself the nature of sin.'

4. The same testimony is given by all other Churches; not only by the Greek and Romish Church, but by every Reformed Church in Europe, of whatever denomination. Indeed some of these seem to carry the thing too far; so describing the corruption of heart in a believer, as scarce to allow that he has dominion over it, but, rather, is in bondage thereto; and, by this

means, they leave hardly any distinction between a believer and an unbeliever.

5. To avoid this extreme, many well-meaning men, particularly those under the direction of the late Count Zinzendorf, ran into another; affirming, that 'all true believers are not only saved from the *dominion* of sin, but from the *being* of inward as well as outward sin, so that it no longer *remains* in them': and from them, about twenty years ago, many of our countrymen imbibed the same opinion, that even the corruption of nature is *no more,* in those who believe in Christ.

6. It is true that, when the Germans were pressed upon this head, they soon allowed (many of them at least), that 'sin did still remain *in the flesh,* but not *in the heart* of a believer': and, after a time, when the absurdity of this was shown, they fairly gave up the point; allowing that sin did still remain, though not reign, in him that is born of God.

7. But the English, who had received it from them (some directly, some at second or third hand), were not so easily prevailed upon to part with a favourite opinion: and even when the generality of them were convinced it was utterly indefensible, a few could not be persuaded to give it up, but maintain it to this day.

II. 1. For the sake of those who really fear God, and desire to know 'the truth as it is in Jesus,' it may not be amiss to consider the point with calmness and impartiality. In doing this I use indifferently the words *regenerate, justified,* or *believers*; since, though they have not precisely the same meaning (the first implying an inward, actual change, the second a relative one, and the third the means whereby both the one and the other are wrought), yet they come to one and the same thing; as every one that believes, is both justified and born of God.

2. By sin, I here understand inward sin; any sinful temper, passion, or affection; such as pride, self-will, love of the world, in any kind or degree; such as lust, anger, peevishness; any disposition contrary to the mind which was in Christ.

3. The question is not concerning *outward sin*; whether a child of God *commit sin* or no. We all agree and earnestly maintain, 'He that committeth sin is of the devil.' We agree, 'Whosoever is born of God doth not commit sin.' Neither do we now inquire

whether inward sin will *always* remain in the children of God; whether sin will continue in the soul as long as it continues in the body: nor yet do we inquire whether a justified person may *relapse* either into inward or outward sin; but simply this, Is a justified or regenerate man freed from *all sin* as soon as he is justified? Is there then no sin in his heart?—nor ever after, unless he fall from grace?

4. We allow that the state of a justified person is inexpressibly great and glorious. He is born again, 'not of blood, nor of the flesh, nor of the will of man, but of God.' He is a child of God, a member of Christ, an heir of the kingdom of heaven. 'The peace of God, which passeth all understanding, keepeth his heart and mind in Christ Jesus.' His very body is a 'temple of the Holy Ghost,' and an 'habitation of God through the Spirit.' He is 'created anew in Christ Jesus': he is *washed,* he is *sanctified.* His heart is purified by faith; he is cleansed 'from the corruption that is in the world'; the love of God is shed abroad in his heart by the Holy Ghost which is given unto him.' And so long as he 'walketh in love' (which he may always do), he worships God in spirit and in truth. He keepeth the commandments of God, and doeth those things that are pleasing in His sight; so exercising himself as to 'have a conscience void of offence toward God and toward men': and he has power both over outward and inward sin, even from the moment he is justified.

III. 1. 'But was he not then freed from all sin, so that there is no sin in his heart?' I cannot say this; I cannot believe it; because St. Paul says the contrary. He is speaking to believers, and describing the state of believers in general, when he says, 'The flesh lusteth against the Spirit, and the Spirit against the flesh: these are contrary the one to the other' (Gal. v. 17). Nothing can be more express. The Apostle here directly affirms that the flesh, evil nature, opposes the Spirit, even in believers; that even in the regenerate there are two principles, 'contrary the one to the other.'

2. Again: when he writes to the believers at Corinth, to those who were 'sanctified in Christ Jesus' (1 Cor. i. 2), he says, 'I, brethren, could not speak unto you as unto spiritual, but as unto carnal, as unto babes in Christ. Ye are yet carnal; for whereas there is among you envying and strife, are ye not carnal?' (chap.

iii. 1, 3). Now, here the Apostle speaks unto those who were unquestionably believers—whom, in the same breath, he styles his brethren in Christ—as being still, in a measure, carnal. He affirms, there was envying (an evil temper), occasioning strife among them, and yet does not give the least intimation that they had lost their faith. Nay, he manifestly declares they had not; for then they would not have been babes in Christ. And (what is most remarkable of all) he speaks of being carnal, and babes in Christ, as one and the same thing; plainly showing that every believer is (in a degree) carnal, while he is only a babe in Christ.

3. Indeed this grand point, that there are two contrary principles in believers—nature and grace, the flesh and the Spirit—runs through all the Epistles of St. Paul, yea, through all the holy Scriptures; almost all the directions and exhortations therein are founded on this supposition; pointing at wrong tempers or practices in those who are, notwithstanding, acknowledged by the inspired writers to be believers. And they are continually exhorted to fight with and conquer these by the power of the faith which was in them.

4. And who can doubt, but there was faith in the angel of the church of Ephesus, when our Lord said to him, 'I know thy works, and thy labour, and thy patience: thou hast patience, and for My name's sake hast laboured, and hast not fainted'? (Rev. ii. 2-4). But was there, meantime, no sin in his heart? Yea, or Christ would not have added, 'Nevertheless I have somewhat against thee, because thou hast left thy first love.' This was real sin which God saw in his heart; of which, accordingly, he is exhorted to *repent*: and yet we have no authority to say, that even then he had no faith.

5. Nay, the angel of the church at Pergamos, also, is exhorted to *repent*, which implies sin, though our Lord expressly says, 'Thou hast not denied My faith' (verses 13, 16). And to the angel of the church in Sardis He says, 'Strengthen the things which remain, that are ready to die.' The good which remained was *ready to die*, but was not actually dead (chap. iii. 2). So there was still a spark of faith even in him; which he is accordingly commanded to *hold fast* (verse 3).

6. Once more: when the Apostle exhorts believers to 'cleanse themselves from all filthiness of flesh and spirit' (2 Cor. vii. 1), he

plainly teaches, that those believers were not yet cleansed therefrom.

Will you answer, 'He that abstains from all appearance of evil does, *ipso facto,* cleanse himself from all filthiness'? Not in any wise. For instance, a man reviles me: I feel resentment, which is filthiness of spirit; yet I say not a word. Here I 'abstain from all appearance of evil'; but this does not cleanse me from that filthiness of spirit, as I experience to my sorrow.

7. And as this position, 'There is no sin in a believer, no carnal mind, no bent to backsliding,' is thus contrary to the Word of God, so it is to the experience of His children. These continually feel an heart bent to backsliding; a natural tendency to evil; a proneness to depart from God, and cleave to the things of earth. They are daily sensible of sin remaining in their heart—pride, self-will, unbelief; and of sin cleaving to all they speak and do, even their best actions and holiest duties. Yet at the same time they 'know that they are of God'; they cannot doubt of it for a moment. They feel His Spirit clearly 'witnessing with their spirit, that they are the children of God.' They rejoice 'in God through Christ Jesus, by whom they have now received the atonement.' So that they are equally assured, that sin is in them, and that 'Christ is in them the hope of glory.'

8. 'But can Christ be in the same heart where sin is?' Undoubtedly He can; otherwise it never could be saved therefrom. Where the sickness is, there is the Physician

> Carrying on His work within,
> Striving till He cast out sin.

Christ indeed cannot *reign* where sin reigns; neither will He dwell where any sin is *allowed.* But He *is* and *dwells* in the heart of every believer, who is *fighting against* all sin; although it be not yet purified, according to the purification of the sanctuary.

9. It has been observed before, that the opposite doctrine— that there is no sin in believers—is quite new in the Church of Christ; that it was never heard of for seventeen hundred years; never till it was discovered by Count Zinzendorf. I do not remember to have seen the least intimation of it, either in any ancient or modern writer; unless perhaps in some of the wild, ranting Antinomians. And these likewise say and unsay,

acknowledging there is sin *in their flesh,* although no sin in their heart. But whatever doctrine is *new* must be *wrong;* for the *old* religion is the only *true* one; and no doctrine can be right, unless it is the very same 'which was from the beginning.'

10. One argument more against this new, unscriptural doctrine may be drawn from the dreadful consequences of it. One says, 'I felt anger to-day.' Must I reply, 'Then you have no faith?' Another says, 'I know what you advise is good, but my will is quite averse to it.' Must I tell him, 'Then you are an unbeliever, under the wrath and the curse of God?' What will be the natural consequence of this? Why, if he believe what I say, his soul will not only be grieved and wounded, but perhaps utterly destroyed; inasmuch as he will 'cast away' that 'confidence which hath great recompense of reward': and having cast away his shield, how shall he 'quench the fiery darts of the wicked one'? How shall he overcome the world, seeing 'this is the victory that overcometh the world, even our faith'? He stands disarmed in the midst of his enemies, open to all their assaults. What wonder, then, if he be utterly overthrown: if they take him captive at their will; yea, if he fall from one wickedness to another, and never see good any more? I cannot, therefore, by any means receive this assertion, that there is no sin in a believer from the moment he is justified,—first, because it is contrary to the whole tenor of Scripture; secondly, because it is contrary to the experience of the children of God; thirdly, because it is absolutely new, never heard of in the world till yesterday; and, lastly, because it is naturally attended with the most fatal consequences—not only grieving those whom God hath not grieved, but perhaps dragging them into everlasting perdition.

IV. 1. However, let us give a fair hearing to the chief arguments of those who endeavour to support it. And it is, first, from Scripture they attempt to prove that there is no sin in a believer. They argue thus: 'The Scripture says, Every believer is born of God, is clean, is holy, is sanctified, is pure in heart, has a new heart, is a temple of the Holy Ghost. Now, as "that which is born of the flesh is flesh," is altogether evil, so "that which is born of the Spirit is spirit," is altogether good. Again: a man cannot be clean, sanctified, holy, and at the same time unclean, unsanctified, unholy. He cannot be pure and impure, or have a new and an old heart together. Neither can his soul be unholy, while it is a temple of the Holy Ghost.'

I have put this objection as strong as possible, that its full weight may appear. Let us now examine it part by part. And (1) 'That which is born of the Spirit is spirit, is altogether good.' I allow the text, but not the comment. For the text affirms this, and no more,—that every man who is 'born of the Spirit' is a spiritual man. He is so: but so he may be, and yet not be altogether spiritual. The Christians at Corinth were spiritual men; else they had been no Christians at all: and yet they were not altogether spiritual; they were still, in part, carnal.—'But they were fallen from grace.' St. Paul says, No. They were even then babes in Christ. (2) 'But a man cannot be clean, sanctified, holy, and at the same time unclean, unsanctified, unholy.' Indeed he may. So the Corinthians were. 'Ye are washed,' says the Apostle, 'ye are sanctified'; namely, cleansed from fornication, idolatry, drunkenness, and all other outward sin (1 Cor. vi. 9-11): and yet, at the same time, in another sense of the word, they were unsanctified; they were not washed, not inwardly cleansed from envy, evil-surmising, partiality.—'But sure, they had not a new heart and an old heart together.' It is most sure they had; for, at that very time, their hearts were *truly,* yet not *entirely,* renewed. Their carnal mind was nailed to the cross; yet it was not wholly destroyed.—'But could they be unholy, while they were temples of the Holy Ghost?' Yes; that they were temples of the Holy Ghost is certain (1 Cor. vi. 19); and it is equally certain, they were, in some degree, carnal, that is, unholy.

2. 'However, there is one scripture more which will put the matter out of question: "If any man be" a believer "in Christ, he is a new creature. Old things are passed away; behold, all things are become new" (2 Cor. v. 17). Now, certainly a man cannot be a new creature and an old creature at once.' Yes, he may: he may be partly renewed, which was the very case with those at Corinth. They were doubtless 'renewed in the spirit of their mind,' or they could not have been so much as 'babes in Christ'; yet they had not the whole mind which was in Christ, for they envied one another. 'But it is said expressly, "Old things are passed away; all things are become new." ' But we must not so interpret the Apostle's words, as to make him contradict himself. And if we

will make him consistent with himself, the plain meaning of the words is this: His old judgement concerning justification, holiness, happiness, indeed concerning the things of God in general, is now passed away; so are his old desires, designs, affections, tempers, and conversation. All these are undeniably become new, greatly changed from what they were; and yet, though they are new, they are not wholly new. Still he feels, to his sorrow and shame, remains of the old man, too manifest taints of his former tempers and affections, though they cannot gain any advantage over him, as long as he watches unto prayer.

3. This whole argument, 'If he is clean, he is clean'; 'If he is holy, he is holy' (and twenty more expressions of the same kind may easily be heaped together), is really no better than playing upon words; it is the fallacy of arguing from *a particular* to *a general*; of inferring a general conclusion from particular premises. Propose the sentence entire, and it runs thus: 'If he is holy at all, he is holy *altogether.*' That does not follow: every babe in Christ is holy, and yet not altogether so. He is saved from sin; yet not entirely: it *remains,* though it does not *reign.* If you think it does not *remain* (in babes at least, whatever be the case with young men or fathers), you certainly have not considered the height, and depth, and length, and breadth of the law of God (even the law of love laid down by St. Paul in the thirteenth of Corinthians); and that *every* ανομια, disconformity to, or deviation from, this law, *is sin.* Now, is there no disconformity to this in the heart or life of a believer? What may be in an adult Christian, is another question; but what a stranger must he be to human nature, who can possibly imagine that this is the case with every babe in Christ!

4. 'But believers "walk after the Spirit" (Rom. viii. 1), and the Spirit of God dwells in them; consequently, they are delivered from the guilt, the power, or, in one word, the being of sin.'

These are coupled together, as if they were the same thing. But they are not the same thing. The *guilt* is one thing, the *power* another, and the *being,* yet another. That believers are delivered from the *guilt* and *power* of sin, we allow; that they are delivered from the *being* of it, we deny. Nor does it in any wise follow from these texts. A man may have the Spirit of God dwelling in him, and may 'walk after the Spirit,' though he still feels 'the flesh lusting against the Spirit.'

5. 'But "the church is the body of Christ" (Col. i. 24); this implies, that its members are washed from all filthiness; otherwise it will follow, that Christ and Belial are incorporated with each other.'

Nay, it will not follow from hence, 'Those who are the mystical body of Christ still feel the flesh lusting against the Spirit,' that Christ has any fellowship with the devil, or with that sin which He enables them to resist and overcome.

6. 'But are not Christians "come to the heavenly Jerusalem," where "nothing defiled can enter"?' (Heb. xii. 22). Yes; 'and to an innumerable company of angels, and to the spirits of just men made perfect': that is,

> Earth and heaven all agree,
> All is one great family.

And they are likewise holy and undefiled, while they 'walk after the Spirit'; although sensible there is another principle in them, and that 'these are contrary to each other.'

7. 'But Christians are reconciled to God. Now, this could not be, if any of the carnal mind remained; for this is enmity against God: consequently, no reconciliation can be effected, but by its total destruction.'

We are 'reconciled to God through the blood of the cross': and in that moment the φρονημα σαρκος, the corruption of nature, which is enmity with God, is put under our feet; the flesh has no more dominion over us. But it still *exists*, and it is still in its nature enmity with God, lusting against His Spirit.

8. 'But "they that are Christ's have crucified the flesh with its affections and lusts" ' (Gal. v. 24). They have so; yet it remains in them still, and often struggles to break from the cross. 'Nay, but they have "put off the old man with his deeds" ' (Col. iii. 9). They have; and, in the sense above described, 'old things are passed away; all things are become new.' A hundred texts may be cited to the same effect; and they will all admit of the same answer.—'But, to say all in one word, "Christ gave Himself for the church, that it might be holy and without blemish" ' (Eph. v. 25, 27). And so it will be in the end: but it never was yet, from the beginning to this day.

9. 'But let experience speak: all who are justified do at that

time find an absolute freedom from all sin.' That I doubt: but, if they do, do they find it ever after? Else you gain nothing.—'If they do not, it is their own fault.' That remains to be proved.

10. 'But in the very nature of things, can a man have pride in him, and not be proud; anger, and yet not be angry?'

A man may have *pride* in him, may think of himself in some particulars above what he ought to think (and so be proud in that particular), and yet not be a proud man in his general character. He may have *anger* in him, yea, and a strong propensity to furious anger, without *giving way* to it. 'But can anger and pride be in that heart, where *only* meekness and humility are felt?' No: but *some* pride and anger may be in that heart, where there is much humility and meekness.

'It avails not to say, "These tempers are there, but they do not *reign*": for sin cannot, in any kind or degree, exist where it does not reign; for *guilt* and *power* are essential properties of sin. Therefore, where one of them is, all must be.'

Strange indeed! 'Sin cannot, in any kind or degree, *exist* where it does not reign?' Absolutely contrary this to all experience, all Scripture, all common sense. Resentment of an affront is sin; it is ανομια, disconformity to the law of love. This has existed in me a thousand times. Yet it did not, and does not, *reign*.—'But *guilt* and *power* are essential properties of sin; therefore, where one is, all must be.' No: in the instance before us, if the resentment I feel is not yielded to, even for a moment, there is no guilt at all, no condemnation from God upon that account. And in this case, it has no *power*. Though it 'lusteth against the Spirit,' it cannot prevail. Here, therefore, as in ten thousand instances, there is *sin* without either *guilt* or *power*.

11. 'But the supposing sin in a believer is pregnant with everything frightful and discouraging. It implies the contending with a power that has the possession of our strength; maintains his usurpation of our hearts; and there prosecutes the war in defiance of our Redeemer.' Not so: the supposing sin is in us, does not imply that it has the possession of our strength; no more than a man crucified has the possession of those that crucify him. As little does it imply, that 'sin maintains its usurpation of our hearts.' The usurper is dethroned. He remains indeed where he once reigned; but remains *in chains*. So that he does, in some sense, 'prosecute the war, yet he grows

weaker and weaker; while the believer goes on from strength to strength, conquering and to conquer.

12. 'I am not satisfied yet: he that has sin in him, is a slave to sin. Therefore you suppose a man to be justified, while he is a slave to sin. Now, if you allow men may be justified while they have pride, anger, or unbelief in them; nay, if you aver these are (at least for a time) in all that are justified; what wonder that we have so many proud, angry, unbelieving believers?'

I do not suppose any man who is justified is a slave to sin; yet I do suppose sin remains (at least for a time) in all that are justified.

'But if sin remains in a believer he is a sinful man: if pride, for instance, then he is proud; if self-will, then he is self-willed; if unbelief, then he is an unbeliever; consequently, no believer at all. How then does he differ from unbelievers, from unregenerate men?' This is still mere playing upon words. It means no more than, If there is sin, pride, self-will in him, then—there is sin, pride, self-will. And this nobody can deny. In that sense then he is proud, or self-willed. But he is not proud or self-willed in the same sense that unbelievers are; that is, *governed* by pride or self-will. Herein he differs from unregenerate men. They *obey* sin; he does not. Flesh is in them both: but they 'walk after the flesh'; he 'walks after the Spirit.'

'But how can *unbelief* be in a believer?' That word has two meanings. It means either no faith, or little faith; either the absence of faith, or the weakness of it. In the former sense unbelief is not in a believer; in the latter, it is in all babes. Their faith is commonly mixed with doubt or fear; that is, in the latter sense, with unbelief. 'Why are ye fearful,' says our Lord, 'O ye of little faith?' Again: 'O thou of little faith, wherefore didst thou doubt?' You see here was *unbelief* in *believers*; little faith and much unbelief.

13. 'But this doctrine—that sin remains in a believer; that a man may be in the favour of God, while he has sin in his heart—certainly tends to encourage men in sin.' Understand the proposition right, and no such consequence follows. A man may be in God's favour though he feel sin; but not if he *yields* to it. *Having sin* does not forfeit the favour of God; *giving way* to sin does. Though the flesh in you 'lust against the Spirit,' you may still be a child of God; but if you 'walk after the flesh,' you are a

child of the devil. Now this doctrine does not encourage to *obey* sin, but to resist it with all our might.

V. 1. The sum of all this is: there are in every person, even after he is justified, two contrary principles, nature and grace, termed by St. Paul, the *flesh* and the *Spirit*. Hence, although even babes in Christ are *sanctified*, yet it is only in part. In a degree, according to the measure of their faith, they are spiritual; yet in a degree they are carnal. Accordingly, believers are continually exhorted to watch against the flesh, as well as the world and the devil. And to this agrees the constant experience of the children of God. While they feel this witness in themselves, they feel a will not wholly resigned to the will of God. They know they are in Him; and yet find an heart ready to depart from Him, a proneness to evil in many instances, and a backwardness to that which is good. The contrary doctrine is wholly new; never heard of in the Church of Christ, from the time of His coming into the world, till the time of Count Zinzendorf; and it is attended with the most fatal consequences. It cuts off all watching against our evil nature, against the Delilah which we are told is gone, though she is still lying in our bosom. It tears away the shield of weak believers, deprives them of their faith, and so leaves them exposed to all the assaults of the world, the flesh, and the devil.

2. Let us, therefore, hold fast the sound doctrine 'once delivered to the saints,' and delivered down by them, with the written word, to all succeeding generations: that, although we are renewed, cleansed, purified, sanctified, the moment we truly believe in Christ, yet we are not then renewed, cleansed, purified altogether; but the flesh, the evil nature, still *remains* (though subdued), and wars against the Spirit. So much the more let us use all diligence in 'fighting the good fight of faith.' So much the more earnestly let us 'watch and pray' against the enemy within. The more carefully let us take to ourselves, and 'put on, the whole armour of God'; that, although 'we wrestle' both 'with flesh and blood, and with principalities, and powers, and wicked spirits in high places,' we 'may be able to withstand in the evil day, and having done all, to stand.'

SERMON XLVII

THE REPENTANCE OF BELIEVERS

This sermon was written at Londonderry on April 24, 1767, and was published at London in 1768 as a separate pamphlet. It was inserted in the 1771 edition of the *Works* as a further elucidation of the previous sermon on Sin in Believers. It is on the same text as Sermon VII, which was one of Wesley's favourites; but it has nothing otherwise to do with it. The *Journal* shows that he reached Londonderry on Friday, April 17, and employed the following Monday, Tuesday, and Wednesday, 'in speaking to the members of the society.' He wrote the sermon on Thursday and Friday, leaving the city on the Monday following. It is a careful and seasonable discourse, and no one can read it without realizing his need of the continual grace of the Holy Spirit. The second part contains a clear statement of the doctrine of entire sanctification. For a full discussion of this, see Sermon XXXV on Christian Perfection.

Repent ye, and believe the gospel.—MARK i. 15.

1. It is generally supposed, that repentance and faith are only the gate of religion; that they are necessary only at the beginning of our Christian course, when we are setting out in the way to the kingdom. And this may seem to be confirmed by the great Apostle, where, exhorting the Hebrew Christians to 'go on to perfection,' he teaches them to *leave* these first 'principles of the doctrine of Christ'; 'not laying again the foundation of repentance from dead works, and of faith towards God'; which must at least mean, that they should comparatively leave these, that at first took up all their thoughts, in order to 'press forward toward the prize of the high calling of God in Christ Jesus.'

2. And this is undoubtedly true, that there is a repentance and a faith, which are, more especially, necessary at the beginning: a repentance, which is a conviction of our utter sinfulness, and guiltiness, and helplessness; and which precedes our receiving that kingdom of God, which, our Lord observes, is

673

'within us'; and a faith, whereby we receive that kingdom, even 'righteousness, and peace, and joy in the Holy Ghost.'

3. But, notwithstanding this, there is also a repentance and a faith (taking the words in another sense, a sense not 'quite the same, nor yet entirely different) which are requisite after we have 'believed the gospel'; yea, and in every subsequent stage of our Christian course, or we cannot 'run the race which is set before us.' And this repentance and faith are full as necessary, in order to our *continuance* and *growth* in grace, as the former faith and repentance were, in order to our *entering* into the kingdom of God.

But in what sense are we to repent and believe, after we are justified? This is an important question, and worthy of being considered with the utmost attention.

I. And, first, in what sense are we to repent?

1. Repentance frequently means an inward change, a change of mind from sin to holiness. But we now speak of it in a quite different sense, as it is one kind of self-knowledge, the knowing ourselves sinners, yea, guilty, helpless sinners, even though we know we are children of God.

2. Indeed when we first know this; when we first find redemption in the blood of Jesus; when the love of God is first shed abroad in our hearts, and His kingdom set up therein; it is natural to suppose that we are no longer sinners, that all our sins are not only covered but destroyed.

As we do not then feel any evil in our hearts, we readily imagine none is there. Nay, some well-meaning men have imagined this not only at that time, but ever after; having persuaded themselves, that when they were justified, they were entirely sanctified: yea, they have laid it down as a general rule, in spite of Scripture, reason, and experience. These sincerely believe, and earnestly maintain, that all sin is destroyed when we are justified; and that there is no sin in the heart of a believer; but that it is altogether clean from that moment. But though we readily acknowledge, 'he that believeth is born of God,' and 'he that is born of God doth not commit sin'; yet we cannot allow that he does not *feel* it within: it does not *reign*, but it does remain. And a conviction of the sin which *remains* in our heart, is one great branch of the repentance we are now speaking of.

3. For it is seldom long before he who imagined all sin was gone, feels there is still *pride* in his heart. He is convinced both that in many respects he has thought of himself more highly than he ought to think, and that he has taken to himself the praise of something he had received, and gloried in it as though he had not received it; and yet he knows he is in the favour of God. He cannot, and ought not to, 'cast away his confidence.' 'The Spirit' still 'witnesses with' his 'spirit, that he is a child of God.'

4. Nor is it long before he feels *self-will* in his heart; even a will contrary to the will of God. A will every man must inevitably have, as long as he has an understanding. This is an essential part of human nature, indeed of the nature of every intelligent being. Our blessed Lord Himself had a will as a man; otherwise He had not been a man. But His human will was invariably subject to the will of His Father. At all times, and on all occasions, even in the deepest affliction, He could say, 'Not as I will, but as Thou wilt.' But this is not the case at all times, even with a true believer in Christ. He frequently finds his will more or less exalting itself against the will of God. He wills something, because it is pleasing to nature, which is not pleasing to God; and he nills (is averse from) something, because it is painful to nature, which is the will of God concerning him. Indeed, suppose he continues in the faith, he fights against it with all his might: but this very thing implies that it really exists, and that he is conscious of it.

5. Now self-will, as well as pride, is a species of *idolatry*; and both are directly contrary to the love of God. The same observation may be made concerning the *love of the world*.

But this likewise even true believers are liable to feel in themselves; and every one of them does feel it, more or less, sooner or later, in one branch or another. It is true, when he first 'passes from death unto life,' he desires nothing more but God. He can truly say, 'All my desire is unto Thee, and unto the remembrance of Thy name': 'Whom have I in heaven but Thee? and there is none upon earth that I desire beside Thee.' But it is not so always. In process of time he will feel again, though perhaps only for a few moments, either 'the desire of the flesh,' or 'the desire of the eye,' or 'the pride of life.' Nay, if he does not continually watch and pray, he may find *lust* reviving; yea, and thrusting sore at him that he may fall, till he has scarce any strength left in him. He may feel the assaults of *inordinate* affection; yea, a strong propensity to 'love the creature more than the Creator'; whether it be a child, a parent, a husband, or wife, or 'the friend that is as his own soul.' He may feel, in a thousand various ways, a desire of earthly things or pleasures. In the same proportion he will forget God, not seeking his happiness in Him, and consequently being a 'lover of pleasure more than a lover of God.'

6. If he does not keep himself every moment, he will again feel the *desire of the eye;* the desire of gratifying his imagination with something great or beautiful, or uncommon. In how many ways does this desire assault the soul! Perhaps with regard to the poorest trifles, such as dress, or furniture; things never designed to satisfy the appetite of an immortal spirit. Yet, how natural is it for us, even after we have 'tasted of the powers of the world to come,' to sink again into these foolish, low desires of things that perish in the using! How hard is it, even for those who know in whom they have believed, to conquer but one branch of the desire of the eye, curiosity; constantly to trample it under their feet; to desire nothing merely because it is new!

7. And how hard is it even for the children of God wholly to conquer the *pride of life*! St. John seems to mean by this nearly the same with what the world terms 'the sense of honour.' This is no other than a desire of, and delight in, 'the honour that cometh of men'; a desire and love of praise; and, which is always joined with it, a proportionable *fear of dispraise*. Nearly allied to this is *evil shame*; the being ashamed of that wherein we ought to glory. And this is seldom divided from the *fear of man,* which brings a thousand snares upon the soul. Now where is he, even among those that seem strong in the faith, who does not find in himself a degree of all these evil tempers? So that even these are but in part 'crucified to the world'; for the evil root still remains in their heart.

8. And do we not feel other tempers, which are as contrary to the love of our neighbour as these are to the love of God? The love of our neighbour 'thinketh no evil.' Do not we find anything of the kind? Do we never find any *jealousies,* any *evil surmisings,* any groundless or unreasonable suspicions? 'He that is clear in these respects, let him cast the first stone at his neighbour. Who

does not sometimes feel other tempers or inward motions, which he knows are contrary to brotherly love? If nothing of *malice, hatred,* or *bitterness,* is there no touch of *envy*; particularly toward those who enjoy some real or supposed good, which we desire, but cannot attain? Do we never find any degree of *resentment,* when we are injured or affronted; especially by those whom we peculiarly loved, and whom we had most laboured to help or oblige? Does injustice or ingratitude never excite in us any desire of revenge? any desire of returning evil for evil, instead of 'overcoming evil with good'? This also shows, how much is still in our heart, which is contrary to the love of our neighbour.

9. *Covetousness,* in every kind and degree, is certainly as contrary to this as to the love of God whether Φιλαργυρια, *the love of money,* which is too frequently 'the root of all evil'; or πλεονεξια, literally, a desire of *having more,* or increasing in substance. And how few, even of the real children of God, are entirely free from both! Indeed one great man, Martin Luther, used to say, he 'never had any covetousness in him' (not only in his converted state, but) 'ever since he was born.' But, if so, I would not scruple to say, he was the only man born of a woman (except Him that was God as well as man), who had not, who was born without it. Nay, I believe, never was any one born of God, that lived any considerable time after, who did not feel more or less of it many times, especially in the latter sense. We may therefore set it down as an undoubted truth, that covetousness, together with pride, and self-will, and anger, remain in the hearts even of them that are justified.

10. It is their experiencing this, which has inclined so many serious persons to understand the latter part of the seventh chapter to the Romans, not of them that are 'under the law,' that are convinced of sin, which is undoubtedly the meaning of the Apostle, but of them that are 'under grace'; that are 'justified freely through the redemption that is in Christ.' And it is most certain, they are thus far right,—there does still *remain,* even in them that are justified, a *mind which is in some measure carnal* (so the Apostle tells even the believers at Corinth, 'Ye are carnal'); an *heart bent to backsliding,* still ever ready to 'depart from the living God'; a propensity to pride, self-will, anger, revenge, love of the world, yea, and all evil: a root of bitterness, which, if the

restraint were taken off for a moment, would instantly spring up; yea, such a depth of corruption, as, without clear light from God, we cannot possibly conceive. And a conviction of all this sin *remaining* in *their hearts* is the repentance which belongs to them that are justified.

11. But we should likewise be convinced, that as sin remains in our hearts, so it *cleaves* to all our words and actions. Indeed it is to be feared, that many of our words are more than mixed with sin; that they are sinful altogether; for such undoubtedly is all *uncharitable conversation*; all which does not spring from brotherly love; all which does not agree with that golden rule, 'What ye would that others should do to you, even so do unto them.' Of this kind is all backbiting, all tale-bearing, all whispering, all evil-speaking, that is, repeating the faults of absent persons; for none would have others repeat his faults when he is absent. Now how few are there, even among believers, who are in no degree guilty of this; who steadily observe the good old rule, 'Of the dead and the absent, nothing but good!' And suppose they do, do they likewise abstain from *unprofitable conversation*? Yet all this is unquestionably sinful, and 'grieves the Holy Spirit of God': yea, and 'for every idle word that men shall speak, they shall give an account in the day of judgement.'

12. But let it be supposed, that they continually 'watch and pray,' and so do 'not enter into' this 'temptation'; that they constantly set a watch before their mouth, and keep the door of their lips; suppose they exercise themselves herein, that *all* their 'conversation may be in grace, seasoned with salt, and meet to minister grace to the hearers': yet do they not daily slide into useless discourse, notwithstanding all their caution? And even when they endeavour to speak for God, are their words pure, free from unholy mixtures? Do they find nothing wrong in their very *intention*? Do they speak merely to please God, and not partly to please themselves? Is it wholly to do the will of God, and not their own will also? Or, if they begin with a single eye, do they go on 'looking unto Jesus,' and talking with Him all the time they are talking with their neighbour? When they are reproving sin, do they feel no anger or unkind temper to the sinner? When they are instructing the ignorant, do they not find any pride, any self-preference? When they are comforting the afflicted, or

provoking one another to love and to good works, do they never perceive any inward self-commendation: '*Now you have spoke well*'? Or any vanity—a desire that others should think so, and esteem them on the account? In some or all of these respects, how much sin cleaves to the best *conversation* even of believers! The conviction of which is another branch of the repentance which belongs to them that are justified.

13. And how much sin, if their conscience is thoroughly awake, may they find cleaving to *their actions* also! Nay, are there not many of these, which, though they are such as the world would not condemn, yet cannot be commended, no, nor excused, if we judge by the Word of God? Are there not many of their actions which, they themselves know, are not to the glory of God? many, wherein they did not even aim at this; which were not undertaken with an eye to God? And of those that were, are there not many, wherein their eye is not singly fixed on God—wherein they are doing their own will, at least as much as His; and seeking to please themselves as much, if not more, than to please God? And while they are endeavouring to do good to their neighbour, do they not feel wrong tempers of various kinds? Hence their good actions, so called, are far from being strictly such; being polluted with such a mixture of evil: such are their works of *mercy*. And is there not the same mixture in their works of *piety*? While they are hearing the word which is able to save their souls, do they not frequently find such thoughts as make them afraid lest it should turn to their condemnation, rather than their salvation? Is it not often the same case, while they are endeavouring to offer up their prayers to God, whether in public or private? Nay, while they are engaged in the most solemn service, even while they are at the table of the Lord, what manner of thoughts arise in them! Are not their hearts sometimes wandering to the ends of the earth; sometimes filled with such imaginations, as make them fear lest all their sacrifice should be an abomination to the Lord? So that they are now more ashamed of their best duties, than they were once of their worst sins.

14. Again: how many *sins of omission* are they chargeable with! We know the words of the Apostle: 'To him that knoweth to do good, and doeth it not, to him it is sin.' But do they not know a thousand instances, wherein they might have done good, to

enemies, to strangers, to their brethren, either with regard to their bodies or their souls, and they did it not? How many omissions have they been guilty of, in their duty toward God! How many opportunities of communicating, of hearing His word, of public or private prayer, have they neglected! So great reason had even that holy man, Archbishop Usher, after all his labours for God, to cry out almost with his dying breath, 'Lord, forgive me my sins of omission!'

15. But besides these outward omissions, may they not find in themselves *inward defects* without number? defects of every kind: they have not the love, the fear, the confidence they ought to have, toward God. They have not the love which is due to their neighbour, to every child of man; no, nor even that which is due to their brethren, to every child of God, whether those that are at a distance from them, or those with whom they are immediately connected. They have no holy temper in the degree they ought; they are defective in everything,—in a deep consciousness of which they are ready to cry out, with M. De Renty, 'I am a ground all overrun with thorns'; or, with Job, 'I am vile: I abhor myself, and repent as in dust and ashes.'

16. A conviction of their *guiltiness* is another branch of that repentance which belongs to the children of God. But this is cautiously to be understood, and in a peculiar sense. For it is certain, 'there is no condemnation to them that are in Christ Jesus,' that believe in Him, and, in the power of that faith, 'walk not after the flesh, but after the Spirit.' Yet can they no more bear the *strict justice* of God now, than before they believed. This pronounces them to be still *worthy of death,* on all the preceding accounts. And it would absolutely condemn them thereto, were it not for the atoning blood. Therefore they are thoroughly convinced, that they still deserve punishment, although it is hereby turned aside from them. But here there are extremes on one hand and on the other, and few steer clear of them. Most men strike on one or the other, either thinking themselves condemned when they are not, or thinking they *deserve* to be acquitted. Nay, the truth lies between: they still *deserve,* strictly speaking, only the damnation of hell. But what they deserve does not come upon them, because they 'have an Advocate with the Father.' His life, and death, and intercession still interpose between them and condemnation.

17. A conviction of their *utter helplessness* is yet another branch of this repentance. I mean hereby two things: first, that they are no more able now *of themselves* to think one good thought, to form one good desire, to speak one good word, or do one good work, than before they were justified; that they have still no kind or degree of strength *of their own*; no power either to do good, or resist evil; no ability to conquer or even withstand the world the devil, or their own evil nature. They can, it is certain, do all these things; but it is not by their own strength. They have power to overcome all these enemies; for 'sin hath no more dominion over them'; but it is not from nature, either in whole or in part; it is the *mere* gift of God: nor is it given all at once, as if they had a stock laid up for many years; but from moment to moment.

18. By this helplessness I mean secondly, an absolute inability to deliver ourselves from that guiltiness or desert of punishment whereof we are still conscious; yea, and an inability to remove, by all the grace we have (to say nothing of our natural powers), either the pride, self-will, love of the world, anger, and general proneness to depart from God, which we experimentally know to *remain* in the heart, even of them that are regenerate; or the evil which, in spite of all our endeavours, cleaves to all our words and actions. Add to this, an utter inability wholly to avoid uncharitable, and, much more, unprofitable, conversation: and an inability to avoid sins of omission, or to supply the numberless defects we are convinced of; especially the want of love, and other right tempers both to God and man.

19. If any man is not satisfied of this, if any believes that whoever is justified is able to remove these sins out of his heart and life, let him make the experiment. Let him try whether, by the grace he has already received, he can expel pride, self-will, or inbred sin in general. Let him try whether he can cleanse his words and actions from all mixture of evil; whether he can avoid all uncharitable and unprofitable conversation, with all the sins of omission; and, lastly, whether he can supply the numberless defects which he still finds in himself. Let him not be discouraged by one or two experiments, but repeat the trial again and again; and the longer he tries, the more deeply will he be convinced of his utter helplessness in all these respects.

20. Indeed this is so evident a truth, that wellnigh all the children of God, scattered abroad, however they differ in other

points, yet generally agree in this: that although we may, 'by the Spirit, mortify the deeds of the body,' resist and conquer both outward and inward sin: although we may *weaken* our enemies day by day; yet we cannot *drive them out.* By all the grace which is given at justification we cannot extirpate them. Though we watch and pray ever so much, we cannot wholly cleanse either our hearts or hands. Most sure we cannot till it shall please our Lord to speak to our hearts again, to speak the second time 'Be clean'; and then only the leprosy is cleansed. Then only the evil root, the carnal mind, is destroyed; and inbred sin subsists no more. But if there be no such second change, if there be no instantaneous deliverance after justification, if there be *none but a* gradual work of God (that there is a gradual work none denies), then we must be content, as well as we can to remain full of sin till death; and, if so, we must remain guilty till death, continually *deserving punishment.* For it is impossible the guilt, or desert of punishment, should be removed from us, as long as all this sin remains in our heart, and cleaves to our words and actions. Nay, in rigorous justice, all we think, and speak, and act, continually increases it.

II. 1. In this sense we are to *repent,* after we are justified. And till we do so, we can go no farther. For, till we are sensible of our disease, it admits of no cure. But, supposing we do thus repent, then are we called to 'believe the gospel.'

2. And this also is to be understood in a peculiar sense, different from that wherein we believed in order to justification. Believe the glad tidings of great salvation, which God hath prepared for all people. Believe that He who is 'the brightness of His Father's glory, the express image of His person,' is 'able to save unto the uttermost all that come unto God through Him.' He is able to save you from all the sin that still remains in your heart. He is able to save you from all the sin that cleaves to all your words and actions. He is able to save you from sins of omission, and to supply whatever is wanting in you. It is true, this is impossible with man; but with God-Man all things are possible. For what can be too hard for Him who hath 'all power in heaven and in earth'? Indeed, His bare power to do this is not a sufficient foundation for our faith that He will do it, that He will thus exert His power, unless He hath promised it. But this

He has done: He has promised it over an over, in the strongest terms. He has given us these 'exceeding great and precious promises,' both in the Old and the New Testament. So we read in the law in the most ancient part of the oracles of God, 'The Lord thy God will circumcise thy heart and the heart of thy seed, to love the Lord thy God with all thy heart, and with all thy soul' (Deut. xxx. 6). So in the Psalms, 'He shall redeem Israel,' the Israel of God, 'from all his sins.' So in the Prophet, 'Then will I sprinkle clean water upon you, and ye shall be clean: from all your filthiness, and from all your idols, will I cleanse you. And I will put My Spirit within you, and ye shall keep My judgements, and do them. I will also save you from all your uncleannesses' (Ezek. xxxvi. 25, &c.). So likewise in the New Testament, 'Blessed be the Lord God of Israel; for He hath visited and redeemed His people, and hath raised up an horn of salvation for us . . . to perform the oath which He sware to our father Abraham, that He would grant unto us, that we being delivered out of the hands of our enemies should serve Him without fear, in holiness and righteousness before Him, all the days of our life' (Luke i. 68, &c.).

3. You have therefore good reason to believe, He is not only able, but willing to do this; to cleanse you from all your filthiness of flesh and spirit; to 'save you from all your uncleannesses.' This is the thing which you now long for; this is the faith which you now particularly need, namely, that the Great Physician, the Lover of my soul, is willing to make me clean. But is He willing to do this to-morrow, or to-day?

Let Him answer for Himself: 'To-day, if ye will hear' My 'voice, harden not your hearts.' If you put it off till tomorrow you harden your hearts; you refuse to hear His voice. Believe, therefore, that He is willing to save you to-day. He is willing to save you *now*. 'Behold, now is the accepted time.' He now saith, 'Be thou clean!' Only believe, and You also will immediately find, 'all things are possible to him that believeth.'

4. Continue to believe in Him that loved thee, and gave Himself for thee; that bore all thy sins in His own body on the tree; and He saveth thee from all condemnation, by His blood continually applied. Thus it is that we continue in a justified state. And when we go on 'from faith to faith, when we have faith to be cleansed from indwelling sin, to be saved from all our

uncleannesses, we are likewise saved from all that *guilt,* that *desert* of punishment, which we felt before. So that then we may say, not only,

> Every moment, Lord, I *want*
> The merit of Thy death;

but, likewise, in the full assurance of faith,

> Every moment, Lord, I *have*
> The merit of Thy death!

For, by that faith in His life, death, and intercession for us, renewed from moment to moment, we are every whit clean, and there is not only now no condemnation for us, but no such desert of punishment as was before, the Lord cleansing both our hearts and lives.

5. By the same faith we feel the power of Christ every moment resting upon us, whereby alone we are what we are; whereby we are enabled to continue in spiritual life, and without which, notwithstanding all our present holiness, we should be devils the next moment. But as long as we retain our faith in Him, we 'draw water out of the wells of salvation.' Leaning on our Beloved, even Christ in us the hope of glory, who dwelleth in our hearts by faith, who likewise is ever interceding for us at the right hand of God, we receive help from Him, to think and speak and act, what is acceptable in His sight. Thus does He 'prevent' them that believe, in all their 'doings, and further them with His continual help'; so that all their designs conversations, and actions are 'begun, continued, and ended in Him.' Thus doth He 'cleanse the thoughts of their hearts, by the inspiration of His Holy Spirit, that they may perfectly love Him, and worthily magnify His holy name.'

6. Thus it is, that in the children of God, repentance and faith exactly answer each other. By repentance we feel the sin remaining in our hearts, and cleaving to our words and actions: by faith, we receive the power of God in Christ, purifying our hearts, and cleansing our hands. By repentance, we are still sensible that we deserve punishment for all our tempers, and words, and actions: by faith, we are conscious that our Advocate with the Father is continually pleading for us and thereby

continually turning aside all condemnation and punishment from us. By repentance we have an abiding conviction that there is no help in us: by faith we receive not only mercy, 'but grace to help in' *every* 'time of need.' Repentance disclaims the very possibility of any other help: faith accepts all the help we stand in need of, from Him that hath all power in heaven and earth. Repentance says, 'Without Him I can do nothing': faith says, 'I can do all things through Christ strengthening me.' Through Him I can not only overcome, but expel, all the enemies of my soul. Through Him I can 'love the Lord my God with all my heart, mind, soul, and strength'; yea, and 'walk in holiness and righteousness before Him all the days of my life.'

III. 1. From what has been said we may easily learn the mischievousness of that opinion,—that we are *wholly* sanctified when we are justified; that our hearts are then cleansed from all sin. It is true, we are then delivered, as was observed before, from the dominion of outward sin; and, at the same time, the power of inward sin is so broken, that we need no longer follow or be led by it: but it is by no means true, that inward sin is then totally destroyed; that the root of pride, self-will, anger, love of the world, is then taken out of the heart; or that the carnal mind, and the heart bent to backsliding, are entirely extirpated. And to suppose the contrary is not, as some may think, an innocent harmless mistake. No: it does immense harm: it entirely blocks up the way to any farther change; for it is manifest, 'they that are whole need not a physician, but they that are sick.' If, therefore, we think we are quite made whole already, there is no room to seek any further healing. On this supposition it is absurd to expect a farther deliverance from sin, whether gradual or instantaneous.

2. On the contrary, a deep conviction that we are not yet whole; that our hearts are not fully purified; that there is yet in us a 'carnal mind,' which is still in its nature 'enmity against God'; that a whole body of sin remains in our heart, weakened indeed, but not destroyed; shows, beyond all possibility of doubt, the absolute necessity of a farther change. We allow, that at the very moment of justification, we are *born again*: in that instant we experience that inward change from 'darkness into marvellous light'; from the image of the brute and the devil, into the image

of God; from the earthly, sensual, devilish mind, to the mind which was in Christ Jesus. But are we then *entirely* changed? Are we *wholly* transformed into the image of Him that created us? Far from it: we still retain a depth of sin; and it is the consciousness of this which constrains us to groan, for a full deliverance, to Him that is mighty to save. Hence it is, that those believers who are not convinced of the deep corruption of their hearts, or but slightly, and, as it were, notionally convinced, have little concern about *entire sanctification.* They may possibly hold the opinion, that such a thing is to be, either at death, or some time they know not when, before it. But they have no great uneasiness for the want of it, and no great hunger or thirst after it. They cannot, until they know themselves better, until they repent in the sense above described, until God unveils the inbred monster's face, and shows them the real state of their souls. Then only, when they feel the burden, will they groan for deliverance from it. Then, and not till then, will they cry out, in the agony of their soul,

> Break off the yoke of inbred sin,
> And fully set my spirit free I
> I cannot rest till pure within,
> Till I am wholly lost in Thee.

3. We may learn from hence, secondly, that a deep conviction of our *demerit*, after we are accepted (which in one sense may be termed guilt), is absolutely necessary, in order to our seeing the true value of the atoning blood; in order to our feeling that we need this as much, after we are justified, as ever we did before. Without this conviction, we cannot but account the blood of the covenant *as a common thing*, something of which we have not now any great need, seeing all our past sins are blotted out. Yea, but if both our hearts and lives are thus unclean, there is a kind of guilt which we are contracting every moment, and which, of consequence, would every moment expose us to fresh condemnation, but that

> He ever lives above,
>   For us to intercede,
> His all-atoning love,
>   His precious blood, to plead.

It is this repentance and the faith intimately connected with it, which are expressed in those strong lines,—

> I sin in every breath I draw,
> Nor do Thy will, nor keep Thy law
>   On earth. as angels do above:
> But still the fountain open stands,
> Washes my feet, my heart, my hands,
>   Till I am perfected in love.

4. We may observe, thirdly, a deep conviction of our utter *helplessness*, of our total inability to retain anything we have received, much more to deliver ourselves from the world of iniquity remaining both in our hearts and lives, teaches us truly to live upon Christ by faith, not only as our Priest, but as our King. Hereby we are brought to 'magnify Him,' indeed; to 'give Him all the glory of His grace'; to 'make Him a whole Christ, an entire Saviour; and truly to set the crown upon His head.' These excellent words, as they have frequently been used, have little or no meaning; but they are fulfilled in a strong and deep sense, when we thus, as it were, go out of ourselves, in order to be swallowed up in Him; when we sink into nothing, that He may be all in all. Then, His almighty grace having abolished 'every high thing which exalted itself against Him,' every temper, and thought, and word, and work 'is brought to the obedience of Christ.'

LONDONDERRY, *April* 24, 1767.

SERMON XLVIII

THE GREAT ASSIZE

PREACHED AT THE ASSIZES HELD BEFORE THE HONOUR-
ABLE SIR EDWARD CLIVE, KNIGHT, ONE OF THE JUDGES
OF HIS MAJESTY'S COURT OF COMMON PLEAS, IN ST.
PAUL'S CHURCH, BEDFORD, ON FRIDAY, MARCH 10, 1758;
PUBLISHED AT THE REQUEST OF WILLIAM COLE, ESQ.,
HIGH SHERIFF OF THE COUNTY, AND OTHERS.

This sermon was added in the 1771 edition partly because of the unique occasion of its delivery, partly because there was no sermon in the original forty-four on this subject. Wesley says of it in his *Journal* for September 1, 1778, 'I cannot write a better [sermon] on the Great Assize than I did twenty years ago.' It was customary for the judges of Assize to attend a service in the parish church of the town in which they were sitting, in all the splendour of their scarlet and ermine, with their trumpeters, javelin-men, and other officers of the Court in attendance; and it was one of the duties of the High Sheriff of the County to make arrangements for the preaching of the sermon. Mr. William Cole, who was High Sheriff of Bedfordshire at this time, was a friend of Wesley, and was his host in November 1759. He lived at Sundon, a village a little to the east of the main road from Luton to Bedford, about five miles north of Luton. He built the first Methodist preaching-house in Luton. Probably he made the arrangements for the Assize sermon when Wesley was at Bedford in November 1757; and on Monday, February 27, Wesley records, 'Having a sermon to write against the Assizes at Bedford, I retired for a few days to Lewisham'—doubtless to the house of Mr. Ebenezer Blackwell. He left London on Monday, March 6, at seven in the morning, and reached Mr. Cole's house at Sundon by three in the afternoon. On the Thursday he rode to Bedford, expecting to have to preach that day; but for some reason, probably because the cases at the previous Assize town had taken more time than was anticipated, the service was postponed to the following day. The service was held in the forenoon at St. Paul's Church, one of the chief architectural ornaments of the town. It stands on the north side of the River Ouse, and has a fine tower and octagonal spire. The old stone pulpit from which Wesley preached is still preserved in the south aisle, and a photograph of it and the church may be seen in the Standard edition of the *Journal,* vol. iv. p. 403. The *Journal* records, 'The congregation at St. Paul's was very large and very attentive. The judge, immediately after sermon, sent me an invitation to dine with him; but having no time I was obliged to send my excuse, and set out between one and two.' He had to reach Epworth for the Sunday, and got to Stilton, about thirty miles, by seven. Next morning he started between four and five, and through frost and flood covered the ninety miles to Epworth by ten that night. He says, 'I was little more tired than when I rose in the morning !'—tough, wiry little man that he was!

The judge on this occasion was Sir Edward Clive, who had been made a Judge of the Common Pleas and knighted in 1753. He was just a year younger than John Wesley, and died in 1771. A caricature of him may be found in Hogarth's plate 'The Bench,' published in this very year, 1758. He is sitting between the Lord Chief Justice Willes and Mr. Justice Bathurst, who has fallen asleep. He is represented with a small head almost lost in his full-bottomed wig, a long thin nose, and a nut-cracker chin. The sermon was published separately by Trye in the same year at the request of the High Sheriff and others, and went through some ten editions in Wesley's lifetime. The Rev. Richard Green calls it 'a model sermon,' and says, 'It is well-formed, plain, practical, earnest; the statements are all supported by apt scripture, and the truth faithfully applied to the conscience.' The title 'The Great Assize' was a familiar name for the Last Judgement; it is found as early as 1340 in Hampole's *Prick of Conscience,* 5514, and several other instances are given in the *Oxford Dictionary,* s.v. 'Assize.' The preliminary note, 'Preached at the Assizes,' &c, in the modern editions is from the title-page of the second edition, also published in London by Trye; it appears in an abbreviated form in the 1771 edition, without the last clause 'Published at the request,' &c.

Two points in the sermon call for criticism in view of recent investigations into the eschatological teaching of the New Testament. First, Wesley identifies without discussion the Day of Jehovah of the Old Testament prophets and the Jewish Apocalyptic writers with the Day of our Lord's second coming, the general resurrection, and the last Judgement, of the New Testament documents; and he uses indiscriminately passages from all these sources to give detail an picturesqueness to his picture. Moreover he adopts the most literal interpretation of them all, the only points at which he baulks being the length of the Day of Judgement, which he thinks 'may not improbably comprise several thousand years'; and the opening of the books, which he says is 'a figurative expression.' It can hardly be doubted that our Lord's teaching was largely influenced by the Old Testament and Apocalyptic conception, especially in His predictions about the destruction of Jerusalem and the Jewish polity; but He added to it the idea of an individual as well as a national judgement, and extended its scope to the whole world.

In the second place Wesley adopts the view that the Last Judgement will take place at some definite time in the future history of the world, when the lives of all men will be reviewed and sentence pronounced upon them. This is certainly the obvious meaning of the teaching of the books of the New Testament which were written before the destruction of Jerusalem by the Romans; but when that tremendous catastrophe had taken place, and it became clear that the General Judgement and the End of the Age had not come, we find in the writings of St. John a new strain of teaching, implying that the Judgement is really continuous and is now going on. Thus 'He that believeth on Him is not judged; he that believeth not hath been judged already. . . . And this is the judgement, that the light is come into the world, and men loved the darkness rather than the light; for their works were evil' (John iii. 18). Again, 'Verily, verily I say unto you, he that heareth My word and believeth Him that sent Me, hath eternal life, and cometh not into judgement. . . . The hour cometh, and now is, when the dead shall hear the voice of the Son of God; and they that hear shall live' (John v. 24). Again, 'For judgement came I into this world' (John ix. 39). Again, 'Now is the judgement of this world' (John xii. 31). At the same time St. John also speaks of a future general resurrection, of 'the last day' and 'the day of judgement.' It seems clear (1) that our Lord spoke in terms of the current national belief of His time, which was derived from the Old Testament prophets and the Apocalypses of the Persian and Greek periods, the time 'between the Books'; (2) that He used the pictorial rather than the abstract method of conveying the truth to His hearers. We may thus safely say that the essential elements of His teaching are (1) that there will be a universal judgement of all men; (2) that He Himself will be the Judge; (3) that the standard of judgement will be His own life and teaching, as far as those who have had the opportunity of knowing it are concerned; (4) that for the heathen the standard will be their own conscience; (5) that the issues of the judgement are decided in this life, and (6) that the decision will be final. But as to the extent to which His representations of the Last Judgement are to be taken as expressing literal physical fact, we shall be wisest if we confess our ignorance and our inability to reach any dogmatic conclusion.

As to the text, the better attested reading is, 'We shall all stand before the judgement seat of God'; indeed, this text is used by some of the Fathers to prove the divinity of Christ, because it is plain from many passages that He will be the Judge; and the Judge is here called God.

We shall all stand before the judgement-seat of Christ.—ROM. xiv. 10.

1. How many circumstances concur to raise the awfulness of the present solemnity!—The general *concourse* of people of every age, sex, rank, and condition of life, willingly or unwillingly gathered together, not only from the neighbouring, but from distant, parts; *criminals,* speedily to be brought forth and having no way to escape; *officers,* waiting in their various posts, to execute the orders which shall be given; and the

representative of our gracious *Sovereign,* whom we so highly reverence and honour. The *occasion* likewise of this assembly adds not a little to the solemnity of it: to hear and determine causes of every kind, some of which are of the most important nature; on which depends no less than life or death, death that uncovers the face of eternity! It was, doubtless, in order to increase the serious sense of these things, and not in the minds of the vulgar only that the wisdom of our forefathers did not disdain to appoint even several minute circumstances of this solemnity. For these also, by means of the eye or ear, may more deeply affect the heart: and when viewed in this light, trumpets, staves, apparel, are no longer trifling or insignificant, but subservient, in their kind and degree, to the most valuable ends of society.

2. But, as awful as this solemnity is, one far more awful is at hand. For yet a little while, and 'we shall all stand before the judgement-seat of Christ.' 'For, as I live, saith the Lord, every knee shall bow to Me, and every tongue shall confess to God.' And in that day, 'every one of us shall give account of himself to God.'

3. Had all men a deep sense of this, how effectually would it secure the interests of society! For what more forcible motive can be conceived to the practice of genuine morality? to a steady pursuit of solid virtue? an uniform walking in justice, mercy, and truth? What could strengthen our hands in all that is good, and deter us from all evil, like a strong conviction of this, 'The Judge standeth at the door'; and we are shortly to stand before Him?

4. It may not therefore be improper, or unsuitable to the design of the present assembly, to consider,—

   I. THE CHIEF CIRCUMSTANCES WHICH WILL PRECEDE OUR
      STANDING BEFORE THE JUDGEMENT-SEAT OF CHRIST;
  II. THE JUDGEMENT ITSELF; AND,
III. A FEW OF THE CIRCUMSTANCES WHICH WILL FOLLOW IT.

1. Let us, in the first place, consider the chief circumstances which will precede our standing before the judgement-seat of Christ. And, first, God will show 'signs in the earth beneath' (Acts ii. 19); particularly He will 'arise to shake terribly the earth.' 'The earth shall reel to and fro like a drunkard, and shall be removed like a cottage' (Isa. xxi v. 20). 'There shall be

earthquakes,' κατα τοπους (not in divers only, but) 'in *all* places'; not in one only, or a few, but in every part of the habitable world (Luke xxi. 11); even 'such as were not since men were upon the earth, so mighty earthquakes and so great.' In one of these 'every island shall flee away, and the mountains will not be found' (Rev. xvi. 20). Meantime all the waters of the terraqueous globe will feel the violence of those concussions; 'the sea and waves roaring' (Luke xxi. 25), with such an agitation as had never been known before, since the hour that 'the fountains of the great deep were broken up,' to destroy the earth, which then 'stood out of the water and in the water.' The air will be all storm and tempest, full of dark vapours and 'pillars of smoke' (Joel ii. 30); resounding with thunder from pole to pole, and torn with ten thousand lightnings. But the commotion will not stop in the region of the air; 'the powers of heaven also shall be shaken. There shall be signs in the sun, and in the moon, and in the stars' (Luke xxi. 25, 26); those fixed, as well as those that move round them. 'The sun shall be turned into darkness, and the moon into blood, before the great and terrible day of the Lord come' (Joel ii. 31). 'The stars shall withdraw their shining' (Joel iii. 15), yea, and 'fall from heaven' (Rev. vi. 13), being thrown out of their orbits. And then shall be heard the universal *shout,* from all the companies of heaven, followed by the 'voice of the archangel,' proclaiming the approach of the Son of God and Man, 'and the trumpet of God,' sounding an alarm to all that sleep in the dust of the earth (1 Thess. iv. 16). In consequence of this, all the graves shall open, and the bodies of men arise. The sea also shall give up the dead which are therein (Rev. xx. 13), and every one shall rise with 'his own body': his own in substance, although so changed in its properties as we cannot now conceive. 'For this corruptible will' then 'put on incorruption, and this mortal put on immortality' (1 Cor. xv. 53). Yea, 'death and hades,' the invisible world, shall 'deliver up the dead that are in them' (Rev. xx. 13). So that all who ever lived and died, since God created man, shall be raised incorruptible and immortal.

2. At the same time, 'the Son of Man shall send forth His angels' over all the earth; 'and they shall gather His elect from the four winds, from one end of heaven to the other' (Matt. xxiv. 31). And the Lord Himself shall come with clouds, in His own

glory, and the glory of His Father, with ten thousand of His saints, even myriads of angels, and shall sit upon the throne of His glory. 'And before Him shall be gathered all nations; and He shall separate them one from another, and shall set the sheep,' the good, 'on His right hand, and the goats,' the wicked, 'upon the left' (Matt. xxv. 31, &c.). Concerning this general assembly it is, that the beloved disciple speaks thus: 'I saw the dead,' all that had been dead, 'small and great, stand before God; and the books were opened' (a figurative expression, plainly referring to the manner of proceeding among men), 'and the dead were judged out of those things which were written in the books, according to their works' (Rev. xx. 12).

II. These are the chief circumstances which are recorded in the oracles of old as preceding the general judgement. We are, secondly, to consider the judgement itself, so far as it hath pleased God to reveal it.

1. The person by whom God will judge the world, is His only-begotten Son, whose 'goings forth are from everlasting'; 'who is God over all, blessed for ever.' Unto Him, being 'the outbeaming of His Father's glory, the express image of His person' (Heb. i. 3), the Father 'hath committed all judgement, because He is the Son of Man' (John v. 22, 27); because, though He was 'in the form of God, and thought it not robbery to be equal with God, yet He emptied Himself, taking upon Him the form of a servant, being made in the likeness of men' (Phil. ii. 6, 7); yea, because, 'being found in fashion as a man, He humbled Himself' yet farther, 'becoming obedient unto death, even the death of the cross. Wherefore God hath highly exalted Him,' even in His human nature, and 'ordained Him,' as Man, to try the children of men, 'to be the Judge both of the quick and the dead'; both of those who shall be found alive at His coming, and of those who were before gathered to their fathers.

2. The time, termed by the prophet, 'the great and the terrible day,' is usually, in Scripture, styled *the day of the Lord*. The space from the creation of man upon the earth, to the end of all things, is *the day of the sons of men*; the time that is now passing over us is properly *our day*; when this is ended, *the day of the Lord* will begin. But who can say how long it will continue? 'With the Lord one day is as a thousand years, and a thousand years as one

day' (2 Pet. iii. 8). And from this very expression, some of the ancient fathers drew that inference, that, what is commonly called the day of judgement would be indeed a thousand years: and it seems they did not go beyond the truth; nay, probably they did not come up to it. For, if we consider the number of persons who are to be judged, and of actions which are to be inquired into, it does not appear that a thousand years will 'suffice for the transactions of that day; so that it may not improbably comprise several thousand years. But God shall reveal this also in its season.

3. With regard to the place where mankind will be judged, we have no explicit account in Scripture. An eminent writer (but not he alone; many have been of the same opinion) supposes it will be on earth, where the works were done, according to which they shall be judged; and that God will, in order thereto, employ the angels of His strength—

> To smooth and lengthen out the boundless space,
> And spread an area for all human race.

But perhaps it is more agreeable to our Lord's own account of His coming in the clouds, to suppose it will be above the earth, if not 'twice a planetary height.' And this supposition is not a little favoured by what St. Paul writes to the Thessalonians: 'The dead in Christ shall rise first. Then we who remain alive shall be caught up together with them in the clouds, to meet the Lord in the air' (1 Thess. iv. 16, 17). So that it seems most probable, the great white throne will be high exalted above the earth.

4. The persons to be judged, who can count, any more than the drops of rain, or the sands of the sea? 'I beheld,' saith St. John, 'a great multitude which no man can number, clothed with white robes, and palms in their hands.' How immense then must be the total multitude of all nations, and kindreds, and people, and tongues; of all that have sprung from the loins of Adam, since the world began, till time shall be no more! If we admit the common supposition, which seems no ways absurd, that the earth bears, at any one time, no less than four hundred millions of living souls, men, women, and children; what a congregation must all those generations make, who have succeeded each other for seven thousand years!

Great Xerxes' world in arms, proud Cannae's host,
They all are here; and here they all are lost.
Their numbers swell to be discern'd in vain;
Lost as a drop in the unbounded main.

Every man, every woman, every infant of days, that ever
breathed the vital air, will then hear the voice of the Son of God,
and start into life, and appear before Him. And this seems to be
the natural import of that expression, 'the dead, small and
great': all universally, all without exception, all of every age, sex,
or degree; all that ever lived and died, or underwent such a
change as will be equivalent with death. For long before that day,
the phantom of human greatness disappears, and sinks into
nothing. Even in the moment of death, that vanishes away. Who
is rich or great in the grave?

5. And every man shall there 'give an account of his own
works'; yea, a full and true account of all that he ever did while in
the body, whether it was good or evil. O what a scene will then be
disclosed, in the sight of angels and men!—while not the fabled
Rhadamanthus, but the Lord God Almighty, who knoweth all
things in heaven and in earth,—

> *Castigatque, auditque dolos; subigitque fateri*
> *Quae quis apud superos, furto laetatus inani,*
> *Distulit in seram commissa piacula mortem.*

Nor will all the actions alone of every child of man be then brought
to open view, but all their words; seeing 'every idle word which
men shall speak, they shall give account thereof in the day of
judgement' (Matt. xii. 36, 37); so that 'by thy words,' as well as
works, 'thou shalt be justified; and by thy words thou shalt be
condemned.' Will not God then bring to light every circumstance
also that accompanied every word or action, and if not altered the
nature, yet lessened or increased the goodness or badness, of
them? And how easy is this to Him who is 'about our bed, and
about our path, and spieth out all our ways'! We know 'the
darkness is no darkness to Him, but the night shineth as the day.'

6. Yea, He will bring to light, not the hidden works of
darkness only, but the very thoughts and intents of the heart.
And what marvel? For He 'searcheth the reins, and understandeth all our thoughts.' 'All things are naked and open to the eyes

of Him with whom we have to do.' 'Hell and destruction are before Him without a covering. How much more the hearts of the children of men!'

7. And in that day shall be discovered every inward working of every human soul; every appetite, passion, inclination, affection, with the various combinations of them, with every temper and disposition that constitute the whole complex character of each individual. So shall it be clearly and infallibly seen, who was righteous, and who unrighteous; and in what degree every action, or person, or character was either good or evil.

8. 'Then the King will say to them upon His right hand, Come, ye blessed of My Father. For I was hungry, and ye gave Me meat; thirsty, and ye gave Me drink: I was a stranger, and ye took Me in; naked, and ye clothed Me.' In like manner. all the good they did upon earth will be recited before men and angels; whatsoever they had done, either in word or deed, in the name, or for the sake, of the Lord Jesus. All their good desires, intentions, thoughts, all their holy dispositions, will also be then remembered; and it will appear that though they were unknown or forgotten among men, yet God noted them in His book. All their sufferings likewise for the name of Jesus, and for the testimony of a good conscience, will be displayed unto their praise from the righteous Judge, their honour before saints and angels, and the increase of that 'far more exceeding and eternal weight of glory.'

9. But will their evil deeds too (since, if we take in his whole life, there is not a man on earth who liveth and sinneth not), will these be remembered in that day, and mentioned in the great congregation? Many believe they will not; and ask, 'Would not this imply, that their sufferings were not at an end, even when life ended?—seeing they would still have sorrow, and shame, and confusion of face to endure.' They ask farther, 'How can this be reconciled with God's declaration by the Prophet, "If the wicked will turn from all his sins that he hath committed, and keep all My statutes, and do that which is lawful and right; all his transgressions that he hath committed, they shall not be once mentioned unto him"? (Ezek. xviii. 21, 22). How is it consistent with the promise which God has made to all who accept of the gospel covenant, "I will forgive their iniquities, and remember

their sin no more"? (Jer. xxxi. 34): or, as the Apostle expresses it, "I will be merciful to their unrighteousness, and their sins and iniquities will I remember no more"?' (Heb. viii. 12).

10. It may be answered, It is apparently and absolutely necessary, for the full display of the glory of God; for the clear and perfect manifestation of His wisdom, justice, power, and mercy, toward the heirs of salvation; that all the circumstances of their life should be placed in open view, together with all their tempers, and all the desires, thoughts, and intents of their hearts: otherwise, how would it appear out of what a depth of sin and misery the grace of God had delivered them? And, indeed, if the whole lives of all the children of men were not manifestly discovered, the whole amazing contexture of divine providence could not be manifested; nor should we yet be able, in a thousand instances, 'to justify the ways of God to man.' Unless our Lord's words were fulfilled in their utmost sense, without any restriction or limitation, 'There is nothing covered, that shall not be revealed; or hid, that shall not be known' (Matt. x. 26); abundance of God's dispensations under the sun would still appear without their reasons. And then only when God hath brought to light all the hidden things of darkness, whosoever were the actors therein, will it be seen that wise and good were all His ways; that He saw through the thick cloud, and governed all things by the wise counsel of His own will; that nothing was left to chance or the caprice of men, but God disposed all strongly and sweetly, and wrought all into one connected chain of justice, mercy, and truth.

11. And in the discovery of the divine perfections, the righteous will rejoice with joy unspeakable; far from feeling any painful sorrow or shame, for any of those past transgressions which were long since blotted out as a cloud, washed away by the blood of the Lamb. It will be abundantly sufficient for them, that all the transgressions which they had committed shall not be once mentioned unto them to their disadvantage; that their sins, and transgressions, and iniquities shall be remembered no more to their condemnation. This is the plain meaning of the promise; and this all the children of God shall find true, to their everlasting comfort.

12. After the righteous are judged, the King will turn to them upon His left hand; and they shall also be judged, every man

according to his works. But not only their outward works will be brought into the account, but all the evil words which they have ever spoken; yea, all the evil desires, affections, tempers, which have, or have had, a place in their souls and all the evil thoughts or designs which were ever cherished in their hearts. The joyful sentence of acquittal will then be pronounced upon those upon the right hand; the dreadful sentence of condemnation upon those on the left; both of which must remain fixed and unmovable as the throne of God.

III. 1. We may, in the third place, consider a few of the circumstances which will follow the general judgement. And the first is the execution of the sentence pronounced on the evil and on the good: 'These shall go away into eternal punishment, and the righteous into life eternal.' It should be observed, it is the very same word which is used, both in the former and the latter clause. It follows, that either the punishment lasts for ever, or the reward too will come to an end:—no, never, unless God could come to an end, or His mercy and truth could fail. 'Then shall the righteous shine forth as the sun in the kingdom of their Father,' 'and shall drink of those rivers of pleasure which are at God's right hand for evermore.' But here all description falls short; all human language fails! Only one who is caught up into the third heaven can have a just conception of it. But even such a one cannot express what he hath seen: these things it is not possible for man to utter.

The wicked, meantime, shall be turned into hell, even all the people that forget God. They will be 'punished with everlasting destruction from the presence of the Lord, and from the glory of His power.' They will be 'cast into the lake of fire burning with brimstone,' originally 'prepared for the devil and his angels'; where they will gnaw their tongues for anguish and pain; they will curse God and look upward. There the dogs of hell—pride, malice, revenge, rage, horror, despair—continually devour them. There 'they have no rest, day or night, but the smoke of their torment ascendeth for ever and ever'! For 'their worm dieth not, and the fire is not quenched.'

2. Then the heavens will be shrivelled up as a parchment scroll, and pass away with a great noise: they will 'flee from the face of Him that sitteth on the throne, and there will be found no

place for them' (Rev. xx. 11). The very manner of their passing away is disclosed to us by the Apostle Peter: 'In the day of God, the heavens, being on fire, shall be dissolved' (2 Pet. iii. 12). The whole beautiful fabric will be overthrown by that raging element, the connexion of all its parts destroyed, and every atom torn asunder from the others. By the same, 'the earth also, and the works that are therein, shall be burned up' (verse 10). The enormous works of nature, the everlasting hills, mountains that have defied the rage of time, and stood unmoved so many thousand years, will sink down in fiery ruin. How much less will the works of art, though of the most durable kind, the utmost efforts of human industry—tombs, pillars, triumphal arches, castles, pyramids—be able to withstand the flaming conqueror! All, all will die, perish, vanish away, like a dream when one awaketh!

3. It has indeed been imagined by some great and good men, that as it requires that same almighty power to annihilate things as to create; to speak into nothing or out of nothing; so no part of, no atom in, the universe, will be totally or finally destroyed. Rather, they suppose that, as the last operation of fire, which we have yet been able to observe, is to reduce into glass what, by a smaller force, it had reduced to ashes; so, in the day God hath ordained, the whole earth, if not the material heavens also, will undergo this change, after which the fire can have no farther power over them. And they believe this is intimated by that expression in the Revelation made to St. John: 'Before the throne there was a sea of glass, like unto crystal' (Rev. iv. 6). We cannot now either affirm or deny this; but we shall know hereafter.

4. If it be inquired by the scoffers, the minute philosophers, 'How can these things be? Whence should come such an immense quantity of fire as would consume the heavens and the whole terraqueous globe?' we would beg leave, first, to remind them, that this difficulty is not peculiar to the Christian system. The same opinion almost universally obtained among the *unbigoted* Heathens. So one of these celebrated *freethinkers* speaks, according to the generally received sentiment,—

> *Esse quoque in fatis reminiscitur, affore tempus,*
> *Quo mare, quo tellus, correptaque regia coeli*
> *Ardeat, et mundi moles operosa laboret.*

But, secondly, it is easy to answer, even from our slight and superficial acquaintance with natural things, that there are abundant magazines of fire ready prepared, and treasured up against the day of the Lord. How soon may a comet, commissioned by Him, travel down from the most distant parts of the universe! And were it to fix upon the earth in its return from the sun, when it is some thousand times hotter than a red-hot cannon ball, who does not see what must be the immediate consequence? But, not to ascend so high as the ethereal heavens, might not the same lightnings which 'give shine to the world,' if commanded by the Lord of nature, give ruin and utter destruction? Or, to go no farther than the globe itself; who knows what huge reservoirs of liquid fire are from age to age contained in the bowels of the earth? Aetna, Hecla, Vesuvius, and all the other volcanoes that belch out flames and coals of fire, what are they, but so ruany proofs and mouths of those fiery furnaces; and at the same time so many evidences that God hath in readiness wherewith to fulfil His word? Yea, were we to observe no more than the surface of the earth, and the things that surround us on every side, it is most certain (as a thousand experiments prove, beyond all possibility of denial) that we ourselves, our whole bodies, are full of fire, as well as everything round about us. Is it not easy to make this ethereal fire visible even to the naked eye, and to produce thereby the very same effects on combustible matter, which are produced by culinary fire? Needs there then any more than for God to unloose that secret chain, whereby this irresistible agent is now bound down, and lies quiescent in every particle of matter? And how soon would it tear the universal frame in pieces, and involve all in one common ruin!

5. There is one circumstance more which will follow the judgement, that deserves our serious consideration: 'We look,' says the Apostle, 'according to His promise for new heavens and a new earth, wherein dwelleth righteousness' (2 Pet. iii. 13). The promise stands in the prophecy of Isaiah: 'Behold, I create new heavens and a new earth: and the former shall not be remembered' (lsa. lxv. 17), so great shall the glory of the latter be! These St. John did behold in the visions of God. 'I saw,' saith he, 'a new heaven and a new earth; for the first heaven and the first earth were passed away' (Rev. xxi. 1). And only

righteousness dwelt therein: accordingly, he adds, 'And I heard a great voice from' the third 'heaven, saying, Behold, the tabernacle of God is with men and He will dwell with them, and they shall be His people, and God Himself shall be with them, and be their God' (xxi. 3). Of necessity, therefore, they will all be happy: 'God shall wipe away all tears from their eyes; and there shall be no more death, neither sorrow, nor crying, neither shall there be any more pain' (xxi. 4). 'There shall be no more curse; but they shall see His face' (xxii. 3, 4),—shall have the nearest access to, and thence the highest, resemblance of, Him. This is the strongest expression in the language of Scripture, to denote the most perfect happiness. 'And His name shall be on their foreheads'; they shall be openly acknowledged as God's own property, and His glorious nature shall most visibly shine forth in them. 'And there shall be no night there; and they need no candle, neither light of the sun; for the Lord God giveth them light: and they shall reign for ever and ever.'

IV. It remains only to apply the preceding considerations to all who are here before God. And are we not directly led so to do, by the present solemnity, which so naturally points us to that day, when the Lord will judge the world in righteousness? This, therefore, by reminding us of that more awful season, may furnish many lessons of instruction. A few of these I may be permitted just to touch on. May God write them on all our hearts!

1. And, first, how beautiful are the feet of those who are sent by the wise and gracious providence of God, to execute justice on earth, to defend the injured, and punish the wrongdoer! Are they not the ministers of God to us for good; the grand supporters of the public tranquillity; the patrons of innocence and virtue; the great security of all our temporal blessings? And does not every one of these represent, not only an earthly prince, but the Judge of the earth? Him whose 'name is written upon His thigh, King of kings, and Lord of lords'? O that all these sons of the right hand of the Most High may be as holy as He is holy! wise with the wisdom that sitteth by His throne, like Him who is the eternal Wisdom of the Father! no respecters of persons, as He is none; but rendering to every man according to his works; like Him inflexibly, inexorably just, though pitiful

and of tender mercy! So shall they be terrible indeed to them that do evil, as not bearing the sword in vain. So shall the laws of our land have their full use and due honour, and the throne of our King be still established in righteousness.

2. Ye truly honourable men, whom God and the King have commissioned, in a lower degree, to administer justice; may not ye be compared to those ministering spirits who will attend the judge coming in the clouds? May you, like them, burn with love to God and man! May you love righteousness and hate iniquity! May ye all minister, in your several spheres (such honour hath God given you also!) to them that shall be heirs of salvation, and to the glory of your great sovereign! May ye remain the establishers of peace, the blessing and ornaments of your country, the protectors of a guilty land, the guardian angels of all that are round about you!

3. You, whose office it is to execute what is given you in charge by him before whom you stand; how nearly are you concerned to resemble those that stand before the face of the Son of Man, those servants of His that do His pleasure, and hearken to the voice of His words! Does it not highly import you, to be as uncorrupt as them? to approve yourselves the servants of God? to do justly, and love mercy? to do to all as ye would they should do to you? So shall that great Judge, under whose eye you continually stand say to you also 'Well done, good and faithful servants: enter ye into the joy of your Lord!'

4. Suffer me to add a few words to all of you who are at this day present before the Lord. Should not you bear it in your minds all the day long, that a more awful day is coming? A large assembly this! But what is it to that which every eye will then behold, the general assembly of all the children of men that ever lived on the face of the whole earth? A few will stand at the judgement-seat this day, to be judged touching what shall be laid to their charge; and they are now reserved in prison, perhaps in chains, till they are brought forth to be tried and sentenced. But we shall all, I that speak and you that hear, 'stand at the judgement-seat of Christ.' And we are now reserved on this earth, which is not our home, in this prison of flesh and blood, perhaps many of us in chains of darkness too, till we are ordered to be brought forth. Here a man is questioned concerning one or two facts, which he is supposed to have committed: there we are

to give an account of all our works, from the cradle to the grave; of all our words; of all our desires and tempers, all the thoughts and intents of our hearts; of all the use we have made of our various talents, whether of mind, body, or fortune, till God said, 'Give an account of thy stewardship, for thou mayest be no longer steward.' In this court, it is possible, some who are guilty may escape for want of evidence; but there is no want of evidence in that court. All men, with whom you had the most secret intercourse, who were privy to all your designs and actions, are ready before your face. So are all the spirits of darkness who inspired evil designs and assisted in the execution of them. So are all the angels of God; those eyes of the Lord, that run to and fro over all the earth, who watched over your soul, and laboured for your good, so far as you would permit. So is your own conscience, a thousand witnesses in one, now no more capable of being either blinded or silenced, but constrained to know and to speak the naked truth, touching all your thoughts, and words, and actions. And is conscience as a thousand witnesses?—yea, but God is as a thousand consciences! O, who can stand before the face of the great God, even our Saviour Jesus Christ!

See! See! He cometh! He maketh the clouds His chariots! He rideth upon the wings of the wind! A devouring fire goeth before Him, and after Him a flame burneth! See! He sitteth upon His throne, clothed with light as with a garment, arrayed with majesty and honour! Behold, His eyes are as a flame of fire, His voice as the sound of many waters!

How will ye escape? Will ye call to the mountains to fall on you, the rocks to cover you? Alas, the mountains themselves, the rocks, the earth, the heavens, are just ready to flee away! Can ye prevent the sentence? Wherewith? With all the substance of thy house, with thousands of gold and silver? Blind wretch! Thou camest naked from thy mother's womb, and more naked into eternity. Hear the Lord, the Judge! 'Come, ye blessed of my Father, inherit the kingdom prepared for you from the foundation of the world.' Joyful sound! How widely different from that voice which echoes through the expanse of heaven, 'Depart, ye cursed, into everlasting fire, prepared for the devil and his angels!' And who is he that can prevent or retard the full execution of either sentence? Vain hope! Lo, hell is moved from beneath to receive those who are ripe for destruction. And the everlasting doors lift up their heads, that the heirs of glory may come in!

5. 'What manner of persons then ought we to be, in all holy conversation and godliness?' We know it cannot be long before the Lord will descend with the voice of the archangel, and the trumpet of God; when every one of us shall appear before Him, and give account of his own works. 'Wherefore, beloved, seeing ye look for these things,' seeing ye know He will come and will not tarry, 'be diligent, that ye may be found of Him in peace, without spot and blameless.' Why should ye not? Why should one of you be found on the left hand at His appearing? He willeth not that any should perish, but that all should come to repentance; by repentance, to faith in a bleeding Lord; by faith, to spotless love, to the full image of God renewed in the heart, and producing all holiness of conversation. Can you doubt of this, when you remember, the Judge of all is likewise the Saviour of all? Hath He not bought you with His own blood, that ye might not perish, but have everlasting life? O make proof of His mercy, rather than His justice; of His love, rather than the thunder of His power! He is not far from every one of us; and He is now come, not to condemn, but to save the world. He standeth in the midst! Sinner, doth He not now, even now, knock at the door of thy heart? O that thou mayest know, at least in this thy day, the things that belong unto thy peace! O that ye may now give yourselves to Him who gave Himself for you, in humble faith, in holy, active, patient love! So shall ye rejoice with exceeding joy in His day, when He cometh in the clouds of heaven.

SERMON XLIX

THE LORD OUR RIGHTEOUSNESS

PREACHED AT THE CHAPEL IN WEST STREET, SEVEN DIALS, ON SUNDAY, NOVEMBER 24, 1765

West Street, Soho, runs north-west from St. Martin's Lane, a little to the south of Seven Dials, to Shaftesbury Avenue, which it strikes just east of Cambridge Circus. On the north-east side of the street is a brick building with four large arched windows, and a door at each end. This is the old West Street Chapel, where this sermon was preached. Next door to it is the Chapel-house, a plain three-storey dwelling. A photograph of it will be found in the Standard edition of the *Journal*, iii. 497. It was originally built about 1680 for the French Protestants of Soho, and was known as La Tremblade. In 1728 it was bought by the parish of St. Clement Danes, and in 1743 was offered to John Wesley, probably by the Rev. Thomas Blackwell, the rector of the parish. It was opened by Wesley on Trinity Sunday, May 29, 1743; he preached on part of John iii, the Gospel for the day, and administered the Lord's Supper to some hundreds of communicants, the service lasting from 10 to 3. The chalices used on this occasion had been presented to the French congregation in 1703 by Peter Fenowillet, and were afterwards in use at Great Queen Street Chapel. In the afternoon he preached on 'Ye must be born again' to 'an immense congregation' at the Great Gardens, Whitechapel; and in the evening met the leaders and the Bands. 'At ten at night,' he says, 'I was less weary than at six in the morning.' It was the second Methodist preaching-house in London; the first being the Foundery near the present site of Wesley's Chapel in City Road, where Wesley began to preach in 1739. See Telford's *Two West-End Chapels*.

On Sunday, November 24, 1765, the *Journal* records: 'I preached on those words in the Lesson for the day "The Lord our Righteousness." I said not one thing which I have not said at least fifty times within this twelve-month; yet it appeared to many entirely new, who much importuned me to print my sermon, supposing it would stop the mouths of all gainsayers. Alas, for their simplicity! In spite of all I can print, say, or do, will not those who seek occasion of offence find occasion?' John Valton in his Journal for October 24 writes: 'Mr. Wesley arrived in perfect health, just in time to step into the pulpit and preach on Ps. lxxxi. 10.' This was at the Foundery, and the sermon was a reply to the phrase 'The imputed righteousness of Christ' in Hervey's *Eleven Letters*. It was doubtless substantially the present sermon, which was published separately in 1766, and passed through five editions before it was placed as No. XX in the edition of the sermons of 1771.

The Rev. James Hervey entered Lincoln College, Oxford, in 1731, when he was only seventeen; and two years later he joined the little company of the Methodists. In 1736 he became curate to Charles Kinchin at the quaint little church at Dummer (see *W.H.S. Proceedings*, xii. 39). After some interruption from enfeebled health, he ultimately became his father's curate at Weston Favel, near Northampton; where he remained until his death in 1758. His *Meditations among the Tombs*, published in 1746, achieved great popularity as a devotional book. But his most important work was the series of dialogues and letters entitled *Theron and Aspasio*, published in 1755. He had become very friendly with Whitefield and had embraced the Calvinist view of predestination and the perseverance of the saints; but this did not prevent him from submitting his *Theron and Aspasio* to John Wesley for criticism before its publication. Its main subject was the Imputed Righteousness of Christ; and whilst Wesley speaks in the warmest terms of much of the teaching of the dialogues, he animadverts rather brusquely on the phrase 'the imputed righteousness of Christ,' which, he rightly says, is unscriptural; and on the tendency of the doctrine towards Antinomianism: if Christ's righteousness is imputed to us, why should we try to supplement it by good works of our own? Hervey himself protests against this perversion of his teaching; but there is no doubt that it is liable to such a misunderstanding, and was, as a matter of fact, used as an argument by the Antinomians who were giving Wesley so much anxiety in his societies. So far Wesley's criticisms were just; but he also assumed, which was not the case, that Hervey believed in reprobation, and attacked not quite fairly some of his statements on that ground. Hervey was already a very sick man, and naturally was grieved with his old friend's blunt remarks; so he made no reply to him. But in the early part of 1758 he began writing a reply to Wesley's strictures, although they had not been published and were merely notes written at his own request. Wesley heard of this, and in self-defence published his remarks in a pamphlet entitled *A Preservative against Unsettled Notions in Religion* in June 1758. Hervey, though he was a dying man, attempted to write a series of letters in reply; and submitted them for revision to William Cudworth the minister of the Independent Chapel in Margaret Street, London, who was at bitter enmity with Wesley. Wesley wrote to him in November, begging him to have nothing to do with Cudworth, whose work he describes as an 'insolent, scurrilous, virulent libel'; and in December, the day before he died, Hervey desired his brother not to publish the letters, as he had not been able to revise more than half of them. But some one (probably Cudworth) issued them from the press surreptitiously in 1764, and in the next year Hervey's brother printed an authentic edition entitled *Eleven Letters from the Late Rev. Mr. Hervey to the Rev. Mr. John Wesley*, on the ground that the other edition was faulty and incorrect, and that Wesley was still publishing his criticism of *Theron and Aspasio*. It was this publication that occasioned Wesley's sermon. He had already, in the preface to his *Treatise on Justification* dated November 16, 1764, answered the charges made in the earlier edition of the *Eleven Letters*, and he there states his conviction that they do not express the 'tender, loving, grateful spirit' of Hervey; 'No,' he says, 'the hand of Joab is in all this. I acknowledge the hand, the heart, of William Cudworth.' The whole business is lamentable; and it is easy to see how mistakes were made on both sides. The first three paragraphs of the sermon show how deeply Wesley regretted it, and his remarks in par. 3 go to the root of the matter. It was a misunderstanding by each of these good men of the views of the other; and when the fire of controversy was once kindled, each of them said things of the other that cooler reflection would have condemned.

The text was taken from the lesson for the day; but was probably suggested by a passage in *Theron and Aspasio,* dial. vi, 'What other righteousness, then, can be meant, but the righteousness of our great Substitute, Surety, and Saviour, who took our nature, discharged our debt, and is therefore styled "Jehovah our righteousness"?'

The *locus classicus* on which this whole controversy about imputed righteousness turns is Rom. iv. 1-12. Now, no one can fail to observe that neither here nor anywhere else in the Scriptures is it said that the righteousness of Christ is imputed to the believer. It is the believer's faith that is imputed to him for righteousness. Moreover, it would save us from a good deal of needless difficulty if we got rid altogether of the word 'imputed,' which has acquired a technical, theological flavour, and substituted for it what the Greek word means—'reckoned' or 'accounted.' Man is unrighteous; but if he believes on Christ, his faith is accounted or credited to him as equivalent for this purpose to righteousness; and so, though he is ungodly, God justifies him. His faith is in Christ, who by His perfect righteousness both in doing and suffering the will of God, His active and passive righteousness, has made satisfaction for our sins; and as long as it is understood that this is what is meant by the imputed righteousness of Christ, we may agree with Wesley not to quarrel about the phrase, though it is very liable to lead to error both of faith and practice.

Error has developed in three main directions. First, the Roman Church, in its anxiety to avoid Antinomianism, taught that good works are a meritorious cause of justification, and that merit can even be accumulated by works of supererogation; so that, in effect, the righteousness of Christ needs to be supplemented by our own righteousness, if we are to be saved. Second, the Mystics, laying all the stress upon the work of Christ *within* the believer, tended to minimize the importance of His work done for the believer by His perfect life and atoning death; and by the emphasis they attached to the inward experience of ecstatic fellowship with God, undervalued, even if they did not denounce, all outward good works and means of grace. Third, the Antinomians, going to the other extreme, so magnified the importance of the imputed righteousness of Christ that they denied the necessity of any good works at all. Christ had done all, therefore we need do nothing; indeed, the Performance of good works was a kind of slur on the absolute sufficiency of the work of Christ. When this notion was associated with the vulgar type of Calvinism, which taught that the elect were saved, do what they would, and the non-elect damned, do what they could, it is plain that there was little motive left for the practice of good works, and the flood-gates were opened to all sorts of self-indulgence. As par. 19 declares, this was the result which Wesley feared from Hervey's teaching; so that we can easily understand his attack upon it. He honestly tries to conciliate his opponents by consenting to use the phrase which they approved—imputed righteousness; but in his *Remarks on Hill's Farrago Double-distilled* (1773) he gives his real and final judgement on the question: 'The thing, that we are justified merely for the sake of what Christ has done and suffered, I have constantly and earnestly maintained above four-and-thirty years. And I have frequently used the phrase, hoping thereby to please others for their good to edification. But it has had a contrary effect since so many improve it into an objection. Therefore I will use it no more. I mean the phrase *imputed righteousness*; that phrase, *the imputed righteousness of Christ,* I never did use'; and he advises all his brethren to lay it aside as ambiguous and unscriptural and liable to be misinterpreted.

This sermon was highly valued by Wesley, and in *Minutes*, 1766, he directs each of the Assistants to have it, and also Sermons XXXVI, XXXVIII, and L, carefully dispersed.

This is His name whereby He shall be called, The Lord our Righteousness.—JER. xxiii. 6.

1. How dreadful and how innumerable are the contests which have arisen about religion! And not only among the children of this world, among those who knew not what true religion was, but even among the children of God; those who had experienced 'the kingdom of God within them'; who had tasted of 'righteousness, and peace, and joy in the Holy Ghost.' How many of these, in all ages instead of joining together against the common enemy, have turned their weapons against each other, and so not only wasted their precious time, but hurt one another's spirits, weakened each other's hands, and so hindered the great work of their common Master! How many of the weak have hereby been offended! How many of the lame turned out of the way! How many sinners confirmed in their disregard of all religion, and their contempt of those that profess it! And how many of 'the excellent ones upon earth' have been constrained to weep in secret places'!

2. What would not every lover of God and his neighbour do, what would he not suffer, to remedy this sore evil; to remove

contention from the children of God; to restore or preserve peace among them? What but a good conscience would he think too dear to part with, in order to promote this valuable end? And suppose we cannot 'make' these 'wars to cease in all the world,' suppose we cannot reconcile all the children of God to each other, however, let each do what he can, let him contribute, if it be but two mites, toward it. Happy are they who are able, in any degree, to promote 'peace and good-will among men'; especially among good men; among those that are all listed under the banner of 'the Prince of peace, and are therefore peculiarly engaged, 'as much as lies in them,' to 'live peaceably with all men.'

3. It would be a considerable step towards this glorious end, if we could bring good men to understand one another. Abundance of disputes arise purely from the want of this: from mere misapprehension. Frequently neither of the contending parties understands what his opponent means; whence it follows, that each violently attacks the other, while there is no real difference between them. And yet it is not always an easy matter to convince them of this; particularly when their passions are moved: it is then attended with the utmost difficulty. However, it is not impossible; especially when we attempt it, not trusting in ourselves, but having all our dependence upon Him with whom all things are possible. How soon is He able to disperse the cloud, to shine upon their hearts, and to enable them both to understand each other, and 'the truth as it is in Jesus'!

4. One very considerable article of this truth is contained in the words above recited, 'This is His name whereby He shall be called, THE LORD OUR RIGHTEOUSNESS'; a truth this, which enters deep into the nature of Christianity, and, in a manner, supports the whole frame of it. Of this undoubtedly, may be affirmed, what Luther affirms of a truth closely connected with it; it is *articulus stantis vel cadentis ecclesiae*: the Christian Church stands or falls with it. It is certainly the pillar and ground of that faith, of which alone cometh salvation; of that catholic or universal faith which is found in all the children of God, and which 'unless a man keep whole and undefiled, without doubt he shall perish everlastingly.'

5. Might not one, therefore, reasonably expect that, however they differed in others, all those who name the name of Christ should agree in this point? But how far is this from being the

case! There is scarce any wherein they are so little agreed; wherein those who all profess to follow Christ, seem so widely and irreconcilably to differ. I say *seem*; because I am thoroughly convinced, that many of them *only* seem to differ. The disagreement is more in words than in sentiments: they are much nearer in judgement than in language. And a wide difference in language there certainly is, not only between Protestants and Papists, but between Protestant and Protestant; yea, even between those who all believe justification by faith; who agree, as well in this, as in every other fundamental doctrine of the gospel.

6. But if the difference be more in *opinion* than real *experience*, and more in *expression* than in *opinion*, how can it be, that even the children of God should so vehemently contend with each other on the point? Several reasons may be assigned for this: the chief is, their not understanding one another; joined with too keen an attachment to their opinions and particular modes of expression.

In order to remove this, at least in some measure; in order to our understanding one another on this head; I shall, by the help of God, endeavour to show,

I. WHAT IS THE RIGHTEOUSNESS OF CHRIST:
II. WHEN, AND IN WHAT SENSE IT IS IMPUTED TO US:

And conclude with a short and plain application.

And, I. What is the righteousness of Christ? It is twofold, either His divine or His human righteousness.

1. His divine righteousness belongs to His divine nature, as He is Ὁ ὤν. He that existeth 'over all, God blessed for ever'; the Supreme; the Eternal; 'equal with the Father as touching His Godhead though inferior to the Father as touching His manhood.' Now this is His eternal, essential, immutable holiness; His infinite justice, mercy, and truth; in all which, He and the Father are one.

But I do not apprehend that the divine righteousness of Christ is immediately concerned in the present question. I believe few, if any, do now contend for the imputation of this righteousness to us. Whoever believes the doctrine of imputation, understands it chiefly, if not solely, of His human righteousness.

2. The human righteousness of Christ belongs to Him in His human nature; as He is the 'Mediator between God and man, the Man Christ Jesus.' This is either internal or external. His internal righteousness is the image of God, stamped on every power and faculty of His soul. It is a copy of His divine righteousness, so far as it can be imparted to a human spirit. It is a transcript of the divine purity, the divine justice, mercy, and truth. It includes love, reverence, resignation to His Father; humility, meekness, gentleness; love to lost mankind, and every other holy and heavenly temper; and all these in the highest degree, without any defect, or mixture of unholiness.

3. It was the least part of His external righteousness, that He did nothing amiss; that He knew no outward sin of any kind, neither was 'guile found in His mouth'; that He never spoke one improper word, nor did one improper action. Thus far it is only a negative righteousness, though such a one as never did, nor ever can, belong to any one that is born of a woman, save Himself alone. But even His outward righteousness was positive too: He did all things well; in every word of His tongue, in every work of His hands, He did precisely the 'will of Him that sent Him.' In the whole course of His life, He did the will of God on earth, as the angels do it in heaven. All He acted and spoke was exactly right in every circumstance. The whole and every part of His obedience was complete. 'He fulfilled all righteousness.'

4. But His obedience implied more than all this: it implied not only doing, but suffering; suffering the whole will of God, from the time He came into the world, till 'He bore our sins in His own body upon the tree'; yea, till having made a full atonement for them, 'He bowed His head, and gave up the ghost.' This is usually termed the *passive* righteousness of Christ; the former, His *active* righteousness. But as the active and passive righteousness of Christ were never, in fact, separated from each other, so we never need separate them at all, either in speaking or even in thinking. And it is with regard to both these conjointly, that Jesus is called 'the Lord our Righteousness.'

II. But when is it that any of us may truly say, 'The Lord *our* Righteousness'? In other words, when is it that the righteousness of Christ is *imputed* to us, and in what sense is it imputed?

1. Look through all the world, and all the men therein are

either believers or unbelievers. The first thing, then, which admits of no dispute among reasonable men is this: to all believers the righteousness of Christ is imputed; to unbelievers it is not.

But when is it imputed? When they believe: in that very hour the righteousness of Christ is theirs. It is imputed to every one that believes, as soon as he believes: faith and the righteousness of Christ are inseparable. For if he believes according to Scripture, he believes in the righteousness of Christ. There is no true faith, that is, justifying faith, which hath not the righteousness of Christ for its object.

2. It is true, believers may not all speak alike; they may not all use the same language. It is not to be expected that they should: we cannot reasonably require it of them. A thousand circumstances may cause them to vary from each other, in the manner of expressing themselves; but a difference of expression does not necessarily imply a difference of sentiment. Different persons may use different expressions, and yet mean the same thing. Nothing is more common than this, although we seldom make sufficient allowance for it. Nay, it is not easy for the same persons, when they speak of the same thing at a considerable distance of time, to use exactly the same expressions, even though they retain the same sentiments: how then can we be rigorous in requiring others to use just the same expressions with us?

3. We may go a step farther yet: men may differ from us in their opinions, as well as their expressions, and nevertheless be partakers with us of the same precious faith. It is possible they may not have a distinct apprehension of the very blessing which they enjoy. Their ideas may not be so clear, and yet their experience may be as sound, as ours. There is a wide difference between the natural faculties of men, their understandings in particular; and that difference is exceedingly increased by the manner of their education. Indeed, this alone may occasion an inconceivable difference in their opinions of various kinds: and why not upon this head, as well as on any other? But still, though their opinions, as well as expressions, may be confused and inaccurate, their hearts may cleave to God, through the Son of His love and be truly interested in His righteousness.

4. Let us then make all that allowance to others, which, were

we in their place, we would desire for ourselves. Who is ignorant (to touch again on that circumstance only) of the amazing power of education? And who that knows it, can expect, suppose, a member of the Church of Rome, either to think or speak clearly on this subject? And yet, if we had heard even dying Bellarmine cry out, when he was asked, 'Unto which of the saints wilt thou turn?'—*Fidere meritis Christi tutissimum* ('It is safest to trust in the merits of Christ'), would we have affirmed that, notwithstanding his wrong opinions, he had no share in His righteousness?

5. But in what sense is this righteousness imputed to believers? In this: all believers are forgiven and accepted, not for the sake of anything in them, or of anything that ever was, that is, or ever can be done by them, but wholly and solely for the sake of what Christ hath done and suffered for them. I say again, not for the sake of anything in them, or done by them, of their own righteousness or works: 'Not for works of righteousness which we have done, but of His own mercy He saved us.' 'By grace ye are saved through faith; . . . not of works, lest any man should boast'; but wholly and solely for the sake of what Christ hath done and suffered for us. We are 'justified freely by His grace, through the redemption that is in Jesus Christ.' And this is not only the means of our obtaining the favour of God, but of our continuing therein. It is thus we come to God at first; it is by the same we come unto Him ever after. We walk in one and the same new and living way, till our spirit returns to God.

6. And this is the doctrine which I have constantly believed and taught, for near eight-and-twenty years. This I published to all the world in the year 1738, and ten or twelve times since, in those words, and many others to the same effect, extracted from the Homilies of our Church: 'These things must necessarily go together in our justification: upon God's part, His great mercy and grace; upon Christ's part, the satisfaction of God's justice; and on our part, faith in the merits of Christ. So that the grace of God doth not shut out the righteousness of God in our justification, but only shutteth out the righteousness of man, as to *deserving* our justification.' 'That we are justified by faith alone, is spoken to take away clearly all merit of our works, and wholly to ascribe the *merit* and *deserving* of our justification to Christ only. Our justification comes freely of the mere mercy of God. For whereas all the world was not able to pay any part

toward our ransom, it pleased Him, without any of our deserving, to prepare for us Christ's body and blood, whereby our ransom might be paid, and His justice satisfied. Christ, therefore, is now the righteousness of all them that truly believe in Him.'

7. The Hymns published a year or two after this, and since republished several times (a clear testimony that my judgement was still the same) speak full to the same purpose. To cite all the passages to this effect, would be to transcribe a great part of the volumes. Take one for all, which was reprinted seven years ago, five years ago, two years ago, and some months since,—

> Jesu, Thy blood and righteousness
> My beauty are, my glorious dress:
> 'Midst flaming worlds, in these array'd,
> With joy shall I lift up my head.

The whole hymn expresses the same sentiment, from the beginning to the end.

8. In the Sermon on Justification published nineteen, and again seven or eight years ago, I express the same thing in these words: 'In consideration of this, that the Son of God hath "tasted death for every man," God hath now "reconciled the world unto Himself, not imputing to them their" former "trespasses." So that, for the sake of His well-beloved Son, of what He hath done and suffered for us, God now vouchsafes, on one only condition (which Himself also enables us to perform), both to remit the punishment due to our sins, to reinstate us in His favour, and to restore our dead souls to spiritual life, as the earnest of life eternal.'

9. This is more largely and particularly expressed in the Treatise on Justification, which I published last year: 'If we take the phrase of imputing Christ's righteousness, for the bestowing (as it were) the righteousness of Christ, including His obedience, as well passive as active, in the return of it, that is, in the privileges, blessings, and benefits purchased by it; so a believer may be said to be justified by the righteousness of Christ imputed. The meaning is, God justifies the believer for the sake of Christ's righteousness, and not for any righteousness of his own. So Calvin (*Institut.*, l. 2, c. 17): "Christ, by His obedience, procured and merited for us grace or favour with God the

Father." Again: "Christ, by His obedience, procured or purchased righteousness for us." And yet again: "All such expressions as these,—that we are justified by the grace of God, that Christ is our righteousness, that righteousness was procured for us by the death and resurrection of Christ, import the same thing; namely, that the righteousness of Christ, both His active and passive righteousness, is the meritorious cause of our justification, and has procured for us at God's hand, that, upon our believing, we should be accounted righteous by Him" ' (page 5).

10. But perhaps some will object, 'Nay, but you affirm that faith is imputed to us for righteousness.' St. Paul affirms this over and over; therefore I affirm it too. Faith is imputed for righteousness to every believer; namely, faith in the righteousness of Christ: but this is exactly the same thing which has been said before; for by that expression I mean neither more nor less, than that we are justified by faith, not by works; or that every believer is forgiven and accepted, merely for the sake of what Christ has done and suffered.

11. 'But is not a believer invested or clothed with the righteousness of Christ?' Undoubtedly he is. And accordingly the words above recited are the language of every believing heart,—

> Jesu, Thy blood and rghteousness
> My beauty are, my glorious dress.

That is, 'For the sake of Thy active and passive righteousness, I am forgiven and accepted of God.'

'But must not we put off the filthy rags of our own righteousness, before we can put on the spotless righteousness of Christ?' Certainly we must; that is, in plain terms, we must repent, before we can believe the gospel. We must be cut off from dependence upon ourselves, before we can truly depend upon Christ. We must cast away all confidence in our own righteousness, or we cannot have a true confidence in His. Till we are delivered from trusting in anything that we do, we cannot thoroughly trust in what He has done and suffered. First, we receive the sentence of death in ourselves: then, we trust in Him that lived and died for us.

12. 'But do not you believe inherent righteousness?' Yes, in its proper place; not as the ground of our acceptance with God, but as the fruit of it; not in the place of imputed righteousness, but as consequent upon it. That is, I believe God implants righteousness in every one to whom He has imputed it. I believe, 'Jesus Christ is made of God unto us sanctification,' as well as 'righteousness'; or, that God sanctifies, as well as justifies, all them that believe in Him. They to whom the righteousness of Christ is imputed are made righteous by the Spirit of Christ; are renewed in the image of God, 'after the likeness wherein they were created, in righteousness and true holiness.'

13. 'But do not you put faith in the room of Christ, or of His righteousness?' By no means: I take particular care to put each of these in its proper place. The righteousness of Christ is the whole and sole foundation of all our hope. It is by faith that the Holy Ghost enables us to build upon this foundation. God gives this faith; in that moment we are accepted of God: and yet, not for the sake of that faith, but of what Christ has done and suffered for us. You see, each of these has its proper place, and neither clashes with the other: we believe, we love, we endeavour to walk in all the commandments of the Lord blameless: yet,—

> While thus we bestow
> Our moments below,
> Ourselves we forsake,
> And refuge in Jesus's righteousness take.
> His passion alone,
> The foundation we own;
> And pardon we claim,
> And eternal redemption in Jesus's name.

14. I therefore no more deny the righteousness of Christ, than I deny the Godhead of Christ, and a man may full as justly charge me with denying the one as the other. Neither do I deny imputed righteousness: this is another unkind and unjust accusation. I always did, and do still continually, affirm, that the righteousness of Christ is imputed to every believer. But who deny it? Why, all infidels, whether baptized or unbaptized; all who affirm the glorious gospel of our Lord Jesus Christ to be a cunningly-devised fable; all Socinians and Arians; all who deny the supreme Godhead of the Lord that bought them; they, of

consequence, deny His divine righteousness, as they suppose Him to be a mere creature; and they deny His human righteousness, as imputed to any man, seeing they believe every one is accepted for his own righteousness.

15. The human righteousness of Christ, at least the imputation of it, as the whole and sole meritorious cause of the justification of a sinner before God, is likewise denied by the members of the Church of Rome; by all of them who are true to the principles of their own Church. But undoubtedly there are many among them whose experience goes beyond their principles; who, though they are far from expressing themselves justly, yet feel what they know not how to express. Yea, although their conceptions of this great truth be as crude as their expressions, yet with their hearts they believe: they rest on Christ alone, both unto present and eternal salvation.

16. With these we may rank those even in the Reformed Churches who are usually termed Mystics. One of the chief of these, in the present century (at least in England), was Mr. Law. It is well known that he absolutely and zealously denied the imputation of the righteousness of Christ, as zealously as Robert Barclay, who scruples not to say, 'Imputed righteousness!— imputed nonsense!' The body of the people known by the name of Quakers espouse the same sentiment. Nay, the generality of those who profess themselves members of the Church of England are either totally ignorant of the matter, and know nothing about imputed righteousness, or deny this and justification by faith together, as destructive of good works. To these we may add a considerable number of the people vulgarly styled Anabaptists together with thousands of Presbyterians and Independents, lately enlightened by the writings of Dr. Taylor. On the last I am not called to pass any sentence: I leave them to Him that made them. But will any one dare to affirm that all Mystics (such as Mr. Law in particular), all Quakers, all Presbyterians or Independents, and all members of the Church of England who are not clear in their opinions or expressions, are void of all Christian experience?—that, consequently, they are all in a state of damnation, 'without hope, without God in the world'? However confused their ideas may be, however improper their language, may there not be many of them whose heart is right toward God, and who effectually know 'the Lord our Righteousness'?

17. But, blessed be God, we are not among those who are so dark in their conceptions and expressions. We no more deny the phrase than the thing; but we are unwilling to obtrude it on other men. Let them use either this or such other expressions as they judge to be more exactly scriptural, provided their heart rests only on what Christ hath done and suffered, for pardon, grace, and glory. I cannot express this better than in Mr. Hervey's words, worthy to be wrote in letters of gold: 'We are not solicitous as to any particular set of phrases. Only let men be humbled as repenting criminals at Christ's feet, let them rely as devoted pensioners on His merits, and they are undoubtedly in the way to a blessed immortality.'

18. Is there any need, is there any possibility, of saying more? Let us only abide by this declaration, and all the contention about this or that particular phrase is torn up by the roots. Keep to this,—'All who are humbled as repenting criminals at Christ's feet, and rely as devoted pensioners on His merits are in the way to a blessed immortality'; and what room for dispute? Who denies this? Do we not all meet on this ground? What then shall we wrangle about? A man of peace here proposes terms of accommodation to all the contending parties. We desire no better: we accept of the terms: we subscribe to them with heart and hand. Whoever refuses so to do, set a mark upon that man! He is an enemy of peace, a troubler of Israel, a disturber of the Church of God.

19. In the mean time, what we are afraid of is this: lest any should use the phrase, 'The righteousness of Christ,' or, 'The righteousness of Christ is imputed to me,' as a cover for his unrighteousness. We have known this done a thousand times. A man has been reproved, suppose, for drunkenness: 'Oh,' said he, 'I pretend to no righteousness of *my own*; Christ is *my righteousness*.' Another has been told, that 'the extortioner, the unjust, shall not inherit the kingdom of God'; he replies, with all assurance, 'I am unjust in myself, but I have a spotless righteousness in Christ.' And thus, though a man be as far from the practice as from the tempers of a Christian; though he neither has the mind which was in Christ, nor in any respect walks as He walked; yet he has armour of proof against all conviction, in what he calls 'the righteousness of Christ.'

20. It is the seeing so many deplorable instances of this kind,

which makes us sparing in the use of these expressions. And I cannot but call upon all of you who use them frequently, and beseech you in the name of God our Saviour, whose you are, and whom you serve, earnestly to guard all that hear you against this accursed abuse of them. O warn them (it may be they will hear *your* voice) against 'continuing in sin that grace may abound'! Warn them against making 'Christ the minister of sin'; against making void that solemn decree of God, 'Without holiness no man shall see the Lord,' by a vain imagination of being *holy in Christ*! O warn them that if they remain unrighteous, the righteousness of Christ will profit them nothing! Cry aloud (is there not a cause?) that for this very end the righteousness of Christ is imputed to us, that 'the righteousness of the law may be fulfilled in us'; and that we may 'live soberly, righteously, and godly, in this present world.'

It remains only to make a short and plain application. And, first, I would address myself to you who violently oppose these expressions, and are ready to condemn all that use them as Antinomians. But is not this bending the bow too much the other way? Why should you condemn all who do not speak just as you do? Why should you quarrel with them for using the phrases they like, any more than they with you for taking the same liberty? Or, if they do quarrel with you upon that account, do not imitate the bigotry which you blame. At least, allow them the liberty which they ought to allow you. And why should you be angry at an expression? 'O, it has been abused!' And what expression has not? However, the abuse may be removed, and, at the same time, the use remain. Above all, be sure to retain the important sense which is couched under that expression: 'All the blessings I enjoy, all I hope for in time and in eternity, are given wholly and solely for the sake of what Christ has done and suffered for me.'

I would, secondly, add a few words to you who are fond of these expressions. And permit me to ask, Do not I allow enough? What can any reasonable man desire more? I allow the whole sense which you contend for; that we have every blessing through the righteousness of God our Saviour. I allow *you* to use whatever expressions you choose, and that a thousand times over; only guarding them against that dreadful abuse, which you are as deeply concerned to prevent as I am. I myself frequently use the expression in question,—imputed righteousness; and often put this and the like expressions into the mouth of a whole congregation. But allow me liberty of conscience herein: allow me the right of private judgement. Allow me to use it just as often as I judge it preferable to any other expression; and be not angry with me, if I cannot judge it proper to use any one expression every two minutes. You may, if you please; but do not condemn me because I do not. Do not, for this, represent me as a Papist, or 'an enemy to the righteousness of Christ.' Bear with me, as I do with you; else how shall we 'fulfil the law of Christ'? Do not make tragical outcries, as though I were 'subverting the very foundations of Christianity.' Whoever does this, does me much wrong: the Lord lay it not to his charge! I lay, and have done for many years, the very same foundation with you. And, indeed, 'other foundation can no man lay, than that which is laid, even Jesus Christ.' I build inward and outward holiness thereon, as you do, even by faith. Do not, therefore, suffer any distaste, or unkindness, no, nor any shyness or coldness of your heart. If there were a difference of opinion, where is our religion if we cannot think and let think? What hinders but you may forgive me as easily as I may forgive you? How much more, when there is only a difference of expression? Nay, hardly so much as that—all the dispute being only, whether a particular mode of expression shall be used more or less frequently? Surely we must earnestly desire to contend with one another, before we can make this a bone of contention! O let us not any more, for such very trifles as these, give our common enemies room to blaspheme! Rather let us at length cut off occasion from them that seek occasion! Let us at length (O why was it not done before?) join hearts and hands in the service of our great Master. As we have 'one Lord, one faith, one hope of our calling,' let us all strengthen each other's hands in God, and with one heart and one mouth declare to all mankind, 'THE LORD OUR RIGHTEOUSNESS.'

SERMON L

THE SCRIPTURE WAY OF SALVATION

This sermon was first published in a separate form in 1765; it is not in the original four volumes, but was placed in Vol. III of the collected *Works* of 1771. It is from the same text as the University Sermon (No. I), but entirely different from it in its treatment of the subject. In that, the text is given as 'By grace are ye saved through faith'; in this, as 'Ye are saved through faith'; and in the *Journal* the sermons are usually distinguished by the form of the text. The first was one of Wesley's favourites, and it is recorded seven times at least in the body of the *Journal,* and several times in the Sermon-Register. No doubt it was not always verbally the same as the Oxford sermon, but it would be on the same general lines of treatment. The earliest notice I have found of the second sermon is in the *Journal,* March 30, 1764. Wesley was at Rotherham, and had found there sixty persons professing to have received the blessing of entire sanctification. 'In the evening I preached in the new house at Rotherham on the sure foundation "Ye are saved through faith." It was a season of strong consolation to many. One who had been some time groaning for full redemption now found power to believe that God had fulfilled her desire, and set her heart at liberty.' On October 7 in the same year he preached 'in Moorfields to a huge multitude on "Ye are saved through faith." ' As we have seen in some other cases, he seems to have liked to preach his sermons, to try them over, so to speak, a time or two, before he printed them; and it is pretty clear from the context that the Rotherham sermon was on entire sanctification, as this is. If the 'five-and-twenty' years of iii. 3 is to be taken as an exact figure, dating from the delivery of the first sermon in 1738, this one would have been written in 1763; but the twenty-five may be a round number, equivalent to 'about a quarter of a century ago.'

The object of the sermon was to correct the erroneous doctrines of the Glasites, or Sandemanians, which had been more or less accepted by Thomas Maxfield and George Bell, and had wrought havoc in the Society in London. John Glas was originally a Presbyterian mmister, but was deposed in 1730, and started a congregation of his own in Dundee, to which others in Edinburgh and Perth were soon attached. His son-in-law, Robert Sandeman, joined him in Perth, and soon became the leader of the sect. He taught that faith was a mere intellectual assent to the truth of the gospel story, and that 'the bare death of Jesus Christ, without a thought or deed on the part of man, is sufficient to present the chief of sinners spotless before God.' He attacked Hervey's account of faith in *Theron and Aspasio,* and Wesley came to the rescue of his old friend, and answered Sandeman in a pamphlet published in 1757, and included in his collected Works. Maxfield and Bell developed the Antinomian tendency of his teaching, and denied that good works were necessary to sanctification, or that the means of grace were of any value; 'God has done,' said Bell, 'with all preachings and sacraments.' At the same time they depreciated justification, affirming that a merely justified person was not born of God, and that he could neither please God nor grow in grace; and asserted that the entirely sanctified believer was absolutely perfect, infallible, inaccessible to temptation, and secure from ever falling. They finally separated from Wesley in 1763 and took with them many members of his Societies. It was to counteract the influence of their teaching that Wesley wrote his *Cautions and Directions to the greatest Professors* (1762), the sermon on Sin in Believers (1763), and this sermon.

Comparing it with Sermon I, we note, (1) the definite place and importance assigned to 'preventing grace' in the work of salvation; (2) the clear distinction drawn between justification and sanctification; (3) the recognition that after justification, sin still remains in believers; (4) hence the necessity for entire sanctification, for which repentance and good works are necessary, though not in the same degree or in the same sense as faith.

Dr. Beet (*London Quarterly Review,* January 1920) draws attention to the great contrast between Sermon XXXV on Christian Perfection and Sermon L on The Scripture Way of Salvation. The latter 'is a compact statement of Wesley's mature thought about the great doctrines which inspired the Methodist Revival; it is of more practical value than all the other sermons put together.' 'He asserts again and again that, as we are justified by faith, so are we sanctified by faith; and very forcibly describes this saving faith. He also urges his readers to accept here and now this great salvation.'

In *Minutes,* 1766, the Assistants are directed to see that this sermon, as well as Sermons XXXVI, XXXVIII, and XLIX, are carefully dispersed in the Societies.

Ye are saved through faith.—EPH. ii. 8.

1. Nothing can be more intricate, complex, and hard to be understood, than religion, as it has been often described. And this is not only true concerning the religion of the Heathens, even many of the wisest of them, but concerning the religion of those also who were, in some sense, Christians; yea, and men of great name in the Christian world; men who seemed to be pillars thereof. Yet how easy to be understood, how plain and simple a thing, is the genuine religion of Jesus Christ; provided only that

we take it in its native form, just as it is described in the oracles of God! It is exactly suited, by the wise Creator and Governor of the world, to the weak understanding and narrow capacity of man in his present state. How observable is this, both with regard to the end it proposes, and the means to attain that end! The end is, in one word, salvation; the means to attain it, faith.

2. It is easily discerned, that these two little words, I mean faith and salvation, include the substance of all the Bible, the marrow, as it were, of the whole Scripture. So much the more should we take all possible care to avoid all mistake concerning them, and to form a true and accurate judgement concerning both the one and the other.

3. Let us then seriously inquire,—

> I. WHAT IS SALVATION?
> II. WHAT IS THAT FAITH WHEREBY WE ARE SAVED? AND,
> III. HOW ARE WE SAVED BY IT?

I. 1. And, first, let us inquire, What is salvation? The salvation which is here spoken of is not what is frequently understood by that word, the going to heaven, eternal happiness. It is not the soul's going to paradise termed by our Lord, 'Abraham's bosom.' It is not a blessing which lies on the other side of death; or, as we usually speak, in the other world. The very words of the text itself put this beyond all question: '*Ye are saved*.' It is not something at a distance: it is a present thing; a blessing which, through the free mercy of God, ye are now in possession of. Nay, the words may be rendered, and that with equal propriety, 'Ye *have been* saved': so that the salvation which is here spoken of might be extended to the entire work of God, from the first dawning of grace in the soul, till it is consummated in glory.

2. If we take this in its utmost extent, it will include all that is wrought in the soul by what is frequently termed 'natural conscience,' but more properly, 'preventing grace'; all the drawings of the Father—the desires after God, which, if we yield to them, increase more and more; all that light wherewith the Son of God 'enlighteneth every one that cometh into the world'—showing every man 'to do justly, to love mercy, and to walk humbly with his God'; all the convictions which His Spirit,

from time to time, works in every child of man—although it is true, the generality of men stifle them as soon as possible, and after a while forget, or at least deny, that they ever had them at all.

3. But we are at present concerned only with that salvation which the Apostle is directly speaking of. And this consists of two general parts, justification and sanctification. Justification is another word for pardon. It is the forgiveness of all our sins; and, what is necessarily implied therein, our acceptance with God. The price whereby this hath been procured for us (commonly termed 'the meritorious cause of our justification'), is the blood and righteousness of Christ; or, to express it a little more clearly, all that Christ hath done and suffered for us, till He 'poured out His soul for the transgressors.' The immediate effects of justification are, the peace of God, a 'peace that passeth all understanding,' and a 'rejoicing in hope of the glory of God' 'with joy unspeakable and full of glory.'

4. And at the same time that we are justified, yea, in that very moment, sanctification begins. In that instant we are born again, born from above, born of the Spirit: there is a *real* as well as a *relative* change. We are inwardly renewed by the power of God. We feel 'the love of God shed abroad in our heart by the Holy Ghost which is given unto us'; producing love to all mankind, and more especially to the children of God; expelling the love of the world, the love of pleasure, of ease, of honour, of money, together with pride, anger, self-will, and every other evil temper; in a word, changing the earthly, sensual, devilish mind, into 'the mind which was in Christ Jesus.'

5. How naturally do those who experience such a change imagine that all sin is gone; that it is utterly rooted out of their heart, and has no more any place therein! How easily do they draw that inference, 'I *feel* no sin; therefore, I *have* none: it does not *stir;* therefore, it does not *exist:* it has no *motion;* therefore, it has no *being*!'

6. But it is seldom long before they are undeceived, finding sin was only suspended, not destroyed. Temptations return, and sin revives; showing it was but stunned before, not dead. They now feel two principles in themselves, plainly contrary to each other; 'the flesh lusting against the Spirit'; nature opposing the grace of God. They cannot deny, that although they still feel

power to believe in Christ, and to love God; and although His 'Spirit' still 'witnesses with their spirits, that they are children of God'; yet they feel in themselves sometimes pride or self-will, sometimes anger or unbelief. They find one or more of these frequently *stirring* in their heart, though not *conquering;* yea, perhaps, 'thrusting sore at them that they may fall'; but the Lord is their help.

7. How exactly did Macarius, fourteen hundred years ago, describe the present experience of the children of God: 'The unskilful,' or unexperienced, 'when grace operates, presently imagine they have no more sin. Whereas they that have discretion cannot deny, that even we who have the grace of God may be molested again. For we have often had instances of some among the brethren, who have experienced such grace as to affirm that they had no sin in them; and yet, after all, when they thought themselves entirely freed from it, the corruption that lurked within was stirred up anew, and they were wellnigh burned up.'

8. From the time of our being born again the gradual work of sanctification takes place. We are enabled 'by the Spirit' to 'mortify the deeds of the body,' of our evil nature; and as we are more and more dead to sin, we are more and more alive to God. We go on from grace to grace while we are careful to 'abstain from all appearance of evil' and are 'zealous of good works,' as we have opportunity doing good to all men; while we walk in all His ordinances blameless, therein worshipping Him in spirit and in truth; while we take up our cross, and deny ourselves every pleasure that does not lead us to God.

9. It is thus that we wait for entire sanctification; for a full salvation from all our sins—from pride, self-will, anger, unbelief; or, as the Apostle expresses it, 'go on unto perfection.' But what is perfection? The word has various senses: here it means perfect love. It is love excluding sin; love filling the heart, taking up the whole capacity of the soul. It is love 'rejoicing evermore, praying without ceasing, in everything giving thanks.'

II. But what is that faith through which we are saved? This is the second point to be considered.

1. Faith, in general, is defined by the Apostle, πραγματων

ελεγχος ου βλεπομενων—*an evidence,* a divine *evidence and
conviction* (the word means both) *of things not seen*; not visible, not
perceivable either by sight, or by any other of the external
senses. It implies both a supernatural *evidence* of God, and of the
things of God; a kind of spiritual *light* exhibited to the soul, and a
supernatural *sight* or perception thereof. Accordingly, the
Scripture speaks of God's giving sometimes light, sometimes a
power of discerning it. So St. Paul: 'God, who commanded light
to shine out of darkness, hath shined in our hearts, to give us the
light of the knowledge of the glory of God in the face of Jesus
Christ.' And elsewhere the same Apostle speaks of 'the eyes of'
our 'understanding being opened.' By this two-fold operation of
the Holy Spirit, having the eyes of our soul both *opened* and
enlightened, we see the things which the natural 'eye hath not
seen, neither the ear heard.' We have a prospect of the invisible
things of God; we see the *spiritual world,* which is all round about
us, and yet no more discerned by our natural faculties than if it
had no being. And we see the *eternal world;* piercing through the
veil which hangs between time and eternity. Clouds and
darkness then rest upon it no more, but we already see the glory
which shall be revealed.

2. Taking the word in a more particular sense, faith is a divine
evidence and *conviction* not only that 'God was in Christ,
reconciling the world unto Himself,' but also that Christ loved
me, and gave Himself for *me*. It is by this faith (whether we term it
the *essence*, or rather a *property* thereof) that we *receive Christ*; that
we receive Him in all His offices, as our Prophet, Priest, and
King. It is by this that He is 'made of God unto us wisdom, and
righteousness, and sanctification, and redemption.'

3. 'But is this the *faith of assurance,* or *faith of adherence?*' The
Scripture mentions no such distinction. The Apostle says,
'There is one faith, and one hope of our calling'; one Christian,
saving faith; 'as there is one Lord,' in whom we believe, and 'one
God and Father of us all.' And it is certain, this faith necessarily
implies an *assurance* (which is here only another word for
evidence, it being hard to tell the difference between them) that
Christ loved me, and gave Himself for me. For 'he that believeth'
with the true living faith 'hath the witness in himself': 'the Spirit
witnesseth with his spirit that he is a child of God.' 'Because he is
a son, God hath sent forth the Spirit of His Son into his heart,

crying, Abba, Father'; giving him an assurance that he is so, and a childlike confidence in Him. But let it be observed, that, in the very nature of the thing, the assurance goes before the confidence. For a man cannot have a childlike confidence in God till he knows he is a child of God. Therefore, confidence, trust, reliance, adherence, or whatever else it be called, is not the first, as some have supposed, but the second, branch or act of faith.

4. It is by this faith we are saved, justified, and sanctified; taking that word in its highest sense. But how are we justified and sanctified by faith? This is our third head of inquiry. And this being the main point in question, and a point of no ordinary importance, it will not be improper to give it a more distinct and particular consideration.

III. 1. And, first, how are we justified by faith? In what sense is this to be understood? I answer, Faith is the condition, and the only condition, of justification. It is the *condition*: none is justified but he that believes: without faith no man is justified. And it is the *only condition*: this alone is sufficient for justification. Every one that believes is justified, whatever else he has or has not. In other words: no man is justified till he believes; every man when he believes is justified.

2. 'But does not God command us to repent also? Yea, and to 'bring forth fruits meet for repentance''—to cease, for instance, from doing evil, and learn to do well? And is not both the one and the other of the utmost necessity, insomuch that if we willingly neglect either, we cannot reasonably expect to be justified at all? But if this be so, how can it be said that faith is the only condition of justification?'

God does undoubtedly command us both to repent, and to bring forth fruits meet for repentance; which if we willingly neglect, we cannot reasonably expect to be justified at all: therefore both repentance, and fruits meet for repentance, are, in some sense, necessary to justification. But they are not necessary in the *same sense* with faith, nor in the *same degree*. Not in the *same degree*; for those fruits are only necessary *conditionally*; if there be time and opportunity for them. Otherwise a man may be justified without them, as was the *thief* upon the cross (if we may call him so; for a late writer has discovered that he was no thief, but a very honest and respectable person!); but he cannot be justified without faith; this is impossible. Likewise, let a man have ever so much repentance, or ever so many of the fruits meet for repentance, yet all this does not at all avail; he is not justified till he believes. But the moment he believes, with or without those fruits, yea, with more or less repentance, he is justified.—Not in the *same sense*; for repentance and its fruits are only *remotely* necessary; necessary in order to faith; whereas faith is *immediately* and *directly* necessary to justification. It remains, that faith is the only condition which is *immediately* and *proxixately* necessary to justification.

3. 'But do you believe we are sanctified by faith? We know you believe that we are justified by faith; but do not you believe, and accordingly teach, that we are sanctified by our works?' 'So it has been roundly and vehemently affirmed for these five-and-twenty years: but I have constantly declared just the contrary; and that in all manner of ways. I have continually testified in private and in public, that we are sanctified as well as justified by faith. And indeed the one of those great truths does exceedingly illustrate the other. Exactly as we are justified by faith, so are we sanctified by faith. Faith is the condition, and the only condition, of sanctification, exactly as it is of justification. It is the *condition*: none is sanctified but he that believes; without faith no man is sanctified. And it is the *only condition*: this alone is sufficient for sanctification. Every one that believes is sanctified, whatever else he has or has not. In other words, no man is sanctified till he believes: every man when he believes is sanctified.

4. 'But is there not a repentance consequent upon, as well as a repentance previous to, justification? And is it not incumbent on all that are justified to be 'zealous of good works '? Yea, are not these so necessary, that if a man willingly neglect them he cannot reasonably expect that he shall ever be sanctified in the full sense; that is, perfected in love? Nay, can he grow at all in grace, in the loving knowledge of our Lord Jesus Christ? Yea, can he retain the grace which God has already given him? Can he continue in the faith which he has received, or in the favour of God? Do not you yourself allow all this, and continually assert it? But, if this be so, how can it be said that faith is the only condition of sanctification?'

5. I do allow all this, and continually maintain it as the truth of

God. I allow there is a repentance consequent upon, as well as a repentance previous to, justification. It is incumbent on all that are justified to be zealous of good works. And these are so necessary, that if a man willingly neglect them, he cannot reasonably expect that he shall ever be sanctified; he cannot grow in grace, in the image of God, the mind which was in Christ Jesus; nay, he cannot retain the grace he has received; he cannot continue in faith, or in the favour of God.

What is the inference we must draw herefrom? Why, that both repentance, rightly understood, and the practice of all good works—works of piety, as well as works of mercy (now properly so called, since they spring from faith), are, in some sense, necessary to sanctification.

6. I say, 'repentance rightly understood'; for this must not be confounded with the former repentance. The repentance consequent upon justification is widely different from that which is antecedent to it. This implies no guilt, no sense of condemnation, no consciousness of the wrath of God. It does not suppose any doubt of the favour of God, or any 'fear that hath torment.' It is properly a conviction, wrought by the Holy Ghost, of the sin which still *remains* in our heart; of the φρονημα σαρκος, *the carnal mind*, which 'does still *remain*' (as our Church speaks) 'even in them that are regenerate'; although it does no longer reign; it has not now dominion over them. It is a conviction of our proneness to evil, of an heart bent to backsliding, of the still continuing tendency of the flesh to lust against the spirit. Sometimes, unless we continually watch and pray, it lusteth to pride, sometimes to anger, sometimes to love of the world, love of ease, love of honour, or love of pleasure more than of God. It is a conviction of the tendency of our heart to self-will, to Atheism, or idolatry; and above all, to unbelief; whereby, in a thousand ways, and under a thousand pretences, we are ever departing, more or less, from the living God.

7. With this conviction of the sin remaining in our hearts, there is joined a clear conviction of the sin remaining in our lives; still *cleaving* to all our words and actions. In the best of these we now discern a mixture of evil, either in the spirit, the matter, or the manner of them; something that could not endure the righteous judgement of God, were He extreme to mark what is done amiss. Where we least suspected it, we find a

taint of pride or self-will, of unbelief or idolatry; so that we are
now more ashamed of our best duties than formerly of our worst
sins: and hence we cannot but feel that these are so far from
having anything meritorious in them, yea, so far from being able
to stand in sight of the divine justice, that for those also we
should be guilty before God, were it not for the blood of the
covenant.

8. Experience shows that, together with this conviction of sin
remaining in our hearts, and *cleaving* to all our words and actions;
as well as the guilt which on account thereof we should incur,
were we not continually sprinkled with the atoning blood; one
thing more is implied in this repentance; namely, a conviction of
our helplessness, of our utter inability to think one good
thought, or to form one good desire; and much more to speak
one word aright, or to perform one good action, but through
His free, almighty grace, first preventing us, and then
accompanying us every moment.

9. 'But what good works are those, the practice of which you
affirm to be necessary to sanctification?' First, all works of piety;
such as public prayer, family prayer, and praying in our closet;
receiving the supper of the Lord; searching the Scriptures, by
hearing, reading, meditating; and using such a measure of
fasting or abstinence as our bodily health allows.

10. Secondly, all works of mercy; whether they relate to the
bodies or souls of men; such as feeding the hungry, clothing the
naked, entertaining the stranger, visiting those that are in
prison, or sick, or variously afflicted; such as the endeavouring
to instruct the ignorant, to awaken the stupid sinner, to
quicken the lukewarm, to confirm the wavering, to comfort the
feeble-minded, to succour the tempted, or contribute in any
manner to the saving of souls from death. This is the
repentance, and these the 'fruits meet for repentance,' which
are necessary to full sanctification. This is the way wherein God
hath appointed His children to wait for complete salvation.

11. Hence may appear the extreme mischievousness of that
seemingly innocent opinion, that there is no sin in a believer;
that all sin is destroyed, root and branch, the moment a man is
justified. By totally preventing that repentance, it quite blocks
up the way to sanctification. There is no place for repentance in
him who believes there is no sin either in his life or heart:

consequently, there is no place for his being perfected in love, to which that repentance is indispensably necessary.

12. Hence it may likewise appear, that there is no possible danger in *thus* expecting full salvation. For suppose we were mistaken, suppose no such blessing ever was or can be attained, yet we lose nothing: nay, that very expectation quickens us in using all the talents which God has given us; yea, in improving them all; so that when our Lord cometh, He will receive His own with increase.

13. But to return. Though it be allowed, that both this repentance and its fruits are necessary to full salvation; yet they are not necessary either in the same sense with faith, or in the same degree.—Not in the *same degree*; for these fruits are only necessary *conditionally*, if there be time and opportunity for them; otherwise a man may be sanctified without them. But he cannot be sanctified without faith. Likewise, let a man have ever so much of this repentance, or ever so many good works, yet all this does not at all avail: he is not sanctified till he believes. But the moment he believes, with or without those fruits, yea, with more or less of this repentance, he is sanctified.—Not in the *same sense*; for this repentance and these fruits are only *remotely* necessary—necessary in order to the continuance of his faith, as well as the increase of it; whereas faith is *immediately* and *directly* necessary to sanctification. It remains, that faith is the only condition which is *immediately* and *proximately* necessary to sanctification.

14. 'But what is that faith whereby we are sanctified,—saved from sin, and perfected in love?' It is a divine evidence and conviction, first, that God hath promised it in the holy Scripture. Till we are thoroughly satisfied of this, there is no moving one step further. And one would imagine there needed not one word more to satisfy a reasonable man of this, than the ancient promise, 'Then will I circumcise thy heart, and the heart of thy seed, to love the Lord thy God with all thy heart, and with all thy soul, and with all thy mind.' How clearly does this express the being perfected in love!—how strongly imply the being saved from all sin! For as long as love takes up the whole heart, what room is there for sin therein?

15. It is a divine evidence and conviction, secondly, that what God hath promised He is able to perform. Admitting, therefore,

that 'with men it is impossible' to 'bring a clean thing out of an unclean,' to purify the heart from all sin, and to fill it with all holiness; yet this creates no difficulty in the case, seeing 'with God all things are possible.' And surely no one ever imagined it was possible to any power less than that of the Almighty! But if God speaks, it shall be done. God saith, 'Let there be light; and there' is 'light'!

16. It is, thirdly, a divine evidence and conviction that He is able and willing to do it now. And why not? Is not a moment to Him the same as a thousand years? He cannot want more time to accomplish whatever is His will. And He cannot want or stay for any more *worthiness* or *fitness* in the persons He is pleased to honour. We may therefore boldly say, at any point of time, 'Now is the day of salvation!' 'To-day, if ye will hear His voice, harden not you hearts!' 'Behold, all things are now ready; come unto the marriage!'

17. To this confidence, that God is both able and willing to sanctify us now, there needs to be added one thing more,—a divine evidence and conviction that He doeth it. In that hour it is done: God says to the inmost soul, 'According to thy faith be it unto thee!' Then the soul is pure from every spot of sin; it is clean 'from all unrighteousness.' The believer then experiences the deep meaning of those solemn words, 'If we walk in the light as He is in the light, we have fellowship one with another, and the blood of Jesus Christ His Son cleanseth us from all sin.'

18. 'But does God work this great work in the soul gradually or instantaneously?' Perhaps it may be gradually wrought in some; I mean in this sense,—they do not advert to the particular moment wherein sin ceases to be. But it is infinitely desirable, were it the will of God, that it should be done instantaneously; that the Lord should destroy sin 'by the breath of His mouth,' in a moment, in the twinkling of an eye. And so He generally does; a plain fact, of which there is evidence enough to satisfy any unprejudiced person. *Thou* therefore look for it every moment! Look for it in the way above described; in all those *good works* whereunto thou art 'created anew in Christ Jesus.' There is then no danger: you can be no worse, if you are no better, for that expectation. For were you to be disappointed of your hope, still you lose nothing. But you shall not be disappointed of your hope: it will come, and will not tarry. Look for it then every day,

every hour, every moment! Why not this hour, this moment? Certainly you may look for it *now,* if you believe it is by faith. And by this token you may surely know whether you seek it by faith or by works. If by works, you want something to be done *first, before* you are sanctified. You think, I must first *be* or *do* thus or thus. Then you are seeking it by works unto this day. If you seek it by faith, you may expect it *as you are*; and if as you are, then expect it *now.* It is of importance to observe, that there is an inseparable connexion between these three points,—expect it *by faith*; expect it *as you are*; and expect it *now.* To deny one of them, is to deny them all; to allow one, is to allow them all. Do *you* believe we are sanctified by faith? Be true then to your principle; and look for this blessing just as you are, neither better nor worse; as a poor sinner that has still nothing to pay, nothing to plead, but 'Christ *died.*' And if you look for it as you are, then expect it *now.* Stay for nothing: why should you? Christ is ready; and He is all you want. He is waiting for you: He is at the door! Let your inmost soul cry out,

> Come in, come in, Thou heavenly Guest!
>   Nor hence again remove;
> But sup with me, and let the feast
>   Be everlasting love.

SERMON LI

THE GOOD STEWARD

This sermon was first published in 1768 at Newcastle, doubtless during Wesley's visit to that city after his return from Scotland in the latter part of May. It is entitled *The Good Steward; a Sermon. By John Wesley, M.A., Chaplain to the Right Hon. the Countess Dowager of Buchan*. It was republished in the same year in London, in Leeds, and in Bristol; and was inserted in the collected *Works* in 1771 immediately after the Standard Sermons.

The Earls of Buchan, a branch of the family of Comyn, played a conspicuous part in the history of Scotland. Their domains lay north-east of Aberdeen, along the coast up to Moray Firth. The Earl of Buchan was one of the Council of Regency in 1286 on the death of Alexander III; but he himself died the same year, and his son John steadily supported Edward I of England in his claim to the overlordship of Scotland. Bruce defeated him at Inverury in 1310, and

> Gert his men burn all Bouchane
> Fra end till end, and sparit nane;
> And heryit them on sic maner,
> That efter that, neir fifty yheir,
> Men menyt the heirschip of Bouchane.

(Barbour's *Bruce,* ix). His Countess, however, was a Macduff; and in spite of her husband, she exercised the hereditary privilege of her clan and went to Scone in 1306 to crown John Baliol; in revenge for which patriotic act Edward I caused her to be hung up in a cage outside one of the towers of Berwick Castle. In the reign of Henry VII the then Earl of Buchan, 'Hearty James,' as he was nicknamed, entered into a plot in 1491 to dethrone James III, and to hand over his heir, James IV, to England; which happily failed. Henry David, the tenth Earl, succeeded his father in 1745. He married Agnes, daughter of Sir James Stewart, of Goodtrees, near Edinburgh, the Solicitor-General for Scotland. He came with his lady to Bath on account of his health, and there, through the influence of the Countess of Buntingdon, heard the preaching of Whitefield, Wesley, Fletcher, and other Methodists in her ladyship's chapel, and became converted to their views. He died there on December 1, 1767, in the full triumph of faith at the age of fifty-eight. His body lay in state in the Countess's chapel for five days, on each of which two sermons were preached by Whitefield and others; and was then taken to Scotland for burial. The young earl, who had also been converted, appointed, by the advice of Lady Huntingdon, Mr. Venn, Mr. Fletcher, and Mr. Berridge as his chaplains; he was twenty-four years of age, and lived till 1829 a life of quiet literary retirement. The Dowager Countess returned to Edinburgh, probably to her old home at Goodtrees, and, on the recommendation of the Countess of Huntingdon, appointed Wesley as her chaplain. He seems to have 'read himself in' with this sermon, which is dated May 14, 1768, and was doubtless preached before his noble patroness in Edinburgh on the following day, Sunday, in the evening. He says: 'In the evening our house was sufficiently crowded, even with the rich and honourable.' One of the congregation was doubtless Lady Maxwell, who had found peace a week or two before, and was a member of the Methodist Society in Edinburgh. The 'House' was the Octagon Chapel in Low Calton, the foundation stone of which had been laid by Wesley on April 24, 1765; it has disappeared to make room for street improvements, and was replaced by the chapel in Nicolson Square. Wesley wrote to thank Lady Huntingdon for her share in securing him this honour. Both Tyerman and Butler date the letter correctly January 4, but others give June 4. This mistake in the date has led to a confusion between the young earl's appointments of his three chaplains and the Countess's appointment of Wesley as her chaplain. See *W.H.S. Proceedings*, vol. x. p. 91.

As to the exposition of the text, it is plain that the parable has to do primarily with the proper use by Christians of worldly wealth; Wesley not unjustifiably extends it to cover all our human powers and talents, and this involves him in a little difficulty when he comes to his second division (ii. 12) and the interpretation of 'Thou mayest be no longer steward.' He finds himself compelled to say of the powers which we shall retain after death, 'The things continue, but our stewardship does not.' Surely we shall still be in the same relation of responsibility to God for their use in the future life as in the present.

The speculations as to the future state in section ii. are interesting, and should be compared with Wesley's last words on this subject in the sermon on Faith (No. CXXII) written on January 17, 1791, only six weeks before he passed into the fuller life of heaven. He there conjectures that the spirits of believers may be permitted to minister to their friends still in the body; that they will swiftly increase in knowledge, holiness, and happiness; that they will forget nothing; that they will have new powers of perception and movement, 'swifter than the light'; and that they will know one another. 'Indeed, sceptics may ask, 'How do disembodied spirits know each other? 'I answer plainly, I cannot tell; but I am certain that they do.'

Give an account of thy stewardship; for thou mayest be no longer steward.—LUKE xvi. 2.

1. The relation which man bears to God, the creature to his Creator, is exhibited to us in the oracles of God under various representations: Considered as a sinner, a fallen creature, he is there represented as a debtor to his Creator. He is also frequently represented as a servant, which indeed is essential to him as a creature; insomuch that this appellation is given to the Son of God when, in His state of humiliation, He 'took upon Him the form of a servant, being made in the likeness of men.'

2. But no character more exactly agrees with the present state of man, than that of a steward. Our blessed Lord frequently represents him as such; and there is a peculiar propriety in the representation. It is only in one particular respect, namely, as he is a sinner, that he is styled a debtor; and when he is styled a servant, the appellation is general and indeterminate: but a steward is a servant of a particular kind; such a one as man is in all respects. This appellation is exactly expressive of his situation in the present world: specifying what kind of servant he is to God, and what kind of service his Divine Master expects from him.

It may be of use, then, to consider this point thoroughly, and to make our full improvement of it. In order to this, let us, first, inquire, in what respects we are now God's stewards. Let us, secondly, observe, that when He requires our souls of us, we 'can be no longer stewards.' It will then only remain, as we may, in the third place, observe, to 'give an account of our stewardship.'

I. 1. And, first, we are to inquire, in what respects we are now God's stewards. We are now indebted to Him for all we have; but although a debtor is obliged to return what he has received, yet until the time of payment comes, he is at liberty to use it as he pleases. It is not so with a steward; he is not at liberty to use what is lodged in his hands as he pleases, but as his master pleases. He has no right to dispose of anything which is in his hands, but according to the will of his lord. For he is not the proprietor of any of these things, but barely entrusted with them by another; and entrusted on this express condition,—that he shall dispose of all as his master orders. Now, this is exactly the case of every man, with relation to God. We are not at liberty to use what He has lodged in our hands as we please, but as He pleases who alone is the possessor of heaven and earth, and the Lord of every creature. We have no right to dispose of anything we have, but according to His will, seeing we are not proprietors of any of these things; they are all, as our Lord speaks, αλλοτρια, *belonging to another person*; nor is anything properly *our own,* in the land of our pilgrimage. We shall not receive τα ιδια, *our own things,* till we come to our own country. Eternal things only are our own: with all these temporal things we are barely entrusted by another, the Disposer and Lord of all. And He entrusts us with them on this express condition,—that we use them only as our Master's goods, and according to the particular directions which He has given us in His Word.

2. On this condition He hath entrusted us with our souls, our bodies, our goods, and whatever other talents we have received: but in order to impress this weighty truth on our hearts, it will be needful to come to particulars.

And, first, God has entrusted us with our soul, an immortal spirit, made in the image of God; together with all the powers and faculties thereof, understanding, imagination, memory, will, and a train of affections, either included in it or closely dependent upon it,—love and hatred, joy and sorrow, respecting present good and evil; desire and aversion, hope and fear, respecting that which is to come. All these St. Paul seems to include in two words, when he says, 'The peace of God shall keep your hearts and minds.' Perhaps, indeed, the latter word, νοηματα, might rather be rendered *thoughts;* provided we take that word in its most extensive sense, for every perception of the mind, whether active or passive.

3. Now, of all these, it is certain, we are only stewards. God has entrusted us with these powers and faculties, not that we may employ them according to our own will, but according to the express orders which He has given us; although it is true that, in doing His will, we most effactually secure our own happiness; seeing it is herein only that we can be happy, either in time or in eternity. Thus we are to use our understanding, our imagination, our memory, wholly to the glory of Him that gave them. Thus our will is to be wholly given up to Him, and all our affections to be regulated as He directs. We are to love and hate, to rejoice and grieve, to desire and shun, to hope and fear, according to the rule which He prescribes whose we are, and whom we are to serve in all things. Even our thoughts are not

our own, in this sense; they are not at our own disposal; but for every deliberate motion of our mind we are accountable to our great Master.

4. God has, secondly, entrusted us with our bodies (those exquisitely wrought machines, so 'fearfully and wonderfully made'), with all the powers and members thereof. He has entrusted us with the organs of sense; of sight, hearing, and the rest: but none of these are given us as our own, to be employed according to our own will. None of these are lent us in such a sense as to leave us at liberty to use them as we please for a season. No: we have received them on these very terms,—that, as long as they abide with us, we should employ them all in that very manner, and no other, which He appoints.

5. It is on the same terms that He imparted to us that most excellent talent of speech. 'Thou hast given me a tongue,' says the ancient writer, 'that I may praise Thee therewith.' For this purpose was it given to all the children of men,—to be employed in glorifying God. Nothing, therefore, is more ungrateful or more absurd, than to think or say, 'Our tongues are our own.' That cannot be, unless we have created ourselves, and so are independent on the Most High. Nay, but 'it is He that hath made us, and not we ourselves'; the manifest consequence is, that He is still Lord over us, in this as in all other respects. It follows, that there is not a word of our tongue for which we are not accountable to Him.

6. To Him we are equally accountable for the use of our hands and feet, and all the members of our body. These are so many talents which are committed to our trust, until the time appointed by the Father. Until then, we have the use of all these; but as stewards, not as proprietors; to the end we should 'render them, not as instruments of unrighteousness unto sin, but as instruments of righteousness unto God.'

7. God has entrusted us, thirdly, with a portion of worldly goods; with food to eat, raiment to put on, and a place where to lay our head; with not only the necessaries, but the conveniences, of life. Above all, He has committed to our charge that precious talent which contains all the rest,—money: indeed it is unspeakably precious, if we are wise and faithful stewards of it; if we employ every part of it for such purposes as our blessed Lord has commanded us to do.

8. God has entrusted us, fourthly, with several talents which do not properly come under any of these heads. Such is bodily strength; such are health, a pleasing person, an agreeable address; such are learning and knowledge, in their various degrees, with all the other advantages of education. Such is the influence which we have over others, whether by their love and esteem of us, or by power; power to do them good or hurt, to help or hinder them in the circumstances of life. Add to these, that invaluable talent of time with which God entrusts us from moment to moment. Add, lastly, that on which all the rest depend, and without which they would all be curses, not blessings; namely, the grace of God, the power of His Holy Spirit, which alone worketh in us all that is acceptable in His sight.

II. 1. In so many respects are the children of men stewards of the Lord, the Possessor of heaven and earth: so large a portion of His goods, of various kinds, hath He committed to their charge. But it is not for ever, nor indeed for any considerable time: we have this trust reposed in us only during the short, uncertain space that we sojourn here below; only so long as we remain on earth, as this fleeting breath is in our nostrils. The hour is swiftly approaching, it is just at hand, when we 'can be no longer stewards'! The moment the body 'returns to the dust as it was, and the spirit to God that gave it' we bear that character no more; the time of our stewardship is at an end. Part of those goods wherewith we were before entrusted are now come to an end; at least, they are so with regard to *us*; nor are we longer entrusted with them: and that part which remains can no longer be employed or improved as it was before.

2. Part of what we were entrusted with before is at an end, at least with regard to us. What have we to do, after this life, with food, and raiment, and houses, and earthly possessions? The food of the dead is the dust of the earth; they are clothed only with worms and rottenness. They dwell in the house prepared for all flesh; their lands know them no more: all their worldly goods are delivered into other hands, and they have 'no more portion under the sun.' 3. The case is the same with regard to the body. The moment the spirit returns to God, we are no longer stewards of this machine, which is then sown in

corruption and dishonour. All the parts and members of which it was composed lie mouldering in the clay. The hands have no longer power to move; the feet have forgot their office; the flesh, sinews, and bones, are all hastening to be dissolved into common dust.

4. Here end also the talents of a mixed nature; our strength, our health, our beauty, our eloquence, and address, our faculty of pleasing or persuading, or convincing others. Here end, likewise, all the honours we once enjoyed, all the power which was lodged in our hands, all the influence which we once had over others, either by the love or the esteem which they bore us. Our love, our hatred, our desire, is perished: none regard how we were once affected toward them. They look upon the dead as neither able to help nor hurt them; so that 'a living dog is better than a dead lion.'

5. Perhaps a doubt may remain concerning some of the other talents wherewith we are now entrusted, whether they will cease to exist when the body returns to dust or only cease to be improvable. Indeed, there is no doubt but the kind of speech which we now use, by means of these bodily organs, will then be entirely at an end, when those organs are destroyed. It is certain, the tongue will no more occasion any vibrations in the air; neither will the ear convey these tremulous motions to the common sensory. Even the *sonus exilis,* the low, shrill voice, which the poet supposes to belong to a separate spirit, we cannot allow to have a real being; it is a mere flight of imagination. Indeed, it cannot be questioned, but separate spirits have some way to communicate their sentiments to each other; but what inhabitant of flesh and blood can explain that way? What we term 'speech,' they cannot have: so that we can no longer be stewards of this talent when we are numbered with the dead.

6. It may likewise admit of a doubt, whether our senses will exist, when the organs of sense are destroyed. Is it not probable, that those of the lower kind will cease—the feeling, the smell, the taste—as they have a more immediate reference to the body, and are chiefly, if not wholly, intended for the preservation of it? But will not some kind of sight remain, although the eye be closed in death? And will there not be something in the soul equivalent to the present sense of hearing? Nay, is it not probable, that these will not only exist in the separate state, but exist in a far greater

degree, in a more eminent manner, than now, when the soul, disentangled from its clay, is no longer 'a dying sparkle in a cloudy place'; when it no longer 'looks through the windows of the eye and ear'; but rather is all eye, all ear, all sense, in a manner we cannot yet conceive? And have we not a clear proof of the possibility of this, of seeing without the use of the eye, and hearing without the use of the ear? yea, and an earnest of it continually? For does not the soul see, in the clearest manner, when the eye is of no use; namely, in dreams? Does she not then enjoy the faculty of hearing, without any help from the ear? But however this be, certain it is, that neither will our senses, any more than our speech, be entrusted to us in the manner they are now, when the body lies in the silent grave.

7. How far the knowledge or learning which we have gained by education will then remain, we cannot tell. Solomon indeed says, 'There is no work, nor device, nor knowledge, nor wisdom, in the grave, whither thou goest.' But it is evident, these words cannot be understood in an absolute sense. For it is so far from being true that there is no knowledge after we have quitted the body, that the doubt lies on the other side, whether there be any such thing as real knowledge till then; whether it be not a plain sober truth, not a mere poetical fiction, that

> All these shadows, which for things we take,
> Are but the empty dreams, which in death's sleep we make;

only excepting those things which God Himself has been pleased to reveal to man. I will speak for one. After having sought for truth, with some diligence, for half a century, I am, at this day, hardly sure of anything but what I learn from the Bible. Nay, I positively affirm, I know nothing else so certainly, that I would dare to stake my salvation upon it.

So much, however, we may learn from Solomon's words, that 'there is no' such 'knowledge or wisdom in the grave,' as will be of any use to an unhappy spirit: 'there is no device' there, whereby he can now improve those talents with which he was once entrusted. For time is no more; the time of our trial for everlasting happiness or misery is past. Our day, the day of man, is over; the day of salvation is ended! Nothing now remains but 'the day of the Lord,' ushering in wide, unchangeable eternity!

8. But still, our souls, being incorruptible and immortal, of a nature 'little lower than the angels' (even if we are to understand that phrase of our original nature, which may well admit of a doubt), when our bodies are mouldered into earth, will remain with all their faculties. Our memory, our understanding, will be so far from being destroyed, yea, or impaired, by the dissolution of the body, that, on the contrary, we have reason to believe, they will be inconceivably strengthened. Have we not the clearest reason to believe, that they will then be wholly freed from those defects which now naturally result from the union of the soul with the corruptible body? It is highly probable, that, from the time these are disunited, our memory will let nothing slip; yea, that it will faithfully exhibit everything to our view which was ever committed to it. It is true, that the invisible world is in Scripture, termed 'the land of forgetfulness'; or, as it is still more strongly expressed in the old translation, 'the land where all things are forgotten.' They are forgotten; but by whom? Not by the inhabitants of that land, but by the inhabitants of the earth. It is with regard to them that the unseen world is 'the land of forgetfulness.' All things therein are too frequently forgotten by these; but not by disembodied spirits. From the time they have put off the earthly tabernacle, we can hardly think they forget anything.

9. In like manner, the understanding will, doubtless, be freed from the defects that are now inseparable from it. For many ages it has been an unquestioned maxim, *Humanum est errare et nescire*: ignorance and mistake are inseparable from human nature. But the whole of this assertion is only true with regard to living men; and holds no longer than while 'the corruptible body presses down the soul.' Ignorance, indeed, belongs to every finite understanding (seeing there is none beside God that knoweth all things); but not mistake: when the body is laid aside, this also is laid aside, for ever.

10. What then can we say of an ingenious man, who has lately made a discovery, that disembodied spirits have not only no senses (not even sight or hearing), but no memory or understanding; no thought or perception; not so much as a consciousness of their own existence! that they are in a dead sleep from death to the resurrection! *Consanguineus lethi sopor* indeed! Such a sleep we may call 'a near kinsman of death,' if it

be not the same thing. What can we say, but that ingenious men have strange dreams; and these they sometimes mistake for realities?

11. But to return. As the soul will retain its understanding and memory, notwithstanding the dissolution of the body, so undoubtedly the will, including all the affections, will remain in its full vigour. If our love or anger, our hope or desire, perish, it is only with regard to those whom we leave behind. To them it matters not, whether they were the objects of our love or hate, of our desire or aversion. But in separate spirits themselves we have no reason to believe that any of these are extinguished. It is more probable, that they work with far greater force, than while the soul was clogged with flesh and blood.

12. But although all these, although both our knowledge and senses, our memory and understanding, together with our will, our love, hate, and all our affections, remain after the body is dropped off; yet, in this respect, they are as though they were not—we are no longer stewards of them. The things continue, but our stewardship does not: we no more act in that capacity. Even the grace which was formerly entrusted with us, in order to enable us to be faithful and wise stewards, is now no longer entrusted for that purpose. The days of our stewardship are ended.

III. 1. It now remains, that being no longer stewards, we give an account of our stewardship. Some have imagined, this is to be done immediately after death, as soon as we enter into the world of spirits. Nay, the Church of Rome does absolutely assert this; yea, makes it an article of faith. And thus much we may allow, the moment a soul drops the body, and stands naked before God, it cannot but know what its portion will be to all eternity. It will have full in its view, either everlasting joy, or everlasting torment; as it is no longer possible for us to be deceived in the judgement which we pass upon ourselves. But the Scripture gives us no reason to believe, that God will then sit in judgement upon us. There is no passage in all the oracles of God which affirms any such thing. That which has been frequently alleged for this purpose seems rather to prove the contrary; namely (Heb. ix. 27), 'It is appointed for men once to die, and after this the judgement': for, in all reason, the word 'once' is here to be applied to judgement as well as death. So that the fair inference to be drawn from this very text is, not that there are two judgements, a particular and a general; but that we are to be judged, as well as to die, once only: not once immediately after death, and again after the general resurrection; but then only 'when the Son of man shall come in His glory, and all His holy angels with Him.' The imagination therefore of one judgement at death, and another at the end of the world, can have no place with those who make the written Word of God the whole and sole standard of their faith.

2. The time then when we are to give this account is, when the 'great white throne comes down from heaven, and He that sitteth thereon, from whose face the heavens and the earth flee away, and there is found no place for them.' It is then 'the dead, small and great, will stand before God; and the books will be opened': the book of Scripture, to them who were entrusted therewith; the book of conscience to all mankind. The 'book of remembrance,' likewise (to use another scriptural expression), which had been writing from the foundation of the world, will then be laid open to the view of all the children of men. Before all these, even the whole human race, before the devil and his angels, before an innumerable company of holy angels, and before God the Judge of all, thou wilt appear, without any shelter or covering, without any possibility of disguise, to give a particular account of the manner wherein thou hast employed all thy Lord's goods!

3. The Judge of all will then inquire, 'How didst thou employ thy soul? I entrusted thee with an immortal spirit, endowed with various powers and faculties, with understanding, imagination, memory, will, affections. I gave thee withal full and express directions, how all these were to be employed. Didst thou employ thy understanding, as far as it was capable, according to those directions; namely, in the knowledge of thyself and Me—My nature, My attributes, My works, whether of creation, of providence, or of grace?—in acquainting thyself with My Word—in using every means to increase thy knowledge thereof, in meditating thereon day and night? Didst thou employ thy memory, according to My will, in treasuring up whatever knowledge thou hadst acquired, which might conduce to My glory, to thy own salvation, or the advantage of others? Didst

thou store up therein, not things of no value, but whatever instruction thou hadst learned from My Word; and whatever experience thou hadst gained of My wisdom, truth, power, and mercy? Was thy imagination employed, not in painting vain images, much less such as nourished "foolish and hurtful desires"; but in representing to thee whatever would profit thy soul, and awaken thy pursuit of wisdom and holiness? Didst thou follow My directions with regard to thy will? Was it wholly given up to Me? Was it swallowed up in Mine, so as never to oppose, but always run parallel with it? Were thy affections placed and regulated in such a manner, as I appointed in My Word? Didst thou give Me thy heart? Didst thou not love the world, neither the things of the world? Was I the object of thy love? Was all thy desire unto Me, and unto the remembrance of My name? Was I the joy of thy heart, the delight of thy soul, the chief among ten thousand? Didst thou sorrow for nothing, but what grieved My Spirit? Didst thou fear and hate nothing but sin? Did the whole stream of thy affections flow back to the ocean from whence they came? Were thy thoughts employed according to My will—not in ranging to the ends of the earth, not on folly, or sin; but on "whatsoever things were pure, whatsoever things were holy"; on whatsoever was conducive to My glory, and to "peace and goodwill among men"?'

4. Thy Lord will then inquire, 'How didst thou employ the body wherewith I entrusted thee? I gave thee a tongue to praise Me therewith: didst thou use it to the end for which it was given? Didst thou employ it, not in evil speaking or idle speaking, not in uncharitable or unprofitable conversation: but in such as was good, as was necessary or useful either to thyself or others—such as always tended, directly or indirectly, to "minister grace to the hearers"? I gave thee, together with thy other senses, those grand avenues of knowledge, sight, and hearing: were these employed to those excellent purposes for which they were bestowed upon thee—in bringing thee in more and more instruction in righteousness and true holiness? I gave thee hands and feet, and various members, wherewith to perform the works which were prepared for thee: were they employed, not in doing "the will of the flesh," of thy evil nature; or the will of the mind (the things to which thy reason or fancy led thee); but "the will of Him that sent" thee into the world, merely to

work out thy own salvation? Didst thou present all thy members, not to sin, as instruments of unrighteousness, but to Me alone, through the Son of My love, "as instruments of righteousness"?'

5. The Lord of all will next inquire, 'How didst thou employ the worldly goods which I lodged in thy hands? Didst thou use thy food, not so as to seek or place thy happiness therein, but so as to preserve the body in health, in strength and vigour, a fit instrument for the soul? Didst thou use apparel, not to nourish pride or vanity, much less to tempt others to sin, but conveniently and decently to defend thyself from the injuries of the weather? Didst thou prepare and use thy house, and all other conveniences, with a single eye to My glory—in every point seeking not thy own honour, but Mine; studying to please, not thyself, but Me? Once more: in what manner didst thou employ that comprehensive talent, money?—not in gratifying the desire of the flesh, the desire of the eye, or the pride of life; not squandering it away in vain expenses—the same as throwing it into the sea; not hoarding it up to leave behind thee—the same as burying it in the earth; but first supplying thy own reasonable wants, together with those of thy family; then restoring the remainder to Me, through the poor, whom I had appointed to receive it; looking upon thyself as only one of that number of poor, whose wants were to be supplied out of that part of My substance which I had placed in thy hands for this purpose; leaving thee the right of being supplied first, and the blessedness of giving rather than receiving? Wast thou accordingly a general benefactor to mankind? feeding the hungry, clothing the naked, comforting the sick, assisting the stranger, relieving the afflicted, according to their various necessities? Wast thou eyes to the blind, and feet to the lame, a father to the fatherless, and an husband to the widow? And didst thou labour to improve all outward works of mercy, as means of saving souls from death?'

6. Thy Lord will farther inquire, 'Hast thou been a wise and faithful steward with regard to the talents of a mixed nature which I lent thee? Didst thou employ thy health and strength, not in folly or sin, not in the pleasures which perished in the using, "not in making provision for the flesh, to fulfil the desires thereof," but in a vigorous pursuit of that better part which none could take away from thee? Didst thou employ whatever was pleasing in thy person or address, whatever advantages thou

hadst by education, whatever share of learning, whatever knowledge of things or men, was committed to thee, for the promoting of virtue in the world, for the enlargement of My kingdom? Didst thou employ whatever share of power thou hadst, whatever influence over others, by the love or esteem of thee which they had conceived, for the increase of their wisdom and holiness? Didst thou employ that inestimable talent of time, with wariness and circumspection, as duly weighing the value of every moment, and knowing that all were numbered in eternity? Above all, wast thou a good steward of My grace, preventing, accompanying, and following thee? Didst thou duly observe, and carefully improve, all the influences of My Spirit—every good desire, every measure of light, all His sharp or gentle reproofs? How didst thou profit by "the Spirit of bondage and fear," which was previous to "the Spirit of adoption"? And when thou wast made a partaker of this Spirit, crying in thy heart, "Abba, Father," didst thou stand fast in the glorious liberty wherewith I made thee free? Didst thou from thenceforth present thy soul and body, all thy thoughts, thy words, and actions, in one flame of love, as a holy sacrifice, glorifying Me with thy body and thy spirit? Then "well done, good and faithful servant! Enter thou into the joy of thy Lord"!'

And what will remain, either to the faithful or unfaithful steward? Nothing but the execution of that sentence which has been passed by the righteous Judge; fixing thee in a state which admits of no change through everlasting ages! It remains only that thou be rewarded, to all eternity, according to thy works.

IV. 1. From these plain considerations we may learn, first, How important is this short, uncertain day of life! How precious, above all utterance, above all conception, is every portion of it!

> The least of these a serious care demands;
> For though they're little, they are golden sands!

How deeply does it concern every child of man, to let none of these run to waste; but to improve them all to the noblest purposes, as long as the breath of God is in his nostrils!

2. We learn from hence, secondly, that there is no employ-ment of our time, no action or conversation, that is purely

indifferent. All is good or bad, because all our time, as everything we have, is not our own. All these are, as our Lord speaks, τα αλλοτρια—*the property of another*; of God our Creator. Now, these either are or are not employed according to His will. If they are so employed, all is good; if they are not, all is evil. Again: it is His will, that we should continually grow in grace, and in the living knowledge of our Lord Jesus Christ. Consequently, every thought, word, and work, whereby this knowledge is increased, whereby we grow in grace, is good; and every one whereby this knowledge is not increased, is truly and properly evil.

3. We learn from hence, thirdly, that there are no works of supererogation; that we can never do more than our duty; seeing all we have is not our own, but God's; all we can do is due to Him. We have not received this or that, or many things only, but everything from Him: therefore, everything is His due. He that gives us all, must needs have a right to all: so that if we pay Him anything less than all, we cannot be faithful stewards. And considering, 'every man shall receive his own reward, according to his own labour,' we cannot be wise stewards unless we labour to the uttermost of our power; not leaving anything undone which we possibly can do, but putting forth all our strength.

4. Brethren, 'who is an understanding man and endued with knowledge among you?' Let him show the wisdom from above, by walking suitably to his character. If he so account of himself as a steward of the manifold gifts of God, let him see that all his thoughts, and words, and works, be agreeable to the post God has assigned him. It is no small thing, to lay out for God all which you have received from God. It requires all your wisdom, all your resolution, all your patience and constancy; far more than ever you had by nature, but not more than you may have by grace. For His grace is sufficient for you; and 'all things,' you know, 'are possible to him that believeth.' By faith, then, 'put on the Lord Jesus Christ'; 'put on the whole armour of God'; and you shall be enabled to glorify Him in all your words and works; yea, to bring every thought into captivity to the obedience of Christ!

EDINBURGH, *May* 14, 1768.

SERMON LII

PREACHED BEFORE THE SOCIETY FOR REFORMATION OF
MANNERS, ON SUNDAY, JANUARY 30, 1763, AT THE
CHAPEL IN WEST STREET, SEVEN DIALS.

In 1677 a number of young men who had been influenced by the preaching of Dr. Anthony Horneck of the Savoy Chapel, Dr. Smithies of St. Michael's, Cornhill, and Dr. William Beveridge of St. Peter's, Cornhill, afterwards Bishop of St. Asaph, formed themselves into a religious society, meeting once a week for prayer and Christian conference. They also made a weekly collection which they applied to the relief of poor families, debtors, orphans, and others. In the reign of James II they fell under suspicion and had to hold their meetings more or less secretly; but at the Revolution of 1689 their numbers greatly increased, and in 1691 they organized themselves for the suppression of public vice, procured a letter from Queen Mary through Archbishop Tillotson requiring the magistrates to enforce the laws against swearing, drunkenness, Sabbath-breaking, &c., and secured the patronage of the Lord Mayor and Aldermen of the City. They published and distributed a summary of the laws against vice and profanity and drew up rules for the conviction of offenders. The result of their efforts was that several Sunday markets were abolished, music-halls and brothels were closed, many offenders were convicted, and above 2,000 prostitutes and keepers of brothels were brought before the courts and punished. A sermon was preached annually before the society, and the preacher in 1698 was Samuel Wesley, the father of John and Charles. The sermon was preached on February 13, in St. James's, Westminster, and repeated at St. Bride's, Fleet Street. The text was Ps. xciv. 16; the sermon was printed in the *Methodist Magazine* for 1814, p. 648. The divisions are (I) That it is difficult to persuade men to engage in the cause of God against wicked persons. (II) That it is the duty of good men to oppose vice and wickedness. Under the second head are three subdivisions: (1) That good men ought to oppose vice and wickedness; (2) that they should do this with united counsels; (3) and with the utmost zeal and prudence. Then come some practical inferences: (1) That we should reprove those who encourage wickedness—and under this head there is a vigorous attack on the 'infamous theatres'; (2) that the members of the society should apply the same prudence and zeal to the regulation of their own conduct as to that of others.

The society continued its work until 1730, when it became defunct. But it was revived in 1757, the father of the movement being, according

749

to Wesley's testimony in his *Journal*, February 2, 1766, Mr. W. Welsh.
The history of it is given in this sermon (I) and need not be repeated;
and the note at the end of the sermon tells of its disastrous termination.
Wesley preached the annual sermon in 1763 at the West Street Chapel
(for the history of which see introduction to Sermon XLIX), and took
the same text as his father had chosen sixty-five years before. On
January 17 he had retired to Lewisham, doubtless to the house of his
friend, Mr. Blackwell, to write the sermon; and he published it as a
sixpenny pamphlet in the course of the year, and embodied it in the
fourth volume of the Sermons in the *Works* of 1771. It is well worth the
study of all those who are engaged in social reform.

Who will rise up with me against the wicked?—PS. xciv. 16.

1. In all ages, men who neither feared God nor regarded man
have combined together and formed confederacies, to carry on
the works of darkness. And herein they have shown themselves
wise in their generation; for by this means they more effectually
promoted the kingdom of their father the devil, than otherwise
they could have done. On the other hand, men who did fear
God, and desire the happiness of their fellow creatures, have, in
every age, found it needful to join together, in order to oppose
the works of darkness, to spread the knowledge of God their
Saviour, and to promote His kingdom upon earth. Indeed He
Himself has instructed them so to do. From the time that men
were upon the earth, He hath taught them to join together in
His service, and has united them in one body by one Spirit. And
for this very end He has joined them together, 'that He might
destroy the works of the devil'; first in them that are already
united, and by them in all that are round about them.

2. This is the original design of the church of Christ. It is a
body of men compacted together, in order, first, to save each his
own soul; then to assist each other in working out their salvation;
and, afterwards, as far as in them lies, to save all men from
present and future misery, to overturn the kindgom of Satan,
and set up the kingdom of Christ. And this ought to be the
continued care and endeavour of every member of His Church;
otherwise he is not worthy to be called a member thereof, as he is
not a living member of Christ.

3. Accordingly, this ought to be the constant care and
endeavour of all those who are united together in these
kingdoms, and are commonly called, *The Church of England*.

They are united together for this very end, to oppose the devil and all his works, and to wage war against the world and the flesh, his constant and faithful allies. But do they, in fact, answer the end of their union? Are all who style themselves 'members of the Church of England' heartily engaged in opposing the works of the devil, and fighting against the world and the flesh? Alas! we cannot say this. So far from it, that a great part, I fear the greater part of them, are themselves *the world*,—the people that know not God to any saving purpose; are indulging, day by day, instead of 'mortifying, the flesh, with its affections and desires'; and doing, themselves, those works of the devil, which they are peculiarly engaged to destroy.

4. There is, therefore, still need, even in this Christian country (as we *courteously* style Great Britain), yea, in this Christian Church (if we may give that title to the bulk of our nation), of some to 'rise up against the wicked,' and join together 'against the evil doers.' Nay, there was never more need than there is at this day for them 'that fear the Lord to speak often together' on his very head, how they may 'lift up a standard against the iniquity' which overflows the land. There is abundant cause for all the servants of God to join together against the works of the devil; with united hearts and counsels and endeavours to make a stand for God, and to repress, as much as in them lies, these 'floods of ungodliness.'

5. For this end a few persons in London, towards the close of the last century united together, and, after a while, were termed, *The Society for Reformation of Manners*; and incredible good was done by them for near forty years. But then, most of the original members being gone to their reward, those who succeeded them grew faint in their mind, and departed from the work: so that a few years ago the Society ceased; nor did any of the kind remain in the kingdom.

6. It is a Society of the same nature which has been lately formed. I purpose to show, first, the nature of their design, and the steps they have hitherto taken: secondly, the excellency of it; with the various objections which have been raised against it: thirdly, what manner of men they ought to be who engage in such a design: and, fourthly, with what spirit, and in what manner, they should proceed in the prosecution of it. I shall conclude with an application both to them, and to all that fear God.

I. 1. I am, first, to show the nature of their design, and the steps they have hitherto taken.

It was on a Lord's day, in August, 1757, that, in a small company who were met for prayer and religious conversation, mention was made of the gross and open profanation of that sacred day, by persons buying and selling, keeping open shop, tippling in alehouses, and standing or sitting in the streets, roads, or fields, vending their wares as on common days; especially in Moorfields, which was then full of them every Sunday, from one end to the other. It was considered, what method could be taken to redress these grievances; and it was agreed, that six of them should, in the morning, wait upon Sir John Fielding for instruction. They did so: he approved of the design, and directed them how to carry it into execution.

2. They first delivered petitions to the Right Honourable the Lord Mayor, and the Court of Aldermen; to the justices sitting at Hicks's Hall, and those in Westminster; and they received from all these honourable benches much encouragement to proceed.

3. It was next judged proper to signify their design to many persons of eminent rank, and to the body of the clergy, as well as the ministers of other denominations, belonging to the several churches and meetings in and about the cities of London and Westminster; and they had the satisfaction to meet with an hearty consent and universal approbation from them.

4. They then printed and dispersed, at their own expense, several thousand books of instruction to constables and other parish officers, explaining and enforcing their several duties and to prevent, as far as possible, the necessity of proceeding to an actual execution of the laws, they likewise printed and dispersed, in all parts of the town, dissuasives from Sabbath-breaking, extracts from Acts of Parliament against it, and notices to the offenders.

5. The way being paved by these precautions, it was in the beginning of the year 1758, that, after notices delivered again and again, which were as often set at nought, actual informations were made to the Magistrates against persons profaning the Lord's day. By this means they first cleared the streets and fields of those notorious offenders who, without any regard either to God or the King, were selling their wares from morning to night. They proceeded to a more difficult attempt,

the preventing tippling on the Lord's day, spending the time in alehouses, which ought to be spent in the more immediate worship of God. Herein they were exposed to abundance of reproach, to insult and abuse of every kind; having not only the tipplers, and those who entertained them, the alehouse keepers, to contend with, but rich and honourable men, partly the landlords of those alehouse keepers, partly those who furnished them with drink, and, in general, all who gained by their sins. Some of these were not only men of substance, but men of authority; nay, in more instances than one, they were the very persons before whom the delinquents were brought. And the treatment they gave those who laid the informations naturally encouraged 'the beasts of the people' to follow their example, and to use them as fellows not fit to live upon the earth. Hence they made no scruple, not only to treat them with the basest language, not only to throw at them mud or stones, or whatever came to hand, but many times to beat them without mercy, and to drag them over the stones or through the kennels. And that they did not murder them, was not for want of will; but the bridle was in their teeth.

6. Having, therefore, received help from God, they went on to restrain bakers likewise, from spending so great a part of the Lord's day in exercising the works of their calling. But many of these were more noble than the victuallers. they were so far from resenting this, or looking upon it as an affront, that several, who had been hurried down the stream of custom to act contrary to their own conscience, sincerely thanked them for their labour, and acknowledged it as a real kindness.

7. In clearing the streets, fields, and alehouses of Sabbath-breakers, they fell upon another sort of offenders, as mishievous to society as any; namely, gamesters of various kinds. Some of these were of the lowest and vilest class, commonly called 'gamblers'; who make a trade of seizing young and inexperienced men, and tricking them out of all their money; and after they have beggared them, they frequently teach them the same mystery of iniquity. Several tests of these they have rooted out, and constrained not a few of them honestly to earn their bread by the sweat of their brow, and the labour of their hands.

8. Increasing in number and strength, they extended their views, and began, not only to repress profane swearing, but of

remove out of our streets another public nuisance, and scandal of the Christian name,—common prostitutes. Many of these were stopped in their mid career of audacious wickedness. And, in order to go to the root of the disease, any of the houses that entertained them have been detected, prosecuted according to law, and totally suppressed. And some of the poor desolate women themselves, though fallen to

> The lowest line of human infamy,

have acknowledged the gracious providence of God, and broke off their sins by lasting repentance. Several of these have been placed out, and several received into the Magdalen Hospital.

9. If a little digression may be allowed, who can sufficiently admire the wisdom of Divine Providence, in the disposal of the times and seasons so as to suit one occurrence to another? For instance: just at a time when many of these poor creatures, being stopped in the course of sin, found a desire of leading a better life, as it were in answer to that sad question, 'But if I quit the way I now am in, what can I do to live? For I am not mistress of any trade; and I have no friends that will receive me':—I say, just at this time, God has prepared the Magdalen Hospital. Here those who have no trade, nor any friends to receive them, are received with all tenderness; yea, they may live, and that with comfort, being provided with all things that are needful 'for life and godliness.'

10. But to return. The number of persons brought to justice,
From August, 1757, to August, 1762, is 9,596
From thence to the present time:—
For unlawful gaming, and profane swearing......... 40
For Sabbath-breaking.. 400
Lewd women, and keepers of ill houses................. 550
For offering to sale obscene prints.......................... 2
In all..10,588

11. In the admission of members into the Society, no regard is had to any particular sect or party. Whoever is found, upon inquiry, to be a good man, is readily admitted. And none who has selfish or pecuniary views will long continue therein; not only because he can gain nothing thereby, but because he would

quickly be a loser, inasmuch as he must commence subscriber as soon as he is a member. Indeed, the vulgar cry is, 'These are all Whitefieldites.' But it is a great mistake. About twenty of the constantly subscribing members are all that are in connexion with Mr. Whitefield; about fifty are in connexion with Mr. Wesley; about twenty, who are of the Established Church, have no connexion with either; and about seventy are Dissenters; who make, in all, an hundred and sixty. There are, indeed, many more who assist in the work by occasional subscriptions.

II. 1. These are the steps which have been hitherto taken in prosecution of this design. I am, in the second place, to show the excellency thereof, notwithstanding the objections which have been raised against it. Now, this may appear from several considerations. And, first, from hence,—that the making an open stand against all the ungodliness and unrighteousness which overspread our land as a flood, is one of the noblest ways of confessing Christ in the face of His enemies. It is giving glory to God, and showing mankind that, even in these dregs of time,

> There are who faith prefer,
> Though few, and piety to God.

And what more excellent than to render to God the honour due unto His name? to declare, by a stronger proof than words, even by suffering, and running all hazards, 'Verily there is a reward for the righteous; doubtless there is a God that judgeth the earth'?

2. How excellent is the design to prevent, in any degree, the dishonour done to His glorious name, the contempt which is poured on His authority, and the scandal brought upon our holy religion by the gross, flagrant wickedness of those who are still called by the name of Christ! To stem, in any degree, the torrent of vice, to repress the floods of ungodliness, to remove, in any measure, those occasions of blaspheming the worthy name whereby we are called, is one of the noblest designs that can possibly enter into the heart of man to conceive.

3. And as this design thus evidently tends to bring 'glory to God in the highest,' so it no less manifestly conduces to the establishing 'peace upon earth.' For as all sin directly tends both

to destroy our peace with God, by setting Him at open defiance, to banish peace from our own breasts, and to set every man's sword against his neighbour; so whatever prevents or removes sin does, in the same degree, promote peace—both peace in our own soul, peace with God, and peace with one another. Such are the genuine fruits of this design, even in the present world. But why should we confine our views to the narrow bounds of time and space? Rather pass over these into eternity. And what fruit of it shall we find there? Let the Apostle speak: 'Brethren, if one of you do err from the truth, and one convert him,' not to this or that opinion, but to God; 'let him know that he which converteth the sinner from the error of his way shall save a soul from death, and hide a multitude of sins' (Jas. v. 19, 20).

4. Nor is it to individuals only, whether those who betray others into sin, or those that are liable to be betrayed and destroyed by them, that the benefit of this design redounds; but to the whole community whereof we are members. For is it not a sure observation, 'Righteousness exalteth a nation'? And is it not as sure, on the other hand, that 'sin is a reproach to any people'; yea, and bringeth down the curse of God upon them? So far, therefore, as righteousness in any branch, is promoted, so far is the national interest advanced. So far as sin, especially open sin, is restrained, the curse and reproach are removed from us. Whoever, therefore, they are that labour herein, they are general benefactors; they are the truest friends of their King and country. And in the same proportion as their design takes place, there can be no doubt but God will give national prosperity, in accomplishment of His faithful word, 'Them that honour Me I will honour.'

5. But it is objected, 'However excellent a design this is, it does not concern *you*. For are there not persons to whom the repressing these offences, and punishing the offenders, properly belong? Are there not constables, and other parish officers, who are bound by oath to this very thing?' There are. Constables and churchwardens, in particular, are engaged by solemn oaths to give due information against profaners of the Lord's day, and all other scandalous sinners. But if they leave it undone; if, notwithstanding their oaths, they trouble not themselves about the matter; it concerns all that fear God, that love mankind, and that wish well to their King and country, to

pursue this design with the very same vigour as if there were no officers existing; it being just the same thing, if they are of no use, as if they had no being.

6. 'But this is only a pretence: their real design is to get money by giving informations.' So it has frequently and roundly been affirmed; but without the least shadow of truth. The contrary may be proved by a thousand instances: no member of the Society takes any part of the money which is by the law allotted to the informer. They never did from the beginning; nor does any of them ever receive anything to suppress or withdraw their information. This is another mistake, if not wilful slander, for which there is not the least foundation.

7. 'But the design is impracticable. Vice is risen to such a head, that it is impossible to suppress it; especially by such means. For what can a handful of poor people do, in opposition to all the world?' 'With men this is impossible, but not with God.' And they trust not in themselves, but Him. Be then the patrons of vice ever so strong, to Him they are no more than grasshoppers. And all means are alike to Him: it is the same thing with God 'to deliver by many or by few.' The small number, therefore, of those who are on the Lord's side, is nothing; neither the great number of those that are against Him. Still He doeth whatever pleaseth Him; and 'there is no counsel nor strength against the Lord.'

8. 'But if the end you aim at be really to reform sinners, you choose the wrong means. It is the Word of God must effect this, and not human laws; and it is the work of ministers, not of magistrates; therefore, the applying to these can only produce an outward reformation; it makes no change in the heart.'

It is true the Word of God is the chief, ordinary means, whereby He changes both the hearts and lives of sinners; and He does this chiefly by the ministers of the gospel. But it is likewise true, that the magistrate is 'the minister of God'; and that he is designed of God to be 'a terror to evil-doers,' by executing human laws upon them. If this does not change the heart; yet, to prevent outward sin is one valuable point gained. There is so much the less dishonour done to God; less scandal brought on our holy religion; less curse and reproach upon our nation; less temptation laid in the way of others; yea, and less wrath heaped up by the sinners themselves against the day of wrath.

9. 'Nay, rather more; for it makes many of them hypocrites, pretending to be what they are not. Others, by exposing them to shame, and putting them to expense, are made impudent and desperate in wickedness: so that, in reality, none of them are any better, if they are not worse, than they were before.'

This is a mistake all over. For, (1) where are these hypocrites? We know none who have pretended to be what they were not. (2) The exposing obstinate offenders to shame, and putting them to expense, does not make them desperate in offending, but afraid to offend. (3) Some of them, far from being worse, are substantially better; the whole tenor of their lives being changed. Yea, (4) some are inwardly changed, even from 'darkness to light, and from the power of Satan unto God.'

10. 'But many are not convinced that buying or selling on the Lord's day is a sin.'

If they are not convinced, they ought to be; it is high time they should. The case is as plain as plain can be. For if an open, wilful breach both of the law of God and the law of the land is not sin, pray what is? And if such a breach of divine and human laws is not to be punished, because a man is not convinced it is a sin, there is an end of all execution of justice, and all men may live as they list!

11. 'But *mild* methods ought to be tried first.' They ought: and so they are. A mild admonition is given to every offender, before the law is put in execution against him; nor is any man prosecuted, till he has express notice that this will be the case unless he will prevent that prosecution by removing the cause of it. In every case, the mildest method is used which the nature of the case will bear; nor are severer means ever applied, but when they are absolutely necessary to the end.

12. 'Well, but after all this stir about reformation, what real good has been done?' Unspeakable good; and abundantly more than any one could have expected in so short a time, considering the small number of the instruments, and the difficulties they had to encounter. Much evil has been already prevented, and much has been removed. Many sinners have been outwardly reformed; some have been inwardly changed. The honour of Him whose name we bear, so openly affronted, has been openly defended. And it is not easy to determine, how many and how great blessings, even this little stand, made for God and His

cause, against His daring enemies, may already have derived upon our whole nation. On the whole, then, after all the objections that can be made, reasonable men may still conclude, a more excellent design could scarce ever enter into the heart of man.

III. 1. But what manner of men ought they to be who engage in such a design? Some may imagine, any that are willing to assist therein ought readily to be admitted; and that the greater the number of members, the greater will be their influence. But this is by no means true: matter of fact undeniably proves the contrary. While the former Society for Reformation of Manners consisted of chosen members only, though neither many, rich, nor powerful, they broke through all opposition, and were eminently successful in every branch of their undertaking; but when a number of men less carefully chosen were received into that Society, they grew less and less useful, till, by insensible degrees, they dwindled into nothing.

2. The number, therefore, of the members is no more to be attended to than the riches or eminence. This is a work of God. It is undertaken in the name of God, and for His sake. It follows, that men who neither love nor fear God have no part or lot in this matter. 'Why takest thou My covenant in thy mouth?' may God say to any of these; 'whereas thou' thyself 'hatest to be reformed, and hast cast My words behind thee.' Whoever, therefore, lives in any known sin is not fit to engage in reforming sinners: more especially if he is guilty, in any instance, or in the least degree, of profaning the name of God; of buying, selling, or doing any unnecessary work on the Lord's day; or offending in any other of those instances which this Society is peculiarly designed to reform. No; let none who stands himself in need of this reformation presume to meddle with such an undertaking. First let him 'pull the beam out of his own eye': let him be himself *unblamable* in all things.

3. Not that this will suffice: every one engaging herein should be more than a harmless man. He should be a man of faith; having, at least, such a degree of that 'evidence of things not seen,' as to aim 'not at the things that are seen, which are temporal, but at those that are not seen, which are eternal'; such faith as produces a steady fear of God, with a lasting resolution,

by His grace, to abstain from all that He has forbidden, and to do all that He has commanded. He will more especially need that particular branch of faith,—confidence in God. It is this faith which 'removes mountains'; which 'quenches the violence of fire'; which breaks through all opposition; and enables one to stand against and 'chase a thousand,' knowing in whom his strength lies, and, even when he has the 'sentence of death in himself, trusting in Him who raiseth the dead.'

4. He that has faith and confidence in God will, of consequence, be a man of courage. And such it is highly needful every man should be, who engages in this undertaking: for many things will occur in the prosecution thereof which are terrible to nature; indeed, so terrible, that all who 'confer with flesh and blood' will be afraid to encounter them. Here, therefore, true courage has its proper place, and is necessary in the highest degree. And this faith only can supply. A believer can say,

> I fear no denial, no danger I fear,
> Nor start from the trial; for Jesus is near.

5. To courage patience is nearly allied; the one regarding future, the other present evils. And whoever joins in carrying on a design of this nature, will have great occasion for this. For, notwithstanding all his unblamableness, he will find himself just in Ishmael's situation, 'his hand against every man, and every man's hand against him.' And no wonder: if it be true, that 'all who will live godly shall suffer persecution,' how eminently must this be fulfilled in them who, not content to live godly themselves, compel the ungodly to do so too, or, at least, to refrain from notorious ungodliness! Is not this declaring war against all the world? setting all the children of the devil at defiance? And will not Satan himself, 'the prince of this world, the ruler of the darkness' thereof, exert all his subtilty and all his force in support of his tottering kingdom? Who can expect the roaring lion will tamely submit to have the prey plucked out of his teeth? 'Ye have,' therefore, 'need of patience; that, after ye have done the will of God, ye may receive the promise.'

6. And ye have need of steadiness, that ye may 'hold fast' this 'profession of your faith without wavering.' This also should be

found in all that unite in this Society; which is not a task for a 'double-minded man'—for one that is 'unstable in his ways.' He that is as a reed shaken with the wind is not fit for this warfare; which demands a firm purpose of soul, a constant, determined resolution. One that is wanting in this may 'set his hand to the plough'; but how soon will he 'look back'! He may, indeed, 'endure for a time; but when persecution, or tribulation,' public or private troubles, arise, because of the work, 'immediately he is offended.'

7. Indeed, it is hard for any to persevere in so unpleasing a work, unless love overpowers both pain and fear. And, therefore, it is highly expedient, that all engaged therein have 'the love of God shed abroad in their hearts'; that they should all be able to declare, 'We love Him, because He first loved us.' The presence of Him whom their soul loveth will then make their labour light. They can then say, not from the wildness of a heated imagination, but with the utmost truth and soberness,—

> With Thee conversing, I forget
> All time, and toil, and care:
> Labour is rest, and pain is sweet,
> While Thou, my God, art here,

8. What adds a still greater sweetness, even to labour and pain, is the Christian 'love of our neighbour.' When they 'love their neighbour,' that is, every soul of man, 'as themselves,' as their own souls; when 'the love of Christ constrains' them to love one another, 'even as He loved us'; when, as He 'tasted death for every man,' so they are 'ready to lay down their life for their brethren' (including in that number every man, every soul for which Christ died); what prospect of danger will then be able to fright them from their 'labour of love'? What suffering will they not be ready to undergo, to save one soul from everlasting burnings? What continuance of labour, disappointment, pain, will vanquish their fixed resolution? Will they not be—

> 'Gainst all repulses steeld nor ever tired
> With toilsome day or ill-succeeding night?

So love both 'hopeth' and 'endureth all things'; so 'charity never faileth.'

9. Love is necessary for all the members of such a Society, on another account likewise; even because 'it is not puffed up'; it produces not only courage and patience, but humility. And O how needful is this for all who are so employed! What can be of more importance, than that they should be little, and mean, and base, and vile, in their own eyes! For, otherwise, should they think themselves anything, should they impute anything to themselves, should they admit anything of a Pharisaic spirit, 'trusting in themselves that they are righteous, and despising others'; nothing could more directly tend to overthrow the whole design. For then they would not only have all the world, but also God Himself, to contend with; seeing He 'resisteth the proud, and giveth grace' only 'to the humble.' Deeply conscious, therefore, should every member of this Society be of his own foolishness, weakness, helplessness; continually hanging, with his whole soul, upon Him who alone hath wisdom and strength, with an unspeakable conviction that 'the help which is done upon earth, God doeth it Himself'; and that it is He alone who 'worketh in us both to will and to do of His good pleasure.'

10. One point more whoever engages in this design should have deeply impressed on his heart; namely, that 'the wrath of man worketh not the righteousness of God.' Let him, therefore, learn of Him who was meek, as well as lowly; and let him abide in meekness, as well as humility: 'with all lowliness and meekness,' let him 'walk worthy of the vocation wherewith he is called.' Let him be 'gentle toward all men,' good or bad, for his own sake, for their sake, for Christ's sake. Are any 'ignorant, and out of the way'? Let him have 'compassion' upon them. Do they even oppose the word and work of God, yea, set themselves in battle array against it? So much the more hath he need 'in meekness to instruct those who thus oppose themselves'; if haply they may 'escape out of the snare of the devil,' and no more be 'taken captive at his will.'

IV. 1. From the qualifications of those who are proper to engage in such an undertaking as this, I proceed to show, fourthly, with what spirit, and in what manner, it ought to be pursued. First, with what spirit. Now this first regards the *motive*, which is to be preserved in every step that is taken; for if, at any time, 'the light which is in thee be darkness, how great is that darkness! But if thine eye be single, thy whole body shall be full of light.' This is, therefore, continually to be remembered, and carried into every word and action. Nothing is to be spoke or done, either great or small, with a view to any temporal advantage; nothing with a view to the favour or esteem, the love or the praise, of men. But the intention, the eye of the mind, is always to be fixed on the glory of God and good of man.

2. But the spirit with which everything is to be done regards the *temper* as well as the motive. And this is no other than that which has been described above. For the same courage, patience, steadiness, which qualify a man for the work, are to be exercised therein. Above all, let him 'take the shield of faith': this will quench a thousand fiery darts. Let him exert all the faith which God has given him, in every trying hour. And let all his doings be done in love: never let this be wrested from him. Neither must many waters quench this love, nor the floods of ingratitude down it. Let, likewise, that lowly mind be in him which was also in Christ Jesus; yea, and let him 'be clothed with humility,' filling his heart, and adorning his whole behaviour. At the same time, let him 'put on bowels of mercies, gentleness, long-suffering'; avoiding the least appearance of malice, bitterness, anger, or resentment; knowing it is our calling, not to be 'overcome of evil, but to overcome evil with good.' In order to preserve this humble, gentle love, it is needful to do all things with recollection of spirit; watching against all hurry, or dissipation of thought, as well as against pride, wrath, or surliness. But this can be no otherwise preserved than by 'continuing instant in prayer,' both before and after he comes into the field, and during the whole action; and by doing all in the spirit of sacrifice offering all to God through the Son of His love.

3. As to the outward manner of acting, a general rule is, Let it be expressive of these inward tempers. But, to be more particular: let every man beware not to 'do evil that good may come.' Therefore, 'putting away all lying, let every man speak the truth to his neighbour.' Use no fraud or guile, either in order to detect or to punish any man; but 'by simplicity and godly sincerity commend yourself to men's consciences in the sight of God.' It is probable that, by your adhering to these rules, fewer offenders will be convicted; but so much the more will the blessing of God accompany the whole undertaking.

4. But let innocence be joined with prudence, properly so called: not that offspring of hell which the world calls prudence, which is mere craft, cunning, dissimulation; but with that 'wisdom from above' which our Lord peculiarly recommends to all who would promote His Kingdom upon earth: 'Be ye therefore wise as serpents,' while ye are 'harmless as doves.' This wisdom will instruct you how to suit your words, and whole behaviour, to the persons with whom you have to do; to the time, place, and all other circumstances. It will teach you to cut off occasion of offence, even from those who seek occasion, and to do things of the most offensive nature in the least offensive manner that is possible.

5. Your manner of speaking, particularly to offenders, should be at all times deeply serious (lest it appear like insulting or triumphing over them), rather inclining to sad; showing that you pity them for what they do, and sympathize with them in what they suffer. Let your air and tone of voice, as well as words, be dispassionate, calm, mild; yea, where it would not appear like dissimulation, even kind and friendly. In some cases, where it will probably be received as it is meant, you may profess the good-will you bear them; but, at the same time (that it may not be thought to proceed from fear, or any wrong inclination), professing your intrepidity, and inflexible resolution to oppose and punish vice to the uttermost.

V. 1. It remains only to make some application of what has been said; partly to you who are already engaged in this work; partly to all that fear God; and more especially to them that love as well as fear Him.

With regard to you who are already engaged in this work, the first advice I would give you is, calmly and deeply to consider the nature of your undertaking. Know what you are about; be thoroughly acquainted with what you have in hand; consider the objections which are made to the whole of your undertaking; and, before you proceed, be satisfied that those objections have no real weight: then may every man act as he is fully persuaded in his own mind.

2. I advise you, secondly, be not in haste to increase your number; and, in adding thereto, regard not wealth, rank, or any outward circumstance; only regard the qualifications above

described. Inquire diligently, whether the person proposed be of an unblamable carriage, and whether he be a man of faith, courage, patience, steadiness; whether he be a lover of God and man. If so, he will add to your strength as well as number: if not, you will lose by him more than you gain; for you will displease God. And be not afraid to purge out from among you any who do not answer the preceding character. By thus lessening your number, you will increase your strength: you will be 'vessels meet for your Master's use.'

3. I would, thirdly, advise you narrowly to observe from what motive you at any time act or speak. Beware that our intention be not stained with any regard either to profit or praise. Whatever you do, 'do it to the Lord,' as the servants of Christ. Do not aim at pleasing yourself in any point, but pleasing Him whose you are and whom you serve. Let your eye be single, from first to last; eye God lone in every word and work.

4. I advise you, in the fourth place, see that you do everyhing in a right temper; with lowliness and meekness, with patience and gentleness, worthy the gospel of Christ. Take every step, trusting in God, and in the most tender, loving spirit you are able. Meantime, watch always against all hurry and dissipation of spirit; and pray always, with all earnestness and perseverance, that your faith fail not. And let nothing interrupt that spirit of sacrifice which you make of all you have and are, of all you suffer and do, that it may be an offering of a sweet-smelling savour to God, through Jesus Christ!

5. As to the manner of acting and speaking, I advise you to do it with all innocence and simplicity, prudence and seriousness. Add to these, all possible calmness and mildness; nay, all the tenderness which the case will bear. You are not to behave as butchers, or hangmen; but as surgeons rather who put the patient to no more pain than is necessary in order to the cure. For this purpose, each of you, likewise, has need of 'a lady's hand with a lion's heart.' So shall many, even of them you are constrained to punish, 'glorify God in the day of visitation.'

6. I exhort all of you who fear God, as ever you hope to find mercy at His hands, as you dread being found (though you knew it not) 'even to fight against God,' do not, on any account, reason, or pretence whatsoever, either directly or indirectly, oppose or hinder so merciful a design, and one so conducive to His glory.

But this is not all: if you are lovers of mankind, if you long to lessen the sins and miseries of your fellow creatures, can you satisfy yourselves, can you be clear before God, by barely not opposing it? Are not you also bound, by the most sacred ties, 'as you have opportunity, to do good to all men'? And is not here an opportunity of doing good to many, even good of the highest kind? In the name of God, then, embrace the opportunity! Assist in doing this good, if no otherwise, yet by your earnest prayers for them who are immediately employed therein. Assist them, according to your ability, to defray the expense which necessarily attends it, and which, without the assistance of charitable persons, would be a burden they could not bear. Assist them, if you can without inconvenience, by quarterly or yearly subscriptions. At least, assist them *now;* use the present hour, doing what God puts into your heart. Let it not be said, that you saw your brethren labouring for God, and would not help them with one of your fingers. In this way, however, 'come to the help of the Lord, to the help of the Lord against the mighty!'

7. I have an higher demand upon you who love as well as fear God. He whom you fear, whom you love, has qualified you for promoting His work in a more excellent way. Because you love God, you love your brother also: you love, not only your friends, but your enemies; not only the friends, but even the enemies, of God. You have 'put on as the elect of God, lowliness, gentleness, long-suffering.' You have faith in God, and in Jesus Christ whom He hath sent; faith which overcometh the world: and hereby you conquer both evil and shame, and that 'fear of man which bringeth a snare'; so that you can stand with boldness before them that despise you, and make no account of your labours. Qualified, then, as you are, and armed for the fight, will you be like the children of Ephraim, 'who, being harnessed, and carrying bows, turned back in the day of battle'? Will *you* leave a few of your brethren to stand alone, against all the hosts of the aliens? O say not, 'This is too heavy a cross; I have not strength or courage to bear it!' True, not of yourself: but you that believe 'can do all things through Christ strengthening you.' 'If thou canst believe, all things are possible to him that believeth.' No cross is too heavy for *him* to bear; knowing that they that 'suffer with Him shall reign with Him.' Say not, 'Nay, but I cannot bear

to be *singular.*' Then you cannot enter into the kingdom of heaven. No one enters there but through the narrow way; and all that walk in this are singular. Say not, 'But I cannot endure the reproach, the odious name of an informer.' And did any man ever save his soul, that was not a by-word, and a proverb of reproach? Neither canst thou ever save thine unless thou art willing that men should say all manner of evil of thee. Say not, 'But if I am active in this work, I shall lose, not only my reputation, but my friends, my customers, my business, my livelihood; so that I shall be brought to poverty.' Thou shalt not; thou canst not; it is absolutely impossible, unless God Himself chooseth it; for His 'kingdom ruleth over all,' and 'the very hairs of thy head are all numbered.' But if the wise, the gracious God choose it for thee, wilt thou murmur or complain? Wilt thou not rather say, 'The cup which my Father has given me, shall I not drink it'? If you 'suffer for Christ, happy are you; the Spirit of glory and of God' shall 'rest upon you.' Say not, 'I would suffer all things, but my wife will not consent to it; and, certainly, a man ought to leave father and mother and all, and cleave to his wife.' True; all but God; all but Christ: but he ought not to leave Him for his wife. He is not to leave any duty undone, for the dearest relative. Our Lord Himself hath said in this very sense, 'If any man love father, or mother, or wife, or children, more than Me, he is not worthy of Me.' Say not, 'Well, I would forsake all for Christ; but one duty must not hinder another; and this would frequently hinder my attending public worship.' Sometimes it probably would. 'Go, then, and learn what that meaneth, I will have mercy, and not sacrifice.' And whatever is lost by showing this mercy, God will repay seven-fold into thy bosom. Say not, 'But I shall hurt my own soul. I am a young man; and by taking up loose women I should expose myself to temptation.' Yes, if you did this in your own strength, or for your own pleasure. But that is not the case. You trust in God; and you aim at pleasing Him only. And if He should call you even into the midst of a burning fiery furnace, 'though thou walkest through the fire, thou shalt not be burned, neither shall the flames kindle upon thee.' 'True; if He called me into the furnace; but I do not see that I am called to this.' Perhaps thou art not willing to see it. However, if thou wast not called before, I call thee now, in the name of Christ: take up thy cross, and follow Him! Reason no

more with flesh and blood, but now resolve to cast in thy lot with
the most despised, the most infamous, of His followers; the filth
and offscouring of the world! I call thee in particular, who didst
once strengthen their hands, but since art drawn back. Take
courage! Be strong! Fulfil their joy, by returning with heart and
hand! Let it appear thou 'departedst for a season, that they
might receive thee again for ever. O be 'not disobedient to the
heavenly calling'! And, as for all of you who know whereunto ye
are called, count ye all things loss, so ye may save one soul for
which Christ died! And therein 'take no thought for the
morrow,' but 'cast all your care on Him that careth for you!'
Commit your souls, bodies, substance, all to Him, 'as unto a
merciful and faithful Creator'!

SERMON LIII

ON THE DEATH OF
THE REV. MR. GEORGE WHITEFIELD

PREACHED AT THE CHAPEL IN TOTTENHAM COURT ROAD,
AND AT THE TABERNACLE, NEAR MOORFIELDS, ON
SUNDAY, NOVEMBER 18, 1770.

George Whitefield died at Newburyport, Massachusetts, thirty miles
north of Boston, on September 30, 1770, in the Presbyterian manse
which is stlll preserved. He was buried in a vault under the pulpit of the
Presbyterian meeting-house on October 2, according to his own wish;
and in 1828 a cenotaph was erected in the church with a suitable
inscription. Under date November 10, 1770, Wesley says, 'I returned to
London, and had the melancholy news of Mr. Whitefield's death
confirmed by his executors, who desired me to preach his funeral
sermon on Sunday the 18th.' [This was his own wish. 'If you should die
abroad,' said Mr. Keen, 'whom shall we get to preach your funeral
sermon? Must it be your old friend, the Rev. Mr. John Wesley?' This
question was often put, and as often Whitefield answered, 'He is the
man.'] 'In order to write this, I retired to Lewisham on Monday; and on
Sunday following went to the chapel in Tottenham Court Road. An
immense multitude was gathered together from all corners of the town.
I was at first afraid that a great part of the congregation would not be
able to hear; but it pleased God to strengthen my voice that even those
at the door heard distinctly. It was an awful season. All were still as
night; most appeared to be deeply affected; and an impression was
made on many which one would hope will not speedily be effaced. The
time appointed for my beginning at the Tabernacle was half-hour after
five, but it was quite filled at three; so I began at four. At first the noise
was exceeding great; but it ceased when I began to speak; and my voice
was again so strengthened that all who were within could hear, unless
an accidental noise hindered here or there for a few moments. Oh that
all may hear the voice of Him with whom are the issues of life and
death; and who so loudly, by this unexpected stroke, calls all His
children to love one another.' On the following Friday he repeated the
sermon at the Tabernacle at Greenwich to an overflowing congregation. Again, on January 2, 1771, he preached at Deptford 'a kind of
funeral sermon for Mr. Whitefield. In every place I wish to show all
possible respect to the memory of that great and good man.'

It must not be forgotten that at this very time Wesley was in the thick
of the controversy with the Rev. Walter Shirley and the Countess of
Huntingdon's preachers about the famous *Minutes* of 1770, in which
Wesley had laid down clearly the differences between his views and
those of the Calvinists. It is much to the credit both of Mr. Whitefield's

friends and of Wesley that this was not allowed to interfere with their invitation to him to preach the sermon, nor with his own affectionate and ungrudging recognition of the greatness and goodness of his departed fellow worker. Indeed, their difference of opinion had never, since the dispute in 1741, been permitted to interrupt their mutual love and esteem; they agreed to differ, and still to love one another.

The sermon was at once published in London; and a reprint was issued in Dublin, also dated 1770, with an additional hymn 'Glory and thanks and love'; and it was placed last in the sermons in vol. iv (1771). A warm attack was made on it in the *Gospel Magazine* of February 1771, probably by Mr. Romaine. He first objected to the text. 'How improper,' he says, 'to apply the words of a mad prophet to so holy a man as Mr. Whitefield!' Of course Wesley's answer was obvious: he did not apply the words to Mr. Whitefield, but to himself; and he humorously says, 'Nothing would be more suitable than for Balaam junior to use the words of his forefather; surely a poor reprobate may, without offence, wish to die like one of the elect!' The more serious part of the attack was on the statement in iii. 5 that 'the fundamental doctrines which Mr. Whitefield everywhere insisted on' were 'the new birth, and justification by faith.' Romaine, on the contrary, affirms 'the grand fundamental doctrines, which he everywhere preached, were the everlasting covenant between the Father and the Son, and absolute predestination flowing therefrom.' Wesley answers '(1) that Mr. Whitefield did not everywhere preach these. In all the times I myself heard him preach, I never heard him utter a sentence either on one or the other. Yea, all the times he preached in West Street Chapel, and in our other chapels throughout England, he did not preach these doctrines at all, no, not in a single paragraph. (2) That he did everywhere preach the new birth, and justification by faith. Both in West Street Chapel and in all our other chapels throughout England, he did preach the necessity of the new birth, and justification by faith, as clearly as he has done in his two volumes of printed sermons.' Wesley was not ignorant of the differences between himself and Whitefield in regard to predestination: but most properly in this sermon, whilst he recognizes (iii. 1) that there are differences of opinion between the children of God, he emphasizes the points of agreement; and whatever Whitefield may have believed about the eternal decrees, no man ever preached a full and free salvation more constantly and effectively than he did. The only solution of this difficulty is to be found in the recognition that the two opposing views represent the two sides of one truth, which our finite understanding is not able to synthesize; but which we may nevertheless accept, just as we accept the Unity in Trinity in the Godhead, or the divine-human person of our Lord.

Incidentally we learn from Wesley's reply to Romaine that one of the hymns sung at the service was Charles Wesley's 'Shrinking from the cold hand of death,' from the *Short Hymns on Select Passages* (1762), now No. 823 in the Methodist Hymn-Book; the other was no doubt the one appended to the sermon, 'Servant of God, well done!' written by

Charles Wesley for this occasion, and published as 'An Hymn on the Death of the Rev. Mr. Whitefield' in the third (posthumous) series of Funeral Hymns. The hymn appended to the Dublin edition of the sermon is No. 42 in the second series of Funeral Hymns, published in 1759 (Osborn's edition of *Poetical Works*, vi. 285).

The Tottenham Court Road Chapel, or Whitefield's Tabernacle, as it was often called, stood on the west side of the road, between Tottenham Street and Howland Street. The site was then surrounded by fields and gardens, and there were only two houses to the north of it. The foundation stone was laid by Whitefield in June 1756, and he opened it on November 7 of the same year. It soon was found to be too small, and was enlarged in 1759. A vault was prepared beneath the chapel, in which Whitefield meant that both he himself and the two Wesleys should be interred; but his wish was not fulfiled. In 1890 the building was taken down and re-erected. It is now known as Whitefield's Central Mission.

The Tabernacle was originally a wooden shed to the north of Upper Moorfields, close to Wesley's Foundery, opened in 1741; in 1753 it was superseded by a brick building, the one in which this sermon was preached in the afternoon. This was used for over a century, and was then replaced by a Tabernacle at the corner of Tabernacle Street and Leonard Street, Finsbury, which occupied the old site. The old pulpit was retained from which Wesley preached on this occasion. The building is now used for business purposes.

Let me die the death of the righteous, and let my last end be like his!—NUM. xxii. 10.

1. 'Let my last end be like his!' How many of you join in this wish? Perhaps there are few of you who do not, even in this numerous congregation! And O that this wish may rest upon your minds!—that it may not die away till your souls also are lodged 'where the wicked cease from troubling, and where the weary are at rest'!

2. An elaborate exposition of the text will not be expected on this occasion. It would detain you too long from the sadly-pleasing thought of your beloved brother, friend, and pastor; yea, and father too: for how many are here whom he hath 'begotten in the Lord'! Will it not, then, be more suitable to your inclinations, as well as to this solemnity, directly to speak of this man of God, whom you have so often heard speaking in this place?—the end of whose conversation ye know, 'Jesus Christ, the same yesterday, and to-day, and for ever.'

And may we not,—

I. OBSERVE A FEW PARTICULARS OF HIS LIFE AND DEATH?

II. TAKE SOME VIEW OF HIS CHARACTER? AND,

III. INQUIRE HOW WE MAY IMPROVE THIS AWFUL PROVIDENCE, HIS SUDDEN REMOVAL FROM US

I. 1. We may, in the first place, observe a few particulars of his life and death. He was born at Gloucester, in December, 1714, and put to a grammar-school there, when about twelve years old. When he was seventeen, he began to be seriously religious, and served God to the best of his knowledge. About eighteen he removed to the University, and was admitted at Pembroke College in Oxford; and about a year after he became acquainted with the Methodists (so called), whom from that time he loved as his own soul.

2. By them he was convinced that we 'must be born again,' or outward religion will profit us nothing. He joined with them in fasting on Wednesdays and Fridays; in visiting the sick and the prisoners; and in gathering up the very fragments of time, that no moment might be lost: and he changed the course of his studies; reading chiefly such books as entered into the heart of religion, and led directly to an experimental knowledge of Jesus Christ, and Him crucified.

3. He was soon tried as with fire. Not only his reputation was lost, and some of his dearest friends forsook him; but he was exercised with inward trials, and those of the severest kind. Many nights he lay sleepless upon his bed; many days, prostrate on the ground. But after he had groaned several months under 'the spirit of bondage,' God was pleased to remove the heavy load, by giving him 'the Spirit of adoption'; enabling him through a living faith, to lay hold on 'the Son of His Love.'

4. However, it was thought needful, for the recovery of his health, which was much impaired, that he should go into the country. He accordingly went to Gloucester, where God enabled him to awaken several young persons. These soon formed themselves into a little society, and were some of the first-fruits of his labour. Shortly after, he began to read, twice or thrice a week, to some poor people in the town; and every day to read to and pray with the prisoners in the county jail.

5. Being now about twenty-one years of age, he was solicited to enter into holy orders. Of this he was greatly afraid, being

deeply sensible of his own insufficiency. But the Bishop himself sending for him, and telling him, 'Though I had purposed to ordain none under three-and-twenty, yet I will ordain you whenever you come'—and several other providential circumstances concurring—he submitted, and was ordained on Trinity Sunday, 1736. The next Sunday he preached to a crowded auditory, in the church wherein he was baptized. The week following he returned to Oxford, and took his Bachelor's degree: and he was now fully employed; the care of the prisoners and the poor lying chiefly on him.

6. But it was not long before he was invited to London, to serve the cure of a friend going into the country. He continued there two months, lodging in the Tower, reading prayers in the chapel twice a week, catechizing and preaching once, beside visiting the soldiers in the barracks and the infirmary. He also read prayers every evening at Wapping chapel, and preached at Ludgate prison every Tuesday. While he was here, letters came from his friends in Georgia, which made him long to go and help them: but not seeing his call clear, at the appointed time he returned to his little charge at Oxford, where several youths met daily at his room, to build up each other in their most holy faith.

7. But he was quickly called from hence again, to supply the cure of Dummer, in Hampshire. Here he read prayers twice a day; early in the morning, and in the evening after the people came from work. He also daily catechized the children, and visited from house to house. He now divided the day into three parts, allotting eight hours for sleep and meals, eight for study and retirement, and eight for reading prayers, catechizing, and visiting the people. Is there a more excellent way for a servant of Christ and His Church? If not, who will 'go and do likewise'?

8. Yet his mind still ran on going abroad; and being now fully convinced he was called of God thereto, he set all things in order, and, in January, 1737, went down to take leave of his friends in Gloucester. It was in this journey that God began to bless his ministry in an uncommon manner. Wherever he preached, amazing multitudes of hearers flocked together, in Gloucester, in Stonehouse, in Bath, in Bristol; so that the heat of the churches was scarce supportable: and the impressions made on the minds of many were no less extraordinary. After his return to London, while he was detained by General Oglethorpe, from

week to week and from month to month, it pleased God to bless his word still more. And he was indefatigable in his labour: generally on Sunday he preached four times, to exceeding large auditories; beside reading prayers twice or thrice, and walking to and fro often ten or twelve miles.

9. On December 28 he left London, It was on the 29th that he first preached without notes. December 30, he went on board; but it was above a month before they cleared the land. One happy effect of their very slow passage he mentions in April following: 'Blessed be God, we now live very comfortably in the great cabin. We talk of little else but God and Christ; and scarce a word is heard among us when together, but what has reference to our fall in the first, and our new birth in the Second, Adam.' It seems, likewise, to have been a peculiar providence, that he should spend a little time at Gibraltar; where both citizens and soldiers, high and low, young and old, acknowledged the day of their visitation.

10. From Sunday, May 7, 1738, till the latter end of August following, he 'made full proof of his ministry' in Georgia, particularly at Savannah: he read prayers and expounded twice a day, and visited the sick daily. On Sunday he expounded at five in the morning; at ten read prayers and preached, and at three in the afternoon; and at seven in the evening expounded the Church Catechism. How much easier is it for our brethren in the ministry, either in England, Scotland, or Ireland, to find fault with such a labourer in our Lord's vineyard, than to tread in his steps!

11. It was now that he observed the deplorable condition of many children here; and that God put into his heart the first thought of founding an Orphan-house, for which he determined to raise contributions in England, if God should give him a safe return thither. In December following, he did return to London; and on Sunday, January 14, 1739, he was ordained priest at Christ Church, Oxford. The next day he came to London again; and on Sunday, the 21st, preached twice. But though the churches were large, and crowded exceedingly, yet many hundreds stood in the churchyard, and hundreds more returned home. This put him upon the first thought of preaching in the open air. But when he mentioned it to some of his friends, they judged it to be mere madness: so he did not

carry it into execution till after he had left London. It was on Wednesday, February 21, that, finding all the church doors to be shut in Bristol (beside, that no church was able to contain one half of the congregation), at three in the afternoon he went to Kingswood, and preached abroad to near two thousand people. On Friday he preached there to four or five thousand; and on Sunday to it was supposed ten thousand! The number continually increased all the time he stayed at Bristol; and a flame of holy love was kindled, which will not easily be put out. The same was afterwards kindled in various parts of Wales, of Gloucestershire, and Worcestershire. Indeed, wherever he went, God abundantly confirmed the word of His messenger.

12. On Sunday, April 29, he preached the first time in Moorfields, and on Kennington Common; and the thousands of hearers were as quiet as they could have been in a church. Being again detained in England from month to month, he made little excursions into several counties, and received the contributions of willing multitudes for an Orphan-house in Georgia. The embargo which was now laid on the shipping gave him leisure for more journeys through various parts of England, for which many will have reason to bless God to all eternity. At length, on August 14, he embarked: but he did not land in Pennsylvania till October 30. Afterwards he went through Pennsylvania, the Jerseys, New York, Maryland, Virginia, North and South Carolina; preaching all along to immense congregations, with full as great effect as in England. On January 10, 1740, he arrived at Savannah.

13. January 29, he added three desolate orphans to near twenty which he had in his house before. The next day he laid out the ground for the house, about ten miles from Savannah. February 11, he took in four orphans more; and set out for Frederica, in order to fetch the orphans that were in the southern parts of the colony. In his return he fixed a school, both for children and grown persons, at Darien, and took four orphans thence. March 25, he laid the first stone of the Orphan-house; to which, with great propriety, he gave the name of Bethesda; a work for which the children yet unborn shall praise the Lord. He had now about forty orphans, so that there was near a hundred mouths to be fed daily. But he was 'careful

for nothing,' casting his care on Him who feedeth the young ravens that call upon Him.

14. In April he made another tour through Pennsylvania, the Jerseys, and New York. Incredible multitudes flocked to hear, among whom were abundance of negroes. In all places the greater part of the hearers were affected to an amazing degree. Many were deeply convinced of their lost state, many truly converted to God. In some places, thousands cried out aloud; many as in the agonies of death; most were drowned in tears; some turned pale as death; others were wringing their hands; others lying on the ground; others sinking into the arms of their friends; almost all lifting up their eyes, and calling for mercy.

15. He returned to Savannah, June 5. The next evening, during the public service, the whole congregation, young and old, were dissolved in tears: after service, several of the parishioners, and all his family, particularly the little children, returned home crying along the street, and some could not help praying aloud. The groans and cries of the children continued all night, and great part of the next day.

16. In August he set out again, and through various provinces came to Boston. While he was here, and in the neighbouring places, he was extremely weak in body: yet the multitudes of hearers were so great, and the effects wrought on them so astonishing, as the oldest men then alive in the town had never seen before. The same power attended his preaching at New York, particularly on Sunday, November 2: almost as soon as he began, crying, weeping, and wailing were to be heard on every side. Many sunk down to the ground, cut to the heart; and many were filled with divine consolation. Toward the close of his journey he made this reflection: 'It is the seventy-fifth day since I arrived at Rhode Island, exceeding weak in body; yet God has enabled me to preach an hundred and seventy-five times in public, besides exhorting frequently in private! Never did God vouchsafe me greater comforts: never did I perform my journeys with less fatigue, or see such a continuance of the divine presence in the congregations to whom I preached.' In December he returned to Savannah, and in the March following arrived in England.

17. You may easily observe, that the preceding account is chiefly extracted from his own journals which for their artless

and unaffected simplicity, may vie with any writings of the kind. And how exact a specimen is this of his labours both in Europe and America, for the honour of his beloved Master, during the thirty years that followed, as well as of the uninterrupted shower of blessings wherewith God was pleased to succeed his labours! Is it not much to be lamented, that anything should have prevented his continuing this account, till at least near the time when he was called by his Lord to enjoy the fruit of his labour? If he has left any papers of this kind, and his friends account me worthy of the honour, it would be my glory and joy to methodize, transcribe, and prepare them for the public view.

18. A particular account of the last scene of his life is thus given by a gentleman of Boston:—

'After being about a month with us in Boston and its vicinity, and preaching every day, he went to Old York; preached on Thursday, September 27, there; proceeded to Portsmouth, and preached there on Friday. On Saturday morning he set out for Boston; but before he came to Newbury, where he had engaged to preach the next morning, he was importuned to preach by the way. The house not being large enough to contain the people, he preached in an open field. But having been infirm for several weeks, this so exhausted his strength, that when he came to Newbury he could not get out of the ferry-boat without the help of two men. In the evening, however, he recovered his spirits, and appeared with his usual cheerfulness. He went to his chamber at nine, his fixed time, which no company could divert him from, and slept better than he had done for some weeks before. He rose at four in the morning, September 30, and went into his closet; and his companion observed he was unusually long in private. He left his closet, returned to his companion, threw himself on the bed, and lay about ten minutes. Then he fell upon his knees, and prayed most fervently to God that if it was consistent with His will, he might that day finish his Master's work. He then desired his man to call Mr. Parsons, the clergyman, at whose house he was; but, in a minute, before Mr. Parsons could reach him, died, without a sigh or groan. On the news of his death, six gentlemen set out for Newbury, in order to bring his remains hither: but he could not be moved; so that his precious ashes must remain at Newbury. Hundreds would have gone from this town to attend his funeral, had they not expected he would have been interred here. . . . May this stroke be sanctified to the Church of God in general, and to this province in particular!'

II. 1. We are, in the second place, to take some view of his character. A little sketch of this was soon after published in the *Boston Gazette*; an extract of which is subjoined:—

'[Little can be said of him but what every friend to vital Christianity who has sat under his ministry will attest.] In his public labours he has, for many years, astonished the world with his eloquence and devotion. With what divine pathos did he persuade the impenitent sinner to embrace the practice of piety and virtue! [Filled with the spirit of grace, he] spoke from the heart, and, with a fervency of zeal perhaps unequalled since the day of the Apostles, [adorned the truths he delivered with the most graceful charms of rhetoric and oratory.] From the pulpit he was unrivalled in the command of an ever-crowded auditory. Nor was he less agreeable and instructive in his private conversation; happy in a remarkable ease of address, willing to communicate, studious to edify. May the rising generation catch a spark of that fame which shone, with such distinguished lustre, in the spirit and practice of this faithful servant of the most high God!'

2. A more particular, and equally just, character of him has appeared in one of the English papers. It may not be disagreeable to you to add the substance of this likewise:—

'The character of this truly pious person must be [deeply] impressed on the heart of every friend to vital religion. In spite of a tender [and delicate] constitution, he continued to the last day of his life, preaching with a frequency and fervour that seemed to exceed the natural strength of the most robust. Being called to the exercise of his function at an age when most young men are only beginning to qualify themselves for it, he had not time to make a very considerable progress in the learned languages. But this defect was amply supplied by a lively and fertile genius, by fervent zeal, and by a forcible and most persuasive delivery. And though in the pulpit he often found it needful by "the terrors of the Lord" to "persuade men," he had nothing gloomy in his nature; being singularly cheerful, as well as charitable and tender-hearted. He was as ready to relieve the bodily as the spiritual necessities of those that applied to him. It ought also to be observed, that he constantly enforced upon his audience every moral duty; particularly industry in their several callings, and obedience to their superiors. He endeavoured, by the most extraordinary efforts of preaching, in different places, and even in the open fields, to rouse the lower class of people from the last degree of inattention and ignorance to a sense of religion. For this, and his other labours, the name of GEORGE WHITEFIELD will long be remembered with esteem and veneration.'

3. That both these accounts are just and impartial, will readily be allowed; that is, as far as they go. But they go little farther than the outside of his character. They show you the preacher, but not the man, the Christian, the saint of God. May I be permitted to add a little on this head, from a personal knowledge of near forty years? Indeed, I am thoroughly sensible how difficult it is to speak on so delicate a subject; what prudence is required to avoid both extremes, to say neither too little nor too much! Nay, I know it is impossible to speak at all, to say either less or more without incurring from some the former, from others the latter censure. Some will seriously think that too little is said; and others, that it is too much. But without attending to this, I will speak just what I know, before Him to whom we are all to give an account.

4. Mention has already been made of his unparalleled zeal, his indefatigable activity, his tender-heartedness to the afflicted, and charitableness toward the poor. But should we not likewise mention his deep *gratitude* to all whom God had used as instruments of good to him?—of whom he did not cease to speak in the most respectful manner, even to his dying day. Should we not mention, that he had a heart susceptible of the most generous and the most tender *friendship*? I have frequently thought that this, of all others, was the distinguishing part of his character. How few have we known of so kind a temper, of such large and flowing affections! Was it not principally by this, that the hearts of others were so strangely drawn and knit to him? Can anything but love beget love? This shone in his very countenance, and continually breathed in all his words, whether in public or private. Was it not this, which, quick and penetrating as lightning, flew from heart to heart? which gave that life to his sermons, his conversations, his letters? Ye are witnesses!

5. But away with the vile misconstruction of men of corrupt minds, who know of no love but what is earthly and sensual! Be it remembered, at the same time, that he was endued with the most nice and unblemished *modesty*. His office called him to converse very frequently and largely with women as well as men; and those of every age and condition. But his whole behaviour towards them was a practical comment on that advice of St. Paul to Timothy: 'Entreat the elder women as mothers, the younger as sisters, with all purity.'

6. Meantime, how suitable to the friendliness of his spirit was the *frankness* and *openness* of his conversation!—although it was as far removed from rudeness on the one hand, as from guile [and disguise] on the other. Was not this frankness at once a fruit and a proof of his *courage* and *intrepidity*? Armed with these, he feared not the faces of men, but 'used great plainness of speech to persons of every rank and condition, high and low, rich and poor; endeavouring only 'by manifestation of the truth to commend himself to every man's conscience in the sight of God.'

7. Neither was he afraid of labour or pain, any more than of 'what man [could] do unto him'; being equally

> *Patient* in bearing ill and doing well.

And this appeared in the *steadiness* wherewith he pursued whatever he undertook for his Master's sake. Witness one instance for all,—the Orphan-house in Georgia; which he began and perfected, in spite of all discouragements. Indeed, in whatever concerned himself he was pliant and flexible. In this case he was 'easy to be entreated'; easy to be either convinced or persuaded. But he was immovable in the things of God, or wherever his conscience was concerned. None could persuade, any more than affright, him to vary, in the least point, from that *integrity* which was inseparable from his whole character, and regulated all his words and actions. Herein he did

> Stand as an iron pillar strong,
> And steadfast as a wall of brass.

8. If it be inquired what was the foundation of this integrity, or of his sincerity, courage, patience, and every other valuable and amiable quality; it is easy to give the answer. It was not the

excellence of his natural temper, not the strength of his understanding; it was not the force of education; no, nor the advice of his friends: it was no other than faith in a bleeding Lord; 'faith of the operation of God.' It was 'a lively hope of an inheritance incorruptible, undefiled, and that fadeth not away.' It was 'the love of God shed abroad in his heart by the Holy Ghost which was given unto him,' filling his soul with tender, disinterested love to every child of man. From this source arose that torrent of eloquence which frequently bore down all before it; from this, that astonishing force of persuasion which the most hardened sinners could not resist. This it was which often made his 'head as waters, and his eyes a fountain of tears.' This it was which enabled him to pour out his soul in prayer in a manner peculiar to himself, with such fullness and ease united together, with such strength and variety both of sentiment and expression.

9. I may close this head with observing what an honour it pleased God to put upon His faithful servant, by allowing him to declare His everlasting gospel in so many various countries, to such numbers of people and with so great an effect on so many of their precious souls! Have we read or heard of any person since the Apostles, who testified the gospel of the grace of God through so widely extended a space, through so large a part of the habitable world? Have we read or heard of any person who called so many thousands, so many myriads, of sinners to repentance? Above all, have we read or heard of any who has been a blessed instrument in His hand of bringing so many sinners from 'darkness to light, and from the power of Satan unto God'? It is true, were we to talk thus to the gay world, we should be judged to speak as barbarians. But *you* understand the language of the country to which you are going, and whither our dear friend is gone a little before us.

III. But how shall we improve this awful providence? This is the third thing which we have to consider. And the answer to this important question is easy (may God write it in all our hearts!). By keeping close to the grand doctrines which he delivered; and by drinking into his spirit.

1. And, first, let us keep close to the grand scriptural doctrines which he everywhere delivered. There are many

doctrines of a less essential nature with regard to which even the sincere children of God (such is the present weakness of human understanding) are and have been divided for many ages. In these we may think and let think; we may 'agree to disagree.' But, meantime, let us hold fast the essentials of 'the faith which was once delivered to the saints'; and which this champion of God so strongly insisted on, at all times, and in all places!

2. His fundamental point was, 'Give God all the glory of whatever is good in man'; and, 'In the business of salvation, set Christ as high and man as low as possible.' With this point, he and his friends at Oxford, the original Methodists, so called, set out. Their grand principle was, There is *power* (by nature) and no *merit* in man. They insisted, all power to think, speak, or act aright is in and from the Spirit of Christ; and all merit is (not in man how high soever in grace, but merely) in the blood of Christ. So he and they taught: there is no power in man, till it is given him from above, to do one good work, to speak one good word, or to form one good desire. For it is not enough to say, all men are *sick of sin*: no, we are all '*dead* in trespasses and sins.' It follows, that all the children of men are, 'by nature, children of wrath.' We are all 'guilty before God,' liable to death temporal and eternal.

3. And we are all helpless, both with regard to the power and to the guilt of sin. 'For who can bring a clean thing out of an unclean?' None less than the Almighty. Who can raise those that are *dead*, spiritually dead in sin? None but He who raised us from the dust of the earth. But on what consideration will He do this? 'Not for works of righteousness that we have done.' 'The dead cannot praise Thee, O Lord'; nor do anything for the sake of which they should be raised to life. Whatever, therefore, God does, He does it merely for the sake of His well-beloved Son: 'He was wounded for our transgressions, He was bruised for our iniquities.' He Himself 'bore' all 'our sins in His own body upon the tree.' He 'was delivered for our offences, and was raised again for our justification.' Here then is the sole meritorious cause of every blessing we do or can enjoy; in particular of our pardon and acceptance with God, of our full and free justification. But by what means do we become interested in what Christ has done and suffered? 'Not by works, lest any man should boast'; but by faith alone. 'We conclude,' says the Apostle,

'that a man is justified by faith, without the works of the law.' And 'to as many as' thus 'receive Him, giveth He power to become the sons of God, even to those that believe in His name; who are born, not of the will of man but of God.'

4. And 'except a man be' thus 'born again, he cannot see the kingdom of God.' But all who are thus 'born of the Spirit' have 'the kingdom of God within them.' Christ sets up His kingdom in their hearts; 'righteousness, peace, and joy in the Holy Ghost.' That 'mind is in them, which was in Christ Jesus,' enabling them to 'walk as Christ also walked.' His indwelling Spirit makes them both holy in heart, and 'holy in all manner of conversation.' But still, seeing all this is a free gift through the righteousness and blood of Christ, there is eternally the same reason to remember, 'He that glorieth, let him glory in the Lord.'

5. You are not ignorant that these are the fundamental doctrines which he everywhere insisted on. And may they not be summed up, as it were, in two words,—the new birth, and justification by faith? These let us insist upon with all boldness, at all times, and in all places; in public (those of us who are called thereto) and at all opportunities in private. Keep close to these good old unfashionable doctrines, how many soever contradict and blaspheme. Go on my brethren, in the 'name of the Lord and in the power of His might.' With all care and diligence, 'keep that safe which is committed to your trust'; knowing that 'heaven and earth shall pass away but this truth shall not pass away.'

6. But will it be sufficient to keep close to his doctrines, how pure soever they are? Is there not a point of still greater importance than this namely, to drink into his spirit?—herein to be a follower of him, even as he was of Christ? Without this, the purity of our doctrines would only increase our condemnation. This, therefore, is the principal thing—to copy after his spirit. And allowing that in some points we must be content to admire what we cannot imitate; yet in many others we may, through the same free grace, be partakers of the same blessing. Conscious then of your own wants and of His bounteous love, who 'giveth liberally and upbraideth not,' cry to Him that worketh all in all for a measure of the same precious faith; of the same zeal and activity; the same tender-heartedness, charitableness, bowels of mercies. Wrestle with God for some degree of the same grateful, friendly, affectionate temper; of the same openness, simplicity,

and godly sincerity; 'love without dissimulation.' Wrestle on, till the power from on high works in you the same steady courage and patience; and above all, because it is the crown of all, the same invariable integrity!

7. Is there any other fruit of the grace of God with which he was eminently endowed, and the want of which among the children of God he frequently and passionately lamented? There is one, that is, catholic love; that sincere and tender affection which is due to all those who, we have reason to believe, are children of God by faith; in other words, all those, in every persuasion, who 'fear God and work righteousness.' He longed to see all who had 'tasted of the good word,' of a true catholic spirit; a word little understood, and still less experienced, by many who have it frequently in their mouth. Who is he that answers this character? Who is the man of a catholic spirit? One who loves as friends, as brethren in the Lord, as joint partakers of the present kingdom of heaven, and fellow heirs of His eternal kingdom, all, of whatever opinion, mode of worship, or congregation, who believe in the Lord Jesus; who love God and man; who, rejoicing to please and fearing to offend God, are careful to abstain from evil, and zealous of good works. He is a man of a truly catholic spirit, who bears all these continually upon his heart; who, having an unspeakable tenderness for their persons, and an earnest desire of their welfare does not cease to commend them to God in prayer, as well as to plead their cause before men; who speaks comfortably to them, and labours, by all his words, to strengthen their hands in God. He assists them to the uttermost of his power, in all things, spiritual and temporal; he is ready to 'spend and be spent' for them; yea, 'to lay down his life for his brethren.'

8. How amiable a character is this! How desirable to every child of God! But why is it then so rarely found? How is it that there are so few instances of it? Indeed, supposing we have tasted of the love of God, how can any of us rest till it is our own? Why, there is a delicate device, whereby Satan persuades thousands that they may stop short of it and yet be guiltless. It is well if many here present are not in this 'snare of the devil, taken captive at his will.' 'O yes,' says one, 'I have all this love for those I believe to be children of God; but I will never believe he is a child of God who belongs to that vile congregation! Can he, do you

think, be a child of God, who holds such detestable opinions? or he that joins in such senseless and superstitious, if not idolatrous, worship?' So we may justify ourselves in one sin by adding a second to it! We excuse the want of love in ourselves by laying the blame on others! To colour our own devilish temper, we pronounce our brethren children of the devil! O beware of this!—and if you are already taken in the snare, escape out of it as soon as possible! Go and learn that truly catholic love which 'is not rash,' or hasty in judging; that love which 'thinketh no evil'; which 'believeth and hopeth all things'; which makes all the allowances for others that we desire others should make for us! Then we shall take knowledge of the grace of God which is in every man, whatever be his opinion or mode of worship: then will all that fear God be near and dear unto us 'in the bowels of Jesus Christ.'

9. Was not this the spirit of our dear friend? And why should it not be ours? O Thou God of love, how long shall Thy people be a by-word among the Heathen? How long shall they laugh us to scorn, and say, 'See how *these* Christians love one another!' When wilt Thou roll away our reproach? Shall the sword devour for ever? How long will it be ere Thou bid Thy people return from 'following each other'? Now, at least, 'let all the people stand still, and pursue after their brethren no more'! But whatever others do, let all of us, my brethren, hear the voice of him that, being dead, yet speaketh! Suppose ye hear him say, 'Now, at least, be ye followers of me as I was of Christ! Let brother "no more lift up sword against brother, neither know ye war any more!" Rather put ye on, as the elect of God, bowels of mercies, humbleness of mind, brotherly kindness, gentleness, long-suffering, forbearing one another in love. Let the time past suffice for strife, envy, contention; for biting and devouring one another. Blessed be God, that ye have not long ago been consumed one of another! From henceforth hold ye the unity of the Spirit in the bond of peace.'

10. O God, with Thee no word is impossible! Thou doest whatsoever pleaseth Thee! O that Thou wouldest cause the mantle of Thy prophet, whom Thou hast taken up, now to fall upon us that remain! 'Where is the Lord God of Elijah?' Let his spirit rest upon these Thy servants! Show Thou art the God that answerest by fire! Let the fire of Thy love fall on every heart!

And because we love Thee, let us love one another with a 'love stronger than death'! Take away from us 'all anger, and wrath, and bitterness; all clamour and evil speaking!' Let Thy Spirit so rest upon us, that from this hour we may be 'kind to each other, tender-hearted, forgiving one another, even as God, for Christ's sake hath forgiven us'!

AN HYMN

Servant of God, well done!
Thy glorious warfare's past;
The battle's fought, the race is won,
And thou art crown'd at last;
Of all thy heart's desire
Triumphantly possess'd,
Lodged by the ministerial choir
In thy Redeemer's breast.

In condescending love,
Thy ceaseless prayer He heard;
And bade thee suddenly remove
To thy complete reward:
Ready to bring the peace,
Thy beauteous feet were shod,
When mercy sign'd thy soul's release,
And caught thee up to God.

With saints enthroned on high,
Thou dost thy Lord proclaim,
And still *To God salvation* cry,
Salvation to the Lamb!
O happy, happy soul!
In ecstasies of praise, ,
Long as eternal ages roll,
Thou seest thy Saviour's face!

Redeem'd from earth and pain,
Ah! when shall we ascend,
And all in Jesu's presence reign
With our translated friend?
Come, Lord, and quickly come!
And, when in Thee complete,
Receive Thy longing servants home,
To triumph at Thy feet!